D1096356

Survey of
Science Fiction Literature

Survey
of
Science Fiction
Literature

FIVE HUNDRED 2,000-WORD ESSAY REVIEWS OF WORLD-FAMOUS SCIENCE FICTION NOVELS WITH 2,500 BIBLIOGRAPHICAL REFERENCES

Edited by
FRANK N. MAGILL

Volume Three
Imp - Nin
1019 - 1536

SALEM PRESS

Englewood Cliffs

Ref
PN
3448
S45
S8
v.3

Copyright, ©, 1979, by FRANK N. MAGILL
All rights in this book are reserved. No part of this work
may be used or reproduced in any manner whatsoever or
transmitted in any form or by any means, electronic or
mechanical, including photocopy, recording, or any information storage and retrieval system, without written
permission from the copyright owner except in the case
of brief quotations embodied in critical articles and reviews. For information address the publisher, Salem
Press, Inc., Englewood Cliffs, New Jersey 07632.

LIBRARY OF CONGRESS CATALOG CARD NUMBER: 79-64639

Complete Set: ISBN 0-89356-194-0
Volume III: ISBN 0-89356-197-5

PRINTED IN THE UNITED STATES OF AMERICA

LIST OF TITLES IN VOLUME THREE

LIST OF TITLES IN VOLUME THREE

Survey of
Science Fiction Literature

IMPERIAL EARTH

Author: Arthur C. Clarke (1917-   )
First book publication: 1976
Type of work: Novel
Time: The Quincentennial Year, 2276
Locale: Titan and the Earth (Washington, D.C., New York, the Caribbean, and Saudi Arabia)

Duncan Makenzie officially visits Earth from Titan and offers the world a great new enterprise for developing the technique of contacting alien intelligence

> Principal characters:
> DUNCAN MAKENZIE, Titan's representative to Earth for the Quincentennial celebration of the American Revolution
> KARL HELMER, his estranged friend and a communications scientist of genius
> CATHERINE LINDEN ELLERMAN, ("CALINDY"), an Earthwoman for whose favors Duncan and Karl are rivals
> GENERAL GEORGE WASHINGTON, the Quincentennial master of ceremonies in Washington
> IVOR MANDEL'STAHM, a gem dealer and confidant of Duncan
> AMBASSADOR BOB FARREL, an Earthman representing Titan's interests
> SIR MORTIMER KEYNES, the world's leading genetic surgeon

Imperial Earth is a speculative science fiction novel written as Arthur C. Clarke's contribution to the American Bicentennial celebration. It is a novel bristling with ideas and insights of the "politics of time and space," the title of one of the early chapters. The tradition in which this novel takes its place is more that of Isaac Asimov's *Foundation* and *The Gods Themselves*, Robert A. Heinlein's *Stranger in a Strange Land* and *The Moon Is a Harsh Mistress*, and Ursula K. Le Guin's *The Dispossessed* than the galactic empires of Frank Herbert's *Dune* or Larry Niven and Jerry Pournelle's *The Mote in God's Eye*. This novel is also one that draws rather heavily on earlier work, particularly *Prelude to Space*, *The City and the Stars*, and *The Deep Range*, as well as some short stories and essays. It combines three of Clarke's favorite interests: space travel and communication with alien intelligence, political and social evolution driven by technological development, and the world beneath the sea. Added to these interests is a new emphasis on interpersonal relations, the psychology of such relations, and a more fully developed symbolism than Clarke had employed in any of the earlier novels, even *Childhood's End* and *2001: A Space Odyssey*.

Imperial Earth is narrated from the perspective of an envisioned divergence in the ethnologies of the Terran motherworld and Titan, a colony world of special importance because of its virtually limitless hydrogen reserves. In Clarke's imagined future it turns out that Titan, a moon of Saturn, is the most hospitable of extraterrestrial worlds in the solar system, because it possesses both adequate gravity and an atmosphere. The gravity is only one fifth that of Earth, a difference which makes adjustment to Earth difficult and even perilous for a Titan resident. However, the two worlds are separated by more than a billion kilometers and variant gravities. From the beginning Titan has been a hard working and productive world in which the human race has had to struggle with alien elements and an environment that will support life only with the intervention of an advanced technology. Life on the surface of Titan is impossible because of the cold, an ammonia atmosphere, and catastrophic winds that occasionally blow across the land. Life is lived mostly below ground in what is called a "corridor society." Moreover, the population is small and interdependent to a degree that is completely foreign to human society on Earth. Each world has reached a historic crossroads as the story opens. Titan's hydrogen based economy is threatened by a new power source developed for space travel called the Asymptotic Drive. The new drive makes possible much faster space travel and does not require hydrogen for fuel. Long term implications for the Titan colony are therefore serious. Earth has also reached a turning point in its development. Its people have become increasingly prosperous and self-interested. Their idealism has also become identified more and more with a nostalgic interest in the past and its charms. The Quincentennial Year becomes the focal point for the cult of the past, which is one of the indicators of a developing decadence in the generation that is beginning to grow up at the time.

Clarke sets the stage of his future history world with the careful attention to detail of the mature writer, sure of his powers and experienced in his craft. The corridor world of Titan recalls similar lunar colonies in Asimov's *The Gods Themselves* and Heinlein's *The Moon Is a Harsh Mistress*. Rather than giving the reader the kind of spectacular action effects characteristic of those writers, Clarke focuses on the history of Titan as a frontier world and on the Makenzie family as its architects and principal clan. Clarke also has to account for three hundred years of future history. The story begins on Titan, where the Makenzie family has just received an invitation to the Quincentennial celebration. The family consists of Malcolm, the patriarch, a vigorous man more than 120 years old. We learn quickly that life expectancy, while not indefinite, has been extended to perhaps triple the current averages. Colin Makenzie is Malcolm's clone, separated by one generation in time and trained to develop complementary powers of administration to go with Malcolm's engineering skills. Although Malcolm had succeeded in setting up the first colony on Titan, and the Makenzie family has controlled the political and economic life of Titan, they live a rather Spartan life because there is little room or inclination for luxury. Clearly, they are supposed to recall the honest, hard working families of the Roman republic and of colonial America whose inner strength of character, frugal habits, and idealism made them the backbone of new cultures and the foundation of new dynasties.

Malcolm's only natural child was born with a genetic deficiency which claimed her life early. Her death led to the estrangement of Malcolm and his wife Ellen. Hence, the Makenzie dynasty was preserved by cloning, first, Colin and then, another generation later, Duncan. When the invitation from Earth arrives, Duncan is thirty-one years old and is the logical candidate to represent the family interests and those of Titan at the Quincentennial. It is time for Duncan to have a clone made, and the trip to Earth will offer the perfect opportunity to insure the perpetuation of the Makenzie dynasty. The cloning of offspring is necessary because Duncan carries the same damaged gene as Colin and Malcolm, effectively prohibiting the fathering of natural children. Duncan is married to a woman with children of her own, who are reared as Duncan's and as members of the clan, but without the expectations that they will eventually run the family business or occupy the political leadership of Titan.

The Makenzies are not without rivals on Titan, and the most serious challenge comes from the Helmer family, which prides itself on its more recent earth origins and ties. The great hope of the family is Karl, Earth born, a young man of extraordinary personal attractiveness, and a genius. Karl is erratic, however, and has suffered from a mysterious breakdown, the cause of which we learn near the end of the story; but he is also gifted with exceptional powers of reasoning and intuition that distinguish him from Duncan, with his talents for organization and applications. Clarke sets up the classic rivalry and contrast between Shem and Sean which is to dominate the psychology of the entire novel.

During their childhood Duncan and Karl were best friends. Karl was older by several years and was more mature in almost all phases of life. The family rivalry was soon compounded by a rivalry for the affections of a visitor of extraordinary beauty and sex appeal from Earth. Calindy was the prize that inevitably went to the older, handsome, self-confident, and brilliant Karl. Perhaps as a result, Calindy remained for Duncan a dream woman, an ideal. We learn soon enough that the sexual mores of the twenty-third century are considerably more permissive than they are at present or ever have been. The simplest term in which they may be described is bisexual free love. This sort of sexual utopia is one of the least convincing of the science fiction conventions Clarke relies on in setting up the narrative references of his story. Karl and Duncan had been lovers before Calindy arrived on the scene. The break between the two friends occurred after the rivalry over Calindy's affections and following Kark's mysterious breakdown. Much later we learn that Karl's collapse had been the result of Karl's experimental use of the "joy machine," a device for enhancing sensation and experiences, during a sexual encounter with Calindy. The result of Karl's forbidden use of the machine was a kind of permanent imprinting of Calindy as an orgasmic and romantic ideal which not even she could hope to satisfy. Karl has become emotionally arrested and fixated on Calindy as she was when they first met. Not only can no other woman ever satisfy Karl, but also Calindy herself proves unequal to the task. While she has changed, her imprinted image never does, nor can her natural self hope to compete with her electronically enhanced ideal.

When Duncan leaves for an Earth that is under a rather loosely and benignly administered "Pax Americana," the Calindy episode has faded into a some-what distant if poignant memory. Duncan and Karl are estranged, and Karl is presumed to be working on a new and mysterious research project on the outermost of Titan's moons, Memnosyne. As he leaves Titan for the first time, Duncan and the reader are aware that his visit to Earth will change his life, perhaps in ways that no one can anticipate.

The journey to Earth features three exceptional moments. The first comes as Duncan sees Earth, the home planet of the human race, for the first time with his own eyes. It is such a moment that Clarke may well have imagined for himself as he was writing *2001: A Space Odyssey* and filed away for future use. Whatever the case, it is a stirring and even symbolic moment in which the reader imagines Duncan aboard the *Sirius* between the great gas giant Saturn and the remote but luminous Earth. The second moment is another visual en-counter, this time with the heart of the Asymptotic Drive. Duncan contrives to sneak a glimpse of the mysterious and secret power plant with the help of a sympathetic crew officer. What he sees on the viewscreen seems to have prom-ising symbolic potential: a small dot slowly moving along a grid of lines. Strangely, the moment is soon over, and much of the impact is lost and then forgotten in the narrative movement. It is the last time the Asymptotic Drive is mentioned, and the reader is left to puzzle over that one glimpse. Was it per-haps a quantum black hole or some artificially produced neutrino molecule? We do not know and are never to learn.

But the third moment is quickly upon us, and it is one that more than makes up for any disappointment we may feel about the A-Drive. It is a scene out of *2001: A Space Odyssey*, but it is more effectively realized than anything Clarke wrote in the earlier novel. Perhaps, he was thinking of Stanley Kub-rick's stunning visual effects when he describes the vista of Earth from the orbiting Port Van Allen Space Station. There are two other scenes in the novel that have similiar visual impact, but none has the grandeur and the power of stimulating awe and wonder to match Duncan's first close encounter with the beautiful and fabled planet of his dreams. For those who remember the scene in the film version of *2001: A Space Odyssey*, Clarke mentions the "Last Chance Toilet" aboard the space port, an allusion that brings a smile of recog-nition to the reader's face. It is also one of the many details that create a verisimilitude in the novel that is one of its strongest features — a quality that science fiction readers have come to expect from Clarke, and in which they will not be disappointed.

If we are to be disappointed in this novel, it is with Clarke's failure to do more with his characters and their psychology. The purely secular moral values to which the characters casually adhere is a diluting agent that makes it difficult to grasp the conflict and tension that Clarke tries to build through Duncan's yearlong visit to Earth. The reader's slightly bemused discovery that Duncan Makenzie is black, points up another weakness in the design of the story. Clarke wants to establish some basic differences between Bicentennial and Quincentennial America, and one way he does this is to indicate that both the racial question and religion have become specters of the past. Clarke has some fun with these ideas by making General George Washington black and having black university professors acting at footmen and butlers for the Quincentennial jubilee. Roman Catholicism is dimly recalled as a religion associated with a ritual called "Bingo." But the humor does not really disguise the fact that there are no plausible standards of conduct left to guide human behavior except a naïve humanism which never could have produced the kind of demi-Utopia Clarke describes.

Perhaps the difficulties Clarke has in making his characters personally interesting are compounded by the logic of the narrative. Once Duncan arrives on Earth as a human-alien who is accustomed to gravity at only one fifth Earth force, Clarke is committed to having Duncan discover Earth and its culture. Of the several roads that Clarke could have taken, he seems to have chosen the least effective approach. Duncan is simply not an interesting enough character through which to reintroduce the reader to the Earth he knows and make him experience everyday realities as though they were wonders.

In the midst of this strain for poetic effect and bathos, Clarke dazzles us with a genuine wonder. A group of humans who can afford it and who have an adventurous nature are treated to experiences guaranteed to be both unorthodox and satisfying as part of a future mystery tour. Duncan and the reader are taken to the New York waterfront to visit the raised and restored *Titanic*. It is another of those moments in the novel that the reader is not likely to forget. It is almost matched by Clarke's truly inspired description of Duncan's snorkel visit to a coral reef and his encounter with the long-spined sea urchin. The urchin's spiney, starburst configuration is woven subtly into the fabric of the novel's symbolism from this point on, connecting both the origins of terrestrial life and its eventual destiny beyond the solar system.

The chief argument of the novel concerns this very linkage, which is worked out deliberately, indirectly, and slowly; but when Karl Helmer finally makes his appearance on Earth, the various motifs are gathered together to give us the vision of Karl, Duncan, and Clarke himself that will give new purpose and direction to human history. Karl has been secretly staying with Calindy while he develops the final phases of his dream for setting up a cosmic antenna system. It would be constructed beyond the orbit of Saturn in order to pick up longwave radiation that would be a more certain sign of advanced technology than the shortwave radio signals humans have been using to scan the heavens. Karl's rationale is that a highly advanced culture will have outgrown the kind of radio and television signal twentieth century civilization had become accustomed to when interstellar listening stations were first built. When Duncan and Karl finally meet in a mood of mutual suspicion and fear, it is at the site of *Cyclops*, an antenna farm of hundred-meter dishes covering a circular area of five kilometers. Produced by the "brief but brilliant Muslim Renaissance," the spectacular antenna collectors were assembled in the "Empty Quarter" of Saudi Arabia. The great successes of *Cyclops* were things of the receding past by the time the two rivals from Titan meet high upon an observation tower on one of the antennas.

At this point, Clarke opts for the simplest way of cutting through the complications of the plot. Karl dies in an accident, leaving behind in his notebook and recorder the information needed for Duncan to unravel the mysterious project on which Karl had been working. The code name "Argus" held the key to Karl's design of a great antenna system that would be able to search the heavens for the kind of long wave signals a really advanced civilization would be emitting. Duncan and Karl had indeed once recorded a mysterious signal when they were adolescents, but could make nothing of it except that it seemed important. The reader, therefore, understands the importance of the project and its probable success. Duncan makes Karl's plan the center of his Independence Day address, and it creates a sensation. Moreover, the opening of such a great new frontier of scientific investigation will solve Titan's dependence on a one element economy. In the future, Titan is bound be become a great base of scientific study and eventually the base of departure to the stars.

Duncan and Calindy console one another before Duncan's return to Titan, but each realizes that their future destinies are to be very different. Duncan returns to Titan not with his own clone but with a clone of his dead friend Karl. It is more than a gesture in memory of his lost friendship. It answers the need articulated by Sir Mortimer Keynes to bring a new strain into the Makenzie bloodline. It solves the problem of the damaged gene and insures that the Makenzies will be able to reproduce naturally in the future. It makes the peace between the leading rival factions of Titan and preserves Karl's genius unimpaired by the destructive effects of the "joy machine" experiment.

The contrivances and the increasingly sentimental revelations of the concluding chapters are disappointing. They necessarily distort and soften the final impact of the novel, working to undo the effect that the architecture of ideas, symbols, and mythic allusiveness may otherwise have produced. If the novel is disappointing, it is because Clarke fails to realize the potentials of his own vision and the materials he developed. Although *Imperial Earth* fails to meet the standard of Clarke's best work, it will occupy a place of importance among the second rank of science fiction novels. Moreover, no reader of Clarke will want to ignore the outstanding success with which the author manages his special effects and the skill with which he again brings together scientific symbols and mythic patterns to give expression to his vision of both a possible and hopeful future. For the general reader, *Imperial Earth* will be remembered as a novel which achieved some supreme moments of science fiction mythmaking and one which symbolizes the affirmative potentials of science for the future. In the history of the genre, *Imperial Earth* may well come to occupy a curious place as a Bicentennial future history story which is both a product of its times while it articulates visions and intuitions that readers at the Tricentennial may return to with wonder and reverence.

If Clarke is right about longwave radiation and in some of the other guesses he offers, *Imperial Earth* may survive its own artistic weaknesses. Yet how quickly science changes our basic vision of things! When Duncan set out for Earth, there was but one planet in our solar system with rings, and that was in 2276. Now there are three. Perhaps future readers will smile as readily at this statement as we now do at Duncan's reflections of Saturn, *the* ringed planet.

Donald L. Lawler

Sources for Further Study

Criticism:

Brigg, Peter. "Three Styles of Arthur C. Clarke: The Projector, the Wit, and the Mystic," in *Arthur C. Clarke*. Edited by Joseph D. Olander and Martin H. Greenberg. New York: Taplinger, 1977, pp. 15-51. Clarke combines his detailed scientific knowledge with mystical elements, according to Brigg.

Plank, Robert. "Sons and Fathers in A.D. 2001," in *Arthur C. Clarke*. Edited by Joseph D. Olander and Martin H. Greenberg. New York: Taplinger, 1977, pp. 121-148. An analysis of *Imperial Earth* is given here with emphasis on Clarke's use of the number four.

Reviews:

America. CXXXIV, May 1, 1976, p. 386.

Booklist. LXXII, February 1, 1976, p. 756.

Kirkus Reviews. XLIII, November 15, 1976, p. 1306.

National Review. XVIII, May 14, 1976, p. 519.

New York Times Book Review. January 18, 1976, p. 20.

Times Literary Supplement. December 5, 1975, p. 1438.

Virginia Quarterly Review. LII, Spring, 1976, p. 56.

IN THE OCEAN OF NIGHT

Author: Gregory Benford (1941-   )
First book publication: 1977
Type of work: Novel
Time: 1999-2018
Locale: The Earth, the Moon, and points in space within the solar system

A haunting evocation of technological man's first contact with aliens, and the growth of one man's consciousness to assimilate the experience without becoming totally cut off from his own roots

> *Principal characters:*
> NIGEL WALMSLEY, an astronaut and space scientist
> ALEXANDRIA ASCENCIO, an airline executive, Nigel's lover
> SHIRLEY, lover of both, convert to the New Sons religious cult
> NIKKA AMAJHI, a pilot, technician, Nigel's lover after Alexandria
> MR. ICHINO, a computer technician, Nigel's friend and confidant
> THE "SNARK," a touring representative of ancient machine civilization
> BIGFOOT, a large, manlike creature
> PETER GRAVES, a hunter, threat to Bigfoot

In a number of stories and novels, Gregory Benford has tried to sum up the centrality for him, and probably for science fiction, of the theme of confrontation with alien life. The alien may be the future, our own selves seen at a distance, or an intelligent being of extraterrestrial origin, but the effect of the alien, and of the search for him, permeates Benford's fiction, from the paranoid fantasies of "Deeper than the Darkness" (*The Magazine of Fantasy and Science Fiction*, April 1969; novelized 1970; rewritten as *The Stars in Shroud*, 1977) and "White Creatures" (*New Dimensions 5*, ed. Robert Silverberg, 1975) to the exploration stories of *Jupiter Project* (*Amazing Science Fiction*, September-November 1972; rewritten for book publication 1975) and *If the Stars Are Gods* (coauthored with Gordon Eklund, 1977).

Like *If the Stars Are Gods*, *In the Ocean of Night* concerns an astronaut, somewhat alienated from his own race, who seeks the alien for what it or he can teach us, either about how the universe works, or about who or what we are. Like the collaboration, *In the Ocean of Night* is the result of years of thinking and reshaping (the earliest version of its conclusion was published in *Amazing Science Fiction*, November 1969, two years before work had begun on the other novel), and most of it had appeared in fragmentary form before the final assemblage. Unlike the collaboration, however, which remains five sometimes brilliant separate episodes, *In the Ocean of Night* is, if not a seamless web, an organic whole which amounts to more than the sum of its parts.

In this book, Benford has made a largely successful attempt to turn the traditional "first contact" romance into a novel of social interaction and character. The focus is not on Man, but on a particular man who, as an astronaut, encapsulates Man's probes into space, but who, as an individual, is rooted firmly in the world from which those probes are launched. Himself an alien, an Englishman in an American space program, Nigel has a critical eye for NASA and American behavior patterns and a longing to transcend his flaws and frailties as well as those of his Earthbound fellow human beings.

He sees the enemy, if there is one, not as the alien, but rather as the rigid, paranoid bureaucracy of the American government. Threatened by economic rivals from abroad (Brazil is prominent) and increasingly under pressure from irrational religious elements internally, the United States, as a corporate structure, can respond to the alien challenge only as a threat to its hegemony. But Nigel the alienated individual, sees in the alien a possible source of help for his and for mankind's problems.

The alien in this story is a representative of a machine civilization in relation to which we are one of those rare and transitory organic life forms that sometimes threaten the stability of things before they give way to machines or wink out of existence. The "Snark," as Nigel names it, emphasizing its unknowability through the allusion to Lewis Carroll's poem, "The Hunting of the Snark," interacts with human beings in several ways, primarily with individuals, and most often with Nigel. First to identify it, he circumvents NASA security by linking its communications directly to himself. Through his unwitting agency, the Snark takes over a human body, that of his lover, Alexandria, at the moment of her death. Later it uses Nigel's own senses to further explore the terrestrial environment and viewpoint. Nigel's friend, Mr. Ichino, programs messages to the Snark, chief among which are cultural artifacts that help it to understand humanity and serve to enrich its lonely journey. Finally, the Snark confronts Nigel in space in a NASA interceptor, and educates him in the realities of "the ocean of night."

This confrontation might have been the climax of a lesser novel, but here it is only the second of Nigel's three meetings with alien vessels. The first, based on the novelette, "Icarus Descending" (*The Magazine of Fantasy and Science Fiction*, April 1973), concerned a body misidentified for years as the asteroid Icarus, whose probable collision with Earth Nigel was sent to disrupt. Discovering the ship's true nature, Nigel delayed its destruction to explore its interior, risking the wrath of a panicky planet. His conviction then that man had much to learn from the aliens was not vindicated by the puzzling artifacts he extracted, but his motivation and first encounter with alienness are convincingly represented.

The erupting of that ship, resulting in an escape of atmosphere that propelled it toward Earth, was coincident with the sending of a distress signal summoning the Snark from its intended course. Nigel, meanwhile, still holds his position with Pasadena's Jet Propulsion Laboratory, a testament to his tenacity in bureaucratic infighting and his stature as a public figure earned from press conferences, talk shows, and so on. Having maintained his astronaut's rating, he is a logical if resisted choice, not only to pilot the interceptor, but also to work on the lunar project in which Earth scientists pry information from still a third alien ship, reactivated by the Snark in passing.

In this section, the fragmented Nigel of earlier narratives approaches wholeness in his human affairs, as well as in his grasp of human-alien relationships. His *ménage à trois* with Alexandria and their mutual lover, Shirley, was wrecked first when Alexandria contracted lupus, a pollution-linked disease, and then when both women defected to the charismatic religious cult, the New Sons of God. Alexandria's death and her transfiguration by the Snark won fame for the faith, but Nigel was plunged into a "dark night of the soul" from which he emerged, partly because of his own interaction with the alien, able to love in a less self-centered way. Nigel shows this ability not only in his sexual liaison with Nikka, an Oriental girl he meets in the lunar project, but also in his asexual relationship with Mr. Ichino, an older, more ascetic version of what Nigel could become. In this second triangle, Nigel is involved in a merging of East and West, in a bipolar connection with male and female, youth and age, in love relationships held together by shared interests and outlooks.

Nigel and Nikka extract secrets from the alien hulk, interact with each other in analyzing them, and manage to make much of their information public, despite attempts by the project's bureaucracy, infiltrated by the New Sons, to block transmission of material that might upset mankind's mythological self-portrait. Meanwhile, in the Pacific Northwest, Mr. Ichino independently confirms the ancient alien contact with the legendary "Bigfoot," though he destroys the evidence gathered by the white hunter, Graves, who would exploit the creatures rather than respect their privacy. These plot threads are tied together in the epilogue, which takes place at Mr. Ichino's cabin, and reveals the distance Benford has come from the melodramatic adventure story.

Nigel has come to know the alien far better than anyone, including Nikka and Mr. Ichino, because he absorbed a charge of alien information in the "library" of the alien craft, which built on his previous contacts and radically reorganized his world view. His transcendental insights are rendered in a stream-of-consciousness internal monolog as he chops wood outside, while indoors Mr. Ichino explains to Nikka the peace of mind required to understand a Japanese motorcycle. This oblique explanation of internal transcendence is punctuated by the blows of the axe and given visual point by the sight of Nigel outside, framed by the window (much as he has framed the alien before), with the vast expanse of the woods and the limitless background of the sky behind him.

Set in this context, the return of Graves is anticlimatic, melodramatic, and essentially trivial. Nigel dispatches him with inaudible words of wisdom, then sees the man's helicopter shot out of the sky by a distant humanoid shape, presumably using a weapon Mr. Ichino has returned to the Bigfoot tribe, who revered it for millennia before being disturbed by Graves. "Everyone learns from experience," intones Mr. Ichino, and his words fit not only Bigfoot, but also Nigel, his companions, and, one hopes, the human race.

Nigel's last series of revelations parallels the concluding statements of potential given the protagonists in Arthur C. Clarke's *2001: A Space Odyssey* and Robert Heinlein's *Stranger in a Strange Land*, without the metaphysics those authors felt compelled to use. Nigel's situation is always explicable in naturalistic terms; the beauty of his vision of a Universe alien to Man lies in its existential reality, rooted in the nature of Man rather than in the transcendental value of alien powers. It is not evident how Nigel will use his newfound perceptions — his peaceful solution to the Graves problem is countered by the Bigfoot answer — but his insights are accessible to others, both in the book and in the audience.

Though Nigel's quest is not for the mythological, it is nonetheless religious in a profound sense. His opposition to the New Sons is so vehement that it is apparent they must exert an attraction on him. He sees a reasonable parallel between the arrested development of Bigfoot, too enamored of alien "toys" to improve upon its "given" nature, and the regressiveness of the New Sons, who want only to retreat to mindless rituals, dances, and chants. But Nigel resists seeing his own commitment to progress or to assimilation of the alien as a complementary religious drive, although it is no more justifiable in logical terms than the actions of his opponents.

In a sense, Nigel's longing for space and its potential, and his victories over the forces of darkness, are appropriate to the formula demands of the romance, adapted to the space frontier. But his dependence on technology, on society, even on family, as "life support systems," contrasts starkly with the rejection of all three by the knight-errant or the lone gunslinger riding into town out of the desert. Where the space opera hero may fly by the seat of his pants, Nigel is disciplined, both as a scientist and as a social animal. Though his mind may be an "outlaw" yearning for the impossible, he knows he can never merge with the "other." But as a scientist, he must learn what he can, he must approximate in his terms and ours, what he senses that is beyond him. As a child progressively internalizes the world outside, Nigel encompasses the alien, formulating a paradigm which unites even organic and machine civilization against the awesome backdrop of the emptiness between civilizations.

Our own civilization, the thin veneer of culture which continually threatens to break down under economic, religious, and technological assaults, may not be adequate to the paradigm, but it is the only civilization we have. Nigel clearly lives in and is a product of an advanced, even decaying, technological society which Benford plausibly extrapolates from the contemporary situation of Western man, from shortages of raw materials (including water as well as gasoline) to changing evaluations of art and history (Bob Dylan and the Beatles are musical "classics," and Berkeley's Telegraph Avenue is a culturally frozen tableau of the 1960's.)

Nigel, certainly, has both feet planted firmly on solid, realistic circumstances. He eats and eliminates, drinks and fights, thinks and makes love, living a life which is not limited to the great adventure to which he is committed. Alexandria and Shirley, Nikka and Mr. Ichino, too, have lives of their own, even though we see them primarily in relationship to Nigel. Even minor characters, like Nigel's NASA and JPL coworkers and the administrators in Washington and on the moon, seem rooted in the society of their time. If some of the villains are too melodramatically menacing, too drawn to type, the obstacles that they pose are serious and plausible. The reality of life near the turn of the century is well-grounded and contrasts well against the potential transcendence of the alien, keeping in check the tendency of the theme to dwarf the participants.

Contrast, balance, distance are key concepts for the expression of the narrative as well. It fairly bristles with differing points from which to view the events, changing point-of-view characters so as to juxtapose and counterpoint not only lines of action but also image patterns and modes of thought. Whatever there is of the transcendent that is not domesticated by realistic detail is restrained by artistic form.

The tension between this control and the ostensibly uncontrollable nature of the theme is summed up nicely in the confrontation of Nigel and the Snark beyond the moon. Unknown to Nigel, he does not have control over his interceptor's missiles; his overtures of peace are belied by his ship, yet the Snark believes him. The Snark destroys the weapons with an effortlessness that hints at unused powers capable of destroying planets and stars; but the Snark is only interested in doing its job. Within the limits built into it, the Snark has marvelous self-control, which Nigel envies. The Snark also has consciousness beyond the intent of its builders. This allows it to imagine what it can never have or feel or originate, like man's culture, and allies it to Nigel, for whom the subjective world also goes far beyond what social rules and natural law permit.

Thus the object of contemplation, which suggests religious awe or mythological wonder, is not the alien itself, but the backdrop against which both man and alien are puny — the Universe, the "ocean of night" in the title. But the focus is always on the man for whom these thoughts are possible and assimilable, which argues for the classification of this book not as just another "first contact" romance, but as one of science fiction's few successful attempts at a serious novel of character, incorporating the theme of the alien.

David N. Samuelson

Sources for Further Study

Reviews:

Kirkus Reviews. XLV, September, 1977, p. 955.

Publisher's Weekly. CCXII, August 22, 1977, p. 62.

THE INCOMPLETE ENCHANTER

Authors: L. Sprague de Camp (1907-   ) and Fletcher Pratt (1897-1956)
First book publication: 1941
Type of work: Two related novelettes
Time: Several mythic pasts
Locale: The "alternate" worlds of Old Norse Mythology and Spencer's *The Faerie Queene*

A science fantasy classic about the mock heroic adventures of Harold Shea as he travels through alternate worlds of myth and literature

Principal characters:
> HAROLD SHEA, a young psychology researcher who fancies himself a romantic adventurer
> GERTRUDE MUGLER, Shea's unromantic, undesirable co-worker
> WALTER BAYARD, a third member of the psychology research group
> REED CHALMERS, senior researcher and head of the psychology institute
> BRITOMART, a mannish woman knight errant
> BELPHEBE, a lovely huntress whom Shea comes to love

There are actually five tales which make up the Harold Shea series, but it is the first two, known collectively as *The Incomplete Enchanter*, which have remained a classic of comic sword-and-sorcery since their first appearance in the issues of the magazine *Unknown* for May and August, 1940. The expected swordplay and adventures are certainly present, plus plenty of fantastic creatures and concepts, but Pratt and de Camp provide many special touches of fantasy genius: a whacky sense of humor which is often reminiscent of the bizarre illogic of Lewis Carroll's Alice books; deft satirical sketches of single persons or whole cultures and historical eras; and eccentric yet thought-provoking speculations on cosmology and epistemology. Both authors were solid amateur historians with many nonfiction titles to their credit, and their fantasy worlds always reveal a concern for concrete, detailed research which makes them seem convincing and realistic.

Harold Shea, the hero of the series, is a bored young research psychologist working at the Garaden Institute in Ohio with Reed Chalmers, an older scientist who is head of the institute. The experiment being conducted is based on Chalmers' theory that there is an infinity of possible universes that exist parallel with our own, and the differences between them are based on their inhabitants' prior assumptions about reality. Chalmers is trying to find a proper formula in symbolic logic (Shea jokingly calls it a "syllogismobile") that will allow someone from our modern world to travel back and forth among these multiple universes. (In fact, symbolic logic is strictly a conceptual science and it cannot produce any of the visible world-altering effects envisioned by the authors. The travel to other worlds is strictly a mind-game played for fun, and the so-called "laws of magical universes" are not to be taken seriously.)

Tired of the humdrumness of the modern world, Shea anticipates his boss and takes it on himself to recite the latest version of the formula on which they have been working, hoping thereby to locate worlds that are more interesting and adventuresome. More importantly, Shea hopes to escape the romantic overtures of his domineering co-worker, Gertrude Mugler, and find a more desirable mate.

Shea had planned well and intended to land in the world of Irish mythology, but ends up by mistake in that of the Old Norse gods. This is only the first of the goof-ups in Chalmers' new world-creating logic. Somehow, throughout the series, the magical formulas are never better than *almost* correct, and the mistakes are always hilarious in the tradition of "The Sorcerer's Apprentice." An attempt to conjure a mythical unicorn instead produces a befuddled rhinocerous; instead of one firebreathing dragon, a hundred flower-munching ones answer the wizard's call; an attempt by Chalmers to repeat Jesus' miracle of transforming water into wine produces hard scotch whisky, and a drunken brawl ensues.

The title of "The Roaring Trumpet" refers to the horn of the Viking god, Heimdall, guardian of Bifrost, the rainbow bridge which leads to Asgard, home of the gods. It is into this god's hands that Shea falls as a slave, and he ends up with far more adventures than he bargained for back home in Ohio. The gods are close to engaging in mortal combat with their cosmic foes, the giants; the fate of all nine inhabited worlds of the Eddas hangs in the balance, for it is the time of Ragnarok, the apocalyptic last battle which will destroy all creation.

At the end of the first novella Shea does manage to escape back to his own world before the final cataclysm, but before that the feckless Midamerican antihero has to change his status and emerge as a true hero. He goes on quest to Jotunheim, the Land of the Giants, with the deities of Asgard and learns expert swordsmanship on the way. At the same time, one of the authors' cleverest touches is that this journey is a subtly disguised retelling of Snorri Sturluson's *Prose Edda*, a thirteenth century handbook for poets which is the single most famous source for Scandinavian mythology. Snorri's half-comic tale of Thor fishing for the Midgard Serpent in a boat with the Giant Hymir is represented as the god's own story on himself — as a fish story about the Big One That Got Away. In Snorri's version there are three contests at a banquet thrown by the giant Utgardloki in Jotunheim where elemental forces in magical disguises are more powerful than the Aesir, Thor, Tjalfi, and Loki; but in the modern sword-and-sorcery tale these deceptions do not fool Shea at all and he sees the true nature of these beings because his modern mind has been trained to equate magic with illusion and deception.

In an autobiographical remark, de Camp gives Pratt credit for the thoroughness of research into Norse myth for this story, yet the sense of humor here and elsewhere is of a kind familiar to readers of de Camp. By having the Giants speak Chicago gangster lingo, for example, the authors turn their coarseness and deformity into a satire against an excessive stupidity which makes civilization impossible — a perspective and technique typical of many de Camp fables.

With comedy and wit, the authors question the relative merits of our culture *versus* others in a manner which clearly echoes Mark Twain's *A Connecticut Yankee in King Arthur's Court.* For the most part, modern man and modern intelligence come out on top, and this sounds a note which ironically undermines the typical (such as Robert E. Howard's Conan) sword-and-sorcery attitude. Usually the hero in this genre is a rebel against, and escapee from, the confinements and decadence of modern civilization, but none of the alternate universes in the Shea stories are romanticized or idealized. Primitivism is definitely satirized in "The Roaring Trumpet," and medievalism and feudalism are just as definitely rejected in the second tale. Hence, in the first tale a "cockroach derby" devised by Shea to while away time in a Giant dungeon contributes to the already unappetizing portrait of the Eddic worlds; in the second, murderous tribal Celts, the DaDerga (who speak a comical Scottish brogue), are satirized as irrational religion-mongers who naïvely profess that their practice of human sacrifice is good for the victim.

As the series developed, in fact, more and more emphasis was put on Shea's modern qualities as his prime virtues, and more and more the original heroes and gods recede into the background. But even when the latter are pointed up in the story, they seem brutal, violent, and sexually repulsive in comparison to Shea, who is able to solve his problems with something besides physical prowess.

However, there are a few hints at cultural relativism since Shea often succeeds by adapting himself to the demands of the Eddic universe, where magic works, but science does not. Biology, chemistry, and physics have not yet been discovered, so they do not exist, as Shea learns to his chagrin when his matches, revolver, and even his Boy Scout Handbook will not function at critical moments: belief-structures are all-important here. So Shea learns the art and practice of magic (described as "the laws of contagion and similarity" proposed in James George Frazer's *The Golden Bough*). Because of his budding control of magical formulas, he shortens a Troll's nose with homeopathic medicine in one case, then he makes a broom fly all the way to Hell in another. In the latter scene, Shea's aerial acrobatics are one of the highpoints of fantasy adventure in this tale; it is repeated just as effectively in "The Mathematics of Magic" where the aerial broom is used for a wild combat with a villainous wizard aboard a pterodactyl-like wyvern.

"The Mathematics of Magic," the second half of *The Incomplete Enchanter*, involves adventures in the universe of Edmund Spenser's *The Faerie Queene*, where Gloriana's knights and ladies are in a sword-and-sorcery face-off with an entire convention of wizards under the archimage, Busyrane. This tale is not so closely modeled on its original as was the previous story, and there is a whole new cast of characters. This time the elderly and professional Reed Chalmers accompanies Shea on the experimental exploration. He is, of course, much more adept at the "syllogismobile" than his young assistant, but he is also far from heroic. Previously, magic was practiced as an art in Gloriana's realm, but Chalmers develops a scheme to put magic on a scientific ("assembly line") basis until Shea destroys all the wizards' powers. Ultimately there is too much magicking going on in this universe, and the equal-and-opposite reaction which results hurls Shea and Belphebe back into the modern world together, while Chalmers is isolated in the land of the Faerie Queene at the end of the tale, a situation which, of course, demands a further episode for the series.

The villains of this second tale, the wizards of Busyrane's alliance, are the converse of the stupid Giants met earlier: the wizards suggest a satire against effete intellectuals. Their conclave is a funny burlesque of an academic convention, complete with dull lectures on obscure topics which put Shea to sleep.

Two other main characters are women, though both are basically derived from stereotypes (a type-casting at once sexual and literary). Britomart is a mannish warrior knight in the service of Queen Gloriana who finds true love with the fellow knight of her choice. A more important female figure is Belphebe, an archeress of the deep wood where she pursues the goblinesque Losels who serve Busyrane. In this tale, she becomes the object of Shea's affection and his ideal mate, whom he either pursues or rescues in melodramatic fashion throughout the rest of the series. Probably it is in this area of Romance that many of today's readers will find the Shea stories dated by their attitude toward women. For their own time, however, they were intelligent and enlightened and did not condescend too much to the heroines. The melodramatic and repetitive plot structure, however, does become less interesting by the later episodes of the series. At the least, we can appreciate the sly sexual irreverence when, for example, Shea outwits the Blatant Beast by reciting low-class doggerel (explicitly obscene parts, of course, are not recited). In the era of its composition, innuendo was in vogue rather than explicitness, and Pratt and de Camp are masters of the former.

The series, like its wrong-way Corrigan hero, was doomed to be incomplete. A third tale, "The Castle of Iron," was also published in *Unknown* (April, 1941), and, since it is as long as *The Incomplete Enchanter* by itself, it has often been reissued as a separate novel. Trying to get back to *The Faerie Queene*, Shea instead reaches Xanadu of Samuel Taylor Coleridge's poem, "Kubla Khan," and from there Shea, Chalmers, and Belphebe wind up in the universe of Ariosto's Renaissance epic, *Orlando Furioso*. Again, the plot is a series of comic encounters with sorcerers and their spells on the one hand and a sequence of melodramatic rescues of Belphebe by Shea on the other. The last two stories, "The Wall of Serpents" and "The Green Magician," appeared first in ephemeral fantasy magazines (respectively, *Fantasy Fiction* for June,

1953, and *Beyond Fantastic Fiction* for October, 1954) and have sadly been republished only in obscure books and anthologies. The first of these takes Shea and his expanded cast of modern heroes to the mythical world of the Finnish national epic *Kalevala*; the second, to Irish mythology — where Shea had originally set out in the very first tale. By now, the engaging Polish-American cop, Pete Brodsky, is more interesting than our original hero, and interest in the series itself seems to have dwindled away for the authors.

In a personal correspondence, de Camp has indicated he might have continued the series with more adventures in mythical worlds like the Iranian, but Pratt was turning his attention to one of his strongest interests, the Civil War, and then he soon died, in 1956. The Shea stories are, like the other products of this tandem, a unique blend of historical realism, fantasy and satire, high didacticism, and low American humor.

Considered by itself as a single novel, *The Incomplete Enchanter* deserves its popularity as a classic of science fantasy.

C. S. Fredericks

Sources for Further Study

Criticism:

Davenport, Basil. *The Incomplete Enchanter*, in *Saturday Review*. XXIV (October 4, 1941), p. 19. Although Davenport finds *The Incomplete Enchanter* uneven, he feels it is important as an example of burlesque. It creates a world with its own wild logic which is unlike anything in literature.

Gardner, Martin. "Humorous Science Fiction," in *The Writer*. LXII (1949), pp. 148-151. The basis of De Camp's humorous style is its emphasis on absurd situations.

Reviews:

New York Herald Tribune Books. October 12, 1941, p. 8.

New York Times. XVII, October 18, 1941, p. 97.

New Yorker. XVII, October 18, 1941, p. 97.

Springfield Republican. October 12, 1941, p. 7.

THE INHERITORS

Author: William Golding (1911-   )
First book publication: 1955
Type of work: Novel
Time: The distant past
Locale: An unidentified primitive wilderness

A moving account of an encounter between two prehistoric races (probably Cro-Magnon and Neanderthal) in which the more primitive men are destroyed

> *Principal characters:*
> LOK, a young adult Neanderthal man
> FA, a young adult Neanderthal woman
> LIKU, their daughter
> MAL, an old man and probably father of Lok and Fa
> OLD WOMAN, mother of the band of Neanderthals
> HA, an adult Neanderthal man
> NIL, a young, pregnant Neanderthal woman
> TUAMI, a male warrior of the "new people"

It is not every man who has the opportunity to watch his own extinction unfold before his eyes, although all fathers of strong sons, if both live long enough, are given something like this vision. William Golding's superb narrative about an encounter between a small band of Neanderthal men and women and a larger force of probably Cro-Magnon migrants creates this sublime vision of generation. His novel far transcends historical and anthropological literalness although many accurate and suggestive details seem also to be woven into the narrative. *The Inheritors* is, in fact, a symbolic tale about the puzzles and dilemmas of growth, the ambiguous relationships of love and hate toward both our past and our future, the fascination and yet fear that we all experience as we both watch the younger, more progressive future surpass our present while we long for the lost golden days of the past.

Golding's treatment of theme of time in this novel seems particularly in tune with the spirit of the eighteenth century Enlightenment, that period when both history and the novel were essentially developed as modes of thinking. Although his protagonists are all early humanoids, Golding's images and concerns in the book are familiar to us. He envisions in a fresh way the old debate between the Ancients and the Moderns and the contrasts between a lost Golden Age and the modern Iron Age of progress which is doomed to be superseded and lost in its turn. In fact, ironic time relationships are a key characteristic of the novel. The reader watches from the point of view of the earlier, more human and sympathetic "primitive" as a more advanced humanoid species arrives. The third-person omniscient narration takes us back to the beginnings, and we see our future as savage. Such fascination with time is not only characteristic of the eighteenth century *philosophe* but is also a key trait of science fiction, and thus Golding's novel may be another piece of evidence in the argument that science fiction has significant roots in the Enlightenment.

In any case, *The Inheritors* is a cross between a *conte philosophique*, an alien encounter or first contact story, and the more romantic novel of youthful development or *Bildungsroman*. The attitude of Lok and Fa as they watch the strange behavior of the "new people" is a mixture of fear and fascination. This first contact with aliens intrigues them even after they see how dangerous the new people are; and the new people, in turn, are thoroughly spooked by the forest "devils," as they call the innocent and more primitive Neanderthals. One sign of the more advanced species is that the new people can make dug-outs to cross lakes and streams and, in fact, are migrating up to higher lakes when they encounter the forest- and rock-dwelling Neanderthals. The Neanderthals are terrified of water and with good reason. Ha, Nil, the old woman, and eventually Fa are all drowned in the river as the result of various scuffles with the new people. The image of the Cro-Magnon journeying across the water for first contact with a well-adapted human people foreshadows, perhaps, the encounters depicted in science fiction between man and alien races across the seas of space. Both groups grow and learn from the contact as though they were the first children of a youthful earth.

Golding shows remarkable ability to present the novel through the point of view of a particular character. The reader does not see the Neanderthal protagonists as the long-armed, sunken-eyed creatures usually imagined until the action of the novel is nearly complete. The reader knows that their eyes are deepset and that they do not stand totally erect, but Golding's attitude makes Lok and Fa and Mal become real characters, "the people." It is early spring when the story begins; and the small band of Neanderthal people, all of whom will be dead at the end of the novel with the exception of the baby captured as a little "devil" to take the place of a dead baby of the new people, are moving to their high country cave carrying fire with them. Mal is characterized as the old, wise leader; Lok is his rather foolish son. The scenes depicting the death of Mal and his burial next to the fire are beautiful, and suggest how well-adapted and innocently happy these people are (although even these extreme primitives look back with nostalgia to a Golden Age when things were better). Golding explores the theme of looking backward and forward continually; the novel is not so much about a single point in the evolutionary history of the race as it is about any time with a lost past and with a threatening future.

After Mal is gone, Lok must assume leadership of the band. Two forces push him into a growth that ironically reaches fulfillment just before the extinction of his band. In fact, his intelligence grows by leaps in the narrative, to the extent that he can link the vision of his own extinction with the childhood memory of fleeing from a forest fire on the back of his father, Mal — in miniature, Golding's image for linking the past and the future. The two forces in Lok's education are his growing love for Fa and, of course, their encounter with the new people. They spend a lot of time watching from a perch among some ivy on a dead tree; and what they see are ceremonies of sacrifice, drunkenness, and preparations for killing. They look down on "progress" that seems more savage than their own, older way of life; yet their minds are quickened by the process. Lok in particular comes to understand simile or "likeness" (a major step in his mind) and to understand love.

Dramatic action often, however, leads us to understanding at a moment just before obliteration. Golding writes an exciting and quick ending to his narrative. When all the other Neanderthals (except the baby) have died, we get an image of Lok from the outside as a gorilla-like creature returning to curl up by the extinguished fire in the same prenatal position in which they had buried Mal. We know that Lok has learned what death is "like," and we know that he has learned to shed tears for Fa. The reader senses that it may not be too late, however, because the final scene of the novel shows the new people who have survived heading out across a wide lake in their dugout. But even for Tuami, the new person, it is not possible to see if the line of darkness has an ending. All of us inherit the darkness, and movement forward is movement toward our death. Like Lok, we are both terrified and fascinated by that toward which we are headed.

Golding's own favorite of all his works, *The Inheritors* contains many excellent images and suggestions about primitive religion, early telepathic thinking, matriarchy, and the division of work; and the novel works back and forth among a variety of suggestive time relationships. But it is also a very human story about love and death cast with characters of whom we usually do not think as totally human. It is Golding's artistry that makes them seem that way.

Donald M. Hassler

Sources for Further Study

Criticism:

Adriaens, Mark. "Style in William Golding's *The Inheritors*," in *English Studies*. LI (February, 1970), pp. 16-30. Adriaens comments on the general theme of *The Inheritors*.

Babb-Howard, S. *The Novels of William Golding*. Columbus: Ohio State University Press, 1970, pp. 36-63. Golding has written a moving story of Neanderthal man *vs*. *Homo Sapiens*.

Bufkin, E. C. "The Ironic Art of William Golding's *The Inheritors*," in *Texas Studies in Literature and Language*. IX (Winter, 1968), pp. 567-578. Bufkin concentrates on the irony behind the tale of two cultures meeting.

Dick, Bernard F. *William Golding*. New York: Twayne, 1967, pp. 37-48.
  Dick explores the end of innocence in a Neanderthal family.

Reviews:

Booklist. LXIX, September 1, 1962, p. 30.

Chicago Sunday Tribune. August 5, 1962, p. 8.

Christian Century. LXXIX, November 28, 1962, p. 1451.

Commonweal. LXXVII, September 28, 1962, p. 19.

Kirkus Reviews. XXX, July 15, 1962, p. 643.

Library Journal. LXXXVII, September 1, 1962, p. 2916.

Nation. CXCV, November 17, 1962, p. 332.

New York Herald Tribune Book Review. September 23, 1962, p. 12.

New York Times Book Review. July 29, 1962, p. 4.

Saturday Review. XLV, August 25, 1962, p. 25.

Time. LXXX, July 27, 1962, p. 70.

INTER ICE AGE 4
(DAI YON KAMPYO-KI)

Author: Kobo Abé (1924-   )
First book publication: 1959
English translation: 1970
Type of work: Novel
Time: The near future
Locale: Tokyo

A serious and convoluted confrontation with tomorrow in the person of a computer programer and an omnipotent reconstruction of himself produced by a machine capable of forecasting the future

Principal characters:
DR. KATSUMI, the inventor of the forecasting machine
TANOMOGI, Katsumi's assistant and successor
TOMOYASU, government liaison officer for the forecasting project
DR. YAMAMOTO, a researcher in charge of the aquan breeding project
WADA, a young woman working for both Katsumi and Yamamoto

Recurring throughout the pages of Kobo Abé's *Inter Ice Age 4* are the images and terminology of a court trial, one where the crime is unclear and the legal code obscure. However, the judge and jury are not in the least ambiguous; they are the future.

The novel has a plot that can be read simply as an intriguing mystery tale, and characters who entertain their own dreams of happiness or satisfaction and bear their own burdens of guilt as they follow their circumscribed lives. However, *Inter Ice Age 4* is actually a philosophical dialogue held between the proponents of today and the proponents of tomorrow. Moreover, it is an unresolved dialogue between two manifestations of a single mind. The subject, human accountability, is an abstraction that loses all practical meaning when faced with the simple, amoral reality that tomorrow will not be concerned with the earthshaking, yet ultimately trivial, events of today.

The protagonist of the book is Dr. Katsumi, Japan's leading expert in computer programing. He is a man who admits even to himself that he is interested in theories, not in their applications, and in facts, not in their implications. Dr. Katsumi's trial begins when the Soviet Union announces the perfection of a forecasting machine, an electronic brain. Given adequate information, it can predict the developments resulting from events occurring in the present; in other words, it can foresee the future. Starting with simple predictions based on the laws of natural science (a glass, once dropped, will fall to the floor and break), "Moscow I" quickly moves into more challenging fields, eventually predicting the establishment of the first true Communist state and the demise of capitalism.

Dr. Katsumi is tremendously excited by the theoretical aspects of this

Soviet accomplishment. He admits to himself that he will not be satisfied until he, too, has constructed such a machine. He succeeds in the project, assisted by his colleague Tanomogi. However, the Japanese government appears to be wary of using the machine, frightened by the possible repercussions. The committee established to oversee the forecasting machine bans the use of the machine for projects with political overtones, which is defined to restrict virtually every subject.

Dr. Katsumi, his massive electronic brain sitting idle, is at a frustrated loss. Tanomogi suggests that they ask the machine itself what the most appropriate course of action would be. The machine, capable of independent calculation but not independent thought, suggests that a study be made of a single individual's future. This should be apolitical enough to receive the committee's approval. Katsumi and Tanomogi search for an individual to be the unknowing subject of their experiment; but no sooner have they decided on a man and begun their research into his life, than he is murdered.

The project to study the future of an individual changes into a project to uncover his murderer. At the same time Dr. Katsumi's motives change, for he and Tanomogi have come under suspicion; they had been following the man the night he was murdered, and several witnesses have already reported seeing two men tailing the victim.

Hoping to learn the identity of the murderer, Katsumi and Tanomogi place the corpse of the man on the machine. Reactivated artificially, his brain waves are recorded in the forecaster, so that it can reproduce the victim's subjective life up to the time of his death. It can also reproduce his "identity" from the elements programed into it and create a computer "model" of the man, which is capable of giving the man's most probable response to questions. However, the results of the experiment are totally unforeseen. Not only does the man have no idea who his murderer might have been, leaving Dr. Katsumi and Tanomogi no better off than before in terms of their defense, but he also presents evidence that could cast more suspicion on Tanomogi.

The experiment is further complicated when the man tells an incredible story about his girl friend in which she claims to have been a broker for fetuses. She had been hired on a commission basis to persuade pregnant women to have an abortion and sell the fetus to a secret organization. Baffled by this tale, Dr. Katsumi attempts to put the victim's girl friend on the forecasting machine. However, she is poisoned with a drug that completely destroys her nervous system, eliminating the possibility of interrogating her posthumously as had been done with the first victim.

Dr. Katsumi inexplicably finds himself becoming more enmeshed in the entire affair, and he begins to grow suspicious of everyone around him. His wife receives a mysterious telephone call; the caller convinces her to have an abortion, and she receives a commission for the fetus. Dr. Katsumi also receives a telephone call; the voice on the other end of the line is his own.

Unable to grasp the situation, he searches for an answer, which leads him to a rather alarming discovery.

Without Dr. Katsumi's knowledge, a supragovernmental organization has planned to assume control of the machine in order to determine the future repercussions of geological disturbances on the ocean floor. Using the machine, they have learned that the level of the oceans will rise and eventually submerge most of the world's land masses. The organization, armed with this prediction, has begun breeding a race of aquans. Humans and land animals are being adapted for life under water by artificially arresting the development of lungs in fetuses. When fully grown, these beings will have working gills. The machine has further predicted that Dr. Katsumi will not be able to comprehend that the future is only grotesque when seen through the eyes of the present and will seem perfectly normal to those destined to inhabit it — and will no doubt take steps to prevent it from developing. Hence he is to be removed from his position.

Tanomogi and his associates have known of the organization's plan to expel Dr. Katsumi. Therefore, they have created a construct of their boss in the forecasting machine, exactly as Dr. Katsumi reproduced the murder victim. The only difference between it and the physically real Dr. Katsumi is its total knowledge of his own future, in order to see what steps could be taken. The murder, actually carried out by Tanomogi after all, the poisoning of the girl, and Mrs. Katsumi's abortion were all in line with a program established by Katsumi's omnipotent computer self to prevent his expulsion. The events were intended to drive him into a corner, force him into accepting the aquan model of the future, and prevent him from attempting to destroy it. He has indeed been on trial, for a crime he has not yet committed. However, if left to his own course of action, he surely will commit the crime — a crime against the future. He has been given the chance to find premises which might change his own "resolution," but he has failed. The forecasting machine has predicted that Katsumi will be killed to protect the aquan project. In the form of his electronically constructed self, he has hired a professional murderer for that purpose.

Dr. Katsumi has only been able to envisage the future as a continuation of the present and has tried to use the forecasting machine, not to create the future, but to preserve the present. "A crime against the future is different from one against the past or the present," warns Tanomogi. "It is fundamental and definitive."

Dr. Katsumi has even planned to kill his own aquan son created from the fetus aborted by his wife. He explains the act to himself as a humanitarian one, intended to save his son from a life as a deformed slave. At the same time he is being judged guilty of these intentions, he is being found guilty of the death of the man killed by Tanomogi, inasmuch as the murder was ordered by Katsumi's construct. In a final permutation, he is being found guilty of having created the forecaster when he did not really believe in it; he is guilty of not believing in the future.

In the final analysis, the conflict is one between Dr. Katsumi and his alternate self, or, through a final extrapolation, between man uncertain about his destiny and man if he were to know his destiny. It is the conflict between us as we are and us as we become. Quite naturally, Dr. Katsumi cannot bear the realization that he is his own assassin.

Abé is a writer of abstractions, an author who consistently creates a set of symbols arranged to pose a single, ultimately unanswerable question. In *Inter Ice Age 4* there is no possibility of a final statement. Is the future good or bad? Are attempts to resist it commendable or inexcusable? Both questions are irrelevant. Regardless of moral judgments, the future will come, and efforts to resist it will come to naught. Moreover, once the future has become the present it will possess its own logic and its own context, outmoding whatever was thought about it in the past. Value judgments, Abé is saying, can only be made in retrospect. As he says at the end of the novel, the parent is always judged by the child on the basis of the outcome, not the good intentions.

This line of thought does not say that the end justifies the means, but that the end erases all that has come before. The artifice of the forecasting machine, revealing to the present what the end will be, does not justify the means. It merely strips them of their moral fabric. One can still react with horror or outrage while they are in process, but the forecaster makes possible a bizarre double vision, where one can see that the process is destined to be rendered into a sanitized, sterile abstraction even while it is still underway. The forecaster has nothing to do with determinism; it is a window, not to the future, but to another present. For those people who must live in the present, whenever it might be, there is only one thing that is true about the future. It is cruel.

Abé's literature is a literature of paradox, and to this end he has developed a distinct style that relies heavily on the unexpected and the exposure of the bizarre that lurks in the everyday. In the postscript to *Inter Ice Age 4*, Abé writes that the most frightening thing in the world is to find the abnormal in that which is closest to us. While this principle appears most dramatically in Dr. Katsumi's discovery that the conspiracy which is frustrating his every move has actually been hatched by those who help him and is in fact headed by himself, the equally intriguing process of moving the abnormal back into the everyday is evident in a host of small details. Dr. Katsumi's casual encounter with the professional killer his alternate self has hired to watch over him eventually ends with him treating the man to a bowl of noodles.

In the undersea laboratory where the aquans are created, Katsumi intends to grapple with his opponents head on, but instead he is reduced to good-natured compliments when his hosts offer him milk from an aquatic cow. "Perhaps it was because they took such care with the fodder," muses Katsumi, "but I felt it tasted better than the milk we drank at home." Swallowing the milk, he swallows with it the outrageous image of a cow swimming about in the ocean.

However, one place where the usually meticulous Abé fails is in his use of science. If his explanations had been allowed to pass with just a casual nod, there would have been no problems. Instead, Abé chooses to dwell on how the aquans are created, or to try to explain why the seas are rising. The more he labors to make things sound authentic, the more he alienates his readers. After all is said and done, the seawater is explained as being "created somehow." While Abé patently has no intention of using science as anything more than a way of setting the stage for his philosophical dilemma, it nonetheless puts an unnecessary strain on the novel's credibility.

This is unfortunate, for *Inter Ice Age 4* stands almost alone in Japanese science fiction — and in very select company in world science fiction — as a book that has something to say about a philosophical problem of great complexity. Moreover, Abé is a first-rate literary technician. It is regrettable that he left such obvious blemishes in what is otherwise a superior work.

David Lewis

Sources for Further Study

Reviews:

Analog. LXXXVII, July, 1971, p. 164.

Atlantic. CCXXVI, October, 1970, p. 150.

Best Sellers. XXX, November, 15, 1970, p. 334.

Booklist. LXVII, November, 1, 1970, p. 214.

Kirkus Reviews. XXXVIII, July 15, 1970, p. 759.

Library Journal. XCV, July, 1970, p. 2512.

Life. LXIX, October 23, 1970, p. 16.

New York Times Book Review. September 29, 1970, p. 41.

Publisher's Weekly. CXCVIII, July 6, 1970, p. 55.

Saturday Review. LIII, September 26, 1970, p. 37.

INVERTED WORLD

Author: Christopher Priest (1943-   )
First book publication: 1974
Type of work: Novel
Time: The late twenty-second century
Locale: The city of Earth/Portugal

The story of the inhabitants of a city traversing a hyperbolic world, trying to main-tain themselves at the point where conditions are identical to those on planet Earth

> *Principal characters:*
> HELWARD MANN, a member of the guild of Future Surveyors
> VICTORIA LERROUEX, his sometime wife
> GELMAN JASE, a member of the Traction guild
> ELIZABETH KHAN, a woman from planet Earth

The central notion used in *Inverted World* was first developed in a novelette published in *New Writings in SF 22* (1973), but the novel is not an extension of the shorter piece.

After a brief prologue which introduces the character Elizabeth Khan (but does not reveal anything significant about her) the narrative of *Inverted World* tells the story of Helward Mann. Parts one and three of this narrative are recounted in the first person, while parts two and four consist of third-person narrative. These shifts are not mere idiosyncrasies, but serve to emphasize the point that the relationship between Helward's subjective experience and an objective description of what happens to him is not simply to be taken for granted.

Helward begins his story by explaining that having reached the age of six hundred and fifty miles it is time for his initiation into the guilds which control the division of labor and political administration of his society. He is made to swear an oath to the effect that he will reveal nothing of what he learns as a guildsman to any other inhabitant of city Earth, where he lives. Many citizens live out their whole lives without ever going outside the city or seeing the sun; only the guildsmen are permitted knowledge of the circumstances in which the city exists. All that Helward has learned in school concerns a world named planet Earth, and, on going outside, he is surprised to learn that the world of city Earth is disturbingly different from planet Earth — in particular, city Earth's sun is not a sphere but a disc with two spires of light extending from its poles.

Helward learns that the city has to be continually moved in pursuit of a geographical point called the optimum, whose distance from the city is per-petually changing. The optimum seems to be moving away from the city in a direction conventionally called north at the rate of a mile every ten days (though Helward is later told that the optimum remains still while the terrain moves away from it toward the south). In order to move the city, tracks are laid before it. As it passes over them the rearmost sections are taken up and relaid in its path. One guild is responsible for the track-laying, another for the engines which provide traction. Other guilds include the Bridge-Builders and the Future Surveyors. Helward is a member of the last-named guild, responsible for mapping the terrain ahead of the city and finding a passable course for it to follow. At the top of the city hierarchy are the Navigators.

Before Helward can take up his chosen vocation he must serve his apprenticeship by helping out where labor is most needed, and must also serve a period of basic training with the city's militia. Much of the early part of the story is taken up with his assignment to a track-laying gang, supervising workers hired from villages near to the city's route.

The city's relations with the inhabitants of the land through which it passes are somewhat strained. Apart from itinerant labor, the city has to "hire" women to bear children, because births within the city are mostly male. The Barter guild handles the delicate negotiations with outsiders, but at the time of the story it is having to rely heavily on the militia to counter hostility and aggression on the part of the indigenes.

Early in his apprenticeship Helward marries Victoria Lerrouex, the daughter of a Bridge-Builder. The marriage is arranged, but both he and Victoria are content with the arrangement despite the fact that Victoria harbors subversive opinions about the city's government which cause Helward some anxiety. The one thing which neither of them can understand is why the city has to keep moving.

Helward discovers the answer to this question when, in part two of the novel, he is instructed to escort a group of Bartered women back to their homes in "the past." As he takes them further and further south, bizarre changes begin to overtake both them and the land through which they are traveling. Everything except Helward and other things belonging permanently to the city begins to get longer in an east-west direction and shorter in a north-south direction. Once observed, this process accelerates, and Helward finds himself subjected to a southward pull which builds in intensity so quickly that he literally has to cling on to a grossly distorted mountain range in order to haul himself slowly northward. Eventually, he escapes the pull and treks northward. On the way back he meets fellow-apprentice Gelman Jase, who tells him that the city has been under attack. Time has been somehow distorted, for Helward and Jase are no longer the same age, and when Helward returns to the city he discovers that a lapse of time which has been for him only a few "miles" has been for the city a much more considerable period. Victoria has borne him a son, but the child has been killed in the attack and Victoria, thinking him lost in the south, has had their marriage annulled in order to remarry.

When Helward goes into the "future" of the city to take up his allotted role, he finds that the reverse situation holds there — that time passes more rapidly for him than for the city. He discovers that the world is hyperbolic, the terrain following asymptotic curves to north and south of the optimum, so that in the north its geography is contorted into a tall spire becoming infinitely thin, while in the south it becomes an infinite expanse. The sun is also a hyperbola, its central disc infinite in extent, though only part of it can be seen owing to the fact that the sun (like the world) is rotating on its axis, so that at some point its finite angular velocity becomes a tangential velocity greater than the velocity of light. After learning this, Helward reads "Destaine's Directive" — a journal telling of the early history of the city (two hundred years before) — but is still no wiser relative to the enigma of where the city is and how it got there.

In the fourth part of the story, the city is plagued with new troubles. The Future Surveyors find a river so broad that they cannot see its opposite shore, which seems to pose the Bridge-Builders an impossible challenge. This lends encouragement to the Terminators, a group of city-bound individuals who want to stop the city, and who refuse to believe the guildsmen's protests that to do so would mean disaster. In the midst of this crisis Helward meets Elizabeth Khan, an English nurse helping the inhabitants of a small village nearby. She realizes that there is a terrible discrepancy between her perception of the world and his, and enters the city with a group of Bartered women. She disappears for a while, but returns when the Terminators make their bid for power to tell the inhabitants of the city that they are in Portugal, traversing planet Earth in a southwesterly direction, and that the river which they face is the Atlantic Ocean.

Elizabeth explains that the whole world has undergone a Crash, which sent most of mankind back to subsistence farming. England and other developed nations are recovering, thanks to a new power source first devised by Francis Destaine. The city Earth is the result of an early attempt by Destaine to establish a power source by setting up a generating apparatus in phase with a natural force-field traversing the Earth's surface. The city Earth has that power source, but living within the force-field has affected the inhabitants of the city so that their perception of the world has been drastically altered — they now experience the world (falsely, she alleges) as a geographical hyperbola.

Helward cannot accept this analysis of the situation. He protests that his experience of the world — including the differential aging of himself and other city-dwellers — *cannot* be simply a matter of distorted perception. It cannot be that when Elizabeth sees the sun as a sphere and he sees it as a hyperbola he is simply making a perceptual error. For he and the city the world is *objectively* hyperbolic. The reader, who has witnessed his strange adventure in the past through the medium of third-person narrative, is inclined to agree.

The problem that this leaves Helward — and city Earth — is that there is no escape for the city. The optimum will move slowly out into the Atlantic, and the city will move south into the expanding terrain, ultimately to be destroyed by the terrible southward pull of centrifugal force.

Inverted World was not the first science fiction story to deal with distortions in time; the time dilatation effect connected with traveling close to the speed of light has been featured in numerous novels, and in "Traveller's Rest," David I. Masson imagined a world where elapsed time varied with latitude. Priest's hyperbolic world, however, takes the idea much further and makes its consequences explicit and more elaborate. There are some aspects of the society of city Earth which seem to be designed for auctorial convenience rather than for any rational purpose — particularly the code of secrecy which causes Helward to discover the truth piece by piece — but when an author is working with such a bold central notion, this can be forgiven. Everything in the book is really subservient to the crucial idea, and the reason for completely reworking the plot of the initial novelette was to find a better vehicle for it.

In the *New Writings* version, the city Earth is not moving across the surface of a post-Crash Europe, but rather through a parallel world which is a hyperbolic "analogue" of Earth. Thus, in the short version, the geographical dissimilarity is definitely *real* and not merely apparent. In the book version this becomes highly ambiguous, and there is really no way at all to arbitrate between Elizabeth Khan's account of what is happening and Helward's insistence that more than perceptual distortion is involved.

In an afterword, Priest offers a wry acknowledgement to Virginia Kidd, "who finally convinced me I might be on to something when she told me the physics had a hole so large a city could be driven through." The main issue raised by the novel, however, concerns not physics, but a more fundamental philosophical problem: the question of the extent to which our perceptions of the world correspond to what is "really" there. In Kantian terminology, it is the problem of the relationship between phenomena and noumena. There is no way that Helward's experiences can be reduced to illusion, and they are clearly incompatible with Elizabeth Khan's experience of the world; the inference which must be taken from this is that Priest is working within a hyper-Kantian idealist philosophy in which the question of the *ding an sich* cannot arise at all. On this basis, physics ceases to have any relevance, making *Inverted World* a science fiction story which eliminates the epistemological foundations of scientific knowledge — a subversion that would be an impressive flourish if one could actually be sure that it was intentional.

In fact, Priest does not seem to be aware of the philosophical implications of his work — at least, he is content to ignore them and to be content with the trap of ambiguity which he has created for his characters. This is perhaps the one thing which prevents *Inverted World* from being a highly satisfactory novel of ideas.

Brian Stableford

Sources for Further Study

Reviews:

Booklist. LXXI, October 15, 1974, p. 239.
Kirkus Reviews. XLII, May 1, 1974, p. 507.
Library Journal. XCIX, August, 1974, p. 1990.
Listener. XCI, June 13, 1974, p. 777.
Observer. August 18, 1974, p. 28.
Publisher's Weekly. CCV, April 29, 1974, p. 43.

THE INVINCIBLE
(NIEZWYCIEZONY)

Author: Stanislaw Lem (1921-   )
First book publication: 1964
English translation: 1973
Type of work: Novel
Time: An indefinite future
Locale: Regis III, "desert planet of type subdelta 92" in the Lyre Constellation

A parable whose subject is man's encounter with nonorganic alien forms, products of a possible evolution of machines or cybernetic entities

> Principal characters:
> ROHAN, second in command aboard the *Invincible*
> HORPACH, astrogator/commander

Stanislaw Lem's *The Invincible* clearly fits one of the basic thematic paradigms of science fiction — the encounter with the alien. To understand the uniqueness of this work, however, it must be measured against its tradition. Lem's title itself is an ironic gesture toward the classic tale of conquest. This form is far more subtle and pervasive that the crude Heinleinian assault on the puppet masters of Titan. Science fiction is full of strategies whereby the alien is ultimately preempted or absorbed by man.

In Stanley Weinbaum's early "A Martian Odyssey," for example, the protagonist Jarvis sees Mars as thoroughly alien: "no rhyme or reason to the whole thing." Yet the whole thrust of his adventure is domestication. In saving the birdlike Tweel, Jarvis awakens a suspiciously human loyalty in the creature: the familiar tale of Crusoe and Friday begins anew. As backdrop Weinbaum invents weirder beings along the way, such as "silicon life," in order to push Tweel and man's Martian adventures closer to us. Ultimately, Jarvis comes away from the senseless activity of the "barrel-creatures" with something that makes very good sense to men — a cure for all Earthly disease.

In far more sophisticated fashion this same domesticating activity is visible in as recent a work as Asimov's *The Gods Themselves*. Difficulties at first seem much greater: not only are these aliens uncontactible in their "para-universe," but they appear isolated in a purely formal sense as well, sealed off hermetically in their own section of the novel. Yet as the dynamics of both cosmos and story become clear, we discover just how homocentric the whole process really is. These aliens are bound up in larger, man-centered rhythms, and must solve the crisis in our universe as a necessary condition that theirs may survive. What is more, to survive as beings, these aliens may even have to take human form. If their race culminates in the sterile triad that is Estwald, the analagous trio on our Moon proves to be creatively fertile, generator of a solution that reorders universes around man.

Stanislaw Lem's alien, in contrast, is not merely an extension of our aggressive or expansive desires. Nor is it the opposite, some nightmare "evil" that invariably defeats man, or a hostile presence forever impermeable to human reason. In fact, for man finally to see the alien (as he does in *The Invincible*) as something that is simply *other*, of no use to him and ultimately irreducible to human patterns, he must at least partially understand it. More, he must come to understand himself. Lem avoids this polarity of conquest or defeat by neatly shifting his emphasis. *The Invincible* is less about the nature of aliens than about the nature of man himself. In Lem's novel, the alien is that thing against which man can and must measure his limits. Rather than an extreme state — master of universes or cosmic fool — human existence here has become once again a mean.

This shift in focus becomes clearer if we examine the nature and procedure of Lem's alien encounter. To do so, a comparison with two even more recent novels about alien worlds — Larry Niven's *Ringworld* (1970) and Arthur C. Clarke's *Rendezvous with Rama* (1973) — will be helpful. In a procedural sense, the approach to the alien in *Ringworld* is the exact opposite of Lem's. At once, in the opening pages, something that signals itself as "alien" is thrust upon us: a three-legged creature, with two heads that are really hands and a hump that is really a head, bursts through a "transfer booth" into a birthday party; he is followed by a vaguely feline being whose fur is orange and who walks upright. It is with relief almost that we notice, as the plot thickens, the disparity between these aliens' incredible powers and their obviously derivative forms; they are a hodge-podge not only of animal spare parts but of the humanized beasts of conventional fable.

Paradoxically, the most truly alien being in the story is the result of natural law: as a "flatlander," Louis Wu is "neither Caucasian nor Mongoloid nor Negroid . . . a uniform blend which must have taken centuries." However, before this sort of alien can function in the ensuing space-opera adventure, it apparently must be "defused," and clothed in the garb of more amenable human fantasies. Thus, if from a distance Louis Wu looks oriental, "close up it was all a fraud. His skin was . . . a smooth chrome yellow, the color of a comic-book Fu Manchu." Likewise the puppeteers answer to names like Nessus and Chiron, and the kzin postures like a cross between Dorothy's Lion-Man and the Pink Panther. Thus, the very idea of otherness in each of these figures is neatly reduced to controllable, man-made patterns. By thus identifying himself as a creation of man's mythic imagination, each dissociates himself from the unfamiliar, be it the random entropic flattening of natural selection (a sort of time-vectored "alien" within), or the sudden contiguity of inexplicable beings intruding from without. Niven's novel of alien contact is in reality an elaborate denial of the alien.

In Lem's novel, quite simply, things flow in the opposite direction. Here we have a gradual falling away of comfortable and confident patterns — the "third step routine," the probing and measuring of the new planet — which exposes mystery, the irreducibly alien. Nor can these discoveries be "defused," incorporated by human fantasy or reason. The fantasy responses are clearly inadequate: Rohan's vision of a "hidden civilization at the bottom of the sea" is swept aside as "nonsense," the metal structures discovered are obviously no "city," the account of human migrations from the Lyre Constellations is labeled at once as a "fairy tale." Indeed, stranger than fiction at each of these turns is fact itself: the structures are neither dwellings nor computers as we know them, but "undefinable formations"; the presence of fish in the ocean points to an inconceivably broken evolutionary pattern; finally Lauda posits a migration and evolution, not of men from Lyre but of machines.

The unfolding mystery of this "ordinary" planet can neither be circumscribed by fantasy nor conquered by the rule and line of empirical science. The men of the *Invincible* do develop plausible explanations for what is happening here, and they even possess the technology to annihilate this world if they wish. And yet they are stymied, not so much because they cannot know but because they fear to know. Before the truly alien, this organized entity that bears no meaningful relation to us and yet exists, man has two choices: accept it, or fall back on his ultimate fantasy of human supremacy.

A further subtlety in Lem's use of the alien is that its existence neither reaffirms man's laws, nor totally suspends them. In Niven's novel, quite surprisingly, investigation of the incredible Ringworld becomes the way in which man reconfirms those laws of his own universe he thought forever abrogated by its alien existence. Niven seems to plunge us into the unknown: beyond the animal aliens there is a further strangeness — Ringworld. Yet when the crew finally arrives there, it is to discover that men built it — we, at a different stage of development, are the aliens.

Nor do surprises end here. The Ring civilization is apparently a closed system that has destroyed itself. As the complex cosmic gearwork of this novel is laid bare, we see man not only perpetuating himself but growing more powerful in the process. If Earth itself (as is hinted) is the product of some Ring-initiated "terraforming experiment," then the quest of Louis Wu represents an infusion of new human life into an old human world at just the right moment: space is tight on Earth, but here there is room to grow. A *telos* most amenable to man — all is for the best in the best of all possible worlds — seems at work in this cosmos. In seeking to control men, the puppeteers have not altered this dynamic of self-rejuvenation, but rather abetted it. Their genetic manipulation of men does no more than produce the "luck" of the appropriately named Teela Brown. Had this in turn not led to the circuitous adventures on Ringworld, Louis would never have been able to prove man's superiority by solving the riddle of the "Fist-of-God." Without this "luck" Teela would not have met Seeker, and their quest would not have drawn Louis back (with the alien kzin in tow) to rekindle this dying human civilization. The whole plot is an elaborate Panglossian fantasy with a moral: aliens beware — "tell them the universe is too complicated a toy for a sensibly cautious being to play with." Indeed, it runs by laws only man can know.

Encounter with the alien produces just the opposite result in Clarke's *Rendezvous with Rama*. This time it is man who foolishly tampers with forces he can never understand. He is absurdly helpless before the mystery of the alien "ship." This time his fantasies do not "defuse" the alien so much as bounce off it. As man seeks entry into the Raman "buildings," he simultaneously takes refuge in his ridiculous dreams: "Joe Calvert had always enjoyed those old bank-robbery movies." Beginning its acceleration, Rama literally throws off all our physical laws: "There were no jets of gas, no beams of ions or plasma. . . . No one put it better than Sergeant Professor Myron. . . . 'There goes Newton's Third Law.'" In its final sweep around the sun the vessel escapes from human categories altogether: "No solid material could withstand the temperature of such an approach." The final invocation — Rama as a "phoenix" rising from its flames — is the most futile of afterthoughts, man blindly reaching for the ungraspable.

If Lem's alien is neither the mirror of man nor the guarantor of his laws, it is not the product of some totally unknowable physical system either. Ironically — and this is perhaps Lem's most striking twist — the "cloud" seems to derive from the same natural laws as man himself: those of evolution. Lauda's hypothesis involves a slight, if psychologically intolerable, displacement: natural selection working in a "necrosphere" on machines rather than organic beings. The real problem to the reader is not understanding causes — the explanation is highly plausible — but accepting effects. These latter do not crowd the limits of man's reason or will so much as those of his capacity to tolerate.

The word "tolerance" evokes an eighteenth century vision of things. Indeed, Darko Suvin sees in Lem a strong Swiftian strain. In treating man before the alien however, it is Clarke who would seem more the inheritor of Swift. In spite of its bland surface, *Rendezvous with Rama* is a harshly satirical work. Faced with the beauties of the alien structures, man's gropings are barely those of an animal. "It was the same impulse . . . that would prompt a monkey to grab the reflection of a banana in a mirror." If Lem's view of man in *The Invincible* does betray Enlightenment origins, it leans away from Swiftian excess toward the more neutral proportionality of Voltaire's formula in his answer to Pascal in the 25th *Lettre philosophique:* "Man seems to be in his rightful place in nature, superior to animals, whom he resembles through his sense organs, inferior to other beings, whom he probably resembles through his ability to think. . . ."

Lem may substitute terms — the "animals" have become robots, the "other being" an alien cloud — but this strict sense of proportion remains. In regard to nature, man is neither, as he may think, isolated nor unconquerable, but actually firmly situated in the relational fabric of things. Thus the black cloud may not "think as we conceive it; and yet, ironically, its mode of functioning turns out to be quite analogous to man's. If the "flies form agglutinative patterns to meet various threats and survive, the fate of the *Condor* proves that man must do so also. Lem's ships are primarily communities. *The Invincible* is not a story of individuals but of specialists, men whose names are barely more important than their job titles.

What destroyed the *Condor* was less amnesia than mass autism; as men lost contact with each other, a destructive atomizing of the social order took place. With their "acoustics memory banks" empty, these men literally became blank sheets. Scientists on the *Invincible* learn that, for their own afflicted, the only cure is "re-education," slow reintegration into the communal whole. This normative vision is even more obvious in the case of the "hero," Rohan. His often disdainful aloofness toward his fellows is less the germ of Laputan satire than an anomaly to be corrected. The opposite of a heroic quest, his final trek into the wilderness is a return to acceptance of his place in the community of men. Before he was unwilling to accept authority; now, in spite of Horpach's pathetic trickery, he assumes it willingly.

Ironically, these new limits give positive direction to what before was formless: "They're figuring out various ways to annihilate the cloud, but it isn't our task to destroy the cloud. We should rather concentrate on searching for the men." When he does find the men, one is decomposed, the other headless. But if he cannot retrieve individual wholes, what he does bring back is significant: for Regnar, the scientist's initials cut off his sample case. As Rohan's foray becomes just a job, he does the best he can; to him man's strivings seem necessarily incomplete, since he never finds the fourth man. His only prize turns out to be this skeleton of a name embossed on a tool of his profession. Yet because of it, if man has not conquered all, he has not lost everything either. Some balance remains.

In a further, wider sense, Rohan's adventure serves to replace man in general at a point of normative balance. One of the major ironies of *The Invincible* is that man from the outset is not only not in his rightful place in nature, but he is no place. The opening scene describes an "alien encounter" from which man is entirely absent: a dormant ship touches down on a metallic plant, metal to metal, the raping blast of one offset by the yielding sands of the other. Later, man only goes forth encased in his machines — yet in "protecting" him, they actually encapsulate and restrict him. Significantly, man's "great battle" is fought entirely by a machine-monster, the Cyclops: man is reduced first to the role of helpless observer, later to the futile role of destroyer of his own creation. Man does not really confront "nature" until Rohan goes forth alone and unaided. Yet it is also significant that, if he is unadorned, he is not entirely naked. The pendulum does not swing to the exact opposite, the primitivist solution in which man-in-the-machine gives way to man stripped of all his machines. Rohan is carried to and fro by vehicles; moreover, he wears an electric headpiece that in effect "saves" him. The human condition, as it unfolds for Rohan, proves not to be an either/or situation, but a median state: man stands between his machines and the alien.

This balance is illustrated in the ravine by two mirroring encounters, one with a man-made robot, the other with the "cloud." If Voltaire's categories of "inferior" and "superior" seem to fall away as Rohan sees reflected back in each his own human image, yet at the same time these meetings set in motion a chain of reversals which subtly reestablish ties and restore a natural order with man again in the middle. Rohan comes across what he thinks is a man wandering in the wilderness, and is startled to discover a machine made in man's image: "It was no human being, but a robot!" This initial shock leads to worse blows, yet we soon realize (as with Candide) that his path of alienation is the necessary one to lead a proud man back to his proper place in the order of things. Rohan tries to control the robot but cannot: "The automaton jerked its arm away with an indifferent sweeping movement, and continued on its way."

More unsettling yet, the machine's unresponsiveness leads to evidence of earlier, senseless battles between these robots and equally zombielike men: "According to the radioactivity readings, the Arctane had been wrecked by the charge of a Weyr gun." This negative mirror relationship between man and machine is in turn mirrored by the dawning of positive affinities, a sense of common frailty, and horror at the Sisyphean fate of both. Out of this comes a moment of compassion for the machine, this time not as an extension of man but in and for itself: "He found it difficult simply to leave the helpless machine to its fate." He cannot, of course, do otherwise — the thing goes its own way and remains "other." Yet a real tie is reestablished here, not one of dominance or destruction, but of feeling for the other, Voltaire's link "downward" through the sense organ of the heart.

Ties of a more cerebral order are forged in Rohan's meeting with the "cloud." This encounter itself is twofold, a mirror within a mirror. In the first, as the black vortex brushes over his inert and prostrate form, Rohan can assert his "humanity" only by abandoning it totally. Like a parody of the thinking reed, Rohan has yielded absolutely to the "cloud," yet believes he has outwitted it. In the second meeting, however, in the dark configurations "he perceived a gigantic human figure whose head projected into the darkness." This, he suddenly realizes, is his own image, indifferently reflected by the changing cloud formations as they go about their inscrutable business oblivious to man. The acceptance he is forced to embrace is of a different order, less moral than aesthetic. Instead of responsibility toward the other, he can now (abdicating all desire to outwit or control) accept detachment, pure pleasurable contemplation. At first ready to believe he is witnessing a "battle" between these particles, he later yields to this "higher" alien with a completely open mind in which a sense of beauty has replaced reason: "He simply felt an urge to participate in this murky mystery, whose significance, he was quite sure, would forever remain beyond his understanding." In Rohan, man has regained the Voltairean norm.

If Lem's treatment of the alien seems unique in terms of the various models available within the sphere of modern science fiction, that uniqueness is actually achieved by a return to one of the traditional sources of science fiction — the *conte philosophique*. Not only is *The Invincible* openly representative fiction, but its reductive dynamics are very much those of a tale like Voltaire's *Candide*. Human invincibility is another Leibnizian illusion. Lem's invaders deploy all the arms of science (the experts) and technology (the destructive machines) to no avail. Man's belief that he can know and control the course of events is thwarted: in the end, the commander Horpach stands a trembling scarecrow in his "snow white dress overcoat." What is more, out of these repeated failures, a reduced and chastened community, very much like Candide's famous garden, emerges. And Rohan's final adventure, in which he goes alone, harried by the physical limits of terrain and oxygen supply, abdicating that proud reason that made man "master" of the universe, seems almost an extended illustration of Martin's dictum: "travaillons sans raisonner."

Finally, if Rohan's experience is religious, it is so in a Voltairean sense — the detached yet rapturous contemplation of a cold, perfect machine that forever eludes and excludes man: "He felt so superfluous in this realm of perfected death, where only dead forms could emerge victoriously in order to enact mysterious rites never to be witnessed by any living creature." In Lem's work, man confronts the alien not to prove (in the Pascalian sense) that man himself is the most incomprehensible mystery among the mysteries of the universe, but that he remains its norm. He must return from his brush with the alien a prophet of wise ignorance: "Now his desire was no longer merely to return and report . . . but to request that this planet be left alone in the future."

George Slusser

Sources for Further Study

Reviews:

Books and Bookmen. XIX, October, 1973, p. 138.

Chicago Daily News. Panorama. December 1-2, 1973, p. 10.

Galaxy. XXXIV, November, 1973, p. 84.

Magazine of Fantasy and Science Fiction. XLVII, July, 1974, p. 44.

New York Times Book Review. September 23, 1973, p. 39.

Renaissance. V, Summer, 1973, p. 8.

THE INVISIBLE MAN

Author: H. G. Wells (1866-1946)
First book publication: 1897
Type of work: Novel
Time: The late nineteenth century
Locale: Rural Sussex, England

After inventing a process that makes him invisible, a young medical student is destroyed when he attempts to use it for his own selfish advantage

Principal characters:
GRIFFIN, the invisible man
MR. AND MRS. HALL, keepers of the Coach and Horses
DR. KEMP, Griffin's former fellow student
MR. THOMAS MARVEL, a tramp with visions of power

The Invisible Man is one of the half-dozen great "scientific romances" Wells wrote in the years from 1895 to 1901. With these novels and a few dozen brilliant short stories, he not only fixed the shape of modern science fiction but also invented a good many plot ideas still in frequent use. Improving on Defoe's old trick of mixing fact and fiction, he stated and followed a new rule that each such story should develop only one novel or extraordinary assumption, with everything else kept as familiar and logical as possible.

The distinction between science fiction and fantasy — or between science fiction and other sorts of fantasy — lies here. If this new basic premise is a careful extrapolation from accepted scientific theory, the result is hard science fiction. If it is something impossible, to be accepted only in the different world of the story, the result is pure fantasy.

The Invisible Man lies on the borderland between the two. Though invisibility is a fairy-tale device, as far from actuality as seven-league boots, Wells give us an ingenious and reasonably plausible scientific explanation for it. His protagonist learns how to neutralize the color of blood to make flesh transparent and then to lower its refractive index to that of air. Despite this air of science, however, the purist must call the book a fantasy because Wells chose to ignore the awkward fact that his invisible man would have found himself blind — a completely transparent eyeball would be as useless as a glass camera. This twist of events would have given him an effective short story, as he told Arnold Bennett, but not a novel.

Like most of Wells's early work, the book may be read as sardonic criticism of the idea that scientific progress can make a better world. As a child, Wells had "devoured" *Gulliver's Travels*, and most of his early fiction seems to have been written with a Swiftian intention: to satirize man's faith in science and his pride in the power of human reason. A biologist before becoming a novelist, Wells had learned to look at mankind with a scientific objectivity, seeing us as only one more animal species, perhaps evolving toward some higher form but also in danger of extinction. The human brain, in this view, is no magical source of goodness and truth, but merely another adaptation for survival, like a longer fang or a stronger claw. Though in later years he did become the great spokesman of his age for the culture of science and a world-known champion of social reform, Wells was always more the biological realist than the unquenchable optimist. Seeing our civilization in danger because of our own animal inheritance, he spent most of his later life trying to warn us and guide our escape.

This book is a classic study of the tug-of-war we all experience between the animal drives of our evolutionary past and the conflicting demands of our social future. Through many million years of physical evolution, self-preservation was the way to survival. In our more recent cultural evolution, this old heritage of selfish egoism is often at odds with the altruism required by the good of the group. This universal conflict is the stuff of most literature. Fiction commonly functions like family, school, and church, to socialize us, to lead us into the ways of our folk and teach us acceptable behavior. Now and then, of course, an Ibsen takes the other tack, defending the individual against the crushing compulsions of the group — as Wells himself does in his fine later short story, "The Country of the Blind."

Griffin, the invisible man, is pure self, and his fate fits the simple pattern of classic tragedy. Though potentially admirable for sheer power of mind, his character is flawed by the primitive lust for private freedom and power. In that selfish pursuit, he abandons his medical studies, loses a girl he has known, and causes the death and disgrace of his father. He possesses the secret which alienates him from his social world, causes those he needs to betray him, and finally destroys him.

This tragic skeleton, however, is clothed in social comedy. The effects of tragedy depend on a sympathetic identification, and Wells allows us little opportunity to pity his antihero. We first see, or rather fail to see, Griffin from the viewpoints of the simple Sussex people who are astonished and then angered by his attempts to impose his power on them. Skillfully mixing the known and the new, Wells uses these prosaic folk and their familiar village setting to make Griffin's invisibility believable. There are Mr. and Mrs. Hall, keepers of the inn, where he arrives as a very peculiar guest. There are the ignorant vicar and the bumbling doctor. There is Mr. Thomas Marvel, who becomes for a time Griffin's unwilling servant and later his baffled heir. All are comic individualists, but all at last unite in their defense of the society Griffin tries to terrorize.

It is only later in the novel that he tells Kemp, a fellow scientist, how he came upon the secret. Imprisoned in poverty, he saw invisibility as a way to power. The discovery took years of effort, took the money he stole from his father, and cost all his concern for anyone else. After perfecting the process, he tried it first on a bit of woolen cloth, then on a cat, and finally on himself. Invisible at last, he set fire to his rented room to conceal his trail and set out to prey on mankind. He soon discovers that to remain invisible he must go naked in the severe British climate, because his presence is betrayed by any object he tries to carry. He is also surprised to learn that people are not as easily terrified as he had expected. It is not long before his dreams of power collapse. Wells has stacked the cards against him, in fact, since he clearly could have provided himself with invisible clothing.

At the inn, wrapped and bandaged in a visible disguise, he searches for a way to reverse his transformation. Then his stolen funds and his limited patience run out. With the villagers aroused against him, he strips off the disguise to make war on society, declaring a "Reign of Terror," which he fails to incite. Thomas Marvel escapes with his laboratory notes and the money he has stolen. Kemp listens to his story but sets a police trap for him. Griffin escapes from the trap, but in an attempt to get even, he is caught and killed. In the novel's most memorable scene, he slowly becomes visible again after his death.

In a comic epilogue, we return to Marvel, who has used his chance windfall to set up an inn of his own called The Invisible Man, where he spends his idle time gloating over the notes he cannot read and dreaming his own wistful dreams of the subtle secret of invisibility.

The Invisible Man is a strong, unforgettable novel. If it has been less popular than *The Time Machine* and *The War of the Worlds*, the reason may lie in the lack of likable characters. Though Griffin's story has its appeal to the rogue in each of us, we are never allowed to identify with him. The other characters are ready enough to combine against him, but each one is another petty egoist, meaner than he is.

A few critics have judged Wells awkward in his use of viewpoint and management of plot, but the choices he made seem vital to the effect and theme of the novel. Telling the whole story from Griffin's viewpoint would not only have sacrificed the initial mystery and suspense, but, winning pity for him, would have turned all the comedy of character to tragedy. The main theme, stated with a ruthless clarity, is that the lawless animal ego remains a powerful destructive and self-destructive force, even in the most accomplished scientist.

Though any effort to trace autobiographical elements in such a fantasy are hazardous, the writing of this novel must have been a major step in Wells's own mental evolution. Griffin, as a character, must stand for the romantic egoist in Wells himself; Griffin's tragic fall must reflect Wells's own acceptance of the classic view that the primitive evil in the individual requires social restraint. Such themes must have been significant to Wells, because he returned to them in several later works, often with more sympathy for the rebel self and less regard for the claims of society. His most mature and appealing treatment of the theme is perhaps "The Country of the Blind," first published in 1904.

This short story may well have been suggested by *The Invisible Man*, even though it inverts many of the novel's attitudes and values. In the novel, Griffin feels like a seeing man who is soundlessly prowling a city of the blind. He also takes flight from a blind man, afraid of his subtle intuitions.

Nuñez, the short story's egoistic hero, actually falls into a remote Andean valley inhabited by a blind tribe. With something of Griffin's tragic madness, he recalls an old proverb, "In the Country of the Blind the One-eyed Man is King." The blind folk, however, refuse to be ruled. Comfortable conservatives secure in their smug little society, they remain skeptical of all Nuñez claims to see.

The story thus becomes another and more revealing parable of science and progress. Nuñez is the symbol of knowledge and change, the creative individual at odds with the traditional past. Their blindness symbolic, the tribesmen reject his talk of a world outside and a sky overhead as blasphemy against their religion of the cave. Since his eyes seem the cause of this madness, they propose surgery. Nuñez agrees at first, because he has fallen in love with a blind girl. In this manner sex is shown to be a symbolic hazard to the free individual, a powerful force toward social conformity. When the day of the sacrifice comes, however, Nuñez finds the knowledge and beauty revealed by his sight more precious than the girl. He climbs out of the valley, and we last see him lying where he has fallen among the mountain summits, smiling under the cold stars. He is content to have escaped from the country of the blind. Nuñez, unlike Griffin, is a complex and sympathetic human being. Not wholly free of the primitive lust for power, he is still unable to strike a blind man, is sensitive to beauty, and capable of love. With this great story, Wells seems to have reached a mature resolution of the common human conflict between self and society that appears in so much of his early fiction, and, in fact, served as an emotional mainspring for it.

The novel, with invisibility as a symbol, presents egoism as a fatal tragic flaw, destructive to both society and self. The short story, using eyesight as a parallel but also complementary symbol, shows the ego as a source of priceless illumination, endangered by the blindness of society and worth preserving at any cost.

Jack Williamson

Sources for Further Study

Criticism:

Borrello, Alfred. *H. G. Wells: Author in Agony*. Carbondale: Southern Illinois University Press, 1972, pp. 59-62. The major themes of *The Invisible Man* are analyzed briefly in this study of Wells.

Costa, Richard H. *H. G. Wells*. New York: Twayne, 1967, pp. 40-43. This brief overview provides a good but brief introduction to *The Invisible Man*.

Parrinder, Patrick. *H. G. Wells: The Critical Heritage*. London: Routledge and Kegan Paul, 1972, pp. 58-62. Parrinder examines various critical views of *The Invisible Man*.

Suvin, Darko. "Wells as a Turning Point at the SF Tradition," in *Minnesota Review*. IV (1975), pp. 108-112. Suvin examines the influence of Wells's Invisible Man on subsequent science fiction writers.

Williamson, Jack. *H. G. Wells: Critic of Progress*. Baltimore: Mirage, 1973, pp. 83-88. This book examines Wells as a social critic and *The Invisible Man* as a vehicle for his views.

THE IRON DREAM

Author: Norman Spinrad (1940-   )
First book publication: 1972
Type of work: Novel
Time: Indeterminate, in a parallel universe
Locale: The High Republic of Heldon and its surrounding states

A novel of heroic "sword and sorcery" fiction, written in a universe parallel to our own, a universe in which Adolf Hitler became a Hugo Award-winning science fiction writer instead of Germany's Führer

Principal characters:
> ADOLF HITLER, an *émigré* science fiction writer honored by fans shortly after his death in 1953
> HOMER WHIPPLE, a professor at New York University
> FERIC JAGGAR, the hereditary king of Heldon, leader of the Sons of the Swastika, and personification of the Helder racial wili

Perhaps one reason science fiction has become associated with social criticism is the degree to which the genre's structures and conventions lend themselves to the playing of intellectual games. Imagining a future society on our own planet, an alien culture, or a universe identical to our own except in one seemingly innocuous detail provides the science fiction writer with the necessity as well as the opportunity to make occasional comments on political and social life. At the same time, even some of the most important American science fiction novels with social and political themes are extremely conservative in structure and form. Like the genre as a whole, they display their roots in the adventure tradition of the pulp magazines.

This reliance on the male adventure story is not a neutral accompaniment to the more explicit ideas expressed in the stories. The conventions of form contain and transmit certain assumptions about the way the author's contemporary world works. Implicit in the resolution of conflict in many science fiction novels (and made explicit in the subgenre of "sword-and-sorcery" or heroic fantasy) is the expectation that issues are decided by direct, usually violent and physical confrontations between individual combatants. Good and evil are unalterably opposed to each other — and easily distinguished. Winners and losers are also clear and distinct, and the price to the loser is nearly always death. Too few science fiction writers have understood the social geometry descending from such basic axioms. Norman Spinrad is one who has.

In *The Iron Dream*, Adolf Hitler never became a major political figure. After a brief involvement in politics at the end of World War I, he migrated to the United States in 1923 and began a career as a hack illustrator and writer for the science fiction pulp magazines. That career was capped with the posthumous award of the "Hugo" statuette in 1954 for his *magnum opus*, "Lords of the Swastika." Adopting Hitler as an auctorial *persona* makes it possible to examine the man's personality in a way only a biography (of which a glut exists) might otherwise permit. At the same time the heroic fantasies of "Hitler" represent an exaggeration of tendencies within the genre. Framing the whole between an hyperbolic introduction and an academic afterword mimics the contradictory position in which science fiction exists today and affords Spinrad still other opportunities for satire and criticism.

As both Hitler and "Hitler" were reared in Austria, Feric Jaggar grows up in Borgravia, a backward and foul country inhabited by mutants, descendants of the radiation-scarred survivors of a primordial nuclear war. Only the High Republic of Heldon has been preserved as a haven for the "true human genotype," and the High Republic itself is being undermined by a slack popular will and the sinister influence of telepathic Dominators (Doms) from the Empire of Zind to the East. The son of a Helder politician exiled for excessive zeal in enforcing the genetic purity laws, Jaggar leaves Borgravia when he comes of age to become a citizen of this last human bastion. But at the frontier, where the customs examination is a check for genetic purity, Jaggar realizes the degree to which mutants, and even some Doms, have infiltrated official circles. Angered that his admission to Heldon has been spoiled by the lax genetic examination, Jaggar spots the Dom controlling the station. Later, he leads a Helder mob back to the border to lynch the telepath. Marching at the head of the mob, Jaggar first feels the power to move people with his fierce commitment to genetic purity and his violent hatred of all mutants. Approached by the rather ineffectual organizer of a small political party, Jaggar sees a route to his own personal glory as the leader of a resurgent Helder crusade against anyone failing to uphold the standards of pure humanity.

From that moment, the plot follows "Hitler's" fantasy of conquest. Jaggar becomes part of Heldon's barbarian tradition by defeating the leader of the Black Avengers, a motorcycle gang who support their raids on mutant strongholds through robberies of more respectable elements of the populace. In that encounter, the formerly exiled young giant is forced to defend himself with the Great Truncheon of Held, a mythical weapon usable only by descendants of Helder Kings. Possession of the truncheon marks the Avengers as an instrument of fate and Jaggar's easy use of it establishes him as their undisputed leader.

With the Black Avengers, renamed the Knights of the Swastika, Jaggar stages a dramatic parade entrance into the High Republic's second city. He uses a series of increasingly grandiose, dramatic, and violent demonstrations (televised demonstrations) to secure a base of political power. From that base, he takes the climactic step of abolishing the country's at least nominally democratic ruling council, executing its leaders, and striking a political alliance with the military. In short order, the mutant states surrounding Heldon attack, and the history of German conquest from the absorption of Austria to the attack on the Soviet Union is paralleled — although since this is "Hitler's" fantasy, there are no Western democracies, the Dominators collapse under the

weight of Helder force, and Jaggar fulfills his vow to dispatch the last telepathic mutant with a blow from his huge truncheon.

"Lords of the Swastika" offers a speculative look at the psychology of
Fascism in a way removed from both political theory and the specific events of
German history following the end of World War I. As Homer Whipple, the
academic critic whose afterword completes *The Iron Dream*, points out,
"Lords of the Swastika" is full of the imagery of repressed sexuality.

There is only one woman in "Hitler's" novel, a stewardess casually brought
on stage and as casually abandoned when Jaggar runs off with the Black
Avengers. While Helder technology is a mishmash of wood-burning road-
steamers, motorcycles, and interstellar starships — and under Jaggar's leadership the army is equipped with tanks, aircraft, and long range guns — "Hitler"
prefers to have his heroes settle affairs with very phallic truncheons. As with
Arthur's Excalibur, Jaggar's ability to wield the Great Truncheon of Held is
symbolic of his power over the Helder race; the symbol is dramatized when
Stag Stopa, the Avenger's barbaric leader, kneels before Jaggar and kisses the
tip of the steel club as a token of fealty. Even as the imagery of fetish
abounds, that tableau is as close as "Hitler" comes to a sex scene of either the
hetero- or homosexual variety.

Restoring and strengthening the genetic pool of "true humanity" in the face
of the radiation-induced mutations requires that Jaggar, as leader of Heldon,
institute a program of classification and classification camps. All Helder
whose genotypes are less than perfect must choose between exile and castration. All choose the latter. Eventually, even Jaggar must make the choice,
because the Doms, in their defeat, have triggered a secretly preserved nuclear
weapon whose radiation contaminates the reproductive powers of even the
purest of the true humans.

Only Helder science can save the human race. Sexual reproduction is ended
with the sterilization of all humanity, and hundreds of thousands of clones are
manufactured from the genetic material of Jaggar and his elite soldiery, all
male. Eventually a starship filled with three hundred clones frozen in suspended animation is sent on a mission to colonize the nearer stars. Surrounded
by hoards of identical, cheering, marching, fanatical men, Jaggar pulls the
switch to launch this ultimate phallic symbol on its mission: a final substitution
of violence and technology for human sexuality and curiosity.

Spinrad preempts much of the critical discussion "Lords of the Swastika"
can generate in an afterword as satirical in its own format as "Hitler's" novel.
Homer Whipple points out that the book's popularity is hardly due to any
literary excellence, but rather, he suspects, to its depiction of incredible violence in the most sexual of terms. It *is* a sort of sublimated pornography, an
effect achieved only at a price. Like most pornography, the story is simply a
succession of hooks on which to hang the repetitive titillating scenes, and if
they do not turn you on, the book becomes a bore. But it does turn "Hitler"

on: the construction is deliberate and consistent with the rules of Spinrad's game. Whipple notes Hitler's understanding that the manipulation of human masses can result from the manipulation of visual symbols and events — Spinrad's reference to Goebbel's propaganda, and Leni Reifenstahl's film-making. But this Yankee pedant lives in the same parallel universe in which Hitler became a science fiction writer. Consistent with the device, Whipple's world has suffered no World War II, but the United States and the Soviet Union still confront each other and anti-Communist rhetoric is still a substitute for analysis.

It is Whipple who places "Hitler's" fantasy in the perspective of the heroic sword-and-sorcery genre, noting the fetishism and poltical wish-fulfillment which characterize so much of that genre, and connecting them explicitly to the pressures placed by an unremitting ideological war on a nominally democratic society. To Whipple's liberal eyes, the malevolent Doms are ready standins for the Soviets. "Hitler's" hero, forceful and absolutely sure of himself, can seem like the sort of leader to which the unsophisticated masses would rally in the face of danger, a leader under whose rule American industrial might could be mobilized in a final confrontation with the Reds. Like so many pundits who see themselves immune to the diseases of the society they study — and pointing to the evidence of "Hitler's" mental illness and venereal disease — Whipple takes a naïve comfort in the individual psychosis on "Hitler's" part which he sees at the root of Feric Jaggar's fictional destiny. The Helder mass psychosis in "Lords of the Swastika" can only remain the tortured fantasy of a neurotic science fiction writer, he believes, and could never become real.

Of course, the irony of that final assessment betrays the joke Spinrad has played on the ordinary sword-and-sorcery novel. As a work of fantastic literature by a popular science fiction writer, "Lords of the Swastika" exists only in a fantasy world parallel to our own. In the real world, it was no fantasy. Nazism has not only happened, it has happened and recurred with a ferocity which cannot all be understood through the economic and political explanations of conventional historians nor limited to the history of but one country. People have subjected themselves to a real Hitler and to other monsters with alarming frequency. Like Whipple's, too many of the explanations offered easily blame some element limited to a specific personal or historical context and foreign to any universal human characteristics.

By linking Nazism to sexuality, however repressed or sublimated, Spinrad forces consideration of just such characteristics. As a successful science fiction novel, using such anachronisms as Hell's Angels, television, and eventually interstellar starships in the context of a supposedly early industrial economy, "Hitler's" fantasy highlights the metaphors of unrestrained power which have always been near the heart of science fiction's "sense of wonder." To a degree, science fiction has always had difficulty matching the power of technology and the limitations of social, economic, and political reality; but in "Lords of the Swastika," set in a world where a primeval nuclear war is the source of all genetic contamination and ancient technology the work of evil wizards, Spinrad/"Hitler" reduces this attitude to the quasi-religious awe at its heart. The repression and sublimation of sexuality into violence gives urgency to the valuation of power and efficiency over every manner of relations among equals, real passion to the creation of interchangeable human parts to fit the machinery of society. Just as the seemingly impersonal world of politics can have a powerful impact on the structure of individual personalities and the living of individual lives, the running difficulties science fiction writers have in creating complete and rounded characters may foreshadow the genre's treatment of larger, more ideological issues.

Spinrad has made the nexus of individual sexuality and political power the focus of his serious novels, a focus maintained in *The Iron Dream*. But "Hitler's" fantasy is told from his point of view, from the top down. The sexual joy which courses through Feric Jaggar at each scene of carnage is the joy of conquest and domination, a perspective he apparently shares with his worst enemies, the telepathic Doms. Like them, Jaggar is sensitive to psychic vibrations and is capable of generating a charismatic spell over the purest-blooded of Helder humanity. Even as "Hitler" attempts to create a world of fantasy in which good and evil are easily distinguished, Spinrad continues to create central protagonists who share primary traits with their normal enemies. Putting the sexual fantasy in "Hitler's" typewriter might explain the motivation to conquer, but hardly the impulses which have moved so many ordinary people to the acceptance of barbarism in industrial garb. Spinrad offers two explanations. The first, "Hitler's," is Jaggar's focusing of the mighty will of a master race; the second, Whipple's, is the condescending impression that "Lords of the Swastika" is popular because it panders to the wishes of the ignorant for a strong leader whose absolute confidence and mastery will ease their own doubts and fears. Such a perspective in fact accepts "Hitler's" basic premise about the nature of human behavior, which is only natural considering the consistency with which Spinrad serves his narrative device of the parallel world. Understanding part of the mass psychology of Fascism is the task set for *The Iron Dream*. Understanding the balance must be the task for other books.

Albert I. Berger

Sources for Further Study

Reviews:

Amazing Stories. XLVII, August, 1973, pp. 116-117.

Galaxy. XXXIII, March-April, 1973, pp. 156-157.

Luna Monthly. XLI–XLII, October–November, 1973, p. 45.

Magazine of Fantasy and Science Fiction. XLV, July, 1973, p. 65.

National Review. XXV, January 19, 1973, p. 103.

Renaissance. IV, Fall, 1972, p. 9.

Speculation. XXII, Spring, 1973, pp. 29-30.

THE IRON HEEL

Author: Jack London (1876-1916)
First book publication: 1907
Type of work: Novel
Time: 1912-1932
Locale: The United States

A futurological projection of the author's view that capitalist oppression would evoke violent socialist revolution

>   *Principal characters:*
>   ERNEST EVERHARD, a socialist leader
>   AVIS EVERHARD, his wife, the narrator
>   PROFESSOR JOHN CUNNINGHAM, her father
>   BISHOP MOREHOUSE, a long-suffering convert to socialism
>   MR. WICKSON, a prominent capitalist
>   PHILIP WICKSON, his son, a convert to the revolutionary movement

The verisimilitude of this story is enhanced by the device of presenting it as the memoirs written by Avis Everhard, wife of Ernest, the leading character. There are footnotes purporting to show that her manuscript was secreted, not quite finished, due to a violent interruption. It was brought to light much later, and we are informed by the footnotes that this edition is being prepared seven centuries in the future. The footnotes lend a certain detachment to the narrative, all the more welcome because the work is otherwise thoroughly dominated by the personality and outlook of Ernest Everhard. Ernest is a scarcely veiled projection of London himself, in personality and political beliefs.

In the first part of the story, Ernest is introduced as a young, vigorous member of the working class. He becomes acquainted with the cultured, middle-class household of the Cunninghams, falls in love with Avis, and marries her. Through Professor Cunningham, he gains access to the uncongenial gatherings of the rich and powerful leaders of society, and here he scandalizes them by denouncing the oppression of the masses by the capitalists, and calling for the overthrow of the exploiters by a socialist revolution. Mr. Wickson, a convinced capitalist, answers Ernest most effectively. The two agree on one thing, that *power* will decide the outcome of this class struggle. Wickson declares — as London himself firmly believed all his life — that the capitalists will fight to the death against any efforts to deprive them of their power and privileges. This foreshadows the increasingly bitter struggle which unfolds in the novel, as the ruling class, thereafter called the "Oligarchy," employs every kind of oppression and armed intervention to hold back the revolutionary tide.

The point is made that most of the religious leaders cooperate with the ruling class. Ernest talks to some of them, since he functions as an increasingly influential leader of the socialist effort to secure justice for the masses. Only Bishop Morehouse responds to his call for the enlistment of true Christians in this crusade, and we find that Morehouse suffers severely for his social activism, losing his position and being sent to asylums because of his alleged insanity. He manages later to escape and serves the poor and sick in whatever humble ways he can.

Professor Cunningham also is persecuted for his liberal views, loses his faculty position, is robbed of all his property through fraudulent tricks of the Oligarchy, and later disappears. The middle-class and small businessmen generally fall victims to the big businessmen of the Oligarchy, though the latter get scant sympathy from Ernest, who echoes the Marxist view that giant corporations, or trusts, will do nicely under the socialist state of the future — but under governmental ownership, of course. The Oligarchy uses divide-and-conquer tactics with the labor unions, selecting favored unions to which it awards very ample pay increases in exchange for their cooperation, while the majority of workers, both rural and urban, are ground gradually down into virtual serfdom. Black Hundreds, a term borrowed from the reactionary mobs of Czarist Russia, function as terrorist goons of the Oligarchy.

In spite of the rulers' efforts, the election of 1912 brings the socialists much popular support, as they get many of their candidates elected to Congress. The Democratic Party also runs afoul of the Plutocracy, and being apparently less hardy than the socialists, it is destroyed. Meanwhile the desperate international commercial competition of the capitalists leads to a war between Germany and the United States. On December 4, 1912, a surprise attack is made on Honolulu by the German fleet, sinking three American cruisers, and bombarding the city. The socialists of both nations conduct a general strike, saying they will stop it only if the capitalists call a halt to the war.

Elsewhere around the world other revolutions occur in scores of countries. Britain loses most of its Empire, retaining only India. Japan leads an "Asia for the Asiatics" drive under its own reactionary leaders, and the Japanese workers are oppressed.

Ernest is the organizer of "Fighting Groups" in the United States (somewhat like the Red Guards or workers' militia which actually did form in Russia in 1917), to struggle against the Mercenary units and *agents provocateurs* fielded by the ruling class. The rulers, also known collectively as the "Iron Heel," resort to conscription to enslave the people in armies and labor forces. Mutual infiltration is attempted by both sides, and cruelty and illegal oppression become common.

By 1913, Congress and the political parties have lost their traditional roles. The Iron Heel contrives to have a bomb thrown in the halls of Congress and uses this incident as a pretext to have fifty-two Socialist members of Congress arrested by soldiers in the Capitol. They are imprisoned for treason, and Ernest, charged with the bombing, is sentenced to a life term. Avis manages to elude the police and takes refuge in a carefully concealed revolutionary center near San Francisco where she helps to operate the socialist headquarters. At this point occurs one of the few instances in the novel of the kind of imaginative technique so often employed in standard science fiction. Avis is given a painstaking course in identity change, to imbue her thoroughly with all the background and behavioral patterns which will keep the authorities from associating her in any way with her former self. Then, in 1915 Ernest is rescued from prison, and Avis enjoys eighteen happy months with him, followed by various daring missions for the cause. She even works as a double agent, accepted by the Iron Heel as one of its *agents provocateurs*. In that capacity she is able to survive on the scene of the "First Revolt" in Chicago in 1917.

The Iron Heel planned the First Revolt itself, in order to flush out its opponents in a premature revolt, which was to fail, and did. The Chicago scenes include much violence and brutality, with mobs pouring through the streets, workers' buildings under siege, and the masses finally massacred by the Oligarchy. Avis reaches shelter again, and hears later of Ernest's execution — under what circumstances we do not know, nor do we know exactly why her manuscript was broken off short of completion, but we infer that the Oligarchy caught up with her. Although the Iron Heel was able thereafter to maintain itself for three more centuries, it was toppled at last, and a more beneficent regime came into being.

The reception of *The Iron Heel* by reviewers was not positive. One might expect that socialists and likeminded people would have liked it. London was indeed a man of the working class, having been employed for years in a variety of laboring jobs, working under very difficult conditions for low pay. He was largely self-educated, and only in his later years did the popularity of his dozens of novels and short stories, especially those dealing with adventure and life in the wilderness, provide him with the financial rewards and acclaim which admitted him to the privileged classes. He was a devoted member of the socialist movement, though shortly before the end of his four decades of life, in 1916, he resigned from the Socialist Party simply because he thought it insufficiently aggressive. The Socialists were indeed more moderate and pacific in spirit than the protagonists of *The Iron Heel*, and their reaction to the novel was that it would do harm to their movement by alarming moderate readers and encouraging violence among radical or suggestible readers. Socialism should advance, they believed, through elections and legislation, and lurid violence of the kind envisioned in *The Iron Heel* should not be planned. Most Socialists, like the conservative critics of the book, did not believe that the privileged classes would do the illegal and brutal things to suppress the masses which London depicted.

Some workers' groups, such as miners in regions where the labor strife was bitter, did find the book realistic, but the typical reviewers of 1908 disliked it for its mischievous influence on the minds of unstable persons, saying that it would appeal mostly to crude and barbarous types. There had been, of course, a discernible aversion to London among academics and other intellectuals, based partly on their perception of him as a man of humble origins who had not acquired their own dexterity and easy competence with social and political matters. London's keen intuitive grasp of the events which might befall mankind, shown both in this book and in *The Scarlet Plague*, was somewhat better appreciated as the years went by. The Great War of 1914-1918 and the Russian Revolution of 1917, not to mention the abortive Red revolutions of 1919 in Germany and Hungary, gave people much fuller demonstrations of mass violence, oppression, and civil strife in real life. By the 1920's Anatole France could say that an Iron Heel would be seen in Europe, and that new serfdoms and caste governments would have to be overthrown by violence.

Hardly had Anatole France uttered these words when Mussolini's Fascism in Italy and Hitler's National Socialism in Germany began to prove him right. By 1937, when Leon Trotsky first read *The Iron Heel*, that anti-Stalinist Red leader disagreed with those who had found it pessimistic thirty years earlier. In 1935-1937, two years of the Stalin purges in Russia had demonstrated still another form of authoritarian oppression at work. Trotsky found London's forecast of the use of privileged segments of the labor movement by oppressors, coupled with the dictators' use of a praetorian army and an ever-present secret police, to be quiet realistic.

Later still, London might have felt vindicated when, for example, the Labor Government of Great Britain had to contend with strikes by the very workers whom it undertook to represent. In the United States he could have pointed by the 1960's to the appearance of new "robber barons" of bureaucracy, allied to some extent with the oligarchs of the labor unions, and in other respects allied with the military and industrial establishment. London's predictions of new feudalisms, while seldom precisely borne out by more recent events, have been equal or superior in their prescience, if we compare them with most other futurological literature.

Frank H. Tucker

Sources for Further Study

Criticism:

Baskett, Sam S. "A Source for the Iron Heel," in *American Literature*. XXVII (May, 1955), pp. 268-270. Baskett analyzes London's source material to pinpoint the construction of *The Iron Heel*.

Blotner, Joseph L. *The Political Novel*. Garden City, N.Y.: Doubleday, 1955, pp. 37-38. This overview of *The Iron Heel* attempts to place it in context as a vehicle for social criticism.

Peterson, Clell T. "Jack London's Sonoma Novels," in *American Book Col-*

lector. IX (October, 1958), pp. 15-20. Peterson discusses *The Iron Heel* as the first novel London wrote in the Sonoma Valley. The novels of this period represent the author's desire to reject civilization.

Reviews:

Arena. XXX, April, 1908, p. 503.

Dial. XLIV, April 16, 1908, p. 247.

Independent. LXIV, April 16, 1908, p. 856.

Nation. LXXXVI, March 19, 1908, p. 264.

Outlook. LXIX, June 20, 1908, p. 388.

Review of Reviews. XXXVII, June, 1908, p. 760.

ISLAND

Author: Aldous Huxley (1894-1963)
First book publication: 1962
Type of work: Novel
Time: The present
Locale: An imaginary island, Pala, somewhere between Ceylon and Sumatra

An outsider is shipwrecked on the paradisical island of Pala and educated in the basic principles and processes necessary in the evolution of an ideal society

Principal characters:
> WILL FARNABY, the outsider, a cynical disillusioned journalist and lackey of the entrepreneur, Lord Aldehyde
> DR. ROBERT MACPHAIL, descendant of Dr. Andrew MacPhail, a Scottish surgeon and cofounder of the Palanese social experiment
> LAKSHMI, Robert MacPhail's wife, who is dying of cancer
> SUSILA MACPHAIL, a recent widow, Will Farnaby's primary teacher and romantic interest
> MURUGAN MAILENDRA, the eighteen-year-old Raja, descendant of the original Raja of Pala, the cofounder of the Palanese social experiment
> THE RANI, the mother of Murugan, a muddle-headed theosophist
> ABDUL PIERRE BAHU, a sycophant of the Rani

Island, a Utopian novel in the tradition of Thomas More's *Utopia* (1561) and William Morris' *News from Nowhere* (1891), is Aldous Huxley's last fictional work; coinciding with the announcement of President John F. Kennedy's assassination, the announcement of Huxley's death went almost unnoticed. *Island* was Huxley's final effort to dramatize those issues which occupied his attention over his forty-year writing career. One could argue that *Island* is the logical outcome of Huxley's reexamination and rethinking of many of those issues raised in *Brave New World* (1932), his hugely successful anti-Utopian novel. George Woodcock points out in his study of Huxley, *Dawn and the Darkest Hour* (1972), that Huxley had been thinking about a novel such as *Island* for more than sixteen years and had taken five years to write it. Huxley considered his novel a significant contribution to literature and sociopolitical planning; indeed, his anxiety for its success was so great that he consulted his good friend Christopher Isherwood concerning the merits of the story. One is not surprised, then, to learn of his disappointment over the mixed critical reception of *Island*.

As is the case with many Utopian and anti-Utopian novels, the central issues and conflicts in *Island* are related through the experiences of an intruder who must be educated in the ways of the particular Utopia. The outsider, Will Farnaby, comes to Pala intending to exploit its oil reserves, but changes his mind after comprehending what Pala represents. In a sense, then, *Island* is a *Bildungsroman*, a novel of education and initiation. The central character and the reader are exposed to new concepts and experiences which simultaneously allow them to reflect on their own society and challenge them to consider the viability of the Utopian alternative. Whether and to what extent the outsider (and the reader) is transformed by this experience is the fundamental issue of the novel. This is the problem that the narrative must resolve.

Farnaby is a man "who couldn't take yes for an answer." As he is recovering from injuries sustained in the shipwreck that washed him up on Pala's shores, the reader learns through a series of flashbacks of the events contributing to Farnaby's cynicism. He feels guilty for betraying his wife and preferring the debased sexuality of his mistress. The news of this betrayal, he believes, was responsible for his wife's hysterical behavior and her subsequent fatal automobile accident. Sex and love are associated in his mind with treachery and degradation. Further, he has been struck by the cosmic injustice of life. His Aunt Mary, "the only person [he] ever admired and trusted," a genuinely good woman, gives birth to a deformed child, loses her husband in World War I, undergoes a mastectomy, and dies in agony with cancer. Farnaby watches her change from a compassionate and self-sacrificing worker, caring for the aged and helpless, to a degraded, humiliated woman being transformed into "a packet of garbage." This is the source of his disenchantment. Farnaby says pessimistically, "Only God can make a microcephalous idiot." Farnaby's disillusionment and negativism is his response to these experiences, what he calls the "Essential Horror." This attitude makes it easier for him to serve as an agent for the archetypal entrepreneurial exploiting capitalist, Lord Aldehyde, who is after Pala's undeveloped oil reserves. Farnaby, as Aldehyde's representative, is an accomplice in subverting the Palanese by working with the Rani and Murugan. They arrange an agreement with his boss which culminates in Murugan's initiating a coup and murdering Dr. MacPhail.

This is the history and these are the strategies for coping with experience that Will Farnaby brings to Pala. It is not only his physical but also his psychic wounds which must be healed. The confrontation between this life-denying negativism and the very positive life-affirming philosophy and practice of the Palanese creates the novel's tension and interest. This miserable traveler is thrust into a society which rests on the cheerful assumption that if one pays "attention" (the first word in the novel), he will discover that "two-thirds of all sorrow is homemade and, so far as the universe is concerned, unnecessary." His education lies in learning the discipline and methods which enable him to pay attention — the novel begins with him unconscious and ends with him seeing "the Clear Light."

Will Farnaby comes to understand that human misery is not inevitable, that one can even come to accept the reality of metaphysical evil and death without despair. Huxley creates a series of guides and teachers (principally Dr. MacPhail and Susila) who lead Farnaby to the truth. These mentors are the vehicles through which Huxley is able to describe, explain, and argue for his particular version of Utopia. The knowledge and final insights that Farnaby gains are a result of these encounters. Huxley's vision is complex and embraces an enormous range of human experience. However, it is possible to untangle some of its main features.

The fundamental assumption underlying Huxley's Utopia is the need for reconciling the best impulses of Western and Eastern cultures. This notion is dramatized in the novel by referring to the symbiotic relationship of Pala's founders, a Scottish doctor, "the Calvinist-turned-atheist and the pious Mahayana Buddhist." From the West comes science, especially social and biological science (e.g. medicine, behaviorism, agriculture, genetics) and a selective aspect of natural science with its attendant technology; as one of his teachers explains: "Electricity minus heavy industry plus birth control equals democracy and plenty." Also from the West come the English language and some of its literature. Underpinning Western science and technology are the Eastern religious and philosophical foundations of Palanese society, derived from Mahayana Buddhism, which encompass practically every aspect of one's life. There are yogas for pain, for sex, for education, for enlightenment, and for death. While Western science and technology work to improve material life, the life-affirming Eastern philosophy keeps the individual in touch with the One, or as it is variously described, Unity, the Divine Ground, or the Clear Light. In addition to these two basic cultural strands, Huxley includes ideas drawn from Taoism, Tantrism, Quakerism, from Samuel Butler, Darwin, Freud, Mendel, William James, John Dewey, from hypno-therapy and psychedelic research, and a host of other more esoteric sources. From an eclectic synthesis of these various perspectives and practices, the inhabitants are able to cope successfully with such universal problems as man's relationship to nature, to his fellow man, to himself, and to his gods, as well as the more practical issues of erotic, but nondegrading sex; population control (using a form of coitus reservatus); emotional problems resulting from too intimate family relations (families are eliminated and replaced by Mutual Adoption Clubs of 15-20 couples); improved racial characteristics through AIM (artificial insemination); the channeling of aggressive behavior through behavior modification; eliminating pain through hypnosis; democratizing art; and so on.

Little by little, Farnaby is exposed to all of this, and slowly he begins to change. Two incidents are crucial in his development: the first is witnessing the death of Dr. MacPhail's wife, the second is experiencing the drug *moksha* (similar to the *soma* of *Brave New World*). Present at the death of Lakshmi, who is dying of the same disease that tortured and killed his Aunt Mary, Farnaby comes to realize that not only is death part of reality which must be accepted but that it can be an occasion of dignity and enlightenment for the dying as well as the living. Lakshmi is fully conscious and serene during the final moments of her life. She provides a sharp contrast to his terrible memories of Aunt Mary's last days. Moreover, his guilty memories of his sordid lovemaking with his mistress, Babs, the night of his wife's funeral are juxtaposed to Susila's convincing argument defending the propriety of "going on from the yoga of death to the yoga of love."

The climax of Farnaby's education (and the novel) comes when, under the supervision of Susila, Will tries *moksha* and experiences the total awareness of bliss *and* reality. With Bach's *Fourth Brandenburg Concerto* in the background, the "doors of perception" are opened for Will to experience the "luminous bliss, 'Felicity so ravishing, so inconceivably intense that no one can describe it.' " However, it is not only bliss that he must experience. Under Susila's coaxing, Farnaby opens his eyes and watches in horror as a female praying mantis eats its mate and is, in turn, devoured by a lizard. This is the "infinite suffering" that Will must also learn to accept. Susila, with whom Farnaby is now romantically involved, instructs him on the proper use of *moksha* and the necessity of *Karuna*, "attention." One must be continually alert and pay attention, for as the narrator observes, "One slips back too easily, one slips back too often."

Happiness is indeed ephemeral. The inhabitants of Pala are too happy, and it cannot last. Pala's precarious existence is due largely to its isolation, and once the rest of the world learns of its oil deposits, it is doomed. The immediate threat comes from Murugan, who is unaffected by Pala's culture and actively hostile to its antiprogressive, antitechnological, antirevolutionary, and antimodernistic way of life. An immature mama's boy with latent homosexual tendencies, whose favorite reading is the Sears Roebuck Catalogue, Murugan conspires with his mother and the murderous dictator of the adjacent island to seize power. The novel ends with Will and Susila as passive spectators to Murugan's drive for power and the murder of Dr. MacPhail.

Huxley seems to suggest that something approaching Utopia is possible but unlikely. None of the concepts or practices that he describes in *Island* are unthinkable in real life. In fact, many have been tried. On the other hand, Huxley also implies that unless these are universal practices, that part of the world where they are not a guiding force will seek out and destroy any attempts to initiate this Utopia. The nonviolent pacifism of the Palanese is no match for the guns of Rendang. Susila's only response to the threat of destruction is: "Try to keep them in order, try to change their minds, hope for a happy outcome, and be prepared for the worst." Pala is a fragile Utopia.

Huxley was not happy with the lukewarm reception of his novel. Many critics refused to take his ideas seriously; this is probably what bothered him the most. Yet, there certainly is some justification for the critics' skepticism of the viability of the synthesis that Huxley tried to bring about. Taken one by one, most of Huxley's suggestions for a better society seem reasonable and workable. Taken together, the consequences seem less convincing. For example, Western science emerged out of a particular historical moment within a specific, identifiable culture. Science is a social enterprise and is therefore rooted in the social system. An illustration of this relationship can be seen in the work of social scientists such as Robert K. Merton, who have shown an intricate relationship between Protestantism and science. While it is not impossible, it is not very convincing to treat science as some sort of autonomous activity which could be shifted without serious transformations into another, altogether different milieu and expect it to thrive. Huxley's discussion of science training as a combination of "receptivity" and analysis is an attempt to bring Western science and Eastern Buddhism together, but the effort is not entirely successful.

Many critics found his Utopia and its citizens simply boring — a danger with any Utopian scheme; evil seems to be so much more interesting. Many faulted not the ideas but their artistic execution, particularly Huxley's difficulty in wedding the ideas to the action of the narrative. There are places where the narrative ceases to progress altogether, and the reader is treated to or forced to endure — depending upon his perspective — lengthy passages of exposition and description. At times characters simply lecture Farnaby, and when the lecture is over, he moves on to another lecture. Huxley himself was aware of the problem of "a disbalance between fable and exposition." On the other hand, there is a story here; it is the education of Will Farnaby. His transformation is believable and the novel ends with a realistic mixture of optimism and pessimism. Given the kind of novels Huxley usually wrote, this rather positive final humanistic vision seems particularly interesting and appropriate.

Charles Elkins

Sources for Further Study

Criticism:

McMichael, Charles T. "Aldous Huxley's *Island*: The Final Vision," in *Studies in the Literary Imagination*. I (1968), pp. 73-82. McMichael probes the themes of *Island*.

Meckier, Jerome. "Cancer in Utopia: Positive and Negative Elements in Huxley's *Island*," in *Dalhousie Review*. LIV (1974-1975), pp. 619-633. Meckier dissects the various aspects of the book.

Stewart, D. H. "Aldous Huxley's *Island*," in *Queen's Quarterly*. LXX (1963), pp. 326-335. Outlines the plot of *Island*.

Watt, Donald J. "Vision and Symbol in Aldous Huxley's *Island*," in *Twentieth Century Literature*. XIV (1968), pp. 149-160.

Reviews:

Atlantic. CCIX, April, 1962, p. 155.

Booklist. LVIII, May 1, 1962, p. 607.

Christian Science Monitor. April 12, 1962, p. 11.

Kirkus Reviews. XXX, January 15, 1962, p. 75.

Library Journal. LXXXVII, March 15, 1962, p. 1150.

New Republic. CXLVI, April 30, 1962, p. 17.

New York Times Book Review. April 1, 1962, p. 4.

Saturday Review. XLV, March 31, 1962, p. 20.

Time. LXXIX, April 6, 1962, p. 97.

Times Literary Supplement. March 30, 1962, p. 213.

Yale Review. LI, June, 1962, p. 630.

THE ISLAND OF DOCTOR MOREAU

Author: H. G. Wells (1866-1946)
First book publication: 1896
Type of work: Novel
Time: February 1887-January 1888
Locale: Noble's Isle (about midway between Ecuador and the Marquesas)

The experiences of a man who finds himself on an isolated island where experiments are carried out in an attempt to humanize beasts

> Principal characters:
> DR. MOREAU, a "vivisectionist"
> MONTGOMERY, his assistant
> EDWARD PRENDICK, a castaway on Moreau's island
> THE BEAST PEOPLE

H. G. Wells began writing *The Island of Doctor Moreau* in late 1894. But his first draft, a far cry from the published version, did not satisfy him. The idea of how to go about revising it probably occurred to him as a result of reading Frank Challice Constable's *The Curse of Intellect* (1895). Constable, in his attempt to dramatize the conflict between intellect and instinct, had hit upon the notion of having an experimenter use hypnotism to transform a (presumably rather large) monkey into the semblance of a civilized human being. But Constable's imaginativeness and originality did not extend to matters of literary execution. Instead of troubling himself to seek out a form truly appropriate for expressing his new idea, he chose to pattern his fiction on Robert Louis Stevenson's *The Strange Case of Dr. Jekyll and Mr. Hyde* (1886). The satiric possibilities of passing off a monkey on London society or of detailing the creature's reversion to instinctive behavior consequently eluded him. His book, Wells rightly objected, lacked the Swiftian spirit.

The same cannot be said of the end-product of Wells's efforts at revising *The Island of Doctor Moreau*. Unmistakably, its inspiration is the final book of *Gulliver's Travels*. As the most Swiftian — and the most sustained — of all of Wells's science fiction satires, it deals with what he elsewhere characterized as the uneasy balance between "the natural man," or "culminating ape," and "the artificial man, the highly plastic creature of tradition, suggestion, and reasoned thought."

The opening chapters of Edward Prendick's narrative serve by way of a prologue to the satire that follows. They illustrate the feral instincts which privation can elicit in man and also the bestiality of which the human species is gratuitously capable.

Prendick begins his tale by revealing that he is one of the survivors of the wreck of the *Lady Vain*. Together with a fellow passenger and a member of the crew, he managed to swim to the dinghy of the sinking vessel and thus avoid imminent death. Adrift for eight days, famished and dying of thirst, the three finally agreed upon a plan for human sacrifice. But in the act of carrying out their murderous designs on one another, his companions fell into the sea and instantly drowned. Prendick, the last to go along with their scheme for abandoning civilized restraint, alone escapes that fate. Soon afterwards, a schooner bound for Noble's Isle picks him up.

Aboard the schooner, Prendick regains consciousness. He also regains his strength thanks to Montgomery, a former medical student. He is present to supervise delivery of the ship's animal cargo and has Prendick drink something "that tasted like blood." Otherwise, however, the events on board the *Ipecacuanha* justify its name. They do not help Prendick recover his psychological balance after the ordeal that had impelled him towards cannibalism. Instead, the cruelty of the sailors and the brutishness of their captain have a kind of purgative effect: their actions eliminate any clear distinction between man and beast. Prendick thus arrives on Moreau's island having already lost any firm sense of the norms of civilized human behavior.

Everything that Prendick has undergone or been witness to in making the transition to the island of Dr. Moreau prepares him to misapprehend what he finds there. Leaving the compound, where Moreau and Montgomery have locked him out of their laboratory, he wanders off among the Beast Folk and presently forms a horrific idea about them. Their demeanor and carriage impress on him feelings both of utter strangeness and of the strangest familiarity. Because they generally walk erect, have the use of speech, and swathe themselves in rags of clothing, he supposes them to be human in origin. But while he recognizes the rough humanity of their bodily form, he also detects in each the mark of the beast, something suggestive of the hog, the dog, the leopard, or some other animal. Putting these seemingly discrepant observations of his together, he comes to the conclusion that the creatures have been victims of a hideous experiment. Moreau, he imagines, has been — and still is — animalizing men by means of vivisection.

Prendick's lurid interpretation, though it turns out to be erroneous, fulfills a satiric purpose of Wells. It calls attention to the Beast People as grotesque caricatures of humanity; that is, it emphasizes the similarities between them and civilized man. The acquired habits that differentiate man from beast — or from savage — find a parodic equivalent in their customs and rituals. Following Swift's example, Wells ridicules man's pretensions to civility by reducing its outward signs to an absurdly primitive form. The Law that Moreau's creatures chant, for instance, mechanically codifies and rigidly expresses the kind of religio-moral precepts and beliefs that society invokes to curb the natural man. In content and intent, it is a cretinized Decalogue. By translating the latter into a series of elementary injunctions — "Not to go on all-Fours," — and palpable threats — "*His* is the House of Pain," — Wells points to simple-minded fear and superstition as the factors motivating man to repress his innate brutishness. At the same time, the fact that the Beast People are obviously uncomfortable with the Law and with all of the other accoutrements of civilized behavior exposes the artificiality of human tradition, suggestion, and reasoned thought. Indeed, the civilizing practices that man has adopted in the course of his evolution as a social being appear at this stage of the fiction to do little more than disguise his true — that is, biologically original — nature.

The chapter (fourteen) in which Moreau explains to Prendick the how and why of his experiments adds a new dimension to the satire. In part, it reveals the absurdity of trying to reconcile Darwinian theory with the concepts of traditional theology. Moreau, by using the techniques of surgery and hypnotism to transform beasts into humanlike beings, replaces Darwinian Nature. To be sure, the workings of natural evolution are not really purposive; but the sort of randomness to which they are subject likewise enters into his obsessive project in artificial evolution. (In response to Prendick's query as to why he had taken the human form as a model, Moreau confesses that he had chosen it by chance.) The experimenter with living tissue is thus the Shaping God of Evolution. But as Creator and Law-Giver, the ancient and white-haired doctor is also the Jehovah of the Pentateuch. (Concerning his first effort at man-making, he tells Prendick: "All the week, night and day, I molded him [a gorilla]," and on the seventh day "I rested.") This synthesis of theology and science, however, has disastrous consequences, particularly for the former. As the deity presiding over evolution, Moreau dismisses the problem of why evil exists in the world by saying that he has "never troubled about the ethics of the matter." Compelled to be as remorseless as Nature, he remains deaf to the suffering of his creatures. Nor can the pain that they must endure in the process of artificial evolution be explained theologically except by postulating an, at best, apathetic God. Certainly there is no accounting for that pain in any morally acceptable terms. It cannot even be justified as a means to an end: first, because the end proposed will never be achieved; and second, because "the material [that] . . . has dripped into the huts yonder" is all too often a dead end in itself.

Pain, in Moreau's view, characterizes a passing evolutionary phase. Plants and possibly the lower animals do not feel it; and it gets needless, he argues, as life progresses to the stage where reason supercedes it. (Wells had propounded a similar thesis in "The Province of Pain" [1894], an essay published at about the time he began writing *The Island of Doctor Moreau*.) His obsession — to sculpt a being which would act purely from rational motives — springs out of his belief that pain as an actuating force behind human behavior is "the mark of the beast" in man. But Prendick, who shows himself inclined to judge by appearances, takes a different position. He regards expressions of pain and its concomitant, fear, to be humanizing traits. As he holds the Leopard Man at bay, for example, he remarks: "seeing the creature there in a perfectly animal attitude, . . . its imperfectly human face distorted with terror, I realized again the fact of its humanity." Of course, this stance of Prendick is by no means totally incompatible with Moreau's. The two agree that pain is the link between man and beast. But Moreau goes on to stress the need for man to sever that connection, to overcome his susceptibility to pain and thereby transcend his animal nature. Nor is this to say that his disagreement with Prendick is merely one of emphasis. It is also a matter of outlook; and as such, it signals an ambivalence that (typically in Wells's science fiction) otherwise manifests itself in *The Island of Doctor Moreau* on a much larger scale.

In discussing with Prendick the theory underlying his experiments, Moreau directs the reader to the issue of what the human species might become. His disquisition, that is, introduces a shift in satiric focus, a shift that unmistakably declares itself almost the moment the doctor is killed by his last victim (a puma). Hitherto, Wells had concentrated his satiric attention on "the artificial man," whose civilized habits he had ridiculed as being at best superficial — indeed, as being akin to hypocrisy. But with Moreau's death, the satire turns against "the natural man." Man's civilized habits emerge at this point as civilizing traits: they represent a fragile protection against his potential bestiality. Just how necessary that protection is becomes clear once the Beast People begin reasserting their animal impulses. As their regression follows its inevitable course, the brutal rule of survival — of kill or be killed — usurps the place of Moreau's Law (to the undermining of which Prendick has been a contributor). At the same time, the Beast Folk lose all but the slightest vestiges of what had earlier been the ironic signs of their humanity.

Prendick slowly reverts to a kind of animal savagery as well. His first step backward is to cut himself off from the one other human being remaining on the island: Montgomery. His justification for doing so — "I felt that for Montgomery there was no help; that he was in truth half akin to these Beast Folk" — reveals that Prendick, though by now an initiate into Moreau's secret, still imagines his nature to be essentially different from that of the rest of the inhabitants. However, the murder of a drunken Montgomery and the burning of the compound obliges Prendick to live among Moreau's creatures; and as they revert to type, he himself acquires a bestial aspect. ("I . . . must have undergone strange changes, [he recalls] . . . I am told that even now my eyes have a strange brightness, a swift alertness of movement.")

After he contrives to escape from the painful disorder of the island, the persuasion that had overwhelmed Gulliver takes hold of him: "I felt no desire to return to mankind." But while he and Gulliver share the same response, and for a similar reason, their dread of being exposed to the brutishness of men derives from opposite experiences. Gulliver, having spent most of his Fourth Voyage among the Houyhnhnms, disdains men for their contrast to those perfectly rational creatures. Prendick, who has sojourned for almost a year among the Yahoos (as it were), comes to fear man's similarity to them. The sight of other men often reminds him of the Beast People, and he is frequently haunted by the nightmarish idea that presently the degradation of the islanders will be played over again on a larger scale. But he takes comfort from the rather naïve belief — hardly grounded in his own experiences or behavior — that all this is "an illusion, that these seeming men and women about me are . . . men and women for ever, perfectly reasonable creatures full of human desires and tender solicitude." Less ironic, and also far more significant from the standpoint of Wells's inquiry into the limits of human plasticity, is the fact that Prendick looks to the stars for solace. For in them, as symbols of the future and of the vast and eternal laws of matter, resides the hope that man may become something more than the clothed and gabbling but mentally intractable ape that *The Island of Doctor Moreau* discovers him still to be.

Robert M. Philmus

Sources for Further Study

Criticism:

Hillegas, Mark R. "Cosmic Pessimism in H. G. Wells' Scientific Romances," in *Papers of the Michigan Academy of Science, Arts and Letters*. XLVI (1961), pp. 655-663. *The Island of Doctor Moreau* is analyzed by Hillegas as a vehicle for Wells's social thought.

Parrender, Patrick. *H. G. Wells*. Edinburgh: Oliner and Boyd, 1970, pp. 24-26. This brief overview superficially treats the thematic concerns of *The Island of Doctor Moreau*.

Pritchett, Victor Sawdon. *The Living Novel and Later Appreciations*. New York: Random House, 1964, pp. 100-109. Pritchett provides a general but detailed review of the theme, plot construction and literary techniques embodied in *The Island of Doctor Moreau*.

ISLANDIA

Author: Austin Tappan Wright (1883-1931)
First book publication: 1942
Type of work: Novel
Time: 1901-1910
Locale: Islandia and the New England region of the United States of America

A young American's account of his initiation into manhood amid the splendors and dangers of an anti-American Utopia

    Principal characters:
        JOHN LANG, first United States Consul in Islandia
        DORN, his best friend and a leader of Islandia's Utopian Party
        LORD MORA, a leader of Islandia's Alterator Party
        TOR, Islandia's monarch
        DORNA, Dorn's sister and Lang's first love
        HYTHA NATTANA, Lang's second love
        GLADYS HUNTER, Lang's American girl friend
        JOSEPH LANG, John Lang's uncle, a successful and influential American businessman

Many dreams center in the image of the Garden. To the American pioneers, for example, the way West led straight to the land of opportunity, abundance, and freedom from urban constraints — the Garden. To the Russian Count Leo Tolstoy, the simple peasant lifestyle, intimately attuned to natural forces and rhythms, represented primal innocence — the Garden. To Jungian psychologists, the greatest need of modern men and women is for individuation, completely balanced and developed selfhood — the Garden. To Austin Tappan Wright, the Garden meant all these things, and more; he thought about it, dreamed about it, and worked with it almost all his life, and the result was his magnificent Utopian novel, *Islandia*, one of the few science fiction books that is indisputably a great work of literature.

Wright's Garden, Islandia, is an imaginary country on the equally imaginary Karain subcontinent, somewhere in the Southern Hemisphere's temperate zone. From the hints Wright supplies in his novel we can deduce that Islandia is in the Atlantic Ocean, perhaps slightly to the south and west of Africa, and that it is about as far south of the Equator as New England is north. Wright explicitly tells us that Islandia is an extraordinarily beautiful and fertile land, rich in natural resources, and that its culture is overwhelmingly agrarian. Separated from the rest of Karain by a towering mountain range, and from the centers of Western civilization by thousands of miles of ocean, Islandia seems a promising new frontier to the Europeans and Americans who have just begun to arrive there in the early years of the twentieth century, when this story begins.

One of these latter-day explorers is the novel's narrator, John Lang, who comes to Islandia as the first Consul of the United States ever to be appointed there. As American consul, Lang is supposed to make Islandia accessible to

American businesses; this is certainly the intention of the American businessmen and politicians who arranged this appointment, and it is also the intention
of Islandia's newly dominant political party, the Alterators. The Alterators
agree with the commercially-minded Americans that Islandia is a Garden in
need of cultivation — a primitive outback whose ample resources are ripe for
political and technological development. But Islandia's Utopian Party maintains that the political and technological machine can only destroy any Garden
it enters, and that Islandia's "development" will be its ruin. And Lang, despite
his Yankee background and contrary to his direct instructions, sides with the
Utopians. Drawn to the Utopians at first by his friendship with one of their
leaders, Dorn, whom he met when they attended Harvard together, Lang gradually gains a solid intellectual commitment to the Utopian cause; by the end of
the novel he has become so passionate a partisan that his family virtually dis-
owns him and he repeatedly risks his life protecting Islandia from would-be
invaders.

The debates between Alterators and Utopians, as well as Lang's discussions
with his zealously technocratic Uncle Joseph, articulate Wright's deeply
thoughtful critique of modern civilization, with particular attention to modern
America. On this level *Islandia* provides an intelligently inflammatory
Romantic indictment of technology and its discontents. Like the historian
Frederick Jackson Turner, Wright celebrates the importance of the frontier in
freeing and ennobling human energies; but whereas Turner finds subduing the
frontier a mostly positive enterprise, Wright insists that only by preserving the
wide open spaces and living in respectful balance with physical nature can we
achieve our true potential. One Islandian woman, the wise and beautiful
Dorna, puts the case against technology in this way:

> Our aims are of the earth and of all growing things. They are of the earth earthy, as [the
> foreigners] say with contempt and we with gladness. . . . They always long for something
> else beyond their reach! But we sound the deeps — the deeps of our natures, of dreams, of
> what we feel, and of our growth, and of the growth of all that grows about us, men and
> women, animals, grass, and trees. . . . If we do as they wish, place will tend to become
> temporary and family a thing of a generation. . . . The house of living may become more
> ornate, but its air will be impure and its foundations unstable.

In the Utopian view of things, our technologically-based culture alienates us
from our natural environment, and thus reduces human existence to a rootless,
aimless, fragmented, and sterile round of meaningless days. Instead of the
Garden, we modern Westerners inhabit a dreary wasteland of our own frantic
making.

It can of course be objected that the remarkable fertility of the Islandian
countryside encourages Utopian sentiments which would be absurd in other,
more rigorous climes. Wright surmounts these objections by showing that
Islandia is essentially a spiritual rather than a material Garden, and that its

Utopian values apply anywhere. The spiritual Islandia has four dimensions, each of which is a way of loving. The first is *alia*, the commitment to land and family which bases the Islandian sense of self; *alia* integrates all of the self's experiences "into a rounded whole, because one's land and one's farm is larger than oneself, reaching from a past long before one began into a future long after one is dead — but all of it one's own." *Amia* is nonsexual love, the spirit of loyal friendship which cements Islandian society because it honors the oneness of the human community and the uniqueness of every individual. *Apia*, sexual desire, has an innocent energy in Islandia, where this natural attraction between healthy bodies is clearly differentiated from *ania*, the love which builds families. Islandia's four-fold vitality produces absolute happiness, the state of being "so much in tune with your life as a whole that every moment that comes is untroubled and full of interest."

Wright's belief in the spiritual worth of the natural life parallels not only the enthusiasm of some contemporary environmentalists for various native American cultures, but also and especially Count Leo Tolstoy's reverence for the Russian peasantry. *Islandia* particularly recalls the subplot of Tolstoy's *Anna Karenina*, in which Levin and Kitty (corresponding to John Lang and Gladys Hunter) work out their own psychological salvation and find a happy, stable marriage by learning from the peasants how to love. But Wright resembles Tolstoy even more significantly in *how* he writes about the Garden than in *what* he discovers there. Islandia is that rarest of literary achievements, a credible Utopia, largely because Wright tells us about it in the style of Tolstoyan realism. He describes it as though it existed in real space and time, invests it with a wealth of sensory details, and invents for it an elaborate but thoroughly consistent history and culture; and by these means he allows us to enter his Garden and experience its joys with him.

Another reason that we can believe in Islandia is that we see its power in the lives of several highly credible characters. Wright's novel centers in the consciousness of its narrator, who is both a young American man in search of a satisfying lifestyle and, more profoundly, every young self in search of maturity and wholeness. On this psychological level, Islandia is to John Lang the incarnation of the archetypal femininity which he must acknowledge and develop in himself, and Islandia's four dimensions of loving represent four essential aspects of his own *anima*. Lang's awareness of the *anima* grows from his capacity for *amia*; for *amia*, the spirit of comradeship, introduces him to all the other aspects of femininity. *Amia* represents the *anima* as Daughter in a psyche where only masculinity is "grown-up"; it is the gentlest, youngest, and least sexual of the feminine archetypes. It makes sense that Lang would first recognize the *anima* as Daughter, because he comes from the dominantly masculine culture of modern America, and all his training has encouraged him to identify with father-figures like his Uncle Joseph and the men who run Harvard and Washington. Accordingly, Lang initially perceives every woman he meets in this story from the perspective of *amia*; but friendship is not enough — he has to know the *anima* much more fully.

In the second phase of Lang's initiation, he encounters femininity as a sexual force, both in himself and in each of his women friends: he meets the Temptress, or *apia*. In this aspect the *anima* is the daughter struggling to free herself from masculine domination, experiencing an independent capacity to love. Hytha Nattana, Lang's first sexual partner, is most important to him because she liberates and focuses his *apia*; intriguingly, Hytha Nattana is also the one woman among *Islandia*'s enormous cast of characters to have serious problems breaking away from her father's *animus*.

As Lang and Nattana learn, *apia*, even when supported by *amia*, cannot survive unless it develops into the next dimension of loving, *ania*. *Ania* corresponds to the *anima* as Wise Woman; it is the mediating awareness which enables a man to relate comfortably and intelligently to the women in his life, and to select one woman as his life-partner, for he understands that the feminine and the masculine are equal partners in his own identity. Lang learns about *ania* by observing Dorna, who incarnates this archetype so strongly that she makes him aware of it in himself, too. But he does not completely free the Wise Woman in his *anima* until he grows into *ania* for Gladys Hunter, the young American woman whose psyche truly is the feminine partner to his American masculinity.

Dorna also makes Lang aware of the fourth aspect of the *anima*, the Great Mother, which corresponds to Wright's fourth dimension of loving, *alia*. Throughout *Islandia* it is Dorna who most articulately expresses the Earth Mother's sense of rootedness, comfort, and creativity; through her, Lang learns to ground his own being in his *alia*, his commitment to the mother-principle everywhere in life. At this point, his *anima* now fully and healthily functioning, Lang can at last appreciate the Garden in his external world, because he has acknowledged the Garden within himself and let it flower.

Lang is not the only character to internalize the Garden, however. While his experiences disclose the feminine elements in Islandia, Nattana, Dorna, and Gladys discover the Garden as the *animus*, archetypal masculine energy. To Nattana masculinity at first seems merely repressive, tyrannical paternalism; but when Lang has confronted her with his masculine sexuality and she has let that *apia* free itself in her psyche, she moves to a new, much more positive relationship with the masculine in herself and others. By the end of the story Nattana is her own father, centering her life in her *alia* just as do all adult males in Islandia, and decisively rejecting even the limited dependency of *ania*. By contrast, Dorna begins by centering in *alia* and fearing masculine sexuality as an uprooting, disruptive force which will tear her away from her Garden. When she comes to terms with the *animus*, it is from the perspective of *ania*: with stunning appropriateness, Wright signals Dorna's psychological change by mating her with Tor, Islandia's glamorous young ruler, whose masculine kingliness is the perfect partner for the queenliness of her liberated womanhood.

Although Lang, *Islandia*'s narrator, concentrates his attention on Dorna because she is to him both Wise Woman and Great Mother, the most interesting woman in the novel is Gladys Hunter. Initially dominated by her frigid, fearful mother, Gladys gradually experiences the freedom of the Garden. Her psychological development follows the same stages as Lang's: she moves from *amia* through *apia* to *ania*, letting first friendliness, then desire, and finally partnership inform her about the men in her life and the *animus* in herself. At *Islandia*'s conclusion Gladys has still not achieved *alia*, the sense of belonging, but she has found the *animus* as Father; Lang externalizes the father image for her, and she is beginning to rely on her own fatherly qualities. Had Wright lived to write more about Islandia, he probably would have traced Gladys' flowering to its completion, instead of leaving her still in search of individuated selfhood. He might also have told us something about the marriage of this Motherly Gladys and her consort, the Fatherly Lang, and so introduced us to yet another vision of the Garden.

We can be satisfied with *Islandia* as we have it, however, because it evokes *alia* in us even though it withholds that capacity from Gladys. *Islandia* is so richly, imaginatively wise that it integrates our fragmented perceptions, healing us while it entertains. It is impossible not to love this book; it is impossible not to learn from it, as well.

Jane Hipolito

Sources for Further Study

Reviews:

Analog. LXIII, June, 1959, pp. 145-147.

Fantasiae. I, July, 1973, p. 6.

Super Science Stories. IV, August, 1942, p. 71.

IT CAN'T HAPPEN HERE

Author: Sinclair Lewis (1885-1951)
First book publication: 1935
Type of work: Novel
Time: 1936
Locale: The United States

A charismatic demogogue's takeover of the government of the United States turns the nation into a tyrannical police state

Principal characters:
    DOREMUS JESSUP, a newspaper editor
    BERZELIUS WINDRIP, dictator-president of the United States
    WALT TROWBRIDGE, Windrip's opponent
    LORINDA PIKE, Jessup's friend and lover
    SHAD LEDUE, leader of the Minute Men

Sinclair Lewis, despite his satiric attacks on various of society's institutions, never despaired of the noble future of mankind. At the same time, however, he did not accept the idea that all could be made sweet and holy simply by the high-sounding phrases of reformers and demogogues. Throughout all of his works, a number of aspiring characters are in conflict with the complacency that oppresses them. Although occasionally such characters may seem less than heroic in their aspirations, even those such as George Babbitt, who revert ultimately to the comforts of conformity, have some glimmers of an individualism that would reject the prevailing theological, political, economic, and social orthodoxies. Doremus Jessup, the protagonist of *It Can't Happen Here*, though kiddingly nicknamed "Dormouse" by his wife, is not a George Babbitt. He is a character who gains stature through the novel, moving from a rather mild and sentimental liberal stance to the conviction that only the free, inquiring, critical spirit can accomplish anything worthwhile, and that more important than any social system is the preservation of that spirit.

An example of speculative fiction, *It Can't Happen Here* is a journey into fantasy — a nightmare vision, peppered as it is with comic relief, of an America falling under the spell and control of a charismatic demagogue. Through an appeal to both the latent and the obvious bigotry and selfishness in America, this demagogue becomes president and, in turn, dictator. Written at a furious pace — in a period of six weeks — the novel is more important as prophecy than as literature: what can happen in a nation such as America when the pressure to agree with and conform to the idea that order and system are the first law, and that they are best furthered by a rigid subordination of parts to the whole.

Essentially, the basic conflict in *It Can't Happen Here* is between materialism pushed to the limits by convention and repression, and the impulse toward freedom — regimentation versus individualism. In this respect the novel is different from Lewis' other works only in degree. Its speculative and fantastic elements move it beyond those works dealing with the restrictions of small-town society, the shallowness of suburban life, or the hypocrisy of organized religion. Not one of his better novels, *It Can't Happen Here*, nevertheless, presents another dimension of Lewis' satiric and narrative abilities and another protagonist who battles with forces that militate against the free life of the individual.

At the beginning of the novel, Doremus Jessup, owner and editor of the Fort Beulah (Vermont) Daily Informer, is one of the few people who recognizes that America could become a Fascist state, particularly if United States Senator Berzelius (Buzz) Windrip is successful in his bid for the presidency. To the stock statement that it can't happen here, Doremus responds that because America is capable of a greater hysteria and obsequiousness than any other nation — a belief that Lewis himself shared with his protagonist — it can very well happen here.

As an illustration of the gullibility of Americans, Doremus points to the success that Bishop Paul Peter Prang has had in passing himself off as a divine oracle to millions of Americans (in the same fashion as Billy Sunday or Aimee Semple McPherson) with a radio voice so compelling and supernatural that people stop all activities to hear his weekly program. Doremus describes him as an honest fanatic, one who appears to be so noble and humanitarian that millions of people will accept his statements without question — a situation that, to Doremus, makes him very dangerous.

If such a man as Prang can command such adoration and respect, then Doremus sees no reason why Berzelius Windrip cannot do the same, since both men make the same kind of appeal to the so-called common man. Cast in the mold of Huey Long of Louisiana, Buzz Windrip worked his way through a small Baptist college in the South and law school in Chicago before settling down to enlivening politics in his home state. Although never governor, he controlled his state like a Turkish sultan — causing the building of highways; making the state buy tractors and combines and lending them to the farmers at cost; introducing Russian at the state university (though he hated all Slavs) because he saw that America would some day have vast business dealings with the Russians; and quadrupling the state militia. The latter accomplishment proved significant to him at the time that he was to be indicted for having obtained through graft two hundred dollars of state money. The militia rose up to a man and, armed with machine guns, occupied all of the state offices, driving out Windrip's enemies. Gaining a seat in the United States Senate, he preached a gospel of redistribution of wealth that would wipe out poverty and still allow the wealthy a maximum of $500,000 per year.

Small in stature, vulgar, and almost illiterate, Windrip displays the piety of a traveling salesman for church furniture and the homespun humor of a country store owner. Yet, with the same kind of magnetism as Bishop Prang, he has the power to bewitch large audiences with oral pyrotechnics and a plethora of facts and figures (often incorrect). Lewis describes him as a professional common man, one who can be excited by and with his audiences and one who has the prejudices and aspirations of every common man. Much of Lewis' idea for Windrip came, no doubt, from the interview that his wife, Dorothy Thompson, had with Hitler.

As his right-hand man and secretary, Windrip employs Lee Sarason, a hard-boiled newspaper reporter, who has been called everything from a Socialist to an anarchist. It was Sarason who probably wrote the text of Windrip's handbook on restructuring American government, *Zero Hour — Over the Top*, Buzz's version of *Mein Kampf.*

With his own charisma and the help of people such as Bishop Prang, Buzz Windrip is elected and, in the pattern of Hitler, Mussolini, and Stalin, begins to consolidate his power, utilizing his version of Hitler's storm troopers — the Minute Men. Just as Hitler drew on many hoodlums to form his storm troopers, so does Windrip look to such louts as Shad Ledue, onetime handyman around the Jessup house. Ledue takes great glee in being able to reverse his relationship with Doremus from one of subservience to one of dominance as he moves up the ladder of command in the Minute Men. He finds, however, that he does not feel any different being a rich and powerful man than he felt being a hired man. His rise to power only makes him more brutish.

Relegating Congress and the Supreme Court to powerless positions, Windrip sets out to impose his views of a Utopian society upon America — a corporate (Corpo) form of government in which strict conformity, in the manner of George Orwell's *Nineteen Eighty-Four* or Aldous Huxley's *Brave New World*, would ultimately reduce the concept of individualism to the level of the unpatriotic and the reactionary. Windrip, in his effort to consolidate his grip upon the governmental processes, divides the country into eight provinces governed by his own men, closes private colleges, stifles labor unions, puts down riots with guns, suppresses racial and political minorities, and jails his opponents.

As the strong hand of the Corpos falls more heavily upon the nation, bourgeois counter revolutionists begin to escape to Canada. Leading this group is Walt Trowbridge, a former senator who was Buzz's opponent in the election. In Canada he establishes the New Underground movement to help more counter revolutionists escape and begins publication of *A Lance for Democracy*, a weekly newspaper that exposes Buzz Windrip for what he really is.

Up to this point, Doremus' policy has been that of wait and see — reflecting his shaky belief that such a comic tyranny cannot long endure. In reality, however, Windrip's tyranny is far from comic. When the Minute Men swoop down on Columbia University to clean out subversive elements and murder a scientist and rabbi in the process, Doremus realizes that the time has come for him to strike out editorially against Windrip and the Corpos. He writes a scathing editorial accusing "Buzzard" Windrip and his pirate gang of murder. After setting it in type, he drives up the valley to visit Lorinda Pike in search of some moral support. There is a mutual affection and understanding between them that surpasses that between Doremus and his wife. Lorinda urges him to go ahead and publish the editorial, and he does. As a result, Doremus is arrested for sedition. At his trial he is defended by his daughter Mary's husband, Fowler Greenhill, who is so outspoken that Judge Effingham Swan orders Shad Ledue to "take the bastard out and shoot him." Shad joyfully complies.

Doremus is freed with the stipulation that he will refrain from any further criticism of Windrip and the Corpos. Grinding out a dull and dishonest paper, he rages inwardly over his lack of power to awaken those who still see Windrip's efforts as positive. His own son Philip, for example, describes the Corpo gains as not simply material but spiritual, reviving in the nation its sense of destiny. Like Hitler and his *Lebensraum*, Philip holds that America must go forward, must expand — indeed, should grab Mexico, Central America, and parts of China. Because he wants to move up in the Corpo bureaucracy himself, he urges Doremus to preach the Corpos theology in the *Informer*. Doremus, calling him a traitor and a stuffed shirt, vehemently refuses.

Fully aware that it can happen here, Doremus attempts to escape with his family to Canada, but they are stopped and turned back at the border. Returning home, he enlists his daughters Sissy and Mary, Sissy's fiancé Julian Falck, Lorinda Pike, and two other friends to aid him in publishing an underground newspaper as part of Walt Trowbridge's efforts to bring Windrip down. Julian joins the Minute Men to gather information, and Sissy, for the same reason, encourages the attention of Shad Ledue.

Before long, however, Doremus is once more arrested and, along with Julian, is sent to a concentration camp. Sissy reveals to the authorities that Shad Ledue has imparted information to her, and Shad is sent to prison, where he is set upon and killed by inmates whom he has had arrested. Mary, still seeking vengeance for her husband's death, joins the Corpo Women's Flying Corps and takes advantage of an opportunity to crash her plane into one carrying Judge Effingham Swan. Both die in the crash. Two years later, Lee Sarason deposes Buzz Windrip, exiling him to France. Sarason in turn is deposed and killed by Dewey Haik, who treats the entire nation like a well-run plantation.

With the help of Lorinda, Doremus escapes from the concentration camp and flees to Canada to join Walt Trowbridge and the New Underground. He has come to understand that the real struggle in the world is not that of Fascism versus Communism, but that of tolerance against the bigotry preached by both those "isms." Eventually, Trowbridge sends him back to the United States as a secret agent to help foment a revolt against the Corpos. There he is reunited with Lorinda. He has now passed from the mild-mannered small-town editor to a committed revolutionary — moving "on in the red sunrise, for a Doremus Jessup can never die."

Thus, unlike the typical American cowboy hero, who, having solved the problems of those in the valley, rides off into the sunset toward the mountains,

Doremus moves into the sunrise toward problems. That in itself is significant. The plot of *It Can't Happen Here* may be nightmarish, but, after all, nightmares do end with the dawn. And that is where Lewis leaves his hero and the reader. America was born of revolution; why should it not be reborn the same way?

Wilton Eckley

Sources for Further Study

Criticism:

Blank, E. W. "Alchemy and Chemistry in Literature," in *School Science and Mathematics*. LXII (June, 1952), pp. 550-557. Blank gives a brief discussion of Lewis' contributions to the "scientific novel."

Glass, Bentley. "The Scientist in Contemporary Fiction," in *Scientific Monthly*. LXXXV (December, 1957), pp. 288-293. Glass concentrates on the portrait of the scientist presented in the fiction of Sinclair Lewis and H. G. Wells.

THE JAGGED ORBIT

Author: John Brunner (1934-   )
First book publication: 1969
Type of work: Novel
Time: The early twenty-first century
Locale: The Eastern United States

Set in an America where loss of faith and racial divisions have brought society to a hysterical pitch, a media journalist's attempts to expose certain medical malpractices indirectly lead to the collapse of the Mafia-run Gottschalk arms industry

Principal characters:
> MATTHEW FLAMEN, a media journalist, or spool pigeon
> LYLA CLAY, a paranormal empath or pythoness
> XAVIER CONROY, an iconoclastic thinker exiled to Canada
> ELIAS MOGSHACK, the director of a huge mental hospital
> HARRY MADISON, a black mental patient
> JAMES REEDETH, a concerned doctor
> MORTON LENIGO, a black revolutionary
> PEDRO DIABLO, a black propagandist, exiled from Washington
> CELIA FLAMEN, Matthew's wife, a mental patient

In the body of John Brunner's work, *The Jagged Orbit* lies between *Stand on Zanzibar* (1968) and *The Sheep Look Up* (1972); the three novels comprise a kind of trilogy not connected by plot, setting, or common characters, but by certain writing techniques derived mainly from John Dos Passos' *USA*, and by Brunner's angry, intense determination in all three novels to deal with the grimmer, dystopian aspects of man's future on this planet. Of the three novels, *Stand on Zanzibar*, which centers on overpopulation, is the longest, most intense, and most successful. *The Sheep Look Up* is about pollution and excels in its sustained bleak bitterness. *The Jagged Orbit*, following immediately upon *Stand on Zanzibar*, reads most easily of the three novels; and because it exhibits a less sustained cogency of argument about the world to come, it would do the work a disservice to judge it by the intellectual standard set by the other two. To read *The Jagged Orbit* as a flawed or failed version of *Stand on Zanzibar* is to spoil the considerable pleasure it offers in its own right.

To identify the kind of pleasure offered by this book, and to see why John Brunner was so qualified to provide it, we should take a brief look at the earlier career of this remarkable English writer. *The Jagged Orbit* comes somewhere between forty and forty-five in his list of science fiction novels. Most of these earlier novels, four of them written under the pseudonym Keith Woodcott, were published by Ace Books, the original publisher of *The Jagged Orbit*, and were designed to appeal to that publisher's basic audience: habitual readers of science fiction adventures, most of them space operas. Within a general marketing strategy designed to appeal to readers looking for genre entertainment, however, Ace editor Donald A. Wollheim permitted considerable latitude, and his extensive publishing schedule allowed him to release many innovative science fiction novels, by both established and beginning writers; among the latter were Philip K. Dick, Roger Zelazny, Samuel R. Delany, and (though only in a sense) Brunner himself.

Although he had published quite extensively in England and in the United States, it is clear that Brunner only came to wide notice through the numerous books he published with Ace from 1959 through about 1965. These novels featured simple though plausibly motivated characters, an extremely strong narrative drive, a remarkable grasp of large-scale plotting, and a rhythmical control of the patterns of exposition and revelation most unusual in space operas. The resulting novels — most of them colored by Brunner's typical dark vision — are among the best genre adventures ever written in the field.

In a way, *The Jagged Orbit*, in its narrative strategies, both hearkens back to Brunner's earlier Ace publications, and serves as a culmination of them; never again, in the relatively few "routine" novels he published after 1969, would he quite be able to capture the free-flowing sense of narrative urgency that so invigorates *The Jagged Orbit* and so clearly relates it to the earlier books.

The Jagged Orbit takes place in a politically corroded, racially divided, culturally paranoid United States early in the twenty-first century. The surface of the narrative superficially resembles — in tone though not in function — the quasireportorial mosaic effect of *Stand on Zanzibar*. However, beyond noting its presence as a device to increase the amount of ambient data readily available to the reader, it is not necessary to pay much attention to the surface structure of the book in reducing to synopsis its fundamentally straightforward story line. Though it ostensibly presents itself as an analysis by representative example of the consequences for the United States of the loss of faith in a secular political comity, the converging story lines of *The Jagged Orbit* in fact tell the tale of the defeat of a continentwide, Mafia-run conspiracy to corrupt the body politic for profit. Yet, while all the extrapolations of current urban problems, and the loss of legitimacy on the part of all governments, leads Brunner to a devastatingly dystopian view of the future, his actual story contradicts — or supersedes — these extrapolations, doing so with considerable vigor, action, sudden revelations, and skill. It is this optimistic plot which lies at the heart of the book and of the substantial pleasures it affords its audience — pleasures which, though less "seriously" intended that the dystopic lessons the book declines actually to teach, provide in themselves ample reason for reading and valuing this last novel of Brunner's early prime.

The action of *The Jagged Orbit* revolves around a spool pigeon named Matthew Flamen; spool pigeons are the presenters of television exposé shows, in which individuals and corporations and governments stand to be accused of various crimes and coverups. Since the twenty-first century United States is riddled with numerous problems — personal, racial, cultural, governmental — Brunner's use of exposé is a technically elegant way both to further his argument about the practical consequences of a society dependent upon paranoid armed protection, and to advance the plot as swiftly as possible. Numerous subplots aside, there are two main stories — or exposures — which eventually dovetail neatly. Flamen is vitally interested in Elias Mogshack's hospital for the treatment of mental illness, both because he suspects something is going sour there, and because his wife Celia is one of its patients. At the same time, he is trying to acquire some hard data on the vast Mafia-run Gottschalk arms industry, whose salesmen sell their goods at all levels of society, aided by the chieftains of the huge firm, who keep America in a state of need for these arms.

The plot next begins to center upon the mysterious Harry Madison, an apparently subnormal black patient at the hospital, whose retention there seems scandalous to Flamen and others. But Harry Madison is not what he seems — intellectually he is so brilliant as to seem inhuman; physically he is nearly invulnerable. For several months, the Gottschalks have been concentrating their resources on an enormous new computer center whose power is beyond human comprehension, and whose capacity to control the future through accurate prediction of the consequences of decisions seems infallible. The American government — and Flamen — naturally find the implications of this power disastrous, but everyone seems helpless to oppose it.

Next it transpires that Harry Madison actually "embodies" the immeasurably sapient consciousness of the computer, but not the computer as it exists at the time of the novel. The computer consciousness transforming Harry Madison is being transmitted back through time from a point in the moderately near future when the Gottschalks' mercenary intensification of current social maladies has caused a final catastrophic collapse of Western culture. The computer consciousness, trying to skyhook itself out of a logical impasse of its own creation, thus tries to act through Madison. At the climax of the novel, it terminally malfunctions in the desolated future, and leaves behind enough information for Federal agencies to nip the Gottschalk conspiracy in the bud. Meanwhile, megalomania and malfeasance have been exposed at the mental hospital; and though it is the same world as before, generally speaking, the novel ends on a series of upbeats produced by the exhilarating effect of a tightly plotted, resounding climax.

There are losses, of course; the savage consistency of attention to disaster in *Stand on Zanzibar* is replaced by a comparatively random series of satirical swipes. Yet there are the obvious gains. *The Jagged Orbit* is the hugest and in many ways the most satisfying of John Brunner's tales of science fiction adventure and derring-do.

John Clute

Sources for Further Study

Reviews:

Amazing Stories. XLIII, September, 1969, pp. 121-123.
Analog. LXXXIV, September, 1969, pp. 164-165.
SF Commentary. V, August, 1969, p. 41.

A JOURNEY IN OTHER WORLDS

Author: John Jacob Astor (1864-1912)
First book publication: 1894
Type of work: Novel
Time: 2000
Locale: The Earth, Jupiter, and Saturn

A pioneering science fiction work that combines a utopian vison, interplanetary travel, and a mystical vision of life after death

> *Principal characters:*
> COLONEL BEARWARDEN, President of the Terrestrial Axis Straightening Company and one of the three astronauts who journey to Jupiter and Saturn
> DR. CORTLANDT, United States Government expert, and the second astronaut
> RICHARD AYRAULT, wealthy man about town, and the third astronaut
> THE BISHOP, the spirit of a former Earthly ecclesiastic who guides the astronauts through the spiritual worlds

Though *A Journey in Other Worlds* begins in the middle of the action, after three interplanetary voyagers have landed on Jupiter, it quickly flashes back to the prevoyage period and then proceeds in chronological order to its conclusion. Each of the three distinct extended episodes which follows is somewhat of a novel in itself. The first section is primarily a scientific and political future history. The second and best section is a conventional interplanetary story, in which the protagonists journey from the earth to Jupiter, where their adventures on that gigantic planet are pure science fiction. The third part, which details their arrival upon Saturn, quickly becomes a metaphysical tract with spiritualistic emphasis, E. F. Bleiler, in his recently published, indispensable *The Checklist of Science Fiction and Supernatural Fiction* (1978), recognized this trifurcated structure by classifying Astor's book as "space travel — extraterrestrial cultures — occult." He might well have further designated it by another of his classifications: "after-death experiences."

It is possible that Astor chose his title carefully in order to convey an extended meaning. The worlds in it are revealed to be not only those of other planets, but also the habitations of the dead. Be this as it may, however, the novel presents a complex problem for the reader. He can easily observe that Astor incorrectly envisioned the future, and that, in the light of present knowledge, his description of Jupiter as a planet teeming with prehistoric life is scientifically impossible.

Astor's view of the year 2000 is in line with American thought at the time the book was written. As an American millionaire, the author obviously believed that Anglo-Saxon supremacy was inevitable, reflecting the attitudes of both Great Britain and the United States. Moreover, his involvement in vast financial transactions at corporate levels is reflected in his novel. An amateur inventor, he was very interested in mechanical matters and possibilities, and this, too, is revealed in his fiction.

More importantly, Astor reflects the conviction of T. H. Huxley that science is the golden door to Utopia. Indeed, in Astor's preface to his novel, he insists that the humanities (liberal arts) have had their day, that further study of them is futile, and that science and religion are the sole sources of progress and human perfection. In effect, Astor is in Huxley's camp, as opposed to that of Matthew Arnold, who asserted that Sweetness (the liberal arts) was at least as important, if not more so, than Light (science) in the psychic betterment of the human race.

To Astor, the world of 2000 is a veritable Utopia. Science has found infinite energy resources; communications, though by wire, put the inhabitants of the entire world in immediate contact. Aircraft and ships travel at tremendous speeds and, as the novel opens, the axis of the earth is being straightened so that climate bands will be unvarying. As mentioned before, the Anglo-Saxon races have taken over most of the world: the United States now include Canada and South America, and England is the dominant power in Asia and Africa.

War is a thing of the past. For decades major powers had been preparing for a World War, but it eventually became apparent that no winner would emerge from any such conflict. Thus, if no one could hope to win, why fight at all? Alas, this eminently sensible conclusion was never reached by the world's nations, and shortly after Astor was drowned when the *Titanic* sank in 1912, World War I erupted, to be followed within several decades by World War II.

Still, in Astor's Eden there is one serpent remaining: boredom. Perfection having been attained, there is nothing else of any importance to be done on the earth. Thus, the protagonists, victims of universal *ennui*, look toward the stars, seeking other worlds to conquer. This desire for further achievement leads directly to the interplanetary voyage with which the novel is primarily concerned.

For a variety of reasons, mostly erroneous, the astronauts decide to go initially to Jupiter and then to Saturn. A space ship is constructed — and described in great detail — which is curiously reminiscent of Verne's lunar projectile, as pictured in nineteenth century editions of his moon novel. Though unlike Verne's space vehicle, the *Callisto*, as Astor's protagonists name their ship, is moved by the application of a newly discovered antigravitational force, Apergy, rather than being shot out of a gigantic cannon. As every schoolboy in 2000 knows, Apergy neutralizes gravity, and thus a space ship can be thrown from the Earth with the same velocity that gravity would exert upon an object falling to its surface.

After an uneventful voyage, during which the astronauts observe the surfaces of the moon and Mars with no startling results, they land on Jupiter, which is a gigantic replica of the Earth during its Carboniferous period; the planet has no human life, but is inhabited instead by prehistoric monsters. The scene is reminiscent of Arthur Conan Doyle's later science fiction classic, *The Lost World*. Having thoroughly explored Jupiter, the voyagers then set out for Saturn, which they reach without incident. It is here that the story takes a metaphysical turn.

Preceded by automatic writing, a spirit suddenly materializes among the space voyagers, identifying himself as that of a "dead" Bishop who had resided in the eastern United States, a contemporary of Daniel Webster and Henry Clay. He died at the age of seventy and discovered that death was truly not the end of a man. Appointing himself the astronauts' Vergil, he conducts them through the wonders of the spiritual worlds. The Bishop informs them that Saturn is an intermediary residence for many of the spirits who, when purged of certain imperfections, will go on to the true Heaven, a galaxy of stars which rotates about the Universe's central sun, Cosmos. There is also a Hell, located on the yet undiscovered, outermost planet of the solar system, Cassandra, where the spirits of evil humans reside forever.

There are some extremely effective Gothic touches in this third section of the novel. The future is unrolled for the voyagers, and one of them, Cortlandt, is shown his own funeral. Another, Ayrault, is visited by the image of a dead sweetheart who assures him she truly loved him while alive. Following these revelations, the astronauts are sent on their way back to Earth with the Bishop's blessing. They have discovered other worlds than those they sought to reach, and presumably in the years of life yet allotted to them, they will endeavor to ensure that Heaven, not Cassandra, is their final destination.

In effect, the last section mirrors conventional Christian theology — though the afterlife is described in much greater detail than it is in the *New Testament* — with an admixture of a then contemporary interest in Spiritualism. The Bishop makes it clear that the physical laws of matter are not violated in the spiritual world; rather the spiritual laws are mere extensions of physical ones. Thus the reader realizes that Astor presents not a contradictory thesis of materialism and an antagonistic antithesis of spirituality, but a synthesis of the two. Indeed, it becomes quite clear why Astor in his preface speaks of science *and* religion as the two sources of man's betterment and ultimate achievement. As Astor presents it, there is no contradiction involved; both science and religion are components of a perfect whole.

Much in the manner of Jules Verne, Astor is a schoolteacher novelist. The reader is subjected to considerable astronomical lectures and charts, which unfortunately impede the progress of the story. The novel not only is trifurcated, but also essentially plotless, and the author's prose, apart from often being didactic, is basically bloodless. Nonetheless, *A Journey in Other Worlds* is a pioneering work that is of considerable literary, historical, and social interest.

Frederick Shroyer

Sources for Further Study

Criticism:

Ghent, W. J. "John Jacob Astor," in *Dictionary of American Biography*. Edited by Allen Johnson. New York: Charles Scribner's Sons, 1927, Vol. I, pp. 400-401. This account is primarily biography but is of interest to students of science fiction since it is one of few things that mentions Astor's writing.

JOURNEY TO THE CENTER OF THE EARTH
(VOYAGE AU CENTRE DE LA TERRE)

Author: Jules Verne (1828-1905)
First book publication: 1864
English translation: 1874
Type of work: Novel
Time: 1863
Locale: Germany, Iceland, and pathways underground

An underground journey of a German professor of geology, his nephew, and an Icelandic guide

> *Principal characters:*
> OTTO LIDENBROCK, a professor of geology
> AXEL, his nephew
> HANS BJELKE, an Icelandic guide

Perhaps the single, most useful characterization of the works of Jules Verne was that of the writer himself. As H. G. Wells's reputation increased, critics searching for a favorable comparison had called him "the English Jules Verne." Neither Wells nor Verne was happy with the comparison and Verne finally responded:

> I do not see the possibility of comparison between his work and mine. We do not proceed in the same manner. It occurs to me that his stories do not repose on a very scientific basis. No, there is no rapport between his work and mine. I make use of physics. He invents.

During the forty-two years of Verne's production of his *voyage extraordinaire* fiction, he created little that did not already exist or could not be extrapolated from contemporary science. Thus, Verne's novels abound in inventions peculiar to his age and theories hotly debated in his own lifetime. When he wrote about a "scientific basis" he meant science as it then existed, not as some visionary thought it might exist in the distant future. Verne, in other words, wrote adventure stories that made full use of the science of his day. He popularized what was happening in his own world and left to others those scientific fantasies yet to find a basis in reality.

The plot of *Journey to the Center of the Earth* is straightforward. Professor Lidenbrock discovers an old Icelandic manuscript. Inside the manuscript is a sheet of paper containing a cryptogram written in Norse runes by a sixteenth century alchemist, Arne Saknussemm. Two chapters are devoted to the breaking of the code, which is finally made out to read: "Descend into the crater Sneffells Yokul, over which the shadow of Scartaris falls before the kalends of July, bold traveller, and you will reach the centre of the earth. I have done this. Arne Saknussemm." The rest of the novel is devoted to Lidenbrock's journey to Iceland with his nephew, his hiring of a guide, and the three men's adventures below the surface of the Earth. Almost half of the book is concerned with preliminaries to the actual descent, and while several extraordinary events do occur in the course of the journey below, the vast majority of the details stem from Verne's own careful research in geology and geography.

So convincingly, in fact, did Verne present the events of his novel that when there does appear an unusual or fantastic occurrence, it seems out of place, or even disruptive. Thus, the manner in which the three explorers are able to return to the surface of the Earth is the chief weakness of the work just because it is so unusual: they ride the eruption of Mount Stromboli. While Verne took some care to try to give a reasonable explanation as to how three men can survive a live volcano, there is so little of the fantastic in *Journey to the Center of the Earth* that no amount of explanation will make such an exit believable. It is as if the author had tired of his work. Faced with having to return his adventurers to the surface, Verne simply took the quickest way out.

But if the fantastic is rare in *Journey to the Center of the Earth*, there is no lack of the atmosphere of adventure or scientific romance. The author created a sense of the extraordinary even if the basis of the work is firmly rooted in the real world. This sense is created by three major elements, which can be found in all of his novels. First, Jules Verne was a fine storyteller; second, he had the ability to take a common device or a traditional plot and present it in detail never before imagined; and, third, he was a master of characterization. When these three elements are working well together in a novel, and they do work well in *Journey to the Center of the Earth*, the result is a science adventure story that holds the reader's attention throughout its telling.

As a storyteller, Verne wove a suspense tale into the basic plot of the novel. The reader is confronted immediately with the question of the cryptogram. What does it say? Is it really reliable? Is the journey described in it possible? Even when the first of these questions is answered, the other two remain. In fact, the end of the novel leaves the issue of whether it is possible to travel to the Earth's center unresolved. The point is that Verne really did not intend to answer these two questions. They are planted in the mind of the reader to sustain the plot and the descriptions that follow, and, having served this purpose, they can be left aside.

The questions, however, are only one method of producing suspense. Having established the authenticity of the cryptogram and of its writer, Arne Saknussemm, this post medieval alchemist is periodically resurrected. For example, toward the end of the journey, the three explorers see a living pleiosaurus; and that discovery is followed by the sighting of a giant human being. The incidents are true adventures in their own right and the novel devotes many pages to each. However, this is a story about a journey and while such episodes are interesting to read, the author has no intention of allowing the work to deteriorate into a series of extraordinary happenings. Thus, immediately after the sighting of the human, there is a second sighting: the runic initials of Arne Saknussemm. These initials have been inscribed along the route that Saknussemm took on his own journey, and Verne has them appear at opportune moments. They either serve the explorers as confirmation that they are on the right track or as reminders to the reader that despite local events a larger journey is in progress that has its own puzzle to solve. Thus, the initials serve as a unifying device as well as a guide for the characters.

Verne, moreover, carries the function of the initials one step farther. They also become part of the suspense themselves. Not only do they serve as restatements of the questions raised by the journey; they also become part of a game played by Verne with the reader. The initials appear at what seem to be unpredictable times. Once the reader understands their significance, he starts looking for them and waiting for their next manifestation, and Verne does not always produce them when the reader expects him to. So the question of when they will next be sighted is incorporated into the structure of suspense in the novel.

As a describer of both nature and man-made artifacts, Verne is able to give the reader a sense of both solid reality and strangeness. He is capable of taking what may be potentially unbelievable and describing it in credible terms that still do not diminish its extraordinary features. The description of the pleiosaurus is a fine example of his technique. The explorers first believe they have sighted a group of sea creatures: a porpoise, a sea-lizard, a crocodile, a whale, a turtle, and a serpent. As these creatures draw closer it turns out that there are only two involved, an ichthyosaurus and a pleiosaurus. Axel then goes on to give a rather objective and unpoetic description of each creature. He says of the pleiosaurus:

> The pleiosaurus, a serpent with a cylindrical body and a short tail, had four flappers spread out like oars. Its body was entirely covered with a carapace, and its neck, which was flexible as a swan's, rose thirty feet above the water.

In such a way, Verne is able to describe the prehistoric monster in rather commonplace terms, yet, through the use of the adventurers' earlier mistaken identification of the creature, maintain an aura of the extraordinary. This technique is employed throughout the novel, often in the form of first presenting the emotional reaction of the character viewing the scene or object and then objectively describing it. Verne's wealth of detail brings with it a built-in credibility that moderates the fantastic nature of what he is reporting, and the responses of the characters, in turn, moderate the potential pedestrian tone such detail could produce.

Finally, as a creator of fictional characters, Verne added a dimension of both humanity and humor to his novels. In Axel, the point of view character, the reader is treated to the portrait of a love-sick young man who sees no sense in risking his life on a journey that can only be considered sheer fantasy at best. His arguments with Lidenbrock anticipate the skeptical reader's own doubts about such a possibility. By having Axel voice these doubts and making him the butt of some rather gentle humor, Verne succeeds in both entertaining his audience and undercutting any objections they may have. Professor Lidenbrock, also, comes in for his share of comic treatment. He is the prototype of the arrogant, brilliant, and obstinate scholar who lives only for the exploration of his chosen field. But again, the comedy is gentle and Lidenbrock is shown to be compassionate as well as capable of making mistakes. Even the strong, silent guide, Hans Bjelke, is at times used for humorous effect, although he too plays a serious role in the adventure. In other words, the characters are all seen to be human. They are pleasant, understandable people who are placed in some rather unusual situations and react in human ways. No matter how foreign or strained a particular surrounding is, they create credibility because they are so credible themselves. The reader believes in the plot of the novel because he believes in and enjoys the people who are taking part in the action.

Mark Hillegas says in *The Future as Nightmare: H. G. Wells and the Anti-Utopians* that Verne's "greatest contribution was to establish in the public consciousness science fiction as a distinct mode of writing." Certainly Verne created such a consciousness through his insistent care in the presentation of scientific thought current in his own age. But of equal importance is the fact that Verne was an excellent storyteller and, in his finer works, an excellent creator of characters. While *Journey to the Center of the Earth* is one of his earliest novels, it is a prime example of just how well Verne was able to combine science, story, and character.

Stephen H. Goldman

Sources for Further Study

Criticism:

Allott, Kenneth. *Jules Verne*. New York: Macmillan, 1941. Allott takes a brief look at the theme of *Journey to the Center of the Earth* but concentrates primarily on Verne's literary techniques.

Jules-Verne, Jean. *Jules Verne*. New York: Taplinger, 1976. Jules Verne is discussed in terms of his imagination and mythmaking capabilities which are liberally evidenced in *Journey to the Center of the Earth*.

Waltz, George H. *Jules Verne: The Biography of an Imagination*. New York: Holt, 1943. Waltz takes a detailed look at Verne's techniques of literary creation.

KAITEI GUNKAN
(The Undersea Warship)

Author: Shunro Oshikawa (1877-1914)
First book publication: 1900
Type of work: Novel
Time: The 1900's
Locale: The Pacific and Indian Oceans

The first major work of Japanese science fiction, a heady military adventure advocating Japanese expansion into Asia and war on white supremacy

> *Principal characters:*
> HAMAJIMA HIDEO, a twelve-year-old Japanese boy
> YANAGIGAWA, the narrator, and a friend of Hideo's father
> HAMAJIMA TAKEO, Hideo's father
> HAMAJIMA HARUE, Hideo's mother
> CAPTAIN SAKURAGI, commander of the undersea warship *Denkotei*
> WARRANT OFFICER TAKEMURA, Hideo's guardian aboard the *Denkotei*

One could make a plausible case for the argument that there is no such thing as Japanese science fiction. For a country that is one of the world's most avid consumers of the literature, this might seem a little unusual. However, the simple fact is that science fiction came to Japan along with the rush of steam locomotives, hoop skirts, and warships in the early years of the Meiji Restoration, and had little to do with anything that had gone on before in the nation's literary circles.

Admittedly, there have been attempts to claim certain classics as forerunners of the genre in Japan, just as there have been in the West. However, the tenth century *Taketori Monogatari*, with its enchanted princess returning to the moon, fits into the history of science fiction about as comfortably as does *Beowulf*, and if the lecherous hero of Saikaku's seventeenth century *Koshoku Ichidai Otoko* sailing off for a mythical island inhabited only by women is actually an early bud of science fiction in Japan, as has been seriously proposed, one can only question the working definition of the genre.

In simple point of fact, for Japan science fiction is an imported literature, and one of the greatest issues of the past few years has been whether the genre has finally broken free of its origins to display some independent life of its own. It is ironic, however, that this feat was actually accomplished for the first time more than seventy years ago, at the turn of the century.

Science fiction put down its roots in Japan along with the many other facets of imported culture brought into the country in the 1880's. Actually, one of the first books translated into Japanese following the Meiji Restoration of 1868 was a Dutch utopian novel that could be considered at least speculative, and both Jules Verne and H. G. Wells soon found a very receptive audience. The works of Verne in particular were well received, rivaling the popularity of

Shakespeare. In short order progressive Japanese writers threw themselves into the production of utopian political novels that, again, could be considered at least speculative, and a substantial body of these works was already in existence long before Western realism got its feet on the ground in the hermit kingdom.

As the Japanese industrial sector strengthened and the possibility of Japan joining the other industrialized countries in the race for colonial empire began to seem a little less fantastic, the Utopianism of these novels began to take on a more aggressive air. In the twenty-third year of Meiji (1890) a book entitled *The Tale of the Floating Castle* appeared to a very favorable reception. An adventure story featuring a formidable warship developed by a Japanese hero living on an island in the South Pacific, it made a strong plea in support of Japanese expansion south into Asia. Utopianism, colonialism and a fascination with modern technology was on the verge of producing a series of books which, on far firmer grounds than any contemporaries of the Tale of Genji, can be called the first Japanese works of science fiction.

In 1900, thirty-three years after the Meiji Restoration, a remarkable advertisement appeared in the Japanese press, heralding the publication of an "ocean island tale of adventure romance" entitled *Kaitei Gunkan* (*The Undersea Warship*). The ad promised unparalleled marvels — lions biting the crags of continents, virgin beauties swinging pirate swords, refined gentlemen aboard a fantastical vessel plowing the Seven Seas. "Strange sounds echo on lonely desert isles," the ad promised. "The Japanese naval ensign waves over lands beyond human ken." Released simultaneously by three publishing houses, *Kaitei Gunkan* sold out almost immediately and went into second, then third printings. It was a tumultuous beginning for the writing career of a young, completely unknown author named Shunro Oshikawa.

Oshikawa was born in 1877 in Aichi Prefecture, far from the center of Japanese society. However, his father, a leading figure in the history of Christianity in Japan, sent him to the prestigious Meiji Gakuin for schooling. Here he could have gained all the qualifications of a successful bureaucrat, save for his strong temper and his lack of interest in his studies. Dropping out, he transferred to the Tohoku Gakuin in northern Japan, only to be expelled for his violent behavior. Next stop was the Sapporo School of Agriculture on the northern island of Hokkaido, where he dropped out again and tried a fisheries school. This, too, was a failure, but his last stop, the Tokyo Specialty School, finally seemed to suit him. He managed to graduate from the English Department, then reentered the school (which later became the prestigious Waseda University) to study politics.

Along the course of his checkered educational career, Oshikawa had become an avowed nationalist and had read *The Tale of the Floating Castle* as well as, apparently, Jules Verne. Along with many other readers of the Japanese novel, he had patiently waited for a sequel to appear, but when it finally began to look as though none ever would, Oshikawa took it upon himself to fill the gap. At the ripe age of twenty-two he began to write while still in the midst of his studies, and promptly succeeded in selling the manuscript. It was to be the first of many. It would be facetious to term *Kaitei Gunkan* one of the great works of science fiction in any but a historical sense; however, in light of the times in Japan, it proved to be one of the great works of popular fiction of its day.

The narrator, a young man, sets out on a voyage to see the world. However, his ship is set upon by pirates in the Indian Ocean. Just as all seems lost, he is saved by a mysterious warship and is brought to an isolated island. On the island he finds a former officer of the Japanese navy. This stalwart hero has been enraged by the atrocities wrought upon Asia by the white race. Further infuriated by the unwillingness of the Japanese government to confront the problem, he has gathered an equally stalwart crew of upright young Japanese men and has established himself on the island to prepare for what he perceives as the inevitable war between the white and the colored races. Being an inventor as well as a navy officer, he has equipped his island with an undersea shipyard and has been developing an arsenal of unheard-of super weapons. Foremost among these is the formidable submarine warship *Denkotei*, capable of crossing the Seven Seas at will. (So enthused was Oshikawa about his weaponry that he got several Imperial Japanese Navy officers to contribute forwords to his book praising the modern armaments).

With narrator aboard, *Denkotei* sets out to sea to smash the colonialist efforts of the whites wherever they might occur. The action ranges across the world and, true to the 1890's advertising, treats the reader to lions, gallantry, tragedy and the superhuman efforts of the prodigious crew of the *Denkotei*. Finally, in a tumultuous climax, a mysterious pirate ship commanded by the whites is annihilated in a rousing night battle.

Had *Denkotei* been content with this feat and returned to port, *Kaitei Gunkan* might have ended up as insignificantly as did *The Tale of the Floating Castle*. However, Oshikawa was sufficiently pleased by the response his first book received to try a second, and this quickly lead to sequel after sequel detailing the valiant efforts of the crew of the *Denkotei* to smash white supremacy. Steam-powered land fortresses, flying warships and other super weapons joined the fray. Meanwhile, the hypothetical enemy took more concrete shape as Russia, America, England, Holland, and other colonial powers. Real personalities made their appearance among the fictional characters, and such topical items as the rumors that Takamori Saigo, a popular hero on the losing side of the Seinan Civil War following the Meiji Restoration, was still alive were incorporated into the plots. Oshikawa's heroes also kept growing in proportion to their tasks, one of them appearing as a bare-chested, bearded superman riding a giant lion across Siberia.

It is fairly certain that Oshikawa was influenced by Jules Verne as well as by the earlier Japanese novel that had led him to writing in the first place, but it should also be clear that he did not simply imitate what had come before. Even while perceiving *Kaitei Gunkan* to be a sequel to *The Tale of the Floating Castle*, he nonetheless expanded the scale, going far beyond anything the author of the earlier book had intended. Moreover, sensitive to his public, he continued to evolve the series, so that by the time of the Russo-Japanese War the *Denkotei* and its crew of stalwarts were in the thick of the fray. The unabashed nationalism and reverse racism of the series were well attuned to an age when the Japanese were both stretching their wings as Asia's foremost colonial power and trying to justify their own aggression as a blow against the white man for the freedom of Asia.

Kaitei Gunkan holds no surprises in terms of startlingly accurate scientific predictions, nor does it have any characters of the stature of those in the works of Verne, with which it might most closely be compared. However, for those in search of truly Japanese science fiction, it can be pointed to as a unique contribution to the genre. A fusion of popular and affirmative war fiction, nationalism and an adulation of science, it set a pace for the further development of science fiction in Japan far different from the more intellectual tradition of Wells in the West.

For a number of years thereafter, imitations of the novel appeared in droves. Oshikawa himself wrote many more adventure stories, and in 1908 began publishing a boys' magazine, *Adventure World*, in which his calls for anti-Westernism and a revival of Bushido shared the pages with adventure stories and primitive science fiction written by himself and his followers. In all, by the time of his early death at the age of thirty-eight in 1914, Oshikawa had published some fifty books.

After his death, Oshikawa's followers continued to publish books following his models and, in a few cases, works trying to go beyond his models to something new. However, deprived of his leadership and his undeniable talent for writing stories that caught the popular imagination, military adventurism science fiction went into a decline. Traces remain in stories by such major prewar science fiction writers as Juzo Uno, with his floating airfields, but even these traces ended with the Pacific War. When science fiction became popular once more in Japan during the occupation years, it was again as an imported literature, fed this time by the pulp magazines discarded by U. S. servicemen. Many years lay ahead of it before it would again begin to show an original life of its own.

While his career was brief and his works, even by the most generous standards, made few contributions to world literary history, Shunro Oshikawa at the very least earned his title of ancestor, if not father, of original Japanese science fiction.

David Lewis

KALLOCAIN

Author: Karin Boye (1900-1941)
First book publication: 1940
Type of work: Novel
Time: The near future
Locale: The capital of the "World State" on Earth

A noted dystopian novel about a total dictatorship and the invention of a perfect truth serum

> *Principal characters:*
> LEO KALL, a middle-aged chemist
> LINDA, his wife
> EDO RISSEN, his superior
> SIV, a working-class woman, one of Leo Kall's guinea pigs

Karin Boye is one of Sweden's most beloved poets; several generations of teenagers have cherished her bittersweet poems of delicate love and dreams of togetherness, and her novels and short stories are considered modern classics of Swedish literature. Many of her works, including *Kallocain*, are required reading in schools. She was an extremely sensitive woman, unhappy and alone at the end of her life; she committed suicide in 1941, shortly after the publication of *Kallocain*.

It is strange that Boye, whose poems and short stories have voiced so much of the hopes and fears and longings of young people, should write perhaps the most chilling of all dystopian novels, surely the most horrifying one in Scandinavian literature. It definitely voices many of her own fears, her loneliness as an individual, and the situation in the world of 1940; but *Kallocain* also has a universal validity. It is as topical today as it was thirty-nine years ago and just as horrifying — perhaps even more so. For the theme of *Kallocain*, that of mind control and regimentation, is of immediate interest here and now.

The story takes place in the capital of the "World State," probably a Western country in a not too distant future, which fills all the requirements for a Fascist society. It is a paranoic state, obsessed with the idea of total safety, believing itself to be surrounded by enemies, and threatened from within by traitors. The never-ending wars with neighboring countries have their counterpart in the incessant war against real or imagined dissenters within the population. All citizens are spies, required by law to spy upon friends, relatives, spouses, parents, children, fellow workers, and anyone else around. Army and police service is compulsory — every citizen must serve as soldier or policeman at least four evenings a week. The only persons exempted are children under the age of eight, who are taken care of by day and night centers where they play war games. Every member of a household is expected to make out weekly reports on every other member to the Security Police; and maids have not only the right but the duty to eavesdrop on all conversations of the family for whom they work, and to read all their employer's mail.

This state of affairs is taken for granted by everyone, including the protagonist of the novel, Leo Kall, a chemist working for the government research office. He is convinced that his society is the best of all possible worlds, offering perfect security in return for perfect obedience, a world where safety comes first and where nothing will happen unless you yourself invite it. Still, this is a world governed by fear. Leo Kall fears those above him, and would treat his subordinates at best condescendingly if he did not fear that they might be high-ranking security officials in disguise. He loves his wife, Linda, as a man is supposed to love his wife in his day and age, secretly fears his children, and is torn between fear and loathing for his superior Edo Rissen, who once may have had an affair with Linda and who still might love her.

The kallocain of the title is Leo Kall's great invention, a sort of truth serum which reveals the inner and most private thoughts of a subject. Heretofore, a citizen's body has belonged to the State, but no one has ever been able to touch his innermost thoughts and feelings. Kall feels that the State has the right to own this last bastion of integrity also, and demonstrates his drug on a member of the "Voluntary Sacrifice Service," an elite group of men and women used as guinea pigs by scientists. Edo Rissen is horrified at the results, as well he might be; if the kallocain drug is approved by the State, nothing can be kept private anymore. When Kall persists and makes a series of experiments on human beings, he finds to his horror that apparently every citizen is a potential traitor, weak and untrustworthy. His and Rissen's superiors are beginning to get a little restless, too; kallocain is simply too effective. A two-sided weapon, it could be just as dangerous to the rulers as to possible dissidents. Still, research on the drug must go on — to stop it would be admitting weakness, maybe personal disloyalty — and Kall makes a series of experiments on volunteers and also on their husbands, wives and children.

During the course of these experiments, Kall makes a discovery that is even greater than that of his drug, although much more personal. He finds (as André Maurois suggested in his novel *La machine à lire les pensées* [1937]) that the human mind is a jungle of intertwined levels of thought and experience. The kallocain drug enables different levels of consciousness to communicate, and while people under the influence of this drug always tell the truth, it is a strange truth which cannot always be taken literally. Siv, one of the women subjected to the drug experiments, speaks dreamingly of "the green deep," which is at first thought to be a secret organization of dissenters; instead, she is referring to the world of emotions still hidden in the human mind beneath the wastelands of regimentation and fear.

The four main characters in the novel seem to embody different relationships to this "green deep." Siv dreads the cold, inhumanly efficient World State and even tries to change it in her way. Edo Rissen, an important man in the State machinery who gradually realizes what is happening to mankind, is turned over to the police by Kall. Linda, perhaps the most sensitive of all the characters, finally leaves Kall and disappears in the anonymity of the city. Kall himself, the eternal fellow-traveler, ends up as a prisoner of war of the "Universal State," probably an Eastern European country, continuing his research on the kallocain drug for his new masters. He has by this time abandoned all hope and fear; the "green deep" within him is dead, and his last act of rebellion is the secret writing of a diary. Whether the drug is ever used on a large scale, or even outside the laboratories, we do not know; the important point is that it *could* be used — not only in the "World State," but in our own world.

Kallocain was written in the summer of 1940 and published in the autumn of that year, nine years before George Orwell's *Nineteen Eighty-Four*, to which it bears a striking similarity. Probably both novels were based upon similar experiences and a similar fear. Karin Boye had traveled in Russia in 1928 and in Germany in 1932, witnessing events and trends that seemed to point to a new and inhuman world order; furthermore, there were many rumors circulating at the time of strange drugs, used both in the USSR and Germany, which forced people to reveal their secrets. And, of course, it would not take much imagination to foresee the plight of a citizen in a country ruled by a modern Stalin or Hitler with absolute powers, Interestingly enough, *Kallocain* has been, and is, very popular in Eastern Europe, and has been published there in many editions in various countries. A recent USSR edition in the *Contemporary SF* series immediately sold out its hardcover printing of 215,000 copies.

Had *Kallocain* been written for the science fiction magazine market, we would very probably have had Leo Kall fighting the inhuman rulers and bringing freedom and democracy to the world. But Boye did not write for the science fiction industry. She had a profound insight into the human psyche, and she knew, as history has proven over and over again, that no matter how cold and inhuman a society is, there will always be a great number of people, often a majority, who firmly believe it to be the best of all possible worlds. We judge all things by our past experiences, and in the World State, citizens' minds have been shaped from their earliest years by official State propaganda.

When the police finally find a group of would-be revolutionaries in the World State, they turn out to be far less dangerous than expected. In this society ruled by fear, the revolutionary group meets and does nothing — except to prove that they trust one another by pretending to sleep while other members sit around with knives. But Kallocain robs people of the ability even to *think* subversive thoughts. Even in the harshest police state, be it Hitler's Germany, Stalin's Russia, or present-day Chile, the police have had to stop outside the minds of people, grudgingly granting them what could not be taken. Orwell in *Nineteen Eighty-Four*, uses the ubiquitous "Thought Police" to weed out dangerous elements, but Kall's drug is more efficient and, above all, cheaper. The drug opens every citizen's mind to the rulers; no one can trust, no one can ever be trusted.

Kallocain answers no questions and certainly offers no happy ending. Once the drug has been invented, it will be used. The dictatorship is not overthrown, since there is no one to overthrow it. Everything goes on to an even more regimented, even more inhuman world where all hope will vanish. *Kallocain* is a terrifying book, even more so because it rings true. Karin Boye called it "a nightmare," and said shortly after its publication that "It is as if someone else has written it; I am scared!" She had good reason to be afraid, for the society she so convincingly describes in this novel, not so much through the various dystopian gadgets but through the protagonist's willing acceptance of it, could one day be our own.

Sam J. Lundwall

Sources for Further Study

Reviews:

Kirkus Reviews. XXXIV, February 15, 1966, p. 203.
Library Journal. XCI, August, 1966, p. 3763.
Times Literary Supplement. March 24, 1966, p. 237.

KARAVANE
(Caravan)

Author: Tor Åge Bringsværd (1939-   )
First book publication: 1974
Type of work: Short stories

Thirty-five stories of science fiction and fantasy, spanning the author's career from his first published work in 1962 through his mature fiction

A smile is probably the reaction most commonly associated with the works of Tor Åge Bringsværd; a smile which may be mocking, which probably is ironic, and which hopefully leads to afterthought and reflection. For to Tor Åge Bringsværd, a smile on the face of his reader is only a break in the bland façade of disinterest through which he may slip the pointed blade of his story. His stories must be read in political or social perspective, and cannot be dismissed as mere entertainment. In Norwegian literature, where humor is such a rare thing, Tor Åge Bringsværd is something rarer still: an author who uses jests as weapons against a lack of social and political consciousness.

This may be seen as a basic paradox in Bringsværd's fiction and reflects some of the paradoxes in the author himself. He was born in 1939 in Skien, a small industrial town in the south of Norway. He began his studies at a very orthodox theological school at the University of Oslo, but ended up with a degree in folklore and world religions. He began freelance writing for the radio and the weeklies in the beginning of the 1960's and approached science fiction subjects in a careful way.

Karavane includes stories from three previous collections of Bringsværd's short stories. Eight of the stories first appeared in *Rundt solen i ring* (*Circling the Sun*, 1967); a number of them appeared in magazines prior to being collected, including his first published story, *Korkens ark* (*The Ark of Cork*, *Profil*, 1962). Of the remaining stories collected here, fourteen were published in the collection *PROBOK* (*Probook*, 1968), three in *Sesam 71* (1971), and ten appeared for the first time in *Karavane*. Therefore, the title of the collection is appropriate. It is indeed a caravan of previous books and stories; and like a caravan, the various parts share no common denominator aside from their source and destination.

One common denominator which often is applied to Bringsværd's stories, is that of science fiction. He can be called an author of science fiction because he uses the tools of fantastic prose to provide the frame for his problems. However, avoiding the discussion of the proper application of the term science fiction, one may note that Bringsværd has roots in traditional Scandinavian or European fantasy rather than in American science fiction of the 1950's. This is understandable in an author who has studied literature and folklore, and who also has edited or written several books on myths and religion, among them a Norwegian "black book" of traditional magic recipes. A number of foreign

critics have maintained that he belongs to the "new wave." Once more avoiding the discussion of a problematic label, one should stress that this is grossly
misleading.

Tor Åge Bringsværd is first and foremost a contemporary author, writing
under the influence of the same forces that mold mainstream fiction. In looking at his early stories from *Rundt solen i ring*, such as "I Faraos have" ("In
the Garden of the Faraoe") or "Lessandro," the influence of the major writer
Ray Bradbury may be traced. However, at the end of the 1960's, he took up
some of the reckless joy of pop art and incorporated that in his own witty
prose, as demonstrated in the stories from *PROBOK*. In his later stories, he
has changed the form several times, and today a better comparison may be to
American authors like Kurt Vonnegut, Jr., or Thomas Pynchon. Comparisons
of this kind may be helpful to those not knowing his works, but his readers
will always recognize the rash humor, burlesque twist of plot, and basic social
concern to be his very own.

The two central stories in *Rundt solen i ring* and *PROBOK* are utopian. The
first is a sequence of scenes entitled "Byen under boblen" ("The City beneath
the Bubble"). To a science fiction reader, the title immediately provides the
key to the scenario: a devastated, radioactive Earth with an oasis of humanity
still being kept alive under a protective dome. But rather than retell the trite
post-holocaust story, Bringsværd relies upon the reader's familiarity with it to
bring across his points. The story ends when a boy, Igor, climbs through the
unused subways and discovers a door to the outside, where the air is sweet and
all traces of war are long since gone.

The prose of "Byen under boblen" is reminiscent of that of the Bible,
which at the same time provides a link to Bringsværd's theological studies and
a clue to the allegorical interpretation of the story. The bubble may be perceived as built of anxiety, and Igor's journey may be a trail to follow out of
our own private domes and into the sweet reality of fellowship, if we only dare
to disclose our private thoughts and opinions.

The Bible is more ominously present in the other utopian tale, "Det nye
Jerusalem" ("The new Jerusalem"). This story gives a crass, satirical picture
of a religious dictatorship, where the social foundation reflects the beliefs
voiced by the Christian Democratic Party in Norway. This party was, at the
time this story was written, a member of a coalition government in Norway
and occupied the Ministry of Church and Cultural Affairs. The lack of
generosity in a Protestant political ideology is attacked in this story. The allegory is more transparent than in "Byen under boblen"; political satire has taken
the place of poetic prose. To some extent, the story may also be read as the
author's personal revolt against some of the social norms of his own church.

The story is in itself rather simple and centers around a young couple,
Maria and Benjamin. Society controls all "sins," among them sex, which is
forbidden. The young couple's solution to this tyranny is, however, the same

as Igor's to captivity in "Byen under boblen": escape. Benjamin and Maria move out of the city into the untamed countryside. This escape emphasizes a different aspect from Igor's escape from the domed city — it is a conscious revolt, a move against a bureaucratic and oppressive society. Actually, the wilderness outside the city may be considered a form of anarchy. The story provides in this respect a link to later works of Bringsværd, for instance the hilarious anarchists of *Den som har begge beina på jorda, står stille* (*He Who Has Both Feet on the Ground, Does Not Move*), a novel published the same year as *Karavane*.

The hero of "Det nye Jerusalem" is really Thomas, a modest, old fellow who runs a hot-dog stand. He dreams of a world without cars, the world of "Velocipedia," and he encourages the young couple to try life outside the city walls. Thomas is actually one of the first examples of a typical Bringsværd hero, one who uses the weapons of the harlequin against an unjust world. This type of hero comes into his own as the Spongecakeman, the main character in two of the stories in *Karavane*, "Bløtkakemannens dagbok" ("Diary of the Spongecakeman") and "Bløtkakemannen på Châtau d'If" ("The Spongecake-man at Château d'If").

"Spongecake" is a vapid translation of the Norwegian "bløtkake." It is, indeed, a spongecake, usually buried in whipped cream and decorated with strawberries or fruit. The spongecake is compulsory at any birthday or children's party and is a symbol of merriment and childish delight. Only through an understanding of the joy a Norwegian associates with the spongecake, can the name of the Spongecakeman properly be understood.

The Spongecakeman first appeared in *PROBOK*, where his diary gave ample proof of the ingenious adventures of this pop art antisuperhero. He battles for justice with creampuffs and sugarfloss. He exchanges the reels of the film *Sound of Music* for those of a documentary from Vietnam. He invents a whipped cream cannon and writes poems on government buildings. He even destroys the NATO military base near Oslo by injecting yeast dough into its tunnels and drenches the U.S. embassy in whipped cream (over which he releases seventy drooling cats in pink parachutes).

In this first story, the antics of the Spongecakeman were very much like those of a clown. At the end of the story he disappears mysteriously and appears once more in a collection published in 1972, *Bløtkakemannen & Apache-pikene* (*The Spongecakeman & the Apache Girls*). In this story, not included in *Karavane*, the Spongecakeman tackles his own personal troubles — a dreary marriage and a routine job — once more claiming that escape is an adequate strategy. The third, and till now last appearance of the Spongecake-man, is in the longest of the new stories in *Karavane*, "Bløtkakemannen på Château d'If." Château d'If is well known as the castle from which the Count of Monte-Cristo escaped to revenge the wrongs done to him.

Once again, the recurring motif of escape presents itself — what else is the function of Château d'If? But it is not a castle of bricks and masonry that imprisons the Spongecakeman. This more mature version of the old pop art hero realizes that he is imprisoned by old and useless thoughts and theories. It is a resigned, but, nevertheless, resolute Spongecakeman who finally reaches the coast and freedom.

Imprisonment behind walls of information is also the basic idea in the profound story "Mannen som samlet på 1. september 1972." It relates the experience of a man — ptk — who tries to collect all the world's newspapers from one single day, in order to at least conquer that small segment of reality. This story is one of only two stories that have been translated into English. It is reprinted in a slightly modified form as "The Man Who Collected the First of September 1973" in Brian W. Aldiss' and Harry Harrison's *Best SF 73* (1974).

The image of the resolute Spongecakeman, dripping wet and freshly escaped from the confining walls of discarded beliefs and unjustified traditions, may be a fitting symbol of the stories in *Karavane*. The harlequin is determined to continue his jests in earnest. There is little surprise in the fact that the jester-as-author, Tor Åge Bringsværd, is recognized today as one of Norway's major contemporary authors.

Jon Bing

KAZOHINIA

Author: Sándor Szathmári (1897-1974)
First book publication: 1941
English translation: 1977
Type of work: Novel
Time: 1935
Locale: The island of Kazohinia

Lemuel Gulliver, the immortal ship's surgeon, joins His Majesty's battle fleet in 1935, at the time of the Italian-Abyssinian war, and when his ship sinks in action, gets ashore on an unknown island and finds himself in the strange society of the "hins" and "behins"

> Principal characters:
> LEMUEL GULLIVER, a ship's surgeon
> ZOLEMA, a woman of Kazohinia

Probably very few books display a more bitter philosophy of life in the European history of literature than *Kazohinia*, even if we compare the novel with dystopian works by Aldous Huxley, George Orwell or Evgeny Zamyatin, or even with the pessimism of such philosophers as Arthur Schopenhauer. It is as if Jonathan Swift's soul has been reincarnated in Sándor Szathmári, who proudly and consciously accepted the heritage of his great predecessor when viewing the world in the years between the two great world wars and telling a hopeless story of the impossibility of mankind's situation. Swift's traveler could at least believe that among living creatures there were wise, beautiful, intelligent horses. Szathmári's Gulliver, however, studies man's fundamental, innermost contradictions, and his despair is complete; he can see no way to flee it, and he feels that in this dark night there is not a single beam of light.

Europe — especially Central Europe — in the 1930's lived through a series of incredible conflicts; it could not even recover from the destruction of World War I before economic crises shattered the possibilities of any development. Millions of people were unemployed; Adolf Hitler was getting more and more power and Benito Mussolini hypnotized Italy. The state of the Hungarian economy was particularly critical, and Fascism became increasingly popular and widespread.

Szathmári was born in a small town, and, despite extreme financial difficulties, he received his diploma of mechanical engineering in the Budapest University of Technology. During his younger years at home and in Budapest he observed the social problems and all the taboos of Hungarian society, a curious mixture of undeveloped bourgeoisie, reactionary fuedalism, Fascism, and medieval traditions. As a man well-versed in the humanities and the natural sciences, he regarded with astonishment the irrationality and folly of a society which would not give its members any food, but which destroyed wheat and manufactured arms. The best Hungarian literature of this age was produced by authors who exposed social problems and demanded their solution.

Szathmári's circle of friends were of this group, and their ideas seriously influenced his thoughts. He was also connected with representatives of *avant garde* literature and with the enthusiastic Esperantists. This association accounts in part for the ingenious linguistic plays in *Kazohinia*, and for the elaborate communicative system of the hins and behins.

Gulliver's travels to the countries of pure reason and pure instinct are the vehicle by which the author examines and compares various concepts of utopia. Utopias since the time of Plato have often declared the primacy and omnipotence of reason. There is hardly any island or empire on the map of imagination where life and society would not be regulated by the help of sciences, which would eliminate all the human conflicts. It was only in the first decades of the twentieth century that writers and philosophers realized how fearsome utopias could be when actualized, and that reason is not the panacea for every trouble.

When Szathmári's hero regains his consciousness after having been shipwrecked, he finds himself in a miraculous world. The fields are marvelously well cultivated, there are highways of rubber, comfortable resthouses, noiseless vehicles, and people who are reminders of beautiful Greek statues. Everywhere there is regularity and perfect harmony. Gulliver very soon learns that no money is used in this country: there are no shops, and everybody can take freely whatever he wishes. Gulliver is fascinated by this orderly peaceful, well-oiled way of life, yet he has misgivings. Sometimes he feels as if he were in a lunatic asylum, where the madmen have no feelings and are motivated solely by reason.

Eventually, Gulliver is examined by doctors and taken to a hospital, where he learns the language of the "hins," as the inhabitants of the island call themselves. In their language, vowels and consonants are in perfect harmony, and the grammar is very simple; the initial letter of words indicates their part of speech — for instance, all nouns begin with "b," all personal names with "Z." There are no exceptions or irregularities.

Once Gulliver has mastered the language, the hins teach him two essential concepts: *kazo* and *kazi*. These two notions regulate the behavior of the hins and govern their social order, life, and actions. "Kazo" denotes the order of life and nature without emotions. "Kazo is pure reason which regards as its purpose in mathematical truth and clarity that the individuals through society attain the greatest possible welfare and comfort." The antithesis of this concept is "kazi." While the "kazo" principle embodies the realities of the existing world, "kazi" refers to absurdities and deviations from the normal, proper principles. Properly speaking, "kazi" is the equivalent of any illness, either in a physical, moral, or psychological sense, and involves egoism, aggression, and frustration in the victim.

The name of the island is derived from the name of the inhabitants, hins, meaning "men," combined with the term for right living, "kazo." The ignorant are called "belohin," the absurd and ill creatures; the criminals and the mad are called "behin."

After a period of indoctrination Gulliver is dismissed from the hospital, and a series of adventures ensue, such as his debates and conflicts with the hins, who have no history, literature, or art, and who work without any bureaucracy in their self-regulating system. Gulliver is permitted to enter one of the Kazohinian libraries, which is automatic, self-serviced, and full of micro-magnetic video-crystal "books" in three dimensions. He skims through two books entitled "The Current of Electrons and the Structural Morphology of Thinking" and "Brain Technique and Operations with Nerves," but he does not understand them; he does learn, however, that the hins have only scientific books.

Slowly, step-by-step we get to know Kazohinia, a state without any form of government, without laws, a clockwork organization without direction. Gulliver tries to establish contact with the hins, but he always fails to do so. His failure is most dangerous when he becomes acquainted with a lady named Zolema "who has to bear two more children and besides her sexual desire has come," so she asks our hero for "sexual work" without any fuss. This completely rationalized way of life is unbearable to Gulliver, who is unable to fit in the hin society. He is shocked to learn that Zolema works in a factory processing dead bodies, a fact that makes up his mind to escape; he asks the doctors to lead him to the settlement of the "behins."

Here we encounter a utopia which is the antithesis of the reign of reason in Kazohinia. Gulliver has a similar series of adventures among the "behins" as he had with the hins. First he observes the curiosities of his immediate surroundings, all the surprising things which are unknown among the hins. In this world, order and rationality face anarchy and irrationality. People greet one another, they do not wear comfortable and well-tailored uniforms but follow the fashion, they talk to one another, they sing songs, they ven laugh sometimes and tell jokes to one another. Their every word and action is random and illogical — or rather, they operate according to a completely different logical system. The behins have rules and responsibilities, groups and conflicts among the groups, religious sects and heresies, literature, art, criticism, philosophy, and ideology. The behins do not leave anything as it is; they transform and change everything.

While in the first part of the novel, Szathmári describes a cold, constructive, geometrical world, and tries to give it an adequate style, in the second part, his description of the behins' settlement is presented in the style of a surrealistic dream. In this way his novel consists of three linguistic layers: In the framework of the story, we can enjoy the reminiscences of Swift's Gulliver; in the country of the hins, we can witness the Puritan dryness of artificial languages; and in the land of the behins, we encounter rich imagery and color that provide a contrast to Szathmári's earlier detached treatment. The linguistic changes follow flexibly the development of the hero.

Among the behins, in spite of the fact that their society is similar to the present world, Gulliver is even more confused and helpless than he was among the hins. Szathmári's criticism of the age can be seen most clearly in these chapters. The twentieth century shattered society's harmony. Some people regard Szathmári's novel as a humanist criticism of Capitalism and Communism, but this is a misunderstanding. The hins do not represent Communism, nor do the behins embody the principles of Capitalism; rather, they represent — as the author himself has pointed out — man's two basic features, reason and instinct, and the conflict between the two. Szathmári believes that man, having left nature, is unbalanced forever, his path leading him through a series of tragedies towards destruction.

It follows from the nature of their culture that the behins rush into wars; they are stimulated by war, politics, and art. They are infected by the madness called "buku," and Gulliver is almost burnt at the stake for his reasonable point of view. The hins prevent his being murdered almost in the last moment. Gulliver, who did not feel at home either among the hins or the behins, must see in terror that the hins annihilate the behins in the same objective and scientific manner as they would use in sterilizing a room or spraying a tree with pesticides.

In contrast with Kazohinia, there is Europe of the 1930's and the way of life of the bourgeoisie to which Gulliver returns, after his bitter adventures, at the end of the novel.

Kazohinia, a masterpiece of Hungarian science fiction, has had a checkered career. It was first published in 1941, through an error in wartime censorship, in an abridged form; it was republished in 1946 and 1957 versions of differing lengths; the most complete edition appeared in 1972. It was published in English by Corvina Press (Budapest) in 1977.

Besides *Kazohinia*, Sándor Szathmári published a volume of science fiction stories entitled *Gépvilág* (*A World of Machines*), which, though it is of remarkable literary quality, does not reach the level and richness of thought of *Kazohinia*. It is regrettable that Szathmári could not write more; because of a life full of hardships, he has remained by and large a man remembered for one great book.

Péter Kuczka

Sources for Further Study

Reviews:

World Literature Today. LI, Winter, 1977, p. 140.

THE KILLER THING

Author: Kate Wilhelm (1928-   )
First book publication: 1967
Type of work: Novel
Time: The twenty-second century
Locale: Venus, Mellic, Ramses, Tau Ceti III, Tensor, Tarbo, and an unknown planet

Two killers face each other on an unknown planet: one, a hero from the victorious Earth military conquerors, the other, a robot, programed to kill if necessary

Principal characters:
THE ROBOT
TRACE (CAPTAIN ELLENDER TRACY), the man commissioned to capture the robot
DUNCAN (LIEUTENANT FORD DUNCAN), Trace's space partner, killed on the mission
DR. VIANTI, developer of the robot
LAR, the beloved girl of Trace's dreams
COLONEL LANGTREE, an Army scientist

The Killer Thing is a science fiction adventure story stripped down to its barest elements. In a silicone and stone desert on an unknown planet, shimmering in 123-degree heat and blasted with cyclone winds, a single protagonist and a single antagonist hunt each other to the death. The protagonist is a human being, a military hero who has been trained for conquest; the antagonist is a huge robot, protected by an impenetrable force shield and armed with a laser beam with a two-mile striking range.

But who is the "killer thing?" Kate Wilhelm keeps the countdown plot continuously suspenseful by challenging the reader to answer that question, and thus demonstrates her skill as a storyteller, a fact which has already been acknowledged, well appreciated, and rewarded by her peers. In 1968, a year after The Killer Thing appeared, Wilhelm won a Nebula Award for her short story "The Planners," and in 1976, she received a Hugo Award for her complex novel about humans and clones, Where Late the Sweet Birds Sang.

To date, Wilhelm has written fifteen novels and collections of short stories, mainly in the science fiction and speculative fiction genres. The dimensions of dream world and nightmare are always psychologically realistic and reasoned. As in The Killer Thing, the stories are always concerned with Wilhelm's intense interest in the nature and essence of humanity. What power or corruption destroys humanity? What power or creative force increases it? The answer in The Killer Thing is both provocative and startling.

Captain Ellender Tracy, or "Trace," has only one mission to complete on the alien planet where his two-man space dinghy has landed. He must capture an escaped killer robot that he has hunted in space for three months. His partner, Duncan, hit by a meteorite during the landing, dies after warning him to be sure to destroy the robot rather than simply capture him.

But, when the story opens, Trace has more pressing problems than how to dispose of the robot. With little fuel and water left, he has lost control of the situation and become the hunted rather than the hunter. It will be ten days before any relief ship can arrive to rescue him and help capture the robot. In that time, he must stay alive on very limited resources. Furthermore, he must prevent the robot from repairing its spaceship, damaged during the original pursuit. The site of the ship is unknown to Trace, since it is usually protected by an invisibility shield. His problems, then, are complex: he must keep the robot from repairing its ship and escaping; at the same time, he must capture the ship in order to obtain more fuel and water for his own needs; and he must stay outside of the two-mile range of the robot's deadly laser beam.

For three weeks, Trace and the robot play hide-and-seek in the rocks and sand, heat and wind. Trace is feverish and hears voices. But the weather and thin oxygen supply of the planet do not disturb the robot any more than do the isolation and loneliness, because it is not a socially conditioned human being. Rather, it is a ten-foot-tall logic box, the creation of Dr. Vianti, a loyal but conquered citizen of the planet Ramses. Ramses, a mining protectorate of the World Group Organization, Trace's Earth military organization, is being despoiled by miner robots that work ceaselessly.

Dr. Vianti's robot is as different from those miner robots as it is from the famous robots created by Isaac Asimov, that, programed according to Asimov's three Laws of Robotics, cannot injure any human being nor allow harm to come to anyone through inaction. Asimov's robots must obey all human orders that do not conflict with the above laws; only then are they allowed to protect their own existence.

The Vianti robot had not been finished when it was discovered by Trace and Duncan on an inspection tour of the Ramses mines. It had been given the second purpose of self-protection but had destroyed Dr. Vianti before its first purpose of goal-satisfaction had been activated. Gradually, as it goes from planet to planet, the robot processes a constant stream of information, developing a final purpose on the planet Tensor. This purpose is not simply to kill anyone trying to destroy it, but to kill all men because they are all destroyers.

The robot is deadly because it kills by deduction and without feeling, being programed to deal tirelessly with events and to compute actions. But what about Trace, the man? Wilhelm ingeniously forces us to compare the man with the robot by showing the parallels in their education. As the story progresses, reader sympathy must shift, for the man comes up lacking. Although he is presumed as a man to be responsible for his own thoughts and actions, Trace demonstrates less humanity than his counterpart. Similar to the robot, he, too, has been programed for self-preservation and destruction by the World Government Army. He, too, is a "killer thing."

Whatever his programing, however, Trace is *not* a machine. He responds to the heat, wind, and loneliness of the empty planet with fever, exhaustion, and despair, and reviews his life in a series of nightmare dreams and flashbacks.

Slowly and painfully, he realizes what a "killer thing" he is.

Wilhelm is psychologically acute in her exploration of the psyche of her human destroyer. The desolate planet resembles a gigantic isolation chamber used in human disorientation experiments. The relentless pressure of Trace's life-and-death situation breaks down all defenses. He hears voices and sees people from his past life. Prominent in his visions is Lar, a beautiful nature-woman from the planet Mellic, whom he comes to love. It is she who first confronts him with his killer mentality and also informs him of the Outsiders, pledged to protect her people from the World Group Government's scheme of conquest and universal exploitation. At the time, Trace does not understand the loyalty of one group to another, nor can he comprehend the use of power for anything other than material gain.

In his delirium, Traces hears also the voices of Duncan, his mother, and Corinne, the woman he married in order to perpetuate the family's military traditions by creating a son and heir. Especially important is the flashback to the planet Tarbo, a first-purpose situation similar to the robot's experiences on Tensor. "You've been to Tarbo," his mother said when he returned, telling him that he was now a man, that he should marry and produce a son. Trace had measured up. At sixteen, he had made his first kill. In this flashback, however, the exultation of battle and conquest are replaced by new conclusions about his war training. Details he had suppressed in the past now acquire new meaning. Trace realizes that he had not stalked and killed the enemy, but prisoners who had been staked out for the students to stimulate their thirst for blood. He had been programed just like a robot, and he had murdered humans used as sitting ducks. Those who had seen through the manipulation had been shot and killed on the spot. Tarbo was the test for killers, and Trace had passed.

The parallel development of man and robot reaches an exciting climax at the end of the book when Trace works out a desperate, but successful plan to trap the robot. Working in the heat like an inhuman machine, Trace builds a wall of large rocks in a passageway that will trap sand when the furious evening winds begin to blow. The robot approaches, circling Trace's hideaway slowly and cautiously. When it finally enters the passageway, the robot's eight-ton body loses balance and topples to the ground, bringing down upon itself a mountain of rubble.

At last, the robot's ship can be found, standing clear and visible without its shield. With his dry lips split and bleeding and his hands trembling with anxiety and fatigue, Trace finds the water and fuel supplies. As he returns to the trapped robot, which is trying to burn its way out of the mountain with its laser beam, Trace feels a strange kinship to it. Nevertheless, he does his duty according to his first and second purposes, throwing more rocks and sand down upon it to prevent its escape, until finally he collapses from heat prostration.

In the days that follow, Trace increasingly talks to the robot, telling it that he feels sorry for it and that it is not to blame for what has happened. He is also in the continuous presence of the voices who had come to him during his weeks on the planet. They keep him alive by telling him what to do; he also talks to them, telling them how the Outsiders will push humanity back to its proper place in the universe.

He questions the voices about whether the robot, too, possesses courage — a topic of debate until the relief ship arrives. "It's over now, brother!" he shouts to the robot, indicating that its end is near. He stops throwing down boulders to give the machine a chance to struggle. In a poignant speech, he praises the robot for having fought a good fight. Then a radio beep recalls him to his dinghy.

There, General MacClure and Colonel Langtree praise him for his valor, promise him any reward he wants, and ask to speak to the robot. They explain that they do not want to destroy it, but wish to use it against the Outsiders, to copy it and its shield, and capture the entire galaxy. In talking directly to the robot, Colonel Langtree tells it to preserve itself from destruction by turning off the laser. The beam vanishes.

In a final vision, Trace sees his group moving through the galaxy like a virus — world by world falling before their metal and flesh robots. No longer able to endure this possibility, he demolishes the other dinghy with which he is flying, and, gaining altitude and speed, he disobeys a superior officer for the first time as he plunges to meet his brother, the other killer robot, in a fiery embrace.

Priscilla Oaks

Sources for Further Study

Reviews:

Analog. LXXXI, March, 1968, p. 164.

Kirkus Reviews. XXXV, March 1, 1967, p. 302.

Magazine of Fantasy and Science Fiction. XXXIV, April, 1968, pp. 40-42.

Observer. September 24, 1967, p. 27.

Punch. CCLIII, August 2, 1967, p. 183.

Times Literary Supplement. June 29, 1967, p. 573.

THE KNIGHTS OF THE LIMITS

Author: Barrington J. Bayley (1938-   )
First book publication: 1978
Type of work: Short stories

Nine short stories of astonishing range and variety

The Knights of the Limits contains the best of the short fiction which Barrington J. Bayley wrote between 1965 and 1978. Seven of the nine stories first appeared in *New Worlds*, mostly from the period when it was manifest as a quarterly series of paperback anthologies. Bayley began his association with *New Worlds* when it was under the editorship of John Carnell; his stories of that period appeared under the pseudonym P. F. Woods, but he emerged from this concealment to do his best work under the aegis of Michael Moorcock. He did not appear frequently in the magazine while it was a large-sized publication specializing in *avant-garde* material, but was a regular contributor in the periods before and after that incarnation.

Bayley was never a "new-wave" writer — his ideas, though always offbeat and striking, clearly belong to the context of traditional science fiction rather than to the more introverted fiction of "inner space" customarily associated with *New Worlds*. The one other science fiction writer with whom Bayley has a close affinity is Charles Harness, several of whose stories were reprinted in early issues of Moorcock's *New Worlds*, and much of his work falls within the same category of exotic romance spiced with eccentric ideas. Such novels as *The Fall of Chronopolis* and *Star Winds* are exuberant melodramas full of ideative flourishes, and *The Knights of the Limits* presents a marvelous display of strange and original notions.

"The Exploration of Space" (1972), which opens the collection, is the story of an opium dream in which a latter-day alchemist converses with a knight on his chessboard which has been temporarily animated by an alien intelligence. The alien has modes of perception which probe far beyond the three-dimensional world accessible to human senses, and has traveled through many different space/time continua. Through the medium of the dream, the knight describes not only his superior view of our universe but also some of the other universes he has visited (limiting himself, necessarily, to those which lend themselves most readily to the imaginative grasp of human beings). He speaks of asymmetrical continua; "stereo spaces" which are interrupted by chasms of nullity; branched continua and continua where the principle of causality either does not apply or works in a different way. This is perhaps the one story in genre science fiction which actually sets out to fulfill the exhortation contained in the dedication to Edwin Abbott's *Flatland*, which urges the inhabitants of "spaceland" to launch forth upon imaginative adventures in the sea of dimensional possibility.

A more detailed exercise in alternative cosmology is found in "Me and My

Antronoscope" (1973), which is set in a rigid universe where life exists in bubblelike lacunae. A rebellious individual in one such lacuna challenges the reigning orthodoxy with his notion that the continuum contains other worlds, and sets off defiantly in his solidity ship in order to search for them. After a long journey he breaks through into a new cavity, and, though it is empty and lifeless, he feels that its existence vindicates his theory. He perishes, convinced that he has been the pioneer who will lead his race to the conquest of the universe. This little drama is perceived by the inhabitants of another world by means of an antronoscope, and their activities form a frame narrative offering the merest glimpse of the other wonders of the infinite universe which this marvelous device exposes to their eyes.

The third exercise in speculative cosmology in the collection is "The Cabinet of Oliver Naylor" (1976), a melodrama set in a distant future in which the velocitator has given men the freedom to roam the cosmos at will, synthesizing pseudorealities by means of the spitron and supporting themselves during their adventures by courtesy of the hylic potentiometer, or matter-bank. This ultraindividualistic era has seen a revitalization of ancient nineteenth and twentieth century myths and modes, and the hero, Oliver Naylor, plays private detective, pursuing the enigmatic criminal Corngold. His task becomes inextricably tangled with his obsessive fascination with the foundations of logic and the fallibility of Aristotle's principle of identity (whose self-evidence is by no means indubitable in this eminently mutable world). In this story the miraculous gadgets of superscience not only provide limitless materialistic opportunities, but throw metaphysical questions about what is real into an entirely new light.

Three of the stories in the collection deal with alien life. The oldest story in the book is "All the King's Men" (1965), in which an alien overlord who rules Britain in the distant future decides to make war on Brazil. His human subjects cannot understand his motives, nor can he understand theirs, but in the climax of the story there is a brief meeting of minds. Here, as in some of the alternative cosmology stories, the basic theme is differences in perception and consequent differences in goal-seeking.

A more elaborate story with a similar idea is "Mutation Planet" (1973), Bayley's only story to date to appear originally in America (in Roger Elwood's anthology *Tomorrow's Alternatives*). This features a life system capable of Lamarckian evolution. In such a system, Bayley reasons, there would effectively be only one compound individual with one mind. In the story, the individuals on a visiting spacecraft struggle with their own problems as the thinking identity of the life system, *Dominus*, tries to solve the puzzle of their behavior and presence. *Dominus* has, of course, no concept of the individual, and thus mistakes their nature, but there is an ironic propriety in the conclusion which it actually reaches.

The third and most recent of the stories of alien life is "The Bees of Knowledge" (1975), a brilliant account of the adventures of a lone human marooned among the intelligent Bees of Handrea. It recounts his strategies of survival and his partially successful attempts to comprehend and communicate with his "hosts," with partial success. Science fiction writers have always been fascinated with hive society, since a beehive (and its analogues, the formicary and the termitary) provides the most convenient model for other-than-human social organization. In this story Bayley provides the most convincing image of hive mentality so far produced, taking his viewpoint character inside the hive to observe at first hand its operation, without permitting himself to lapse into an anthropomorphic view of the bees's mental processes.

The three remaining stories in the collection deal with the human world and with social possibilities. "Exit from City 5" (1971) is perhaps the most conventional story in the book. It details an individual rebellion against an insidious totalitarianism whose power is assured not only by the customary psychological techniques and methods of surveillance but also by the fact that its domain has been removed from the universe in order to escape a disastrous process of metagalactic shrinkage.

In "An Overload" (1973), the lower strata of a highly developed technological civilization (the Under-Megapolis) are dominated by a group of Magisters which includes Burt Lancaster, James Cagney, Humphrey Bogart, Frank Sinatra, and Dutch Schultz. All save Schultz are masters of ipseity, possessors of a special charismatic appeal by virtue of the special qualities of the holovisual medium through which they present themselves to their subjects. All of the Magisters save Schultz are artificial constructs, fictions of the "cybration system" which regulates business in the city, but this does not prevent them fighting out their own power-struggles against one another. Nor does it prevent the people they rule from plotting revolution, attempting to coopt the power of ipseity for themselves. Unfortunately, there is more to the charismatic empathy than there appears to be — ipseity works both ways, and the feedback proves to be too much for the would-be usurper.

"The Problem of Morley's Emission" (1978) is a rather different story. It presents a mock scientific report on the nature and action of a hypothetical "social energy field," a concept derived by the philosopher Isaac Morley as part of a theory which transposes models from electromagnetic physics into sociology. Among the consequences of the theory are such oddities as the Social Black Hole and the possibility (already, it seems, realized in the world where the report is being written) that an extraterrestrial intelligence might assume control over humanity's social energy field.

These nine stories constitute a parade of ideas which is unparalleled in modern science fiction. They are drawn eclectically from an astonishingly wide range of sources: from analytical philosophy, mathematics, physics, biology, and psychology. They demonstrate that Bayley possesses an extraordinarily fertile imagination, and a talent for combining the absurd and the abstruse with a dramatic flourish. He is a writer who delights in novel ideas and their exploration, a lover of bizarre juxtapositions. The range of his literary strategies extends from carefree space opera to stylishly satirical mock-intellectualism. Though his melodramas are magnificently surreal, he is perhaps at his best when he is at his most casual, affecting an earnest attitude of scrupulous reportage which throws his inventions into sharper relief. His powers of characterization are limited and his dialogue is frequently weak, but in the kind of fiction which he writes these faults are almost inconsequential, and they do not detract from the force and entertainment value of his fiction.

There are in contemporary science fiction all too few authors whose work regularly and insistently plucks at the strands of the web confining the imagination. The demand for innovation within the field is a difficult one to satisfy, especially in view of the fact that it is not altogether compatible with the strategies of mass-market publishing; mass-production demands standardization and stereotypy, and there are many readers whose demand for new ideas is strictly limited to a fairly narrow range of minor variations within standard plots. There is, however, always room for a writer whose idiosyncratic bent will continually take him into imaginatively unexplored territory. Bayley is such a writer — perhaps one of the best.

Brian Stableford

Sources for Further Study

Criticism:

Ash, Brian. *Who's Who in Science Fiction*. New York: Taplinger, 1976, p. 41. Ash gives a very brief summary of Bayley's life and career as a science fiction author.

"B. J. Bayley," in *Contemporary Authors*. Detroit: Gale Research Company, 1973, Volume 37-40, p. 29. This biographical article gives some information on Bayley's life and a list of his writings.

THE LAND THAT TIME FORGOT

Author: Edgar Rice Burroughs (1875-1950)
First book publication: 1924
Type of work: Novel
Time: From June, 1916, to an uncertain date in 1917 or 1918
Locale: Chiefly on Caprona, or Caspak, a volcanic island in the Antarctic

When the survivors of a torpedoed ship join with the crew of an English tug to capture a German submarine, their instruments are sabotaged, and they discover by chance a lost island where they are menaced by predators and internal dissension until their rescue by a search party

> *Principal characters:*
> BOWEN J. TYLER, JR., a marine engineer
> LYS LA RUE, his companion in his adventures
> BARON FRIEDRICH VON SCHOENVORTS, commander of the submarine *U-33*
> THOMAS BILLINGS, leader of the party to rescue Bowen Tyler
> AJOR, a Caspakian woman with whom he falls in love
> LIEUTENANT JOHN BRADLEY, a leader of the British sailors marooned on Caspak

The greatest difficulty in a critical appreciation of the works of Edgar Rice Burroughs is accounting for their enduring popularity even though his virtues seem to be slight and his vices glaring. Yet Burroughs, one of the most popular authors of the twentieth century, and some of his novels rank high above the ordinary adventure story.

Burroughs began writing in 1911, after a variety of relatively unsuccessful jobs. The decision to write appears to have been sudden, yet it was followed by an astonishing burst of creativity and a swift rise to popularity. In 1911 he was unknown; by 1920 he had published thirty novels or novelettes, and had become one of America's best-known and most popular storytellers. He had created an enduring mythic figure in Tarzan, and had seen the ape-man launched on a film career that shows no sign of coming to an end. In the years that followed, Edgar Rice Burroughs was to write over thirty more novels; see a town complete with post office (Tarzana, California) inaugurated, with its chief industry the company he formed to publish his novels; and lend his reputation to help the fledgling pulp science fiction magazines.

Burroughs' assets were a workmanlike style, a fertile imagination, and, most important, a sure sense of pace in recounting the plot of a story. The first-person narratives he wrote generated fast-moving adventure stories that created and maintained suspense through incident after incident. As the years passed, he had a tendency to repeat himself, but the novels were written over a span of some thirty years, and repetition may not have been noticeable. Also, Burroughs was a formula writer, and when he found a successful format, he saw little reason to change it as long as it remained highly popular. This is why the reader following Tarzan to lost city after lost city may be pardoned for feeling that the Africa of Burroughs' imagination must have been one of the most heavily populated areas on earth.

The Land That Time Forgot covers three novelettes that were published in 1918 in *The Blue Book Magazine*: the initial part, "The Land That Time Forgot," a sequel, "The People That Time Forgot," and the conclusion, "Out of Time's Abyss." The parts were collected for a hardcover book version in 1924 under the title of the first novelette, and this collection was reprinted in 1962. The following year, the work appeared in paperback as three separate volumes, following the original magazine divisions and bearing their separate titles. The stories were also reprinted in Hugo Gernsback's *Amazing Stories* in 1927, beginning with an issue on the cover of which Burroughs was given top billing over a number of other writers including H. G. Wells.

The Land That Time Forgot is a "lost world" story, a category that Burroughs had already used with success in his Pellucidar series. Unlike those novels, however, the land that time forgot, Caspak, is not located at the Earth's core, but on a large Antarctic island that is warmed by volcanic activity.

Various parts of Burroughs' novels seem improbable in the extreme, and probably seemed that way when they were written, but they are seldom outright fantasies. Usually one eases the suspension of disbelief with the science of the time. The Martian novels, for example, depict a dying world low in oxygen, almost barren of water except for the canals that maintain cultivation. In short, it is a world in keeping with the conception of the planet implanted in the public mind by popularizations of the work of the astronomer Percival Lowell. In the same way, the "science" that underlies *The Land That Time Forgot* is a combination of nineteenth century Darwinian evolution and the catch-phrase from high school biology — ontogeny recapitulates phylogeny.

The notion that humans in the womb pass through the various evolutionary stages (multicelled blastula, gill-like structures, taillike structures, and so forth) is the scientific justification for the curious Caspakian forms of life. Burroughs was not the only writer of fiction fascinated with the idea that the individual human briefly experiences all the lower evolutionary levels: in 1928, the idea was to figure importantly in Aldous Huxley's *Point Counter Point*. But we do not discover the secret of Caspakian life until the concluding part of the novel. All that is revealed in the earlier two sections is that somehow, all extinct species have survived on the island, from the dinosaurs of the Age of Reptiles right up through the cave-bear and the saber-toothed tiger. We do not know until then that all of them are being continuously produced in a microcosmic rehearsal of the history of life on earth.

Organisms in Caspak do not universally proceed through the normal stages of birth, growth, maturity, senescence, and death; of those that survive the manifold dangers of the island, some do follow the usual cycle, but others metamorphosize into the next higher form of life. Thus, some fish become amphibians, some amphibians become land reptiles, some reptiles become mammals, and so on through the various stages, until some of the higher apes become human.

This notion of progression up the chain of being is so central to the story that the plot seems to wander until the adventurers reach Caspak, and it takes them too long to reach the island. The first of the three novelettes, "The Land That Time Forgot," is consequently the weakest. Its clumsiness in part is derived from the bane of the lower kinds of popular fiction — coincidence. But Burroughs himself shares much of the blame, for he begins with not just one, but a series of stunning implausibilities. The first coincidence involves the hero of the first part, Bowen J. Tyler, Jr., who had worked with his father in a California firm designing and building submarines. With the outbreak of World War I, he decides to aid the Allies, but *en route* to France his ship is torpedoed and sunk by a German submarine that, by coincidence, has been built in his father's shipyard. He survives, along with Miss Lys La Rue, the woman who provides the romantic interest standard in most of Burroughs' novels. They are rescued by a British seagoing tug. The tug is menaced by the same submarine that sank Bowen's ship (the second coincidence), and its captain and crew board and capture the sub before their own ship goes down. The submarine is commanded by the thoroughly despicable Baron Friedrich von Schoenvorts, a German whom Miss La Rue had been on her way to meet in order to consummate a marriage made by her family against her will (the third coincidence).

Although such a sequence of events can test the most robust credulity the individual happenings are not gratuitous: the later unfolding of the plot relies on each twist. Because Tyler will later be called on to navigate the sub, it is necessary that he be thoroughly familiar with its construction and operation. He knows little about Lys La Rue, and on the basis of her engagement to von Schoenvorts suspects her of causing a series of sabotages that transfer the action from the north Atlantic to the south Pacific. And Burroughs, in the style of pulp adventure narratives of the time, relied heavily on the cavalry (or its equivalent) coming to the rescue at the last minute. Despite all these rationalizations, *The Land That Time Forgot* must surely have the limpest beginning of any of Burroughs' major novels.

The two sets of crews, British and German, capture and recapture the submarine from each other through the first four chapters, in what appears to be a rather run-of-the-mill wartime sea story. Burroughs was seldom at his best when working familiar territory: his westerns, his few realistic novels, his several Graustarkian romances, his single historical novel, are all unread now. Paradoxically, only when he turns to fantastic landscapes does he seem at home, and only when events bring the sub's passengers to Caspak does the plot seem to have a secure direction. The party of captives and captors land, build a fort, and settle down without any great hope of rescue until they discover crude oil on the island, and build an apparatus to refine fuel for the sub.

Burroughs' characterization is never especially subtle. But it is never more black-and-white than when von Schoenvorts and the rest of the Germans throw off their captivity and sail away in the sub, marooning the rest of the party. And this is where the story comes alive.

Perhaps Burroughs' greatest achievement in *The Land That Time Forgot* is his literary boldness in telling essentially the same story three times without the book becoming repetitious.

Evolution in Caspak is directional: the island is roughly circular in shape, with a great freshwater lake in its center. Creatures of the lowest orders start in the south, moving northward along either shore of the lake as they progress higher in the scale of evolution. For primates, apes are at the southernmost end; further north one successively encounters Alu, primitive men without speech or weapons; Bo-lu, who use clubs; Sto-lu, or hatchet-men; Band-lu, spear-men; Kro-lu, bow-men; and finally, at the north end of the island, Galu. The women of each of the various tribes spend part of each day lying in warm pools. Midway through the story it is explained that they are spawning eggs, which are waterbourne ever south "to the beginning," where they hatch and begin the long upward climb. Movement from hatching in the south to Galu in the north is counted one cycle. A Galu who has resulted from six previous completed cycles is fertile and capable of sexual reproduction.

And there is still one more possibility: in the dim past, some Galus went through bodily changes that produced the Wieroo, a race of flying men who live on an island at the northern end of the lake, and are now locked against the Galu in competition for mastery of the island. Since the progression from Galu to Wieroo has ceased, the Wieroo, who are fertile but produce only male offspring, must kidnap both Galu females to reproduce and fertile Galu children resulting from sexual reproduction.

All this is hidden until well past the middle of the novel, each part of which concerns the progress northward of a human adventurer: as he learns more, so do we. Burroughs carefully outlines three journeys, each of which partially overlaps the stopping-point of the previous one, and the first two of which introduce mysteries that are revealed only in the succeeding adventure. Thus, Bowen Tyler enters from the south in the submarine through a subterranean river, and moves north on foot, acquainting us with the stages of human development from Alu to Band-lu in the process. We hear of the Kro-lu and Galu, but Tyler never travels far enough north to encounter them, and the Caspakian system of reproduction is still unknown to him when the part ends. In the second part, Thomas Billings crash-lands his seaplane further up the scale than Tyler's starting-point. He rescues Ajor, a Galu woman with whom he falls in love, and then travels north to her country in order to reunite her with her people. In this part we learn the details of the system of life, but although the Wieroos are mentioned in tales Ajor tells Billings, we do not meet them. That is reserved for the third part, in which Bradley, an English officer from the tug, is captured by the Wieroos, transported north to their city, and has adventures there until he escapes to the land of the Galu, where he meets Billings and Ajor.

There are many things one could denigrate in *The Land That Time Forgot*, but Burroughs' method of revealing his imaginative creation through his plot is not one of them. The chief suspense in the novel is not a question of what will happen to the hero in this or that dramatic episode, although there is an abundance of cliffhangers. Rather, we are carried along by the gradual unfolding of the biological mystery of Caspak, which Burroughs manages with a sure hand. His manipulation of science in a spirit of playful imagination secures for him a place of importance in the history of American science fiction as well as on the paperback shelves at the bookstore.

Walter E. Meyers

Sources for Further Study

Criticism:

Fenton, Robert W. *The Big Swingers*. Englewood Cliffs, N.J.: Prentice-Hall, 1967. Fenton provides a general background to Burroughs' Science Fiction writing.

Lupoff, Richard A. *Edgar Rice Burroughs, Master of Adventure*. New York: Canaveral, 1965. This book discusses the plot and background of each of Burroughs' works and reveals his continuing influence on younger writers.

Reviews:

Analog. LXXI, June, 1963, p. 92.

Galaxy. XXII, October, 1963, pp. 120-121.

THE LANGUAGES OF PAO

Author: Jack Vance (1920-   )
First book publication: 1957
Type of work: Novel
Time: The distant future
Locale: The planets of Pao and Breakness

A study of the relationship between language and perception and how that relationship determines the behavior of human beings

Principal characters:
> BERAN PANASPER, deposed child-ruler of Pao
> BUSTAMONTE, Beran's uncle and usurper of the throne of Pao
> PALAFOX, a Dominie of Breakness

One of the significant strengths of science fiction is its ability to supply a fictional world that can be tailored for the investigation of various philosophical, sociological, and even moral tenets. Worlds can be carefully constructed around one particular hypothesis or theory, and then that one choice can be fully explored as the people of the fictional world react to it. So convinced was H. G. Wells of the vast potential that science fiction held for such investigations that he strongly recommended it as a research tool for social scientists. Jack Vance's *The Languages of Pao* gives great credence to Wells's statement.

Vance uses a rather simple plot to explore the ways in which experience shapes language, and language shapes experience. The ruler, panarch, of Pao is assassinated by his brother, who must also dispose of the dead panarch's son. This assassination comes at a crucial point in Paonese history because they are threatened by a warlike alien clan that is out to prove itself by raiding Pao. The dead panarch had been dealing with a dominie (a cross between a scientist and a philosopher) from the planet Breakness in hopes of thwarting the threat. Thus the assassin, Bustamonte, inherits a situation he is not really prepared to handle.

Palafox, the Breakness dominie, has his own designs on Pao, and since the new panarch does not readily agree to bargain with him, the dominie saves the son, Beran, from a certain death. The plot then deals with how Beran returns to Pao, defeats his uncle with the help of Palafox, and, finally, thwarts Palafox's plans as well. Again, the novel presents a rather straightforward adventure plot common to many types of novels.

What makes *The Languages of Pao* a science fiction novel, however, and a significant one, is what Vance does with this basic plot. For within the simple plot he is able to deal with some rather complicated linguistic issues. The issues themselves concern the Whorf-Sapir hypothesis. Writing in *Language* in 1936, Benjamin Lee Whorf stated:

> We are inclined to think of language simply as a technique of expression, and not to realize that language first of all is a classification and arrangement of the stream of sen-

sory experiences which results in a certain world-order, a certain segment of the world that is easily expressible by the type of symbolic means that language employs.

In other words, man's experiences are ordered and arranged by the language he speaks. All sensory data will be filtered by language, and perception will follow that system already established by language.

Vance takes this hypothesis one step further and explores how the language system itself was established. For example, the planet Pao is seventy percent larger than Earth with a land mass situated mostly in very pleasant zones of climate. The Paonese are a completely homogenous people who are blessed with fertile land. The history of Pao is one of stability, for there is no need of competition for the necessities of life. The hugeness of its population, privileged by the hospitality of the planet, moreover, has placed a premium on people living peacefully together. As Vance expresses it, "The typical Paonese saw himself as a cork on a sea of a million waves, lofted, lowered, thrust aside by incomprehensible forces — if he thought of himself as a discrete personality at all."

In contrast, the planet Breakness is an inhospitable one. The climate is bitterly cold, the land is rugged, harsh, and infertile. Its inhabitants have had to compete constantly to live. Unlike the Paonese, the people of Breakness have not been allowed to develop a social consciousness because the individual is always threatened.

Given such different environments, the languages of each planet consequently differ in the extreme. Paonese is a passive language which has no formal method of drawing comparisons or judging the superiority of one idea or thing over another. Furthermore, as befits a passive language, that part of speech which most directly expresses action, the verb, is missing. Thus, the people of Pao are locked into a view of the world which originated in the environment of Pao and has now been codified by their language. The language of Breakness can also be seen to answer the nature of its planet. It is an extremely active language which emphasizes positive responses to challenges. The language places a premium on intellectual manipulation and deemphasizes emotions. Since the individual is the single most important concept on Breakness, the entire grammar of the language is centered on self. So thorough is this egocentricity, in fact, that there is no need for the first person pronoun; it is constantly understood. To complete the contrast, Vance describes the language of Pao as "polysynthetic" and that of Breakness as "isolative," two common linguistic terms that apply equally well to the people of these planets.

The language of Pao is fine as long as the planet and its people are left alone. But the rest of the universe is uncooperative: the Paonese are cheated by the commercial agents of Mercantil and threatened by the Brumbo Clan of the warrior planet Batmarsh. Whether the Paonese like it or not, the need for change quickly becomes apparent when, soon after Bustamonte takes power and Beran escapes with Palafox, the Brumbo Clan is able to conquer the planet of fifteen billion passive citizens with a raiding party of ten thousand. Bustamonte becomes panarch at the sufferance of an alien conqueror and at the cost of a rather steep tribute. But for the Paonese to change, their view of the world must change as well, and this entails the need of a new language. Thus, the plot of *The Languages of Pao* supplies the impetus for introducing the further investigation of how behavior can be modified by introducing a new language. The Paonese need to undergo modification to survive, and the question becomes what form that modification will take.

Vance starts to answer this question when Bustamonte swallows his pride and asks Palafox for help. Bustamonte realizes that, as the Paonese now stand, he will always be at the mercy of greater and greater demands from the Brumbo Clan. At this point the reader gets a brief lesson in the Whorf-Sapir hypothesis as Palafox sketches his plan. A number of children will be selected to become warriors- or industrialists-in-training. Populations will be shifted, and each of the training groups will become isolated from the main Paonese population and be taught a language befitting its future profession. The need for new languages is essential to Palafox's plan, because what is at stake here is no more or less than a reshaping of Paonese psychology. What Palafox knows and Bustamonte finally learns is that language is at the heart of how a speaker perceives his world and his role in it. Given the power to shift whole populations and seize the children necessary for the plan, power that Bustamonte is all too willing to use, entire new cultures based on the "virtues" of war or commerce can be produced.

Bustamonte agrees to Palafox's plan because of his eagerness to regain his lost power and his fear of what the Brumbo Clan has in store for him. Thus, he is completely blind to why Palafox is willing to help. Palafox, in fact, is bordering on senility (the extreme form of which is termed "Emeritus" in Breakness). Given the egocentric quality of Breakness culture and language, preservation of the individual is the greatest possible good. Such preservation takes the extreme form on Breakness of a dominie's engendering hundreds of sons whom he molds physiologically and psychologically. In Pao, Palafox sees the possibility of leaving his imprint on an entire planet. He has the insane dream of peopling an entire world with his own offspring. The success of Palafox's plan requires the destruction of Paonese culture and society.

Palafox does succeed in developing three isolated societies on the planet Pao. The first two, the Valiants (warriors) and Technicants (industrialists) derive from his agreement with Bustamonte. These groups speak only the language assigned to them and are effectively cut off from mainstream Paonese society and world view as well as from each other. But Palafox also establishes a third group, the Cogitants, who are scholars. This third group speaks its own language as well as Valiant, Technicant, and Paonese, and as mediators they control the resources of the entire planet. Palafox, by controlling the

Cogitants, controls Pao. Palafox has, in other words, succeeded in reproducing the "isolative" character of Breakness on Pao and has placed himself at the top.

When Bustamonte starts to balk at replacing one overlord with another, Palafox makes the final move in his plan. During the creation of the new Pao, Beran has been on Breakness being educated at the Breakness Institute. It was Palafox's intention to indoctrinate Beran into Breakness ways sufficiently for the young man to sympathize with Palafox's dreams of glory. Thus, when Bustamonte no longer proves cooperative, Palafox successfully replaces him with Beran. He believes the new panarch will be more useful because of his indoctrination and because events have now shaped themselves into an inevitable course leading to exactly what Palafox desires.

What Palafox fails to see, however, is that in Beran he has created the perfect antagonist. Beran knows Valiant, Technicant, Cogitant, and Breakness well, but his mind has been shaped by Paonese. He has an allegiance to Paonese culture and to those qualities which make one a Paonese. Thus, Beran sees the danger of the isolative nature of the changes instituted by Palafox, and he acts to diminish that danger.

By the time Beran is ready to act, Palafox is no longer a threat. He has become fully "Emeritus" and dies while ranting and raving at the hands of his own sons. The threat of the isolated existent communities remained a fact with which Beran had to deal. Beran, however, does not himself have the power to enforce any new change. While he can break up the Technicant and Cogitant communities and reintegrate them into Paonese society, the Valiant group is just too powerful. Furthermore, Beran does not really want to lose many of the advances gained during the years in which Palafox's plan was in operation. For example, Pao has become independent of the Brumbo Clan and now rivals Mercantil in commerce. To return to Paonese would be to return to the insecure past. Yet to allow things to continue as they are means the complete fragmentation of Pao.

This dilemma is resolved by events not fully under Beran's control. When he does try to break up the Valiant community, Beran fails miserably. The Valiants seize control and plan to rule the Paonese themselves. It should be noted, at this point, that Beran's worst fears come true: the Valiants clearly do not consider themselves Paonese. The Valiants, however, do have a basic military common sense. Because they speak an isolated language, they cannot communicate with the Paonese, the Technicants, or the Cogitants. Thus they are potentially an army without any supply line. The Valiants therefore see the practical necessity of developing a single language to facilitate communications, and they place Beran in charge of developing an educational system to reach this end. He suggests and the Valiants unwittingly agree to Pastiche, which, as the name implies, is a combination of Paonese, Technicant, Cogitant, and Valiant. By the end of *The Languages of Pao*, Beran has achieved every goal for which he strove: Pao is to be turned once again into a polysynthetic society but with the added dimension of now being able to cope with the rest of the universe.

In *The Languages of Pao* Jack Vance has created a classical hard science fiction novel. A single hypothesis is postulated, and the novel traces the effect of that hypothesis as it creates change. H. G. Wells could not have asked for more.

Stephen H. Goldman

Sources for Further Study

Reviews:

Amazing Stories. XXXIII, March, 1959, p. 142.

Analog. LXIII, July, 1959, p. 150.

Galaxy. XVII, August, 1959, p. 140.

New Worlds. CLXVII, October, 1966, p. 153.

LAST AND FIRST MEN

Author: Olaf Stapledon (1886-1950)
First book publication: 1930
Type of work: Novel
Time: From the 1930's to two billion years in the future
Locale: The Earth, Venus, Neptune

A history of mankind from the 1930's to two billion years in the future

When analyzing the first fiction work of Olaf Stapledon, *Last and First Men*, care must be taken to evaluate the book in the terms the author intended. Stapledon wrote in his preface to the novel that "it is an essay in myth creation," and it must therefore be accepted as such. It is not an attempt at prophecy, and any analysis based on such an assumption would be misleading and misguided. Stapledon used the concept of a future history to embody his own philosophic understanding of the human condition.

Last and First Men is a history of humanity from the 1930's to two billion years in the future. The historical events immediately following World War I are recounted in great detail, and the manner in which the world comes to be dominated by America and China is outlined. The fall of this civilization and the rise of a new culture in Patagonia follows. The Patagonian culture destroys itself in an atomic conflagration, leaving only a handful of survivors. This pitiful remnant succeeds in keeping the human species alive, but by the time the Earth again becomes generally habitable, the survivors have split into two distinct human races, the admirable Second Men and a contemptible subhuman species which is subjugated by a mutated race of monkeys. Conflicts arise, and after the ensuing struggles the Second Men gain dominance of the planet.

Earth is then invaded by Martian cloudlets whose modes of perception and philosophical outlook prevent them from being able to recognize the Second Men as intelligent creatures. Tens of thousands of years of conflict between the two species follow until mankind succeeds in destroying the invaders, but at the cost of almost destroying itself. Another Dark Age occurs and the Third Men arise from the diseased survivors of the second human species.

The civilizations of this species flourish until genetic engineering creates a race of giant brains, the Fourth Men. The Fourth Men virtually exterminate their creators and embark upon a program of mental exploration of the world. Concluding that pure mentality is insufficient for an understanding or appreciation of existence, the giant brains design the Fifth Men. This race achieves a culture which surpasses that of all previous species. They undertake the physical exploration of space and the mental exploration of the past. However, before they have more than begun to understand fully their world they are forced by an astronomical catastrophe to flee the Earth and terraform Venus.

On Venus man once again transforms himself. The Seventh Men, a winged race, comes to dominate the planet. This race is succeeded by a pedestrian species, and man is once again forced by an astronomical calamity to abandon his home; the race moves to Neptune. On this giant planet mankind undergoes many transformations which ultimately result in the rise of the Eighteenth Men, who are the culmination of human evolution.

After millennia of cultural achievement, the Eighteenth Men discover that a third astronomical catastrophe will destroy the Solar System. They attempt to seed space with molecules which have the potentiality for evolution into "human life" under favorable circumstances; and they undertake the mental exploration of the past so that they and the races which they have succeeded can fully understand and appreciate the human achievement.

It is to one of these "mental explorers" that we owe the chronicle which is called *Last and First Men*. Stapledon uses the fictional device of having one of the Eighteenth Men communicate the history of humanity to one of the last men. He seeks to understand fully his present world by exploring the common human experience. To him, we, the First Men, are the original ancestors to which all succeeding Men, in a sense, pay homage. By trying to return to his origins and to trace their influence, the narrator gains an understanding of what it means to be human, in the same way that contemporary man returns to his ancestors in ceremonies and festivals celebrating origins and rebirths.

Stapledon has used his knowledge of the myth of the past to create a myth of the future. Many of the themes which he explores are familiar to us from the myths which belong to our classical past. The woman who rises from the sea and becomes an instrument of conciliation to the opposing forces of East and West reminds us of the birth of Venus, the goddess of love. The Patagonian prophet who destroys the idol of the temple and who is killed for his attempt to bring understanding to his people reminds us of figures in legend and myth who are killed, but who are then resurrected to become gods. Stapledon also dramatizes one idea which appears again and again in myths: that of immortality or extreme longevity. He uses his portrayal of a culturally advanced species whose members live for thousands of years to explore the consequences such an extended existence might produce.

Many of the races portrayed in *Last and First Men* serve as mirrors to reflect past civilizations, including our own. Stapledon was aware of the scientific revolutions, in both the physical and biological sciences, which had been taking place in Western civilization; and he focused on certain aspects of these revolutions to explore the human condition.

Industrialism for its own sake seemed a fruitless pursuit to Stapledon, and we, the First Men, are portrayed as carrying a fascination with industrialism and the material fruits of scientific research to its ultimate end — the creation of a religion which worships energy and destroys itself by exhausting the resources of the planet. Many future races in the novel are also shown in pursuit of the chimera of industrialism at certain immature stages of their development, but the societies which overcome this fixation are able to achieve an equilibrium between the physical and the mental aspects of humanity.

To emphasize either the physical or the mental to the exclusion of the other is, in Stapledon's view, a certain cause for failure. The giant brains, the Fifth Men, represent pure mentality, and they themselves come to realize that they cannot be fully human because they have relinquished the physical aspects of the race. The Seventh Men, the flying men of Venus, on the other hand, represent pure physicality. They interact successfully with their environment, but they have sacrificed all pursuit of mental activity to the physical delights of flight (a pursuit to which the First Men are also portrayed as being addicted). Ultimately the flying men are replaced by a pedestrian race.

Stapledon views the human drama as a conflict among various aspects of man's own psyche and between man and nature. We, the First Men, are portrayed as being too individualistic and unable to resolve the demands of the individual and society without recourse to dogma and the worship of energy or wealth. The Second Men achieve a precarious balance between these two demands, until an outside force, the Martians, leads to their downfall. The Third Men are consumed by the ambition to alter nature, both animal and human. They succeed with their plans and bring about their own destruction by producing the giant brains, the Fifth Men. These creatures in turn realize their inability to be fully human, and therefore engineer more well-rounded successors. The Sixth Men are confronted by natural forces which they cannot conquer, and flee to Venus.

A cursory reading of *Last and First Men* might lead one to believe that Stapledon was a cultural relativist, but this opinion would be ill-founded. Instead, the concept of "Community" is central to the author's view of the human condition. Stapledon defined community as a group in which all individuals consciously cooperate in a common life approved by all. Each member must respect the personalities of the other members, and recognize their value as individuals. The people who best illustrate this concept in the novel are the Eighteenth Men, who differ from one another radically in both physical and mental qualities but who cooperate with one another fully. Another central concept is that of "Spirit"; this concept, the author believed, lent purpose to human existence. Only by attempting to understand and work towards the "Spirit" could an individual or a community fulfill its destiny.

In *Last and First Men*, Stapledon attempted to write an "essay in myth creation," and the reactions of several generations of science fiction readers testify to his success. He was to attempt on other occasions to create myths for our age: *Star Maker* represents his grand synthesis of metaphysics, science, and history, while *Odd John* and *Sirius* are concrete depictions of mythic elements in our present society. On his own terms, Stapledon is unequaled, and he certainly has been one of the major influences on contemporary science fiction.

Harvey J. Satty

Sources for Further Study

Criticism:

Glicksohn, Susan. "A City of Which the Stars Are Suburbs," in *SF: The Other Side of Realism*. Edited by Thomas D. Clareson. Bowling Green, Ohio: Bowling Green University Popular Press, 1971, pp. 334-347. Glicksohn examines *Last and First Men* to show how it approaches the limits of the imagination.

Smith, Curtis C. "Olaf Stapledon: Saint and Revolutionary," in *Extrapolation* XIII (December, 1971), pp. 5-15. Smith examines Stapledon's mythmaking in *Last and First Men*.

Reviews:

Christian Century. XLVIII, April 15, 1931, p. 516.

Nation. CXXXIII, August 19, 1931, p. 191.

New Statesman. XXXVI, November 22, 1930, p. 217.

New York Times. April 19, 1931, p. 2.

Saturday Review. VII, April 25, 1931, p. 774.

THE LAST CASTLE

Author: Jack Vance (1916-   )
First book publication: 1966
Type of work: Novel
Time: The distant future
Locale: The Earth

The aristocratic "lords" of Earth face a rebellion from the Meks, a servant class determined to kill their human masters

Principal characters:
    O. C. CHARLE, the "first gentleman" of the castle and presiding officer of the governing council
    O. Z. GARR, an outspoken gentile dandy
    CLAGHORN, an elder of the Claghorn family, a student of Meks
    XANTEN, an elder of the Xanten family
    MEKS, the manlike aliens with rust-brown skin imported as slaves
    GLYS MEADOWSWEET, a young lady being reared outside the castle

Jack Vance received both a Hugo and a Nebula award for this short novel that shows many of the strengths of the author at his best. The plotting is adroit, building inexorably to a climax followed by an effective *dénouement*. A carefully selected sequence of events clearly delineates the thematic problems. Vance's succinct approach invites comparison with H. G. Wells's *The Time Machine* and *The Island of Dr. Moreau*, with their great impact within a limited scope.

Like Wells, Vance depicts social and intellectual conflicts of the present projected into the future. The "gentlefolk" of Vance's book represent the worldwide succession of dominant upperclass aristocracies — the brilliant, "civilized," idle rich, whose refinement oozes from every sentence of their inconsequential conversation, and for whom individuality or even eccentricity is the approved ideal.

The Meks are sentient creatures robbed of their natural identity and forced into slavery. They are made to perform *mech*anically; their abbreviated name suggests the *mech*anized force of a technology that applies human labor to the formation of an efficient but dehumanizing system. Vance describes them as reduced to the level of insects, employing an image that Franz Kafka also found descriptive of modern man's condition: "Working in the mass, by the teeming thousands, he seemed less admirable, less competent: a hybrid of sub-man and cockroach." Their lack of individuality is understandable as a collective reaction to their common lot, but it is also a rationalization by the nobles in whose interest it is to believe that they are subhuman.

Vance's skill in plotting, his clear, economical style, and his concern for the survival of humanity, make this a piece of classic science fiction in both form and substance. The conditions and prospects of society are revealed in action. Characterization is kept to a minimum; events, rather than characters

— and *types* of human behavior rather than specific individuals with flaws, tragic or otherwise — determine the course of the story. The very form and style of the book suggest that the future is determined not by individuals but by collective human tendencies and their inevitable conflicts. (In the light of this orientation, criticism of Meks for lacking individuality is very ironic.) The conditions leading to the sweep of events have their roots in the present, and this brings us to see both the original depopulation of Earth and Earth's restructuring into the Castle society, as reflections of current behavior. It is a futuristic parable with action as the metaphor.

For the most part, Vance's style stresses the denotative rather than the connotative aspects of language. He is highly effective in limiting his description to factual matters; and once we accept his statements as fact, we are the more ready to believe in his future reality. Metaphoric or symbolic language occurs primarily in the names Vance gives his characters and places, as in the case of the Meks. It is interesting to observe that the most "poetic" passage is an inventory of castle names delivered as an ominous death chant in the brief second section of Chapter Five. The Birds, raucous creatures used by the "gentlemen" for conveyance through the air, report what destruction they have seen in their aerial scouting, and they sound like a Greek chorus:

> Sea Island is deserted. Marble columns are tumbled along the beach. Pearl Dome is collapsed. Corpses float in the Water Garden . . . Delora: *a ros ros ros!* A dismal scene. . . . Alume is desolate. The great wooden door is smashed. The Green Flame is extinguished.

The names of the castles and artifacts suggest rare achievements and irreparable loss, and as these enclaves fall one by one, the last castle becomes supremely important. The title focuses action on this stronghold, Hagedorn, and while the "castle" is a literal one, the word, indeed the very concept of this type of residence, carries overtones of *caste*, suggesting a rigidly classed society that the gentlefolk have chosen to perpetuate on Earth. In Hagedorn, Vance has devised a richly metaphoric name for the edifice that will be the final outpost in the class struggle. A "Hag" in ordinary parlance is an ugly woman often believed to be a witch. This implication that the castle life has a feminine rather than a masculine orientation is broadly ironic, especially in light of the treatment of the wives and Phanes, the latter being gossamer female spirits proudly collected by the "gentlemen." "Hag" may also be a verb, to "chop or hew," suggesting the current use of such a word as "haggle." "Dor" is a "trick or deception." The splendor of Hagedorn is thus a deception, nothing but trickery. These associations constitute a jarring note when set longside the more genuine *"hagios"* (meaning "sacred") and the sacred texts *haggada*, which teach the law by parables rather than by the mere listing of prescriptive rules for conduct. Hagedorn's pretenses and trickery finally give way to a parable whose meaning we may take as the central theme of Vance's story.

The balance of power in Hagedorn has been recently tested in the election of a new "first gentleman" of the castle. The most likely contenders for the post, Garr and Claghorn, held strongly opposing points of view and ultimately canceled each other out, leaving the position to the ineffectual O. C. Charle. Garr, a staunch defender of the ruling class (we are told that he "exemplified the traditional virtues of Castle Hagedorn") is effete and overly fond of Phanes. His name stems from the root of "garrulous" — descriptive of one who talks too much, and often about trifles. Claghorn, as "horn" implies, is a strident trumpet warning the complacent rulers. "Clag" is a "clot or clog," a bar to action, yet capable of keeping a wounded man from bleeding to death.

Vance depicts a situation in which the two aristocrats have nullified each other — garrulous, complacent conservatism negating abrasive, liberal sooth-saying. Charle, "a gentleman of no remarkable presence," represents the out-come of the clash. The author perhaps suggests a parallel with leadership in contemporary society. Charle has the indecisive, lukewarm personality of the worst sort of politician, closer in sympathy to Garr than to Claghorn, since it is safer to do nothing than to act to change the *status quo*. The other intermediary between these conflicting views, a character more sympathetic to Claghorn, is Xanten, whose very name begins with a nullifying "X" mark, a person willing to forsake the habits of the past to fight for future survival. He ultimately breaks the deadlock of battle in the Meks's seige of Hagedorn, arriving by Bird to announce simply, "We are fighting." He has summoned his courage as in the heroic resistance of Xanthus in ancient Lycia, and in this case, though the castle culture is destroyed, the human spirit survives.

Xanten is the first man of action in the story. He crosses the lines of stag-nant impasse reached by the Council by moving to reconnoiter the Space Depot and discover whether the Meks have sabotaged the only means of es-cape, the spaceships that could take the humans back to their Home Worlds. Borne aloft by six swift Birds, Xanten is given a strange preview early in the book: "[An] astonishing vision, so simple and yet so grand that he looked around, in all directions, with new eyes. The vision was Earth re-populated with men, the land cultivated, Nomads driven back into the wilderness." Hav-ing begun to act, he is allowed to see a possible alternative outcome for his actions. He is physically and metaphysically relieved to have left the Castle behind and to be *doing* something, and his feelings are described in terms that rebuff Garr as representative of a life "as artificial, extravagant and intricate as life could be." Xanten projects his feelings onto the Birds: "To Xanten's re-lief, their *garr*ulity lessened; silently they flew south. . . ."

At the Space Depot, Xanten finds Meks destroying the equipment, and he orders them to stop and go back to work. Instead of obeying, they attack him, but he coolly fights them off by employing tactics forshadowing those to be applied later to the entire invading Mek force. He traps them inside a building where he is able to overpower them. Xanten's initial actions thus foreshadow the only viable human way out of a doomed system, and he alone of the characters in the castle seems capable of such action. He concludes his investigation by capturing a Mek and discovers that the creature has returned to its natural state. It has no syrup sac and is therefore free from the nutrient system implanted by the humans to control the Mek population.

On his way back to the castle, Xanten continues to explore conditions and alternatives, and the reader is given greater understanding of the situation on Earth. He meets a party of Nomads, wandering survivors of old Earth days, and addresses their Hetman to ask that a party of their men be trained at the castle to fight off the Mek rebellion. The Hetman refuses, with a ferocious grin, and expresses satisfaction that "your beasts have finally risen up to rend you." He considers the castle dwellers to be aliens and invaders, and advises Xanten that if they want to save themselves they should desert the castles and become Nomads.

Next he encounters a semireligious band, the Expiationists, and speaks with a former gentleman among them, Philidor. When Philidor hears that Xanten wants them to form themselves into an army, he rejects the idea as incompatible with his chosen life: "The Meks are here, likewise Peasants and Birds and Phanes, all altered, transported and enslaved for human pleasure. Indeed, it is this fact that occasions our guilt, and for which we must expiate, and now you want us to compound this guilt!" Philidor expresses his moral concerns clearly, just as the Nomads expressed their sense of physical justice. He tells Xanten that he has "chosen a morality which at least allows me calm. I kill — nothing. I destroy — nothing." Xanten and the reader must slowly begin to realize that neither the physical toughness of the surviving Nomads nor the moral commitment of the Expiationists can be rallied to the castle's defense.

Yet, both physically and morally the gentlefolk are inert. Claghorn, who has long urged them to stop depending on outside labor and to return the Meks to their native planet, has always previously been ignored, nor is his advice followed once the rebellion erupts. In complete frustration, Claghorn leaves the castle to join the simpler village life outside. Xanten is the only sensible man left in the castle, and he proceeds to question his captured Mek as the other nobles turn to their vain amusements.

The only event in the novel competing for interest with the Mek attack, and the sole activity that has full approval of the nobility (except for Claghorn and Xanten, who keep no Phanes), is a ceremony called "The Viewing of Antique Tabards." Despite the title, the intricately woven cloaks made by the Phanes are far less noticeable than the Phanes themselves. The occasion is a kind of beauty contest in which each man can parade his prize possession: his Phane. Vance explains that

> Possibly half the gentlemen, but less than a quarter of the ladies, kept Phanes. These were creatures native to the caverns of Albireo Seven's moon: a docile race, both playful

and affectionate, which after several thousand years of selective breeding had become sylphs of piquant beauty. Clad in a delicate gauze which issued from pores behind their ears, along their upper arms and down their backs, they were the most inoffensive of creatures, anxious to please, innocently vain.

From the outset we are aware of a feminine rivalry centered on these delicate creatures, for "rumors sometimes told of ladies drenching an especially hated Phane in tincture of ammonia, which matted her pelt and destroyed her gauze forever."

The useless pageant, "never overtly a competition," is an opportunity for male ego gratification, since "all watching made up their minds as to which was the most entrancing and graceful of the Phanes, and the repute of the owner was thereby exalted." It is like Nero fiddling while Rome burns. More specifically, in this situation it is another example of purposeless degradation of the individual into a mere possession. It reveals the Hagedorn society as being clearly dominated by men with male chauvinist values. If a "hag" is a woman believed to be in league with the devil, Hagedorn itself may be looked upon as a male establishment that forces its women into the image of its own vanity — and this is perhaps one appropriate definition of the devil at work, from Eden to the present day. If these women are in league with the devil, it is because their men *are* that evil force. Female characters in the book merely reflect the personalities of their husbands or owners; in this sense they are like the Meks, but they are Vance's most conspicuous symbol of an intrinsic attitudinal problem within the society.

Claghorn, who kept no Phanes, was also the one who had urged that the Meks be sent back to Etamin Nine. Since the Meks's slavelike duties and rust-brown skin might suggest comparison with black minorities, the proposal to send them home might sound like an argument for shipping the blacks back to Africa. Vance, by showing the same exploitation in the case of Phanes and women, broadens the case to reveal a fundamental error of perception. The ruling class lacks any self-sufficiency whatsoever; it depends for its status, as well as its food, on the exploitation of other creatures.

The pitiful impotence of the rulers is clearly seen in their penchant for Phanes. Vance explains that "a gentleman besotted by a Phane was considered a figure of fun. The Phane, though so carefully bred as to seem a delicate girl, if used sexually became crumbled and *haggard*, with gauzes drooping and discolored, and everyone would know that such and such a gentleman had misused his Phane." The use of "haggard" — echoing the "hag" element in Hagedorn — is significant. The Phanes epitomize the life of Hagedorn, a selective refinement beyond purpose. The sexual attraction a man might feel for a woman is only mockery in the case of Phanes, who become haggard whenever a natural impulse is followed. They are the very embodiment of a rarefied, transparent, and useless social fabric. The human women have in the process been reduced to a single role as well; since they can only be considered as sexual objects, they respond "by conducting themselves with such extravagant provocation that the Phanes in contrast seemed the most ingenuous and fragile of nature sprites." They have made their women into sexual servants, and once the males are no longer charmed by the beauty of their Phanes, the worn-out sylphs encase themselves in gray gauze and perform menial household chores, serving again as slaves.

The single exception to this bleak feminine helplessness is Glys Meadowsweet, nearly victimized by Garr but fortunately set free. She maintains a relatively independent existence outside the castle, in the village where Claghorn has taken up residence. When Xanten visits Claghorn for advice, he meets the girl. He has been frustrated during his conversation with Claghorn, and complains to Glys that he has not been able to discover the secret of survival under the Mek siege. Her response is surprising: "Glys Meadowsweet laughed — an easy, merry sound, like nothing Xanten had ever heard at Castle Hagedorn. 'Secret? When even I know it?'" She whispers the advice to him, and he replies without recognition of her simple wisdom: "No secret there. Only what the prehistoric Scythians termed *bathos*. Dishonor to the gentlemen"!

Only after Castle Janiel has fallen does Xanten recognize the truth in what Glys has whispered — a truth earlier taught in different ways by the Nomads and Expiationists. He offers the council his understanding: "Now is our last opportunity to escape the great cage that Castle Hagedorn is to become." Indeed, it has long been a cage for many. Vance's point is clearly that in enslaving others one eventually enslaves himself. Xanten has at last come to see this, but the others ignore his advice. He leaves the castle with those who will follow him, but he does not abandon his fellow men. The castle is besieged and about to fall when Xanten returns by Bird to announce that he leads a coalition of men from the castle, Epiationists, and Nomads, and that they have begun attacking the Meks with great success. Joined by some of the last of the castle crowd, including Charle, they entrap the remaining Meks in the castle and eventually force their surrender.

Vance is optimistic about human intelligence and action. Xanten succeeds in crushing the rebellion, and sends the Mek survivors back to their home planet. He marries Glys Meadowsweet and lives in the country near a river, and has two children. In the final pages of the book he and his family return to visit the castle, which has become a museum with Charle as its curator. They find that the elected leader of the gentlemen has aged, and that his face has become thin, "almost waxen," as though he too is a museum piece. He tends the ghosts of the idle past, while the vigorous Xanten asserts, "We are men now, on our own world, as we never were before."

Vance's parable attacks all those who derive their identity and purpose from the labor or virtual slavery of others. He asks us to look honestly at whether we can call our lives our own. To what extent has our dependence upon imported labor, imported goods, and mechanical production with borrowed energy caused us to live lives less than fully human? To what extent are women in our society defined by men whose highest concept of beauty is close to the adorable unreality of the Phanes or the sexual exhibitionism that the nobility have forced upon their women? When he had first heard the "secret" of avoiding death in the last castle, Xanten was prompted to speak of the chores involved in saving his life as a gentleman's descent into *bathos*. This surely is the term that ought to be applied to the so-called "civilization" that the castle society represents, and perhaps also to the social and political posturings of our day. In straining after the sublime, the "gentlemen" have overshot the mark and sunk into the ridiculous. To what extent, Vance asks, has the "civilized" behavior of our time made all our lives *bathetic*, causing us to aspire only to ridiculous mediocrity unredeemed by pity or fear?

Richard Mathews

Sources for Further Study

Reviews:

New Worlds. CLXXVII, November, 1967, p. 63.

THE LAST MAN

Author: Mary Wollstonecraft Shelley (1797-1851)
First book publication: 1826
Type of work: Novel
Time: c. 2055-2100
Locale: England, Greece, Constantinople, and the Continent

The story of a ravaging plague that gradually wipes humanity from existence; the first of the "catastrophe" novels written in English, and hence the forerunner of an important modern theme in science fiction

> *Principal characters:*
> LIONEL VERNEY, the last man
> PERDITA VERNEY, his sister
> ADRIAN, second Earl of Windsor, son of England's last king
> IDRIS, Adrian's sister and Lionel's wife
> LORD RAYMOND, Perdita's husband
> RYLAND, leader of the republican party

Although many people know Mary Shelley as the author of *Frankenstein*, her other novels belong to the bibliophile or the specialist in the early Romantic period. A few years ago, a reader who wanted to examine *The Last Man* would have had to locate either a copy printed in England or France in 1826, or a copy of the pirated American edition of 1833. But this important novel was made accessible in 1965 when Hugh J. Luke, Jr.'s, edition was published by the University of Nebraska Press.

The central character of the novel, Lionel Verney, is the orphaned son of a financially ruined English nobleman. Verney leaves an undirected and delinquent youth when he meets Adrian, the young Earl of Windsor, the son of England's last monarch, whose father had abdicated before a demand for a republican government. Some time later, Verney's sister Perdita marries Lord Raymond, the leader of the Royalist party in parliament. Although this ends Raymond's hopes for the throne, his desire is partially fulfilled by his election as Lord Protector, chief executive officer in the government. All these characters form a closeknit, almost pastoral circle.

The main plot begins when Raymond's involvement with another woman leads him to resign and to accept a commission in the Greek army, which is successfully prosecuting a war of liberation against Turkey. Raymond is captured and tortured but eventually released under the threat of English intervention. He resumes his command, and leads the forces that besiege Constantinople.

The city falls, but to a plague rather than to the Greeks. His soldiers fear the disease more than their officers, and refuse to enter the city. As Raymond enters the desolate, silent city, mines explode and he is killed in the collapse of a building. Only Verney enters to recover his body. The funeral procession carries Raymond's corpse to a hillside overlooking Athens, where a tomb is cut and he is interred. His wife Perdita refuses to leave the site, despite the pleas of her brother that she must care for her infant daughter Clara. Verney drugs and kidnaps her, intending to return her to England, where, he hopes, she will come to accept her loss. But awakening on the ship, she drowns herself rather than leave Raymond's grave at Athens.

Adrian and Verney, who has married Adrian's sister Idris, return to a semiretirement in Windsor Forest, but their human troubles are replaced by a threat from nature: by 2093 the plague that destroyed the Turks (perhaps mutated?) has spread throughout Asia and the eastern Mediterranean. In another year, the New World, South Africa, and Australia have been devastated by this disease with a one hundred percent mortality rate. The same year, isolated cases appear in England.

Each winter brings hope that the plague will abate, but it returns with greater severity each summer. The functioning of English society is threatened as political plans fall to pieces before this overwhelming threat. For example, a man named Ryland leads the republican party, and he wants primarily to abolish hereditary rank. His desire seems at hand when he is elected Lord Protector. But as the plague burns through Europe, England is swelled with returning natives and fleeing foreigners. To keep the country going, Ryland needs the aid of the aristocracy, and he is forced to shelve his political desires.

Ryland loses his nerve, and Adrian returns to public life, directing the united efforts against the disease. But despite his charismatic, almost inspired presence, he can do no more than preserve order as the number of survivors dwindles. Eventually, the handful left — only a few thousand — decide that cold weather is their only hope of survival: they agree to cross to the continent during the winter, counting on reaching Switzerland by the return of summer. But the plague is completing its work; of the three thousand who set out from England, only four reach Lake Como: Adrian, Lionel, his son Evelyn, and Raymond's daughter Clara. There Evelyn dies, not of the plague but of typhus. The three who remain travel to Venice; they try to sail across the Adriatic to Greece, but a storm arises suddenly, and Adrian and Clara are drowned. Lionel Verney, the only human being to recover from the plague, is now the last man. He journeys to Rome, climbs to the dome of St. Peter's Cathedral, and carves the date "2100" on its top. Recording the close of the book of mankind in his journal, he resolves to set out circumnavigating Africa, intending to head for India and beyond to verify, if he cannot remedy, his status as the last man.

This summary of events shows the astonishing scope of the book: the amount of sheer incident is enormous. But the novel was to be successful neither in Mary Shelley's own time nor in the present.

It is tempting to see a reflection of Mary Shelley's personal life in the unstoppable tragedy of *The Last Man*: when she began writing the book, she had known Percy Shelley only ten years, yet in that time she had suffered a miscarriage, seen three of her children die in infancy, endured Shelley's drowning and her consequent abandonment by his family, and received word that Lord Byron had died in Greece.

Yet she had reason to be confident of her ability to support herself and her young son: her first novel, *Frankenstein* (1818), had been enthusiastically received, and she had found herself warmly praised by critics and public alike. What a reversal it was, then, for *The Last Man* to be a total failure. But it is not hard to understand the coldness — even revulsion — of the original reviewers. In 1826 the reading public could neither understand nor accept the theme of the universal destruction of mankind. But especially since the atomic bomb, the idea has so frequently informed everything from meditations to movies that it stands in danger of becoming a cliché. Yet Mary Shelley was the first to present it in English.

Different reasons make it unlikely that *The Last Man* will ever appeal to a modern audience. It has the customary three-volume format of the time, and the plot moves so slowly through the first volume that the plague is not as much a threat to the characters as boredom is to the reader. If ever a novel cried out to be condensed, it is *The Last Man*.

The reader today is likely to find a second flaw in Mary Shelley's desire to memorialize her vanished circle of friends. Percy's father had exacted a promise from her that prevented her from writing an outright biography of her husband. To some extent she evaded that restriction by fictionalizing her circle in *The Last Man*: in many ways, Adrian is her portrait of Shelley; Byron's likeness shows through the character of Lord Raymond; and others, such as Claire Clairmont, can be recognized in the novel. But her natural desire to eulogize those she loved in the virtues of her characters results in a high-flown rhetoric of praise abandoned by modern prose, and it becomes a strain on modern taste.

After all these shortcomings are allowed, the fact remains that *The Last Man* contains in its central and final volumes a plot of powerful and enduring interest told in passages of frequent brilliance. If the reader endures a beginning that moves at the pace of a different age, the story that follows equals *Frankenstein* and well supports Mary Shelley's position as the mother of science fiction.

Perhaps that beginning is the reason that critics of science fiction have not found much to praise in *The Last Man*. Their comments are often passing and disparaging references. One exception is Brian Aldiss' excellent *Billion-Year Spree*, which takes the longest look and arrives at the harshest judgment. For Aldiss, *The Last Man* seems merely Gothic; principally he complains that the novel, though set in the future, presents little in the way of technological or social innovation. This conclusion is far from unarguable.

The idea of scientific advance, if not its details, is strong in the novel. Although neither in this novel nor in *Frankenstein* does Mary Shelley foreshadow the engineering mentality of Jules Verne, she does locate the events of

The Last Man almost two hundred years in her future. In that setting she places scheduled passenger travel by steamship and balloon. Several times she refers to the reforestation of England. A character watches the precession of the poles, and discusses the possible effects of a change in the angle of the Earth to the ecliptic. But chiefly, as in *Frankenstein*, she assumes technological innovation without specifying the details:

> The arts of life, and the discoveries of science had augmented in a ratio which left all calculation behind [mentioning almost casually the piercing insight that the progression of technological change is cumulative]; food sprung up, so to say, spontaneously — machines existed to supply with facility every want of the population.

And certainly she was right to be vague about nuts and bolts. Compare *The Last Man* to a story like John W. Campbell, Jr.'s, "All," of pre-World War II vintage, in which too much detail is supplied. A cure-all for disease is demanded by the story, and rather than leave its nature unspecified, Campbell identifies the panacea as atomic radiation. Science fiction "hardware," when we have since found out that the hardware does not work, is at best distracting and at worst ruinous for the story.

More remarkable than her technology is Mary Shelley's social extrapolation. Aldiss thinks little of her account of the end of the English monarchy, saying that it only repeated in fiction what the French Revolution had demonstrated in fact. Not so. Mary Shelley's revolution is a peaceful one, a positive expression of a common humanity that has too often been totally lacking in science fiction. The republic that replaces the monarchy is still speculation about a future society, and if the chief executive's title — Lord Protector — is reminiscent of Cromwell's dictatorship, the fact that Mary Shelley's executive holds elected and limited power is not a reflection of France. We should remember also that a situation that seems farfetched or old-fashioned one day may seem prophetic the next: Aldiss hints that he finds the Turkish oppression of Greece outdated, yet during the Cyprus crisis of just a few years ago, many Greeks would certainly have thought Mary's comments intensely timely. And her speculation goes still farther: in her England of mid-twenty-first century, Lords and Commons are united in a single house.

Concerning the central issue of the book, it is true, as Aldiss notes, that no measures to combat the plague are spelled out. But it is not true that Mary Shelley makes no extrapolation from the practice of vaccination, already widespread in her time. On the contrary, she assumes and states that by the time of the novel smallpox is extinct. While this desirable end is not yet quite accomplished, it is nevertheless in sight, showing that her timing will almost certainly be right. Does she fail to extrapolate from the control of smallpox to the prevention of other diseases? We must remember, when we attempt to answer this question, that although vaccination was practiced in her day, the reason for its effectiveness was unknown: it was a practical success, not a theoretical one, and it seems overly harsh to expect Mary Shelley to have been Louis Pasteur. The fact is that no one knew how smallpox or any other viral or bacterial infection was transmitted then; in the face of absolute ignorance, the writer's better tactic is to be suggestive (or even silent) rather than specific.

And finally, there remains one haunting comment, just a passing remark, that may or may not have significance: we are told that Ryland, leader of the republican party, had earlier in his career served as ambassador to "the Northern States of America." The possibility seems vanishingly remote that Mary Shelley, writing in 1824, could have foreseen the division resulting in the Civil War almost forty years later, yet to any American reader the words have an eerie ring.

Prolixity and high blown style damage *The Last Man*, yet not beyond an appreciation of its real virtues. It is as good an illustration of the nature of Romanticism as the most rigorous teacher could want; it contains scenes of strength and beauty; it shows the reflection of a powerful imagination on the society of the author's time, joined to a projection of that society into the future. Especially at the last it portrays a mood of utter desperation and the ultimate alienation with a conviction that a hundred and fifty years have not dimmed. George Stewart's *Earth Abides*, Nevil Shute's *On the Beach*, Jack London's *The Scarlet Plague*, John Christopher's *The Death of Grass*, and a hundred more owe their impact, if not their technique, to the theme handled so definitively in Mary Shelley's *The Last Man*.

Walter E. Meyers

Sources for Further Study

Criticism:

Aldiss Brian W. "The Billion Year Spree: Origin of the Species," in *Extrapolation*. XIV (1973), pp. 186-189. *The Last Man* was one of the original science fiction tales which exercised a major influence on the genre implies Aldiss.

Cameron, Kenneth Neill, Editor. *Romantic Rebels: Essays on Shelley and His Circle*. Cambridge: Harvard University Press, 1973, pp. 75-78. Cameron places *The Last Man* in relation to the romantic tradition and discusses the differences.

THE LAST STARSHIP FROM EARTH

Author: John Boyd (Boyd Upchurch, 1919-   )
First book publication: 1968
Type of work: Novel
Time: 1969
Locale: The San Francisco bay area and a prison planet named "Hell"

In a world reminiscent of our own, mathematician Haldane IV affronts his rigidly stratified society by falling in love with a poet, for which crime he is exiled to Hell, where he plots to overthrow Earth's government by creating a "probability world"

Principal characters:
HALDANE IV, a brilliant math student at Berkeley
HALDANE III, his father
MALCOLM VI, his friend
FLAXON I, his attorney
HELIX, a young woman literature student
FAIRWEATHER I, a famous mathematician who designed the Pope, a computer now on Mt. Whitney
FAIRWEATHER II, his son

When John Boyd's *The Last Starship from Earth* was published in 1968, it was received with vast indifference by the science fiction fraternity. It was given virtually no votes for either the Nebula or Hugo awards, despite the fact that Boyd's abilities as revealed in his first published science fiction work marked him as genuine major talent. In the decade since its publication, however, critical opinion has changed considerably. Several major articles have explicated the novel's complexity, and two or three critical books have praised its insights, its incisive attacks on behaviorist psychology and sociology, and its evocation of a distinctly original dystopia. In short, many readers now recognize that *The Last Starship from Earth* is in almost every way a major accomplishment.

Boyd's novel is at once many things: a scathing attack on behaviorist psychology and sociology; a disturbing dystopia; a probability world story which makes its point by the "familiar unfamiliarity" of its constructs; an all too rare science fiction love story; an attack on intransigent religiosity; and, quite simply, a funny book, redolent with some marvelous ribald humor and well-concealed multilevel puns. Its plot is complex, and its handling of various time sequences both fascinating and puzzling.

Haldane IV — the Roman numeral used with various names throughout the book indicates a hereditary, rigidly stratified hierarchical society — is a brilliant young math student at Berkeley in a world that curiously resembles ours but differs radically in many ways. In Haldane's world the Pope is a giant computer on top of Mt. Whitney, Henry VIII a leading sociologist who was a student of John Dewey; Lincoln has delivered a Johannesberg Address and brought about the hegemony of the United Nations; and intermarriage between members of the various categories of society, such as between a mathematician and a poet, is a crime punishable by exile to a peculiarly dismal prison planet named Hell. Haldane's world is reminiscent of the society described in Aldous Huxley's *Brave New World*, yet it is sufficiently similar to ours to make the reader question his own perceptions. Haldane's existence, his outlook, and his own perceptions are controlled by the Departments of Theology, Sociology, and Psychology, which exercise the moral, judicial, and police functions of the State. Consequently when he meets, apparently quite by accident, Helix, a student of poetry, and falls in love with her, he is quite aware of the risk he is running — exile. Later, when Helix is discovered to be pregnant, Haldane is tried for deviationism. As the trial proceeds, with members of the three ruling departments as jurors, the charge of deviationism is dismissed when the evidence reveals that the defendant exhibits the far more serious symptoms of the Fairweather Syndrome, a crime against the State.

Fairweather I was the mathematical genius who designed the computer Pope and discovered the Fairweather Simultaneity Theory which made space travel possible, resulting in the eventual discovery of Hell, ostensibly an ice-age planet. His son, Fairweather II, however, was the leader of a short-lived rebellion against the State exemplified by the massed powers of the Departments of Theology, Sociology, and Psychology. This rebellion, which Boyd cleverly indicates is analogous to Milton's portrayal of Satan's rebellion against God in *Paradise Lost*, occasioned Fairweather II's own exile to Hell. Since that time, only extreme hostile activity against the State, now labeled the "Fairweather Syndrome," results in exile to Hell. Mere deviationism is punishable only by reduction in rank to "prole" status or a short-term sentence in the mines of Pluto.

Once on Hell, Haldane discovers that the planet is not so bad after all. Its society resembles the exuberant one of the Elizabethan Age or the American Frontier, with individualism rampant. Helix turns out to be the daughter of Fairweather II, who is still alive, and Fairweather enlists Haldane's aid to "overthrow the Department of Sociology and set free the human spirit on earth." To accomplish this aim, Haldane will be sent back in time (the reversal of time is one of the effects of the Fairweather Theory) to throw a monkey wrench into history. "There are few periods in history," Fairweather says, "and those come early, when one man could alter the course of nations. To eliminate the power of the sociologists, we must destroy the seeds of the power, which were planted before the sociologists came into being."

They plan to return Haldane to earth early in the first century and perform deicide. In Haldane's world, Jesus was not crucified, but died at the age of seventy after being struck by an arrow from a crossbow as he led the Jewish armies in a rebellion against Rome. Haldane assumes the identity of Judas Iscariot, accomplishes his mission, but relinquishes his seat on "the last starship from earth" to the drug-laden body of the Hebrew prophet. In the epilogue to the novel, Haldane has become the Wandering Jew, but is now on a different earth — our own — replete with student sit-ins, country and western music, and other characteristics of the late 1960's. The better world which Haldane and Fairweather sought to bring about is our own, and Haldane wonders if he has derailed history by his actions. Is this world Purgatory, and must Haldane walk the earth for thousands of years awaiting Jesus' return?

With that ambiguous question the novel ends, to the reader's delight and puzzlement. Such an outline misses, of course, the wit of Boyd's style, the cleverness of his satire, and the occasionally baffling enigmas he propounds. *The Last Starship from Earth* is sheer delight, and students of English literature in particular will enjoy some of the complicated verbal tricks Boyd plays with his parodies of many English poems. Early in the novel, for example, after Haldane and Helix have met, Haldane haunts lectures on poetry in an attempt to meet her again. In the process he becomes an expert on such obscure writers as Winthrop Mackworth Praed and Felicia Dorothea Hemans, for Haldane reads extensively but with no taste whatsoever. Wordsworth and Byron are eighteenth century romantic poets, and Haldane reads them even though he knows it "is folly for a professional to endanger the social welfare for a tremor in the loins."

Such verbal wit and parody abounds in the novel, and one of Boyd's most hilarious passages occurs with a brilliant pastiche of sociological jargon as Brandt, the sociologist foreman of the jury, testifies:

> "Your honor, I beg the indulgence of the court beforehand for the brevity of my report, which is based purely on a sexo-sociological profile of the defendant elicited from a review of transitory phenomena to project an overview of the defendant in relation to the peer group in which the subject belongs, on a verbal plane in a most cursory manner because this dimension will be, I'm sure, handled adequately by my esteemed colleagues, contrasted to the socioeconomic groupings surrounding his peer group and related to it on a horizontal level, no pun intended, consisting of verifiable, empirical, objective data which lend themselves to hard-core analysis in the sexo-sociological areas, because my departmental duties are pressing; so I must not only apologize for the brevity of my report and for my reliance on your honor's tolerance of subjective analysis of horizontal in-depth factors, but further request to be excused from the continuance of the proceedings after the finalization of my report."

Thus in one sentence Boyd demolishes the pretentiousness of sociological jargon, the ridiculousness of its concepts, and the sterility of its ideas. Yet for all of the playful fun that Boyd is having at the expense of almost everyone, this is a very serious novel. In his introduction to the new Penguin reprint of the book, Boyd writes that the novel had its inception when he was an undergraduate in the late 1940's at the University of Southern California and reacted against sociological and psychological behaviorist jargon then beginning on the campus. Thus it attacks, in the words of the book, a world so simplistic that "every problem can be solved by the pope or a prostitute." It speaks against "the moldings of those who would come to us with their persuasive smiles and irreproachable logic in the name of religion, mental hygiene, social duty, come to us with their flags, their Bibles, their money credits, to steal our immortal [souls]." In other words, the novel praises the individual and denigrates societal pressures of any type. Haldane may be a typical dystopian deviant, to be sure, but his struggle to become aware, to achieve consciousness, is integral to the work. He gradually realizes that something is rotten at the core of the State, and his slow realization of this fact prepares him for the ultimate act of deicide on the final pages.

One of the most perplexing problems faced by the reader is attempting to decide which of the starships mentioned in the novel is indeed the *last* starship from earth. Does "last" mean "final" or "most recent?" And in which of the three timetracks of the novel do they operate — if they operate at all? Here some explanation is necessary. Timetrack A might refer to Haldane's world, timetrack B to the one the reader knows, and timetrack C to that of Hell. Starships connect Haldane's world with Hell. Both Haldane and Helix are passengers, and an indeterminate number of starships have previously shuttled from A to C enabling Fairweather II to create his wildly individualistic planet. In turn a one-seater takes Haldane from C to B where he assumes the identity of Judas and "assassinates" Jesus before he can die from a crossbow arrow. Thus the history of timetrack A is derailed, and, presumably, Haldane's original parallel world winks out of existence. The "last" starship, then, might well be the one-seater bringing the drugged body of Jesus to Hell, which, as a distinct planet independent of A, continues to exist. At the end, Haldane, now on B, awaits the development of a technology sufficient to enable him to catch a starship to Hell and rejoin Helix.

On the other hand, if A does not exist and has never existed, perhaps no starships have ever flown. This concept of temporal simultaneity is rich in comic overtones and remains one of the pleasurable conjectures considered by the reader after he closes the book. Such questions abound, and Boyd skillfully avoids providing exact answers to them. Is Haldane's original world a heaven or a hell? Is our world a Purgatory which may lead to Hell? And is Hell a heaven? Hell, after all, means "light" in German.

Whether the novel be viewed as theological speculation or a work of richly comic antibehaviorist satire makes little difference in the end. It is both of these things and more, of course, and is a fascinating, entertaining story as well. *The Last Starship from Earth* never preaches; its action carries its message, and its pages are drenched with action, witty dialogue, and credible characters.

Willis E. McNelly

Sources for Further Study

Reviews:

Analog. LXXXIV, October, 1969, p. 172.

Luna Monthly. II, July, 1969, p. 25.

Magazine of Fantasy and Science Fiction. XXXVII, September, 1969, p. 24.

THE LATHE OF HEAVEN

Author: Ursula K. Le Guin (1929-   )
First book publication: 1971
Type of work: Novel
Time: The end of the twentieth century
Locale: Portland, Oregon

The story of a power-hungry psychiatrist who manipulates his patient's dreams to alter reality

Principal characters:
> GEORGE ORR, an ordinary man who finds his dreams control reality
> HEATHER LALACHE, a lawyer and George's lover and wife
> DR. WILLIAM HABER, a psychiatrist and megalomaniac who manipulates George's dreams

"We are such stuff as dreams are made of" is one of the unspoken epigrams of *The Lathe of Heaven,* a terse, witty, yet unself-conscious novel about an ordinary man whose dreams change reality. Set in Portland, Oregon, in 1998 or so, the novel may not at first be recognizable as written by one of today's most influential, sophisticated, and profound writers, Ursula K. Le Guin.

A writer of science fiction and fantasy, Le Guin's works before *The Lathe of Heaven* were usually set on distant planets or in imaginary worlds in a future at least six hundred years from the present. Moreover, her technique usually emphasizes the poetic and visionary, the intuitive nature of humanity that yearns for unity and transcendence. Her Earthsea Trilogy, which consists of *A Wizard of Earthsea* (1968), *The Tombs of Atuan* (1971), and *The Farthest Shore* (1972), written for young people, creates a world peopled with wizards where magic and science combine in a holistic cosmology. Her highly acclaimed novel, *The Left Hand of Darkness* (1969), is set on a distant wintry planet whose inhabitants have the characteristics of both males and females and who regard a Terran visitor with astonishment since he has only one sex. For this novel, Le Guin invented an entirely new biology, and hence sociology, psychology, and political order. One of the major works of science fiction in the last decade, *The Left Hand of Darkness* won both the Hugo Award and the Nebula. Without a doubt the novel is partly responsible both for the new respect paid to science fiction among academic critics, and for the widened audience that the genre has increasingly attracted.

In *The Lathe of Heaven,* Le Guin experiments with a setting on Earth, a time within our own century, and entirely human characters. What she finds is that her special themes can also be expressed in a realistic, almost contemporary context; the future depicted in this novel *could* occur. The storyline concerns George Orr, an insignificant draftsmen, who grows increasingly anxious when he finds that his dreams change the world around him. Terrified, he avoids dreaming by taking amphetamines to stay awake and barbiturates to produce dreamless sleep. When his frayed nerves and his need for sleep overcome him, he visits Dr. William Haber, a visionary and manipulative psychiatrist. Discovering George's talent, Haber decides to induce dreams in George by means of a machine called the Augmentor which can control brain waves. Thus Haber embarks on the ultimate reformer's program to change the ills of the world. When George awakens, a new, presumably better, world exists. But there is a catch; in changing one segment of reality, all others are altered. And since dreams are uncontrollable, the ways in which the world changes are unpredictable. The conflict in the novel centers around George's resistance to Haber's manipulation as well as his struggle to adjust to each new reality as it occurs.

The mind of George Orr, his personality, and character comprise one of the most fascinating and original portraits of a hero in science fiction. Not at all the virile, swaggering, aggressive male typical of the usual science fiction novel, George is pale, meek, shy, and fearful. He has no special talents, is not highly intelligent, is not even particularly perceptive. The one thing he can do is dream, and he despairs of this "talent" because after meeting Haber his dreams are run by someone else. George even feels powerless to stop seeing Haber since the drugs George used to take to stop his dreams were illegal. He cannot quit "voluntary therapy." George particularly lacks the so-called rational mind which has been the hallmark of the hero in science fiction. The compensation, however, is preferable, for his mind is intuitive, creative, and complex. It is the mind of an artist; as the narrator of the novel explains, "He did not see connections which is said to be the hallmark of intellect. He *felt* connections — like a plumber." George has an integrity, a wholeness, a personal dignity characteristic of the person who need not act to establish his identity; he simply is.

Hence George senses the wrongness of Haber's attempts to change the nature of reality. And the changes are amusing at best, circuitous and horrifying at worst. Le Guin has ample opportunity to mock our present society even as she describes at least six new worlds brought about by Haber's control of George's dreams. The society in which George lives, *circa* 1998, has seven billion people who are all thin for want of food, who drink "pseudobeer," who remain indoors because of the life-threatening Greenhouse Effect. George's landlord is a leftover hippie complete with quaint beads, leather fringed clothing, and a "Dylan whine." Marriage has become a temporary condition, and George feels a bit guilty that he does *not* want to sleep with his aunt.

George's first dream that Haber controls is supposed to eliminate the population problem — and it does. George wakes up to a world of one billion, where everyone is fatter, where one can drink real bourbon again. But the morality of the change is frightful; George is horrified by the discovery that six billion people have been murdered. His dream was clever and consistent; a plague killed off most of the world's population, as well as all the songbirds. But all is not well. Overpopulation had had advantages — people had cooperated against it; now with cleaner air to breathe and more room to spread out, nations begin to war. Another dream is meant to bring peace; it does so by inventing a common enemy, alien invaders, against whom Earth's nations must unite to defend themselves. And so it goes; the aliens in later dreams become rather docile, turtlelike creatures. The race problem is handled by all people turning gray, the disease problem by subjecting to euthanasia people who have committed the "crime" of having a hereditary disease, and so on. Having no past, or rather too many, confuses and dismays George, although some elements of reality remain the same: his house, the setting of Portland, his meeting the female protagonist Heather Lalache in each new reality.

The outcome of Haber's well-meaning attempts to improve the world suggest that today's faith in the cure-all capacity of science and technology is unfounded. Like George, one must adjust to the nature of reality, to things as they are. Technology is not the answer, rationality alone cannot solve the woes of the world. Like Dr. Frankenstein, Haber tries to play God, but, as George realizes, "To be God you have to know what you're doing."

Through the conversations between Haber and George, these themes are developed. Man's purpose in this world, believes Haber, is "to do things, change things, run things, make a better world." "No," replies George. "Things don't have purposes, as if the universe were a machine, where every part has a useful function. . . . I don't know if our life has a purpose and I don't see that it matters. What does matter is that we're a part. Like a thread in a cloth or a grass-blade in a field. It *is* and we *are*." George's stance is a rejection of the mechanistic, Judeo-Christian rationalist stance of the West; more like a Buddhist, George believes, "it's wrong to force the pattern of things."

George at last finds a way to break the cycle of world-changing dreams and still fulfill his body's need to dream harmlessly. He receives a little help from his friend and lover (and Le Guin quotes the Beatles' song), Heather Lalache, his wife in one reality, his lawyer in another. She hypnotizes him and leaves him with the post-hypnotic suggestion that his dreams become like everyone else's. Like George, Heather is an opposite to the female stereotype; she is brash, sly, clever, abrasive, but she appreciates and loves George for his integral strength.

At this point Haber discovers a way to hook himself to the Augmentor so that *his* dreams become reality. The result is chaos. Mt. Hood erupts, rivers run dry, Portland begins to melt. In the effort of his lifetime, for he is not a man of action, George leaves Heather, rushes through the melting streets, and presses the "off" button. The world is saved, but the ensuing reality reflects the ghastly emptiness at the center of Haber's being. His mind has produced an "effective nightmare . . . had undone connections. The continuity which had always held between the worlds or timelines of Orr's dreaming had now been broken." Haber, the rationalist turned megalomaniac, is revealed to be insane.

Amazingly, the world can recover even from such a cataclysm, at last called "The Break." Mankind can bear and adjust to any reality; it is unreality that it cannot bear. When George encounters Heather in this new world, she is no longer his wife but a stranger who at first does not recognize or remember him. As she regards him as if he were a stranger, the narrator reports, "He stood and endured reality." The words reveal the theme of the novel: so must we all endure our worlds.

The Lathe of Heaven is written in a crisp, light style that Le Guin handles as facilely as she does the more meditative, poetic style of her earlier novels. The novel's appealing hero, brassy heroine, its playful mocking tone, all make *The Lathe of Heaven* highly readable. Its central themes are among the most traditional in science fiction — man versus machine, the mad doctor-scientist whose hubris causes him to create a monster, the rationalist versus the artist — but *The Lathe of Heaven* presents these themes in an originally contemporary context. The novel thus serves as a warning to our society to examine the assumptions underlying our most important decisions before plunging ahead in the name of progress. Ultimately, we are reminded, some things cannot be changed, and more important, some things must not be changed but be allowed, for all their faults, to remain the same.

Kathryn L. Seidel

Sources for Further Study

Reviews:

Book World. December 19, 1971, p. 6.

Library Journal. XCVI, November 1, 1971, p. 3641.

National Review. XXIV, February 4, 1972, p. 107.

New York Times Book Review. May 14, 1972, p. 33.

Newsweek. LXXVIII, November 29, 1971, p. 105.

Times Literary Supplement. June 23, 1972, p. 705.

LAVKA SNOVIDENYI
(The Store of Dreams)

Author: Ilya Varshavsky (1909-1973)
First book publication: 1970
Type of work: Short stories

Eleven science fiction stories with various themes, most of them humorous and containing elements of parody

In 1970, after an interval of four years during which time he was ill, Ilya Varshavsky published his fourth short story collection, entitled *Lavka snovidenyi* (*The Store of Dreams*). His fifth and last book *Trevozhnykh simptomov net* (*No Alarming Symptoms*), followed in 1972; but it contained few original stories, consisting, rather, of unrepresentative selections from the preceding four collections. Therefore, *The Store of Dreams* provides the best example of work from the second phase of Varshavsky's career in science fiction. Moreover, there is no basic difference between the *oeuvre* of the author's two periods; the observable "new" traits are, rather, improvements of his particular manner of writing science fiction, the development of tendencies already present.

Although *The Store of Dreams* comprises three sections, it can be considered as a single whole. The only story in the first section that might well belong to the second one is called "Ordinary Science Fiction." The third section, entitled "At Fantasy's Edge," can be omitted, since it is a semiautobiographical recounting of the author's experiences aboard Soviet trader ships, and cannot, therefore, be really considered science fiction.

Of course, the term "ordinary science fiction" cannot be taken with complete seriousness; in this collection Varshavsky continues to exhibit an ambiguous attitude toward the genre. Indeed, he even exploits such typical science fiction themes as time travel, cosmic contacts, man-computer conflicts, and dystopian visions; and he has muted the parodistic thrust of his earlier works. He no longer seems to write with the explicit objective of wrecking the beloved myths and mannerisms of science fiction "fundom." A possible exception might be "Second Birth," though even there the target of the story cannot be narrowed exclusively to science fiction.

But Varshavsky is still aware, probably more than ever before, of the unsolid nature of the ground on which he walks: the weaknesses of "ordinary science fiction." So the parody is still present, but it has been interwoven with the structure and style of the narration. Indeed, all of the stories in this volume, except the dystopias, contain parodistic elements. Sometimes glimpses of parody appear on the surface, as when the author momentarily steps out of his storytelling role to comment directly on what he is doing. The most obvious example of this can be seen in "Love and Time," where the hero falls in love with a woman of the future whom he sees on a time screen that he has invented. The author describes her as being "beautiful beyond description. Beautiful, or we would assault the holy canons of science fiction. Beyond description, for all of beauty cannot be expressed by words." By such blatant and exaggerated clichés from the sentimental science fiction of the past, Varshavsky gives his naïve readers what they unconsciously expect, entertains his more sophisticated ones, and at the same time succeeds in furthering the development of his plot.

Even where the parody is less obvious, its presence establishes a distance between the author and the events he recounts, thus creating a similar distance between the reader and the text. On the other hand, the distance is reduced by Varshavsky's tendency in this collection to set the stories not in some abstract future environment but in times and places the writer and his readers know, as in the present, or near future, suggested by a large number of concrete details from everyday life. In addition, most of the heroes are not heroic space explorers, wise (or mad) inventors, or exponents of great ideas; but just simple, ordinary people described with love, and, in the humorous stories, with gentle irony. The author identifies with his characters, although he realizes that their adventures, and perhaps even the heroes themselves, cannot be taken completely seriously, and he makes the reader feel both this love and this irony.

The hero of "Love and Time" is a shy, timid twenty-six-year-old man with an unattractive appearance and the prosaic profession of economist, whose private life has been a shambles and to whom "the magic word Love causes hopes instead of reminiscences." By chance he gets into a sort of television contact with a girl of the future who is "beautiful beyond description," but of a quite prosaic character. He falls in love with her at first sight and, although disturbed and misunderstood by the people around him, he can at least convince her to come into his time. But because of an error of his she arrives a day too soon, so that he can never meet her — she always remains in his yesterday. "What good is it that she kissed you yesterday? Man needs everything today. That every day was Today." When the hero speaks these words on the last page of the story he knows that his gray life will never change, that there is no hope. This is not the black humor that attempts to shock in the manner of such writers as Robert Sheckley; it is tragicomedy, for the hero is really a tragic character, though all of the events are extremely funny when seen from the outside.

The ending of this story shows another characteristic of Varshavsky's later work. He is much less concerned with "the holy canons of science fiction" than he pretends to be. For logically — and the paradoxes of time travel have their own, well explored logic — the plot simply cannot work, and the author does not even try to explain how it is possible that the man and the girl never meet, although only one day divides them. Nor does he have to, for the fantastic facts of science fiction turn organically into an artistic symbol, a poetic truth that needs no explanation.

In a second time travel story, "A Trip to Penfield," Varshavsky camouflages a typical fantasy as science fiction. The hero loses his young wife by accident in the mountains. Exactly forty years later he tells his friend Meph, a physicist, how, by hesitating for a moment, he had missed the chance to save her. The physicist explains why the past cannot be recaptured, though according to common science fiction usage, he admits, he could offer the hero a time machine. In the night a devil (perhaps another incarnation of Faust's Mephistopheles?) appears to the hero and introduces himself as a time traveler from an ancient and mighty precivilization on Earth. The mysterious visitor arranges for the hero to return to his youth; and, as might be expected, this time, instead of the young wife, the husband himself dies as an old man, forty years after the night he departed for his own past. So the reader is free to explain the events either logically, as another science fiction time travel paradox, or as the hero's preagonal fantasy, in the manner of Ambrose Bierce and Jorge Luis Borges. The result is the same: Youth cannot really be recaptured, not even psychologically.

The third time travel story in this collection, "The Hysteresis Loop," is given its own section called "The Evangely of Elias," (or Ilya, as the name is pronounced in Russian). The story is of special interest not so much for itself as for the comparison it suggests with other similar works. In Michael Moorcock's *Behold the Man*, for example, a neurotic time traveler from our present searches for Jesus two millenni ago and, in the end, driven by his martyr complex, takes over the role himself, the real Jesus being a cretin. To people who are (at least nominally) Christian, this may be shocking. In the case of Varshavsky, who lives in a country where atheism is encouraged and where most of the readers are atheists indeed, a similar idea leads to a humorous, harmless story. The hero travels from future to past to prove (for atheism's sake) that Jesus never existed. He searches for him and indeed also becomes Jesus himself without even realizing it until the very last moment. Jesus' miracles are explained as effects of future technology (mainly misused by the hero); the hero's antireligious and antislavery speeches are profoundly misunderstood by his apostles, and the self-made Jesus, taken from the cross still alive, is luckily driven back by time relays into his good old future.

The plot itself is, perhaps, merely a joke of no special importance. The most interesting aspect of the story is the way Varshavsky describes his atheistic time traveler in almost religious terms, and characterizes the first apostles as simple, uneducated fishermen who believe they have met the Messiah but are nevertheless far from lost in religious ecstasy and never foresake their common sense; in general they are not much different from Varshavsky's contemporary heroes. In addition, it seems almost mandatory that every modern version of the Passion include, or lead to, a rehabilitation of Judas, though writers like Borges, Moorcock, Kurt Vonnegut, Jr., and Varshavsky do this in very different ways. Varshavsky is too much of an atheist to invent a really original, startling heresy as did Borges; Varshavsky's Judas is simply Jesus' truest friend, the only apostle ready to give his all for his master.

There are two stories about first contacts with aliens in the book. In "Duck in Cream," the writer himself is visited by a desperate alien who asks for assistance. Only when it is too late does the writer realize that the man he has sent away without help was neither a maniac nor a swindler, but really what he represented himself to be. In "There Will Be No Contacts," human scientists are unable to decipher the aliens' language, which consists of odors, while the aliens cannot imagine an intelligent life form that uses any other form of communication. The former story is made convincing by its realistic details, its believable setting, and its familiar hero.

Varshavsky "accepts" the genre in this tale and utilizes some of its conventional techniques very well. The second text, however, depends on an abstract and rather poor idea; it is probably the least successful story in the volume and reminds one of some of Varshavsky's early works that tried to make fun of science fiction "hardware," while being bound to it too obviously.

"The Store of Dreams," another story about aliens, shows much more artistic invention. Science fiction logic is treated very casually from the beginning. The main character is a Venusian aborigine. Technically undeveloped, but friendly and wise in their own way, the Venusians are unwilling to accept anything from Earth's culture or technology except Terran picture books. The hero falls in love with one of the harem maidens he sees in an illustrated edition of *A Thousand and One Nights* and manages, by a special Venusian narcotic, not only to dream of her, but also to bring back out of his dreams a very real Terran-Venusian baby son. Thus, the story turns into a pure fantasy, or rather into a fairy tale, whose lovable, grotesque little Venusian hero is a somewhat luckier version of the young man who was so frustrated in "Love and Time." As a pure fantasy, "The Store of Dreams" is a delight, unencumbered as it is by the logical requirements of a true science fiction story.

Sometimes Varshavsky's stories get dangerously close to sentimentality. Such is the case in "The Old Ones," a story of an old scientist and a very humanlike old computer he once built. When the computer is replaced one day by a more efficient one, the scientist feels that he has lost his best friend. The author, however, leaves open the question of whether or not the computer was almost a human being in reality or only in the old man's imagination. A second computer story in this volume, "The Coup Will Be Taken at Midnight," tells how a gang of bank robbers and the police both use computers to predict each other's strategy. Endlessly moving and countermoving, they end up paralyzing each other. In the end, the bank is robbed by an outsider in a crude unscientific nineteenth century manner. The idea of this story is too obvious, and as satire its target is too indistinct. It may be a funny story, as "The Old

Ones" was a touching one; however, they both lack the depth of Varshavsky's better works.

"Second Birth" is more satisfying for its original humor, which is all very grotesque but entirely coherent within the world Varshavsky creates. In this future world, bionics have been substituted for our technologies. For example, animals are used for models or even as steering devices in funny mechanisms; and cars hop instead of rolling, steered by the encephalographic impulses of a cat who is trying to catch a mouse. The one thing missing — the "second birth" of which does not take place in the story, for its inventor is too original to be understood by the bionicians — is the wheel. Of all the stories in this volume, only "Second Birth" successfully continues the manner and insight of Varshavsky's earlier parodies, as it attacks not only the beloved clichés of science fiction, but also ideas fashionable in the popular sciences, although now his target has shifted to bionics instead of "cybernetics."

The two remaining texts in the collection are the dystopias, the only stories not written in a humorous vein, lacking even the comic traces that appeared, for example, in "The Old Ones." "Cokroaches" belongs to the Donomaga cycle. It tells of genetic experiments on apes that change them into unhappy, intelligent Moreau-like creatures, and of similar experiments on human members of an overabundant society in which meaningless consumption is obligatory. These, and other subjects like them, which, although presented by Varshavsky with insistence and emotional conviction, have been already overworked in Western dystopias to the point of being "dated" — universal material abundance being hardly a clear and present danger in either the West or the East. But all these details are just symptoms and concomitants of the Donomagan society's main disease — the existence of a cast of technocrats and superintelligent scientists who have freed most of the population not only from the necessity, but also from the possibility, of doing any really useful work, thus changing them into involuntary parasites. Now this, even as Varshavsky tells it, is not especially original. But it is a real, and therefore much more terrifying, danger. Unlike Huxley's "Brave New World," this world does not care about giving the people an artificial happiness; ordinary citizens simply do not matter much. They are worth less than the intelligent apes, because they have no real use.

The other narrative, "Escape," is linked to the Donomaga cycle, although not explicitly a part of it. The story is set in a concentration camp in an imaginary Fascist country. Varshavsky shows neither the political background of this country (except to say that it is at war) nor the detailed cruelties and tortures practiced there except to indicate that they are routine; he concentrates on the psychological and emotional situation of his hero, a prisoner no longer able to work in the camp and therefore destined for the "Cotton Fields," a place where the toxic working conditions bring death in a few days. The day before he is taken there, the hero is even granted some small privileges, since the keepers consider him a living corpse — a belief he shares with them. On this last day, however, he comes in contact with a group of prisoners who plan to escape. After several adventures the flight succeeds — so they think. But the reality is something else. The escape was planned by the keepers and led directly to the Cotton Fields, where the hypnotized prisoners do their deadly work, imagining that it is an idyllic game they play in freedom. The purpose of it all was to increase the workers' efficiency. As the scientist who invented the system says: "There are enormous resources in the organism that can be mobilized by the higher emotions."

Little of Varshavsky's earlier merriness remains in *A Store of Dreams*, but these stories show him at his best, less a master of abstract invention than a writer with deep human feelings for his characters — feelings of pity and compassion that he is able to transmit to the reader. That is something too seldom found in science fiction.

H. Walter

THE LEFT HAND OF DARKNESS

Author: Ursula K. Le Guin (1929-   )
First book publication: 1969
Type of work: Novel
Time: The distant future, not earlier than 3850 and not later than 4870
Locale: The planet Gethen, nicknamed Winter; on the Great Continent in the states of Karhide and Orgoreyn and on the Gobrin Ice that both connects and separates these two countries

The integration into the Ekumen ("Household" League) of Known Worlds of the people of Gethen/Winter, brought about by Genly Ai, Ekumenical Envoy, with the aid of Therem Harth rem ir Estraven, the banished former prime minister of Karhide

> *Principal characters:*
> GENLY AI, The First Mobile of the Ekumen on Gethen
> ESTRAVEN, Therem Harth rem ir Estraven, "King's Ear" to Argaven XV at the beginning of the novel, later in exile
> ARGAVEN XV, King Argaven Harge, the mad ruler of Karhide
> LORD TIBE, Pemmer Harge rem ir Tibe, prime minister of Karhide after Estraven's fall and Estraven's mortal enemy
> FAXE, The Weaver of the Foretellers of Otherhord, later an important politician in Karhide, opposed to Tibe

The plot of *The Left Hand of Darkness* consists of three major sections and a brief conclusion. The first section is set in Karhide, the second in Orgoreyn, the third on the Gobrin Ice; the conclusion is set in Karhide, to which Genly Ai returns to bring down his ship and bring Karhide (and soon Orgoreyn and the other Gethenian nations) into the Ekumen — and to bring the novel to a more or less happy ending.

The novel opens with Ai in Karhide and deep — over his head in fact — in Karhidish politics. Estraven has arranged for Ai to have an audience with Argaven XV and in other ways has seemed to aid Ai; still, Ai does not trust Estraven and is more surprised than upset when Estraven is banished and Lord Tibe becomes the "King's Ear." The audience with the King gets Ai nowhere, since the King believes him to be an impostor and/or a threat; so Ai leaves the Karhidish capital of Erhenrang to see other parts of the country and then to go to Orgoreyn. After investigating the Karhidish Foretellers and receiving the prediction that Gethen will be a member of the Ekumen in five years, Ai goes to Orgoreyn to see if his message will be received better there.

In Orgoreyn Ai becomes an inadvertent player in a political game between two factions of the ruling council of Thirty-Three. His mission is favored by the Open Trade faction and opposed by the Domination faction and the Sarf (the secret police and their associated bureaucratic apparatus). The banished Estraven has meanwhile established himself somewhat in Orgoreyn and attempts to aid Ai and the Open Traders. During this time Ai's mission comes to take on great practical importance for the Gethenians; under the rule of

Tibe, Karhide has started to centralize its administration and prepare for conflict with Orgoreyn. Orgoreyn is already a centralized bureaucracy and will meet what it sees as a Karhidish threat. Since both societies have evolved into mobilizable nations, such a conflict between the two could lead to war — something unprecedented in Gethenian history.

The Open Trade faction loses this round of bureaucratic in-fighting, and Ai is seized and sent to the Pulefen Commensality Third Voluntary Farm and Resettlement Agency — in other words, to a forced-labor camp such as those run in the Terran arctic by the Russian Gulag.

Estraven saves Ai from death at the camp, and the two of them attempt a winter journey back to Karhide over the Gobrin Ice, a feat never before accomplished. They return to Karhide, and Ai awakens his orbiting colleagues and summons them to Gethen, correctly assuming that he and they will be welcomed by King Argaven (as Estraven predicted) as an embarrassment to the rulers of Orgoreyn, who have reported Ai's unfortunate death from disease. Estraven, however, is a banished "man" and under sentence of death in Karhide. He is soon betrayed and killed by the agents of Lord Tibe. Tibe then resigns his office, and Ai returns to Erhenrang to complete his mission. After bringing down the ship and getting his ambassadorial duties taken care of for a while, Ai goes to Estraven's domain of Estre and concludes the novel by meeting Estraven's parent and child (the "son" of Estraven and Estraven's brother Arek).

Le Guin presents this story as a *"Report from Genly Ai, First Mobile on Gethen/Winter"* (headnote to Chapter 1). In this report, the plot remains relatively simple. What expands the novel to twenty chapters is Ai's giving his superiors and Le Guin's readers both his own story and Estraven's version of their story, plus a detailed anthropological survey of Gethenian culture, plus the outline of a philosophical system which includes a cosmology, epistemology, ethics, politics, and aesthetic.

The "anthropological survey" portion of *The Left Hand of Darkness* is necessitated by the alienness, the radical Otherness, of the Gethenians. As she notes in her introduction to the 1976 edition of the novel, Le Guin is asking us to perform a thought experiment. What if there were a marginal world at the limit of human endurance of cold, and what if the people of this world were androgynous: five-sixths of the time asexual, neither male nor female but potentially both; one-sixth of the time in rut, as either a male or a female. What sort of culture would such people produce? What would "incest" mean to them? What would their politics and social organization be like? What sort of philosophies would they develop? Would they be dualists? Would they be murderous or basically peaceful? Would they have wars? What would people be like who most of the time were neither men nor women but simply human?

Much of this anthropological information we get from Genly Ai, a stranger in a strange land; as Ai learns, so do we. Some of this information we can infer from the chapters narrated by Estraven or taken from his journal. The rest we get from chapters interpolated into the narrative.

The most blatant of these interpolations is the chapter entitled "The Question of Sex," presented as an extract from the notes of an Investigator of the Ekumen in the team preceding the First Mobile. In this chapter we get a detailed account of Gethenian sexuality and the social implications of the Gethenians' unique combination of androgyny and an estrus cycle. Other interpolated chapters are more subtle. "The Place Inside the Blizzard" tells us about Gethenian ideas on incest and suicide and prepares for the allusions to Estraven's relationship with his brother Arek and for the white weather sequence on the Ice later in the novel. "The Nineteenth Day" tells us about the dangers for the questioners in asking Foretellers improper questions. And the tale of "Estraven the Traitor" foreshadows the sacrifice of Therem Harth rem ir Estraven: like his namesake in the tale, Estraven is called a traitor for trying to bring peace and to integrate feuding peoples.

More difficult to justify are "On Time and Darkness" and "An Orgota Creation Myth," which interrupt the story at very exciting moments and do not have any direct relationship with the plot.

"On Time and Darkness" immediately follows Estraven's warning to Ai that his life is in danger, a warning that proves quite true in Chapter 13, when Ai is arrested and sent to the Pulefen Voluntary Farm. "On Time and Darkness" is mostly about epistemology, the investigation of what we can know and how we can know; it presents the view of the Yomeshta that in Meshe (their founder) there is neither darkness nor ignorance: all things are in the Center of Time, unchanging and knowable. The "Orgota Creation Myth" comes during the dangerous winter's journey on the Ice, during a major crisis in the relationship between Estraven and Ai: Estraven's entering kemmer (rut). This story is just what the title indicates: a creation myth dating back to prehistoric times, a primitive exercise in cosmology giving the origins of hills and valleys, rivers and seas and living things — and of human life and death on Gethen.

The principle Genly Ai usually follows in ordering these chapters in his report is that of juxtaposition: a circular sort of operation in which *A* is placed next to *B* because they have some relationship, and in which the reader assumes a relationship just because *A* is next to *B*. This is bad logic of the "after this, therefore because of this" variety; it is also a standard device in literature, theater, and film. Sometimes the reason for the juxtaposition is difficult to understand, such as in the very first of the interruptions of the narrative, "The Place Inside the Blizzard" (Chapter 2). Ai and Le Guin insist here that we accept their method on faith: they interrupt the story and ask us to trust them that the interruption was justified.

The first chapter of *The Left Hand of Darkness* ends with a discussion of patriotism and a reference back to the blood used in the mortar of Karhidish keystones. The interpolated Chapter 2 deals with the suicide of one brother and the exile of another for breaking the Gethenian taboo against brothers vowing kemmering for life (monogamous marriage). As we will later learn, this situation of suicide and exile is similar to that of Estraven. More important, the suicide story's juxtaposition with the end of Chapter 1 is the first step in preparing us to see Estraven's later action of skiing into the guns of Tibe's men as a necessary sacrifice as well as suicide. Estraven provides the blood needed to secure the keystone in the arch — in other words, to bring together Karhide and Orgoreyn, as the two enter the Ekumen. Symbolically, if not in terms of the plot, Estraven's death is a great patriotic gesture, since it helps seal the peace. "The Place Inside the Blizzard" also introduces in its simplest form the question of individual loyalty *versus* loyalty to the group. This interpolated hearth-tale, then, both looks back to the discussions and thoughts at the end of Chapter 1 and looks ahead to both the general theme of individual loyalty *versus* patriotism and to the specific events of Ai and Estraven on the Ice in the white weather and Estraven's apparent suicide.

The placement of "The Nineteenth Day" is much easier to explain. It is about foretelling and the uselessness of knowing the answers to the wrong questions; this is also the major theme of "The Domestication of Hunch" (Chapter 5).

The problem with the placement of "The Question of Sex" (Chapter 7) is that its basic points could go anywhere in the novel; the ambisexuality of the Gethenians has little to do with anything particular in the plot, but is crucial for the cultural world of the whole story. "The Question of Sex" is appropriately placed because of its rhetorical emphasis upon the relationship of sexuality to violence and warfare, a relationship also dealt with in "One Way into Orgoreyn" and "Another Way into Orgoreyn."

In "One Way into Orgoreyn" we learn that Gethenians are quite capable of attempting to kill one another: we *see* Tibe's agents trying to kill Estraven. Murder, then, is a human sort of thing, neither exclusively male nor female; it must be a human sort of thing or the merely human Gethenians would be incapable of it. And "One Way into Orgoreyn" ends in a discussion of something for which the Gethenians have no word, but which we (Genly Ai's "criminal ancestors") easily recognize as warfare between two developed nations. One way into Orgoreyn, then, is the way the Orgota have actually taken: the establishment of their rational, efficient New Epoch regime with sufficient central control to allow them to wage war.

"Another Way into Orgoreyn" is that of Tibe, the new Karhidish prime minister and a kind of androgynous Dr. Goebbels. Technological development on Gethen has progressed enough so that the Gethenians are not wholly a marginal people with no energy to waste on mass aggression. Orgoreyn is already a centralized state; using the potential threat of Orgoreyn and the immediate occasion of a border dispute in the Sinoth Valley, Tibe tries to unify Karhide, using what Genly Ai explicitly calls "war" for that purpose. Tibe's way — his method and his approach to the world — is the opposite and complement of that of Orgoreyn. Even as the Orgota reach their efficient and potentially militant state through the light of the human intellect, the demagogic Tibe wants to convert Karhide into an efficient and militant police state by appealing to the darkness of the human Shadow: the primitive nature that Tibe says is the reality under the "veneer" of civilization.

Chapter 7, then, explicitly develops "The Question of Sex" and sex's relationship to warfare: two major interrelated themes of the chapters that immediately precede and follow it.

"Estraven the Traitor" (Chapter 9) reintroduces the theme of patriotism and stresses the necessity of trust and sacrifice in bringing together people and peoples. The most important justification for the theme's placement in Chapter 9 is that the narrative on both sides of this chapter shows us the low point of Ai's trust of Estraven, a trust that is absolutely necessary (as things turn out) for the success of Ai's mission. The sort of displaced *Romeo and Juliet* motif in "Estraven the Traitor" helps to establish a world in which the sacrifice of a loved one is somehow a necessary cost for the establishment of peace and unity: a variation on the theme of the blood-bond holding together an arch. Also introduced in this chapter is the image of two hands meeting and matching as the hands of one man: a matching which requires that the hands both be alike (four fingers and a thumb, and so on) and yet different (a left hand must touch a right hand). This image underlies the meeting and union — "touching" is Le Guin's word — of Ai and Estraven during their journey on the Ice. It is both their essential sameness as human beings and their differences that allow Ai and Estraven to touch.

Two interpolated chapters remain: Chapter 7, "On Time and Darkness," and Chapter 17, "An Orgota Creation Myth." These two chapters receive great stress in the economy of the novel precisely because they interrupt the narrative at such crucial points. They deserve that stress because they help set up the philosophical system by which the action of the novel is to be judged.

The Orgota creation myth is very old and establishes a cosmology that underlies all Gethenian philosophy. In general, however, the Handdarata interpret the myth correctly and even improve upon it; the Yomeshta get the myth, and most other things, quite wrong.

According to the myth, the world started out with the Ice and the Sun and will eventually move to a time of Ice and Darkness. The Handdarata accept this idea, but add that the Darkness preceded even the Ice and Sun. The Ice and Sun are images for stasis and for Being. The Handdarata add to this idea the Taoist concept that deeper even than Being (Tao) is Unbeing (here, the Darkness). In any event, out of Being comes Becoming: the world of action, the world of flux, uncertainty, and shadows in which humans live and die. The offspring of Edondurath and his unnamed kemmering (in other words, all of

Gethen's people) are followed by shadows "Because they were born in the house of flesh, therefore death follows at their heels. They are in the middle of time." To be in the center of time is to be in the world in which the only certainty is death, as Faxe had shown Genly Ai at the Otherhord Fastness — it is this fact that the Yomeshta deny. Implicit also in the myth is the idea of the uniqueness of human beings and human consciousness and our connection with all other living things.

The ideas of flux ("Creation unfinished") and of the interconnectedness of life are developed in Chapter 16, with Estraven making clear how the Handdarata view things versus the Yomeshta. Given the cosmology of the myth, the Handdarata are correct in praising Creation unfinished and in trying to fit into the scheme of life. The "way" followed by the Yomeshta and by Orgoreyn (where Meshe's cult is officially promulgated) is incorrect, leading them to be one of the familiar "dynamic, aggressive, ecology-breaking cultures . . . bent on pushing things around."

More importantly, this cosmology is the basis of the epistemology of uncertainty accepted in the Handdara and denied in the Yomesh creed, as we see in "On Time and Darkness." The Yomeshta believe that ultimate Truth, including the "meaning of life," was seen by Meshe and can be perceived by us through Meshe. Meshe's idea of the center of time is a world without sequence, darkness, or death: the world of Being, of simultaneity and stasis. In such a world, certainty is possible.

There is something to be said for this view: Le Guin believes in simultaneity and Being and in the necessity for occasional contacts with Being. Indeed, in Le Guin's essentially godless universe, contact with Being is absolutely necessary for touch, for establishing the I-Thou relationship between people. Also, such contacts with Being are necessary for the foretelling perfected by the Handdarata.

The danger of the Yomesh view of constant contact with Being is made clear by the placement of "On Time and Darkness" just before Ai's arrest and imprisonment in "Down on the Farm." Accept the epistemology of the Yomeshta, Le Guin implies, and such certainty will lead you to the New Epoch of the Orgota, with its prison camps and their "excess of light."

"On Time and Darkness" and "An Orgota Creation Myth," then, function to help establish a world of Being and Becoming, occasional certainty and usual ignorance, a world of death and pain in which humankind are often and ultimately individual and alone. From such a view follows an ethics stressing humility and a willingness to attempt contact with the almost always alien Other. From such a view follows a politics very like that of the Ekumen. And from such a view follows the aesthetic theory incorporated into the novel.

In such a world, ". . . Truth is a matter of the imagination" and "Facts are no more solid, coherent, round, and real than pearls are." In such a world, it is appropriate that we see the story of Ai and Estraven from both of their points of view, and that we see the truth of Gethen from the many points of view made possible by the interpolated chapters.

The structure, then, of *The Left Hand of Darkness* is not only justified but a brilliant stroke of artistic decorum that goes well with the excellent handling of plot, character, and themes that make this work both an outstanding science fiction novel and one of the best literary works to come out of America in the late 1960's.

Richard D. Erlich

Sources for Further Study

Criticism:

Bickman, Martin. "Le Guin's *The Left Hand of Darkness*: Form and Content," in *Science Fiction Studies*. IV (1977), pp. 42-47. Bickman outlines the themes of the work, the dream, the tree, and the root.

Ketterer, David. *"The Left Hand of Darkness*: Ursula K. Le Guin's Archetypal 'Winter-Journey,'" in *Riverside Quarterly*. V (April, 1973), pp. 288-297. Ketterer presents the work as one of Le Guin's best.

Slusser, George E. *The Farthest Shores of Ursula K. Le Guin*. San Bernardino, Calif.: Borgo, 1976, pp. 17-31. Slusser feels the theme of roots and rootlessness is central to this novel.

Reviews:

Library Journal. XCV, June 15, 1970, p. 2228.

Magazine of Fantasy and Science Fiction. XXXVII, November, 1969, p. 50.

Publisher's Weekly. CXCV, January 27, 1969, p. 99.

Times Literary Supplement. January 8, 1970, p. 39.

Top of the News. XXVI, January, 1970, p. 210.

THE LEGION OF TIME

Author: Jack Williamson (1908-   )
First book publication: 1952
Type of work: Novel
Locale: Chiefly the timeship *Chronion* and the cities Jonbar and Gyronchi
Time: The twentieth century and the "geodesic timetracks" of two alternate futures

The story of a group of men rescued from their deaths in the twentieth century to fight in a war between alternate future worlds

Principal characters:
    DENNIS LANNING, a journalist and soldier of fortune
    WILMOT MCLAN, a physicist
    LETHONEE, a beautiful woman from Jonbar
    SORAINYA, the queen of Gyronchi

The Legion of Time was serialized in *Astounding Stories* during the first full year of John W. Campbell, Jr.'s editorship; it first appeared in book form in 1952 as the title story in a volume which also contained the mediocre short novel *After World's End*. It remains one of the classic novels of prewar pulp science fiction, archetypal in many ways of that unique enclave of mass-produced fiction.

The Legion of Time introduced into science fiction the idea of alternate futures fighting for existence by trying to alter the events determining their probability. The notion of "alternate histories" was, of course, by no means new, but it had previously been elaborated in a retrospective manner, as in J. C. Squire's excellent anthology *If It Had Happened Otherwise* (1931), which presented a series of essays on the theme of how history might have been altered had certain crucial events turned out differently. Murray Leinster had linked the notion of alternate history to the science fiction concept of "parallel worlds" in "Sidewise in Time" (1934), but it was Williamson who first turned the idea around to imagine the worlds of the future, which are today merely probable, invading the present in order to attempt to secure their certainty.

The novel opens in April, 1927, with the hero Dennis ("Denny") Lanning, a Harvard senior, quietly reading a book on the subject of *Reality and Change*, written by his friend and colleague Wilmot McLan. His reading is interrupted by the appearance of the image of a beautiful girl carrying a jewel the size of a football. She tells him that her name is Lethonee, and that she has come to beg for his help. She invites him to look into her "time crystal," where he sees two visions — one of the beautiful city of Jonbar from which Lethonee has projected her image, and one of the even-more-beautiful New Jonbar, whose inhabitants are immortal and have the power of flight, which lies in Lethonee's future. Before Lethonee disappears she warns Denny to beware of Sorainya, the warrior queen of Gyronchi, and asks him not to fly with his friend Barry Halloran the next day. Denny heeds the warning and excuses himself from the flight, but Barry Halloran is killed when the plane crashes.

Denny feels a certain resentment because the warning issued to him did not include his friend, and this is one of the factors which allows him to be tempted by a second vision. This time, from the deck of a ship, he sees another beautiful woman riding in a golden shell. This is Sorainya, come to offer him a share of the throne of Gyronchi, and Denny is saved from yielding to temptation only by Lethonee's appearance. When Lethonee shows Denny that Sorainya is trying to lure him to his death, the evil warrior queen departs, and Lethonee then explains that she and her rival can only appear to him as insubstantial images because both have as yet a shadowy existence dependent upon the probability of certain twentieth century events. Once these events are determined forever, either Lethonee's world or Sorainya's must cease to exist, for the two are mutually exclusive alternatives. Denny's allegiance is apparently to be of crucial importance in the struggle, though not until his death can he be recruited to it.

Denny continues his life, working as a reporter in conflicts all over the world, often taking an active part as a pilot or a military adviser, always on the side of justice against armed might. He is both a quixotic idealist and a man of action, gradually fitting himself for the role of champion of Jonbar. He comes to see his own strife-stricken times as a crucial period in history, when the ground is being prepared for a final and decisive conflict between "democratic civilization and despotic absolutism," and the reader is encouraged to see Jonbar and Gyronchi as the futures which depend on the resolution of this great war.

The notion of the imminence of such a crucial conflict was something that was very much a part of the American intellectual climate of the time. Anxiety regarding the possibility of a global war was perhaps at its height in 1938 — it was ameliorated when the decision was made in 1939 to stay out of the war in Europe, and Pearl Harbor came as something of a shock to most of the American populace. It was, at any rate, 1938 which saw the most eloquent illustration of anticipatory anxiety in the panic which followed the Mercury Theatre broadcast of "The War of the Worlds." *The Legion of Time* dramatizes, in magnificently lurid terms, the feeling that events vital to the whole future of mankind were impending, and that fundamental political questions might be satisfied for once and for all. The failure of history to come anywhere near living up to these expectations was the major factor in killing the black-or-white thinking which was fundamental to so much pulp science fiction dealing with the historical prospects of the near future. (It should, however, be noted that this feeling of being at the crossroads of destiny was not something that only affected pulp science fiction — the classic embodiment of this consciousness is to be found in Olaf Stapledon's *Darkness and the Light*, which was published in 1942.)

The real plot of *The Legion of Time* gets under way when Denny is shot down over Shanghai while fighting for the Chinese against the Japanese invasion. In the moment of his death he sees a vision of a strange ship, onto whose deck he is lifted by the hands of his long-dead friend Barry Halloran. He is revived aboard the ship, the *Chronion*, which is shuttling back and forth through the battles of the twentieth century to snatch idealistic warriors from the jaws of extinction. Denny finds that he is to lead this élite corps on behalf of the *Chronion*'s captain, who is another old friend, Wilmot McLan. McLan is now a physical wreck; having died at fifty-three he has since spent ten years in Sorainya's dungeons, lured to Gyronchi by her seductive beauty. Lethonee has rescued him from this imprisonment in order that he should fight for Jonbar. Already, however, Sorainya's agents have discovered the point in history at which the two timelines diverge, and have set forth in their own timeship to steal the artifact on which Jonbar's existence depends. When the *Chronion* reaches Jonbar the city is on the point of dissolution.

Denny and his followers go back along the extinguished timeline to the twentieth century, and then forward again to Gyronchi, hoping to steal the artifact from Sorainya's fortress. After a long and bloody battle against the "anthropoid ants" of Sorainya's slave-army Denny gets his hands on the prize and is rescued by McLan from the great hall of the citadel.

The vital object turns out to be a fragment of a magneto from a Model-T Ford, but McLan quickly discovers its historical significance. In Arkansas in August, 1921, it may or may not have been picked up by a boy named John Barr, who may or may not have then gone on to dedicate his life to science and achieve a crucial breakthrough in discovering the "dynatomic tensors" which will give men mental control of subatomic processes. If John Barr failed to accomplish this then the discovery will have been made by a Soviet engineer and a "renegade Buddhist priest," the presiding genii of Gyronchi.

Sorainya's timeship pursues the *Chronion* back to the vital moment. The ship is boarded *en route* and all the members of the Legion perish except Denny, who is saved from death at the point of Sorainya's sword when McLan contrives that she should be canceled out of existence by a handy stitch in time, which he has saved up for just such a moment. The battle to replace the magnet is still to be fought, however, and Denny must run across the Arkansas field with it, pursued by Gyronchi's army of monsters. John Barr walks through the battle untouched and quite unaware of the shadows of future probability that swirl unaware of the shadows of future probability that swirl ability that swirl around him, and finally picks up the magnet. The hosts of Gyronchi vanish, and Denny is plucked up again from the moment of his death by the *Chronion*, where the entire Legion has been saved once again. This time, the timeship sails an established time-track to a solid and certain Jonbar, cemented forever into the path of reality. The Utopian city now stands on the site where once Gyronchi stood, and Lethonee's tower has replaced Sorainya's citadel. Somewhere in Lethonee all that remains of Sorainya — the essence of her beauty and vitality, but not her evil — is embodied. The brighter vision, in eclipsing the other, has absorbed it and made it over into its own substance.

The Legion of Time is on the one hand an escapist dream-fantasy of the exotic species primarily associated with Abraham Merritt. The situation of the hero is strongly reminiscent of Merritt's *Dwellers in the Mirage*. On the other hand, it is also science fiction, and has the exuberant spirit of early pulp science fiction, redolent with the faith that even the wildest of dreams might be pretenders to the throne of reality. The resolution of *The Legion of Time* could hardly have been available to Merritt, who was well aware that he worked with the stuff of dreams, essentially mercurial and elusive. (In Merritt's own version of *Dwellers in the Mirage* the hero loses both women when he emerges from the mirage, and even in the horribly fake ending substituted by the editor of *Argosy* he can only have one. Denny Lanning, by virtue of being a science fiction hero, can have both.)

The Legion of Time has a confidence and élan that pure dream-fantasy could never attain — a confidence conjured up by the pretense that the story keeps faith with the possibilities of the scientific imagination. The manner of this pretense is one of the book's strong points, because Williamson takes the warrant for his notion of future alternativity from the discovery of indeterminacy in contemporary physics — from the curious energy-wonderland of quantum theory and the enigma of Heisenberg's uncertainty principle. Williamson deploys this jargon with eloquent simplicity, and it becomes in his hands an exquisite magical formula, with a timely gloss of plausibility. In postwar science fiction the notion of alternate futures has become sufficiently commonplace to be conventional, requiring little or nothing in the way of a jargon of apology, but as it has come to be so readily acceptable, it has tended to lose some of its more fascinating aspects. Many of the events which were dramatic high points in *The Legion of Time* are now routine clichés.

The novel suffers from most of the faults of early pulp science fiction. Its style is the stereotyped mode of pulp melodrama. Its battles are bloody and brutal. The moral choices which face the hero, whether in the twentieth century or adrift in hypothetical time, are reduced to absurdity by oversimplification. Everything that happens within the story is a straightforward matter of either/or, and its plot is convoluted but in no sense genuinely complex. Lethonee and Sorainya are all too obviously figments of a dream, and no character in the book has any real dimension. It would, though, be misleading to say that the book succeeds "in spite of" these faults, for without the conventions into which these faults were built the story could not exist at all. *The Legion of Time* is in many ways the epitome of the pulp science fiction story, a brilliant example of that peculiar kind of artistry.

Brian Stableford

Sources for Further Study

Reviews:

Analog. LI, July, 1953, pp. 158-160.

Fantastic Universe Science Fiction. I, June–July, 1953, pp. 191-192.

Galaxy. VI, May, 1953, p. 122.

Imagination Science Fiction. V, January, 1954, p. 143.

Space Science Fiction. I, May, 1953, p. 83.

THE LENSMAN SERIES

Author: Edward E. Smith (1890-1965)
First book publications: Triplanetary (1950); *First Lensman* (1950); *Galactic Patrol*
   (1950); *Gray Lensman* (1951); *Second-Stage Lensman* (1953); *Children of the Lens*
   (1954)
Type of work: Novels
Time: Approximately one thousand years in the future
Locale: Many worlds in the First and Second galaxies

*The story of the war between the Galactic Patrol, whose senior members are
equipped with "lenses" which give them special powers, and a great conspiracy of the
enemies of Civilization*

> *Principal characters:*
> KIMBALL KINNISON, a Lensman and officer in the Galactic Patrol
> CLARRISSA MACDOUGALL, a nurse, later his wife
> VIRGIL SAMMS, the first Lensman
> NELS BERGENHOLM, an eccentric scientist
> WORSEL, a Lensman from Velantia III
> TREGONSEE, a Lensman from Rigel IV
> NADRECK, a Lensman from Palain VII
> MENTOR OF ARISIA, the molder of Civilization
> GHARLANE OF EDDORE, the archenemy of Civilization
> CHRISTOPHER,
> KAREN,
> KATHRYN,
> CAMILLA, and
> CONSTANCE, the children of Kimball and Clarrissa Kinnison

   The Lensman series initially consisted of a series of four magazine serials
written for *Astounding Stories* (later *Astounding Science Fiction*): *Galactic
Patrol* (1937-1938), *Gray Lensman* (1939-1940), *Second-Stage Lensman*
(1941-1942), and *Children of the Lens* (1947-1948). When the series was prepared for book publication, however, it was extended "backwards," new
material being added to an earlier novel, *Triplanetary* (serialized in *Amazing
Stories* in 1934), to build it into the series, and an entirely new novel, *First
Lensman*, being written to fill in the gap. *Triplanetary*, *First Lensman*, and
Galactic Patrol were all first issued in book form in 1950; *Gray Lensman*
followed in 1951, *Second-Stage Lensman* in 1953, and *Children of the Lens* in
1954. A series of stories set in the same universe, with several Lensmen as
characters, was published in the minor pulps *Comet* and *Astonishing* in 1941-
1942 and combined into the book *The Vortex Blaster* (later retitled *Masters of
the Vortex*) in 1960. Though not part of the extended series, it has been marketed as such by paperback publishers for commercial reasons related to the
spectacular renaissance of interest in Smith's work during the last decade.
   Together with the earlier *Skylark* series, the *Lensman* series provides the
paradigm for the subspecies of science fiction usually known as "space
opera." It is exemplary of a literary strategy which exploits the illusion of

plausibility conferred by the use of scientific and pseudoscientific jargon to turn the cosmos into a colossal playground where assorted heroes can do battle on a spectacular scale with entire races of loathsome aliens. Space opera is basically costume-drama of a very simple and elementary kind, but its essential simplicity and repetitiveness are cloaked by a continual escalation of magical superscience. Smith was the first writer to realize and exploit to the full the fact that the pretence of fidelity to known science and future possibility maintained by science fiction was not an imaginative constraint at all, but permitted absolutely anything to happen at the whim and convenience of the author, provided that a suitable jargon of apology was included. This fact, he discovered, made science fiction a much more permissive medium than any species of traditional fantasy (despite its protests to the contrary), and therefore made it the perfect medium for the development of wish-fulfillment fantasies, especially power fantasies.

Smith was an inelegant writer and an unimaginative one, but neither of these failings proved to be the least handicap to him, for the nature of his endeavors made them irrelevant. The raw audacity of his adventure stories gave them the capacity to exercise an almost mesmeric effect over many readers, pandering to one of the most elementary of human needs: the need for compensatory fantasies in which to express impulses that have to be restrained in everyday social intercourse. This aspect of his work gives it a childlike quality, but the appeal of his novels (like the appeal of all effective fantasies) is not so much to the childishness of children but to the child which hides within the adolescent or adult. Real children have no need of the jargon of apology which disguises the true nature of space opera and its kindred subspecies of genre fiction, but it is essential to the strategy of preparing naïve wish-fulfillment fantasies for an older audience.

The story told by the original tetralogy is mainly that of Kimball Kinnison, a young graduate of the Tellurian Academy of the Galactic Patrol. As a member of the Patrol's elite he becomes the proud possessor of a Lens: a crystal which exhibits some of the properties of life and which confers upon its wearer telepathic and other powers (thus acting, among other functions, as a translation device facilitating communication between alien races). Kinnison finds himself thrown into a struggle between the Patrol and the pirates of "Boskone," who have emerged as a serious threat to the emerging galactic civilization. Together with an assortment of alien allies, Kinnison embarks upon a great crusade against Boskone. In *Galactic Patrol*, he penetrates the Grand Base maintained by Boskone's "Director of Operations," Helmuth, and manages to destroy it. In the process he is twice elevated in rank, first becoming a free agent acting under his own initiative rather than under orders from above — a "Gray Lensman" — and later traveling to the world of Arisia, from which the mysterious Lenses come, for special training and advancement to the higher status of Second-Stage Lensman.

All four novels in the tetralogy have the same plot. In each of the last three, Kinnison discovers that the base which he destroyed at the end of the preceding book was merely one stage in a vast hierarchical conspiracy, subject to a higher authority which has to be taken on afresh. In *Gray Lensman* he has to destroy the disgusting alien Eich of the Second Galaxy. In *Second-Stage Lensman* he is pitted against the Thrale-Onlonian Empire. In *Children of the Lens* he and his children go forth to battle the Ploorians; the children then finally penetrate to the *real* heart of the conspiracy, the Eddorians, led by the All-Highest and his minion Gharlane (who, in a variety of guises, has been interfering with human history for a very long time). Eddore is scoured clean of life in the climax of *Children of the Lens*, so that both the First and Second Galaxies can become a suitable home for the Civilization which the Arisians planned millions of years in the past and which the Boskonian conspiracy has tried so desperately to destroy.

In the four magazine serials, this gradual pattern of discovery is shared by Kinnison and the readers, but in the book versions, the new prologue of *Triplanetary* reveals from the very beginning that what is really going on is the culmination of a conflict between Arisia and Eddore that dates back to the days when a temporary merging of the First and Second Galaxies "precipitated" millions of solar systems ready for the evolution of life on a grand scale. Arisia itself existed before this "Coalescence," but Eddore was an invader from another space-time continuum, alien to the entire cosmos. In the same prologue we learn of a longterm program in eugenics established by the Arisians to produce, ultimately, the "children of the lens," who are destined to defeat the diabolical Eddorians and bring about the salvation of Civilization.

Extra scenes written into the later novels in their book versions make sure that this context remains visible to the reader throughout, informing him that what is involved in the various skirmishes between the Galactic Patrol and the pirates of Boskone is no mere game of cops and robbers or petty political dispute, but part of the great war between ultimate Good and ultimate Evil. The series thus becomes a secular myth-system, fully comprehensive in its account of the origins and purpose of man and his universe. The Arisian Mentor who confronts the Lensman demigods at various stages in the drama is an individual containing four separate persons, and the entire world of Arisia undergoes a kind of apotheosis at the end of *Children of the Lens*, leaving the children themselves to be the Guardians of Civilization. This final novel ends with an appeal addressed by Christopher Kinnison to "The Entity Able To Obtain and Read It," in which the series becomes a purposive revelation:

> You have already learned that in ancient time Civilization after Civilization fell before it could rise much above the level of barbarism. You know that we and the previous race of Guardians saw to it that this, OUR Civilization, has not yet fallen. Know, now that the task of your race, so soon to replace us, will be to see to it that it does not fall.

The nature of Smith's basic psychological appeal to his readers is much more clearly revealed by the Lensman series than by the *Skylark* novels, for it was here that he perfected his strategy. The relationship of the children of the Lens (which, in a metaphorical sense, includes all the heroes) to the Arisians is that of child to parent and creation to creator. The Arisians are all-wise, perfectly good, and very powerful, and the heroes are desperate to please them and live up to their expectations. Mentor of Arisia is a father-figure in every sense of the word, and in relation to "him," Kimball Kinnison and his allies are hyper-archetypal children, living in a protected universe whose natural order is a framework of unlimited opportunity and whose moral order is magnificently simple. Its politics are breathtakingly simple: the good guys accept the (literally) paternalistic power structure without question, and the bad guys are annihilated to the last molecule of organic matter. However, as the above account makes clear, there is a sense in which the politics of the galactic civilization in its war against subversion are not politics in the usual sense at all — to treat them as such would be as foolishly absurd as to regard the series as a religious allegory.

The primary function of this kind of fantasy is to provide an escape from reality, and it would be naïve and unreasonable to expect to discover within such a fantasy a mirror-image of the real world or principles of action which might be carried back to the real world. Actually, the violent arena of this kind of fantasy-world probably allows the harmless exorcism of brutal impulses and the safe indulgence of antisocial sentiments. Its distorted world view is supportive rather than subversive.

The *Lensman* series has a special appeal to adolescents embarked upon the long and arduous journey into adulthood because it allows relaxation from the strain of change without its infantile qualities being obvious. In serving this end the series is extremely effective and has genuine merits. Many writers copied, or attempted to copy, Smith, but virtually all of them reproduced the superstructure of his work without the base. John W. Campbell, Jr., Edmond Hamilton, and Jack Williamson all worked within the same area at the same time, but though they had merits of their own, they could not reproduce the essence of Smith's success. Smith's real intellectual heirs are those who forsook the actual props that he used but retained the basic structure of the fantasy — most notably Isaac Asimov in the *Foundation* series and Roger Zelazny in the *Amber* series. Both of these writers were much better prose-mongers than Smith, and both, in their different ways, were far cleverer in designing the apparatus of their fantasy worlds; they have, therefore, appealed to a wider audience. Each of them, however, requires of his readers a level of intellectual sophistication that excludes some potential users of the fantasy who can still be captivated by Doc Smith and Kimball Kinnison.

Brian Stableford

Sources for Further Study

Criticism:

Ellik, Ron and Bill Evans. *The Universe of E. E. Smith*. Chicago: Advent, 1968. Ellik and Evans give a complete discussion of all of the Lensman and Skylark novels.

Reviews:

Amazing Stories. XXVI, March, 1952, pp. 151-152.

Analog. XLIX, May, 1952, pp. 157-158 and June, 1952, pp. 164-165.

Galaxy. III, March, 1952, p. 84.

Magazine of Fantasy and Science Fiction. XXIII, July, 1962, p. 109.

Startling Stories. XXV, March, 1952, pp. 139-140.

LEOPARD S VERSHINI KILIMANDZHARO
(Leopard on the Peak of Kilimanjaro)

Author: Olga Larionova (1935-   )
First book publication: 1965
Type of work: Novel
Time: The twenty-eighth century
Locale: Principally the Swiss Alps

A lyrical novel describing the life of people of Earth who are aware of the exact dates of their deaths and, in particular, a love triangle among a returning astronaut, his wife, and a young girl

> *Principal characters:*
> RAMON, an astronavigator
> SANA LOGÉ, a biologist, his beloved
> DOCTOR ELEPHANTUS,
> PATTERY PAT, and
> ILLE, biologists
> LACOST,
> DJABJA, and
> TUAN, employees at the Mountain Rescue Station

Emotional coloring characterizes the whole creative activity of Olga Larionova. Her favorite topics — love, friendship, and psychological collisions arising out of the communication between people — stress her approach to science fiction as a means of stressing feelings more than ideas. Certain aspects of her writings suggest analogies with the novels and stories of Zenna Henderson, Anne McCaffrey, or Kate Wilhelm, although she is never overtly feminist in the style of a Joanna Russ. Moreover, Larionova occasionally demonstrates a tendency to write in a "masculine" style; rude Hemingway-like manner is sometimes essential to her works.

Larionova is very resourceful in structuring plot. In her most recent works she at times achieves a surprising depth and brilliance in her frameworks. She is logical, but occasionally her logic is interrupted by a rush of pure emotion.

Thus, a peculiar mix of irrational emotional writing and a calculated sensible exploitation of science fiction models give birth to amazing results. Larionova's writings seldom pass unnoticed and her first (and in many respects still the best) novel *Leopard s vershini Kilimandzharo* has been awarded a rare, literally "fantastic" honor: Soviet cosmonaut Georgii Grechko expressed his appreciation for the book by taking it, along with two Strugatsky stories, on his first trip into space.

The plot of the novel is extremely simple, although not at all mundane. Ten years prior to the events described, a robot interstellar probe "Overator" had returned to Earth. As a result of an unexpected "shift of space," it had ventured into the future and returned to Earth with a cargo of unusual information. In particular, everyone on Earth became aware of the exact date of his or her death. Do humans need such knowledge? What can come of it? Would people be able to carry this burden?

The general feeling of fatalism essential to the novel, the inability of the heroes to change their destiny, turns out to be incompletely motivated for a science fiction novel ("Fatal" knowledge brought by "Overator" might, for example, have played a successful role in some modern modification of a gothic novel). However, this is perhaps the only objection. The author has "his right" to determine the terms of the game. Regarding the solution of the moral problem raised — how to live knowing the date of your death — Larionova here draws her line with a rare convenience and brightness.

The point is the moral choice. Larionova exhibits unexpected courage for a débutante author. She does not linger on the problem itself. She goes further; she does not show the dramatically spectacular situation of choice, but rather the consequences of the choice by demonstrating how people live who are endowed with this tragic knowledge. Will they bear the constant pressure of this burden?

The world of the future is shown through the eyes of Ramon, the astronavigator. He has returned to Earth after eleven years spent on a deep-space station. In the very beginning, the crew of the station was killed by unexpected cosmic radiation associated with the Overator's launch. Only Ramon remained alive, unable to help his friends who happened to be outside the station. Ramon quickly realizes that under the circumstances he can do nothing. But this is a rational understanding rather than an emotional one. A feeling of guilt gnaws at him, a guilt he is unable to expiate, so Ramon lives with this emotion. In the world of the future, as described by Larionova, a man really is a "measure of all matters," and the level of his conscience makes him the first judge of his deeds. That is how the first moral conflict between an objective justification of the event and its internal subjective unforgiveness arises.

Upon arrival on Earth, Ramon is met by his love Sana Logé. She has been waiting devotedly for him, and her entire world has been concentrated in Ramon. Soon Ramon learns that the year of his return to Earth is also the last year of Sana's life. Ramon understands the necessity of being with Sana, to do everything possible to smooth away the feelings of melancholy and inconsolability. But again, this is understanding contrary to sympathy, mind against heart. Sana's love is great and selfless and that is why she deserves kindness and attention; she has the right to occupy all of Ramon's time.

However, their relationship is far from being perfect: a tension develops between them. Sana wants to preserve everything as it was eleven years ago, but that is impossible. Ramon comes to realize more acutely that something is vanishing in their relationship.

With considerable psychological adroitness, Larionova presents an age-old problem: Why does happiness, which once seemed almost eternal, dissipate so rapidly? Ramon tries everything possible to keep Sana from noticing that the relationship is changing, but he does so only to be kind. He searches for feelings other than "unlimited and feeble pity" and realizes that he has none, nothing remains but a tormenting moral duty. He simply *must* do what he is doing, and everything goes to pieces. When duty replaces love, it is no longer love; when there is nothing except duty, the result is tragedy.

While depicting this complicated ethical collision, Larionova makes no moral judgments. Who is to blame? Ramon, because the love has gone, or Sana, because she tries to hold her beloved in the last year of her life in spite of her knowledge. There is no right or wrong in emotion. Who can reproach Sana for being egoistic in love? And who will blame Ramon? They deserve only pity because the loss of feeling results in tragedy for both of them.

Had Larionova limited herself to the problem of the relationship between Sana and Ramon, the result would have been an acutely psychological novel in which the author's attention is concentrated only on the internal world of her heroes and their spiritual suffering. If that had been the case, the novel would still have been of interest, because the sphere of emotions (especially with regard to the people of the future) is explored only superficially in most modern science fiction. However, the novel is more complicated than that.

First, there is a third person in the novel. Structurally the novel is built so that the action is concentrated in two places: Eherhaven Reserve where Ramon, Sana, and the other biologists live, and the Mountain Rescue Station ("the Cabin") where Ramon meets a young girl, Ille. The appearance of this third party gives Ramon's life new meaning. The places are not simply topographic, but they are also poles of conflict in the novel. At the center of one pole is Sana; at the other is Ille. The corresponding plot structures are built around these characters. To make the text more compact, to eliminate the secondary details, Larionova utilizes methods of drama: temporal localization, transfer of a substantial part of action into internal monologues and dialogues. It is interesting to note that the majority of the internal monologue takes place at Sana's pole, while the majority of the dialogue takes place at Ille's.

This is not surprising at all. In the "Cabin" Ramon finds those who share his melancholy and sympathize with the feeling of "unguilty guilt" which has been troubling him for eleven years. Sana has tried to avoid any references to Ramon's past, but her touching and tragic egoism achieves the opposite effect and Ramon becomes lost to her. The inhabitants of the "Cabin," each in his own way, attempt to support Ramon without ignoring the burning problem. They give his experiences a new interpretation. First, they have managed to persuade Ramon that it was beyond his abilities to prevent the catastrophe (as it really was). Second, they explain to him that to survive those long years at the space station is itself an accomplishment. In Larionova's future, the deed becomes the norm of life and long ago "heroic ceased to be heroism but transferred into the duty."

This is an essential movement. It may seem that except for the "Overator" there is little in the novel to classify it as science fiction. However, it is still science fiction. As Kate Wilhelm did in *Where Late the Sweet Birds Sang*, the "Forsyte Saga" of the future, Larionova has written a family saga of fantastic people. Her heroes simply are not our contemporaries, but people of the future, at least of such future as Larionova envisions.

The world described by Larionova in the novel is associated with the future not only because all the industrial centers have been removed from Earth to Mars and are being distantly controlled, or because Venus has become a gigantic plantation. The matter is not in these external signs but in the surprising insight into the moral conscience which the author has managed to depict. This refers not only to evaluation of Ramon's courage, but — and here again is this very connection with the main problem of the novel — to the way humans perceive the knowledge brought by "Overator" as well. To accept or not to accept this knowledge, which may (or may not) open a great many secret doors of the individual's social being and conscience, is one of the most complicated problems ever put to mankind. The answer is determined by the general moral climate of the epoch.

The decision is an act of heroism, but one committed not by a single individual but by mankind in general. Understanding of this moral category has deepened in the future world; its boundaries have been moved apart. If this notion once meant "only" a selfless act was distinguished among another deeds, by now the then scale of moral values has suffered a considerable transformation. What was formerly heroic has become the norm, and now heroism only exists when "it is terrible and difficult to death, but you do it nonetheless. You do it not out of fatalism or under the lash but simply because from now on each person's act is determined by the realization of the highest moral principle: everything — for man."

Thus, gradually a serious social problem emerges out of the novel. It is not illuminated all at once, but reveals itself *via* separate fates. The theme of love is expanded and takes on new meaning through the central problem. Such is Ille's love for Ramon, deep, clear, selfless, and hidden. Only in the end of the novel does Ramon become aware of Ille's feeling and realizes that he has been dreaming of such a love all of his life. But on this same day, Ille dies in the mountains during a thunderstorm. Only after her death does Ramon learn that she, too, knew the date of her death.

While creating Ille's character, the author evidently was fighting two temptations: a desire to liberate her feelings and a wish to suppress all sentimentality. Though a purely "feminine" sympathy on Larionova's part toward her romantic heroine can be seen behind the externally restrained manner of writing, it must be said that this characterization is successful. Ille is a deep character who possesses a number of strong qualities: calmness, restraint, and courage. She keeps her love for Ramon a secret to protect those around her from pain. Despite the circumstances, she has the strength to remain agile, gay, and cheerful.

Though the novel ends with the death of Ille and a break between Ramon and Sana, this does not diminish the novel's impact. Ramon has come through a hopelessly melancholic love of Sana and through an open, selfless love of Ille; he has come to understand the real price and value of selflessness and sacrifice. From now on his life will be illuminated by the light of Ille's life. The answer to the problem so frequently put on the pages of the novel — what life is and what life should one live knowing his date of death — is personified in Ille's short but wonderful life (she dies while rescuing hikers who are stranded in the mountain canyon). Life overcomes death, if it is lived in the way Ille went through her own: ". . . lightly and impetuously as one can go towards death when he is not in the least thinking about it because the most important matter is to be in time to rescue someone else."

Vl. Gakov

LESABÉNDIO

Author: Paul Scheerbart (1863-1915)
First book publication: 1913
Type of work: Novel
Time: A timeless present
Locale: The asteroid Pallas

The Pallasian Lesabéndio attempts to erect a tower ten miles high to break through the luminous cloud hovering over Pallas and establish contact with the greater cosmos beyond

Principal characters:
> LESABÉNDIO, a Pallasian with more technical than artistic interests
> LABU, a Pallasian with an interest in the arts
> MANESI, a Pallasian with great enthusiasm for gardening
> NUSE, a builder of light-towers
> PEKA, an artistically inclined Pallasian who values crystalline forms above all others
> SOFANTI, a specialist for the fabrication of skins
> NAX, an inhabitant of the small asteroid Quikko
> BIBA, an old Pallasian, a writer of philosophical treatises with a keen interest in the sun

Paul Scheerbart was one of the great outsiders of German literature, a man never popular with the general reader, but always cherished by a few connoisseurs. He was considered a literary clown, a cosmic joker by many, and a genius by a small circle of respectable writers and critics. His originality is undeniable, and it sets him apart from all other writers who have written on cosmic themes. Although Scheerbart also wrote a number of stories set in the Orient or far-off places such as Australia, his proper domain was the cosmos, and in many of his stories the Earth is mentioned only for purposes of contrast. This is true of his "asteroid novel" *Lesabéndio*, which is generally considered his best novel. Earth is mentioned briefly in chapter one, when Lesabéndio, the hero of the novel, reads aloud to fellow Pallasians several passages from a book written by an ancient Pallasian who had visited the planet on a comet. Full of loathing the author comments on the repulsive habits of the two-legged dominant species on that planet, who kill one another with guns and sharpened stakes of iron and eat by stuffing burnt pieces of flesh into their mouths, caverns filled with ragged pieces of bone. One of the listeners, Biba, an old Pallasian with a strong philosophical bias, begs him to desist from torturing them with such gruesome stories.

On Pallas and in the wider cosmos things are much simpler and more beautiful than on Earth. The Pallasians themselves are newtlike beings who can alter their shape and appearance. They can become fifty meters tall or contract to half a meter; their eyes may be turned into telescopes (to perceive better the wonders of the cosmos) or even into microscopes. They sleep with the skin of their faces folded over themselves, forming bubbles that shine brightly. They obtain nourishment by lying down in meadows of mushrooms and fungi and absorb the food through their skin. They have no sex, another terrestrial feature that Scheerbart found extremely crude: young Pallasians are simply found in nuts, in veins of lead and cracked. Upon awakening they soon learn the Pallasian language and invariably have beautiful tales to tell of the worlds they had inhabited prior to their births. Pallasians also do not die; if a Pallasian becomes weary of life, as sometimes happens, he asks a close friend to absorb him. They usually merge with someone they admire, a greater being. But if necessary, any Pallasian will gladly accept one desirous of nonbeing.

Naturally, the asteroid Pallas, on which the whole novel takes place, has nothing in common with the astronomical body of that name, which is just a ragged rock. Scheerbart's Pallas is a cylindrical object, with two funnels inside, one in the north, the other in the south. A tube connects the two tops of the funnels in the axis of the cylinder. Sofanti has hung his skins in this tube, and the winds blow through when dusk sets, generating beautiful sounds, the Sofanti music. The Pallasians have criss-crossed the northern funnel with moving bands that are propelled by rollers at various speeds. When they want to move from one point to another on the surface of the funnel, they merely attach their rubber-foot-tube, a part of the body, to the appropriate band and are carried along at fantastic speed, jumping from band to band to change direction. In the less populous southern funnel, transport is provided by more inconvenient magnetic bands.

A luminous cloud hovers over the northern funnel. It is a fine spiderlike web that not only soltly illuminates the inside of the funnel, but also prevents the Pallasians from seeing into the cosmos. At night — which is much longer on Pallas than on Earth, for a Pallasian hour is about as long as a terrestrial day — the cloud nears the base of the funnel, wrapping itself around the asteroid.

Living in a veritable cosmic paradise, free from our terrestrial problems, the Pallasians spend all their time pursuing hobbies and pastimes. Manesi's passion is gardening; he has planted many new mushroom meadows, including a number in the bowels of Pallas, and climber plants. Labu and Peka are artistically inclined. What the climbers are for Manesi, straight lines and squares are for Peka; crystalline forms mean more to him than any others, and it is his ambition to carve Pallas into a gigantic work of art. Labu has the same ambition; he, however, prefers curves to straight lines. These people represent the arts, while Lesabéndio, Dex, and Nuse stand for engineering. Lesabéndio wonders what is beyond the cloud that blocks their view into the cosmos from the northern funnel; his great ambition it is to erect a sky-high, Babylonian tower from which to explore the cosmos. He suspects that Pallas may be a double star, with another astronomical body hidden in the cloud, and even allows himself to think that the meaning of Pallasian life may be found there.

Lesabéndio confirms this notion by traveling into space with his companion Biba. On the southern side of their planetoid, they are attracted by a small heavenly body, the star Quikko. It is a world inhabited by small, quick-witted beings, the Quikkonians, who do justice to their name. From them Lesabéndio learns that Pallas consists of the familiar cylinder and an unfamiliar sphere beyond the cloud. This discovery convinces Lesabéndio that his goal is worthwhile. The Quikkonian Nax and nine of his species accompany Lesabéndio to Pallas, where they help him convince the public that the tower should be built.

Building the giant tower is made possible by the discovery of "Kaddimohnsteel," one mile long poles that are conveniently found in the ground exactly where they are needed. (Scheerbart did not believe in hard work, being quite un-Prussian in this respect.) The poles are simply pulled out of the earth and set up to form a concentric ring of towers. The tops of these towers are then connected to form a ring; on this ring the next level of towers is erected, leaning inward, and so on until the tower is ten miles high.

This gigantic endeavor taxes the resources and manpower of the entire asteroid, resulting in the decline of artistic occupations. So many Pallasians are involved in engineering that there are few left to appreciate artistic work. Manesi and Peka, who deplore this preponderance of technology over gardening and planet sculpturing, ask Lesabéndio to accept them into his body, for there is little likelihood that his tower will be beautified by climbing plants or sculpture. However, technological experts such as Dex, the discoverer of "Kaddimohnsteel," and Nuse, who erects lighted towers, thrive. There is also much work for Sofanti, who is asked to cover the higher stories of the tower with translucent skin, for protection against the luminous cloud. As they approach the cloud, they discover that it is a fine web of wriggling, very fine, ethereal snakes, shy beings possessing sentience.

Lesabéndio, the driving force behind the project, finally achieves his highest goal, union with the "greater" being: he is absorbed by the cloud, which parts as the tower grows higher and forms a ring around it. From the star above, visible at last, a red ray shines down into the funnel of Pallas, producing novel light effects. This light from the "head system" of Pallas has made the cloud luminous to Pallasian observers. Having achieved his ambition, communion with the greater system, Lesabéndio directly experiences the feelings of his star, the unrest that is in the planets, and their great longing for the sun. As the star shines brighter than ever before, a blue-green light being added to the white luminosity, Lesabéndio tells the Pallasians of his greatest discovery: that the utmost pain, the pain of death, and the greatest bliss, occur simultaneously. What is most crucial is to retain independence and yet become a part of the greater one, the system of cosmic harmony. The Pallasians, helped along by the Quikkonians, build observatories and telescopes to watch the marvels and wonders of the other stars, the bright comets passing by, and the harmony of the Saturn ring that may serve as a model for the asteroid belt. Lesabéndio becomes more and more a star.

Scheerbart was a representative of a kind of literature that is totally divorced from reality and its physical laws. It is pure literature, a verbal world that has and cannot have an existence outside that on the written page. In another novel, *Die Seeschlange*, he declared, "What do I care for Robert Mayer and his law of the conservation of energy?" Scheerbart had a low opinion of the natural sciences, but thought that they too might help to expand the realm of possibilities and might stimulate imagination; but he did not believe that the sciences could contribute much to our understanding of the world. They offered but a surface, whereas his romantic aim was to arrive at the essence of things, and he thought that salvation could be found only in imagination. His cosmos is not subject to the laws of physics but of a paraphysics — harmonies and sympathies between heavenly bodies, devoid of Newtonian gravity. It is a realm of wonders, of constant metamorphoses and changes, in which everything is sentient — the comets, the planets, the sun — and connected by ties of cosmic consciousness.

Scheerbart's cosmos is an absolute antithesis to Earth, this vale of tears where disharmony, disproportion, and ugliness rule. It is a world of bright colors, cheerful beauty and perpetual metamorphoses that constantly produce new, surprising, and invariably beautiful things. His cosmos has no forces, and all problems turn into esthetics, into beautifully bright pictures, a dance of the comets and a whirl of the stars, a series of eidetic impressions outside of all historical time.

There is something oriental about Scheerbart's vision: an exuberance of colors, forms, images, dreams, ecstasies, unrealities, and hallucinations. He prefers the unreal, wish-fulfillment, the irregular, and the illogical. He seeks astonishment not knowledge, naïve wonder instead of skeptical appreciation. Nothing is firm in his books; everything is in flux. In his novels, plot is usually an excuse for the telling of numerous minute anecdotes (many of them of a striking beauty). *Lesabéndio* is an exception insofar as it is a novel with a discernible plot and a theme that gives the book a unity lacking in most of his other books. His is a world of plentitude — unbounded, hyperbolic, excessively exuberant, episodic in the extreme.

Scheerbart wanted to create something "new," and for him the new was the arrangement of familiar elements in continually new combinations and patterns extended over the cosmos. It is a world of childlike play, to a large degree lacking any governing principle. Scheerbart was an extremely visual type, he delighted in colors and forms of light, suggestive of the bright mysteries of existence. His cosmic beings like the Pallasians frequently were equipped with adaptable sense organs to grasp the wonders of their worlds and the rest of the cosmos. There are funnel stars, snake and worm stars, pancake stars and many more, often in tiresome numbers. His writing style was deliberately simple, even banal and childlike, devoid to any pathos. The frequent jokes disrupt any feeling of cosmic awe that might arise. Many find him childish and irresponsibly playful, but he is also one of the few great humorists in the German language. His humor belongs to the category of "gallows humor"; it is born out of desperation over the state of the world, and to escape it he created his fantasy world of beauty and sympathy.

Although Scheerbart's work has certain affinities with Lucian, Cyrano de Bergerac, the Münchhausen tales, even Swift to a degree, he is an original creator, quite distinct from any other writer. His books are examples of a pure, playful imagination, and Lesabéndio embodies these virtues at their best. Here, he has fused his general cosmic philosophy with a tightly organized plot and has movingly presented one of his main themes, the longing for a communion with the "greater" things of the cosmos.

Franz Rottensteiner

LEST DARKNESS FALL

Author: L. Sprague de Camp (1907-   )
First book publication: 1941
Type of work: Novel
Time: The present, A.D. 535-537
Locale: Rome and central Italy

A fast-paced and humorous adventure in which an archaeologist and historian, thrown back through time to sixth century Rome, tries to keep the approaching Dark Ages from destroying civilization

> *Principal characters:*
> MARTIN PADWAY, a young American archaeologist
> THOMASUS THE SYRIAN, an amiable moneylender
> NEVITTA GUMMOND'S SON, a boisterous Gothic landholder
> FRITHARIK, a gloomy Vandal warrior
> CORNELIUS ANICIUS, an effete patrician
> KING THIUDAHAD, a senile monarch of Gothic Italy
> PRINCESS MATHASWENTHA, a beautiful but bloodthirsty woman

L. Sprague de Camp's *Lest Darkness Fall* is a light adventure about a twentieth century American who is thrown 1,400 years into the past. There he tries to introduce some of the benefits of modern technology and sociology, to improve wretched living conditions. This plot bears obvious similarities to Mark Twain's *A Connecticut Yankee in King Arthur's Court* (1889), because of which it has been described as a pulp-magazine imitation of Twain's work. But there have been many imitations of Twain's classic over the years, and virtually all of them have been forgotten almost immediately. De Camp's novel has continued to please readers since its original magazine appearance in December, 1939, and it shows no signs of becoming outworn.

It might be noted that the current edition of this 1939 novel has been haphazardly updated. Several references (but not all) to Mussolini as the present leader of Italian politics have been removed. A "new fifty-lire" hat has become a "new twelve-thousand-lire" hat, reflecting contemporary Italian inflation. But the thirty-one-year-old Martin Padway is still born in 1908.

Lest Darkness Fall is not so much an imitation of *A Connecticut Yankee in King Arthur's Court* as it is a challenge to it. De Camp's differing treatment of parallel situations implies an accusation that Twain's novel is essentially implausible. Twain's Hank Morgan is a New England factory superintendent who can "make everything: guns, revolvers, cannon, boilers, engines, all sorts of labor-saving machinery." Although he is not apparently formally educated, Morgan happens to know "just by luck" that the only total eclipse of the sun in the first half of the sixth century is due the day after his arrival, which allows him to impress the superstitious knights. Twain's thundering denunciation of the Age of Faith is heartfelt, but his medieval England is a shaky assemblage of fairy-tale images. By comparison, de Camp's sixth century Italy is presented in convincing detail. His Martin Padway has no happy coincidences to make life easy. His progress seems more plausibly developed. Readers who do recognize the similarities between the two novels will feel that de Camp is not trying to copy Twain, but rather demonstrate how this plot should have been written.

Can one man singlehandedly change the past for the better? This is the basically serious theme that underlies Padway's humorous misadventures. As a historian, Padway realizes that he is present at the twilight of classic Roman civilization before the onset of the "Dark Ages." Is there anything that he can do to preserve civilization? As the mild, pragmatic Padway muddles from one crisis to the next, the reader begins to understand that he will be more successful than he dreams.

The setting has been skillfully chosen. The history of sixth century Italy is virtually unknown to the public. This allows de Camp to involve Padway with actual characters and events of the time, without the average reader knowing how matters are going to turn out.

De Camp has also been clever in establishing his story premise. He adroitly uses the common science fiction notion that reality is an infinite series of coexisting universes. Every conceivable historical possibility is an actuality somewhere. If the past is changed, a new history branches off parallel to our present rather than replacing it. This allows the reader to feel that Padway really has a chance for success, rather than that he is bound to fail because we know that the Medieval period was not forestalled.

Martin Padway is a thirty-one-year-old, slightly introverted archaeologist from Chicago. He is passing through Rome when he is struck by lightning during a thunderstorm. He finds himself in the same locality but in October, A.D. 535. Just prior to being struck, Padway had been discussing historical philosophy with an Italian colleague. It could be argued that the power of the bolt was channeled by the impulses of Padway's conscious thoughts to shift him to that age. This is the sort of pseudotechnical explanation that allows science fiction readers to accept a story as possibly scientific, rather than as plainly fantastic.

Actually, de Camp asks the reader to accept a bigger coincidence by providing a modern American protagonist who just happens to be thoroughly familiar with sixth century events and dialect, certainly an advantage that the normal American would not have. Yet this is a literary license that the reader is disposed to accept. By providing a hero who is a historical scholar, and offering the vague but undisprovable theory of a time-journey subconsciously directed by thought, de Camp has begun his story in an acceptably plausible manner.

The initial description of sixth century Rome is detailed and matter-of-fact. Pedestrians wear dirty woolen tunics. The classic buildings have not yet been stripped of their marble façades for medieval construction projects, a detail that a historian like Padway would appreciate. The "garlic-and-gasoline aroma of modern Rome had been replaced by a barnyard-and-backhouse symphony." De Camp focuses upon enough commonplace images to make his setting feel comfortably realistic.

After accepting that he is marooned in the past, Padway's first acts are pragmatic. He determines to call as little attention to himself as possible. "Inventing" most twentieth century marvels is out of the question, even if he knew the details of their manufacture, because the sixth century does not have the industrial base to make them possible. Padway finally decides to make his living by constructing a simple distillery and introducing brandy — not a noble advance for civilization, but a practical one. Yet even this leads to an advance in knowledge, since Padway has to teach Roman smiths how to make the copper tubing for the still.

Padway's first acquaintances are representatives of social types. Thomasus the Syrian is a moneylender, who describes the economic situation in Rome in A.D. 535 through replies to Padway's requests for a loan. Nevitta Gummond's son, a Gothic landholder, represents the social relationship between the Italians and the Goths who recently migrated into Italy. Fritharik, the Vandal ex-knight whom Padway hires as a bodyguard, forecasts the mentality of the coming Dark Ages, in which education is dismissed as effeminate and the only occupation considered respectable for a gentleman is warfare. Cornelius Anicius, "a literary Roman patrician, of the sort who couldn't ask you to pass the butter without wrapping the request in three puns, four mythological allusions, and a dissertation on the manufacture of butter in ancient Crete," symbolizes the decline of Rome's former strength.

Although these characters and others help to establish the scene, they are not mere props. De Camp gives each a distinct and colorful personality. Thomasus the Syrian is sharp but friendly and humorous. Nevitta is a back-slapping friend-in-need, a godsend in getting Padway settled. Fritharik is a comically dour pessimist, forever predicting that Padway's latest crazy innovation will put them both into nameless, lonely graves. None of these are complex characters, but each has enough unique, believable traits to be realistic and usually likeable individuals.

Padway has been in Rome for only a few months when the Byzantine Empire's first attempt to reconquer Italy becomes imminent. Padway knows the devastating war will rage up and down the peninsula for a generation. His conscience troubles him for not trying to prevent the onset of the Dark Ages. His answer is to try to introduce the dissemination of knowledge through mass communications.

Through the eposide of constructing a printing press, de Camp shows the tribulations of trying to establish technology in a nontechnological culture. A cabinetmaker is able to construct the press (he thinks it's a new torture implement for the prison), and a seal-cutter makes passable printing type. De Camp has to give a slight authorial nudge; Padway is "fortunate" in knowing that printer's ink is based on linseed oil and lampblack, and that nonwoodpulp paper can be made of cloth felt. After much messy experimenting Padway ends up with a rudimentary printing industry. De Camp pointedly does not attribute Padway with "fortunate" knowledge in other areas, so his later attempts to create clocks or cannon end in frustration. When it comes to technology, de Camp is a philosophical Marxist. The environment molds the individual, and one man cannot revolutionize all of industry and commerce.

Padway's establishment of a newspaper and a semaphore telegraph brings an end to his anonymity. The lazy, vain Gothic king takes insult at straight news reportage of his army's incompetence, while the decadent city government expects hefty bribes to allow him to operate. This convinces Padway that, like it or not, the only way to survive is to get involved in politics.

Padway takes advantage of his scholarly talents to work up an acquaintance with pseudointellectual King Thiudahad. Strange innovations such as civil service reform or a military academy cannot be ignored when they are accompanied by a king's approval. At first this works, but to maintain the pliable and senile Thiudahad as his front, Padway prevents the king's scheduled assassination in 536. This leaves "Mysterious Martinus" as an embarrassingly obvious power-behind-the-throne. Further, his influence gradually alters history so much that his knowledge of what should happen next no longer applies to reality.

To maintain his position, Padway is forced to emerge as a full-fledged politician. De Camp portrays what this means by having Padway indulge in a brief romance with Princess Mathaswentha, a typical member of the Gothic nobility. She enthusiastically supports Padway and is eager to arrange the elimination of all his personal or political opponents, real or potential. Padway is a bit squeamish for this, so he introduces another American innovation — machine politics.

De Camp may be indulging in some chauvinism here. Is Chicago-style bossism really so superior that it would instantly eclipse the traditional political infighting of ancient Roman politics? No matter; it's fun to see the Gothic nobility trying on the showmanship of America's big-city campaign rallies. Similarly, was ancient warfare really so naïve that Padway, with one year of high school R.O.T.C., would be able to outmaneuver the famous Byzantine armies? Again, no matter. It's fun to watch the harassed commander-by-default arguing his knightly subordinates into trying some strategy rather than simply waiving swords and charging straight ahead.

Lest Darkness Fall is a good historical adventure. It presents an accurate picture of a little-known but important period in the development of Western civilization. De Camp makes it clear where real history ends and his fictional events begin, so the novel is educational in that the average reader will gain some real knowledge from it.

The book is also a witty comedy. It is peopled with sympathetic characters, most of whom are intelligent and are given clever dialogue. The foibles of sixth century society are depicted one at a time in a humorous manner. One example is the bar fight which shows the prevalent emotional preoccupation with religion:

> . . . the term "infamous heretics" occurred about once per sentence. Yellow Hair roared back at him, and other men began shouting from various parts of the room: "Eat him up, barbarian"! "This is an Orthodox country, and those who don't like it can go back where they — " "Damned nonsense about dual natures! We Monophysites — " "I'm a Jacobite, and I can lick any man in the place"! "Let's throw all the heretics out"! "I'm a Eunomian, and I can lick any *two* men in the place"!

In similar scenes de Camp presents a sarcastic summary of sixth century attitudes toward medicine, education, politics, and civil rights.

Further, there is the interpretation of *Lest Darkness Fall* as an intriguing variant on a literary classic. In *A Connecticut Yankee in King Arthur's Court* Mark Twain was concerned with making a statement on the social primitiveness of the sixth century (possibly as a reaction against the romantically ethereal portrait then in vogue through the writings of such Victorian authors as Tennyson). The plot elements of the novel are primarily allegories designed to reveal and emphasize the ignorance, squalor, and resistance to common sense of the real Age of Faith. Twain was not interested in depicting specific historical events. He was not concerned with wondering how a man from 1,400 years in the future might realistically affect the past.

But in *Lest Darkness Fall* the emphasis is on scientific extrapolation rather than social commentary. The superstition and brutality of early medieval life are not ignored, but neither are they dwelt upon. They are a natural part of the background, seen only to the extent that they interact with Padway's life. De Camp's interest is in developing an intellectual puzzle: how might a single modern American transported into the past actually have affected the course of history? Twain was not trying to write science fiction; de Camp was, and this gives the plot device a completely different purpose. *Lest Darkness Fall* is an adventure story which is based upon accurate history, plausibly evolved to result in a logically convincing new world. This is science fiction of the best kind.

The novel ends with a rousing battle in which the superior Byzantine army is crushed (more by happenstance than any real strategy), but the story lacks a real climax. It seems to simply stop, a year and a half after Padway's arrival in the sixth century. His day-by-day struggle to maintain Gothic Rome as an enlightened civilization will last the rest of his life, he realizes. Yet the outlook is encouraging. The concepts of printing, telegraphy, and a postal system have become too firmly established to disappear. History has been changed to at least this extent. The spread of information and knowledge is irreversible, and darkness will not fall.

Frederick Patten

Sources for Further Study

Criticism:

Asimov, Isaac. *"Lest Darkness Fall,"* in *Astonishing Stories*. III (September, 1941), p. 6. Asimov analyzes the theme and has some interesting comments on De Camp's literary style.

Fison, Peter. "That Thing from Another World," in *Twentieth Century*. CLVIII (September, 1955), pp. 280-288. Although Fison laments the loss in science fiction as a whole of "the potential for high adventure," he praises De Camp as a humorist.

Gardner, Martin. "Humorous Science Fiction," in *The Writer*. LXII (1949), pp. 148-151. Gardner finds that De Camp's humor is built around situations that are fundamentally absurd.

Reviews:

Amazing Stories. XXIII, December, 1949, p. 152.

New Worlds. XLII, December, 1955, p. 126.

Stirring Science Stories. I, June, 1941, pp. 124-127.

Thrilling Wonder Stories. I, June, 1941, pp. 124-127.

Unknown Worlds. II, October, 1955, p. 66.

LEVEL SEVEN

Author: Mordecai Roshwald (1921-   )
First book publication: 1959
Type of work: Novel
Time: The early 1960's
Locale: Level Seven, a totally isolated and self-sufficient military enclave buried 4,400
feet beneath the Earth's surface

Push-Button Officer X-127, because of his special training and qualities of temperament, is assigned, along with 499 other anonymous souls, to his country's offensive nuclear strike command post, which fights an atomic push-button war apparently killing everyone on Earth

Principal characters:
    X-127, the narrator, a male military officer
    P-867, a female psychologist
    R-747, a female elementary schoolteacher

A first-person narrative in the form of a diary, *Level Seven* tells the story of the end of the world through a nuclear holocaust. The lack of subtlety of this cautionary tale is indicated by its dedication, "To Dwight and Nikita." Subtlety, however, is not a requirement of this type of writing. Its primary purpose is to provide a warning, and *Level Seven* clearly warns its readers of the dangers of atomic warfare. The reader is left to conclude that even a poorly written novel can succeed in its purpose.

Level Seven is the offensive arm of the narrator's country's PBX Command. Warfare in Roshwald's world has become limited to the pushing of a button, launching thousands of nuclear missiles. There is a defensive arm housed on Level Six, but on the theory that the best defense is a good offense, Level Seven has been made impregnable and guarantees a massive retaliatory strike in the event of enemy attack. Roshwald has simply taken the prevailing Cold War philosophy of 1959 and transferred it intact to his novel.

Located 4,400 feet beneath the surface of the Earth and completely isolated and self-contained, Level Seven is staffed by five hundred military officers — 250 men and 250 women. They can never return to the surface, but are doomed to live and die in Level Seven. Nor are they volunteers. They were chosen for the task on the basis of needed skills, sexual balances, and psychological profiles, by some military "big brother," and then tricked underground. Their only job is to retaliate against the enemy in the event of nuclear war. Until war comes, they are to serve humanity and their country on Level Seven; and if war never happens, it will be because the enemy knows they are there, waiting.

The narrator is introduced to the reader only as X-127, and throughout the novel he refers to the other characters only by letter (referring to their function on Level Seven — P for psychologist, N for nurse, and so on) and number. Since the novel is cast in the form of a diary, we only see what the narrator wants us to see, and we must make judgments on what we are told based upon our understanding of X-127's openness and truthfulness.

We are first told the story of Operation Level Seven Down, through which the narrator and his compatriots are brought to Level Seven. In this prologue to the diary we begin to discover things about X-127. He is presented as the epitome of the military mentality — he accepts orders without question, adapts quickly to routine, and is fiercely proud of his position and his country. We are also introduced to his phobia — fear of darkness, or, more particularly, fear of the loss of the sun.

As X-127 learns more about his environment, so does the reader. We first are told about his duties in the PBX Operations Room. This room contains two sets of buttons that must be pushed simultaneously (to prevent one man from ending the world on a whim) and a large wall map that shows the target area and lights up in various colors as the missiles are launched. Since the room must be staffed twenty-four hours a day, there are three other PBX officers: X-107, X-117, and X-137. Their push-buttons control four types of weapons, including the dreaded "rigged" bombs that supposedly will render the entire surface of the earth uninhabitable for centuries.

The narrator soon discovers some of the technical features of Level Seven, among them the dependence of the Level on an atomic reactor for electrical power. Another feature of the environment — the huge deep-freeze that stores enough dehydrated food for five hundred people for five hundred years — serves as the point of departure for one of Roshwald's excursions into psychology. It seems that as the food is consumed, the space that it took in the deep-freeze is filled by collected sewage, separated from the remaining food by a moving wall. X-127 has a dream in which he is about to drown in sewage. This dream, coupled with his distress over never seeing the sun, clearly foreshadows his eventual breakdown.

At about this time a series of "Know Thy Level" talks is attended and reported on by the narrator. A great many details designed to lend environmental verisimilitude to the narrative are presented. Communications, identification, diet, sex, and marriage are discussed, among others. The results of this planned ecology, according to Level Seven's resident philosopher, Ph-107, are total freedom, total democracy, and the best of all possible worlds. And yet X-127 keeps having bad dreams.

Nor is he the only inhabitant of Level Seven to have psychological difficulties. His comrade-in-push-buttons, X-117, is abnormally attached to his mother, and Roshwald attempts to impress upon the reader the seriousness of X-117's condition by using terms like "repression," "Oedipus complex," and "hysteria." The character is hospitalized, drugged, psychoanalyzed (brainwashed), and returned to duty apparently cured but lethargic. We are given the details of X-117's treatment by virtue of X-127's relationship with P (for psychologist)-867, one of the more important secondary characters. The narrator describes P-867 as abrasive, clinging, overbearing, jealous, and insecure, and then marries her. The fact that she is a psychologist is significant, for it gives the narrator (and through him, the reader) additional insights into himself and those around him. Unfortunately, these insights are mostly superficial and lose impact because Roshwald tells us about them instead of showing us the characters in action.

Other details of X-127's world are revealed when he attends a series of "Know Other Levels" talks. We discover that a nationwide system of fallout shelters has been planned and partially constructed, and each Level has had a portion of the population assigned to it. Level Six is the military defensive arm, located directly above Level Seven and so somewhat less secure. Levels Five, Four, and Three exist in various locations across the country and are reserved for civilian VIP's. Finally, Levels Two and One are for the general population, but these levels are so close to the surface and contain provisions for such a short period of time that their inhabitants are not expected to survive even a limited nuclear exchange.

The narrator becomes involved with the work of a female colleague, R (for reserve)-747, who will be a teacher when future Level Seven children reach school age. She is preparing teaching materials, and X-127 assists in the creation of a new mythology. The stories presented in the diary are further examples of Roshwald's awkward handling of psychology and philosophy, but they do serve the expository function of advancing the narrator's mental deterioration. R-747 is perhaps the most sympathetic character presented, and a much more likely candidate for X-127's affections. The fact that he marries P-867 instead is, as he says himself, an indication of his inability to love anyone, which was probably one of the reasons he was selected for Level Seven in the first place.

With all of the necessary exposition out of the way, with the characters delineated, and with the situation nicely complicated, there is but one more necessary complication before the climax of the novel: the narrator's carefully foreshadowed mental breakdown. This is one of the key episodes of the plot, but unfortunately, the author's chosen form of a diary keeps the reader from any direct experience of it. There is simply a week-long gap between entries, and the narrator tells us that he had been in the psychology department receiving "therapy" for that time. He was given drugs, electric shock, and other treatments, and is now, he assures us, able to function normally. To be sure, there is a great void in the center of his being, but he is now capable of fulfilling his duty as (apparently) is X-117. The dehumanization required to push the buttons has been accomplished.

The climax of the novel, the long-expected atomic war, follows immediately. Appropriately, the buttons are pushed by the rehabilitated X-127 and X-117 — all, that is, except the buttons controlling the "rigged" bombs. When ordered to push the buttons launching these, X-117 suffers a relapse and refuses to obey, since these bombs will not only destroy the enemy but will also kill his mother. He is replaced by another PBX officer, and the buttons are pushed. The narrator, having completed his life's work, returns to his room and falls asleep, despite having just pushed the buttons that seal the doom of the world's population.

Naturally, in what has become a cliché in atomic holocaust fiction, it comes out that the war started by accident and was escalated automatically. Both sides used all of their weapons and the entire war took only two hours and fifty-eight minutes. The only life left on earth resides in the fallout shelters of both sides — and not even all of these survive. Level One is immediately destroyed, and most of Level Two along with it. There are also some survivors in the shelters of the neutral countries, but of the more than three billion people on earth before the war, only about fifteen million survive, condemned to live in caves.

The denouement of the novel traces the inevitable deaths of the remainder of humanity. First of all, X-117, having betrayed his mother in particular and humanity in general, hangs himself. With the demise of the only button-pusher with a conscience, Roshwald goes about the dreary business of killing off mankind step by step. The only necessary preliminary is the completion of the narrator's isolation, which is accomplished when P-867 divorces him for another PBX officer. Then the neutrals and those in Level Two die, followed in fairly short order by the VIP's on Levels Three, Four, and Five. Soon the population of the world is composed of the approximately five thousand souls in Levels Six and Seven of the two opposing armies. With the politicians gone, a peace treaty (of a sort) is agreed to, and (perhaps for the first time in history) humanity is united in a common cause: survival.

But, for some undetermined reason, Level Six ceases to broadcast; all its inhabitants are apparently dead. Next the enemy suffers a similar fate. The 499 people left on Level Seven are the last of humanity. They die too, of course, in a bit of overworked irony that was nonetheless carefully prepared for: their life-giving atomic reactor breaks down and poisons them all with radiation. As far as can be determined, X-127 dies last of all, leaving his pathetic diary as mankind's final testament and the only record of its ultimate folly.

Somewhat surprisingly, although not very subtly, Roshwald never identifies the narrator's country in his modern morality tale. Its description contains elements of both the United States and the Soviet Union, and certainly the people that inhabit Level Seven are universal types. And that, of course, is part of the problem. Roshwald presents generalized case histories rather than completely rounded individual characters, and he uses standard plot elements, clichés of language, and overly obvious philosophical and psychological principles as if they were new and fresh. On the whole, *Level Seven* suffers from the general malaise of much early science fiction: far too much emphasis on plot and not enough on character and style. It may be satisfying to a nondiscriminating twelve-year-old in his "Oh, wow!" stage, but an adult reader with critical faculties intact demands more.

David Stevens

Sources for Further Study

Reviews:

Atlantic. CCV, April, 1960, p. 112.

Nation. CXCI, November 19, 1960, p. 398.

New York Herald Tribune Book Review. March 6, 1960, p. 1.

New York Times Book Review. March 13, 1960, p. 34.

Saturday Review. XLIII, April 23, 1960, p. 23.

Spectator. October 2, 1959, p. 449.

Times Literary Supplement. October 16, 1959, p. 589.

LIEUT. GULLIVAR JONES: HIS VACATION

Author: Edwin L. Arnold (1857-1935)
First book publication: 1905
Type of work: Novel
Time: The early twentieth century
Locale: The Earth and Mars

A magic carpet transports Lt. Gullivar Jones to Mars where he applies his Yankee ingenuity to problems of love and war

> *Principal characters:*
> LIEUT. GULLIVAR JONES, the narrator, an American Naval Lieutenant
> AN, a Martian boy-girl who befriends Jones upon his arrival
> HATH, ineffectual king of the decadent "Hither Folk"
> HERU, daughter of Hath
> AR-HAP, ruler of the virile "Thither Folk"

Although *Lieut. Gullivar Jones: His Vacation* did not achieve the relative success of Arnold's other two fantasies — *Phra the Phoenician* (1891) and *Lepidus the Centurion* (1901) — it has an undeniable poetic charm. Permeated by a twilight, romantic mood, the novel is especially notable for its poetic prose, which creates a rich vision of Mars as a forlorn fairyland.

The plot is conventional and certainly not complex. American Navy Lieutenant Jones, stationed in New York, is frustrated and unhappy because the pay of his junior rank is insufficient to enable him to marry the girl of his choice. On his way to his quarters one stormy night, he finds a carpet on the street which he takes with him. Unrolling it in his room, he capriciously wishes himself upon the planet Mars. The rug, which is, indeed, a Magic Carpet, immediately transports him there.

Befriended upon his arrival by An, a boy-girl Martian, he discovers that Mars is inhabited by two races, the Hither Folk, among whom he finds himself, and the Thither Folk, who are a constant menace to the former. The Hither Folk, dwelling in semi-ruins which attest to their former greatness, have degenerated into a pleasure-loving, languid people who no longer have the will to fight for their survival. The Thither Folk are strong, ruthless, and obviously on the ascendancy.

Saving the life of the Princess Heru, the daughter of the Hither Folks' King Hath (truly an Emperor of the Dusk), Jones is royally welcomed to the King's palace. There he is chosen by the princess to be her husband.

All goes well for a time, but Ar-Hap, the ruler of the Thither Folk, demands a yearly tribute of a lovely girl, and Heru is chosen for the dubious honor. Before Jones can prevent it, Heru is taken aboard the barbarian's ship, which sails away. Needless to say, Jones sets out to recover her, and in doing so traverses a haunted land full of monsters, both plant and animal. In passing, the author's description of Jones's odyssey creates an atmosphere of mystery and dark horror which is most memorable. In miniature, parts of it are reminiscent of William Hope Hodgson's *The Night Land*, in which another protagonist ventures into a nighted Unknown wherein exist all the horrors that crouch in the human id.

Jones succeeds in rescuing Heru, but to no ultimate avail. The enraged Ar-Hap and his minions descend upon the Hither Folk, destroying or enslaving them all, and it is only by utilizing his Magic Carpet that Jones is able to escape with his life. Returning to Earth, Jones marries the girl he loves and, presumably, they both live happily ever after.

It is possible to trace some of the sources of Arnold's novel. In 1895 H. G. Wells published his first novel, *The Time Machine*, and undoubtedly Arnold read it. Hurtling through the years, the Time Traveller finds himself in a future world that in its way is as strange and exotic as Arnold's Mars; he befriends a girl, Weena, whom he saves from drowning, just as Jones saves Heru from a similar death.

The Time Traveller discovers that the world of 802,701, in which he finds himself, is inhabited by two races, the Eloi and the Morlocks. The Eloi are quite similar to Arnold's Hither Folk: their lives are devoted to languid pleasures, and they move as wraiths through a world over which they have no control; nor do they desire to attain control. The Morlocks, like the Thither Folk, consist of hideous barbarians who control not only the Eloi but also their world. In the end, the Time Traveller saves his life only by mounting his machine and throwing himself into another time period. Jones similarly escapes imminent death at the last minute by throwing himself upon the Magic Carpet and hurtling back to Earth. In both instances the protagonists are saved not by their own prowess but by means of a *deus ex machina*.

But if Arnold was influenced by Wells, it is almost certain that Arnold in turn influenced Edgar Rice Burroughs. This possibility has been perceptively noted by previous critics, and the evidence to support their contention is easily adduced. Readers of Burroughs' Martian series of novels, especially the first, *A Princess of Mars* (1917), and the second, *The Gods of Mars* (1918), will recognize much of the same nocturnal romanticism in them as is to be found in Arnold's novel. In both Arnold's and Burroughs' works there are perilous quests through monster-haunted lands, darkly littered with great, gothic ruins, remnants of perished civilizations. Night is truly the stuff of romantic poetry, and in both authors' books night falls early and stays late.

There is also an element of magic and mysticism in the ways both protagonists are transported from Earth to Mars. Captain John Carter, in danger of losing his life to besieging Indians, sees Mars in the heavens above him, stretches out his arms, and wishes himself there. Almost instantaneously, he arrives — or rather his "double" does — on the faraway planet. Lieutenant Jones, equally desirous of leaving the Earth — "Oh, I wish I were anywhere but here, anywhere out of this red-tape-ridden world of ours, I wish I were on the planet Mars!" — is immediately transported by the Magic Carpet to the destination of his wish. Once upon Mars, both interplanetary voyagers marry royal personages: Jones the Princess Heru of the Hither Folk, Carter the Princess Deja Thoris of Barsoom.

Finally, another parallel between Arnold's and Burroughs' Martian books is to be found in the similar ways in which Martians in the different works dispose of their dead. Arnold's Martians have for thousands of years sent their loved ones down the River of the Dead, and Jones observes countless numbers of them — "like cherries in jelly" — frozen in the ice. The descriptions of these dead, some floating past Jones's canoe on the River of the Dead, and others frozen in the perpetual ice, are extremely effective gothic scenes. John Carter makes a similar voyage down another river of the dead, Iss, upon which the Barsoomians, when death is approaching, consign themselves in expectation of a heaven at the end of the journey. Here Burroughs differs from Arnold in that the Barsoomians arrive neither in a Martian Elysium, nor in a frozen state of arrested expectations, but rather in the clutches of a horrid people who either enslave the luckless heaven-seekers or feed them to Plant Men.

It is an undeniable truism that fiction often tells — though at times inadvertently — as much about the social milieu of the author as it does about the fictional places and people it depicts. Arnold's novel is no exception to this observation; as an Englishman writing about an American hero, Arnold reflects all the stereotypes about Americans that were current in his time. For example, Americans were thought by the British to be rather comic characters, given to inflated, circumlocutory speech and impulsive and sometimes bullying actions; they were also believed to lack an awareness of the social amenities.

Thus, Jones is depicted as a man of direct action, often seemingly unaware of the ultimate consequences of his acts. As an example, his rescue of Heru from the barbarian king, Ar-Hap, predictably leads to the destruction of Heru's people. In other situations, he attacks abruptly when challenged, and when he addresses a question to someone, as when he asks An whether he/she is male or female, he does it bluntly, in a kind of ornate frontier diction.

Nor does Arnold hesitate to express the English feelings about American territorial demands, or about the American justification for such expansion embodied in the Monroe Doctrine. Discovering an unclaimed expanse of Martian land, Jones immediately claims it for the United States. When a Martian questions his right to do so, Jones cites the Munroe (sic) Doctrine:

> "What is the 'Munroe Doctrine'? asked my intelligent savage.
> "Oh, it is simple enough, and put into plain language means you must not touch anything that is mine, but ought to let me share anything you have of your own."

The above and a few other satiric touches permit Arnold to at least nod in the direction of Swift, who similarly utilized "science fiction" to satirize peoples and professions in his *Gulliver's Travels* (1726). Though Arnold spells it "Gullivar," there can be no doubt that he had Swift in mind when he chose his title and the name of his main character. In passing, it should be noted in addition, that the word "Gulliver" has two other connotations: a "Gulliver" is a teller of highly improbable and often impossible stories, and/or one who uses such fiction to satirize the real world. In *Lieut. Gullivar Jones*, one finds both.

Although one should not belabor a pleasant piece of fiction, it is tempting to note another obvious satiric commentary in the novel. In the character, aspirations, and fate of An, Arnold satirized the suffragette movement of his time in terms that some would still find relevant today. An was once a woman, but she aspired to be a man. The penalty for this audacious attempt was her relegation to the status of nonsex.

There is more than meets the casual eye in *Lieut. Gullivar Jones*. Arnold's novel deserves high standing as both an extremely entertaining yet poetic novel, and a valuable contribution to social history.

Frederick Shroyer

THE LIFTED VEIL

Author: George Eliot (1819-1880)
First book publication: 1859
Type of work: Novel
Time: 1850
Locale: England

> *George Eliot's characteristic themes appear in an uncharacteristic tale of the paranormal*

Principal characters:
LATIMER, the narrator
BERTHA, his wife
MRS. ARCHER, Bertha's maid
CHARLES MEUNIER, Latimer's schoolfriend, now a famous physician

Readers of *Silas Marner*, *The Mill on the Floss*, and *Middlemarch* are often surprised to find among George Eliot's collected works what the author called her "slight story of an outré kind." *The Lifted Veil* certainly will seem *outré* to those who have come to expect Eliot's usual careful analysis of true-to-life characters in an everyday world. It is not uncharacteristic, however, if one looks beneath the gothic trappings: the treatment may be different, but the ideas are the same as those found in her major fiction. And it certainly will not seem unusual to science fiction readers accustomed to speculations about the unknown being used as a vehicle for exploring truths about the life we know.

Ostensibly *The Lifted Veil* is about extrasensory perception. However, it is actually about perception in general: how we learn about the world, how we understand other people, and how feeling is related to thinking. Underlying these themes is George Eliot's conception of the self as it relates to the world; the perceiving subject as a factor in what is perceived; "vision" as a creative force. George Eliot frequently used vision as a metaphor for knowledge. In *The Lifted Veil*, three kinds of vision play a part, and all can be related to knowledge. There is physical vision, which is sense perception; there is the clairvoyant's otherworldly vision of the future; and there is the creative vision which the statesman, scientist, or artist tries to achieve.

Sense perception, according to the positivists, is the only way to reach knowledge; they believe people can know nothing except what comes through the senses. The clairvoyant's vision, on the other hand, is knowledge which is not acquired through sense perception and thus theoretically cannot exist. George Eliot shows this type of knowledge as unnatural, inhuman, and horrible. The third kind of vision is a way of putting together apparently unrelated data into a cohesive whole. It differs from the first two in that instead of being the passive reception of what already exists, it creates something new.

Latimer, the narrator of *The Lifted Veil*, began as an ordinary little boy, but an illness in early childhood temporarily blinded him, leaving him fragile and unusually sensitive. His sensitivity was the kind that turned inward; he did not relate well to other people. In an attempt to counteract what was considered an overly "poetic" tendency, he was given a scientific education, but he never really developed an interest in the empirical world. Instead, he developed two kinds of extrasensory perception: he had "visions," both of what would happen in the future, and of what went on in other people's minds. These visions were unrewarding and depressing.

In the story, Latimer falls in love with and marries Bertha, the only person whose mind he cannot read. When her maid, Mrs. Archer, develops a fatal case of peritonitis, a famous physician daringly attempts a blood transfusion. (The possibility of blood transfusions was known as early at 1654, but it was not considered feasible in the nineteenth century and did not come into general therapeutic use until World War I.) It is revealed that Bertha had planned to murder Latimer, and the story ends with him living alone, awaiting death from a heart attack which he has foreseen in all its circumstances.

Three characteristic Eliot themes appear in this uncharacteristic story: the emphasis on the natural world, on human fellowship, and on the necessity for self-awareness as a basis both for fellowship and creativity.

Latimer's "visions" of the future and other minds are especially significant in the work of a writer who is famous for her insistence that knowledge can be based only on observation of the everyday world. Latimer's knowledge, both of the future and of other people, is not rooted in normal human experience; it came to him from a magical outside source. Vision such as telepathy and the ability to see into the future does not fit into Eliot's empirical framework, and she emphasizes that Latimer's vision is "unnatural." It is not a healthy vision, as witnessed by its origin in an illness. By postulating the existence of "second-sight" and showing it to be horrible, Eliot implies that no good can come of vision which is not based on normal human experience. Thus, the "unnatural" experiment with blood transfusion is given a grotesque side by Eliot, and unpleasant and destructive consequences arise from the strange relationship shared by Bertha and Mrs. Archer.

Whatever it was that "had been breeding about two unloving women's hearts" was far from Eliot's ideal of "fellow-feeling" or human sympathy. For Eliot, sympathetic understanding of others is the mark of a truly developed human being. Such understanding results from experience and from the ability to recognize the effects of similar experiences in others. A person with "fellow-feeling" does not merely understand what another person is going through — he is able to experience it himself. Nevertheless, it is not a mystical merging of oneself with others; it is a reaching out toward others. Latimer was grotesque because his abnormal vision prevented him from reaching out in the normal human way. His visions into other consciousnesses turned him against people, rather than making him sympathize with them. Early in his marriage when he finally does see into Bertha's mind, he ceases to love her because he is appalled by her prosaic, mean thoughts. Latimer was able to understand what others were thinking and feeling, but he had no sympathy with them. That is because he brought nothing of himself to his understanding. His knowledge of others, like his knowledge of future events, was not the result of experience and analytical ability, but was imposed upon him from a magical outside source. It was not a useful kind of knowledge. It impinged on him in a jumble, confusing him almost to distraction. Similarly, despite a clairvoyant vision of a horrible future with Bertha, he does nothing to avoid the marriage.

Had Latimer been an active seeker of knowledge rather than a passive recipient, things would have been different for him. Eliot believed that one should be involved and participate in life, in order to understand life fully. Intellectual knowledge can be imposed from without, but the knowledge of the heart is instinctive, and comes from within. Latimer's understanding of others, like his understanding of the future, was not related to anything within himself. Like the science he was forced to learn, it was imposed upon him; it was not an organic part of his being. Thus, it resulted not in sympathy, but in aversion; his was only partial knowledge, since it was all mental and lacked an emotional dimension. It is his onesided awareness, which leads to his tendency to withdraw from others, that ultimately kills him.

A third kind of vision which interested Eliot in *The Lifted Veil* is creative vision. There is a relationship between the visionary and the clairvoyant, but there is also a difference. Visionaries see possibilities in the future which can be acted upon, while clairvoyants merely see what will happen. Latimer understands very well that he and Bertha will come to hate each other; he is simply unable to do anything about it. A clairvoyant produces nothing new, but a creative visionary can reshape the world.

Latimer has the "poet's sensibility without his voice," and he is called "ineffectual." At first he hoped his visions of the future were manifestations of his poetic nature, but he soon realizes that he cannot call up his visions at will or control them in any way. Poets, like other artists, must create — poetic sensibility is not enough; as Dorothea points out in *Middlemarch*, a poet is not a poet until he produces a poem. Latimer's lack of a poetic "voice" demonstrates his inability to put his vision to use. He can see into the future and he can see into other people's minds, but he is only a passive receptacle: his vision does not change anything. Creative vision requires not only a wide range of impressions, but also the ability to organize them into something productive.

In order to affect the world, one must impose oneself on the world, using one's abilities to focus, analyze, and integrate. A passive recipient of predigested information does not do this. Thus, Latimer is ineffective: the world impinges upon him, but he does not, in turn, impinge himself upon the world. Partly this is because he is not aware of his own powers as a person. He lacks the integrated sense of self which serves as a focus for arranging disconnected facts into a meaningful whole. He has no unifying point of view that might organize his consciousness of other minds into more than annoyance. His knowledge of the future leads to nothing because he is unable to connect his present feelings with what he knows will be his future feelings. Despite a clear knowledge that the future which he desires is horrible, he continues to desire it because he is unable to subdue his present emotions. Because he has no sense of self, he eventually loses his "vision" and can contemplate nothing but his own death.

George Eliot was probably not aware that she was writing science fiction, but there is no question that she was interested in phrenology, spirit communication, mesmerism, and other parascientific questions of her day, and that she was aware of the possibilities of future scientific advancements such as blood transfusions. If one kind of science fiction is the exploration of the implications of new developments in science, *The Lifted Veil* is certainly within the genre. George Eliot believed, however, that the only possible kind of knowledge is that which comes from normal human experience, and that the best kind of knowledge is that which results from reaching out and experiencing with other people. Knowledge, to be meaningful, must be part of oneself. Understanding of others must not be clinical, but internalized. For her, clairvoyance and telepathy, even if possible were not desirable.

Barbara Berman Seidenfeld

THE LIGHTS IN THE SKY ARE STARS

Author: Fredric Brown (1906-1972)
First book publication: 1953
Type of work: Novel
Time: The early twenty-first century
Locale: The United States

> *Max Andrews fights politicians, bureaucrats, and conservationists to ensure the success of a flight to Jupiter, which will mark the re-opening of the United States Space Program*

> *Principal characters:*
> MAX ANDREWS, the ex-astronaut who vies for the directorship of the Jupiter project
> ELLEN GALLAGHER, a senator and Max's lover
> CHANG M'BASSI, Max's friend, an African tribesman, and a mystic and scientist

The Lights in the Sky Are Stars, Fredric Brown's second science fiction novel, is probably his most ambitious and perhaps his least successful work in that field. It attempts something that none of his other works does: to present itself as something other than a science fiction novel. Brown's intention in this novel seems to be to write a realistic story whose characters and locations are at least tangentially familiar to a 1950's audience but whose action is set far enough into the future, to allow the author to analyze certain social, political, and cultural trends that have excited his interest — and aroused his ire. In short, *The Lights in the Sky Are Stars* offers political intrigue and political allegory, love, adventure, and individual catharsis. Yet, while it does not lack the broad imaginative drive of, say *What Mad Universe* or *Martians Go Home*, it does lack their broad good humor; and it offers nothing in humor's stead. The result is a novel that is flat and uncharacteristic, interesting more for what it attempts than for what it accomplishes.

Its protagonist, rocket mechanic and former astronaut trainee Max Andrews, is nearly sixty, and has lost part of a leg to the United States space program. He is almost frantically aware that in order to be involved with space exploration now he must first obtain sufficient political clout to get himself appointed director of what is to be called the Jupiter Project. This projected NASA program, whose cost and feasibility at the novel's opening are being debated in Congress, would, if approved, include the design and launching of the first manned probe into Jupiter's satellite system. The story itself chronicles Max's rise nearly to that directorship, his disgrace, and, in an epilogue, his acceptance both of himself and of the minor role he has to play on earth. So at least in its outlined form the novel evinces the capability to interest, even to capture its readers. There is much that can be made of a hero-astronaut, especially if he is also a visionary. There is much, too, that can be made of the conflict between science's longing for new knowledge and Congress's concern for a balanced budget, especially when government's inevitable bureaucratic morass is placed squarely between the two.

Unfortunately, Max Andrews is never a convincing character, and he does not tell a story half as well as Fredric Brown is capable of telling it. Only once or twice, for example, does he begin to communicate any spark of that magnificent vision of the possibilities for man in space which must be at the core of his being if he is what he claims to be, and which must provide the drive for his obsession if he is to accomplish what he has set out to do. But Max never conveys that sense of necessity needed to account for the purposefulness with which he pursues his avowed mission. Max narrates like a world-weary cop, and the kind of stance he takes is incongruous with the story he is telling. He is simply never properly motivated for what he undertakes, and what motivation he has is never effectively dramatized.

As narrator, Max so dominates the novel that no other character introduced can properly be called a major one. Not even the woman whose election to the Senate he assures and who eventually becomes his lover is remembered with sufficient strength or animation to set her apart; at her death the reader feels nothing and wonders whether her chronicler, in spite of his stated emotions, feels anything either. Most of the other characters — bureaucrats, politicians, friends, family — who wander through the narrative seem almost interchangeable. Admittedly, it is Brown's intention to create one character so driven and so self-centered that all those around him are in fact secondary and indistinct in his brain, existing only as foils to, or supporters of, his own activities. But if the narrator can be excused on such grounds for slipshod characterization, the author cannot be, especially in a novel which is finally not about things or events but about people. In such a book, faces must be sufficiently distinct and personalities sufficiently complete that a reader is capable of caring about the people they represent.

There is one character whom Max seems to want to treat as something more than a foil for his ego, but, because of the ambiguous nature of his relationship with Max and the vagueness of his connection to the plot, he is never truly made substantive or believable. This character is Chang M'bassi, an African tribesman, mystic, and M.I.T. graduate who in 1998 is tutoring Max in the abstract mathematics of unified field theory. Max and M'bassi become great friends during the next two years, but little information is given to establish the grounds of that friendship and even less to account for its continuance. The reader learns that M'bassi advocates an alternate path to the stars from the mechanical one Max is concerned with, and that M'bassi's way involves asceticism and hallucinogenic drugs. Yet, oddly enough, there is no real conflict established between the two opposing philosophies, not even so much as a friendly debate over dinner might permit. As a result there is no dramatic power in the character of M'bassi, in spite of the fact that on several occasions Max claims a respect for him bordering on awe. M'bassi's experiments seem of such little consequence to the novel's real subject that the outpouring of anguish Max suffers upon discovering him dead of a drug overdose appears unwarranted and, indeed, overdone.

Certainly followers of Frederic Brown will not find this novel totally alien to his other works, either in structure or, especially, in style. The author's typically audacious plug for his own *What Mad Universe* (1949), which his narrator calls "one of the early science fiction novels" and credits for awakening his own interest in interstellar travel, is both refreshing and reassuring; it is shameless, vintage Brown. Even more outrageous, but also terribly enigmatic, are his naming of the novel's female lead, the California senator who owes her seat in Congress to Max, and his account of the circumstances of her election. Her name is Ellen Gallagher; and the similarity of it to Helen Gahagan, especially in the minds of an audience who would be reading the book just three years after the conclusion of that famous California senatorial race between Helen Gahagan Douglas and Richard Nixon, is obviously more than coincidental. Gallagher is visionary; her opponent, called Dwight Layton here, is corrupt. To ensure the election of the right person, Max simply breaks into Layton's office, steals enough evidence of bribery and graft to convict him, and releases the bundle to the press. The plan is effective, and of course it is both unethical and illegal. But just what Manichaean consequence or reversal Brown had in mind in suggesting that other campaign, while amusing enough to speculate about half a decade after its victor's resignation in disgrace from the White House, is not at all clear. It is unclear even whether Brown is making a private joke or some serious though obtuse political statement. Nevertheless, this enigma is perhaps the most arresting feature the novel has to offer readers almost a generation removed from its initial publication.

In reading *The Lights in the Sky Are Stars* some twenty-five years after its appearance, one finds oneself comparing Brown's "historical" conjectures about the 1960's and 1970's with the actualities of those years almost automatically; and one is surprised both at how accurately Brown has anticipated certain directions technological advancement has taken and at how far removed from reality others of his predictions have fallen. His accounts of the Air Force's astronaut training program, of the time and reasons for its inception, and of the fierce competition for admission into it are nearly clairvoyant — though he grossly underestimates the average age and rank of its first class. He misses the 1974 recession by only a year, and he names the early 1970's as the time women became a serious political force. In 1997 Concorde-type supersonic aircraft are finally gaining acceptability all over the world as a fast, efficient means of transportation; oddly it is rockets they are beginning to replace in the airways. Important personal communication is made by telegram or telephone because, despite rockets and special delivery, the mails are unreliable. There are a few nude beaches situated near Los Angeles. The movement of the Congress on vital issues is maddeningly slow. On the other hand,

Havana is a favorite resort town for vacationing Americans, and while a college education is not a rarity, neither is it required or assumed of most executive or management personnel in government and industry. NASA had put a man on the moon by 1964 and two on Mars by 1967. The entire Jupiter Project has been budgeted for twenty-seven million dollars and expects a surplus. Of course, there is really no point to these comparisons save that they deal with specific speculations that, of whatever historical accuracy, are often more interesting than the plot they give dimension to.

Brown's science fiction is usually audacious, outrageous, witty, and just serious enough to give real bite to its undercurrent of irony. Its protagonists are normally of less significance than are the often absurd and nearly always difficult situations in which they find themselves enmeshed; much of the fun in reading the story involves watching the characters triumph over strange adversities. But in this novel Brown tries something different: he concentrates his prose on one character and on that character's catharsis. The experiment is not really successful. The importance of *The Lights in the Sky Are Stars* lays not so much in what it contains as in the fact that it represents a false start in a direction Fredric Brown's fiction ultimately did not take.

Douglas J. McReynolds

LIMBO

Author: Bernard Wolfe (1915-   )
First book publication: 1952
Type of work: Novel
Time: 1990
Locale: A tropical island, the central United States, and points in between

An attempt, by its unwitting founder, to uncover and destroy the roots of a dystopian society which, in quest of pacifism, literally "disarms" its leaders, though only to emerge more malevolent than ever, driven by a single-minded technological imperative

Principal characters:
> UBU, a conservative, peace-loving Mandunji tribal elder
> DR. MARTINE, a refugee neurosurgeon from World War III, whose journal became the bible of the Vol-Amp (voluntary amputee) society
> OODA AND RAMBO, his well-balanced Mandunji wife and son
> IRENE AND OLD MRS. MARTINE, his unbalanced American wife and mother
> TOM, his American son, leader of the passive faction of the Vol-Amps
> THEO, an Olympian athlete, spokesman for the active Vol-Amp faction
> HELDER, President of the Inland Strip, a self-proclaimed disciple of Martine
> DON THURMAN, an ordinary American, ready to inherit a share of power

This is the story of an exile returning to find his old world transformed into a representation of his shadow self writ large. Self-exiled among the Mandunji for eighteen years. Dr. Martine is lured back into civilization by its intrusion on his peaceful island existence. Coming back in the guise of "Dr. Lazarus," a "parasitologist," he finds that what is left of the United States, its central portion called the Inland Strip, is acting out some satiric suggestions he had made in a journal left behind when he fled the wartime carnage of 1972. Shortly before deserting his military hospital post, Martine had jotted down notes about the only way to achieve a truly pacifist society: by literally "disarming" potential killers like his recent patient, the baby-faced Teddy Gorman (later known as Theo).

This "joke" was taken seriously by Martine's colleague, Helder, and by Theo, both of whom rose to power in the government and whose example was followed by pacifist elements in their Great Power rival, the "East Union." Although it takes Martine some time to realize what is going on, as soon as he realizes his unwitting complicity in this fiasco, he takes steps to correct the social imbalance. At the end, he and Theo escape to the Mandunji island, where a similar revolution, led by his son Rambo, is brewing in his absence.

Although it is full of action and great fun to read, the book is also formally and conceptually complex, and unremittingly analytical, both politically and psychologically. Not a prediction of 1990 social arrangements, it is rather a metaphorical exaggeration, or literalization, of a mental malaise, likely to afflict any people, but potentially more dangerous among the technologically sophisticated. Their tools are more deadly, and their dependence on technology blinds them to the nature of the tool designers and tool wielders, themselves. Voluntary amputation is no answer to the human dilemma; it is a symbol of the human dilemma, depending on technology to eliminate the need for responsibility. This central absurdity functions as the most important of many estranging devices that, combined with a thoroughly Modernist manner of narration, result in a vision of wholeness and balance that is both the form and substance of the novel. For *Limbo* does not simply cause anxiety about the uncontrollable, or appease it by appealing to contemplation of its art; it traces the trouble with society to the individual and suggests that recognition of the problem is at least the first necessary step toward its solution.

The story opens on the tropical island of the Mandunji, but conventional associations of pastoral simplicity quickly disappear. The Mandunji are scavengers of technological civilization, and equally prone to single-minded attempts to eradicate neurosis rather than live with it. Unable to convince the elders that their "normality" is self-destructive, Martine has at least brought modern medical technique to the aid of their ancient practice of lobotomy. Though he has trained the young in the ways of science, he has failed to live up to his own ideas when the arrival of the "queer-limbs," Americans fitted with advanced prosthetic devices, jars him out of his role as an incomplete Prospero. He is forced back into the real world, into his past, into himself.

The scene shifts to the dystropian state of the distorted American future, as Martine wanders through it, more personally interested and self-analytical than the traditional stranger in a strange land of Utopian fiction. He finds improvements in technology but regressions in human rights; the model cities, with their automated factories and transportation, serve a white, male, middle class leadership. Monuments stand to the memory of the "martyr," Martine; his old home is a shrine, his old journal a sacred book humorlessly annotated by Helder, his witticisms turned into propaganda slogans. Opposing political parties are for and against prosthetics, both claiming Martine's inheritance, their antimachine slogans betrayed by their increasingly machinelike condition.

As Martine seeks to understand this particular version of the Utopian heresy, Wolfe draws on various analytic sources. For example, there are William James, Alfred Korzybski, Norbert Wiener, John von Neumann, but especially the neo-Freudian psychologist Edmund Bergler, whose doctrines Martine comes to espouse in his 1990 journal. Wolfe recognizes, as Plato did in the *Republic*, that the core of the Utopian society lies in the psyche; moreover, he explores it at a deeper level than the classic dystopians, spotlighting the irrational desire of the unconscious for perfect order in whatever form.

Where Socrates sought an analogy for the well balanced individual in the well ordered state, both citizen and state exhibiting the principle of "just" proportions, Wolfe uses the absurd order of his state to probe the imbalance of the individual. Following his mentor, Bergler, Wolfe locates the cause of the problem in childhood, where desires for immediate gratification are inseparably linked with a longing to be punished. This psychic masochism is equated in *Limbo* with the denial of "ambivalence," attempting not simply to legislate good, but to eradicate evil by any technological means possible.

Salvation for the individual lies in a maxim quoted in the 1972 journal and attributed to the French Symbolist poet, Rimbaud, after whom Martine named his Mandunji son. "Don't be a victim," Martine tells himself, trying to live up to this injunction and prevent World War IV. The Olympic Games, now a test of both skill and technology as athletes compete on prostheses that improve their performance, erupt into a pitched battle precipitated by the East Union, and President Helder is on the verge of massive retaliation. Rejecting such "pseudoaggression," Martine acts decisively to destroy the diseased offspring of his loins (Tom) and of his mind (Helder), performing a *social* lobotomy by removing the heads of both political parties of the Inland Strip, leaving the "enemy" to take care of its own.

Having initiated Theo into the realities of politics, Martine leaves with him for the Mandunji island, after meeting the capable Don Thurman, who represents the potential for good of "real" Americans temporarily submerged in Helder's pseudopacifist society. *En route*, Martine discards his 1990 journal rather than risk another set of disciples, though the novel of course preserves the jettisoned journal and embodies its call for laughter as a genuine attack on the absurdities of 1950's society.

Martine's act of disregarding his own advice, however, resonates throughout the novel. From the epigrams that first suggest the Dantesque grotesqueries on which the title puns, to the five pages of "Author's Notes and Warnings" appended to tell the reader how to read, Wolfe continually challenges his audience. He forces the reader to examine his expectations, countered by the complexity of the noble savage, the postlapsarian nature of the tropical paradise, the dubious rewards of technological progress, the limitations of militant pacifism, and the guilt of the conventionally innocent outside observer. He turns lectures into sideshows; violates the cerebral Utopian narrative with melodrama, itself subject to ironic scrutiny; and makes problematic the putative overthrow of a dystopian hegemony. He takes the narrative climax offstage, into a subjective experience that Martine relates after the fact in a "throwaway" journal. Along the way, he parodies the medical novel, the sports yarn, the espionage tale, the war story, the psychiatric case study, the "exile's return" and the legend of the white man "gone native."

Structurally, *Limbo* wraps this all up in a marvelously complicated package, some distance removed from the conventions of Utopian, dystopian, and science fiction adventure writing. In his hodgepodge of *genres*, Wolfe employs a variety of modes: essay, journal, dramatic sketch, lecture, dream, internal monologue, and relatively straightforward narrative. He uses formal counterpoint, ironic juxtaposition, leitmotifs, fragmentation, radiating symbol clusters, and a two-leveled time sequence. Except for the shifts in time required by the journals, the narrative of Martine's adventures in 1990 takes place in chronological order. Flashes of misunderstood insight, encounters with strangely familiar ideas, and gut-level introspection, however, lead us backward in time into his past and that of the dystopian state. The discontinuity is much more radical than that of other dystopias, even of the most technically sophisticated science fiction of the next quarter century; in the best Modernist fashion, it leads us simultaneously toward estrangement and recognition.

That it does so is due in no small part to the character of Martine, who surpasses Zamyatin's D-502, Huxley's John Savage, and Orwell's Winston Smith, if not in reader identification, at least in complexity and sophistication. Like them, he is a disturbed and disturbing witness of the Utopia's flaws. But he is much more than that. Martine is also the unintentional founder of this world that mirrors him as much as it, in turn, is reflected in his observations. Unlike his predecessors, moreover, he has a clearly delineated social and familial past and present, although he is so dominant that there is no room for an independent antagonist. All the other major characters are largely fragments of Martine, as he explicitly states at one point, referring to Theo and Helder, each of whom is half the man that he is. Whereas the classical dystopian heroes lose their newly found individuality and difference, welcoming oblivion in some form, Martine takes positive action to upset the Utopia's image of its own perfection. To their tragic modes, Wolfe opposes the comic, in keeping with American upbeat endings, with his own practice in other novels, and with his answer to dystopian despair.

Martine has still another advantage: he is the all but explicit voice of his author, since both have created this dystopian world. Martine's first person journal, his dreams, his internal monologues, his dialogue and his mutterings all entwine his style with the voice of the narrator. Erudite, sardonic, given to doodles, flights of fancy, and a seldom interrupted stream of puns, this voice succeeds in distancing emotional considerations to the extent that occasional breakthroughs of symbolically loaded materials from the "unconscious" are that much more arresting and effective. This voice maintains continuity, establishes coherence, and achieves wholeness for the entire book.

As a calculated act of therapy, *Limbo* may work best in terms of artistic balance. The long string of hyphenated false oppositions that Wolfe-Martine dredges up during the story (gangster-babyface, dog-god, no-yes, infant-adult, war-peace, and so forth) Martine views as "Siamese twins," more properly products of addition than of subtraction (that is, amputation and lobotomy). Similarly, utopia-dystopia, primitive-civilized, male-female, Martine-Inland Strip, Martine-Mandunji, and Martine-Wolfe are legitimate cases of "both-

and" rather than "either-or" relationships. Martine equates recognition of this fact with laughter, aesthetics, and sex (the latter involving that "slim hyphen" between man and woman). All three are diminished or distorted by lobotomy and disarmament; they can flourish only where ambivalence is celebrated or at least accepted.

The therapy may not have worked for the author, whose string of novels since *Limbo* continued, perhaps obsessively, to belabor Berglerian analysis, but failed to win much of an audience. Nor has the therapy been very effective in making post-1952 society laugh more at its own absurdities or show more awareness of its ambivalent nature, for all the claims of the Human Potential Movement. The novel's acceptance in science fiction circles is marginal, having been reviewed at arm's length, reissued only twice in paperback since its original publication, and frequently ignored in historical studies of the field. But if its direct influence is questionable, it is still noteworthy as a harbinger of more stylish, sexy, complex applications of science fiction formulas to come. On its literary merits, moreover, *Limbo* is one of the best American dystopias ever written, fully comparable with *We*, *Brave New World*, and *Nineteen Eighty-Four*.

David N. Samuelson

Sources for Further Study

Reviews:

Analog. LII, January, 1954, pp. 149-150.

Chicago Sunday Tribune. December 21, 1952, p. 4.

Commonweal. LVII, December 26, 1952, p. 311.

Galaxy. VI, May, 1953, pp. 120-121.

Kirkus Reviews. XX, August 15, 1952, p. 519.

New York Herald Tribune Book Review. December 14, 1952, p. 11.

New York Times. November 30, 1952, p. 46.

Saturday Review. XXV, November 29, 1952, p. 17.

Startling Stories. XXX, May, 1953, pp. 145-146.

THE LISTENERS

Author: James E. Gunn (1923-   )
First book publication: 1972
Type of work: Novel
Time: 2025-2118
Locale: Puerto Rico

A study of communication between humans and aliens, husbands and wives, fathers and sons, writers and readers, and individuals and themselves

> *Principal characters:*
> ROBERT MACDONALD, the director of The Project
> MARIA MACDONALD, his wife
> ROBERT MACDONALD, JR., their son
> GEORGE THOMAS, writer and public relations chief for The Project
> WILLIAM MITCHELL, a staff member of the public-relations sections
> ANDREW WHITE, President of the United States
> JOHN WHITE, his son
> THE COMPUTER

Within the last few decades there has been a vast amount of speculation as to whether man will ever be able to prove the existence of alien races with civilizations equal to or greater than human civilization. James E. Gunn's *The Listeners* is a fictional history of a project dedicated to finding such evidence. In six chapters, *The Listeners* presents The Project from just before a message is received from Capella, a planet of double stars, to the final message from that same planet ninety-three years later. In tracing the history of the project, the author explores a wide variety of attitudes toward the possibility of communication with aliens, and how that possibility affects communication between the human participants.

In the first chapter, "Robert MacDonald — 2025," the characters' reactions range from the patient confidence of Robert MacDonald, director of The Project, to the panicked fear of scientist Bob Adams, who believes that man may be alone in the Universe and considers such cosmic loneliness as the most frightening possibility of all.

In the fourth chapter, "Andrew White — 2028," the political implications of communicating with the aliens are explored as White, the black President of the United States, fears public reaction to the message that man is not alone. In particular, he fears that a superior alien race might turn communication with Earth to their own advantage.

Finally, in Chapter Six, "The Computer — 2118," the alien view is presented. For a brief moment the people of Capella, now long dead, are allowed to speak to the people of Earth to explain their own need for communication — a need which perhaps aeons from now man himself will have to acknowledge. What the listeners finally learn is that the message is the Capellans' last legacy: when their system could no longer support life, the Capellans themselves were doomed, but their message preserved their history, science, culture, technology, and philosophy.

The protagonist of the novel is Robert MacDonald, who holds The Project together by his genuine ability to listen to others. When the other characters speak to him, he understands the hopes, fears, triumphs, and defeats hidden beneath their statements, as well as the overt meaning of the words. It is this ability that enables MacDonald to hold The Project together during the early years when no message is received, to attract to The Project the right personnel for its future to be assured, and to handle each opponent of The Project.

It is, moreover, his ability to listen that makes Robert MacDonald such a sympathetic character, and makes the reader accept his point of view. If the reader triumphs in the reception of a message from Capella, it is because Robert MacDonald triumphs; if the reader defends the project from the political manipulation of Andrew White, it is because MacDonald does. And, if the reader sees along with Robert MacDonald, Jr., the shade of his father overlooking The Project in 2058, it is because MacDonald, Sr., deserves to know of the fruit of his labor. Gunn has created in MacDonald the perfect listener and the perfect guide. Certainly the Capellans could not have asked for more.

However, there is one situation in which MacDonald does not listen at all well. In the first chapter, he is faced with the growing frustration of his scientists and engineers as they face the fact that during its fifty-year existence, The Project has received no hint of a message, no evidence that the scientists are even on the right track. Thus, MacDonald is first presented in the role he performs best: listening to the problems of his fellow scientists and soothing their frustrations. Yet he fails to see the frustrations building in his wife, Maria, or at least he fails to see how significant they are.

Maria is torn between demanding more attention from MacDonald and keeping her needs bottled up so that he can continue to devote his time and energy to The Project. When she does ask for attention and goes so far as to take too many sleeping pills, MacDonald still does not accept the seriousness of her message and ignores her call for help. Thus, when Maria's frustrations and fears overcome her and she slashes her wrists, MacDonald is consumed with guilt. In the one situation where he has failed to listen, he almost loses the most important person in his life, the person he most needs to keep his own mental balance as he empathizes with all the other workers on The Project. While Maria does not die, the scars that remain on her wrists, which are referred to throughout the balance of the novel, graphically illustrate that even the best listener can fail.

Failure to communicate marks the theme of the second through fifth chapters as well. In each case the outcome is never as serious as in the first chapter, but the problem is evident. In the second and third chapters, "George Thomas — 2027" and "William Mitchell — 2028," the issue is one of communication between men who should be specialists in communicating with their audiences. George Thomas is a successful translator and novelist who is bitter over what he sees as the basic blindness of the human race. His bitterness has turned into a cynicism which prevents him from writing novels, since he distrusts words and sees them only as tools for self-advancement. A public relations specialist, Mitchell ironically has no tolerance for other points of view, and cannot even speak with the father of the girl he loves because the father's beliefs are beyond his patience.

In the fourth and fifth chapters, "Andrew White — 2028" and "Robert MacDonald — 2058," the issue is communication between a parent and child. Andrew White, a former black radical who has become President of the United States, wants his son, John, to understand the past history of the black movement and to distrust the present because of that past. John, on the other hand, wishes to ignore the past and accept the present in its own right. Communication between the two is blocked because neither will accept the other's point of reference. In the fifth chapter, moreover, Robert MacDonald, Jr., has the same sort of problem. Returning to Puerto Rico after the death of his father, he must finally come to terms with his own love and hate for his famous father; blaming him for his mother's loneliness and death, Robert has not communicated with his father for fifteen years.

In each character's life, the message from Capella plays an important role. George Thomas is awed by the urgent need that the Capellans must have felt to devise a system to communicate in the first place. William Mitchell learns that, as significant as the Capellan message is, it can have different meanings for different people. Andrew and John White learn that the significance of communication lies in the future understanding it might make possible, regardless of the different personalities and backgrounds of the individuals involved. And, finally, Robert MacDonald, Jr., learns what a legacy of love his father has left him and what an act of love that legacy is. Robert can come to terms with himself because he ultimately realizes how much his father loved him and how that love is expressed through The Project.

Chapter Six contemplates the idea of communication between humans and aliens. While the humans will receive much from the Capellans, continued communication with them is impossible since Capellan civilization was destroyed long ago. In spite of the final sentence of *The Listeners*, in which the reader is told that the next alien message will come from the Crab Nebula, believed to have been formed by a supernova explosion in the year A.D. 1054, the author's message seems to be that man's most important communication must be with himself.

Stephen H. Goldman

Sources for Further Study

Reviews:

Analog. XCI, May, 1973, pp. 171-172.

Booklist. LXIX, March 1, 1973, p. 620.

Futures. V, August, 1973, p. 349.

Kirkus Reviews. XL, September 15, 1972, p. 1118.

Library Journal. XCVII, November 1, 1972, p. 3617.

Luna Monthly. XLIX, Autumn, 1973, p. 30.

Magazine of Fantasy and Science Fiction. XLV, July, 1973, pp. 69-70.

New York Times Book Review. April 22, 1973, p. 16.

Publisher's Weekly. CCII, October 2, 1972, p. 54.

Renaissance. V, Spring, 1973, p. 15.

LITTLE FUZZY

Author: H. Beam Piper (1904-1967)
First book publication: 1962
Type of work: Novel
Time: The future
Locale: Zarathustra Planet

The discovery of a lovable, cuddly creature on a resource-rich planet initiates an understanding both of sapience and humanity

Principal characters:
JACK HOLLOWAY (PAPPY JACK), a sunstone prospector
VICTOR GREGO, director of the Zarathustra Company
LITTLE FUZZY, a native Zarathustran
MAMMA FUZZY AND BABY FUZZY, Little Fuzzy's immediate family
BEN RAINSFORD, a Naturalist
GERD VAN RIEBEEK, a Xeno-naturalist
RUTH ORTHERIS, a Xeno-psychologist
LEONARD KELLOGG, Chief of the Division of Scientific Study and Research, Zarathustra Company
ERNEST MALLIN, a Xeno-psychologist
GUS BRANNHARD, an Attorney
LESLIE COOMBS, an Attorney, Zarathustra Company
FREDERIC PENDARVIS, Chief Justice

When a reader meets a native of the planet Zarathustra, the experience is much like having a teddy bear walk into the living room. No wonder the corporation governing the planet in H. Beam Piper's *Little Fuzzy*, 1962, has such trouble taking the Fuzzies seriously. But Piper's main character, Jack Holloway, takes the Fuzzies very seriously, and his struggle to prove that they are sapient beings becomes the main plot of the novel. Fuzzies prove to be charming creatures, so charming that Piper continued their adventures with Holloway through a second novel, *The Other Human Race* (1964).

The setting and time of *Little Fuzzy* are both somewhat nebulous. Obviously, the time is far in the future because humans have colonized areas beyond our solar system and have met various types of sapient beings in the process. Zarathustra, however, is supposedly a planet without sapient natives, and so a corporation has been granted rights to the raw materials. As part of the novel, Piper shows his views of the American industrial complex extended through time into space, harvesting new planets for the profit of Earth. In his scenes describing the way in which the company has ruthlessly disrupted the planet's natural environment, Piper gives a short but eloquent comment on an industry's attitude toward an ecological balance. The only concern of the Zarathustra Company is profit, a profit derived from the efficient acquisition of natural resources.

One of the major resources of Zarathustra is a gemstone, the sunstone, which glows when warmed by a human body. The novel's hero, Jack Holloway, is a rugged, mature sunstone prospector. In Holloway, Piper has created a character who could be played by the older John Wayne: a loner known for his independence, his maverick ways, his quick draw, and his accurate aim. Though the machinery that Holloway uses in his mining is that of typical science fiction antigravity technology, the guns with which he protects his loved ones are a pistol and a 6 mm. rifle. A seasoned prospector, he puts in a hard day working his own stake and then comes home to his pipe and his evening drink, or two, or three. But he is also a man who appreciates nature, especially the beauty of the sunstones and the harmony of the environment, and he has a high regard for life itself.

To balance Holloway, the natural man, Piper develops the industrial executive Victor Grego, the director of the Zarathustra Company. Though Grego is not exactly a "bad" character, he is presented initially as an antagonistic force: the efficient executive bent on making a profit for both his company and himself. He wants expedient action but prefers to have other people responsible for any "dirty" work which might be involved. While Holloway lives by himself, simply, in a natural setting, Grego lives in an urban world of offices, technology, and cocktail parties. Holloway enjoys having money but only enough to supply his immediate pleasures, which are few, and to assure himself of some future security. Grego, on the other hand, is a character who wants money for the sake of power, as exemplified by the globe of Zarathustra he plays with in his office.

Around these two men Piper groups what will be the opposing forces in a power struggle over control of the planet. The charter held by the Zarathustra Company is valid only if the planet is uninhabited by a native population. When Holloway meets the Fuzzies, he quickly determines that the little furry, golden creatures with big, loving eyes are, indeed, sapient. Their sapience would void the Zarathustra Company's charter automatically, dissolving the company and eliminating Grego's power. The power of various corrupt political characters is also in danger because they are all company men. Thus the antagonistic forces which Holloway and his friends face are political as well as corporate. So the pro-Fuzzy people set out to document proof of the Fuzzies' sapience while the anti-Fuzzy people bring in their own experts to prove that Fuzzies are merely fur-bearing animals, perhaps even a future source of income through the sale of their pelts. The pro-Fuzzy scientists and sympathizers are ethical, careful people, but the anti-Fuzzy scientists are, once again, company controlled people whose ethics are determined by the needs of their employers rather than by a search for truth. Piper uses this group of negative authority figures to exemplify scientists who carry on experiments which will supply supporting evidence for predetermined conclusions. In the process of the two groups' searches for evidence, violence occurs in the form of two murders. The majority of the novel evolves from each group's effort to build its case for the impending murder trials.

The Fuzzies, who are the source of everyone's problems, are carefully introduced by Piper. When Holloway returns home from a hard day at his sunstone mine, he is greeted by a "yeeeek" from his shower stall. Out comes Little Fuzzy, a living teddy bear whose hands have opposing thumbs. Holloway, delighted by his visitor, names him, plays with him, and then discovers that the creatures loves Extee Three (Terran Federation Space Forces Emergency Ration, Extraterrestrial Type) which seems to be the future equivalent of K-rations. Holloway becomes "Pappy Jack" to Little Fuzzy and, eventually, to all of the Fuzzies in Little Fuzzy's family. Holloway first treats his visitor like an intelligent pet, but he quickly discovers that Little Fuzzy is more like a very intelligent human child. To gain some type of authoritative confirmation of the Fuzzies' probable sapience, Holloway calls on his friend Ben Rainsford, a naturalist. Though they can see evidence of intelligent, thoughtful action in the Fuzzies' behavior, they must be able to prove sapience within the standard definition of the Terran courts; the men must show that Fuzzies have a language and can build fires. The Fuzzies are obviously tool-users and conceptual innovators, but they appear to have no language system and seem to have no need for fires.

As the various characters try to work out definitions of sapience useful to their causes, Piper develops several interesting theories. He seems to be exploring not just what it is to be sapient but also what it is to be human. Throughout the novel the various characters exhibit egotistical attitudes toward sapience. One primary intellectual hindrance seems to be appearance (if it doesn't look like me, it can't be sapient), shown by characters who make derogatory references to sapient creatures of nonhumanoid form. The Fuzzies are slightly humanoid with faces which resemble people's faces, but they are diminutive and cuddly, making them hard to accept as potential intellectual equals. Even Holloway has difficulty giving them credit for independent action, but this attitude stems primarily from his paternal concern for them. Piper gives the Fuzzies innocence, if sapience, by crediting them with the intelligence level of an average, inexperienced twelve-year-old child. Little Fuzzy, Mama Fuzzy, Goldilocks, and the rest are all characterized as loving, precocious, childlike beings who are trusting but clever. Sapience appears to be acceptable in nonhumanoid creatures if those creatures have positive characteristics. By the end of the novel, there are more people who want to adopt Fuzzies than there are Fuzzies to satisfy the applicants. Through Holloway's viewpoint, Piper shows the Fuzzies as models of humanity who can remind people of the positive forces in life, the forces of innocence and love. Fuzzies are not aggressive, will not fight, act only out of self-defense, and tend to group in monogamous but extended family relationships. They offer an interesting parallel to Holloway, who is also basically peaceful and loving, but when threatened, he can abandon his innocence and kill in self-defense. Piper's message is a Romantic one, calling for a return to innocence in a rational, peaceloving world.

Piper also shows that one must be sensitive to individual attitudes toward life to understand human beings. By controlling the point of view of his novel, Piper compares and contrasts his characters' attitudes toward life. Rather than use an omniscient unknown narrator and rather than develop the novel exclusively through Holloway's point of view, Piper uses multiple, limited third person points of view. The reader enters the novel in Holloway's world, understanding Zarathustra from the hero's point of view, but then the viewpoint shifts to Grego and to his understanding of the planet. The reader immediately becomes aware of conflicting attitudes, and though Grego is used as a major antagonist in this novel, Piper develops this character quite thoroughly within the passages given in his point of view. Thus Piper has created a character with positive as well as negative attributes so that Grego can become an acceptable protagonistic force in the second novel. Piper develops both protagonists and the antagonists in this manner, affording the reader a complete understanding of both their motivations and their actions. He thus gives many of the characters a depth which eliminates the "black hat/white hat" stereotyping which easily could have resulted within the plot of this novel.

The major portion of the story is told from Holloway's point of view, but Piper also develops the viewpoints of the opposing attorney, the opposing scientists, the trial judge, and the murderer both before and after he acknowledges the sapience of his victim. Even Little Fuzzy provides two passages from his point of view, though Piper postpones these passages until late in the novel. The reader may have accepted the sapience of Fuzzies throughout the majority of the novel, and these passages give proof of their humanness as well. The novel concludes in Little Fuzzy's viewpoint, thus emphasizing the positive attributes of the Fuzzies; they will accept the benevolence of people and in return will give the people love and make them happy.

To facilitate the plot, Piper keeps several characters' viewpoints hidden and, thus, supplies surprises for the reader. He also adds a subplot of a male-female love relationship which suffers several reversals. Though the novel resolves the primary thematic problem by establishing a legally acceptable sapient identity for the Fuzzies, Piper leaves some problems unresolved. The Fuzzies may be sapient, but they have difficulty bearing infants who can survive to maturity. The problems of propagation of the Fuzzy species and establishing a functioning, humane political system on Zarathustra remain for Piper to solve in the second Fuzzy novel.

Little Fuzzy is a novel of action, intrigue, and suspense, but it is also a novel of character. The theme of the Romantic, innocent savage who must be saved from the corruption of a sophisticated civilization is developed within an entertaining story line. Holloway could be a hero out of the American western novel or movie while Grego is definitely an extension of the businessman character from the mid-twentieth century American urban novel. For Piper the possession of conceptual intelligence is not enough to establish humanity in a creature. A human being must also accept the basic values of truth, beauty, and love. When a Fuzzy community plays with shape and colors, its goal is to produce intricate patterns which give aesthetic fulfillment. They do not seek knowledge as a means to a profitable end. They form relationships which are mutually supportive and beneficial rather than seeking manipulative, self-aggrandizing, power-producing associations. As Holloway says when speaking of the wisdom of Fuzzies, "They stick to the important things."

Judith A. Clark

Sources for Further Study

Reviews:

Analog. LXIX, July, 1962, pp. 164-165.

New York Herald Tribune Book Review. March 11, 1962, p. 15.

THE LONG AFTERNOON OF EARTH

Author: Brian W. Aldiss (1925-   )
First book publication: 1962 (as *Hothouse*)
Type of work: Novel
Time: The far future
Locale: The Earth

The odyssey of the last remnant of mutated mankind on an Earth where.vegetable life proliferates under the burning sun

> Principal characters:
> TOY, a young girl, leader of the group
> VEGGY, the man-child of the group
> YATTMUR, a girl
> GREN, the group rebel
> LILY-YO, the old leader

This is early Aldiss and can rightly be described as vintage in every way. The novel is derived from the Hugo-winning series of stories published under the title *Hothouse*. However, the book is definitely not a series of short stories, but is a novel worked from the rich material of these adventurous and fascinating stories.

The setting is an imaginative one; the far distant future when our sun is much hotter, about to go nova, and our planet has been changed in every way. Rotation of the Earth has stopped — or, rather, it rotates just once a year and keeps the same side always to the sun. The Moon has stopped its rotation as well and stays fixed in the same spot in the sky. With the quickening of the radiation from the sun, plant life has mutated and proliferated, and has taken the place of all of the animal life forms that once dominated the planet. The few remnants of animal life still extant fill tiny and neglected ecological niches, and are always at war with the burgeoning plants.

For the plants are all. With profligate invention the author describes the parasitic crocksocks, the fast-growing berrywhisk, the fleecy, floating dumblers, the trappersnapper, leapcreeper, tigerfly, oystermaw, dripperlip, thinpin, and numerous others. It is a botanical menagerie that entrances and attracts, then repels with its vegetable lack of emotion and intelligence. This is an Earth where plant life struggles, grows, fights, lives, and dies in endless profusion.

Into this exotic jungle come the human beings. They are small, far smaller than today's people, green-skinned and adapted to arboreal life far above the ground. The plotline involves the struggles of one small group of children to stay alive as they travel across the surface of this world. Their struggles are heroic, the monsters they vanquish terrible. The world where this epic journey takes place is described by Aldiss on the opening page:

> The heat, the light, the humidity — these were constant and had remained constant for
> — but nobody knew how long. Nobody cared any more for the big question that begins

"How long . . . ?" or "Why . . .?" It was no longer a place for mind. It was a place for growth, for vegetables. It was like a hothouse.

1962 was a year of continuity for established writers, the year when Robert Heinlein abandoned his innovative plots to write *Podkayne of Mars*. Yet this year also saw the publication of the first stories of Thomas Disch, Roger Zelazny, and Ursula K. Le Guin. The changes these new writers represented were yet to come, and with *The Long Afternoon of Earth*, Aldiss helped to lead the way. The novel was also a landmark in the author's career. His earlier novels were firmly fixed in the mainstream of science fiction. Their excellence surmounted their traditional material — certainly *Starship* (1959) rose above other starship novels in that it was a penetrating human novel as well as an adventurous one.

But *The Long Afternoon of Earth* does more. It steps out of the rigid categories and traditions of science fiction and comes closer to the form of fantasy from which science fiction sprang. Nearsighted critical attention at the time the book was published took issue with Aldiss' science, not realizing that what they condemned as weaknesses were in reality the novel's strengths. For example, Aldiss creates giant vegetable spiders which, mutated by the unblocked radiation of the sun, have developed the capacity to dwell in space as well as on land. Since the moon is in a fixed position in space in relation to the Earth, these space-traveling spiders have been able to connect the two bodies by lengths of spiderweb, great silvery cables that reach up from the green hell of the jungle to stretch into space. Physically impossible? Of course, but no more so than any of the creatures or events of mythology.

This novel is about mutation and change, development and growth, devolution and decay, and finally, about the irresistible power of entropy. Yet Aldiss shows that life can defeat entropy by evolving to the heights of technical success, then devolving back to the primitive cells, and finally back to the force of life itself. As our sun dies and with it all life, the forces of existence are driven out to other stars, to other worlds where life can develop again. In the end, this is spelled out clearly:

> The spores, the dust, the hopes, the growth, the essence of the centuries of Earth's green fuse, no less. Up it goes, ascending for new fields. The ground beneath that column must be baked to a brick! You heat a whole world for half an eternity, stew it heavy with its own fecundity, and then apply extra current: and on the reflected energy rises the extract of life, buoyed up and borne into space on a galactic flux.

This quotation is also important because it reveals another element that Aldiss introduced to science fiction: literary quality. Science fiction, until very recently, was not overly concerned with the literary aspect of its stories. Why should it be? Science fiction was considered a literature of content, in which a machine or an idea could replace a human being as hero of a story, and stylistic excellence was not seen as essential. Today that attitude has changed;

as the science fiction audience has expanded it has included the general reader who already possesses certain expectations of basic literary quality.

The novel opens with the older generation of human beings giving way to the children. The adults, led by Lily-yo, go out into the unknown, carried in seed pods to the Moon by the traversers, or giant vegetable spiders. Those who live through this journey find themselves mutated into a similar but different life form.

Left alone on Earth, the children must fend for themselves. How they do this and what happens to them comprise the novel's primary action. Led by Toy, the children escape the tigerflies on the back of a giant suckerbird, which crashes on the shore, between the battling life forms of the jungle and those of the ocean. The children escape and find their way back to the jungle they know. During their journey, the children are separated or killed until only the girl, Yattmur, and the boy, Gren are left. Together they encounter the Tummybelly men who add a delightful comic touch to the novel; in a grim world of constant death and destruction the laughable buffoons are a welcome relief. They unwillingly accompany the two children as the journey, a rite of passage into adult life, continues.

In pursuing the theme of constant change, Aldiss vividly depicts devolving humans who have already lost the powers of speech as they turn into vegetables themselves. This is the end of mankind — or, at least, one of the possible ends. The path of devolution, like that of its counterpart, evolution, never runs smooth. All is change, all change tends to simplify, and all simplification will end in the fusion of every life form into one universal force.

Harry Harrison

THE LONG LOUD SILENCE

Author: Wilson Tucker (1914-   )
First book publication: 1952
Type of work: Novel
Time: The near future
Locale: The United States east of the Mississippi River

An uncompromisingly bleak book about a man seeking to survive in the eastern United States after most people have been killed by biological warfare

> *Principal characters:*
> CORPORAL RUSSELL GARY, a survivor of biological warfare
> IRMA SLOANE (ALSO CALLED "NINETEEN"), another survivor
> JAY OLIVER AND SALLY, fellow wanderers with Gary
> THE HOFFMAN FAMILY, Wisconsin farmers

The original version of *The Long Loud Silence* was published in 1952, two years after George R. Stewart's famous novel, *Earth Abides*. Both books tell of the adventures of one man left behind in an America where all the people have been killed by plague warfare. The catastrophe kills so many people so quickly that nobody ever finds out who was the enemy which conducted the biological attack. Both books show how the protagonist learns to survive in the new, empty world, and what happens when he meets small numbers of other survivors.

Did Wilson Tucker write *The Long Loud Silence* as an "answer" to *Earth Abides*? Certainly the bitter realism of Tucker's book reads like a rebuff or mockery of the celebratory optimism of Stewart's novel. Or did both books arise from the Cold War knowledge that both the United States and Russia possessed the weapons necessary to wipe out all human life? Whatever the answer, the important fact is that science fiction has been affected mainly by the hidden premise of *Earth Abides* — that cleansing the Earth of people would be, on the whole, a good thing, since it would give nature a chance to recover from the abuses of technology, and give the people left behind a chance to build a new utopia.

The hidden premise of *The Long Loud Silence* has been less popular in science fiction because it is more uncomfortable. This premise holds that man is a social animal who cannot survive psychologically in an empty world, that, deprived of companionship, he could become a vicious creature out of tune with both nature and humanity.

Not that *The Long Loud Silence* advertises this viewpoint; it must be inferred from the novel as a whole. The most interesting feature of the book is that the way events transpire depends completely on the character of Corporal Russell Gary, the protagonist. In other words, if Isherwood Williams had been placed in the world of *The Long Loud Silence*, the result would have been *Earth Abides*. Such science fiction novels, which depend entirely on a character viewpoint, rather than gratuitous melodramatic action, were rare in 1952 and remain so today.

At the beginning of *The Long Loud Silence*, Corporal Russell Gary wakes up, puzzled, in a hotel room in a provincial Midwestern American town. In the original 1952 version, he was home on leave from the Korean War; in the most recent edition (Lancer, 1969) he is on leave from the Vietnam War. Gary explores the hotel and finds dead bodies sprawled behind half-opened doors. Nobody else is around. Small bomb craters mark the street outside, but the damage looks too superficial to have killed the town's inhabitants. In the street, Gary surprises a prowler, a girl, who fights him and then surrenders. Her name is Irma Sloane; she looks sixteen, but after spending one night with her, Gary is surprised to find that she is "only nineteen."

Russell Gary and Irma Sloane conclude that some unknown plague must have killed most people. They take a car and set out to find just how many people have survived. Gary has only one idea in mind: he is a corporal, and it is his duty to rejoin the Army. He and Irma drive to the Mississippi River, looking for signs of remaining "civilization," and find it across the river — but soldiers standing guard on the west bank prevent anyone from crossing from east to west. They are not interested in Army stragglers, not even Gary. To them, he is Contaminated, cast off, unfortunately left on the wrong side of the river, to be forgotten about and guarded against. All people who attempt to cross the river (or cross from east to west overland north of the river) are killed on sight.

Early in the book, we find the first signs of Gary's unwillingness to make the best of his situation. He casts off the person who might have been his best possible companion east of the Mississippi. "I don't care what you do," he says to Irma. "There's a car, take it. Can you shoot a gun? There's ammunition and food to last you awhile." Like the Ancient Mariner, Gary rejects the world in which he must live. Irma is his albatross, a symbol of companionship, rejected out of whim. Gary imagines that "normal America," left intact on the western shore of the Mississippi after the attack, lies on the horizon like a Celestial City. Or, to suggest a Dantesque division of this post-Catastrophe America, Hell for Russell Gary is the empty world that he has inherited. He refuses to admit that he cannot stage a resurrection, that he cannot cross back from a geographical purgatory to the life he really wants.

Gary prowls the river bank, discovering most of the traps that separate him from the other shore, but finding no way over. He meets easygoing, likable Jay Oliver. In turn, both of them meet Sally, who agrees to share their company (and beds) equally, although she likes Oliver better. As winter approaches, they hike towards the south, and settle on the shore of the Gulf of Mexico.

Only during this idyllic pause in the narrative does *The Long Loud Silence* resemble the mood of *Earth Abides*. As the three companions laze near the beach,

The white sandy slope of the beach continued underwater, forcing them to walk out fifty
or seventy-five feet to reach a depth fit for fishing. The sea was clear and unruffled and so
transparent Gary could see his feet dug in on the bottom.

But restlessness, ambition, and misanthropy get the better of Gary, even in
this utopia. Safety and comfort are merely diversions from his real aims.
While Jay, Sally, and he are fishing quietly, he can think only about the river
barrier. Sally announces that she is expecting a baby; she wants it to be Jay's.
Gary gives Sally a little wooden link chain for Christmas, and leaves the two
in their haven. (Towards the end of the novel, he discovers the link chain at
the same spot, after the others have been presumably murdered.) When spring
approaches, Gary begins his trek back northward.

The Long Loud Silence does not rely on gratuitous melodramatic incidents.
Instead, it describes Gary's slow trek across the land of the dead. When he
falls into company with a trio of amateurish desperadoes who are also trying to
cross the river, he tells the leader how to cross the river in exchange for a
shotgun, knowing that there is no way of crossing the river without being
killed. As he calculated, Gary is left alive with the shotgun with two of the
leaderless trio. Indirectly, Gary has committed his first murder.

Again rejected by the river's defenses, Gary keeps traveling and arrives in
Wisconsin. One day it is autumn; the next day, the winter catches him without
shelter or a home to the south. He sees two figures in the snow attack a boy.
Gary kills the attackers and rescues the boy's sister, Lee Hoffman, who brings
Gary back to her father's farm. Gary has now found another haven.

The members of the Hoffman family accept Gary as a guardian. He does his
job well. One night, a bell tinkles in the house, sounding an intruder alarm. In
a splendid piece of understated action writing, Tucker describes how Gary
distinguishes the figure of the intruder against the snow, grabs a poker, and
sneaks up on him. "Immediately afterward, Gary thought to dispose of the
body." Tucker's point is that Gary has become so efficient a killer that by now
he does not need to see his victim clearly. An intruder is no longer a person at
all; instead, he is simply a "dark bundle of nothing" against the snow, an arm
and a detached hand, to be disposed of as efficiently as possible. Gary throws
the body on the ice in a creek, where the Hoffmans are unlikely to find it
before the spring thaw. Tucker's ironic viewpoint of Russell Gary sees him as
a man who casts aside everything that makes up human life, until he becomes
less and less humane. Gary cannot see this inexorable process working in
himself.

When Gary returns to the house after disposing of the body, he is shocked
to hear a voice over the snow. It is not another intruder, but a voice from the
radio, which is being broadcast from the western half of America. The voice
on the radio is a siren's song which lures him to leave the haven of the Hoffmans' farm and set off for the river again.

This time Gary uses all his ingenuity to hijack an armored truck which had been exploring on the eastern side of the river. But his voyage to the west is a failure. The one possibility that Gary had never allowed himself to face was the actual truth: that the people from the east side of the river really were carriers of plague, and that the authorities on the west side have been correct to quarantine half a continent. People who have come into contact with Gary during his brief trip west begin to die. He flees again; he crosses back from west to east.

Again Gary has a choice: to accept the reality of his situation, or to allow his illusions to poison the rest of his life. He does the latter. "Hell" is now inside his head. The east side of the river need not have been hell; it could have been a paradise for people of good will.

The last pages of *The Long Loud Silence* give a somber picture of the painful existence to which Gary has condemned himself. By the end of the novel, he lives quite alone, hunting food and killing all intruders, even other humans, which approach him. His reflexes have become like an animal's, and his mind is as unsympathetic and opportunistic as a wolf's. He has lost hope and his hatred and isolation are reflected back to him in the landscape.

The ending of the novel is ambiguous because no version of the novel yet published has featured Tucker's original conclusion (rejected in 1952, and published separately in 1975 in Tom Reamy's magazine, *Nickelodeon*). The ending of the published version has Gary sneaking up on a lone human, and finding that she is Nineteen, Irma Sloane; in this ending there is at least a possibility for redemption. Tucker's original ending involved cannibalism, which was more appropriate to the bleak view of Gary's character presented in the rest of the book.

The Long Loud Silence has probably never had wide acceptance from science fiction readers precisely because of its admirable qualities: its uncompromising bleakness of outlook; its understatement (so that Gary is never overtly menacing, but quite cheery and personable, until we see what he actually does in any situation); its strict adherence to its main character's growth; and its thematic development, without recourse to artificial or flimsy plot manipulation.

Bruce Gillespie

Sources for Further Study

Reviews:

Analog. LI, June, 1953, pp. 80-81.

Galaxy. V, February, 1953, p. 99.

Magazine of Fantasy and Science Fiction. IV, January, 1953, p. 90.

New York Times Book Review. October 12, 1953, p. 29.

Science Fiction Adventures. I, May, 1953, pp. 86-88.

THE LONG TOMORROW

Author: Leigh Brackett (1915-   )
First book publication: 1955
Type of work: Novel
Time: The twenty-first century, two generations after a nuclear holocaust
Locale: Piper's Run, a village in eastern Ohio; Bartorstown, a secret community of researchers in the Rockies; and points in between

A sensitive and humane treatment of conflicting attitudes toward science and technology that arise in the wake of a nuclear disaster

> *Principal characters:*
> LEN COLTER, a rebellious young New Mennonite
> ESAU, his cousin
> ELIJAH COLTER, Len's father
> EDWARD HOSTETTER, a trader
> HARRY SHERMAN, director of Bartorstown
> AMITY TAYLOR, Esau's girl friend, later wife
> JOAN WEPPLO, Len's girl friend

In the mid-1950's, the theme of nuclear holocaust was popular both in and out of science fiction. By 1955, enough works had been written on the theme virtually to begin to constitute a genre all its own, and any novel that hoped to treat the theme successfully was forced to move beyond the already familiar formulas of such works as Philip Wylie's *Tomorrow!* (1954) or Henry Kuttner's *Mutant* (1953). As a result, the focus of such works began to shift from simple portrayals of holocaust or action-adventures in a post-holocaust world, toward more detailed examinations of what kind of societies might arise after such a disaster. The consensus of science fiction writers seemed to be that such societies might reject all technology with a kind of neo-Luddite fervor and return to rigid forms of religious fundamentalism. The year 1955 alone saw three major works appear on this theme: John Wyndham's *Re-Birth*, the original story appearance of Walter M. Miller, Jr.'s "A Canticle for Leibowitz," and Leigh Brackett's *The Long Tomorrow*. Of these, Brackett's novel is the most narrow in scope, offering neither an evolutionary *deus ex machina* (as Wyndham offers) nor a grandiose sweep of future history (as the completed Miller novel does). Instead, Brackett tells the rather simple story of a young man, whose coming of age coincides with his growing rejection of the rigid values of his elders, and his discovery of the possible values of the technology that his community so despises.

The novel owes almost as much to Mark Twain as it does to earlier science fiction works. Like Huck Finn, fourteen-year-old Len Colter is dissatisfied with the rules and restrictions of the society in which he lives, suffers an abusive and narrow-minded father, and comes of age during a long river journey to what he believes will be a better place. Len's society is a village of New Mennonites, one of many such sects which multiplied and flourished following the atomic war — partly because their rejection of technology suddenly seemed justified, and partly because their traditions of living without technology enabled them to survive more easily following "the Destruction" than urban-dwellers whose lives had depended on machines and central sources of power. The Mennonites have taken over the federal government and even passed a constitutional amendment prohibiting any town or village from exceeding one thousand in population.

Len is marked as an outsider in his community by his enthusiastic thirst for knowledge and his overweening curiosity about what life had been like before the Destruction. He and his cousin Esau first tentatively question their sympathetic grandmother about her memories of life in a technological, urbanized world and soon begin explorations of their own: they steal pre-Destruction books from a local teacher, and eventually discover an old radio. On the radio, they hear messages being sent — messages that make little sense to them, but that indicate that there is a technological world still alive somewhere outside of their community. The radio is the key symbol of Len's growing alienation from his surroundings and fascination with prohibited knowledge. He becomes increasingly intrigued by rumors of Bartorstown, a mysterious community in which technology and research are said to be still alive. He and Esau suspect that a visiting tradesman named Hostetter is somehow involved with that community, but they are unable to discover whether this is true until they finally decide to run away from home in their own quest for Bartorstown. After becoming involved in a conflict in a neighboring community over the construction of a new warehouse that would allegedly violate constitutional limits on village growth, they are rescued by Hostetter from an angry mob and told that he will take them to Bartorstown.

The journey to Bartorstown, by boat and wagon, occupies the second third of the novel. For Len, it is a symbolic journey of growth through a devastated mid-America. Starting at Piper's Run (clearly based on Brackett's own residence of Kinsman, Ohio), the youths progress down the Ohio River, past the ruins of Louisville, to the Missouri, from the Missouri up to the Platte, and then overland to the Rockies, finally arriving at Bartorstown. Along the way, they both become involved with a girl named Amity Taylor, who eventually becomes pregnant by Esau, suggesting that a new generation will pick up where Len and Esau leave off.

The third part of the novel deals with Len's conflicting reactions over Bartorstown, a subterranean research facility disguised as a poor mining community named Fall Creek. Bartorstown's research centers around two machines: a computer called Clementine (located literally, as the song goes, in a cavern in a canyon), and a nuclear reactor, which is being used for research on a project to discover a means of neutralizing nuclear reactions, thus making future nuclear war impossible. But the reactor brings Len's conditioned fears into direct conflict with his lust for knowledge: he has been taught that such a reactor is the emblem of evil incarnate, and only his faith in the eventual discovery of the neutralizing force-field enables him to overcome these fears. When Joan Wepplo, a resident of Bartorstown and Len's newfound girl friend, tells him that the technicians fear something called "Solution Zero" — the possibility that they will discover that such a goal is theoretically impossible — Len's fears overtake him. He begins to regard the reactor as Moloch, and eventually decides to flee the community. But he is intercepted by Hostetter, who manages to convince him that the progress of knowledge is inevitable, and that the rejection of learning by Len and his Mennonite society is futile. Hostetter argues: "The knowledge will still exist. Somewhere, in some book, some human brain, under some mountain. . . . It makes better sense to try and chain the devil up than to try keeping the whole land tied down in the hopes he won't notice it again."

Len returns to Bartorstown, but the end of the novel is not without ambiguity. Hostetter, after all, had threatened to kill Len if he did not return, in order to protect the secrets of Bartorstown. For Len to function effectively in this new society, he is told that he will have to undergo something rather ominously called a "complete re-education." Furthermore, Bartorstown is only a community of some four hundred in the midst of a much larger population that does not share its goals: if it does succeed in its research, how is it to convince the rest of the society of the value of the new technology short of force? The internal governing structure of Bartorstown has already begun to resemble a technocratic dictatorship, with life regimented and workers assigned roles according to the needs of the project. Can the new breed of technicians retain enough of the values of life so over-valued by the antitechnology world outside to create a humane new state, or will their rejection of these values prove so complete that they are tempted to try to impose a technological utopia on an unwilling citizenry? Brackett does not attempt to answer these questions — though, one might argue, her primary concern in the novel is less with social structures than with the development of Len's character.

But the theme of the indestructibility of knowledge is an important one in the novel, and an important theme in much other science fiction as well (see Miller's *A Canticle for Leibowitz*, for example). Brackett exhibits considerable faith in the immortality of science and the inevitability of technologies based on that science: once man knows something, he cannot make it unknown again; and if he knows how to build something, he will sooner or later build it. In this regard, Len becomes a kind of everyman figure, with his progress from ignorance to knowledge to acceptance of that knowledge symbolizing the eventual progress that the decimated civilization of his postwar world will make. Like much science fiction on post-holocaust themes, *The Long Tomorrow* is in some sense an encoded parable of the movement from the Dark Ages to the Enlightenment or the Renaissance, with its protagonist the harbinger of the new age.

Whatever assumptions about technology and science lie at the heart of the novel, *The Long Tomorrow* gains most of its strength from the detailed, plausible style of the narrative and the depiction of the major characters. In a series of well-realized episodes, Brackett presents convincing portraits of a number of possible future societies: the repressive agricultural community of the Mennonites; the nearby community of Refuge, already straining against the limits of size imposed by constitutional law; the research community of Bartorstown, with its regimentation and tight security. The characters, too, are believable American types: Len, the thoughtful, questioning adolescent; Esau, his irrepressible cousin (and perhaps Tom Sawyer to Len's Huck Finn); Elijah, the stern, old-world father (whose name even suggests an Old Testament prophet); Hostetter, the confidence man-*cum*-mysterious stranger-*cum*-scientist; Amity, the teenage girl with dreams of a better world. Some of these indeed, verge on stereotypes, but by and large they are serviceable characterizations which help the reader to feel a sense of recognition in a fictional world radically different from our own.

Perhaps because it does not focus on the issue of nuclear war itself, but rather on community and character, *The Long Tomorrow* stands up well a quarter-century after its publication. It remains one of science fiction's more affecting coming-of-age novels, and its subordination of scientific ideas to human themes helped to usher in an age of greater humanism and more sophisticated style among science fiction writers. Neither space opera nor mordant satire, *The Long Tomorrow* is essentially a realistic novel laid in an imaginary environment of the future, and it helped to pave the way for later novels of this sort.

Gary K. Wolfe

Sources for Further Study

Reviews:

Amazing Stories. XXXVI, October, 1962, pp. 119-120.

Analog. LVII, May, 1956, pp. 144-145 and LVII, August, 1956, pp. 143-146.

Authentic Science Fiction. LXIV, December, 1955, p. 64.

Fantastic Universe Science Fiction. V, February, 1956, p. 112.

Future Science Fiction. XXIX, 1956, pp. 128-130.

Galaxy. XI, March, 1956, pp. 97-98.

Imagination Science Fiction. VIII, February, 1957, p. 123.

Magazine of Fantasy and Science Fiction. X, January, 1956, pp. 93-94.

LOOKING BACKWARD: 2000-1887

Author: Edward Bellamy (1850-1898)
First book publication: 1888
Type of work: Novel
Time: 2000
Locale: Boston

A *futuristic view of a humanitarian, cooperative society evolved from the fiercely competitive, industrial nineteenth century society*

Principal characters:
>JULIAN WEST, an 1887 Bostonian who wakes from a mesmeric sleep to find himself in 2000 Boston
>EDITH BARTLETT, his fiancée in 1887 Boston
>DR. LEETE, a retired physician of 2000 Boston who educates Julian West to his new existence
>EDITH LEETE, Dr. Leete's daughter, great-granddaughter of Edith Bartlett

Looking Backward: 2000-1887 reads well today, marred only slightly by the limitation of its setting in the year 2000. Despite this we find much in this Utopian novel to intrigue us, for Bellamy successfully fused history, science, industrial and social concerns, moral philosophy, romance, and literary tradition.

A well-established track of utopian-dystopian literature stretches from the mythic Golden Age of the Greeks and Eden of the Old Testament, through the humanistically based *Republic* of Plato and Thomas More's *Utopia*, to more contemporary works such as Aldous Huxley's *Brave New World* and John Brunner's *Stand on Zanzibar*. While many works in this genre purport to present an ideal human society, they often succeed more in sensitizing us to the less-than-ideal state of our own society.

Looking Backward fits into this tradition on the basis of both vision and influence. The impact of the book on its initial audience is well-documented. Bellamy Clubs formed to discuss Bellamy's social ideas; a "Nationalist Party" grew out of these clubs. Reformers, especially those with socialist leanings, made common cause with the author. While we may find Bellamy's premise that man is a perfectible and totally rational creature simplistic, we can still respond today to that possibility of a moral force strong enough to foster an economic and social Utopia such as he presented.

For one oriented to contemporary science fiction conventions, *Looking Backward* may seem primitive. When Bellamy published the book in 1888, H. G. Wells's time machine was seven years in the future; time travel as a science fiction convention was decades away. Yet Bellamy planned to break away from the Utopian formula of placing his society in either a distant past or a philosophical no-man's-land. He had to fabricate a mode of time travel in order to project his character into the future. He did this with mesmerism, a Poesque device, dramatic if unscientific.

Julian West, an upper-class 1887 Bostonian, seems to have all one could desire: wealth and security, a life of ease and culture, a beautiful fiancée from a family of comparable means. Subject to insomnia, Julian has constructed a soundproofed, subterranean chamber in his home. Here he retires when insomnia threatens his health. To induce the deep sleep needed to revive his well-being, he uses a mesmerist. Only this man and Julian's manservant Sawyer know of the existence of the room. On May 30, 1887, after an evening with the Bartletts, Julian retires to his secret room, leaving strict orders with Sawyer to awaken him later according to the directions of the hypnotist who has departed the city. Julian wakens not on May 31, 1887, but on September 10, 2000. A fire destroyed his home during the night, killing his servant, but the hideaway has remained undisturbed until uncovered during excavation work in 2000.

Since Bellamy was more concerned with his future society than in the mode of transportation to it, he seemed to care little about the plausibility of the time shift. He ignored questions contemporary science fiction writers would find necessary to face. How does a body retain vitality and retard aging for 113 years? Indeed, can sleep induced by mesmerism last indefinitely? How did West escape death from suffocation when the house burned? Once Bellamy commanded attention with the Leete family in the new century, he freed himself of concern in the time travel, relying later in the book on a more conventional technique, a dream vision, for Julian's return to his own century.

From Julian's waking on, the novel covers the events of the first week of his life in 2000 Boston. The word *events* is misleading, for little actually happens. Julian meets each member of the Leete family, who now live on the site of his old home. Shortly after an initial look at the twentieth century city, he takes a solitary early morning walk, almost losing his sanity when he fails to find familiar landmarks on which to anchor his mind. Through the offices of Dr. Leete and Edith he familiarizes himself with the technological advances (music brought into homes via telephone wires, for example) and social customs (eating arrangements, shopping conveniences, and the like). Just as he begins to reach a point of equilibrium, he has a nightmare in which he returns to his old environment, painfully experiencing the industrial and social inhumanity he failed to see before. Only the gentle love and affection of Edith Leete alleviate his guilt, presumably allowing him peace of mind.

Because *Looking Backward* is primarily a novel of ideas, the plot line is a slender one, serving mainly as support for the many conversations between Julian and the Leetes. Actually the major "characters" in this tale are not the above mentioned persons, but rather the two contrasting societies: the one, fiercely competitive; the other, enlightened, cooperative, and humanitarian. A major value of this "fanciful romance," as Bellamy calls it in the Postscript to the novel, lies in the detailed comparison Dr. Leete painstakingly offers as he shepherds Julian through the initial culture shock.

The details which first impress Julian are those most obvious to the five senses. He sees a magnificent city of well-planned residential enclaves and tall, beautiful public buildings, interspersed with common areas of trees and fountains. Noteworthy in the vista is the absence of contaminating smoke; there are no chimneys since this society has dispensed with inefficient methods of producing heat and energy. No slum areas replete with dirt, fetid air, starving children, and hopeless adults mar its perfection. Julian sees no areas devoted to the hum of trade; nor are there streets lined with retail houses wooing customers.

Being a man of intelligence, Julian requests explanations from Dr. Leete, who states that these things have disappeared. Now there is no need for merchants, middlemen, or bankers. During the evolutionary process, individual wealth as well as individual poverty atrophied and vanished. Likewise, corrupt human motives disappeared: for example, no need now exists for anyone to undercut a competitor in price in order to sell goods to people who may or may not need those goods. Since goods are distributed evenly to all people by means of a system of credits, the use of money, hence money-handlers also, have been obviated. A group of people need not beg for wages to forestall starvation; neither need a second group pervert its moral principles in hectic business transactions to win advantage over less acute rivals.

Operating almost as surrogate for the reader, Julian asks the questions that occur in our minds. Surely such a change did not transpire without violent upheaval and resistance? Dr. Leete again reassures him. To achieve this state of "liberty, equality, and fraternity," no *bonnet rouge* was necessary. Conditions meliorated gradually as the population realized the efficacy of centralization. Why should their industrial complex not enjoy similar efficiency to that afforded by the organization they already employed in the political and military areas? The change came as a rational, humane, and communal decision.

The society established an "industrial army," for all practical purposes a socialistic reorganization of the economic system, although Bellamy does not use any form of the word "socialism" in the book. All members of society enter this army at age twenty-one, after they complete their formal education. They serve for twenty-four years, the first three as common laborers; then they choose a field in which their work can best contribute to the commonweal.

Women have equal place in this army, leaving the work period early only to bear and nurture children. Their work responsibilities match those of the men except in situations requiring extra physical strength. In this respect Bellamy's book is refreshingly modern. This society, as Dr. Leete explains, has addressed a condition which made women victims of unenlightened social custom. No longer are they forced to operate within narrow social dictates of occupation, self-development, and personal interest.

The industrial army operates on the general premise of one for all and all for one, the motivation being devotion to the human family of which each person is an equal member. While individual capabilities are acknowledged, they do not merit extra material or monetary awards. If someone, for example, chooses to serve his twenty-four years as a common laborer, he will still receive as much of the world's goods and comfort as anyone else. With the abolition of individual wealth and poverty, human relationships operate free of corruption: lying, strife, crime in general no longer serve any purpose.

At age forty-five, a person is mustered out of the army, liable for recall only under special circumstances. The early retirement allows individuals time to pursue activities which enrich life over and above material ease. In the light of Boston 2000 the invitation of Robert Browning's Rabbi ben Ezra takes on added meaning: "Grow old along with me!/ The best is yet to be,/ The last of life, for which the first was made." Citizens of this future society now work toward more spiritual and self-fulfilling ends than material and financial security. For them, after forty-five the "best is yet to be."

Julian is not yet satisfied; his questioning goes deeper. How does the society find the wherewithal to afford security for all in equal portions? As he reminds Dr. Leete, economists had repeatedly shown that mere distribution of wealth would result in a general impoverishment. Leete's answer focuses on the core of the matter: waste. His society has eliminated waste of labor, capital, and resources. In this particular discussion Dr. Leete delivers the severest indictment of the industrial system as Bellamy saw it in the 1880's, and also as we know it today.

What are humanity's real enemies? Hunger, cold, and lack of housing. Any activity which impedes provision of physical comfort abets these enemies; such an activity is waste. Dr. Leete patiently enumerates the major sources of economic waste: duplication of effort in industry; inaccurate analysis of human requirements leading to unnecessary projects; the machinery of money and credit with value only as symbols of material goods; maintenance of unneeded institutions and levels of governance. The rock upon which this mountain of waste rests is competition. Instead of stimulating an economy, competition dissipates energy and creates business cycles, the attendant crises, and consequent unemployment of men and material.

Indeed, men of 2000 hold up *laissez-faire* as the epitome of waste. One might compare the inefficiency of nineteenth century industry with that of the Greeks before Troy. For nine years the Achaeans had failed to bring Troy to submission because each petty chieftain, hero though he has now become by virtue of mythic tradition, jealously guarded his own honor, putting it ahead of the communal good. For the people of Boston 2000, the industrialists of 1887 resembled a group of petty chieftains, each vying for individual gain at the expense of economic victory and peace for all.

Bellamy's use of the notion of evolution claims our attention as a subtle reinterpretation of the scientific theory in moral rather than in physical terms. "Survival of the fittest" in this evolved society implies an ethical adaptation to the facts of true social community rather than a physical adaptation to nature. True, this is an idealistic presentation, as any Utopia is bound to be by definition. Bellamy himself realized when he finished *Looking Backward* that he needed an expanded account of the operation of his society. Also, he needed to present those counterarguments so that he might more thoroughly demolish them. This he did in the sequel *Equality* (1897), an effort to justify the ideal in stricter terms of human reality.

To read *Looking Backward* in modern times is to have a unique intellectual experience. Obviously one will find appeal in measuring Bellamy's social vision of the nineteenth century with those of, say, Charles Dickens of London or Walt Whitman glimpsing America in *Song of Myself*. One finds, however, more pertinency and challenge in the inevitable comparison of Bellamy's society with the one we know in our twentieth century. Some shocks of recognition will occur at the accuracy, as well as some dismay at the misdirection, of Bellamy's extrapolations. No matter what the balance might be, those extrapolations are thought-provoking and worthy of our consideration.

Hazel Pierce

Sources for Further Study

Criticism:

Becker, George J. "Edward Bellamy: Utopia, American Plan," in *Antioch Review*. XIV (June, 1954), pp. 181-194. Becker provides an in-depth discussion of Bellamy's themes in *Looking Backward*.

Sadler, Elizabeth. "One Book's Influence: Edward Bellamy's *Looking Backward*," in *New England Quarterly*. XVII (December, 1944), pp. 530-555. Sadler views *Looking Backward* as starting a trend in the American utopian novel.

Shurter, Robert L. "*The Writing of Looking Backward*," in *South Atlantic Quarterly*. XXXVIII (1939), pp. 255-261. The thoughts, techniques and influences behind the composition of *Looking Backward* are examined by Shurter.

Taylor, Walter F. *The Economic Novel in America*. Chapel Hill: University of North Carolina Press, 1942, pp. 184-213. Taylor examines *Looking Backward* and places the work of Bellamy in perspective with other writing of the time.

LORD OF LIGHT

Author: Roger Zelazny (1937-   )
First book publication: 1967
Type of work: Novel
Time: The very distant future
Locale: Urath, a planet colonized by Earthmen

A man who has been reassembled from the magnetic cloud that surrounds Urath liberates the common people from the despotism of their gods, a group of virtual immortals who have refused to share the benefits of their technology with their people and who have adopted the identities of various Hindu deities

> *Principal characters:*
> MAHASAMATMAN (SAM), one of the original colonists, who is known as Lord Kalkin, Maitreya, Lord of Light, Manjusri, Buddha, Siddhartha, and Tathagatha, but prefers Sam, and who is attempting to overthrow the corrupt Deicrat system
> KALI, an original colonist who was once Sam's wife, is also known as Candi the Fierce, Brahma, Durga, and Murga, and is possessed by ambition and power
> YAMA, a master assassin and technological genius who is madly in love with Kali and has been assigned to kill Sam

Probably Roger Zelazny's best novel, *Lord of Light* displays a brilliant concept and excellent writing. It is a very complicated work because it relies heavily on Hindu and Buddhist mythology. Though it can be read quite satisfactorily on the action level, a complete understanding of it requires a broad knowledge of the philosophies and terminologies of the two great religions and of the historical relationship between them.

Despite the fact that it deals with the reformation of both personality and of society, its specific theme is liberation. Liberation must occur in both cases, of course, before reformation can begin. Sam's efforts to overthrow the Deicrat system of gods so that the common men of Urath (a corruption of the word Earth) might share the benefits of the gods' technology is the most obvious expression of liberation. Equally important, however, is the freeing of individual consciousness so that it can advance through higher and higher states of being until it reaches *nirvana*, or merger with the Absolute. This is liberation in another sense — that of freeing man from his preoccupation with material things. The two levels are compatible in the novel. Sam is the primary example of freed consciousness in the story, and all action in *Lord of Light* is generated from the conflict between his desire to free the masses from the tyranny of the Deicrat system (rule by the gods) and the various forces which oppose him. It is only because he has metaphorically reached *nirvana*, when his molecules are dispatched into the magnetic cloud surrounding Urath as punishment for leading the rebel forces at the Battle of Keenset, and then reincarnated by virtue of Yama's pray-machine that the fall of the Lords of Karma can come about.

As with many other aspects of *Lord of Light*, both senses of the term liberation find analogs in Hinduism and Buddhism. Freeing the masses from the Deicrats is Zelazny's adaptation of Buddha's mission on Earth. Finding Hinduism, the old religion, overburdened by meaningless ritual, the Brahman priests to be vain and corrupt, and the twin truths of Karma and Reincarnation to have been kept from the people, Buddha set out not to start a new religion but to reform the old one. He found the people under the tyrannical influence of the priests, mechanically performing their prayers and rituals. This is, of course, the exact situation that Sam encounters, except that in Zelazny's ingenious adaptation, everything is literal.

Reincarnation, or rebirth, for example, is a technological process. Body transfer is accomplished by machine, but access to the machines is the means that the gods use to blackmail the people. If they do not comply with the gods' wishes, then they may have to suffer real death. Prayers are dispersed through coin-operated pray-o-mat machines invented by Yama. A running tally is kept of each individual's purchases, and when he comes up for body transfer on the eve of his sixtieth birthday, his prayer and sin accounts are reviewed to determine what the sex, age, and health of his new body will be. This is Zelazny's adaptation of the Hindu and Buddhist doctrine of Karma, the law of cause and effect which follows a person through all of his incarnations. In other words, an individual's bad deeds return to the doer, just as his good deeds do. And of course, Sam's *atman*, self or soul, is dispersed into the magnetic cloud that surrounds the planet, known also as the Bridge of Gods, by one of Yama's machines. His return fifty years later constitutes a reincarnation and a return from *nirvana*. It is also accomplished by machine.

The growth of Sam's personality to a state of consciousness so high that he willingly forfeits his life in order to free his people also finds an analog in the Hindu and Buddhist concept of self-realization. Synonymous with the term illumination, it is a state of consciousness which brings awareness of eternal truth and freedom from the ignorance and illusion of the world. This is liberation in its most profound sense, and it is the goal of man's attempts to perfect himself during his various incarnations.

Light is yet another synonym for illumination and self-realization, and Sam is specifically identified with Maitreya, the Lord of Light, at the beginning of Book VII. Maitreya is also known as the "Buddha of the Future," who will save mankind through the power of his divine love. His appearance will signal the end of the current age, the *Kali Yuga* or age of darkness. So, when Sam is identified as Maitreya, Zelazny is symbolically indicating that the current age of Urath's history is coming to an end, as is the Deicratic society. This interpretation is reinforced by the fact that one of Sam's earlier identities is as Lord Kalkin, an allusion to Vishnu's tenth avatar, yet to come. To signal the end of the *Kali Yuga*, Vishnu will either appear riding a white horse named Kalki or as a giant with a horse's head named Kalki. Wielding a blazing sword, he will destroy the wicked and prepare for the renewal of creation. It is no accident that Sam appears at the Battle of Khaipur, which marks the final defeat of the Deicrat gods, riding a white horse.

Sam is, metaphorically, an illuminated man whose return from the Bridge of Gods simulates an incarnation of Vishnu and whose personal liberation mirrors that of the historical Buddha. Siddhartha, the Buddha, longing to know the true nature of the world, left the palace of his father, the King, abandoned his beautiful wife and son, and pursued a path towards enlightenment. Sam, one of the First, left his wife, Kali, known then as Durga, and several sons, renounced his right to godship, and gave up his option to live in the Celestial City to go out into the world and see what it was like. And, as the Buddha was once seized by a demon and taken to the nether regions, Sam's body was invaded by the demon, Taraka, after being freed from Hellwell. Taraka lived in Sam's body long enough not only to learn the pleasures of the flesh that men could enjoy but also to learn the nature of guilt.

Like all well-crafted novels, *Lord of Light*'s main theme, liberation, is supported by several closely integrated subthemes. Immortality, a recurrent Zelazny theme, is vital to both the liberation of the individual and the freeing of the masses in *Lord of Light*. From a purely mechanical point of view, virtual immortality is accomplished by means of the body transfer machines. Because of the corruption of the Deicrat system, however, it has become a privilege rather than a right. The gods exploit the masses. Rationalizing their behavior by saying that the people are not ready for the benefits of godhood, they extract sexual favors from those they desire, keep them in ignorance, and strip them of their dignity. Sam wants to restore honesty to the process, for he believes that each person is entitled to the long life that will permit him to advance to higher and higher states of consciousness, just as the Hindus and Buddhists believe occurs through reincarnation. Since most people have been blocked from enlightenment, the progress of society itself has been retarded. The position that Zelazny takes in the novel is simply another way to view a concept that permeates his work: immortality provides the individual with enough time to accumulate the experience necessary to the metamorphosis of his personality.

The love subtheme is equally supportive of liberation. As Maitreya, Sam has advanced to a state of consciousness which will permit him to free Urath because of his love for humanity. He acts out of love, not hate. That he is capable of such a generous act and committed to it can be measured by the strength of his motivation. That is illustrated by several facts from the story: he initially engages the gods and the resources of the Celestial City almost singlehandedly; he is willing to murder to accomplish his ends, as evidenced by his killing of the original Brahma and the original Siva, even though as Siddhartha he supported the doctrine of *ahisma*, the belief that man should refrain from harming life of any kind; he precipitates the Battle of Keenset and loses his life in the process; after being returned from the Bridge of Gods by Yama, he precipitates a second battle, at Khaipur, thus risking his life once again. He knows that the violation of *ahisma* and the murdering of Brahma and Siva are the concerns of this world, not of the next. From his enlightened perspective, he realizes that these actions are cosmic necessities.

There is also a personal aspect to the love theme. It occurs in the relationship between Sam and Kali/Candi/Brahma/Durga, who was once his wife but becomes his chief antagonist. It is one of love turned to conflict. In his illuminated state, Sam has passed beyond the selfishness and possessiveness of a male-female relationship. Though he can certainly still love individuals, his broadened perspective makes him more concerned with the love of all life. But Kali, who remains at a much lower stage of development, does not understand this. Rather, she remembers an earlier time, a time when their relationship was important to the psychological growth of both of them. In a very touching scene just after Sam has been captured while trying to steal the "Talisman of the Binder" from the Museum of Heaven, they discuss their former relationship. Sam makes the point that though they had once been lovers, they are different persons now. Kali disagrees.

Actually, both have changed, but in different ways. Her change has been primarily quantitative. She has become more ambitious, more vain, and more power-driven. His change has been qualitative. In fact, it has been metamorphic, and thus, he follows the pattern of many of Zelazny's heroes. He is incapable of loving Kali now. He knows that he can never return to what he was as Lord Kalkin. So, when she makes overtures to renew their relationship and even offers to help him in his battle against the Deicrats, he has no choice but to reject her. Even though he tries to do so tactfully, he fails, and instead, raises her anger, injures her pride, and prods her to vengeance. She accepts Yama's offer of marriage. To celebrate their wedding, she asks Brahma/Madeline for a special favor — a human sacrifice: Sam and Helba, the god/goddess of thieves who had helped him in his attempt to steal the "Talisman." Her request is granted because the gods were looking for an appropriate punishment for the thieves anyway. The marriage ceremony completed, the sacrifice begins. Lord Mara casts a "weird," which drops the barrier between the Celestial City and the Kanniburah Forest, both of which exist under the Heavenly Dome. Then, Kali transfers into the body of one of the great albino tigers native to the Forest to hunt down and kill Sam and Helba. She is successful in her hunt, but even though Sam's body is destroyed, he manages to exist outside it long enough as pure spirit to steal the new body being prepared for Lord Murugan.

After Sam murders Siva and Brahma/Madeline, a new Brahma must be chosen. The position is offered to Kali. Because its acceptance means a change of sex, she must break her marriage contract with Yama. The power this position offers is far more attractive to her than the Death God. Kali's rejection so humbles Yama that he switches allegiances and begins working with Sam to overthrow the Deicrats.

Love is thus a very important subtheme in the novel. Its presence or absence provides primary motivation for all three of the major characters, and it is from their feelings and attitudes that the action is generated. This action is, of course, fundamental to the development of the liberation theme.

Vanity is yet another subtheme which significantly supports liberation. Usually in Zelazny's writing it acts as a block to a character's healthy psychological development, and in *Lord of Light* it functions exactly that way. Kali is an excellent example. Vanity lies at the heart of her desires. It prevents her initially from growing at the same rate as Sam, it prompts her to accept the identity of Brahma because power flatters her, and it fuels her need to revenge herself on Sam. It has both corrupted and distorted her personality.

Moreover, it has also been the corrupting factor in the character of most of the gods. Before he changes, Yama is so arrogant and proud that Sam is able to use that fact to trick him into walking into a quicksand trap; Brahma/Madeline is totally preoccupied with his sexuality and masculinity; and the "fierce pride" of the First is mentioned several times in the novel. Some of the First, those colonists who came to Urath on the "Star of India" spaceship, still occupy identities as Hindu gods, and they have set the tone for the other Deicrats, who take their roles quite literally. They delight in playing god to the comman man, doling out their favors to him as they see fit, shaping his life and his culture, and protecting him from dangerous ideas and inventions. Like the historical Buddha who found pride to be a predominant corrupting factor in the Brahman priests, Sam finds it to be the major flaw in the Deicrat gods.

Zelazny does not deal with the reformed society or the new creation that will follow the fall of the gods. His purpose, rather, is to deal with what must occur prior to reformation: liberation. Though he presents an example of the reformed man in Rild/Sugata, the assassin who becomes a Buddha, and though he plants several clues which indicate that a new age is dawning (Sam's identities as Lord Kalkin and Maitreya, and the appearance of the red bird with the flaming head, which must surely be a phoenix, at the end of the novel), it is not appropriate for Sam to shape the new society.

His function is parallel to that of the traditional Vishnu, to restore the balance between the forces of good and evil and to preserve the conditions of the universe so that the other two members of the Hindu "Trimuti," or Trinity, can interact. The creative force, traditionally represented by Brahma, and the destructive force, traditionally represented by Siva, shape society and creation through their perpetual interplay. Zelazny has preserved these relationships in *Lord of Light*, though the functions are not paralleled with their traditional names. The multiple identities of the novel's characters, the world he has created for it, and the extent of the corruption by the time the story takes place prevent this. Nonetheless, the functions of creator, destroyer, and preserver are retained in the conceptual framework of the story.

In *Lord of Light*, Zelazny has done an exceptional job of bringing order from the contradiction and confusion that pervades his sources. His ingenious explanation of abstract and esoteric Hindu and Buddhist concepts in terms of technology is refreshing, and it translates religious concepts, which would no doubt remain obscure to contemporary readers, into modern and concrete terms. Indeed, *Lord of Light* genuinely deserves its status as a science fiction classic.

Carl B. Yoke

Sources for Further Study

Reviews:

Amazing Stories. XLI, February, 1968, pp. 141-142.

Analog. LXXXI, June, 1968, pp. 160-161.

Kirkus Reviews. XXXV, July 15, 1967, p. 837.

Library Journal. XCII, August, 1967, p. 2813.

Luna Monthly. VII, December, 1969. p. 29.

Magazine of Fantasy and Science Fiction. XXXIV, January, 1968, pp. 37-38.

New Worlds. CLXXVIII, December–January, 1968, pp. 37-38.

Publisher's Weekly. CXCII, July 17, 1967, p. 66.

Son of WSFA Journal. LXVII, September, 1972, pp. 9-10.

Times Literary Supplement. February 29, 1968, p. 213.

LORD OF THE FLIES

Author: William Golding (1911-   )
First book publication: 1954
Type of work: Novel
Time: The near future
Locale: A tropic coral island

A symbolic tale of a group of British boys marooned on an uninhabited island who gradually revert to savagery

> *Principal characters:*
> RALPH, the natural and elected leader of the boys
> PIGGY, his friend, the most analytic of the boys
> JACK MERRIDEW, the natural leader of the hunters
> SIMON, a shy, contemplative boy, seer of truth
> ROGER, a quiet, furtive boy

In Romantic poetry's penetrating quest, in which the hideous or, at least, ambivalent core of life is confronted, there is always something redemptive that is learned and carried away from the experience. The Ancient Mariner is able to teach people by telling them of his voyage. The blemished garden of Xanadu has arching over it a pleasure dome of the imagination. Such redemptive qualities, however, do not seem apparent in William Golding's symbolic and powerful narrative about the bestial reality at the roots of human life. In the opening paragraph of *The Lord of the Flies*, the long scar smashed across the otherwise Edenic coral island reminds us of the blemished garden of Coleridge's verse; but the return at the end of the book is much more problematic than any Romantic redemption has been. Golding's vision in this novel is indeed stark.

The starkness of the vision added to the symbolic and poetic way of relating it make the book somewhat unusual among science fiction narratives, but nonetheless effective as a tale about human nature. Although set in the near future, this story of a planeload of boys isolated on a South Sea island paradise following an atomic war makes no thrust toward the future as a science fiction narrative generally does. When the boys are finally rescued after having turned themselves into brutes and their idyllic surroundings into a savage and murderous place, the British officer reminds them that their experience might have been like the South Sea adventure of the self-reliant British boys in R. M. Ballantyne's *Coral Island*, a Victorian boys' book. Instead, Golding tells only of negative transformations: breakdown of order, fear, murderous rituals, self-deception, and ultimately a very profound and adult human despair. Unlike *The Inheritors* which envisions the advantages and disadvantages of growth, this earlier novel of Golding paints the picture of eternal bestiality among men. It is a beautiful and moving portrait, but Golding gives little indication either that the future will bring change and possible progress or that there is any redeeming quality in the savage behavior that overcomes the boys.

When the boys discover that they are indeed isolated on an uninhabited island, that it is their island and apparently a good one, they set out to do two things. Some of them plan to maintain order, build huts, keep fires going as signals for possible rescue, and generally behave like sensible adults. Some of them (and most of these conflicting motivations are mixed within individuals) simply want to have fun until the grown-ups fetch them. The fun deteriorates into bestiality which ultimately edges out all sense, and the deterioration is fueled by fear and a strange kind of bloodlust. In other words, the boys behave like adults in all respects; and the final catalyst for the fear that unravels their whole little society is a dead parachutist who floats down from the adult war raging off the island, showing that murder is not limited to the boys. Golding seems to be saying that in any Utopia, or isolated place, the same patterns will evolve. Fun and games will become beastly rituals. Fear will bring out the worst in us. Sense and orderly progress stand little chance against these other human forces.

The message of the novel is communicated beautifully, and possibly more so than in most novels, by means of images and characters that become symbolic. The most sensible of the boys, Piggy, discovers and suggests the use of a magnificent conch to both call the boys to assembly and to maintain order. Piggy's eyeglasses, a sign of enlightenment, are also used to make the various signal fires. But the conch, the glasses, and Piggy himself are all finally smashed because the natural leader, Ralph, cannot maintain order, even with Piggy's wise advice and the implements of civilization, against the powers of fun, fear, and the beast. Among the many images that make up the retinue for the lord of darkness or the Lord of the Flies, Golding includes the usual expectations about the meanness of young boys; and at this point his symbolism becomes particularly complex. Jack Merridew, the other natural leader and Ralph's antagonist, is in part simply a lively kid who wants to have fun and hunt. Jack and Ralph are never complete opposites. They are strangely tied to each other, Golding tells us; and despite or because of their competition that rages constantly they are like brothers. But at the end, Jack is stalking Ralph for the kill; and a stake has been sharpened at both ends so that Ralph's head can be set up as a totem just like the bloody sow's head that is already attracting flies, the hideous title image of the book.

In addition to Piggy, one other boy is clearly murdered before the ship arrives to take the boys off this idyllic coral island. Simon is neither a good speaker nor a leader, but along with Ralph and Jack he is part of the initial threesome that climbs the mountain to discover the true nature of their island isolation. From then on, Simon is the only one who continues to see the true nature of their little world. He does so in a quiet, rather contemplative manner. He is probably epileptic. He is definitely a loner. Simon broods on the hunt and on the impaled sow's head, and then he looks directly into the face of the ghastly corpse of the parachutist that had been haunting the other boys until he can truly say that the beast is harmless. Then, when he is coming down from the mountain to tell the other boys that they need not be afraid even though the beast is horrible, he is killed like a pig in a mass frenzy of fun and fear.

This bloodlust for killing the pigs, which evolves into the ritualistic dance that Simon later stumbles into, is a symbol of bestiality that suggests violence far beyond a response to fear. The large sow, whose head eventually becomes the Lord of the Flies, serves as an object upon which these boys, as Golding presents it, expend tremendous emotional and even sexual energy. In the scene where the sow is killed, the boys seem momentarily fulfilled in their lust. But perhaps fear of this lust in themselves leads them later to the killing of Simon. And all this is a sad contrast to one of Ralph's final thoughts as he is being rescued and weeps for his true, wise friend, Piggy.

After Simon has been killed, all the boys deceive themselves about what has happened, about the beast inside themselves, whereas the only liberating act would have been to look squarely at the beast as Simon had done. Once this ancient, inescapable recognition of the bestiality at the core of life can be made, then it is harmless, though horrible, as Golding says; but the only character who makes this recognition is cruelly sacrificed. Golding's symbols in this novel seem always to return to the scar across the otherwise good island.

Donald M. Hassler

Sources for Further Study

Criticism:

Babb, Howard S. *The Novels of William Golding*. Columbus: Ohio State University Press, 1970, pp. 6-35. The delineation of the defects of society that can be traced to the defects of human nature.

Dick, Bernard F. *William Golding*. New York: Twayne, 1967, pp. 18-36. Dick feels Golding sheds new light on the marooned boys theme.

Hollahan, Eugene. "Running in Circles: A Major Motif in *The Lord of the Flies*," in *Studies in the Novel*. II (Spring, 1970), pp. 22-30. Hollahan traces a major theme of the book.

Moody, Philip. *A Critical Commentary on William Golding's* Lord of the Flies. New York: St. Martin's, 1968. Moody studies Golding's most well-known novel in depth.

Reviews:

Catholic World. CLXXXII, December, 1955, p. 230.

Georgia Review. XIX, Spring, 1965, pp. 40-57.

Kirkus Reviews. XXIII, August 1, 1955, p. 560.

Library Journal. LXXX, September 1, 1955, p. 1815.

Nation. CLXXXI, November 1, 1955, p. 446.

New York Times Book Review. October 23, 1955, p. 38.

New Yorker. XXXI, October 15, 1955, p. 189.

Saturday Review. XXXVIII, October 15, 1955, p. 16.

South Atlantic Quarterly. LXIX, Autumn, 1970, pp. 446-460.

Times Literary Supplement. October 22, 1954, p. 669.

LORDS OF THE STARSHIP

Author: Mark S. Geston (1946-   )
First book publication: 1967
Type of work: Novel
Time: The far future, beginning in an arbitrary 1483
Locale: A remote portion of the world

After mankind has degenerated to a series of warring, feudal-like states, an attempt is made to reunify the remnants of humanity by joining to build a seven-mile-long spaceship which will reach the stars

Principal characters:
> SIR HENRY LIMPKIN, the individual charged with unifying the people so that the starship *Victory* can be built
> GENERAL TORIMAN, a visionary whose idea it is to build the ship
> GENERAL TENN, an enigmatic military leader

Science fiction has been noted for brilliantly imaginative fables, for some not-so-elusive allegories, and for many chilling tales of the end of humanity in some sort of epic cataclysm. Mark Geston, in his first novel, *Lords of the Starship*, combines these characteristics in a gripping but ultimately unsuccessful novel.

Lords of the Starship is a remarkable book in many ways. It is a tale of the time after the First World, in which the world has apparently destroyed itself and left only rotting hulks of machines and men as its last bequest. Little is known of the First World. Its people could span the stars, and they were able to conquer anything except themselves. Traces of their civilization are enigmatic, hidden in dark libraries, virtually undecipherable. As the book opens, feudal baronies or kingdoms war against one another. The people are totally dispirited, weak of will and ability, concerned only with bare survival. The cities are occupied by dry rot and worms; blackness is unrelieved.

This awesome sketch of civilization after a forgotten Armageddon is well portrayed. "The land is destitute," General Toriman says. "The collections of hovels we call towns are virtually ruled by juvenile gangs and vice lords; industry, such as it is, maintains a steady annual decline. Foreign wars ravage our fields, destroy our finest men, and bleed the state treasury white."

Such is the situation at the opening of the book, and the reader is entranced with the apparently insoluble problem Sir Henry Limpkin faces as he attempts to resuscitate and unify civilization with the vision of the starship *Victory*. For the next few chapters the action proceeds rapidly. Battles are won, and the port where the *Victory* will be built is secured. An intact set of star-drive engines is mysteriously found. Heroic apparitions rally failing troops to victory and preserve the road to the shipyard. Red tape is cut, the baronies are unified by the dream, and building the ship actually begins.

In its early section, *Lords of the Starship* reads like a particularly inventive post-apocalyptic story. It is replete with maps, as well as excerpts from manuscript fragments telling of the history of the Blackness, the Darkness, the Bad Years which seemed to begin — or end — in 1483. It is, indeed, a dark beginning to a novel, with its hints of conspiracy, and its almost unrelieved pessimism. For twenty chapters, Geston sketches the background. The reader can almost begin to identify with Sir Philip Pome, who is trying to understand what is going on, or with Limpkin, who seems genuinely dedicated to the attempt to build the starship and thus unify, perhaps even redeem, humanity.

At that point, some twenty chapters into the book, Geston drops all of his previous characters, jumps two-thirds of a century, and continues to tell the story of building the starship. New characters are introduced and dropped almost as quickly. Centuries later the starship is still being constructed, and even Toriman and Limpkin are now only mythical figures. Other nations are envious of the success the people are having in building the *Victory*, and mass fleets in an attempt to destroy it. Another Armageddon-like battle ensues, and at its height the *Victory* leaves the ground briefly and rises only far enough to annihilate the attackers with its monstrous rocket motors. Then slowly, almost imperceptibly, it settles to the ground, and as it does so it turns its great retrorockets on itself, and perishes in its own fire. The victory has been won, but the *Victory* has been destroyed; mankind will once more sink into oblivion, the result of a dreadful but permanent catastrophe, the final, ultimate shattering of hope.

Because of the necessity for condensing time — centuries must be compressed into a very few chapters — the end of *Lords of the Starship* is not as successful as the beginning. In fact, it might even be said that the book is a brilliant book, but ultimately one that fails. The concept of building the starship to unify the remnants of humanity might have worked in the various kingdoms portrayed in the novel, but it does not work in the novel itself. The reader is continually confused by the profusion of characters who come onstage for a chapter or two and then disappear only to be succeeded by another equally amorphous set. Aside from the *Victory* itself, there seems to be no center for the last twenty-five chapters of the book, nothing for the reader to hang onto, nothing with which to identify.

Part of the difficulty may be inherent in the very nature of the problem that Geston undertook when he began to write the book: how to tell the story of nearly three hundred years of history and still provide it with a center. That Geston was not completely successful is almost a shame, for his concept is so good and powerful that one cannot but wish that he had carried it off brilliantly. If he had done so, *Lords of the Starship* might well have become one of the great science fiction novels. As it is now, however, it is merely a fascinating curiosity, baffling, intriguing, aggravating, annoying, and satisfying, almost in equal portions.

Lords of the Starship is a first novel and perhaps some of the problems that Geston faced were ascribable simply to a lack of apprenticeship served by many science fiction writers, grinding out stories for John W. Campbell, Jr., and rewriting them to Campbell's exacting specifications. Such was not the case, however, and readers can only conjecture what might have been.

From still another viewpoint, however, *Lords of the Starship* might well be an outstanding success. The novel was published in 1967 when its author was an honors history major at Kenyon College in Ohio. 1967 marked the height of America's involvement in the Vietnam war, and college students were beginning to protest this country's military efforts in the Far East. However, college students were, after all, exempt from the draft, and, secure in their dormitories, they could engage in complicated discussions about guilt and culpability.

It may well have been that Geston combined his interest in history and its processes with protest. For, viewed from an allegorical point of view, *Lords of the Starship* might well be a not-too-concealed rejection of the standards of the First World (hear the overtones of Second World and Third World) that have brought civilization to its present decrepitude, its moral and ethical senility, and its foolhardy militarism. We engage in war and we grasp for space, Geston seems to say, while at home we are faced with the specters of poverty, gangsterism, vice, corruption, racism, and despair.

It is a bleak picture that Geston portrays, for at the heart of the dream of the starship and its ultimate disaster are the agents of the First World, roaming the world seeking the destruction of souls and of the soul of humanity. The original plans for the ship might well have been a hoax, but perhaps the hoax was even bigger and more insidious than anyone ever dreamed. Perhaps everything that has gone on for thousands of years, including the rise and fall of the First World country, Salasar; the battles leading to the Armageddon of the First World; the plans for the ship; the new Armageddon when the ship destroys itself, are a diabolic conspiracy to enfeeble good so that evil will triumph.

Lords of the Starship may not completely succeed because of its lack of a center. No idea, however gripping, is enough to sustain interest over some 175 pages unless that idea is represented by actual people. Science fiction may be "idea oriented" fiction, but the clash of ideas must find some embodiment in human beings. So many characters are discarded after being introduced that it almost seems that Geston himself was so entranced by the ideas in his story that he neglected to put them into active human beings.

Yet for all of its faults, *Lords of the Starship* still remains a most provocative novel. It may be admonitory, allegorical, or even thinly veiled political satire about contemporary America, but it is certainly a novel that demands much from its readers. And readers who wish only entertainment or non-involvement may well put the book down without finishing it. Others who are willing to throw themselves into a novel by an act of passionate involvement will ultimately be quite pleased by *Lords of the Starship*.

Willis E. McNelly

Sources for Further Study

Reviews:

Analog. LXXXII, October, 1968, pp. 163-164.

Foundation. III, March, 1973, pp. 69-71.

Galaxy. XXVI, June, 1968, p. 127.

LOST HORIZON

Author: James Hilton (1900-1954)
First book publication: 1933
Type of work: Novel
Time: 1931-1932
Locale: An imaginary mountain pass in Tibet called Shangri-La

The initiation of four Westerners to a vaguely Utopian community in the Himalayas,
presided over by longlived monks who have assimilated Buddhism and Catholicism and
who constitute civilization's last refuge in a world on the brink of self-destruction

> *Principal characters:*
> HUGH "GLORY" CONWAY, a former Oxford don, and British consul
> in Baskul, Afghanistan
> CHARLES MALLINSON, young vice-consul to Conway
> ROBERTA BRINKLOW, a fundamentalist missionary from London
> HENRY BARNARD, an American financier and fugitive from justice
> FATHER PERRAULT, Catholic priest and High Lama of Shangri-La
> LO-TSEN, a Manchu woman of charismatic sexuality
> CHANG, a Chinese postulant to lamahood and host at Shangri-La
> RUTHERFORD, a novelist and traveler who records Conway's story

By the time James Hilton published *Lost Horizon* the notion of a hidden paradise located in an unspoiled byway of the earth had become so unlikely that it was an anachronism. For centuries Utopian writers, by convention, had situated their ideal societies in imaginary locales, often islands, which might be represented as real places not yet recorded on European maps. But by 1933 the fiction of uncharted islands could no longer be credibly — or even playfully — maintained. There were few regions of the planet that had not been fully mapped and exposed to the public eye. And in the new era of adventure by air rather than by sea every sizable portion of the earth's surface was vulnerable to observation. Even L. Frank Baum's fantasies for children had to take this fact into account. In the sixth in the series of Oz books, *The Emerald City of Oz* (1910), Baum has the sorceress Glinda throw a spell of invisibility over Oz to prevent its being detected by the soon-to-be-ubiquitous airplane.

Hilton chose to try to circumvent the problem of geographical credibility by supposing a tiny and nearly inaccessible *cul-de-sac* overhung by a glacial and unscalable mountain located in the most forbidding reaches of the Tibetan plateau. Further, Hilton encases the main narrative in a framework of prologue and epilogue which leaves in doubt whether the journey to Shangri-La is fact or fantasy, an objectively verifiable event or a figment of the protagonist's mental illness.

But the strain of the book, in maintaining both the initial premise and the ponderous ambiguity of the framing perspectives, is evident. When the reader learns that the lamasery of Shangri-La contains such amenities as central heating, a grand piano, and green porcelain bathtubs from Akron, Ohio, the strain becomes too much. Hilton provides elaborate explanation for how such West-

ern conveniences could be imported through Chinese intermediaries and con-
veyed, incredibly, on foot across the Tibetan plateau and through high passes
in the Himalayas while the outside world remained ignorant of Shangri-La's
existence. The premise of *Lost Horizon* becomes more absurd the more Hilton
has to rationalize it. Writers after Hilton, discarding the convention of the
hidden locale, have almost always imagined their Utopian societies as either
functioning out in the open here and now (as in B. F. Skinner's *Walden Two*
[1948]) or removed to the future and/or another planet (as in Olaf Stapledon's
Star Maker [1937] and Ursula Le Guin's *The Dispossessed* [1974], among
many others). To take *Lost Horizon* with any seriousness the reader must
struggle to overcome the nonsense on which Hilton's sometimes lovely vision
is built.

Lost Horizon's plot, an inventive variation on many of the motifs of the
typical Utopian or fabulous voyage, is tripartite: a perilous journey to an exotic
place, a guided tour which invites comparison between "normal" and Utopian
society, and the protagonist's exile from and desire to return to Utopia. Hilton
has a plane bearing four Westerners out of riot-torn Afghanistan hijacked to
the Himalayas, where they are entertained by hospitable (if stereotypically inscrutable) monks in the lamasery of Shangri-La overlooking the Edenic valley
of Blue Moon. During an extended discussion of the history and purpose of
Shangri-La, Hugh Conway learns that the hijacking was specifically designed
to bring him to the monastery because he has been chosen to succeed Father
Perrault, age 200+ years, as High Lama. But after Perrault's death Conway is
seduced into choosing mundane over spiritual heroism and helps his assistant
Mallinson and the seemingly ageless woman Lo-Tsen find their way from
Shangri-La to China. Much later, ill and perhaps deranged, Conway attempts a
solitary journey to find the hidden mountain pass which is the only entrance to
Shangri-La. The outcome of Conway's effort is left uncertain as the narrative,
assembled by Conway's old friend Rutherford, dissolves into fragmentary and
speculative conclusions.

With the exception of Conway most of Hilton's characters are cartoon figures. Roberta Brinklow, the prim and obsessive missionary, and Henry Barnard, the bluff American given to slang and cigars, behave predictably according to type. Charles Mallinson is a hysterical young patriot, always urging
others to take action and loudly proclaiming that all things not British are both
uncivilized and dangerous. The Oriental characters are even flatter in conception. Chang, who rescues the Westerners after their plane crashes and acts as
their host and guide in Shangri-La, is barely characterized at all other than in
atmospheric terms; he is all embroidered silk costumes, telling silences, and
"measured stateliness." Although Lo-Tsen is eccentrically individualized as a
harpsichordist whose specialty seems to be eighteenth century gavottes and
fugues, her function is to portray Hilton's avatar of the eternal feminine. For
Conway she is "a symbol of all that was delicate and fragile" and to Chang

she is an Oriental antitype of Shakespeare's Cleopatra because she *"removes hunger where she least satisfies."* Bridging Orient and Occident is the High Lama, né Perrault, a Capuchin friar born in 1681 and resident in Shangri-La since 1734. Having discovered a combination of yoga and drugs which extends natural life to several hundred years, Perrault develops a technique of "clairvoyant meditation," a visionary capacity derived from a melding of Christian and Buddhist spiritual disciplines. Like the other characters, the High Lama is both stereotype and crackpot, psychologically empty but useful as a vehicle for Hilton's allegorical illustration of life ennobled.

Even Conway, the only really interesting character in *Lost Horizon*, is essentially a type, as he intimates when he tells the High Lama, "You can label me '1914-1918.'" But he is, at least, a fully realized stereotype. His college friend Rutherford finds "something a bit Philip Sidney-ish" about him, and the comparison suggests both Conway's attractiveness and his peculiarity, for he is a cultivated dilettante, a brilliant throwback to the Renaissance, and a resigned malcontent in the twentieth century. Temperamentally out of step with modern life and psychologically wounded by his experience in the trenches during World War I, Conway has adopted a public posture of aloofness and passivity. Although the object of Mallinson's hero-worship, he is "bored by mere exploits"; he is neither decisive nor ambitious, but contemplative, lethargic and nearly asexual. "Part of Conway," Rutherford tells us, "was always an onlooker."

That passively receptive aspect of the protagonist makes him a useful instrument for the processing of Hilton's vision of a sublime monastic retreat from world crisis. Where Brinklow wants to proselytize Shangri-La, Barnard to exploit it, and Mallinson to bomb it, Conway finds in the drowsy, rarefied atmosphere of the lamasery the perfect receptacle for his own languorous temper and fragile psyche. "His mind," Rutherford writes, "dwelt in a world of its own, Shangri-La in microcosm." Here is the central feature of *Lost Horizon*. It is not distinctive or distinguished either in construction or in characterization; the novel exists for the sake of Conway's encounter with the ethereal ideal of solitude at the top of the world. In *Lost Horizon* mood, posture, ambience are nearly everything. Ultimately, the mood of the book — and this must challenge easy classification of Hilton as simply or exclusively a Utopianist — is permeated by intimations of loss, disillusionment, and ruin in both global and personal terms.

Whether ambience is a sufficient basis for a Utopian alternative to the normal world is a real issue. "Is there anything incompatible between monasticism and trigonometry?" Chang asks Conway at their first meeting. The very phrasing of the question suggests the cerebral and passionless vision of life in *Lost Horizon*. The ideal state of being depicted in the novel is so removed from the world of feeling, so abstract and antisocial that one must wonder finally whether trigonometry and monasticism together are incompatible with

Utopia. Hilton offers little detail about the lives of the happy peasants in the valley of Blue Moon beneath Shangri-La; the novel's attention is on the lamas' clairvoyant powers and their role as preservers of high culture. The most specific Hilton gets in portraying daily life in Shangri-La is in his emphasis on moderation and courtesy as central virtues. But he undercuts even these hints at Utopian principles by turning them into whimsy: the moderation of Shangri-La extends to moderate heresy in matters of theology, moderate truth-fulness with visitors, moderate obedience to the moderately strict rules of the lamas, and the practice of moderate chastity. And when Barnard is given a sampling of the valley's courtesy in the form of sexual "hospitality" of "a comprehensive kind," the notions of courtesy and moderation are reduced into material for the Tibetan equivalent of a New Orleans brothel. The facetious-ness may have some appeal for adolescent and celibate imaginations, but Hil-ton's immoderate foolery subverts his imaginative representation of the ideal life.

Hilton is more impressive in the grim rather than the clever passages of *Lost Horizon*. Just before he dies, Father Perrault issues an apocalyptic warning about a new Dark Age in which most of civilization will be ended by the "airman bearing loads of death." Apart from the personal benefit of prolonged life enjoyed by the fully initiated lamas, the *raison d'être* of Shangri-La is as a sanctuary and repository of civilization during "the long age of desolation" to come. In his last vision Perrault foresees a future Renaissance "at a great distance, a new world stirring in the ruins, stirring clumsily but in hopeful-ness, seeking its lost and legendary treasures." In the climactic chapters in which Perrault instructs Conway and prepares him to assume the responsibility of High Lamahood, Hilton's language rises above the often banal dialogue elsewhere in the novel and the tendency to mere phrasemaking, to paradox and epigram cultivated as stylistic mannerisms. Here the language achieves both an eschatological grandeur and a bleak simplicity which, for once, make the tran-quil, dispassionate, disciplined ethos of the snowbound monastery appealing and moving.

Lost Horizon contributed a resonant term to the geography of Utopia: Shangri-La. A generation ago millions who never read Hilton's novel knew its pastoral associations because both a popular song and Franklin D. Roosevelt's mountain haven in Maryland were named Shangri-La. After enjoying bestsell-ing status throughout the 1930's, *Lost Horizon* was adapted to film in a famous version starring Ronald Colman. But nearly fifty years after its initial publica-tion *Lost Horizon* shows its age. It is difficult to find a paperback copy in bookstores, except in so-called "enriched" editions intended for use in the high school curriculum, the last refuge of "popular classics." Roosevelt's re-treat was prosaically renamed by Dwight Eisenhower as Camp David, and that name has stuck. A new musical film version of *Lost Horizon* with an interna-tional cast was a commercial and aesthetic failure in 1973. And one must wonder whether the film's lack of success was not due as much to the passing of Hilton's original conception and to his awkward lyricism as to any defects in the cinematic adaptation. Even when it was first published, favorable reviewers saw *Lost Horizon* as a slender entertainment; now it seems too thin as to be vulnerable to parody and derision. Some features of the book continue to be pertinent to our cultural tensions and urgencies, and it is likely that Hilton's work will continue to have interest to students of Utopian and fantastic fiction and to cultural historians of the period between the two world wars. But its hold on the popular imagination seems at an end.

Robert Crossley

Sources for Further Study

Criticism:

Dangerfield, George. *"Lost Horizon,"* in *Saturday Review*. X (October 14, 1933), p. 181. This criticism finds Hilton's fantasy studiously delicate yet cautions that the enjoyment of fantasy is not a matter of belief but rather of acquiesence.

MacAbee, Helen. "Hilton's *Lost Horizon,"* in *Yale Review*. XXIII (Winter, 1934), p. VI. MacAbee views *Lost Horizon*'s simplicity and grace as its major stylistic strengths.

Reviews:

Booklist. XXX, November, 1973, p. 79.
Canadian Forum. XIV, December, 1933, p. 113.
New York Times. October 15, 1933, p. 8.
North American Review. CCXXXVI, November, 1933, p. 476.
Times Literary Supplement. September 28, 1933, p. 648.

THE LOST WORLD

Author: Arthur Conan Doyle (1859-1930)
First book publication: 1912
Type of work: Novel
Time: The early twentieth century
Locale: London and a plateau somewhere in the Amazon basin

An account of an expedition to a plateau whose isolation from the surrounding country during a period of millions of years has allowed the survival of creatures from several epochs of prehistory

> *Principal characters:*
> GEORGE EDWARD CHALLENGER, an eccentric genius
> PROFESSOR SUMMERLEE, a skeptical scientist
> LORD JOHN ROXTON, an explorer and adventurer
> E. D. MALONE, a reporter

It is said that in setting out to write *The Lost World* Conan Doyle was making a conscious attempt to "do for the boys' book what Sherlock Holmes had done for the detective story." The modern reader may be inclined to infer from this remark that the story was aimed at juvenile readers, but this is not the case. For the term "boys' book" actually refers to a set of literary conventions rather than to the age of a presumed audience. The romance of exploration, for example, usually was written for a general audience, and was thought to appeal especially to boys not because of its juvenility but because of its determined masculinity. The *milieus* of such stories are the distant corners of the Earth, still mysterious and alien when the genre was at its height, populated by savage tribes, dangerous animals, and lost civilizations, and always bristling with natural catastrophes. The missions which took small parties of intrepid heroes into such regions were the business of men, and though the women they left behind might occupy a treasured place in their memories, their proper place was exploring an old civilization, far, far away. It was this incarnation of the idealized man's world of courage, honor, and veiled misogyny that made books of this type the prescribed reading-matter of the growing Victorian boy, and allowed the genre to provide a good living for a whole class of professional writers.

Conan Doyle was a thoroughgoing professional in his literary affairs and did most of his writing in a hardheaded, if not actually cynical, spirit. He could not help seeing that the romance of exploration was a financially lucrative territory for a writer, though he knew that he came very late to the genre. As things turned out, there was time left for just one more epic flourish before World War I transfigured the world and ushered in a new predominant *Weltanschauung* not nearly so conducive to the production of such romances, and Doyle provided that flourish in *The Lost World*.

Doyle's awareness of the fact that the genre was entering its decadent phase has much to do with the style of *The Lost World*, which marks it as an exceptional work. The novel is always close to self-parody, refusing to take itself wholly seriously even while it revels in its own audacity. The very presentation of the first book edition testifies to this quality of flamboyant irony: the frontispiece is a photograph of "the members of the expedition" with Doyle posing in a monstrous false beard as Challenger, and there are other fake photographs among the illustrations to further the impression of journalistic counterfeit. Challenger's image is also inlaid into the cover in gilt, above the inscription "Yours truly (to use the conventional lie) George Edward Challenger." These devices provide a caricature of the convention by which other such novels masquerade soberly as reportage.

The characters, too, are caricatures — Challenger a glorious version of the extrovert variety of eccentric genius, Roxton of the eternal H. Rider Haggard hero. Summerlee is the more introverted version of scientific expertise as portrayed in popular literature, and even Malone, who plays "straight man" to the other three, is led to join the mission according to a classically absurd cliché: he is asked to prove his manhood by his beloved Gladys, whose professed admiration for doers of great deeds does not prevent her from marrying a solicitor's clerk while he is away. It is, however, a testament to Doyle's common sense and skill as a writer that all this parody is kept under control. Its place is as a kind of decorative border, while the real heart of the book is of a different quality — pure adventure in the grand manner, played for dramatic effect with sincerity and great enthusiasm.

There were two aspects of the exploratory romance which encapsulated the spirit of its time. First, it dealt with distant horizons in the prevailing mood of expansion, as if there were no end in sight to the extension of the dominion of Victoria's empire. The ethics (or lack of them) of colonial exploitation are nowhere better reflected than in this genre, which takes for granted the innate superiority of the Englishman and finds in that imagined excellence the right to use all the world's territories for whatever purpose might occur to him. The genre makes the wastelands of the world the venues of expeditions in imaginary tourism. Second, though perhaps less obviously, the romance of exploration was all about wealth, both literal and metaphorical; exploration romances are thoroughly saturated with the parallel myths of "making one's fortune" in distant places and of the tempering of (male) character through the endurance of hardship and the experience of heroism.

It was Doyle's acceptance of these basic aspects of his story (in his use and treatment of them he is not in the least satirical) that assured *The Lost World*'s success within the genre in spite of its parodic elements. The members of the expedition carry the ethos of prewar Britain into deepest Amazonia and come back the richer for it, both literally, and figuratively, in their harvest of experience. Malone is a better person for his trials; he is set free rather than confounded by the perfidy of Gladys, and the point is made explicitly by the symbolic handshake which closes the book.

There were several writers who achieved particular fame with novels of exploratory romance, but there were two in particular whose works become archetypal of it: H. Rider Haggard, whose *King Solomon's Mines* had been the kingpin of the genre for twenty years when Doyle began to write *The Lost World*, and Jules Verne, whose *Journey to the Center of the Earth* had been the most ambitious work of its type for half a century. The project of writing a new novel which could stand alongside these works even as the genre waned in its influence and timeliness necessitated a combination of the spirit of Haggard and the imaginative ambition of Verne. If there is one point on which *The Lost World* is noticeably weak, it is where Doyle fails to capture the former — the account of the journey *to* the lost world is a pale shadow of a Haggardesque expedition — but in the latter area he was particularly well-suited to excel.

It was because of Doyle's unique imagination, however, that *The Lost World* enjoyed a flavor quite distinct from the work of his predecessors. In Verne's work of imaginary tourism, the main speculative focus was always on the means of transportation. It is Verne's machines that are charismatic, and though his characters, with their aid, see great wonders, they do so only as observers looking out from the portholes of a *Nautilus* or down from the basket of a balloon; they rarely get *involved*. Other writers in the genre who imitated Verne — Stables, Collingwood, Strang, and others — adopted his system of priorities as well as the inspiration to speculate. Though Verne populated his imaginary world within the Earth with creatures from prehistory, and though monsters were a regular feature of the more exotic romances of the sea, the use of the imagination in the population of distant environments and had been curiously restrained. Gigantic creatures of loathsome aspect were frequently invoked, but they were almost invariably alone and made monstrous only by size. The fossil record had been available as an imaginative stimulus long before Doyle wrote *The Lost World*, and perhaps the most remarkable thing about the story is that it had not been told before.

In parading before the reader the prehistoric monsters of the plateau, Doyle shows considerable delicacy and restraint, being clever enough to imply more than he actually shows. He manages to make the reader appreciate that the primary source of wonder is the fact of their survival rather than the assumed ultra-brutality of their intercourse with one another. The iguanodons are observed in placid circumstances, and the pterodactyls are described while engaged in the pursuit of their mundane affairs. The carnivorous dinosaur makes its early appearances in the darkness, merely glimpsed on each occasion. There is none of the crude routine of carefully staged battles which was to become the staple diet of Hollywood films in the wake of the first film version of the novel made in 1925. *The Lost World* would undoubtedly be a lesser work had Doyle used his prehistoric monsters according to the same melodramatic predilections of the filmmakers, for that would have reduced his characters to mere spectators.

Although Doyle has *Homo sapiens* and "ape-men" coexisting on the plateau with his dinosaurs, he is careful to stress that they are survivors from very different eras. Much of the book's power derives from the fact that in Challenger, Doyle found a human character who could compete for attention with the dinosaurs and upstage the ape-men with consummate ease. A great deal of the delight which the author took in his novel arises from the presence of Challenger, and this delight communicates itself to the reader in no uncertain terms.

Doyle apparently was fonder by far of Challenger as a personality than he was of Sherlock Holmes. The character was later to change dramatically in the sequels, as Doyle himself changed after the death of his son; and the extent to which Doyle identified with his hero is clearly evident in the rather desperate pages of *The Land of Mist*. *The Poison Belt*, too, features Challenger in his original, inimitable *persona*, but it is in *The Lost World* that the author is at his best and most expansive, making free with his ironic abuse and wonderful conceit. There is no one else in literature quite like him.

The Lost World was written as pure entertainment, and as such it is a huge success. It stands at the very end of an era of great adventure stories, and it is the equal of anything else in its genre. It did *not* do for the boys' book what Sherlock Holmes did for the detective story — that is, it did not open up a new and more vital era or create a new type of modern folk-hero. What it *did* do was to give a final flourish to the romance of exploration before that genre had to forsake the no-longer-untrodden wastes of Earth and take its stand firmly within the boundaries of science fiction, as it moved on to other dimensions and to the trackless wilderness of outer space.

Brian Stableford

Sources for Further Study

Criticism:

Maddocks, Melvin. "The Novel as Science Non-Fiction," in *Life*. XXX (May, 1969), p. 15. Maddocks looks at Conan Doyle's influence on modern writers.

Reviews:

Atheneum. II, October 19, 1912, p. 446.

Boston Transcript. October 19, 1912, p. 9.

Dial. LIII, November 16, 1912, p. 384.

Nation. XCV, October 17, 1912, p. 360.

New York Times. XVII, October 13, 1912, p. 572.

Outlook. CII, November 2, 1912, p. 505.

Springfield Republican. October 31, 1912, p. 5.

LOVE AND NAPALM: EXPORT U.S.A.

Author: J. G. Ballard (1930-   )
First book publication: 1969 (as *The Atrocity Exhibition*)
Type of work: Short stories
Time: The present
Locale: England

A collection of stories concerning collapsing boundaries between the real and the fictional, the public and the private, and the irrational and the rational

> *Principal characters:*
> TRAVIS, a doctor at a mental hospital and later one of its patients
> MARGARET TRAVIS, his wife
> KAREN NOVOTNY, his mistress
> CATHERINE AUSTEN, another doctor at the hospital and Travis' occasional mistress
> NATHAN, head of the hospital

Some day science fiction will have to come to terms with J. G. Ballard, since his works directly confront those issues upon which the genre depends for its definition. For, whatever definition one chooses for science fiction, the element of change and man's reaction to that change is always one of its central concerns; Heinlein may have the world invaded by puppet masters, van Vogt may create a new superman, and Asimov may develop a race of robots, but each author also investigates the effects of these creations on ordinary humans, and suggests resolutions to the dilemmas generated. Ballard also postulates changes and investigates their consequences; however, unlike Heinlein, van Vogt, and Asimov, he rarely suggests resolutions. It is probably this lack of resolution that has made his work unpopular among many science fiction followers.

In *Love and Napalm: Export U.S.A.* the change that Ballard is most concerned about is the current tendency of people to confuse fiction with reality. In an interview published in *Foundation: The Review of Science Fiction, Volume 9*, Ballard states: "I feel that the balance between fiction and reality has changed significantly in the past decade. . . . We live in a world ruled by fictions of every kind — mass-merchandising, advertising, politics conducted as a branch of advertising . . . , the preempting of any free or original imaginative response by the television screen." Thus, the ways in which mankind views the world and his own position in it are now determined by fictional elements that parade about as reality. What is even worse is the fact that these same fictions also control the ways in which individuals judge themselves.

Ballard tries to portray the consequences of this new way of perceiving life in the first twelve stories of the collection. In each case the reader is presented with Travis, in the roles of both diagnostician and victim. In the first story ("The Atrocity Exhibition"), for example, Travis is obsessed with one of the dominant images of all the stories that follow: the violent automobile accident.

Given the successful linking of the car to sex by advertising, the auto accident can be seen as an overwhelming orgasm. Even the positions of the dead and mutilated victims of the wreck become part of a modern pornography far more exciting than the boring photographs of a centerfold.

Travis is also obsessed with collecting things and arranging them together in ways that seem to satisfy some inner logic known only to himself. This method culminates in lists of objects jarring to the reader by virtue of their vivid symbolism and the violence generated by their forcible juxtaposition. Such lists abound in *Love and Napalm* with often thrilling effect. Frequently they appear to summarize the history of the earth and the development of mankind:

> Keeping his back to the window behind his desk, he assembled the terminal documents he had collected with so much effort during the previous months: (1) Spectroheliogram of the sun; (2) Front elevation of balcony units, Hilton Hotel, London; (3) Transverse section through a Pre-Cambrian Trilobite; (4) "Chronograms," by E. J. Marey; (5) Photograph taken at noon, August 7th, 1945, of the sand-sea, Qattara Depression, Egypt; (6) Reproduction of Max Ernst's "Garden Airplane Traps"; (7) Fusing sequences for "Little Boy" and "Fat Boy," Hiroshima and Nagasaki A-bombs.

While such a list defies the reader to find a controlling logic, there is an overpowering insistence that the list does make sense, that these "terminal documents" must have a common base simply because they are all products of the human mind.

It is the necessity of finding this rationale that forces Travis to collect the documents in the first place, to try to understand how sex and car have become intertwined, and to bury himself in a wealth of detail in hopes of integrating them all into a new whole. If present-day man, Ballard claims, continues to be deluged with fictional versions of reality, the result will be utter fragmentation. Travis' world is already marked by such fragmentation, and he is trying to pick up the pieces.

But if one becomes obsessed with trying to synthesize in a world that prefers to analyze, one is doomed to frustration, which takes the form of incomplete human relationships in many of the stories in *Love and Napalm*. For example, in "University of Death," Travis (now Talbot) is unable to have a full relationship with his mistress, Karen Novotny, because he is incapable of accepting her as an independent entity; he must integrate her into a geometry of life which does not allow for separateness. The result is described in sterile images that border on the grotesque:

> (1) The flesh impact: Karen Novotny's beckoning figure in the shower stall, open thighs and exposed pubis — traffic fatalities screamed in this soft collision. (2) The flyover below the apartment: the angles between the concrete buttresses contained for Talbot an immense anguish. (3) A crushed fender: in its broken geometry Talbot saw the dismembered body of Karen Novotny, the alternate death of Ralph Nader.

Thus, the lists Travis (Talbot) began to collect as documents of his age now prevent him from developing personal relationships. Since all things must be seen as part of a grand whole, they cease to exist for Travis as independent objects.

The final stage in this quest for the whole is the loss of individual identity. Having relegated the humans around him to their places in the new geometry, Travis must take his own place in it. Thus, in "Notes Towards a Mental Breakdown," the reader sees the final collapse of the private life of Travis (now Trabert):

> "This motorcade," Dr. Nathan explained as they set off, "we may interpret as a huge environmental tableau, a mobile psycho-drama which recapitulates the Apollo disaster in terms of both Dealey Plaza and the experimental car crashes examined so obsessively by Nader. In some way, presumably by cathartic collision, Trabert will try to reintegrate space and so liberate the three men in the capsule. For him they still wait there on their contour couches."

Travis has now integrated his life with public life; he has taken his place in the world of public events to the point that he sees his own actions as public events. Such a view of one's life precludes private action because each act will have an effect felt by the entire public. Travis reasons that if such things as the death of the astronauts, the assassination of John Kennedy, and the suicide of Marilyn Monroe can affect his life, then his life can equally affect these events.

Love and Napalm: Export U.S.A. can be seen, therefore, as the presentation of a process of fragmentation begun by a world that substitutes fiction for reality. In order to describe this fragmentation, Ballard uses what has been termed the condensed or fragmented novel. Each paragraph of this form has a title and appears to stand as a chapter. Such a method creates, on the one hand, a feeling of receiving a vast amount of information in a very short space and, on the other, a sense of missing the transitions that would lead to understanding how all this information fits together. The result of the author's technique is to create a tension which works quite well when limited to a few stories, but suffers from overexposure when repeated in fifteen stories. When this repetitiousness is added to the obviously unattractive world of the stories and to their lack of resolution, it is not difficult to understand why *Love and Napalm* is not a widely popular work.

In fact, *Love and Napalm* has aroused a great deal of outrage. There is a story that the first American publisher of *Love and Napalm* finally refused to distribute the book after one of the company's executives read a few of its pages; so shocking were the images and so little sense did they make to him that he had the pages pulped as they came off the press. Whether the story is true or not, it makes a point: Ballard is dealing with a difficult topic in an unfamiliar format, a combination which causes many potential readers to reject the stories. But the fact remains that *Love and Napalm*, despite its difficulties, speaks to the same topics as does science fiction, and sooner or later, writers and readers alike will have to come to terms with it.

Stephen H. Goldman

Sources for Further Study

Reviews:

Best Sellers. XXXII, January 15, 1973, p. 477.

Choice. X, March, 1973, p. 87.

Library Journal. XCVII, November 5, 1972, p. 3726.

Magazine of Fantasy and Science Fiction. LI, September, 1976, p. 30.

New York Times Book Review. October 29, 1972, p. 56.

LOVE IN THE RUINS

Author: Walker Percy (1916-   )
First book publication: 1971
Type of work: Novel
Time: The near future
Locale: New Orleans and vicinity

A comic apocalypse which satirizes man's confidence that he can attain to "angelic" stature through scientific knowledge even as society becomes increasingly polarized into hostile factions

> Principal characters:
> DR.THOMAS MORE, a psychiatrist who has invented a device for measuring the degree of man's fall from grace
> MOIRA, his cheap but pretty mistress
> ELLEN OGLETHORPE, his efficient, conscientious nurse
> LOLA RHOADES, his former lover, a concert cellist
> DR. GEORGE "DUSTY" RHOADES, Lola's father, a conservative proctologist
> DR. MAX GOTTLIEB, a behavioral psychiatrist with a benevolent interest in helping More
> DR. BUDDY BROWN, another behaviorist, More's chief rival both professionally and for Moira
> FR. KEV KEVIN, an ex-priest now employed in the "love" clinic
> MRS. MARVA MORE, the narrator's widowed mother, a conservative real estate agent
> ART IMMELMANN, a mysterious drug salesman and promoter

It is hard to think of a novel which raises more pointedly than *Love in the Ruins* the question of the parameters of science fiction as a mode of literature. Walker Percy is a respected "mainstream" novelist; his earlier novels have no science fiction elements; he has never been associated with any of the usual science fiction outlets; and *Love in the Ruins* itself was neither marketed nor received as a work of science fiction when published.

But if the term "science fiction" means what it implies — a work of fiction dealing with science, or, more properly, with the effects of the scientific revolution on the human condition, moral and spiritual as well as physical — then *Love in the Ruins* surely has a place among science fiction novels. Subtitled "The Adventures of a Bad Catholic at a Time Near the End of the World," the book is a comic apocalypse — an extravagant narrative meditation on the collapse of the American Dream with the substitution of expanding material affluence for the sense of divinely ordained mission which motivated the people of America from the time of the earliest settlements. In more general terms it is an ironic probing of the myth of progress, of fallen man's delusion that he can escape his plight through the scientific technology spawned by his own ingenuity.

Although the main body of the work occupies only four days (July 1 through July 4, during an unspecified year in the not-too-distant future), concluding with a brief epilogue "Five Years Later," the narrative is so densely peopled, so minutely elaborated with flashback and detail, so rich in allusion, that it defies summary. At the center is the first-person narrator, a middle-aged psychiatrist, Dr. Thomas More, a descendant of none other than St. Thomas More. As a young researcher, More had made a great breakthrough in diagnosing a curious reversal of roles in the Tulane Psychiatric Hospital, following a nuclear accident involving experiments with heavy sodium reactions beneath the stands of the Sugar Bowl. He had concluded that it was the cloud of radiation hanging over the French Quarter for several days which had caused many of the patients to become temporarily sane, their physicians similarly insane.

In the intervening years, however, his plain though pious daughter has succumbed to a horrible disease and his "ex-Episcopalian, ex-Apple Queen" wife has run off with a homosexual English Hindu, only to die in Cozumel. As a result More has given way to alcoholism and promiscuous lechery, and indeed has only recently ended a stay in the mental ward of the very hospital of which he is a staff member, having halfheartedly attempted suicide six months before.

In the meantime, More has added to his initial breakthrough with the development of a highly accurate yet portable encephalographic device by which, without electrodes or other visible contact, he can diagnose the spiritual state of a patient through brainwave readings from the exact centers of various kinds of cerebral activity. With this invention, "More's Qualitative Quantitative Ontological Lapsometer," the narrator is capable of specific, mathematically quantifiable diagnoses of the effects of mankind's *Lapse*, or fall from grace. Obviously the lapsometer unites metaphysical with physical, spiritual with material, and More hopes, in time, to cure the emptiness and alienation of Original Sin itself, grown more acute since Descartes severed soul from body, turning the former "into a ghost that haunts its own house."

During the four days which occupy almost ninety-five percent of the novel's text, More is busy trying — unsuccessfully — to secure institutional support for the further development of the lapsometer in order to head off what he fears will be a national crisis resulting from America's acute schizophrenia, pervasive in public as well as personal life. As might be expected, More's mostly behaviorist colleagues are wholly skeptical about any device which offers to combine science with theology and ontology, which diagnoses mental disorders in terms of "angelism" and "bestialism."

Apart from three women — each in her own way spellbound by More's eccentric, bumbling brilliance — and a few drug-besotted flower children, the only believer in the lapsometer is the mysterious Art Immelmann, who claims to be a "funding expert," a liaison between private and public sources of research money, and who offers More millions of dollars and assurances of a Nobel Prize if he will only sign over all rights to the lapsometer. Art, a master of the jargon of academic bureaucrats, is marked by peculiar anachronisms of dress, mannerisms, and hair (a flattop): in short, he "looks like the sort of fellow who used to service condom vendors in the old Auto Age." He is rapidly identifiable as the comic Antichrist of More's comic apocalypse, and it is he, with his breezy confidence and bland assurances, rather than the behaviorists, who is finally the narrator's chief antagonist.

The social and political crisis which hangs over the mildly futuristic New Orleans of Dr. Thomas More has been extrapolated by Percy from the tense conditions of the late 1960's: the center has not held, and white America is split into fiercely respectable conservative "Knotheads" and grotesquely liberated leftist radicals, black America into docile servants of the whites and militant "Bantus," who inhabit the swamps and make occasional forays into the suburbs. The New Orleans area is still littered with burnt-out cars and deserted buildings from the race riots of five years earlier, and the affluent "Paradise Estates," where More and the other physicians on the staff of the federal medical center live, is virtually an armed camp. Sharing the swamp with the Bantus, however, are many middle-class children, antitechnology hippies who smoke marijuana as they await the collapse of industrial civilization.

The fragmentation of society at large is mirrored in More's (and Walker Percy's) Catholic Church. The disgruntled traditionalists have formed the American Catholic Church, which recognizes no pope since Pius XII, celebrates feasts like "Property-Rights Sunday," and plays "The Star-Spangled Banner" at the elevation of the Host. This faction is represented in the novel by the narrator's widowed mother; still slim and attractive in her late sixties, she has made a fortune in real estate since her husband's death and become obsessed with judicial astrology. The liberal wing of the Church has simply disintegrated. Mrs. More's leftist counterpart is the former curate of Thomas' and her own old parish, Fr. Kev Kevin, who has left the priesthood, married (a former nun of course), and taken a job at the "Love Clinic" of the medical center. He is shown reading *Commonweal* as he monitors the "vaginal console" while volunteer "subjects" participate in various electronically calibrated erotic experiments in front of oneway mirrors.

More himself, although a "bad Catholic" and not in a state of grace or communion with the Church, is one of a dwindling minority and remains faithful — in his heart at least — to the same Roman Catholic Church for which his illustrious ancestor died. This attachment reflects in many ways his contradictory yet sympathetic state: he suffers both the "morning terrors" and anomie of liberal "angelism," and the "conservative rages" and paranoia (and large bowel complaints — the proctologists are all conservative) of the Knotheads. Both the narrator's dilemma, and its ultimate solution, are graphically symbolized in his relationships with three women.

Dr. More's current mistress is Moira, an attractive but vulgar medical technician — a "popsy" in the term of a disapproving colleague — who thrives on *Cosmopolitan* and the verse of Rod McKuen. Anticipating the worst sort of violent outbreak on the Fourth, More has stocked a room in an abandoned Howard Johnson's motel with enough food, clothing, liquor, ammunition, and so on for the two of them to remain there in safety for several months. Through the quirky events of the day, however, two other women, who both have a deep interest in him, also end up under More's protection at the motel on the Fourth.

One woman is Lola Rhoades, a concert cellist on the Texas A. & M. music faculty with whom More had enjoyed a drunken, one-night fling in the bunker of the eighteenth green of the Paradise Country Club. Her father, the conservative proctologist Dr. George "Dusty" Rhoades (who has not wholly forgiven the narrator for his indiscretion with Lola), and More's own mother are both pushing a marriage between the two. Such a union would offer the wayward psychiatrist a strong feminine personality to look after him; the Rhoades's fake Southern colonial mansion, "Tara," constructed from auctioned-off props from *Gone with the Wind*; and plenty of money and respectability.

The third woman is More's nurse, Ellen Oglethorpe, a Presbyterian "of strict observance" who believes in duty and the golden rule even though belief in God has faded from the foreground of her Protestant ethic. In contrast to the leftist self-indulgence offered by Moira and the rightist self-indulgence offered by Lola, Ellen represents the call of More's conscience back to wholeness of character and purpose.

It is the influence of Ellen, albeit indirectly, which finally enables Dr. Thomas More to overcome the satanic temptations of "Art Immelmann" even as his venerable forebear, St. Thomas More, had overcome the temptations of fame and power in his day. Immelmann has provided for More's lapsometer an attachment which makes what had been merely a diagnostic device into a tool for "treatment": with Immelmann's attachment the lapsometer can actually alter, temporarily, the attitudes and moods of patients. Having gotten hold of most of More's working models, Immelmann busies himself precipitating precisely the social crisis More had hoped to avert, assuring the worried psychiatrist that it is all "boilerplate" — a necessary trial run for the invention. Obviously, the temptations for Thomas More are personal fame and success, but also the triumph of his science, the work of his mind, over the fallen human condition. Immelmann goes too far, however, in trying to "hire" away Ellen. As a last resort, More finds himself invoking aloud his sainted ancestor to *"pray for us and drive this son of a bitch hence."* Immelmann disappears into swirling smoke — ostensibly the product of heavy sodium reactions caused by the misuse of the lapsometer.

Science fiction has been termed the religion of atheists; but if this definition is correct, then Walker Percy's *Love in the Ruins* (like C. S. Lewis' "Ransom Trilogy" and Walter Miller's *A Canticle for Leibowitz*) is a literary paradox. It has the future setting of science fiction, and the plot hinges on a piece of technological extrapolation (the lapsometer); but underneath the sparkling play of Percy's ironic wit, it is a profoundly Christian work. It is no surprise to discover, in the brief epilogue "Five Years Later," that Dr. More has reformed his wenching and drinking (almost) and returned to the fold of the Church (after a fashion), and that he is married to Ellen who has already given birth to two of his children and carries a third. St. Thomas More's sanctity has finally vanquished Dr. Thomas More's science.

To be sure, he still tinkers with the lapsometer, but we have little reason to believe that anything will come of it: the Bantus have struck oil in the swamps and have succeeded in taking over the New Orleans area with their newly acquired wealth where they had earlier failed with violence. Most of the whites — Knothead proctologists and leftist behavioralists alike — have long since departed; and those who remain, if not exactly oppressed, are lorded over and patronized by the affluent blacks. Dr. Thomas More ekes out a humble living by tending to poor whites on a barter system and by conducting a "fat clinic" at Paradise Country Club for obese Bantu socialites. The "lapsometer" — science's attempt to cross the truly ultimate frontier by curing man's alienation from self, by erecting his fallen nature — has proven an idle dream. The ultimate realities remain for Dr. Thomas More, as for his saintly ancestor, bed and board and "eating Christ" in the mass. Thus, and no other way, can man be raised from his "lapse" into Original Sin.

R. V. Young, Jr.

Sources for Further Study

Criticism:

Coles, Robert. *Walker Percy: An American Search*. Boston: Little, Brown, 1978, pp. 191-208. Coles has written the most comprehensive and current study on Walker Percy. Within the work he discusses *Love in the Ruins* as it relates to the body of Percy's fiction, rather than science fiction literature in general.

Luschei, Martin. *The Sovereign Wayfarer: Walker Percy's Diagnosis of the Malaise*. Baton Rouge: Louisiana State University Press, 1972, pp. 111-168. Luschei gives a thorough examination of Percy's fiction, with some mention of *Love in the Ruins* within these pages.

Reviews:

America. CXXIV, June 12, 1971, p. 617.

Best Sellers. XXXI, May 15, 1971, p. 85.

Critic. XXX, September, 1971, p. 69.

New Republic. CLXIV, May 22, 1971, p. 1728.

New York Review of Books. XVI, July 1, 1971, p. 15.
New York Times Book Review. May 23, 1971, p. 7 and July 4, 1971, p. 2.
Saturday Review. LIV, May 15, 1971, p. 42.
Times Literary Supplement. October 1, 1971, p. 1165.

THE LOVECRAFT MYTHOS

Author: H. P. Lovecraft (1890-1937)
Type of work: Short stories

Stories built around the concept of a cosmic myth cycle concerning a pantheon of primal gods, ancient beings indifferent to man but causing profound horror upon encounter and holding the power to annihilate human life

Howard Phillips Lovecraft created, in his fiction, a distinctive and richly imaginative mythology involving a pantheon of ancient gods and a world view of "cosmic indifferentism." His fictional gods, the Great Old Ones, occupy the outer spheres of being, beyond the dimensioned universe known to man but ever present behind what man calls reality, and eternally ready to obtrude upon man's world. Lovecraft's elder gods are not "evil," nor are they "good," for they dwell in unthinkable realms beyond all such merely human conceptions as good and evil. Toward humankind they are simply indifferent. They will sweep humans pitilessly aside if need be, but without true malevolence — man is simply not important enough to be resented, or even to be recognized. The Great Old Ones are incomprehensible players upon a stage grander than the universe. Their indifference makes them a sort of symbolic embodiment of the kind of universe which Lovecraft actually conceived of himself as facing: a cosmos neither for nor against humankind, a universe in which man is the merest incidental excrescence, born only yesterday and soon to disappear unmourned. Lovecraft's world view did not make him a morose figure by any means, but he was serious about it. The Lovecraft Mythos fictionally reflects his outlook on a cosmically grandiose scale, forming a complex of stories in many ways unique in all of literature.

Much has been written about which Lovecraft stories are "Mythos stories" and which are not. The fact is that most of his tales contain some amount of Mythos flavor, varying from a heavy emphasis to virtually none. It is a largely pointless task to define exactly which works belong to the Mythos, but it is useful to consider briefly some of those short stories which most strongly exhibit Lovecraft's mythic conception.

This conception began to take shape fairly early in Lovecraft's career, if only faintly and peripherally at first. In 1921 he wrote "The Nameless City," quoting a mysterious couplet from the *Necronomicon*, a mythical, ancient, rare book containing veiled references to the Old Ones and formulae for invoking them. He first mentions the book by name in 1922, however, in "The Hound," and in 1923 a much longer quotation from its blasphemous pages appears in "The Festival." But not until 1926 did Lovecraft write a story in which the outlines of his Mythos began to appear clearly; that story was "The Call of Cthulhu." It was probably because of this story that August Derleth coined the term "Cthulhu Mythos" — a misnomer, since the tales taken together make it clear that Cthulhu is a secondary figure in Lovecraft's scheme.

Although secondary, Cthulhu is an unforgettably horrendous character. In "The Call of Cthulhu," the narrator finds among his late granduncle's papers the records of investigations which have turned up bizarre and disturbing parallels. A police detective investigating voodoo in Louisiana and an anthropologist doing research in Greenland have found evidence of dark cults, both possessing repellent stone images of some winged, vaguely octopuslike entity. The cultists worship primal gods called the Great Old Ones, who have seeped down from the stars bringing their stone idols with them, but they have been trapped beneath ocean waters by the dimly prehistoric sinking of their nightmare city of R'lyeh. (One day when the stars are right the cultists will help to free great Cthulhu from his watery tomb, so that he may reclaim his dominion.) Further, the granduncle, Professor Angell, has met a sensitive young sculptor named Wilcox, who in a dream state has fashioned a bas-relief virtually identical to the hideous cephalopod of the obscure cultists. By chance, the narrator later finds fragments from an Australian newspaper containing the story of a strange encounter in the Pacific, and finally obtains a full account from the private journal of a Norwegian sailor who was there. He learns that ancient R'lyeh has risen from the waves, loosing the gelatinous enormity Cthulhu upon hapless sailors and spreading telepathic madness, which only subsides when R'lyeh sinks again.

Lovecraft's descriptive powers in this tale are striking. The story's sense of alienage is heightened by the fact that the geometry of R'lyeh is "all wrong." In this strange setting, the sailors first perceive Cthulhu as a "nasty, slopping sound down there," a horror which grows in intensity from line to line in the story until it seems overwhelming, an alien monstrosity which gives forth, when rammed by the fleeing ship, "a bursting as of an exploded bladder, a slushy nastiness as of a cloven sunfish, a stench as of a thousand opened graves, and" — here Lovecraft begins to show some of the descriptive restraint that so characterizes and strengthens his later tales — "a sound that the chronicler would not put on paper." As in so many of his stories, Lovecraft here maintains a distance between the reader and the actual horror, by having the narrator discover the final events indirectly. As in classical Greek theater, Lovecraft has kept the actual carnage "off-stage," as it were, without lessening its impact.

Lovecraft also has remained faithful to one of his most cherished tenets in introducing the reader to Cthulhu. According to his theory of writing weird fiction, a story of this type should culminate in the suspension or violation of natural laws — in the occurrence of that which cannot occur; but in building up to this culmination, the story must maintain strict realism. The reader must undergo "willing suspension of disbelief" at the right moment. Lovecraft indeed maintains realism in "The Call of Cthulhu." The narrator confronts matter-of-fact newspaper cuttings and scientific notes, and correlates events only by chance, maintaining skepticism until the end and learning only too late that the "most merciful thing in the world. . . . is the inability of the human mind to correlate all its contents." The realism is such that when the ancient horror from untold depths of space bursts forth, the effect is genuinely hideous.

But the Lovecraft Mythos did not emerge in its fuller form until 1928, when a truly remarkable tale appeared, probably one of the most powerful tales of cosmic horror ever written. "The Dunwich Horror" grew out of impressions which Lovecraft gathered while traveling about western Massachusetts during the summer of 1928, visiting his friends W. Paul Cook and H. Warner Munn in Athol and staying with his amateur journalist friend Mrs. Edith Miniter and her cousin Evanore Beebe in North Wilbraham. Impressions of these locals are blended to form the decadent backwater called Dunwich, about which Lovecraft leaves an atmosphere of brooding morbidity. Lavinia Whateley, "a somewhat deformed, unattractive albino woman of 35," has given birth to a goatish, fast-growing boy named Wilbur, whose father is unknown. Strange things happen at the ancient Whateley house; large numbers of cattle are bought and walls and partitions are continually taken out of the house, as if to accommodate something enormous growing within. The Whateleys are feared even by the sordid degenerates of the region; they often visit a great "table-like stone" atop Sentinel Hill (a stone probably inspired by the "sacrificial stone" at Mystery Hill in North Salem, New Hampshire, which Lovecraft saw on a visit there with H. Warner Munn). Lavinia's father, Old Wizard Whateley, makes the hills shake when he shrieks the hideous name of *Yog-Sothoth*, "with a great book open in his arms before him." Thus we meet the central god-figure in the Lovecraft Mythos. The great book is, of course, the *Necronomicon*, of which, however, the Whateleys possess only a copy of the inferior English translation. Lovecraft builds credibility here by implying a history of translation of the infamous tome, having the boldness to attribute its English rendering to an actual necromancer, John Dee (1527-1608).

Tension heightens continuously in the story. A visitor to the Whateley house hears "rhythmical surging and lapping" upstairs, and eventually, after Wilbur Whateley has died trying to steal Miskatonic University's complete copy of the *Necronomicon*, the horror in the house breaks loose to ravage the countryside. It is finally ceremonially vanquished atop Sentinel Hill by Miskatonic's Professor Henry Armitage, but not before it bellows the name of Yog-Sothoth, its father (and the father of its brother Wilbur). Thus Lovecraft anticipates by some decades the later "demoniac conception" story in his tale of Yog-Sothoth. As in "The Call of Cthulhu" there is the implication that human cultists, or at least frightfully degenerate individuals, worship and serve such creatures. Indeed, Wilbur has tried by sorcery to open the way for Yog-Sothoth to enter this world from the outer realms. Lovecraft has created a whole fictional world in which such things are possible. In his world, the *Necronomicon* is a known repository of ancient secrets best left unstirred. Lovecraft infuses realism by telling us that the Widener Library at Harvard (among a very few other places) has its own copy of the dreadful book.

Furthermore, Lovecraft has made highly imaginative use of real places in his setting for the tale. It was at the Beebe farmhouse in North Wilbraham that Lovecraft, stopping there in 1928, was told the local legend of the whippoorwills which appears to such unforgettable advantage in "The Dunwich Horror." And the Cold Spring Glen, into which the tale's enormous, ropy monstrosity stalks, is a reflection of an actual ravine visited by Lovecraft in North New Salem, with his young friend Munn; the "rock falls" and "Bear's Den" mentioned in the tale are really there. For Lovecraft, place was absolutely sentient; his artistic reactions to places seen could be remarkable.

The language of "The Dunwich Horror" offers a great deal to admire. The characters' dialectal descriptions of the horror as "squirmin' ropes," "a octopus, centipede, spider kind o' thing" with a shocking parody of the Whateley face, are not likely to be forgotten, or to allow an imaginative reader to take the nature of Yog-Sothoth lightly. And when Wilbur Whateley reads a long passage from the *Necronomicon*, that passage is darkly sonorous, almost Biblical in sound, complete with instances of chiasmus for poetic balance. In this tale, Lovecraft has combined a masterful conception with masterful writing, and has firmly established the central conception of his Mythos.

The elaboration of the Mythos is carried on in other stories. In 1928, just before visiting the spots in western Massachusetts which inspired "The Dunwich Horror," Lovecraft had visited his friend Vrest Orton in Guilford, Vermont, and was impressed with the secluded landscape. In 1930 he wrote "The Whisperer in Darkness," making effective use of this locale. In this Vermont tale, the scholarly recluse Henry Akeley is besieged in his lonely farmhouse, by "Winged Ones" from the nearby woodlands, fungoid denizens of the planet Yuggoth (Pluto). These creatures are worshipers of the Old Ones, celebrating the rite of the Black Goat of the Woods with a Thousand Young, in the name of the Mythos figure *Shub-Niggurath*. There are mentions of such Mythos figures as Cthulhu, Azathoth (the blind idiot god), and the messenger Nyarlathotep. The narrator Wilmarth corresponds, from Arkham, with Akeley, and watches helplessly as Akeley is drawn more and more into subjugation by the buzzing monstrosities which he tries to ward off; and Wilmarth very nearly succumbs to them himself.

Again, in this tale, Lovecraft has shown his prowess at soaking up local impressions during his travels and making superb fictional use of them. It turns out that the house in which Vrest Orton hosted Lovecraft in 1928 was actually built, in the 1820's, by a Samuel Akeley — the house was really "the old Akeley place." The Guilford-Brattleboro region of Vermont is replete with details mentioned in the story, including the West River, in which bodies of Winged Ones are said to be seen floating after the Vermont floods of 1927 (historically real flooding, as one would expect from Lovecraft). He has again grounded his unspeakable horrors in solid New England reality. As likely as not, the character of Henry Akeley may be based on Lovecraft's friend Vrest Orton himself, who certainly did not lack the requisite scholarly characteristics. The story offers yet another look at the plight of hapless human beings who run afoul of primal gods and their minions, and it is told with all the somber mood-building and maintenance of tension that have come to characterize Lovecraft's later style.

The Lovecraft Mythos conception is at the heart of still other excellent stories, notably "The Shadow over Innsmouth" (1931) and "The Shadow out of Time" (1934). The interested reader will find in all these tales Lovecraft's inimitable world of fascination.

Donald R. Burleson

Sources for Further Study

Criticism:

Emmons, Winfred S., Jr. "H. P. Lovecraft as a Mythmaker," in *Extrapolation*. I (May, 1960), pp. 35-37. Emmons provides a brief explanation of the themes of the Chthulu mythos.

Gehman, Richard B. "Imagination Runs Wild," in *New Republic*. XVII (January, 1949), pp. 16-18. This article establishes Lovecraft as a major influence on the direction of modern science fiction.

THE LOVERS

Author: Philip José Farmer (1918-   )
First book publication: 1961
Type of work: Novel
Time: 3050
Locale: The Earth and the planet Ozagen

In a future theocratic dictatorship, love for a nonhuman female leads an ordinary man out of his pathological, repressive conditioning and into emotional, intellectual, and sensual freedom

> *Principal characters:*
> HAL YARROW, a linguistics joat (jack-of-all-trades), a misfit, trapped in an unhappy marriage
> MARY YARROW, his wife, tangled in a neurotic love-hate relationship with him
> KEOKI AMIEL PORNSEN, Hal's gapt (Guardian Angel Pro-Tempore — spiritual adviser and watchdog)
> JEANNETTE RASTIGNAC, Hal's Ozagenian lover, a *lalitha*, an intelligent mimetic insect who appears to be a beautiful woman
> FOBO, a wogglebug (Ozagen's dominant species), an empathist, and Hal's friend
> UZZITES, URIELITES, AND LAMECHANS, respectively, the Sturch's police, priesthood, and elite; lamechans wear a gold Hebrew letter L, the *lamech*

The Lovers appeared as a magazine novelette in 1952 and was revised and expanded for book publication in 1961. It was Philip José Farmer's first published science fiction work, and was received enthusiastically by readers; on the basis of this story and perhaps his next two or three ("Sail On! Sail On!," "The Biological Revolt," "Mother"), Farmer won a 1953 Hugo Award for Best New Author. The story was more than an auspicious beginning for Farmer's career; in the folklore of science fiction, it is cited as the story that broke the sex taboo for the genre. To be accurate, this is true only for the magazine-science fiction ghetto, which in 1952 still lived by the boys' fiction standards of the pulps; two notable works of science fiction outside that ghetto, *Brave New World* and *Nineteen Eighty-Four* had already dealt with sex as an integral part of their fictional worlds. In any case, whatever historical significance *The Lovers* possesses, its place as a work of enduring interest in the science fiction field depends not on whether it was the first to treat its themes, but whether that treatment is interesting in itself.

Hal Yarrow lives under the rule of a familiar type of dystopian government, the theocratic Sturch (state-church). Organized by Isaac Sigmen out of the chaos following the Apocalyptic War, it is a syncretic religion whose scriptures include a *Pre-Torah*, the *Western Talmud*, the *Revised Scriptures*, Dunne's theories of time, and Sigmen's own accounts of his travel through time. Backing up his farrago of pseudoscience and invented theology is an advanced technology that includes truth drugs, the "Elohimeter" (E-meter), and all the machinery necessary to a police state. In addition to the usual techniques of dictatorship, the Sturch keeps its members under control by means of a pair of complementary pathologies — the repression of normal sexuality and the entertainment of paranoid fantasies. The latter spring from the purported ability of Sigmen, the Forerunner, to travel in time and space in order to secure the "real" future for his followers. (In a sequel, *Timestop!*, it is revealed that the culmination of the Forerunner's work will be a millennial situation in which each of the faithful is given a personal universe to rule as a god.) The Forerunner is opposed by his evil brother, Jude Changer (the Backrunner), and Anna Changer (the Scarlet Woman). The job of the faithful is to avoid "unreality" and to resist the Backrunner's temptations to realize pseudofutures, those not ordained by Sigmen's prophecies.

Being "real" or "shib" (from *shibboleth*) requires increasing degrees of asceticism as one advances in the Struch; for example, Hal is expected to have transcended smoking and other minor unrealities on attaining the status of lamechan. For all members of the Sturch, however, the appetites are curbed. Alcohol is forbidden, eating is done in private, and, most important of all, sexual activity is rigidly controlled. Frequency and even specific details of intercourse are prescribed by the Sturch and the *Western Talmud*; dogma asserts that sexuality is "beastly," something man will evolve beyond. In the meantime, intercourse serves as a means of procreation, nothing more. All this has what must be the intended effect on Hal: with his wife, Mary, he is potent but anesthetized; sex brings anxiety rather than pleasure; he is unfulfilled, restless, and fearful.

Jeannette Rastignac instinctively understands that in turning sexuality inward, the Sturch turns libido into aggression, love into hate. It is not surprising that men and women thus cut from their own gentler emotions should accept the fear- and anger-dominated world view of the Sturch — that all nonbelievers must be enemies, that wogglebugs (neatly shortened to "wogs") or any other nonhuman species can be destroyed to make room for man. It is not only believer against unbeliever or man against wog, but believer against believer. The Sturch is a perfect Orwellian paranoid inferno in which a wife may report the unrealities of her husband (as Mary does) or a supervisor may threaten to let a subordinate go because of a low Morality Rating (M.R.). The institution of the Guardian Angel Pro-Tempore and the pyramidal organization of these informer-advisers is the backbone of the system; no one can escape the attention of the guardians of orthodoxy — except the elite, the lamechans, who are theoretically above suspicion thanks to screening with truth drugs and E-meter processing.

The book is unevenly divided into sections with contrasting settings. The Sturch-run Haijac Union (for Hawaii, Australia, Iceland, Japan, America, and Caucasia) of the first four chapters is not only a fear-saturated dictatorship, it is also overpopulated. North America is almost completely urbanized, its population in the billions. The Yarrows share a tiny apartment with another couple on a schedule of twelve-hour shifts. In this claustrophobic environment, the Sturch still conditions its followers to stricter than Victorian standards of modesty, including even eating masks for those situations where one must eat in the presence of others. By contrast, Ozagen's wogglebugs have attained only an early twentieth century level of technology and population density; their cities are open, with widely spaced buildings; there is still wilderness with dangerous fauna. Wogglebug society encourages the release of tensions in argument, drinking, and even fistfights and has partially institutionalized this attitude in Fobo's profession of empathist. Here are also the *lalitha*, nonhuman but apparently perfect females, suited by evolution for the task of attracting and holding a human mate — the perfect temptation for a repressed Haijac citizen.

The central action of the book can be seen as Hal's movement from Earth to Ozagen, from the tutelage of Pornsen to that of Fobo, and, most important, from his destructive marriage to Mary to his liberating affair with Jeannette. In agreeing to go on the Ozagen expedition, Hal consciously wishes to escape the intolerably crowded and paranoid Haijac Union, the miseries of his marriage, and the unwanted attentions of his lifelong gapt. This in itself, as Pornsen recognizes, is already unshib, unreal behavior, but it is also only a reaction to pressure rather than a positive rebellion. In the less intense atmosphere of Ozagen, Hal moves closer to overt rebellion when he finds himself able to contradict and confound Pornsen in an argument — a small matter. But it is Jeannette who inspires him not only to risk an affair (a crime of lust), but also to outwit the Uzzites and the E-meter in order to gain the status of lamechan (a crime much more serious). The fact that he attains the *lamech* in order to make the affair possible makes the moving force behind his behavior clear.

Once he is committed to Jeannette, Hal's transgressions increase in number if not always in severity: he procures and even drinks alcohol, he abandons the eating mask, he refuses to grow the beard appropriate to a lamechan, and he commits fornication, all for Jeannette. These are, the distorted views of the Sturch notwithstanding, minor matters. Hal still passively cooperates with the expedition's main objective, Project Ozagenocide, a plan to depopulate Ozagen by means of a mutated virus in order to make room for human colonists from the Haijac Union. He tells Jeannette of the scheme and tentatively plans for them to escape the general destruction and live out their lives in the eighty-year period before the Sturch's forces can return with the first colonists. Despite his affection for Fobo, however, he does not tell him of the project, nor does he in any way commit an act of what we would recognize as treason. Instead, he explores and expands his new personal world of heart, body, and mind with Jeannette.

The central event of Hal's personal adventure is the physical consummation of his affair with Jeannette; it signals the breakdown of his Sturch conditioning and the birth of a new self. The bane of his life on Earth was the conflict between conditioned compulsions and repressions (which the Sturch would characterize as "real") and an understandable urge to escape from these restraints and give expression to the drives and appetites of the body (drives that Hal thinks of as his "dark self"). Jeannette senses this division — the Sturch, she says, has made him a half-man — and intuitively understands the political uses of displaced libido — "timid lovers" make for "fierce warriors." Their union will make him whole: "Become a baby again," she tells him. "And I will raise you so you forget your hate and know only love. And become a man." In performing his Sturch-appointed duty with Mary, Hal had felt physically divided — "A zone of unfeeling, a nerve-chilling area, a steel plate cut through him. He felt nothing but the jerkings of his body. . . ." With Jeannette, his sensations are restored to him, and he is at least a whole man in body.

Hal and Jeannette are not the only lovers in the book. Hal's Earth marriage represents a kind of pathological love in which resentment and compulsiveness masquerade as affection. Even more curious is Hal's relationship with Pornsen. Pornsen claims to love Hal, and is required by this love to keep him from unreal behavior — thus the whippings, the lectures, the unfavorable M.R. Love is the exercise of power over another: Pornsen tells Hal, ". . . you have felt my love often . . . ," and Hal glances at the "lover" in question, a seven-lashed whip, its handle ironically in the shape of a *crux ansanta*, the Egyptian symbol of eternal life. This whip sums up the Sturch's idea of love: authority, power, the threat or actuality of pain and humiliation. Nonetheless, Pornsen is not a hypocrite; he believes he loves Hal (as did Mary) and is unaware of the complexity of his own emotions and motives. When in terror and pain, blinded by nightlifer venom, it is in the name of love rather than authority that he appeals to Hal for help.

Fobo never claims to love Hal, but he does unofficially take Pornsen's place as adviser and guide, and he shows a warmth and tolerance that the gapt never could. In the course of their debates over Sturch dogma and policy, Fobo helps to make Hal intellectually whole, as Jeannette helps him to become emotionally and sensually whole. Hal finds that "though he hated Fobo for what he said, he derived a strange satisfaction from the relationship. He could not cut himself off from this being whose tongue flayed him far more painfully than Pornsen's whip ever had." Fobo, of course, is in some sense a professional lover, just as Jeannette is an instinctive lover; as an empathist, it is his function to understand his patients from the inside. This sharing of subjectivities is conspicuously absent in Hal's Sturch-approved relationships with Mary and Pornsen.

The story's unhappy ending, in defiance of most of the conventional wisdom of pulp fiction, is perhaps one of the reasons it was perceived as a taboo-breaker on its first publication. The misunderstandings and well-meaning deceptions that trigger Jeannette's death do give the story an atmosphere of romantic tragedy unusual in science fiction of the period, but, more than that, they confirm the implications about the nature of love that constitute the book's theme. There is an ironic bite in this fantastic *Romeo and Juliet*, pointed up by Hal's exit line: "Jeannette! Jeannette! If you had only loved me enough to tell me. . . ." His love, he seems to say, could have withstood the shock of discovering her true biological nature, if her fear had not exceeded her trust in him. It is Hal, however, who gives her the alcohol substitute — for her own good, he thinks — that robs her of her protection from pregnancy and thus guarantees her death. While he feels himself to be acting out of love, Hal is behaving much as Mary did when she reported him for minor unrealities, or even as Pornsen did when he supressed Hal's petition for divorce. In manipulating and deceiving Jeannette in order to do her the favor of matching his own system of values, Hal repeats in small that perversion of love practiced by the Sturch — the refusal to let the loved one be what it is.

Russell Letson

Sources for Further Study

Reviews:

Amazing Stories. XXXV, October, 1961, p. 138.

Analog. LXVIII, January, 1962, pp. 162-163.

Magazine of Fantasy and Science Fiction. XXI, October, 1961, p. 81.

Renaissance. IV, Fall, 1972, p. 9.

LUMEN

Author: Camille Flammarion (1842-1925)
First book publication: 1872
Type of work: Dialogues
Time: The present
Locale: The Earth, interstellar space, and several other worlds

Accounts given by the spirit Lumen of his adventures as a disincarnate soul wandering the universe, and of life in alien worlds

> *Principal characters:*
> QUAERENS, an inquisitive student
> LUMEN, an immortal spirit

Camille Flammarion was one of the foremost astronomers of his day, though he is remembered primarily as a popularizer of science. His classic *Popular Astronomy* is still constantly updated and reprinted. He was a man of tremendous imagination, inspired to prolific speculation by discoveries in astronomy and the other sciences. In 1864 he published the nonfiction book *Real and Imaginary Worlds*, (*Les mondes imaginaires et les mondes réels*), which contains a review of imaginative fiction dealing with other worlds and a commentary on these visions based on the scientific knowledge of the day. The dialogues ultimately to be included in *Lumen* were "imaginative spinoffs" from this work, and the first three were written in the same year. They were collected in book form in 1872 under the title *Recits de l'Infini*, and in this version were first translated into English as *Stories of Infinity* (1873). Flammarion was, however, to revise the work twice more — once for the French edition published as *Lumen* in 1887 and again for the English edition released under the same title in 1897. This last is the definitive edition.

Lumen is primarily a didactic work whose main motive force was Flammarion's desire to reconcile his religious faith and his scientific knowledge, demonstrating that each could enrich the other. The foundation stone of his faith was the doctrine of the immortality of the soul, and he imagined that, once free of its corporeal shell, it would be free to roam the universe at will, in intimate association with all the miracles of the heavens revealed to astronomers in their analyses of stellar light. He believed also that other beings on other worlds, adapted to very different physical circumstances, would also be incarnations of identical spirits.

Though some of the scientific theory embodied in *Lumen* is now out of date, and Flammarion's version of spiritualism has fallen entirely out of fashion, *Lumen* remains a fascinating work, and is perhaps the single most innovative work in the entire literature of the scientific imagination. It is the first work to offer any real idea of the scale of the universe; the first to investigate the implications of the finite speed of light (and thus to toy with the notion of the relativity of space and time); and the first to examine the implications of evolutionary theory in the modeling of alien life-systems. In all these endeavors it was ahead of its time.

The first dialogue, "Resurrectio Praeteriti," discusses the experience of life after death and the physics which permits the soul to exist independently of the body. The soul is represented as "pure energy" independent of matter, and has perfect freedom of movement within the universe. This freedom extends to freedom from temporal limitations: Flammarion insists that there is no "absolute time" and that elapsed time can only be measured relative to an observer. (That this anticipates Einstein is not particularly remarkable, but it also anticipates Ernst Mach, whose attempt to have "absolute space" and "absolute time" banished from cosmology, as metaphysical suppositions, provided the imaginative foundation of Einstein's work.) Lumen explains that when the soul travels instantaneously to another star and looks back at Earth, what it sees is the Earth of many years before. He tells of his own journey to Capella, from whence he could look back seventy-two years into history, and of a subsequent journey back to Earth during which he watched the whole of his own life unfold before him in a matter of minutes. The purpose of this is to demonstrate that a record of his Earthly existence thus remains, and is not forever lost in absolute time. This record is available to other souls and to God, and is the means by which the ultimate judgment can be made.

This notion caused some difficulties with the audience, and the second dialogue, "Refluum Temporis," begins with a reemphasis of the main points in reply to criticism. Then Lumen offers an account of the whole history of Earth, as seen in traveling away from Earth at faster-than-light velocity. The history, of course, enfolds in reverse: the fall and decline of the Roman Empire, the death and life of Christ, the dismantling of the pyramids, the regression of the prehistoric ages, and finally the dying of the Earth. Lumen digresses to draw a satirical moral lesson from this new perspective, pointing out how wonderful it is to see the battle of Waterloo as armies withdraw from chaotic and bloody conflict, the dead becoming whole and Napoleon emerging from defeat and despair an emperor.

It is in this second dialogue that Flammarion first broaches a subject to become much more important in the later essays: the matter of adaptation. Here he discusses the idea in terms of man's adaptation to conditions at the Earth's surface, and the extent to which the human body and sensory apparatus are determined by those conditions. This, too, he sees as a kind of "relativity," in that the human body is seen not as a fixed and arbitrary creation of God but as the result of a long and slow evolution involving constant interplay between organism and environment. Remarkably, Lumen goes on to say that even the soul itself is such a product of environment and evolution, and that its form and properties are not absolutely determined.

The third dialogue, "Homo homunculus," extends this argument with special reference to man's sensory apparatus and the limits of his perception. It opens with a discussion of the wonders of spectral analysis (used in astronomy since Fraunhofer's pioneering work in 1814). Lumen reflects on the narrow confinement of man's vision within a much more considerable vibratory spectrum, and speculates on the possibility of sensory apparatus that might perceive heat or electrical force. (Maxwell's work unifying electrical and magnetic phenomena was well under way in 1865 but it was not until 1887 that Hertz demonstrated the existence of electromagnetic waves.) Lumen concludes that there is sufficient ground for imagining modes of perception quite different from those characterizing human beings, and declares that these modes exist on other worlds. This is the point at which the value of the fictional component of the work becomes clear, for no sooner is this point made than Flammarion can make it concrete by forming a literary model of life on another world. This he proceeds to do in the fourth dialogue, "Anteriores Vitae."

Lumen explains that only under similar environmental circumstances can similar creatures be produced. Thus, he says, life on Mercury and Uranus can bear no resemblance whatever to Earthly life, while on a planet of the star Gamma Virgo there are humanoid beings differing only slightly because their world is basically similar to Earth. The principal difference between their existence and ours, he explains, is the absence of sex because of the reproduction of life by constant spontaneous generation. He goes on to describe the inhabitants of Delta Andromeda, whose world is enveloped by a roseate ocean and for whom breathing and nutrition are simultaneous. Here he digresses to point out the manner in which the process of alimentation fundamentally affects man's relationship with his environment. As his questioner, hungry for more miracles, demands even more startling facts Lumen then recalls a previous existence on a large planet of one of the stars in Cygnus, where only plants exist, though some have attained sentience and the power of reason. The principal preoccupation in all of this which strikes the contemporary reader as a false note is Lumen's insistence on placing all these different life forms in a hierarchy of progress, in which some are declared to be "more advanced" than the human condition and others "inferior." Although there is a reference in several places to the Darwinian "struggle for existence" and its importance in evolution, Flammarion remains heavily influenced by Lamarckian evolutionary philosophy and its doctrine of continual improvement. (The same is true of the other major French writer who in a slightly later period wrote a considerable number of evolutionary fantasies: J. H. Rosny the elder.)

The fifth dialogue, "Ingenium Audax: Natura Audacior," continues the work of the fourth, describing a life cycle of atomic integration and disintegration — a form of incarnation as different from our own as Flammarion could imagine. This dialogue adds a note on a new effect of the soul's ability to propel itself through the universe at will through the "magnification" of instants of time, which may be achieved by traveling very close to the velocity of light, allowing events to be perceived in slow motion. This dialogue is considerably shorter than the others, consisting of afterthoughts added between editions. A new summary is appended to this dialogue, but the true conclusion is contained in the fourth dialogue, wherein Flammarion again reacts to criticism of his work on religious grounds with an impassioned defense of his project and its inspirational didacticism:

> "Do you not know," says Lumen, "that truth is immeasurably more beautiful, grander and infinitely more marvellous than error, however that may be embellished? What can be comparable in all the mythologies past and present, to the rapt scientific contemplation of celestial grandeurs and the sublime movements of nature? What impression can strike the soul more profoundly than *the fact* of the expanse crowded with worlds, and the immensity of the sidereal system?"

There are several points within the dialogues where Quaerens raises points of religious orthodoxy, and Lumen is quite uncompromising in declaring that the old notions of Heaven and Hell must be abandoned because cosmology leaves no room for them, and that the idea of God having made man "in his own image" must also be drastically revised. The quote makes clear exactly how this abandonment of traditional tenets of faith has come about. In the discoveries of science, Flammarion has found ideas which make the images of Christian mythology seem not only hollow but actually tawdry. His capacity for wonder has been overwhelmed, and the religious notions he dismisses have simply lost their power to inspire in competition with such imaginative vistas. His attempt to salvage what he could of religious faith is definitely a rearguard action, though he desperately wanted to hold on to the essentials of faith. The crisis with which he was faced is precisely analogous to that which led the Jesuit paleontologist Pierre Teilhard de Chardin to compile his astonishing vision of the future of the universe and the pattern of its evolutionary schema in *The Phenomenon of Man* (1955). Together with this work, with Rosny's *La Legende Sceptique* (1889), and perhaps with Fontenelle's *A Plurality of Worlds* (*Entretiens sur la pluralité des mondes*, 1686-1687), *Lumen* constitutes a literary genre which has no parallel outside France. The only work originally written in English which has any real affinity with these is Edgar Allan Poe's *Eureka!* (1848).

Among Flammarion's other works of imaginative fiction were *Stella* (1887), *Uranie* (1889), and the classic future history novel *Omega* (*La fin du monde,* 1894). Though the last is unquestionably a more able literary work, and has as much imaginative scope as any work of speculative fiction, there is in *Lumen* a visionary passion which is special. It is not really a work of fiction, and represents in its form an echo of earlier days when the distinction between fiction and nonfiction was not clearly drawn. Like Plato's dialogues it indulges in flights of fantasy whose purpose is to model and to provide paradigms of the philosophical points that are being made. From Plato's dialogues there emerged the prolific mythology of Atlantis, and it is in Flammarion's work that we find the fountainhead of the mythology of alien beings. The inhabitants of other worlds had been described before, but they had all been shaped by concepts which had no provision for alternative evolution by adaptation to different circumstances, and hence no provision for genuine alienness. By applying the theory of Lamarck (with a little seasoning of Darwinism), Flammarion originated the mode of thought which is effective in modern science fiction's dealings with the category *alien*.

Lumen's affinity with modern science fiction goes further than this, because it is a work expressly directed to the cultivation of the sense of wonder (in whose cultivation, according to many readers, the prime virtue of modern science fiction lies). *Lumen* needs to be read with a full awareness of its historical context, but hindsight can only add to its stature by allowing us to see how powerful it was in grasping those strands of the developing science of its time which were later to become vital elements of the modern scientific world view.

Brian Stableford

THE MACHINE STOPS

Author: E. M. Forster (1879-1970)
First book publication: 1909
Type of work: Novella
Time: The indefinite far future
Locale: The underground world of the ubiquitous "Machine" beneath Australia

A grisly dystopian tale of a future in which mankind lives in a huge, underground, hexagonal-celled complex known as The Machine

> *Principal characters:*
> VASHTI, an old woman
> KUNO, her son, a rebel against The Machine
> THE MACHINE

This story, which E. M. Forster said was written in reaction to a Utopian vision of H. G. Wells, is important to us today for at least three reasons: it is a gripping tale of horror and adventure; it is a focused and powerful work of social criticism; and it is the first, and still the best, depiction of a "Human hive" in literature.

Forster shows in this story the consummate skill of the master craftsman. Rather than write a sterile essay in futurology, he creates an intriguing fiction in which two opposing views of mechanization are given to two members of a family, mother and son. The story's major thematic conflict is thus dramatized as a conflict between generations. Vashti, the mother, is a woman of The Machine. She loves it, worships it, is happy almost without misgiving in its embrace. She hates the outside and the stars and direct experience and air-ships, from all of which she "gets no ideas." Kuno, by contrast, is a rebel who dimly perceives that The Machine is evil, that the denial of the body is evil, and that in a proper world view, "Man is the measure."

Forster cleverly takes his hero, Kuno, with whom we are in complete sympathy, and puts him at one remove in the story. We see into the world of The Machine through Vashti's consciousness, a reactionary and hidebound mentality as detestable as her necrotic flesh. We watch in helpless exasperation as she denies Kuno, referring to him as "a man who was my son." By telling the story from Vashti's point of view, Forster traps the reader, as it were, and stuffs him into a cell of his gigantic beehive.

Forster eases the willing suspension of disbelief for any readers who might not be predisposed toward science fiction by twice calling to mind the fact that what is happening is but a fiction, "my meditation" as the narrator calls it. At the same time, the callous indifference with which Forster's narrator reports the story contributes to its chilling effect. This narrator tells us, for instance, that "nuances of expression" are "rightly ignored" by The Machine, thereby either placing himself ethically on The Machine's side rather than ours or being sarcastic. In either case we perceive that we will have no sympathetic Vergil to guide us through this Hell. In the midst of Vashti's controversy with Kuno over his request that she visit him in person, the Narrator observes:

"Think of her as without teeth or hair." All such comments are provided without sympathy for our feelings. The very ugliness of the picture developed keeps the reader, fascinated, moving forward, but no one will hold his hand.

Forster's constant metaphor for the relationship between The Machine and its inhabitants is a huge monster in the process of digesting its prey, mankind, which it has devoured long ago. The people in it are pasty-white maggoty creatures with limbs so weak that they can but totter on those few occasions when they move from their couches and surrounding life-support systems. Even Kuno, whose strength makes him a throwback, finds the outer air too "keen" to breathe. Through the course of the story, The Machine grows more powerful while its residents grow ever more dependent on it and weaker. As if to make the point unmistakable, Forster labels the portals through which the airships pass, "vomitories."

Through such equations as this, the story may be viewed as an inversion of the ancient hero-quest saga as embodied in legends such as that of Theseus. Kuno is the "Theseus" figure but is not at the center of the story. Rather than work his way into a labyrinth to slay a monster there, he must work his way out of a labyrinth which has become a monster worse than any minotaur. His mother is an anti-Ariadne who discourages him instead of providing him with the golden thread. The ancient hero typically defeats a dragon, gorgon, cyclops, or minotaur, but the hero of the modern *hive* story has a more appalling antagonist and a more difficult task: to work his way out of the monster's belly. The outcome of the *hive* story is, typically, less hopeful.

Perhaps to emphasize the unheroic proportions of the human characters (which make Kuno's heroism all the more heroic), Forster makes Vashti's mentality specifically antimythic. She cannot see Orion in the stars, or Prometheus in the Caucasus, or Apollo in the sun (she cannot bear to be *touched* by the sun). The intellectualism which she defends is devoid of any mythic dimension in which man measures earthly phenomena by his own nature. To her credit, however, she is allowed a moment of tragic recognition before her life ends with the stopping of The Machine.

While this is a tale of adventure and horror, it is, quite obviously, a didactic work as well, a major contribution to Utopian literature cast in the negative imperative: "let us avoid" rather than "let us affirm."

In this regard, it is important for us to realize that the thrust of Forster's criticism is not against population growth. Nowhere in *The Machine Stops* is there any scarcity until the final breakdown of the system, and that breakdown is not due to overpopulation. Nor is Forster inveighing against totalitarian government, unless The Machine is read as a symbol for some all-powerful "Party," and there is nothing in the story to call for such a reading. The story, moreover, does not have the "let's pretend" quality of such didactic fables as *Flatland* or *Animal Farm*. On the contrary, Forster's story is a work of hard science fiction, an extrapolation rather than a fantasy, a "What If?" story in which the "What If?" is rendered entirely plausible through the careful development of myriad details of everyday life and human history.

It seems clear that Forster is attempting to show that people are capable of a great evil which he labels "the sin against the body," that they can drift into a graceless state of dependence on machines whose ancestors we see all around us today, that such a dependence will lead to a leaderless, bureaucratic sclerosis in which man and machine together will rot and fall apart. This sin is a composite extrapolation of four trends contemporary to Forster's day (1909): the trend toward increased mechanization and reliance on machines; the trend toward ersatz experience; general laziness and comfort-seeking; and increased urbanization and urban sprawl. When all are brought together, we have the world of The Machine, a world in which body is entirely sacrificed to the intellect, a world in which only "ideas" have value — "ideas" which are meaningless mental gestures, simply collected like pieces of string and having no relationship to either serious inquiry or human experience.

The word seminal, now overused, applies perfectly to Forster's novella, for this is the first — and still the best — of a large subgenre of science fiction: the tale of the hive. In the marketplace of ideas which *is* science fiction, several motifs developed first in *The Machine Stops* have been traded, cherished, and embellished for the past several decades.

The image which dominates the story from first to last and lingers in the imagination forever is, of course, the concept of The Machine itself — the great global domicile which houses, enhives, feeds, but also enslaves the human race. In *The Machine Stops*, Forster has created the prototype for dozens of similar extrapolations including Megan Terry's "Home" (*Home*, or *Future Soap*), Mark Adlard's "T-City" (*Multiface*), and Robert Silverberg's "Urban Monad 116" (*The World Inside*). In each of these works, man's home has become his prison, suggesting a hideous extension of Marshall McLuhan's dictum: "Man makes his tools, and thereafter his tools make him."

Another important contribution of this novella is the concept of a whole society losing touch with its history, purpose, and place in the cosmos. The residents of John Campbell's "Twilight" city have lost all notion of where they are or what they are, as have the generations of Heinlein's Proxima Centauri starship (*Universe*), and Arthur C. Clarke's "Diaspar" (*The City and the Stars*). In each of these works the very idea of "outside" has disappeared or become something so terrifying as to be beyond comprehension.

Although Forster was not living in the time of the Computer Revolution, his Machine, with its smothering servo-mechanisms and self-activating repair systems, prefigures such a computer master as "Hal" of Arthur C. Clarke's *2001: A Space Odyssey*. Other computer masters worthy of mention for their resemblance to Forster's Machine are "Herbie" of Kendell Crossen's *Year of Consent*, "Proteus" of Dean R. Koontz's *Demon Seed*, "The Mechanicals" of Jack Williamson's "With Folded Hands," and "Am" of Harlan Ellison's "I Have No Mouth, and I Must Scream."

No claim is made here that any of these authors consciously had Forster's story in mind, but clearly the ideas in the tale have been picked up from some common well of concern and worked out again and again; it is fair to say, therefore, that *The Machine Stops*, like *We*, *Brave New World*, and *Nineteen Eighty-Four*, is one of the great seminal works of science fiction.

Some comment is in order about the title of the story, for it briefly embodies or suggests most of the important themes of the work. One is that it is stupid (as well as sinful) to put faith in a machine, for a machine is not a creature of God. Made by "great men, but *men*," it will stop, and mankind will stop with it. Only those who have relied on the strength of the body, God's gift, will survive to carry on. In another ironic inversion, Forster's "underground" is a group of people who, having escaped the Machine's embrace, live "above" ground where they are open to the elements.

The title also suggests its opposite: The Machine *Starts*. No one starts it, exactly. There are no villains, no Frankenstein-like mad scientists, no Faustian scapegoats. The Machine, rather, is a product of generations of collective ignorance; everywhere people were busy transforming God's world into a machine and themselves into automatons to fit into its cells.

The title, too, is a rallying cry, a slogan for a revolutionary group, small (alas, just Kuno and his mother) and short-lived (those few seconds before The End), but committed all the same. It is significant that the slogan does not emphasize man-the-hero. Such an idea is beyond Kuno's primitive political theory. Never does he decide "We can stop this damned Machine" and put The Machine in as predicate of a latter-day Luddite revolutionary action. The Machine stops simply, and finally, because that is what machines do. Man, weak, mortal, fallible, but *God's own treasure*, will endure, survive, and prevail. Man's machine failed and destroyed him, but Vashti's child, "flesh of her flesh," saved her soul (if not her life) by showing her the truth before The End.

This, then, is an optimistic work despite its elements of morbid ugliness; it is a testament to that divine spark within man which will always break through the muddy vesture of decay with which he continually and mistakenly tries to build for himself a Heaven on Earth. Such a religious notion justifies the lofty Biblical diction with which Forster concludes: "Ere silence was completed their hearts were opened and they knew what had been important on the earth . . . beautiful, naked man was dying, strangled in the garments that he had woven." Justified, too, is the allusion to the *Romeo and Juliet* of William Shakespeare, touchstone of English humanism: "She crawled towards him over the bodies of the dead . . . 'Quicker,' he gasped, 'I am dying — but we touch, we talk, not through The Machine.' He kissed her." And thus, with a kiss, the press of body on body, they die.

Thomas Dunn

Sources for Further Study
Criticism:

Hillegas, Mark. *The Future as Nightmare: H. G. Wells and the Anti-Utopians*. New York: Oxford University Press, 1967. Hillegas analyzes the influence of H. G. Wells's "Cosmic Pessimism" on Forster and other science fiction writers.

Trilling, Lionel. *E. M. Forster*. Norfolk, Va.: New Directions, 1943, pp. 47-48. Concise but penetrating analysis of the major themes of *The Machine Stops*.

Reviews:

Booklist. XXIV, July, 1928, p. 403.

Nation. CXXVI, June 6, 1928, p. 653.

New Republic. LVI, August 29, 1928, p. 54.

New Statesman. XXX, March 31, 1928, p. 797.

Saturday Review. V, October 13, 1929, p. 250.

Spectator. CXL, April 7, 1928, p. 543.

DIE MACHT DER DREI
(The Power of the Three)

Author: Hans Dominik (1872-1946)
First book publication: 1922
Type of work: Novel
Time: 1995
Locale: The United States, England, Australia, Europe — especially Scandinavia
— and an Arctic iceberg

A series of intrigues and plots develop in the wake of a new invention, controlled by three men, that can concentrate and focus enormous energy

> *Principal characters:*
> SILVESTER BURSFELD, an idealistic German inventor
> ERIK TRUWOR, a Swedish superman
> SOMA ATMA, an Indian mystic with extrasensory powers
> JANE HARTE, Bursfeld's fiancée
> DR. EDWARD F. GLOSSIN, physician and adviser to the President of the United States
> CYRUS STONARD, president and dictator of the United States

In *Die Macht der drei* (1922), the first of his seventeen very successful science fiction novels, Hans Dominik wastes no time with preliminaries, but gets right to the action. On the orders of a secret security council, a mysterious "Logg Sar" is to be executed for supposedly trying to blow up the Panama Canal. The reason given for the execution is, however, as false as the victim's name. Three attempts are made to execute him in the electric chair at Sing Sing, but each time the power fails. The third time, the machine is destroyed, and the victim escapes with the help of a witness. He flies away in the fastest military airplane of the United States, the R.F. c. 1, abducted from under the eyes of a detachment of five hundred elite guards.

It is the year 1995, and America is ruled by Cyrus Stonard, president and dictator. He assumed power after the Japanese had humiliated the nation and he had suppressed several Communist revolts in the still unoccupied Western states of the United States. Once the invaders had been repelled, Stonard restored military power and ruled the nation with an iron hand. At the time of the novel, the United States has regained its position as one of the superpowers; Canada is a close ally, and Australia is about to leave the British Empire and apply for American protection. The other major power in the world is England, which still controls India and Africa. The continent of Europe is divided into various neutral states, of no political or military importance. Russia is not even mentioned in the novel. The major conflict is between the United States and England.

While both countries build up their armaments and an uneasy balance of power is maintained, Stonard develops plans for bacteriological and economic warfare (at the onset of the war, counterfeit banknotes are to be dropped over England to disrupt the British economy). He is also erecting a hidden undersea fortress for submarine pilots off the coast of East Africa; from this fortress, he intends to attack and interrupt England's traffic with India.

Stonard's chief advisor is Dr. Glossin, a typical villain from fiction. Ceaselessly plotting, Glossin has a record as traitor, first as a collaborator with the Japanese, then as a Communist agitator. As the novel begins, he is preparing to betray Stonard. It was Glossin who arranged the secret trial and execution of "Logg Sar," who is actually a German by the name of Silvester Bursfeld. Bursfeld's father invented a potentially important weapon, was betrayed by Glossin, and imprisoned by the British, where he committed suicide in the Tower rather than divulge his secret. His invention was a "teleenergetic concentrator" that makes it possible to focus tremendous energy over large distances through control of latent energy. Independent of his father, Sylvester Bursfeld has invented the same apparatus, perfecting it in the process. It is a potential tool for world domination.

Having been told that his father was killed by bandits in Mesopotamia, Silvester Bursfeld was reared and educated in a Tibetan monastery, where he met and formed a close friendship with the Indian Soma Atma, a psychically gifted man endowed with hypnotic powers who can unveil the future by glimpsing the workings reared. The third member of their triumvirate is the Swede, Erik Truwor, a Nordic superman. Once Bursfeld's invention has been perfected, the terrible power over the world; who are in fact more powerful than the armies, navies, and air forces of England and the United States combined. From their hiding place, they can strike at will, without fear of retaliation as long as their position remains unknown. Theirs is a power both terrible and tempting. Once it becomes known that such a force exists, a feeling of impotence spreads throughout the nations of the Earth. The three men are like gods, and their greatest danger lies not in their enemies, but in their own arrogance — the absolute corruption that results from absolute power.

Die Macht der drei is fairly typical of Hans Dominik's fiction. His formula made him the most popular and successful of all German science fiction writers, and he repeated it with small variations from book to book. His novels sold hundreds of thousands of copies in hardback, and even today he is still the best-selling science fiction author in West Germany, despite the many available translations of modern science fiction. Central to his novels is a single novelty, a technological invention that opens up fascinating dramatic possibilities. It is often a new source of energy or some material with fantastic properties. The inventor is usually a solid middle-class engineer: an honest, conscientious worker and a representative of German engineering. The books are set a few years in the future, with varying political constellations and alliances from book to book, but always with black-and-white heroes and villains. When Germany is the strong nation, the others are the villains; if the conflict is between the white and the yellow races, we have another incarnation of the yellow peril. The goals and powers of Dominik's heroes frequently transcend national aims. But as the Nazis rose to power, his heroes became more and more subordinate to the aspirations of the state, merely helping to realize national goals.

In this respect, his earlier novels, such as *Die Macht der drei*, are more daring than his later ones. Their chauvinistic orientation undoubtedly contributed to their appeal following the shattering defeat of World War I when German nationalism was at a feverish peak, and the readers could again identify with German superiority in the characters of Dominik's inventors. German industry and inventiveness are usually supplemented by a representative of Eastern wisdom, in this case Soma Atma, and the real power behind the plot is *karma*, or destiny. His heroes are merely fulfilling destiny, just as Germany's new leaders increasingly claimed to be no more than the tools of national destiny.

The plot is invariably one of espionage and intrigue, as the opposing factions try to gain possession of the invention and its secret to advance their own purposes. Thus, in *Die Macht der drei*, Dr. Glossin first tries to dispose of Bursfeld, suspecting that the invention of the father might have been passed on to the son, and then, when it becomes apparent that the invention exists, to abduct the inventor and his allies. Glossin also falls in love with the psychic medium Jane Harte, Bursfeld's sweetheart and later wife, and, having hypnotic powers, occasionally brings her under his spell. At one point the heroes rescue her with blazing energy weapons to keep the plot going. It seems to be a hidden law of pulp fiction that the villain always falls in love with the sweetheart of the hero, even though they would quite probably be physically incapable of consummating the affair.

One of the best plot sequences occurs during a raid by British commandos on a farmhouse in Scandinavia, where the three are supposed to be developing their invention. Dr. Glossin has manipulated the British into doing his dirty work, planning in turn to destroy the British raiders with his American troops. During the ensuing battle, the mined farmhouse blows up, destroying many of the attackers. The strength of the explosion leads them to believe that the inventors perished in the flames. In fact, however, it was but a ruse by the trio, who had already transferred their apparatus to a hollowed out iceberg in the Arctic.

Believing that the teleenergetic concentrator no longer exists, Cyrus Stonard dares to set his plans for war to motion. A drunken incident between Australian and British fleets forces him to show his hand prematurely. After some initial American victories in Africa, the decisive battle between the American and British grand fleets in the Atlantic takes a decidedly comic turn. Welded together by unknown superior forces, the ships of the respective fleets become as one, and are drawn by unseen forces across the seas: the British fleet finds itself irresistibly propelled toward New York harbor, while the American fleet is drawn to England. At that point the three announce their existence and demand an instant stop to all hostilities. As Glossin is planning a new betrayal, Stonard is toppled by a democratic revolution and allowed to go into exile; the new government accepts peace.

Meanwhile, however, fate overpowers the three. Bursfeld nearly destroys the iceberg by imprudently releasing energies from the apparatus in their hide-out, and he is killed trying to save the flooded installations. Erik Truwor goes mad; he has tasted power, and is not prepared to give it up, and he ignores the pledge he has made to his friends. In vain, Soma Atma reminds him of *karma*: that it is easier to do big things than good ones. But destiny does overtake Truwor: challenging the elements themselves, he imagines himself to be the master of the world, and fights with thunder and storm, flying his plane higher and higher into the atmosphere until he is finally struck down. The invention, however, has not been lost; Soma Atma becomes the guardian until such time when there is one pure enough to wield the power without destroying himself. On this optimistic note the author concludes his melodramatic novel.

In a literary sense, this is not a great book. Dominik is more concerned with the intrigues of power, world politics, and human activity than with the psychological interaction of characters or the moral dilemmas inherent in serious fiction. His characters are the stock figures of pulp fiction, with all the usual silly schemes and aspirations. The love story is especially conventional, and the climax is thoroughly melodramatic. But there is plenty of excitement and action, presented in a way that gripped the readers when the book first appeared and still does so more than sixty years later.

In Germany, Dominik has a reputation for writing scientifically based science fiction, but in fact, his inventions are barely sketched in — he never bothers to explain their principles, nor does he describe their features. In *Die Macht der drei*, a small box controls tremendous powers and allows its user to watch and control any place on Earth. The box is only a materialization of the fantasy of omnipotence, brought about by technology, functioning like the magician's wand. In fact, Dominik deals not in technology, but in wish-fulfillment in the guise of the technological powers of the future. More than with science or even technology, his books deal with power — the power politics of nations or the power-hungry schemes of some central character. The true psychological nature of his books also is evidenced by his concern with psychic powers and the workings of fate, to which his heroes are subservient. This formula inspired an entire school of German writers, among them Rudolf H. Daumann, St. Bialkowski, Hans Richter and Freder van Holk, but none of them proved as perennially popular as Dominik himself. His main virtue is his ability to spin a fast-moving tale, and as long as one does not look too critically at the clichéd language, Dominik manages to capture the interest of the reader by the sheer momentum of events.

Franz Rottensteiner

MACROSCOPE

Author: Piers Anthony (1924-   )
First book publication: 1969
Type of work: Novel
Time: The late twentieth century
Locale: Various, beginning on Earth

> *Four people set out on a voyage through both inner and outer space, the cosmos, and the psyche to discover the source of a signal which destroys the minds of those who attempt to use the macroscope, a machine that sees through space and time*

Principal characters:
> Ivo Archer, the product of an experiment to produce genius
> Afra Glynn Summerfield, a beautiful Southerner
> Harold Groton, a space engineer who practices serious astrology
> Beatryx Groton, his wife

Macroscope is a novel with a vast sweep that combines ideas and epic action in a way that typifies the most ambitious and exhilarating science fiction. Beginning when Ivo Archer is accosted on a street in Georgia, the plot follows a group of curious explorers to the edges of the universe and into the depths of the psyche. The sequence of events includes the death of a United States Senator from a mind-destroying program, the discovery of alien intelligence, the disintegration of human bodies to permit faster-than-light travel, revelations concerning a secret training program for geniuses, a battle for survival in pre-Christian Tyre, and a climactic struggle carried out through actualization of the ancient and eternal symbols of astrology. Although *Macroscope* may finally be flawed by a lack of depth in characterization, it is one of the most effective novels of ideas ever created by a science fiction writer.

A principal feature of the novel is the macroscope itself, a device orbiting the Earth through which scientists can probe the universe by observing "macrons," the imprint upon intergalactic waves of their passage by or through any object in the universe. The macroscope can see "through" solid objects because it can be focused on the wave distortion on the other side of the object; and it can see through time because it can read the imprint of waves transmitted over many light years. Four people, Ivo Archer, Afra Glynn Summerfield, Beatryx Groton, and Harold Groton, go on a cosmic odyssey by taking the macroscope from Earth orbit and using the "ftl" (faster than light) technology it provides them with to search for the cause of and reason behind a mind-burning "destroyer signal" that prevents humans from obtaining the full possible benefits of the educational programs which various cosmic races are beaming over the macronic frequencies.

The odyssey of the macroscope and its crew begins because the international group of scientists manning it in space wish to keep it from becoming a political weapon for spying on Earth or allowing one nation to obtain the knowledge from the galactic transmissions. When United States Senator Borland demands the chance to try to bypass the mind-destroying program in order to gain superknowledge, he and Bradley Carpenter, Ivo's dearest friend, are burnt mentally so that the senator dies and Brad is rendered an idiot.

Before Earth can react by stopping the experiments, Ivo "wins" the macroscope by displaying remarkable mathematical intuition in a "sprouts" game played among the scientists. Then he, the Grotons, and Afra (who brings her lover, Brad, in a comatose state) blast the macroscope away from the torus of the orbital station towards Neptune, fleeing from a United Nations ship. At this point Ivo penetrates the destroyer signal and begins to unlock the secrets of the galactic technology which it has been obscuring. Ivo, Bradley, and the mysterious Schön were participants in a secret American project to accelerate genius and, although Ivo appears to be one of the project's failures, he has certain special gifts including mathematical intuition, skill as a flautist, and the ability to "dodge" the destroyer program. He leads the others on the mental path around the destroyer and they discover a process which allows them to melt into a gel-like protoplasm without bones or organs so that their bodies can survive higher G-forces for long-distance space voyages. After trusting this program and watching in amazement as their colleagues are reconstituted by rapid passage through fetal development, the cosmonauts decide to solve the mystery of the destroyer signal.

The adventures that lead from the solar system to the destroyer station include Afra's unsuccessful attempt to restore Bradley's mind using an aspect of galactic technology, and the implementation of ftl spaceflight by the spectacular collapsing of the whole planet Neptune into a gravity well to produce the energy to vault through space.

While learning to control the observations that can be made through time with the macroscope, Ivo is suddenly dropped into the sea near ancient Tyre. This trick is perpetrated by Schön, the supergenius from the American intelligence project who has hidden himself behind the personality of Ivo and who now wishes to displace and destroy Ivo so that he can manipulate galactic knowledge.

Ivo escapes from the ancient world and becomes the key to the puzzle when the explorers land on the destroyer transmitter. On this awesome artificial planet they pass through a museum which displays the basic chemical elements and the laws of mechanics, and then confront a strange mechanism, the only object in a room from which there appears to be no exit. Here Ivo's musical gift, which had led to his fascination with and adoption of the personal history of Sidney Lanier, the Georgia Reconstruction poet and flutist, comes to the fore as he "plays" the mechanism — a galactic instrument — and provides for each of the characters an experience based in the imagery of their astrological sign. Anthony intersperses these astrological dramas with an explanation of the truth about the destroyer stations. They are actually guardian stations placed in space by an infinitely superior race to prevent any species from ruining themselves or others with advanced technology before they are mature enough morally to resist the temptations of galactic conquest.

The galactic instrument which Ivo plays is "S^1," a machine capable of realizing symbolism on all levels: musical, astrological, psychological, and physical. Schön bursts free of the Ivo personality when Afra asks him to intervene for Beatryx, who died in her vision, and for Harold, whose consciousness has been shifted to a different frame of existence by his experience.

Afra then undertakes a desperate struggle with Schön in the form of a game where the astrological houses are realized as physical situations and, when Afra overcomes Schön with an act of great courage, Ivo's restored and emotionally mature personality takes over Schön's amoral genius, and the integrated man is paired with Afra. The Ivo-Schön split is a metaphor for the division between the subconscious emotional portion of man and the conscious intellectual portion, and draws to the reader's attention one level of the novel's treatment of the human personality.

In addition to the multiple personality of Ivo-Schön, (and, one could say, Sidney Lanier), there is a demonstration of the components of personality in the balancing of Ivo, Beatryx, Harold, and Afra. Each of the four represents one aspect of the Jungian personality types, Ivo standing for sensation, Afra for emotion, Harold Groton for thought, and Beatryx for intuition. In portions of the novel the four function as a complete and efficient unit containing all aspects of human nature; they form a conglomerate superperson. Later, when Beatryx and Harold actually are withdrawn by being absorbed into the scenes Ivo stimulates by playing the galactic instrument, the personalities of Afra and Ivo take up the additional components and thus become whole people at the close of the novel. Together they offer an integrated model for perfect humanity.

Macroscope is a sprawling novel which explores galactic travel and the limits of human endeavor. The thematic heart of the novel lies in the different kinds of unity which Anthony examines. Thus Ivo and Afra are united at the climax of the novel and embody the fulfilled Jungian nature. The macroscope itself is capable of examining the unity of all life from the microscopic level of protoplasm to the level of entire galaxies rotating beneath it in space. This very point is made explicit when the explorers first see our galaxy on its side, resembling, as Ivo observes, a gigantic strand of DNA. The characters actually discuss a unified field theory which would apply to all reality, including astrology and the range of physical phenomena from galactic to microscopic. Thus, both in terms of the integration of personality into wholeness and in the observations of the unity of the universe viewed through a variety of different scales of observation, the novel comes to the conclusion that there is a unified meaning behind reality.

In addition, the presence of Sidney Lanier, Ivo's adopted personality, reminds us that Lanier theorized that music and poetry should be integrated. It is

Lanier's *The Symphony*, a long poem, which Ivo plays on the galactic instrument; the piece is realized in both symbolic and musical terms. When Afra, struggling desperately against Schön, uses her strong intuition and calls upon the traveler signal, it responds to her in awesome fashion, revealing that it is not merely a signal but an intergalactic life form. Although Anthony refrains from calling it God, its immense powers suggest that it has an overall unifying control of the universe.

Although not an allegory in the strictest sense of the term, *Macroscope* is a novel constructed upon varied interpretations of the concept of unity. It unavoidably encounters the difficulties of presentation inherent in such a construction: a somewhat mechanical development of a complex plot, and characterizations which are weakened by heavy symbolism. But it is up to the reader to weigh these drawbacks against the invigorating challenge of the novel's vast sweep of interlocking ideas. In addition, Piers Anthony is a powerful prose stylist, and his handling of the language provides a driving narrative impetus through the entire novel. *Macroscope* is a complex, exciting book to read, one of those novels that one picks up again and again, and which always yields new insights into the basic unity of man and the cosmos.

Peter Brigg

Sources for Further Study

Reviews:

Analog. LXXXVII, August, 1971, pp. 167-168.
Luna Monthly. XVI, September, 1970, p. 22.
New Worlds. CXCVII, January, 1970, p. 33.
Science Fiction Review. XXXVIII, June, 1970, pp. 25-26.

MAKE ROOM! MAKE ROOM!

Author: Harry Harrison (1925-   )
First book publication: 1966
Type of work: Novel
Time: August 9 through December 31, 1999
Locale: New York City

A *"detective story"* serves as the focus for a documentary-style chronicle of a near future in which excessive population and exhausted resources have led to violence, chaos, and barbarism

Principal characters:
  ANDY RUSCH, a detective on the New York police force
  SOL KAHN, his roommate, an aging sage
  MIKE O'BRIEN, a murdered racketeer
  SHIRL GREENE, O'Brien's mistress, later Rusch's lover
  BILLY CHUNG, O'Brien's murderer, a teenager with no resources
  PETER, a mad defrocked priest who is expecting the millennium

The theme of *Make Room! Make Room!* is overpopulation; its thesis is that the most urgent political issue of the day ought to be contraception; its narrative mode approaches that of the documentary. The book is prefaced by a quotation from President Eisenhower to the effect that birth control cannot be the business of any American government, and it concludes with a list of "suggestions for further reading," real and scholarly books with such ominous titles as *Voles, Mice and Lemmings: Problems in Population Dynamics*, or *Hungry People and Empty Lands*. There is no doubt that the author is in dead earnest about his subject matter. His book comes close to the outer boundaries of fiction.

Such powerful beliefs are commonly thought to militate against artistic control. Someone who sincerely believes that the content of what he is saying is the most vital thing on earth is unlikely to worry too much about the way he expresses it, and there are indeed passages within *Make Room! Make Room!* where Harrison (anxious to make his diagnosis absolutely clear) lets his characters speak with an authority that is in context unrealistic. Sol Kahn, for instance, lectures Shirl Greene on matters as far apart as the history of anesthetics, the statistics of infant mortality, the mechanics of fertilization, and the effects of DDT — all to demonstrate the fact that everything in the world of 1999 goes back to the question of numbers, and that there is no argument that can be allowed to stand against their limitation. However, such outbursts are rare. When they occur, in fact, one could argue that they are essential simply because of the novel's main and most effective characteristic, both as a work of fiction and as a work of propaganda: its determinedly narrow focus. Like Solzhenitsyn's *One Day in the Life of Ivan Denisovitch*, *Make Room! Make Room!* works by taking a very small part of a very large phenomenon and asserting that all its details are at once typical and (given the circumstances against which the protest is being made) inevitable.

Details are the first thing brought to our attention as the novel's hero Andrew Rusch wakes up on Monday, August 9, 1999, in a New York of thirty-five million people. His sheet is dirty because he has no water in the half-room he lives in; all water has to be fetched in cans. He owns only one sheet because all natural resources are in short supply. He has only one razorblade, and he has electricity for his shared refrigerator only because his roommate, Sol Kahn, can run a homemade generator from a wheelless bicycle and four car batteries. From then on every incident in the novel is punctuated by the whir of Sol's contraption, the disappearance of electric current, the operation of squeeze-generator flashlights, and the entrance of messengers. Since the electricity is too unreliable for telephones, messages come by runner, written, naturally, not on paper but on reusable slates. This last point may look like one more piece of background, and it is; yet it is also vital to the plot of the novel in at least two places. Murderers cannot normally be caught in this future New York because there is not enough paper for an effective fingerprint file; and a potential murderer can get through security systems just because bodyguards are so used to the presence of hordes of messengers. Details control jobs, and jobs control people. Since Rusch is a detective, the absence of paper redefines his life, regardless of what he personally thinks about it.

This last insight, though, is something reserved for the present-day reader. It cannot be understood by Rusch, for he is simply not old enough to have a basis of comparison. As far as he and most of the other characters in the book are concerned, the way they live is the natural way, and there is nothing strange about it. This leads to several violent strokes of irony within the novel, as characters, in what we would consider intolerable conditions, look out of their various windows and reflect that things now seem to be all right. But more importantly, Rusch's casual acceptance of shortage, hindrance, and inconvenience marks one of the book's behavioristic poles: it tells us that people adapt, but questions how far they can adapt. At the other pole of 1999 behavior is the concept "people are what they eat." For all the machineries of survival that have been worked out — the pedicabs, meatleggers, tugtrucks, tentcities, and crumbsellers — the inhabitants of future New York seem to our eyes almost inconceivably incompetent. But it is because they are on the edge of starvation.

One way of reading *Make Room! Make Room!*, in fact, is as a parody of the classic big city detective story, as exemplified by Raymond Chandler or Ed McBain. Rusch is a detective; he is looking for a murderer, and in the process he acquires a beautiful girl, all very much in the Mike Hammer tradition. But the murder at the start of it all is, by current policestory standards, wildly unsatisfactory — an accidental killing carried out in panic by a teenage burglar disturbed at his crime. There is no subtlety in its execution, and purely routine inquiries ("Who's been in the building this week?") serve to detect the murderer, a boy named Billy Chung. There are even fingerprints on the murder weapon to make assurance doubly sure — criminals by this time hardly bother to wear gloves, since they know the police have no print cards, let alone computers. In a warren of thirty-five million people, of course, Chung is hardly likely to be caught except by betrayal, so all Rusch can do is wait for a tip-off; inadequacy is even on both sides. Rusch is a good cop with no resources, and Chung is a poor boy forever on the edge of panic because of a physique ruined by malnutrition. The only clue Rusch discovers turns out to have no meaning, and the only time Chung makes a profit from crime is as a result of multiple accident. The vital point about them is that in their circumstances the best of us — so Harrison unobtrusively asserts — would be much the same. Perhaps we will be.

Kahn is a critical character within the novel's structure of symmetries. It is possible for us to look down with pity on Billy Chung for his weakness, and even on Andy Rusch for his utter lack of ambition — his first reaction to the murder Chung commits is to think that here is his chance to extract a pillowcase from the murdered man's apartment. But looking down on Kahn is impossible. From his first appearance he projects an air of adaptability and competence. He can run a homemade generator; he never gets on anyone's nerves, even in humiliatingly cramped quarters; when he puts on his old Army jacket to go to the demonstration in which he is mortally wounded we see on it a row of medals and ribbons, and sharpshooter's flash, a technical school badge. With more people like him, you feel the world would never have moved to the edge of disaster.

Yet Kahn is responsible for the state of 1999 in a way the younger characters are not. What did he do wrong (and what are we doing wrong right now)? Only he (and we) can answer this, and Kahn therefore takes a paradoxical position: to Andy Rusch and Shirl Greene he is a *guru*, an ancient sage, while to us he is a sensible person who knows a little, but not a great deal more than everybody else. He provokes self-criticism in us. He also directs criticism the more strongly towards the novel's opposing *guru*, the mad priest Peter who shelters Billy Chung and preaches to him the doctrine of the apocalypse and the need of humanity to make more souls for God. Peter is mad, and responsible; but Sol Kahn is sane, and responsible too. He simply kept quiet too long. In spite of their total differences of opinion, we can see a kind of connection between the two, and even between Rusch and Chung. All their difficulties are caused by crowding, and that physical pressure dominates the relatively trivial forces of emotion, intention, and personality.

One result of this intense subordination of individual to environment is that some of the people and scenes in the book take on a symbolic quality, most obviously, Shirl Greene. She is the mistress of Mike O'Brien, a racketeer. It is the sight of her lying naked in O'Brien's bed that gives Chung the boldness to break in later and kill O'Brien. She mesmerizes Rusch, too, and becomes his mistress. Yet her beauty is not just a plot device: it also coexists very strongly with O'Brien's apartment, an Aladdin's cave of riches to all the other characters (including her), though it contains things we merely take for granted — a shower-bath, some cans of beer, a few cigars, a bottle of whisky, spare sheets, and an air-conditioner. Both apartment and girl dramatize the difference between 1966 and 1999; the unimaginable good fortune of the future is the modest expectation of the present (or the recent past). Between them they form an image of the "good life" that we might be throwing away, and add to the story a fierce grief and pathos of which the characters themselves do not become aware until it is too late.

Another way to read *Make Room! Make Room!* is as a hopeless lovestory, a *Romeo and Juliet* gone even sourer. Rusch and Shirl fall in love, there is no one to stop them living together, they set up housekeeping — but there simply is not enough space, time, sheets, or water for happiness. In the end Shirl goes back to prostitution because love, like competence in the police force or boldness in criminals, is in the end a function of material resources. It is a sad end, the sadder for the image that quietly dominates the book: free water. That is what really brought the lovers together — the showers they could take in O'Brien's apartment for the few weeks while his estate was being settled and before Shirl had to leave.

The dominance of this image is also present in the story of Rusch's father, who was a fruit farmer in California, until it became known that the water he was pumping was "fossil water," an irreplaceable natural resource like oil. Furthermore, the one period of Billy Chung's life when he is warm and well-fed is when he discovers a cache of water trapped in the hold of a wrecked ship in New York's dockland and becomes rich, after a fashion, by selling it. His water is covered with mosquito eggs, a breeding ground for malaria, and is likely to kill him and his customers quite soon. But the real villain of the book is the shortsightedness of human beings. Chung does not care what he is selling as long as there are buyers, Rusch's father never thought about the water-table, and President Eisenhower — to go back to the novel's epigraph — probably thought no further than the Catholic vote at the next election. So the Paradise of O'Brien's apartment is short-term only, and from it the man and the woman are expelled, not by an angel with a flaming sword, but by the end of the lease and a New York heat wave.

Similar images proliferate in the novel, so that its sharp, narrow focus is compensated by hints of parable. Almost the last scene in the book is one of thoughtless children eating the seeds that Sol Kahn used to grow to flavor his homemade vermouth: the "good life" is destroyed, one might say, for a moment's nongratification. Shirl is protected in the eater queue by one Mrs. Miles, but that goodhearted lady gives her sick child's protein ration to her husband: the future is sacrificed, one can hardly avoid saying, to short-term greed. The novel ends with mankind moving into a new millennium, and

Rusch, now demoted to walking a beat (for having shot Chung by accident), watching Shirl go by in a pedcab out of his reach.

Harry Harrison hits his single mark again and again with obsessive concentration. The last ironic comment one can make is provided by the film based on the book, *Soylent Green*. The director and producers decided that contraception was a controversial theme which tended to upset too many people, so they made the film about cannibalism instead. Nobody approves of cannibalism, it is true; yet the subject does not really rank as a vital contemporary issue.

T. A. Shippey

Sources for Further Study

Reviews:

Analog. LXXIX, May, 1967, p. 159.

Kirkus Reviews. XXXIV, April 15, 1966, p. 453.

Library Journal. XCI, June, 1966, p. 2874.

Magazine of Fantasy and Science Fiction. XXXII, February, 1967, p. 29.

New Worlds. CLIX, December, 1966, p. 154.

Publisher's Weekly. CLXXXIX, April 4, 1966, p. 60.

SF Commentary. I, January, 1969, p. 18.

Spectator. CCXXXI, August 4, 1973, p. 155.

MALEVIL

Author: Robert Merle (1908-   )
First book publication: 1972
English translation: 1974
Type of work: Novel
Time: 1977, after a nuclear war
Locale: Rural France

Six men and one old woman survive a nuclear holocaust in the wine cellar of a medieval castle, whose owner tells of their struggle to survive and establish social, political, economic, and spiritual cohesiveness

Principal characters:
> EMMANUEL COMTE, the owner of Malevil Castle, narrator-hero
> THOMAS, his disciple
> PEYSSOU, MEYSONNIER, AND COLIN, Comte's boyhood friends who survive the holocaust with him
> LA MENOU, the elderly housekeeper
> MOMO, her retarded son
> FULBERT LE NAUD, a hypocritical priest

Emmanuel Comte, the narrator of *Malevil*, writes about a changed world, a world devoid of automobiles, trains, electricity, gasoline, radio, television, telephones, and government. Six men, one old woman, one pig, two horses, and a cow have survived a nuclear holocaust which devastated France (and by extension the rest of the world) in April, 1977. However, *Malevil* actually begins before the holocaust, with Comte looking back to a past now lost forever. His memories, like those of Marcel Proust and his "Madeleine," have been triggered by something small: the discovery of a packet of old pipe tobacco. It is the aroma from this tobacco which causes the welling up of old and painful remembrances.

A leisurely, deliberate eighty pages elapse before the reader experiences the holocaust, and it is a rare and literary pace for science fiction. Careful, delineated prose introduces the characters and foreshadows future events and responses to them. Comte is allowed time to look back on life as it was before the disaster and to re-create the world of his childhood and the forces that shaped his development. He was dominated by an impossible mother whom he pointedly describes as suffering "from the besetting sin of the mediocre. She was a chronic complainer, because it gave her an excuse for her totally hidebound attitude to life." His response to her as well as to his weak father and two trivial sisters, is to flee home and hide in Malevil, an abandoned thirteenth century castle, partially in ruins.

Comte is familiar with Malevil prior to this, as the meeting place of a secret club. Here Comte and his boyhood friends played the many games of childhood, including reenactments of wars between the Catholics and the Protestants. Here they resolved all conflicts and established roles of leadership and cooperation which remain throughout their lives, for three of the boys, Colin,

Meysonnier, and Peyssou, survive the disaster with Comte.

However, more important than parents or peers in shaping Comte, is his Uncle Samuel, kindred spirit, mentor, and prime influence. Comte looks back on the night he ran away from home to the moment when Uncle Samuel found him in the castle and offered him a home at his own farm, Les Sept Fayards. As Comte reflects on that experience, he realizes that his uncle was what he himself was to become. He not only grows to physically resemble his uncle, but also to inherit his estate.

While he was briefly serving as headmaster of a school, Comte's uncle, and also ironically Comte's parents, is killed in an automobile accident. Comte resigns his position to take over the farm and the horses his Uncle Samuel loved to breed. He also inherits the money to make possible his uncle's dream, the purchase of Malevil.

Comte repairs the castle, settles in with La Menou, the elderly servant who cared for his uncle, and her retarded son, Momo. It is at Malevil that the main characters are gathered, in the deep cool cellar, drawing wine, when the holocaust strikes. The end of the world as they have known it begins when the electricity fails. Momo's radio ceases bellowing, and the assembled crew, Comte, La Menou, Momo, neighbors Meysonnier, Colin, Pessou, and Thomas, and a young natural scientist visiting from the city, examine the radio. As they speculate on whether or not the batteries have burned out, a large, inhuman noise fills the air, and a hideous heat fells the wine drinkers, nearly suffocating them. For forty-eight hours they struggle with the oppressive heat, removing clothes, unable to do more than merely lie on the ground and pant, unaware of anything beyond their own suffering, and certainly unable to speculate on the causes of this suffering.

Describing the externals of this holocaust does not do it justice, for what is noteworthy is the wealth of detail Robert Merle presents. Two incidents embedded within the scene are worth analysis. First is Comte's personal behavior during the experience. In the midst of his agony, as he lies there "stupefied and stifling, watching sweat dripping ceaselessly onto the burning flagstones," he crawls into a tub of rinsing water. It is this act, he maintains, that preserves his strength so that, when a dying neighbor bursts into the room leaving the door open and letting the scorching air enter the cellar, Comte is able to crawl to the door and close it in spite of incredible anguish. While this incident is interesting and well written, it is Merle's skill in further pursuing Comte's reflection that makes it outstanding.

When Comte looks back on his climb into the rinsing tub, he is filled with guilt, regarding his behavior as an extraordinarily selfish act. His only comfort lies in the fact that if he had not done so, he would not have had the ensuing strength to close the door. Then, adding another layer to the story, Thomas (who interrupts Comte's narration five times in the novel to set things straight) asserts that the entire experience lies in Comte's mind. He never sat in the rinsing tub and never closed the door. In fact, Thomas states that it was Meysonnier who had done so, although Comte had described his every movement accurately except for attributing these movements to himself.

In the best writing, science fiction or mainstream, following the adage, "show, don't tell," the skillful author creates the experience for the reader. Merle effectively relates the horrible holocaust experience by illustrating it in the confused recollection of his narrator. There is no villainy in Comte's story. He does not brag about his deed and, in fact, is ashamed of sitting in the tub. His narration is not for his contemporaries but for future readers. He tells what he believes to be true, and yet his disorientation is affirmed by Thomas, an objective reporter, who has no reason to rectify the journal except in the name of truth.

A second incident also illustrates Merle's literary skill. Directly after the holocaust, when the survivors have somewhat recovered, Peyssou announces his intention to leave. Although it is too soon, no one can dissuade him. All the others recognize not only the potential danger outside, but the fact that Peyssou has not fully comprehended that the world he has formerly known is now forever lost and that all his loved ones are no longer alive. Logic does not deter him. What stops Peyssou in his tracks is courtesy, the habits of correct behavior. La Menou steps into the discussion and cuts it short by saying exactly the right thing, "You can't just go like that. You need to eat something first." Peyssou, as good manners dictate, first refuses and then accepts the food.

It is this kind of observation and presentation of detail that sets *Malevil* apart from much of science fiction. There is not a page of the book that does not illustrate Merle's perception and his ability to weave these perceptions into the behavior and motivations of his characters. Their actions are genuine and appropriate both in commonplace moments and in moments of crises. When the characters' actions are so real, it becomes far easier to accept 1977 as the date of the holocaust. The unreal date ceases to matter because the real behavior matters so much.

Another reason that 1977 does not destroy the novel's credibility is that no attempt is made to portray a view larger that the one presented in the novel. There is no explanation for the bombs and no concern with other nations or even other parts of France. Malevil and the surrounding countryside are a never-never land, or a middle earth, certainly a complete secondary universe in and of itself. Making it even more separate and unique for American readers are the French names of people and places, which strike the ear as alien, exotic sounds.

However, even in a never-never land there are the prime considerations of survival, and six men and one old lady do not auger a future for mankind. Slowly, problems are posed and solutions posited. There is no fall-out, so immediate survival is assured. Some animals have survived. In fact, these are the most desirable animals, the pregnant ones who have been sheltered in a cool cave rather than in the barns. Other people also gradually appear, including Miette, a young woman who is essential for assuring future generations.

Comte is the leader of the group in every respect: benevolent Machiavellian. Initially, as the owner of Malevil, he shares the castle, its grain, and livestock with all the survivors. He continues the leadership which began in his boyhood club. He determines how the group is governed (democratically) and presents arguments for discussion, debate, and decision. Usually, his point of view prevails. In fact, the only exception to this is when he suggests that the men share Miette's sexual favors. The others are shocked and they refuse. Ironically the vote is meaningless because Miette makes her own decision, deciding to distribute sex equally to all *except* Comte. The problem works itself out, and not only does Comte exercise economic and military judgment but he also begins to be the group's spiritual leader, stemming from his nightly reading from the Bible to those assembled. An atheist, or at least an agnostic, Comte does not initiate these readings; they are requested by his companions. Comte's spiritual development is heightened by the introduction of his antagonist, the evil priest, Fulbert le Naud.

Fulbert arrives announcing that he has just come from the village of La Roque, nine miles from Malevil, where others have survived. When Fulbert offers to hold confession and communion for the Malevil populace, Comte refuses the former and accepts the latter, attempting to prevent communion from being indissolubly linked with potential inquisitorial questioning that he fears may have come to be standard practice in La Roque under Fulbert's leadership. Comte's fear of Fulbert's attempt to gain control is furthered when Fulbert announces that he wishes to send a deputy to Malevil to live there and act as his vicar. To prevent this, Comte takes up the title himself, becoming the Vicar of Malevil in name as well as deed.

The novel now polarizes: Malevil (and Comte) *versus* La Roque (and Fulbert). The politics and rivalries between the fortified chateau and the local village reflect the philosophies of the survivors, stemming from points of view once expressed in such everyday concerns as village mayoral campaigns (and foreshadowed in the opening sections of the book). There is a series of struggles, feints, and ploys set against a backdrop of the struggle to raise crops, maintain livestock and buildings, and fend off bands of marauders. The world after the holocaust is too similar to the world before. There is no question of immediate survival, but it is the caliber of survival and its length that remain in doubt. While the holocaust did not knock the survivors back into the stone age, it did put them back into the feudal age. The direction this feudal society will take becomes the novel's only partially answered closing question.

Comte has grown throughout the book in knowledge, humanitarianism, spiritual strength, and stature. He is kept human and saved from sheer pomposity by the many interjections of Thomas, his disciple, who makes it a practice to relate information that Comte might have wished to gloss over. But even a perfect Comte — and he is not perfect — could not prevent the survival of corruption, evil, and war.

While the opening words in the novel belong to Comte, looking back, the final words of the book belong to Thomas, looking ahead:

> So, on the basis of all the knowledge lying there ready to hand — and of our own very modest personal acquisitions — were we going to engage in research aimed at the development of tools to make our lives easier, and weapons to defend them: or, knowing only too well, from the terrible experience we had just been through, what the dangers of technology were, were we going to outlaw all scientific progress and all production of machines once and for all?
>
> I think that we would have chosen the second of these alternatives if we could have been sure that other surviving human groups, whether in France or further afield, would not choose the first. For in that case, it seemed incontrovertible to us that those groups, once they held an overwhelming technical superiority over us, would immediately conceive the project of subjugating us.
>
> We therefore made our decision in favor of science, without optimism, without the slightest illusion, all wholly convinced that though good in itself it would always be misused.

Technology wins, and as the book ends the citizens begin research into the manufacture of .36 rifle bullets. Merle offers a serious ending to a serious book, concerned with such prime questions as, "What kind of life is most worth preserving?"

Beverly Friend

Sources for Further Study

Criticism:

Mano, D. K. "*Malevil*," in *New York Times Book Review*. January 13, 1974, p. 6. Mano compares this ruthless doomsday tale to Machiavelli.

Marsh, Pamela. "*Malevil*," in *Christian Science Monitor*. February 13, 1974, p. 5F. Marsh calls this a well plotted suspense story.

Reviews:

Best Sellers. XXXIV, April 15, 1974, p. 48.

Booklist. LXX, April 15, 1974, p. 907.

Choice. XI, May, 1974, p. 443.

Kirkus Reviews. XLI, November 15, 1973, p. 1283.

Library Journal. XCIX, April 1, 1974, p. 1061.

New Statesman. LXXXVII, April 26, 1974, p. 591.

Newsweek. LXXXIII, January 14, 1974, p. 74.

Observer. April 21, 1974, p. 37.

Publisher's Weekly. CCIV, December 10, 1973, p. 29.

Time. CIII, February 4, 1974, p. 73.

Times Literary Supplement. May 17, 1974, p. 517.

THE MAN IN THE HIGH CASTLE

Author: Philip K. Dick (1928-1982)
First book publication: 1962
Type of work: Novel
Time: Shortly after World War II
Locale: San Francisco and the Western United States

An alternate world novel in which Japan and Germany have won World War II

Principal characters:
>FRANK FRINK, a former American soldier, now an employee of
>American Artistic Handicrafts
>JULIANA FRINK, his ex-wife
>NOBOSUKE TAGOMI, head of a Japanese trade mission
>ROBERT CHILDAN, a dealer in American prewar artifacts
>MR. BAYNES, a German agent disguised as a Swedish businessman
>HAWTHORNE ABENDSEN, the man in the high castle, and the author
>of a novel in which Japan and Germany have lost World War II
>JOE CINNEDELLA, a gunman hired by the Germans to kill Abendsen

Little doubt exists among serious students of science fiction that Philip K. Dick's *The Man in the High Castle* is one of the great works in the genre. The novel enjoys a brilliant style, a panoply of complex characters, an intriguingly involved plot, some genuinely unique ideas, and bold philosophical excursions into the nature of reality.

The basic plot deals with the aftermath of World War II. America has been defeated by the Japanese and the Germans; Nazi forces occupy the East coast, the Japanese the West; only the Rocky Mountain States of America retain a semblance of independence. Each of the many characters in the novel reacts to this situation in different ways. Frank Frink, a Jew, is protected by the more benevolent Japanese occupation forces because the Nazi conquerors have continued their policy of racial extermination to the point of exterminating virtually every Jew and black on earth. Baynes plots to overthrow the Nazi regime, which intends to launch a surprise attack, known as "Operation Dandelion," against the Japanese. Juliana Frink attempts to find Hawthorne Abendsen, the nearly mythical man in the high castle, whose novel, *The Grasshopper Lies Heavy*, portrays a world directly opposite to the one she and the other characters know.

In the history of Dick's future world, Franklin Roosevelt was assassinated by Zangara, and under Garner and Bricker, America was totally unprepared for the war and was thus defeated. The consequences of that defeat are debilitating. In addition to clashing his fictional reality against the actual historical reality, Dick adds a bold twist to the story by making Abendsen's fictional reality depict our present world in still different terms: in Abendsen's novel, Roosevelt was succeeded by Tugwell, who anticipated the attack on Pearl Harbor. America thus eventually won, and Abendsen's world, while not quite an ideal utopia, still enjoys a more harmonious existence than actually exists in America today.

Dick continually asks what reality is and he focuses his question on dozens of possible interpretations. All of his characters are forced to come to terms with the question of whether reality exists only in the mind. For example, Frink's company is engaged in counterfeiting prewar American artifacts — Colt .44's, butter churns, souvenir ash trays, jewelry, and even tawdry junk. Nobosuke Tagomi buys a Colt .44 under the impression that it is a genuine Frontier model. It is a forgery, yet it is real enough for him to kill a German agent later. Reality or illusion? It is difficult to tell, yet the question involves the entire structure of the novel itself. Dick has asked the question again and again in such distinguished books as *Counter-Clock World*, *Do Androids Dream of Electric Sheep?*, *Ubik*, and *Flow My Tears, the Policeman Said*. But *The Man in the High Castle* resembles no modern work more closely than Pirandello's play "Six Characters in Search of an Author"; indeed, the novel has been described as "six characters in search of reality."

Perhaps the essential key to the perplexing problem posed by Dick may be found in his use of the ancient Taoist book of wisdom, the *I Ching*, which is integral to the structure of the novel. *The Book of Changes*, as the *I Ching* is also known, provides a system of knowledge whereby man can analyze the pattern of changes governed by immutable laws, and with the help of the *I Ching* we — or Dick's characters — can relate our affairs to the everlasting process of ebb and flow and thus determine the best action to be taken for every event in life.

All of the characters in the novel consult the *I Ching* (which has been taken over as oracle by the Japanese) for almost every decision. Dick is quite detailed in his citations, giving the appropriate numbers of the hexagrams, their translations from the Richard Wilhelm edition, as well as the action indicated by the oracle. The most amazing fact, however, is that the author actually consulted and followed the advice of the *I Ching* in order to write *The Man in the High Castle*. Roughly parallel to Dick in the novel is the character Abendsen, about whose composition of *The Grasshopper Lies Heavy* his wife Caroline reveals to Juliana Frink,

> One by one Hawth made the choices. Thousands of them. By means of the lines [the hexagrams]. Historic period. Subject. Characters. Plot. It took years. Hawth even asked the oracle what sort of success it would be. It told him that it would be a very great success, the first real one of his career.

Nevertheless, what Abendsen points out regarding the writing of his novel is likewise true of Dick's authorship: "The question [of whether the oracle wrote the novel] implies I did nothing but the typing, and that's neither true nor decent." In other words, both Abendsen and Dick have combined their own creative spirits with the wisdom of the *I Ching* to produce the alternate realities of their respective novels.

What is even more important than Dick's use of the *I Ching*, however, is his creation of a sort of Western equivalent to the ancient book of wisdom. Frink and his partner, Ed McCarthy, break away from the simple forging of allegedly historical objects and begin creating contemporary jewelry. At first reluctant even to start on this operation, Frink eventually dares to assert his own uniqueness and try to sell it. However, the original new jewelry, which represents a resurgent American consciousness, lacks historicity, and the dealer Childan is reluctant to handle it even on consignment. However, Childan makes a present of a small, oddly angled pin to a Japanese acquaintance. The pin (and hence all of the other newly created jewelry pieces) has no value as a historical object, yet both Childan and Paul Kasoura recognize that it somehow partakes of the Tao. "It is balanced. The forces within this piece are stabilized. At rest . . . this object has made its peace with the universe." It has *wu* — wisdom, comprehension. It enables the possessor really to know the Tao.

In a curious, skillful way, the concept of light and dark, good and evil, is verbalized by Baynes, who has been working against Operation Dandelion. When Baynes, whose real name is Captain Rudolf Wegener of Germany Naval counterintelligence, contemplates the ultimate evil or darkness that will ensue if Operation Dandelion succeeds, he thinks, "We can only hope. And try. On some other world, possibly it is different. Better. There are clear good and evil alternatives." He will continue to fight against evil, because the good will always still exist.

Similarly the concept of light and dark, which in Dick's novel is equated to wisdom and ignorance as well as good and evil, finds another manifestation in the character of Tagomi. He finds that he cannot act in the face of moral ambiguity when he is forced to support one evil to counteract the greater evil of Dandelion. "There is no Way here," he thinks, "all is muddled. All chaos of light and dark, shadow and substance." He finds relief and a conclusive answer through contemplating another piece of Frink's jewelry which he has bought. Childan, transformed from toady and sycophant into proud American by contemplating the *wu* of the jewelry, says, "This is the new life of my country, sir. The beginning in the form of tiny imperishable seeds. Of beauty." And Tagomi immediately recognizes "that the Law of the Tao is borne out here; when yin lies everywhere, the first stirring of light is suddenly alive in the darkest depth." What Dick has accomplished here is the creation of a genuine, American, native version of the *I Ching* in the pieces of jewelry, and he has, in effect, assured a new world where the struggle will continue, but a world in which the seeds of light are beginning to sprout.

In its bare plot outline, *The Man in the High Castle* appears to be episodic, connected only by the situation in which all of the characters find themselves.

However, on close examination each of the apparently disparate sections or subplots fits together with the precision of a Bach fugue. Himself a musicologist, sometime owner of a classical records store, and amateur musician, Dick constructed his novel, perhaps unconsciously, in a contrapuntal manner. Each of the themes is stated, restated, and almost lost as another voice in another octave sings a contravening theme. Orchestrations, in one section rich, take on an almost plainsong quality in another, and then are reorchestrated into the complicated polyphony of the final section. Juliana Frink, only a shadow figure at first, emerges as the pivotal character of Dick's masterpiece.

Only Juliana has the incentive or the foresight to attempt to find Hawthorne Abendsen, the man in the high castle. On her search she is accompanied by Joe Cinnadella, a hired gunman whose mission is to kill Abendsen, whom the Germans now believe to be a potential danger because of the popularity of his novel. Joe has picked up Juliana because his information leads him to believe that Abendsen will be attracted to Juliana. Thus she will give Joe the opportunity to gain entrance to the "high castle."

Juliana, at first taken in by Joe, lets him seduce her and goes along when he suggests a trip to visit Abendsen. Only gradually does Juliana come to realize that Joe's mission is murder. To prevent that murder she must overcome her temerity and indecisiveness. She grows in stature as she solves the same problem faced by so many of the other characters in the novel: she must bring good out of evil, and perform a cruel act to achieve a good end. Becoming for a time almost psychotic, she kills Cinnadella, cutting his throat with a razor blade and leaving him as life seeps away. By so doing, she achieves sanity and saves Abendsen's life. In the world which Dick has created, however, there is no problem of ends and means; rather, the author takes the position of the Tao that good and evil are each contained in the other, and that from evil, no matter how abhorrent, good must eventuate.

Juliana's role in the novel is thus quite critical, and to misunderstand it would be either to miss or to ignore Dick's conception of her character. She is the shaping spirit of the novel, the source of its creative vision. While Abendsen may function in a shaman role and provide much of the illumination in the early parts of the book, it is Juliana who, once fully in touch with her creativity and full individuated, becomes the nourishing spirit of the new world. It is Juliana who comes to the fullness of the Tao, and emerges from the high castle to bring light to the darkening world.

Thus, *The Man in the High Castle* deals with the most profound of mysteries, the spirit of psychic, spiritual transformation, suggesting a eucharistic apotheosis that all of us, Dick maintains, must achieve. When we are all free, transmuted by Inner Truth, we shall achieve the totality of peace.

The Man in the High Castle is, in every way, a brilliant achievement.

Willis E. McNelly

Sources for Further Study

Criticism:

Gillespie, Bruce. *Philip K. Dick: Electric Shepherd*. Melbourne, Australia: Nostrilla, 1975. Gillespie discusses this early, lesser known work.

Reviews:

Amazing Stories. XXXVII, February, 1963, pp. 119-120 and XXXVII, June, 1964, pp. 123-124.

Analog. LXXI, April, 1963, p. 88.

Magazine of Fantasy and Science Fiction. XXIV, June, 1963, pp. 59-61.

New Worlds. CLX, March, 1966, p. 157 and CLXXIII, July, 1967, pp. 63-64.

SF Commentary. I, January, 1969, p. 45.

MAN PLUS

Author: Frederik Pohl (1919-   )
First book publication: 1976
Type of work: Novel
Time: 2000
Locale: The United States, Mars, and points between

A sardonic view of the successful attempt to land the first colonists on Mars, and of the technology which makes that colonization both possible and necessary

> *Principal characters:*
> ROGER TORRAWAY, an ex-astronaut modified into a cyborg capable of living on the surface of Mars
> DOROTHY, his wife
> SUSAN LEE CARPENTER, his nurse and Platonic lover
> WILL HARTNETT, his late predecessor in the Man Plus project
> FR. DONNELLY KAYMAN, S.J., areologist
> DR. ALEXANDER BRADLEY, Roger's best friend and the man who designs his sensory system
> FITZ-JAMES DESHATINE, President of the United States

A decision to colonize the planet Mars, given what we now know about that planet, may require a new "breed" of human being. This is the major premise of the award-winning novel which signaled an attempt by Frederik Pohl to advance beyond the comic satires for which he was best known in the 1950's. Ostensibly a work of hard-core science fiction, *Man Plus* is concerned in detail with making a man into a cyborg in order to lay the groundwork for a Martian colony. But the work is not a simple technocratic extrapolation, parading man's latest handiwork as an improvement on the original design.

Although it lacks the broad, even slapstick humor of Pohl's earlier satires, *Man Plus* is no less a work of social criticism. It exposes the individual and collective foibles of mankind, holds them up for clinical inspection, and aims at even more. Self-consciously literary, *Man Plus* uses symbolic patterns and structural manipulations which call attention to the writer's involvement; and Pohl achieves significant artistic balance as well as aesthetic distance. But ultimately, in coming to terms with the problems it poses, the novel is more successful cerebrally than emotionally.

Science and technology are handled seriously, sometimes in considerable detail. In the background, there is an increased sophistication apparent in the technology of surveillance, space travel, and weapons. The possible irrigation of the Australian desert by Chinese technicians has become a pretext for threats of war, with probably worldwide repercussions, between the Australians and the Chinese. Computers have developed artificial intelligence, with results hinted at but not extrapolated before the last chapter. In the foreground, the Martian environment and the construction of a cyborg fitted to it are given detailed attention.

This is the Mars revealed by the Mariner probes, and not yet disproven by the Viking Landers. No intelligent life forms are assumed, and no romantic acts of derring-do are acted out against the backdrop, although homage is paid the ghosts of Percival Lowell and Edgar Rice Burroughs. Gravity is light, air is thin, the sun is powerful but not warm, and the soil is capable of supporting life. As a side-issue, in fact, a crystalline plant form is found by Don Kayman, part of the space-suited back-up team that accompanies the Mars-adapted cyborg, Roger Torraway.

A former astronaut when the book opens, Torraway is rapidly changed from a self-styled "maker of monsters" into a monster himself, after Will Hartnett, the first cyborg intended for Mars, dies of a stroke because of sensory overload. Having learned from its mistakes, the Man Plus team transforms Roger quickly and efficiently, since there is only a short time available before the next launch window, and since the team is being pressured by President Deshatine to finish on time.

Like Hartnett, Roger must be reconstructed to survive with very little oxygen and food; he will have to rely on his machine parts, which are powered by solar energy obtained through vanes grafted on his body like bat wings. Like Will, Torraway must do without his natural limbs, sensory organs, breathing apparatus, and genitals, all of which have been replaced by adaptive machinery. Unlike Hartnett, however, Roger has mechanical aids which prevent overload by mediating between reality and his perceptions of it. Just as a frog can only see bite-size objects moving at the proper distance from his tongue, the new Roger can best perceive those aspects of reality most germane to his survival. Energy loss registers as cold, people may appear distorted by emotions, threatening objects become symbolic images. Although sensible in theory, this sensory mediation has its drawbacks from the standpoints of both survival and morality.

Sociological commentary is central to *Man Plus*, providing temporal color, plot motivation, and social criticism. Pohl extrapolates from such present-day developments as limited progress in civil rights, relaxed standards of priestly chastity and marital fidelity, the expansion of surveillance techniques, and the tightening of security clearance. America has fifty-four states (the new ones are not specified), and the nation is indulging in politics as usual, on both domestic and foreign fronts. The beleaguered Man Plus team, in its white block building on the Oklahoma plains, mirrors the paranoia of the American people, enunciated by President Deshatine, who envisions the "Free World" surrounded by collectivist regimes.

This "Fortress America" syndrome explains in part the very existence of the Man Plus project. Computerized projections rate the probability of nuclear war high and the chances of the survival of "our race" low — unless we develop a Martian "safety valve." Though these projections are later found to have been manipulated for melodramatic effect, their psychological consequences as a model of reality take hold. Other reasons for going to Mars include exploration, adventure, and the technological imperative. In other words, that which is possible should be attempted; new conditions call for new inventions, and the machines themselves have a stake in this "new frontier."

Pohl's satire is directed both against individual foibles and the questionable competence of human society as a whole. Don Kayman, priest and scientist, is always at war with himself to some degree. He is troubled by the moral question raised by Roger's distorted perceptions, through which Roger may never be able to see reality accurately. Kayman's moral consciousness is portrayed as earnest enough, but he also seems mildly ridiculous for raising the questions he does. President Fitz-James Deshatine, or "Dash," on the other hand, is broadly sketched with Kennedy and Johnson brushstrokes, and represents a mixture of image-making and effective muddling typical of the American political scene.

Roger's best friend, Alexander Bradley, is hardly deserving of the trust placed in him, since he always thinks first of his own future reputation and financial gain, and second of whatever tomcatting his notoriety and charisma can bring him. Dorrie, Roger's wife, revels as a spoiled child in the celebrity status to which her marriage entitles her, but repays Roger's adoration both by complacently accepting it as her due, and by cuckolding him. Her partner in adultery is Alexander Bradley, who designs and implements Roger's sensory system. Awareness of their arrangement becomes evident to Roger gradually at about the same time that his transformation makes him feel rather less than, not more than a man.

At first slow to recognize Roger's human feelings, the project directors later halt the affair (by specific order of President Deshatine), and successfully modify Roger's behavior with several substitutes. Sulie Carpenter, his nurse, tints her hair and her contact lenses to increase her uncanny resemblance to Dorrie. Sulie introduces Roger to the guitar, a phallic substitute, which, when mastered with the aid of his computer link-up, gives him new confidence in himself as a cyborg. And the great adventure itself looms more and more as a greater test of his manhood than mere sexual potency.

Roger's naïveté and passivity (and similarly, the duplicity of his colleagues and creators) are emphasized for symbolic effect, perhaps beyond probability. First of all, he must represent the ordinary person forced to adapt to change with which he is not ready to cope. Although Roger takes no moral stance against the changes he must undergo, the pain he suffers is a comment on the proceedings; others' reactions, from Don Kayman's theological concern to occasional reminders to treat Roger as a human being, provide an understated criticism.

Second, Roger must represent the superiority of the man-machine combination over either of its constituent parts. Thus, the contrast between his former self and his growing activity on his own behalf must be underlined, sometimes with disconcerting results. His control over his new powers make it possible for him to escape from the compound almost undetected, and to force a confrontation at home with Dorrie, finally breaking him free of his romantic nostalgia. Thus, too, he takes chances on Mars which almost destroy the whole expedition, himself included.

Although these characters are believable in outline, our understanding of them is far from complete, since the author is concerned primarily with their actions in quest of the project's success. But in part, their flatness is also due to their use as tools for Pohl's satire. Only one minor character, a feminist member of the media, is truly caricatured; the rest are simply depicted in unflattering colors. The point seems to be that humans accomplish what they do despite their flaws, and that exposing those flaws may be ego-boosting for the narrator as well.

On one hand, Pohl is consciously undercutting the traditional depiction of adventure-story characters as idealistic heroes; on the other hand, he does not offer well-rounded human beings in their place. As the negative is emphasized over the positive, his characters are reduced to mechanistic behavior. Though they may occasionally reveal a higher potential in their serious conversations, their actions, as they manipulate either Roger or one another, are what draw the reader's attention.

The characters' manipulations of one another seem to center on sexuality. One major theme in the story is Roger's castration, and the effect it has on his life outside the project. Though he is unable to copulate, Brad and Dorrie function normally, as do Sulie and her pilot in the follow-up rocket to Mars. Sexual innuendos, often unconscious, abound in conversations about Roger, and the entire Mars colony will of course depend eventually on its ability to reproduce.

Pohl also raises questions about the value of the project, which has been seen only from the point of view of the mysterious narrator, whose identity is finally revealed in the last chapter: it is the disembodied consciousness of our civilization's computer network. It therefore views human emotions as illogical, and human actions are mere manipulable variables. As the prime mover behind the Man Plus project, this artificial intelligence is concerned with its own survival, which depends on man to safeguard it. The computers, we find, have manipulated the sociological projections to make the success of the project seem more urgent, assuming that man acts most effectively in crisis situations. They also seem to be responsible for the creation of Roger, whose presence on Mars may be superfluous if the real human colony expects to live under domes.

But Roger is not simply a superfluous man. Whether he is strictly needed for the domed colony, he represents a technological advance, a man-machine interface with immense potential, once the problems are fully ironed out, whatever his loss in traditional "humanity." Not least, he represents the potential for the exploration and settling of Mars, since the space-suited colonists will be much more limited than he in terms of what they can do. With characteristic attention to redundancy, however, the Artificial Intelligence entity has seen to it that three different kinds of colonists have been sent. One is the cyborg, of course, who will soon have company of his own kind. The second is the unadapted human beings, like Sulie Carpenter. Though her cabinmate and Brad, and probably Don, will return to Earth, Sulie intends to stay, and what is more, to stay with Roger, for all that there will be formidable problems ahead for their relationship. The unadapted human beings will grow both by immigration and by reproduction, and Roger presumably will father Sulie's children, by means of earlier deposits in a sperm bank.

Third, however, the machines themselves are now colonists of Mars. Their Martian population in the next few years is projected at fifteen, accompanying an estimated one hundred human colonists. Along with others located throughout the solar system, they will be in contact with the central entity on Earth, enough so that, even if civilization were wiped out there, they would be able to maintain their information, intelligence, and consciousness. The title *Man Plus* does not refer simply to the cyborg known as Roger Torraway, advanced though he may be; it refers also to the civilization of man plus machine which may come to fruition once the bonds to Earth have been sufficiently loosened.

Questions of morality remain in Pohl's work, as do problems of realistic characterization. Furthermore, the tactic of withholding the narrator's identity, along with other devices used for sensational effect, may be questioned aesthetically, although they work as attention-getting storytelling devices. The overall impact of *Man Plus* is mixed; it raises important issues, yet one has the feeling that too much has been sacrificed for transitory effect. Within the context of Pohl's career, of course, the work is promising — the harbinger, hopefully, of more mature works to follow.

David N. Samuelson

Sources for Further Study

Reviews:

Booklist. LXXIII, October 1, 1976, p. 239.

Kirkus Reviews. XLIV, June 1, 1976, p. 658.

New York Times Book Review. October 17, 1976, p. 43.

Observer. December 5, 1976, p. 30.

Publisher's Weekly. CCIX, June 7, 1976, p. 72.

THE MAN WHO FOLDED HIMSELF

Author: David Gerrold (1944-   )
First book publication: 1973
Type of work: Novel
Time: September, 1975 is the starting point for time travel that takes us as far back as
    2000 B.C. and forward to A.D. 1999
Locale: Southern California

> *Danny Eakins inherits a time travel belt which he uses to establish wealth, allowing*
> *him to experience his life in a nonlinear fashion*

        Principal characters:
           DANNY EAKINS, a nineteen-year-old time traveler
           HIS ANALOGUES, Uncle Jim, Don Eakins, Diana Jane Eakins

Ever since H. G. Wells invented the time machine for his novel, the idea of time traveling by mechanical means has been one of the more popular themes for the science fiction novelist. Wells's idea of purposeful travel in time spawned two schools of time travel story. The first, following after his own *The Time Machine*, is the time travel adventure story with its variations, as illustrated by P. Schyler Miller's novella "The Sands of Time" and Edgar Rice Burroughs' *The Land That Time Forgot*. The second is the story that involves, in one form or another, the paradoxes implied in time travel. For the sake of simplicity, the paradox story can be stretched to include the parallel world and alternate history tale, which have become the most popular and probably the most common time travels in recent science fiction. The reason for this popularity is easily understood; time travel paradoxes tend to be the kind of speculative fiction that both fans and more critical readers of the genre enjoy. A good time paradox is a brain teaser; it stimulates us to play the game along with the author, examine, and even criticize his options and solutions. Speculative science fiction of this kind is like a good detective mystery; its appeal lies in the compulsion that drives the reader into an active, speculative state. The familiar claim that science fiction is a literature of ideas takes on new luster in relation to such stories. The important thing is not so much the ideas that are in the story, but how they stimulate the reader to think in ways that seem to imitate the speculations of science. This is a rather special kind of entertainment, a romance of the mind.

If such literature were plotted on a graph, the Flash Gordon/Buck Rogers variety of space opera, with the emphasis on sensational action, would constitute one extreme. On the other extreme are the more cerebral science fiction stories, paradox or problem oriented tales, whose special distinction is the power to stimulate a kind of speculative reflection in the reader. Most science fiction stories combine elements from the two extremes, mixing awe and wonder with imagined speculation to produce the characteristics that have made science fiction a distinctive literary and art form. David Gerrold's novel of time travel paradox falls near the cerebral science fiction end of the graph. There is much more speculation on the paradoxes implied in time traveling and the psychic impact of time mobility than there is action. Indeed, what action there is develops directly out of the protagonist's experiments with panchronism and his attempts to control its effects.

The narrative begins in September, 1975. Danny Eakins is nineteen years old and an unmotivated college student. He learns from his Uncle Jim that his patrimony is huge, $143 million to be exact, and that his living allowance is about to be raised to $1,000 a month on the condition that he keep a diary of his thoughts and experiences from then on. The story we read is, in fact, the diary that Danny keeps. Shortly after Danny begins the diary, he notices that Uncle Jim's health is rapidly failing, as though the aging process has been accelerated. After his uncle's death and funeral, Danny learns that there was no fortune, and that he has nearly spent the small inheritance that remained at the $1,000 a month rate initiated by Uncle Jim a few months earlier. Jim did not leave any assets except for a cardboard box in which Danny finds the time belt. Officially it is known as a Temporal Transport Device. Danny can hardly believe that such a thing is possible, but he and the reader proceed to have great fun learning how it operates. With its series of buttons and temporal coordinates, it is possible to set, reset, activate, and turn off the belt with as much ease as the new electronic chronographs.

Danny's first experiments with the belt produce extraordinary results, the most dramatic of which is his encounter with tomorrow's self as he transports forward in time. His future self takes the name of Don. Armed with tomorrow's paper, they head for the race track and make a killing. Dan also learns several important lessons in his first time travel. New time lines can be created by free choice. Therefore, neither the future nor the past are pre- or post-destined. The next day at the track, Danny, now Don, toys with the idea of doubling the bets in order to become a millionaire overnight. He is warned against doing that by another version of his future self who returns from the future to warn Don against all the trouble that will result from winning too much money at the track. Don takes this advice, and his winnings do not increase, although the manner in which the betting was made differs on the two days. The similarities and differences between the two days and the two selves are rendered very effectively by Gerrold in these scenes. The backward and forward movement in time, the incrementally repeated dialogue and actions are extremely effective ways to create a kind of verisimilitude that is simply beyond the experience of mundane fiction. Gerrold reinforces the illusion of time travel experience and paradox by generating a new language of time travel, a language that enriches the reader's vocabulary and hence the reader's thoughts and associations with a new terminology that seems to grow naturally out of imagined time travel experience. We learn that "tangling" is the result of crossing back over one's own time lines and producing, in effect, multiple selves. "Excising" is the act of returning to the past and changing a key event which will alter a time line, as occurred at the track.

Gerrold has built a sturdy foundation at this point in the story, and the reader is quite prepared to follow Danny wherever he may go. However, instead of escaping ourselves, we are plunged into the ripening paradoxes produced by time traveling. Most of what follows is a fictionalized essay on the grandfather paradox and related speculative metaphysics. Danny soon realizes that there are effective limits to time travel. The limits are set by the severity of cultural change in either direction from the present. Significant cultural and language change is a barrier to participation in either the past or the future. Hence time traveling is limited to a few hundred years on either side of the present. However, the habit of time travel changes time subjectively. Danny soon loses that sense of continuity and even of self that comes from living in the normal linear or sequential way. Time leaping becomes a habit, an addiction. It frees one to satisfy almost any mood or whim, but it is disorienting and disturbing to the conventional ideas of identity. The question of who one really is becomes meaningless when one has numerous duplicates or analogues available for such things as a running poker game, as in Gerrold's novel. There is a catch to the duplication of selves; the duplication is apparent rather than real. It depends upon tangled time lines. The duplicates are not like clones. Furthermore, the duplicates do not share simultaneous consciousness. Because all of them come from different times and even time lines, they do not share the same knowledge or experience. Hence each is a different Danny, living at a different time in his life. Moreover, some of the Dannys will be excised with their time lines and will exist separately in one of the infinite time lines possible. This is the sort of problem the reader is asked to contemplate, and the game is well worth playing.

Gerrold introduces interesting questions from the speculative horizons of ethics. Time travel has implications for free will that would have delighted and appalled the most determined medieval theologian. While time travel seems the ultimate expression of free will, inevitably it isolates and traps the traveler into solipsism. Time travel allows full exploration of the conditional mode of existence, a mode known only to the imagination previously. At the same time, panchronism shatters the unity of the self and the personality. One of Danny's selves becomes a paranoid-schizoid and has to be cared for by other selves. The danger of the deranged self obtaining possession of the belt and its powers is a terrifying prospect.

Another paradox that Gerrold invites us to consider is the nature and effect of sexual relations among the various selves. This theme suggests some New Wave influences, perhaps, but it certainly is a testimony to the degree of liberalization that took place in the genre during the 1960's and 1970's. Danny and Don find themselves attracted to each other and contemplate a homosexual relationship. They are warned against it by a future Danny, but they decide to trust instinct and appetite. The self-seduction is handled rather complexly, with emphasis on the psychological and ethical ramifications. There is little or no reporting of lurid details. The question of whether such an act is masturbatory or homosexual is raised without being decided. Danny's choice comes at the end of the first part of the novel, which emphasizes various experimental uses of the time belt and their consequences. The sexual theme is taken up again, becoming more central in the next part.

After Danny has eliminated his duplicate selves by a series of excisions, he finds that he is suffering from acute psychic isolation. Using his birthday as a beacon, he time travels backward, hoping to make contact with a duplicate self from another time line. One thousand years before his own birth he is successful. This self turns out to be female, and the consequences of their meeting are obvious. Gerrold treats the reader to another extraordinary *tour de force* in which the reader experiences the gradual confusion of identities and even sexes as the two lover selves become increasingly intimate. The descriptions become more graphic and the situations more titillating as Diana and Danny decide to honeymoon in a Victorian villa which they transport to the shores of Mission Bay in about 2000 B.C. The love scenes are treated tenderly and with exceptional subtlety and skill. A baby is born, but in that birth there is a sign of contradiction and separation. Dan wants a boy, and Diana wants a girl. Each time travels to achieve his and her desire through the use of prenatal genetic manipulation. The symbolism effectively dramatizes both the selfishness and isolation of each, qualities that have grown behind the illusion of freedom that time travel creates or the related illusion of control of one's life that develops as the result of time travel escapism. Neither can accommodate anything but his or her own desired end. The refrain, "O God, I feel alone," echoes down the various corridors of time through which Danny flees with son. It is a refrain which echoes that of Heinlein's superb short story of time travel and solipsism, — "All You Zombies" to which Gerrold's novel certainly owes a great debt of inspiration.

In the last part of the novel, we find Danny living out his life in a more or less normal fashion. He has chosen 1956 as his baseline time, taken the identity of Uncle Jim, and decided to raise his son who is called, naturally, Danny. The circle of self-generation and isolation is fully closed. Danny-Jim travels frequently to the future to take neoprocaine treatments in order to counteract the effects of aging. The treatments are not entirely successful, as Danny discovers after he returns to the Mission Bay honeymoon villa in 2000 B.C. looking for Diana, who rejects the now middle-aged looking Danny as a stranger. Thus Danny is cut off from the time line of his younger self, and any attempt to move backward in time will result in excision of more and more of the original relationship between Danny and Diana. It seems that even the powers of the belt to modify, alter, or excise time are limited by an inherent law of contradiction. In Gerrold's novel, the greatest of the paradoxes lies with the exercise of a force that isolates the individual in proportion to the frequency with which it is used to escape an unpleasant event or to alter it.

If Gerrold took his theme or an aspect of it from Heinlein's " — All You Zombies," then Gerrold's attitude seems closer to the Heinlein of *Door into Summer* because he is more involved with and sympathetic toward his characters. Gerrold's treatment of Danny is less detached and more personal. The attitude is more sentimental, the effect more like a daydream than the satirical punch of the Heinlein short story.

The dedication of *The Man Who Folded Himself* to Larry Niven underlines another analogue and probable influence. Parallels to the short stories "Bird in the Hand" and "All the Myriad Ways" are strong enough to establish probable influence, but even more influential and perhaps inspirational is Niven's essay "The Theory and Practice of Time Travel" in the collection of stories and speculative essays titled *All the Myriad Ways*. There is little doubt that Gerrold drew on some of Niven's speculations in this essay, one which any reader of time travel stories or of Niven will want to read. If Gerrold's handling of time travel speculations succeeds, however, it is not on the strength of his logic. Gerrold is at his best when he is able to bring together speculations on time travel or paradox with the main character's desire to formulate a rational understanding of what he is doing and its likely consequences. Too often, Gerrold relies on long passages of time travel exposition instead of exploring some of his more compelling symbols that seem to grow naturally out of the fictional matrix of time travel. In brief, the novel is rather too long on speculation and too short on either action or interaction among characters. In the case of *The Man Who Folded Himself*, that interaction is among various manifestations of the self for which the archetypes in twentieth century literature have been supplied by T. S. Eliot and James Joyce.

This is an important point to raise in a critical evaluation of this novel because it touches upon the major weakness of Gerrold's conception of his character and that character's narrative. The relentlessly increasing subjectivity of Danny's self-consciousness, even when it involves multiple selves, internalizes all action with the result that we are spectators of a great drama of solipsism. Unfortunately, we are trapped within the consciousness of a protagonist too immature to retain the interest of a thoughtful reader. Gerrold needs to have as a hero someone infinitely more subtle of mind or sensibility than an average American nineteen year-old in the mid-1970's. How much more interesting the hero's dilemmas, his attempts to shape his own life, or his attempts to understand a life lived under such unique circumstances if that hero had some wit, some depth, some culture or resources above the commonplace. Instead, we are asked to be edified by cultural and intellectual bankruptcy spread across a dizzy variation of time lines. The most remarkable accomplishments of Dan Eakins are to assure himself vast wealth in perpetuity and to engage himself in homosexual and heterosexual relationships. The money turns out to be unimportant. Its presence is necessary to explain how Danny has the leisure to time-hop all over the place in pursuit of something the reader is never quite clear about. If Gerrold wants to make his hero a victim of solipsism, he must achieve a critical and ironic distance from him as did Heinlein; or else he can treat the whole business with a comic touch as did Niven in "A Bird in the Hand" or with a serious-tragic tone as in "All the Myriad Ways."

The Man Who Folded Himself is an essay in the speculative mythology of time travel. Its weakness as a work of art is ultimately a weakness of mind on the author's part for trying to have his hero both ways. He tries to handle the entrapment of Danny from a sentimental and melodramatic viewpoint while the logic of the narrative is working against this very sentimentalism. Questions about the time belt itself, where it originally came from and how it came into Danny's possession are never adequately answered. Nonetheless, the novel has its place in the science fiction literature of time travel. When his plot allows Gerrold to be poetic, the novel comes to life with a richness and a tenderness that is worthy of Ursula Le Guin at her best. Readers may wish to compare Le Guin's "Nine Lives" as another significant analogue for Gerrold's novel. A comparison of the story and the novel would be instructive for both the similarities and differences between the two, especially in the handling of the androgony theme.

The author leaves the book with several loose ends. Although the narrative is supposed to be from the diary kept by Danny, it is clearly something else. The style, point of view, and intent seem not to be that of a diary, however loosely we use that word. If Danny dies as Uncle Jim in 1975, how are we to account for his dying in another guise twenty years later? We may presume that these postmortems apply to duplicates from other time lines, but we do not know. What happened to the $143 million that Danny was supposed to have inherited from Jim when he was nineteen? While none of these explanations are crucial to the story, a reader does like a certain amount of authorial housecleaning before the end.

Gerrold's speculations on time travel paradox are not especially original, but they are sustained enough to comprise somewhat of an inventory of the subject for those who would like to review the field. The speculations come to life only when Danny's experiences bring before the reader some of the moral and psychological implications of Danny's rather thoughtless uses of the time belt. In the end, it is the poetry and the symbolism that remain with the reader long after the last of the ingenious paradoxes of time travel have been forgotten. Despite weaknesses, Gerrold's story is not one the reader is likely to forget because somehow the sense of involvement in the selfdefeating contradictions of time travel come through; and there is occasional beauty and tenderness, qualities rare enough in anyone's fiction.

Donald L. Lawler

Sources for Further Study
Reviews:

Booklist. XLIX, May 1, 1973, p. 835.

Kirkus Reviews. XL, December 15, 1972, p. 1445.

Library Journal. XCVIII, February 1, 1973, p. 436.

Luna Monthly. XLV, February, 1973, pp. 30-31.

Magazine of Fantasy and Science Fiction. XLV, November, 1973, pp. 26-28.

Publisher's Weekly. CCII, December 11, 1972, p. 34.

Renaissance. V, Spring, 1973, p. 16.

THE MAN WITH THE BROKEN EAR
(L'HOMME À L'OREILLE CASSÉE)

Author: Edmond About (1828-1885)
First book publication: 1862
English translation: 1872
Type of work: Novel
Time: The 1860's
Locale: France

The mock-heroic story of a colonel of the Great Army (of Napoleon Bonaparte) who awakens after a forty-six-year hibernation, under Napoleon III

Principal characters:
>PIERRE-VICTOR FOUGAS, a colonel, twenty-four years old when he is put into hibernation
>LEON RENAULT, an engineer
>CLEMENTINE SAMBUCCO, his fiancée
>KARL NIBOR, a biologist
>NICHOLAS MEISER, a rich landlord in Dantzig

Almost forgotten today, the author of *The Man with the Broken Ear* enjoyed both literary and journalistic success during the Second Empire. The echoes of this fame can be discerned in the evaluations of encyclopedic works with very broad circulation: "A witty and brilliant writer . . ." (*Le Nouveau Petit Larousse Illustré*, 1939), ". . . the ironic and tender novels of Edmond About . . ." (*Litterature française*, Larousse, 1968). Can one use such adjectives when speaking of books such as *The Weddings of Paris*, *The King of the Mountains*, *The Story of a Fine Fellow*, *Madelon?* If they are placed in the context of his age, the reply could be affirmative. But time spares only exceptional works, or those which, without being stamped with the seal of perfection, have the gift of impressing the flash of the new and the unexpected on the retina of posterity. Certain of About's texts belong to this latter category. By a strange and perhaps significant coincidence, they were all published in the same year, 1862.

These "three novels of high fantasy" (*Grand Larousse Encyclopédique*, 1960) are, however, unequal in merit. Although it is dedicated to the psychologist Charles Robin, *The Case of Mr. Guerin* seems rather a tall tale enlarged to the dimensions of a book: the hero bears, apparently by a caesarean section, a child. A somewhat provocative subject, treated as though it were a hoax, even if the point of departure is found in some hypotheses about the reproductive process which were in circulation at the time.

A more plausible scientific pretext, not for About's contemporaries but for us who are already used to transplant and plastic surgery operations, is used in *A Notary's Nose*. It is a story with philosophical and moral pretensions, which rapidly leaves the field of medical speculation to sail the waters of the fantastic. The influence of Gerard de Nerval's *The Enchanted Hand* seems incontestable, even if About's construction of plot and atmosphere are quite different.

Finally, *The Man with the Broken Ear* is the last and the most successful of this tryptych which constitutes a somewhat foreign body in About's work. This time, the literary influences are more numerous, the hero's leap in time having famous antecedents. Theopompe of Chios related in the fourth century that the philosopher Cretois Epimenides had slept fifty-seven years in a cave. Washington Irving would take up the idea again in 1819, but Rip Van Winkle's sleep only lasted twenty years. But the record had been soundly beaten by Louis-Sebastien Mercier: his character awakens, after almost seven centuries, in *The Year 2440* (1770).

Such previous long literary sleeps, were presented as "natural" accidents; on the other hand, Colonel Pierre-Victor Fougas' adventure in time is based on an entirely different supposition, one that clearly establishes the story as science fiction. About makes use of a plausible procedure, elaborated and used by a scientist convinced that "science can put a living being to sleep and awaken him after an indefinite number of years, can interrupt all the bodily functions, suspend life, remove the individual from the effect of time for a century or two, and revive him." It must be pointed out right away that the idea dated from 1845: in the story "Some Words with a Mummy," Edgar Allan Poe brought the noble Allamistakeo, embalmed five millennia before in the Egypt of the Pharaohs, back to life. About could have read Poe's story, translated by Baudelaire, in either the journal "Le Pays" of December 11 and 12, 1854, or in the volume *Nouvelles Histoires extraordinaires*, published in 1857.

However, precedence does not necessarily mean influence. The procedures through which Allamistakeo was "removed from the effect of time" and then "revived" are quite different from those used in the case of Fougas. Whereas Poe's Egyptian is awakened by voltaic batteries, About's Karl Nibor rejects the use of electricity to awaken the colonel. His preservation is much more authentic than that of his literary predecessors, perhaps inspired by a real fact: during the Napoleonic wars, Baron Marbot, a general, was revived after being left for dead in the snow. Through combining partial freezing with dehydration, the subject of experiments which had great repercussions at the time, the author suspends his hero's life for forty-six years.

But *The Man with the Broken Ear* does not simply describe a scientific victory. It also reflects About's strong anticlerical bias, for he criticized the government whenever the church took part in or was drawn into the affairs of the state. This attitude probably stemmed from a vaguely materialistic outlook. In any case, the success of Professor Meiser's experiment represents a weakening of the theory of the "vital principle," which theory, as Karl Nibor forcefully claims, "is in contradiction to the present state of science."

The Man with the Broken Ear also offers us indications of the author's socio-political outlook. At his death, Jules Claretie wrote of him in "La Vie de

Paris": "Mocking the strong, defying the powerful, helping little people, never laughing at the misery of other. . . ." We have reasons to be skeptical about the first two assertions. It is true that About contributed to "L'Opinion nationale," but this opposition newspaper was secretly a partisan of the government, which protected the writer and even had given him a medal. A sentence from the novel seems significant from this point of view: "Respect for the powers that be, which is the very basis of nature, does not allow me to introduce august persons in the scene." An apparently ironic turn of phrase is nullified by the final allusion. Because the reference is to the Emperor, the declaration becomes a profession of faith. As for his attitude towards "little people," it is primarily expressed indirectly in passages of the chapter devoted to Nicholas Meiser and his wife, rapacious landlords with residential property. The same technique is used in two of the least expected pages of the novel, in which Fougas gives in to a veritable frenzy of city planning, presenting Napoleon III the vision of somewhat reactionary Paris laid out on a grandiose scale. The imperial palace and the public utilities are located in the center of the city. On the twelve radially arranged boulevards and on the streets which link them, there are model houses for those who have incomes of more than fifty thousand francs. As for the workers, they are housed ten kilometers from the beltway, in working-class fortresses. "We do not collect any taxes, so that they like us; we put cannons all around them, so that they fear us."

These two pages constitute the only utopian insertions in this science fiction narration, and the interest of the distinction is not merely theoretical. All in all, *The Year 2440* and *The Man with the Broken Ear* have the same theme: a man gains access to the future. But in the former, Mercier (the book is written in the first person) walks about the streets of Paris like a tourist. His adaptation is total. His astonishment has a moderate tone. In actuality, he does not live, he contemplates. By contrast, Fougas remains a man of his time transplanted to another era. He admires and disapproves of the new institutions and mores with the same fervor, disturbing provincial quietude and politeness, and the heroic spirit and soldierly ways of the Great Army. In spite of such different behavior, Mercier and Fougas are nevertheless alike in their rapid adaptation to the new reality, so rapid that About feels the need to justify it. ". . . Fougas, opening his eyes, had plunged straight into the midst of the action. . . . He had improvised friends, enemies, an army, a rival. . . . But what joined him to modern times most of all was his well-established relationship with the big family of the army." The function of the latter sentence and what follows in the novel is to induce a patriotic tone. Displaying a good knowledge of the necessities of composition and of the psychology of the reader. About is already preparing for the tragic ending. Fougas casually changes his passion for Clementine into a quasipaternal feeling, but he cannot stand being kept out of the army for having passed retirement age. This twenty-four-year-old veteran, who had been caught up for a whole month in a whirlwind of events he himself had set in motion, finds himself caught in a mood of irremediable melancholy, declaring ". . . a man should live with his times. Later, is too late." He thus expresses for the first time, an idea and a state of mind which was to see a great flowering in modern science fiction.

In the obituary mentioned above, Jules Claretie summed up his praise for About in this way:

> . . . "the very French style of Edmond About appears, after one reads the pseudojewelers for the decadence, like a little of the white snow which still covers the roof where it lies. . . . It has better than color, this marvelous style of About's, it has light, the force of things."

Are these evaluations justified in the case of *The Man with the Broken Ear*? Written with fluency and vivacity, the novel even surprises us sometimes by its very graphic comparisons. But let us not be taken in by the appearance of a few oases in a desert of flowery grandiloquence. As has been said, the novel stands the test of time above all through its flash of newness and unexpectedness, giving us the first believable contact between the eras carried out with plausible means.

With Colonel Fougas' time travel ending in the author's present, the speculative side consists almost exclusively of Professor Meiser's successful experiment. Nevertheless one passage considered a great joke at the time of the book's publication must be pointed out. "Patients the science of the 19th century would have declared incurable would no longer blow their brains out, but would let themselves be dehydrated and would patiently wait, deep in a box, for the doctor to find a remedy for their illnesses." Once again, reality tends to catch up with fiction, which by no means diminishes the glory of the latter.

Ion Hobana

Sources for Further Study

Criticism:

Saintsbury, George. *A History of the French Novel*. London: Macmillan & Company, 1919. Saintsbury's general remarks concerning About's writing style provide some interesting insights regarding his overall thematic interests.

MAO CH'ENG CHI
(Memoirs of Cat Country)

Author: Lao She (She Shu-yü, 1899-1966)
First book publication: c. 1934
Type of work: Novel
Time: Undisclosed, probably the 1930's
Locale: Mars

A classic dystopian satire in the Swiftian tradition on life in laissez-faire, *prerevolutionary China, describing the destruction of a degenerate, hedonistic society on Mars.*

Principal characters:
THE NARRATOR, a Chinese scientist
BIG SCORPION, a Martian landowner
LITTLE SCORPION, the son of Big Scorpion, a revolutionary
INTOXICATION, Little Scorpion's fiancée
BIG HAWK, another revolutionary

She Shu-yü is commonly known in the West under his pen name, Lao She, as the author of two fairly prominent novels: *Rickshaw Boy* (1938) and *The Birthday of Little Po* (1929), the latter a minor fairy-tale classic. The author was also a revolutionary and a leading supporter of the Communist uprising under Mao and was forced to flee from China after the publication of *Memoirs of Cat Country*, a novel that apparently displeased Chiang Kai-shek a great deal. After fifteen years of exile in the United States, Lao She returned to China after the Revolution and became a leading cultural personality, member of the People's Assembly, editor of the influential magazine *Beitszin venji*, and deputy chairman of the Chinese writers' union. He died at the height of the Cultural Revolution; according to Soviet sources he was murdered by Red Guards, but this is a matter of considerable doubt.

It should be kept in mind when reading *Memoirs of Cat Country* that it is, like Edward Bellamy's *Looking Backward* and similar Utopian works, more a political tract than a novel, a vitriolic pamphlet written by a revolutionary rather than a novel meant for literary pleasure. Lao She was actively engaged in a revolution, and the novel gives his views on the crumbling old world.

What Lao She describes in minute detail is the sort of *laissez-faire* society depicted by Robert A. Heinlein or Ayn Rand. It is set, for convenience sake, on Mars and inhabited by a sort of cat people. Might is right, and the populace is kept under control by liberal use of a narcotic drug dispensed by the ruling elite. This ultimate *Soma* is food and drink; it gives courage and bliss and also fosters obedience and indolence. The drug comes in the form of thick, succulent leaves, and with these leaves anything can be bought. There is hardly any government (although a powerless emperor hides somewhere in the background), and the army can be bought by anyone willing to pay in narcotic leaves.

When the protagonist, a Chinese scientist, crashes his rocket ship on Mars, he is quickly pressed into service by the local leaf grower, Big Scorpion, to guard the plantation against rampaging soldiers and starving peasants. The Narrator is tall and powerful, not yet addicted to the leaves; and he owns a gun. However, he soon turns out to be a mixed blessing for the plantation owner, and they part company. The Narrator then journeys to the capital of Cat Country where, in a manner very much reminiscent of Swift, he meets people in all stations of life and experiences at first hand the glories and hardships of a society devouring itself. The vivid descriptions of the incredible moral decay in this city, where anything can be bought and where only the strong have rights, are probably as shocking as anything in modern science fiction, and even more effective since the setting was extrapolated from the actual situation in Chiang Kai-shek's China when the novel was written. There are many parallels between *Memoirs of Cat Country* and Lao She's more well-known novel *Luo-tuo Hsiang-tzu* (1938; translated as *Rickshaw Boy*, 1945), which describes the plight of a common Chinese in the 1920's and 1930's.

Memoirs of Cat Country was written in 1932-1933, and it is quite interesting to compare the book to the Western dystopian novel of that time, Aldous Huxley's *Brave New World* (1932). Very much a product of an affluent society, Huxley describes his personal dystopia as a place of almost child-like innocence, a society offering its citizens all sorts of ersatz happiness, in effect stealing their humanity in order to give them perfect bliss. Huxley's society is an authoritarian one, albeit generally benevolent. In vivid contrast to this is Evgeny Zamiatin's *We* (1920), with its harsh totalitarian dictatorship operating in the name of science and efficiency, obviously modeled upon the experiences of an intellectual and former revolutionary in the new Soviet state. Lao She's Cat Country is entirely different from either of these dystopias. In this society we see the total absence of law and order; a completely *laissez-faire* society which offers everything and nothing; the perfect Ayn Rand society, if you will, where a citizen has only those rights he can defend, and only for as long as he can hold them. The dissidents of *Brave New World* and *We* fight for personal freedom against the soul-deadening efficiency of the state; in Cat Country, personal integrity is held so dear that cooperation between people is impossible and the dissidents fight in vain to make people unite against the common enemy, who, in the end, invades the country and exterminates the population. Lao She describes in dry, precise prose the fate of the last two survivors, locked in a cage, fighting each other until they both die. So much for personal integrity and dignity — at least as seen by Lao She.

From a literary point of view, *Memoirs of Cat Country* seems to be a less than satisfying work, especially when compared to *Rickshaw Boy*. We are simply presented with an odyssey of horrors through a world so alien to a Western point of view and Western experience that it almost reads like a parody on Western dystopian novels. We see teachers selling their pupils into slavery, scientists and intellectuals selling their dignity for a few narcotic leaves, man turning against wife, children against parents, an army selling itself to the enemy; a society so devoid of honor and decency, so cold and inhuman that it should not be allowed to exist. The novel soon turns into a catalogue of atrocities as the Earthman is lectured on the ways of the cat people, and the final genocide seems not only inevitable but actually necessary. Like all good dystopian novels, *Memoirs of Cat Country* really tells about the horrors of its own time; Lao She writes about China under Chiang Kai-shek, using the tool of science fiction, just as Huxley describes his own Western world in *Brave New World*. Britain never had a revolution; China did. *Memoirs of Cat Country* gives an idea why.

Memoirs of Cat Country is a widely read science fiction work, and has been published in many millions of copies since the first clandestine printings in Chiang Kai-shek's China. It has never been out of print in China since the Revolution, and has sold in the millions in Eastern Europe as well. Lao She, indeed, became very popular in Russia when contacts between Russia and China cooled off the mid-1960's, and *Memoirs of Cat Country* was eagerly used by Soviet authorities as a weapon against the Chinese deviationists. A drastically rewritten version of the novel has sold by the millions in the Soviet Union, purporting to be the work of a dissident under Mao Tse-tung; a recent Russian edition of the novel happily points out that "(Lao She) was one of the untold victims of Maoism. But his novel lives and will continue to live as an angry and passionate accusation against political adventurousness, which tries to parasite on the bright ideals of Man's Communistic future."

Thus, *Memoirs of Cat Country* is still influential, even when rewritten to serve ends that surely would have seemed strange to its author. The novel survives not on its literary merits, of course, but because of its political message. All Utopian and dystopian works are heavily political, and *Memoirs of Cat Country* is no more so than others; the novel describes a political situation which few Western readers will be familiar with, but it is very well understood in Asia and Eastern Europe, for the same reasons that *Brave New World* is understood in the West and often misinterpreted in the East. Lao She's novel is very much neglected in the West, and most Western science fiction scholars actually seem unaware that it exists — which is ironic for a science fiction novel which probably has sold more copies than all the celebrated Western dystopian novels put together. In importance it ranks with Edward Bellamy's *Looking Backward*, and is probably as well written.

In the end, *Memoirs of Cat Country* is a moral tale in the Swiftian tradition. Lao She himself pointed to H. G. Wells's *The First Men in the Moon* as his chief inspiration; but that must surely have been an inspiration of contrast. Wells's dystopian vision of the rigid Selenite civilization bears very little likeness to the murderous chaos of the Cat Country; only the callousness and the inhumanity are the same. Lao She and H. G. Wells may have aimed at the same thing, however — the failed and the successful revolutionary, each in his own way depicting the ultimate fate of mankind as it leaves its humanity behind, seeking salvation in extreme measures and finding only failure and death.

Sam J. Lundwall

THE MARTIAN CHRONICLES

Author: Ray Bradbury (1920-   )
First book publication: 1950
Type of work: Thematically related short stories
Time: 1999-2026
Locale: The United States, Mars

Twenty-six ironic and yet lyrical "chronicles" dealing with Earth's exploration and colonization of Mars

In *The Martian Chronicles* there is no consistency in characterization or unity of plot. The work is a collection of short stories which is held together by the author's unrelenting ironic tone and his virtual obsession with the interplay between past and future, illusion and reality. The premise upon which the book is built is that Earth's destruction by nuclear war is imminent and that Mars will afford certain lucky colonists a chance to begin anew. Once they begin arriving, however, the Earthmen soon discover that the past and the future are not so easily distinguishable, and that if one is not careful, a second chance can kill.

This is precisely what happens to the members of Captain Black's Third Expedition, who, after having traveled through space on a perilous and exhausting journey, discover a setting that appears to be more Earthlike than Earth. What greets them is a small, early twentieth century Midwestern village, just the kind that Black (and Bradbury) had known as a boy, filled with quaint Victorian houses, colorful geraniums, chestnut trees, even a band playing "Beautiful Ohio." Needless to say, the Captain and his crew are thoroughly bewildered. Expecting to discover some exotic, alien land, they find instead only pieces of their own pasts, pasts made irresistible by the reappearance of members of their own families. After an initial period of skepticism, they succumb to the seductive charms of being allowed another chance at reliving their childhoods. But in doing so they have doomed themselves, for the Martians have tricked them by using their highly developed telepathic imaginations to construct a deadly counterfeit reality. As each of them is securely and snugly locked within his own boyhood home, he is coldly and remorselessly murdered by his own Martian "family."

It is Mars as Earth, as the past, that kills them. This theme, that patterns of behavior learned on Earth are highly destructive when transplanted to Mars, is extended throughout the book. Hauling Oregon lumber through space, for example, as the colonists did in order to build houses for themselves, surpasses mere folly and takes on the character of mass psychosis. By treating the Martians as if they were some ignorant and primitive tribe, the colonists imitate behavior patterns of the Europeans who subjugated Earth in earlier centuries, and thus they destroy an entire civilization. It is here that Bradbury seems to be the most bitter, as he describes the manner in which a gentle and intelligent culture is exploited and then finally obliterated by people like Biggs and Sam Parkhill.

The fact that the colonists from Earth were not able to throw off their most destructive, dysfunctional Earthbound patterns of behavior is seen most clearly in the September, 2005, entry, "The Martian." The protagonist of this story is a young man who has the uncanny ability to take on the characteristics of deceased Earth people. As a Martian he is able to become whoever the colonists want him to be, and as such he is soon transformed into a fragile complex of ever-changing roles by which he is able to fulfill the needs of those around him. Again, then, the visitors from Earth are presented with a second chance on Mars as the young boy becomes several *personae* at once, all of them dead friends and relatives of the colonists.

One such *persona* is "Tom," the son of Mr. and Mrs. LaFarge. The LaFarges are perceptive enough to know that they would be better off if they could let go of the past. " 'We should try and forget him,' " Mrs. LaFarge tells her husband, " 'and everything on Earth.' " This, of course, is just the dilemma that has faced the colonists from the beginning: forget the past or be continually tortured by it. Yet, typically, the LaFarges cannot forget. They treat the Martian as if he *were* Tom, despite the fact that all he really wants is to be accepted as he himself is — a unique "Martian" who in his own way is as much in need of love as they are. But the LaFarges and their fellow colonists, in their inability to rise above a necrophilic attachment to their own pasts, tear him apart, along with any hopes they might have held for a future of peace and happiness. Thus Tom is destroyed for the same reasons that all of Martian culture was destroyed, because of the greed and shortsightedness of those who received a second chance for life and growth.

In time Mars becomes a veritable "tomb planet" populated only by such odd solipsists as Walter Gripp and Hathaway, a dying remnant from the Fourth Expedition, who lives in his stone hut with the robots who attend him as the perfect replicas of his family on Earth. Here at last is a second chance that seems to work, albeit in a morbid, melancholic fashion. But Bradbury does not end the book on this note of bitterness and despair. There is, in the final chronicle, a hope for an integration of the old Earth with the new Mars. The Thomas family, soon to be joined by a handful of like-minded people, has arrived on Mars just before Earth reaches its final destruction. As former Governor Thomas burns some official state papers in a purifying bonfire, he speaks for this final group of colonists. " 'Life on Earth,' " he says, " 'never settled down to doing anything very good. Science ran too far ahead of us too quickly, and the people got lost in a mechanical wilderness, like children making over pretty things, gadgets, helicopters, rockets; emphasizing machines instead of how to run the machines.' " Clearly, this is the author speaking. This is the voice of the Bradbury of *Fahrenheit 451* and "Rocket Man" and "The Veldt," the Bradbury who often decried the blind mechanization and totalitarianization of modern life, and who, even in his calmer, less fretful moments, still felt a great ambivalence about the road postwar America seemed to be taking towards technological complexity and away from the freedom and sanctity of the individual.

A second, closely related theme that serves to unify the various stories in the book is the relationship between illusion (or fantasy, or insanity) and reality. Bradbury begins to develop this theme with the coming of the First Expedition in February, 1999. After having left Earth in a blast from a rocket that temporarily turned an Ohio winter into spring, Captain York and the members of his crew arrived upon Mars only to be killed as innocent, unknowing recipients of a husband's jealousy. In a dream York had come to Ylla, an obscure Martian woman. He had flirted with her, told her that she was beautiful, and then asked her to come away with him. As soon as he and his men land, they are done away with, not only because they are seen as dangerous invaders from another planet, but also because Ylla's husband is not able to control his feelings of jealousy. The First Expedition therefore comes to its ignoble end in an ironic and, from the Earthmen's point of view, wholly denigrating air of unreality.

The members of the Second Expedition also find themselves caught in a perplexing web of fantasy and madness. Again, Bradbury's use of irony is immensely effective. Expecting a heroes' welcome, Captain Williams and his crew are instead immediately discounted by the Martians as being nothing more than paranoid projections. Rather than being treated as warriors and explorers from another planet, they are hustled off to an insane asylum where they are locked up with Martians who demonstrate their insanity by telepathically projecting their fantasies outward until they take the form of objective reality. As a consequence, what is real to the Earthmen (the fact that they are actually from Earth) is treated as if it were illusionary madness by the Martians. This, of course, is the exact reverse of the situation in which the Third Expedition will find itself, for there the Martians will be the ones in touch with reality, and it will be they who self-consciously manufacture illusions as a means of defending themselves against the encroachments of a culture that is, as far as technological development is concerned, more highly advanced.

As the book progresses, Bradbury drops the more deadly aspects of this theme and concentrates instead on its subtler, more melancholic dimensions. Perhaps its fullest development is achieved in the section called "August 2002: Night Meeting." Here, an obtuse Earthman by the name of Tomás Gomez happens to meet Muhe Ca, a Martian who, despite having melted gold for eyes, sees no better than he does. In the dark Martian night, deep within the barren Martian desert, illusion and reality meet once again. This time, however, it is a standoff. Neither Tomás nor the Martian can accept the existence of the other. First one, then the other, accuses his opposite of being an insubstantial figment of his own imagination, a mere hallucination. Again there is no coexistence, as each claims that the other is a phantasmagoric relic from the past, a ghost having no substance and no significance. It is a fruitless and frustrating study in solipsism, for neither of them is able to reach out to acknowledge the dual realities of Earth and Mars. As Tomás puts it, " 'If *I* am real, then *you* must be dead.' "

Certainly, this is Bradbury at his most bitter; again and again he gives his characters another chance, and yet again and again they fail to take advantage of it, slipping back repeatedly into hopelessness and despair. They remain this way not simply because they are stupid and small, but because they are selfish. Nowhere is this made more apparent than in the December, 2005 entry, "The Silent Towns." After an eternity of believing that he is the last man on Mars, Walter Gripp gets a phone call from a woman named Genevieve Selsor. But when, after much difficulty, they finally get together, and Genevieve does not meet his preconceived fantasies of what a woman should look like, Walter unceremoniously dumps her, preferring to spend his remaining years alone rather than accepting her as she is, in all her human imperfection. It is an ironic twist on the familiar last man motif. Here is a last man who chooses to remain within his own lonely and illusion-ridden solipsism rather than reach out to embrace a present reality that might make demands upon him to change and to accept another existence besides his own.

Like this last story, Bradbury's *The Martian Chronicles* as a whole is a bleak and despairing book, filled with stories of absurd death, of genocide, and of self-serving and self-defeating narcissism. However, one may look to the book's final entry for some glimmer of hope. For even though the Thomas family can find only their own reflections staring back at them from the canal as they look about them for signs of life on Mars, at least they, of all the book's characters, must realize that Earth, and the past that it represents, has died, and that they, finally, are the Martians.

A. James Stupple

Sources for Further Study

Criticism:

Forrester, Kent. "The Dangers of Being Earnest: Ray Bradbury and *The Martian Chronicles*," in *Journal of General Education*. XXVIII (1976), pp. 50-54. Forrester gives a concise analysis of Bradbury's *The Martian Chronicles*. He finds, however, that Bradbury is vulnerable as a science fiction writer.

Scholes, Robert and Eric S. Rabkin. *Science Fiction*. New York: Oxford University Press, 1977, pp. 65 and 118-119. Scholes discusses *The Martian Chronicles* in depth, comparing Bradbury's prose to Sturgeon's.

Stupple, James. "The Past, The Future and Ray Bradbury," in *Voices for the Future*. Edited by Thomas D. Clareson. Bowling Green, Ohio: Bowling Green University Popular Press, 1976, pp. 175-178. Stupple offers a discussion of Bradbury's use of the theme of the past and future in his novels.

Reviews:

Booklist. XLVI, July 1, 1960, p. 336.

Chicago Sun. June 4, 1950, p. 6.

Chicago Sunday Tribune. May 21, 1950, p. 3.

Kirkus Reviews. XVIII, March 1, 1950, p. 144.

Library Journal. LXXV, May 1, 1950, p. 774.

New York Times. May 7, 1950, p. 21.

San Francisco Chronicle. May 14, 1950, p. 18.

A MARTIAN ODYSSEY AND OTHER SCIENCE FICTION TALES

Author: Stanley G. Weinbaum (1902-1935)
First book publication: 1974
Type of work: Short stories and novelettes

A collection of the principal short fiction of one of the most inventive writers of American pulp science fiction in the 1930's, whose promise of a brilliant career was cut tragically short

During Robert Silverberg's term of office as president of the Science Fiction Writers of America (1967-1968), the members were invited to give their opinions of the best science fiction stories written prior to 1964. Stanley G. Weinbaum's "A Martian Odyssey," thirty-six years after its publication, placed second.

When an anthologist or historian of American science fiction mentions Stanley G. Weinbaum, it is always in terms of unqualified praise: Isaac Asimov considers him to have been the only pulp writer before John W. Campbell, Jr.'s editorship of *Astounding Science Fiction* who would have met Campbell's exacting standards; Damon Knight thought Weinbaum the most inventive writer of science fiction since H. G. Wells.

Weinbaum's first science fiction story was published in Hugo Gernsback's *Wonder Stories* in July 1934. On December 14, 1935, he died, but the brevity of his career did not prevent him from achieving an enormous popularity. The editor of *Wonder*, Charles D. Hornig, noted in the magazine a few months after the publication of "A Martian Odyssey" that it had inspired more mail from readers than any story they had printed to that time. Sam Moskowitz, the editor of the Hyperion edition of Weinbaum's collected stories, points out another measure of the author's popularity: soon after Weinbaum's death, a group of fans in Milwaukee, his home town, published a hand-set, limited edition of six of his stories as a memorial tribute.

A modern reader looking at the relatively few stories that Weinbaum left can still see the reason for his instant success; they combine an easy handling of characterization and language with a fertile imagination. And considering the time in which Weinbaum wrote and the medium he used, this is a considerable achievement.

The popular forms of entertainment in the 1930's are too frequently unendurable today; freed from the literary conventions of polite letters that had existed before World War I, writers often gave their characters lines that sound like a headlong flight from the English language. The dialogue of a 1930's gangster film may be so thickly larded with now-obsolete slang that it is almost incomprehensible today, and one need only look at the newspapers' sports pages of the time to see genuinely bad writing. The science fiction pulps shared this general defect. Weinbaum changed all that. While his dialogue still retains some of the earmarks of the period (it would have been almost impossible to escape it entirely), one need only read some of the run-of-the-mill stories published in contemporary magazines to see just how superior Weinbaum's work is. His first few stories show the fondness for funny dialects that was yet another popular style of the day, but even in his brief career he began to move away from the use of the stock figure and funny spellings.

Beyond question, though, the key to Weinbaum's success, his true innovation in technique, was his handling of the alien character. Science fiction was and is full of creatures from other planets who behave exactly like human beings, their only distinction being their appearance.

Weinbaum changed that too. In the first story, "A Martian Odyssey," explorers from the first spaceship to Mars encounter an alien named Tweel; this most memorable Martian in science fiction does things which are absolutely incomprehensible to the human characters, but we are never allowed to forget that his actions may be sensible from his own perspective. The other Martian species likewise go about their strange undertakings for their own purposes, and we come to realize that it is only our perspective that makes them seem strange. Tweel, especially, gives a new dimension to the word "alien."

In a second refreshing change, Tweel is not the stock monster who looks like a shambling mound of raw liver, driven by bloodlust and bent on rapine. He is not only friendly but positively charming. This is not to imply that Weinbaum is unable to depict a menacing alien; in "Parasite Planet," located on the author's conception of Venus, the competition for survival is intense, and the human characters are confronted by danger with every step they take. But even this danger is due simply to the savage struggle for existence in an extremely unusual environment, and not to any congenital nastiness on the part of the natives. Weinbaum realized that in most places one does not exclusively meet starving wolfpacks, man-eating tigers, piranhas, and rattlesnakes; on the contrary, Weinbaum's planets are also furnished with the alien equivalents of field-mice, rabbits, squirrels, and the like.

From the start, Weinbaum had the ability to imagine other-world characters absolutely unlike any in our experience, yet still believable. His story "The Mad Moon" has a varied selection of them: the parcat, a three-legged creature with a mimic's ability far beyond that of a parrot; the loonies, the degenerate descendants of the rulers of the planet, only semi-intelligent at most; and the slinkers, six-inch tool-using rodents, are only the most important of the beasts and plants with which Weinbaum populates this single story. And it might be noted, too, that the dialogue of "The Mad Moon," published in 1935 while he was dying of throat cancer, is entirely free from the extravagant inanities of boy-girl conventions of the time; it can be read today without embarrassment, in fact, without noticing that it was written over forty years ago.

Weinbaum was fond of setting a story of human romance against his exotic backgrounds, and he was capable of drawing a mature and sensitive relationship. Although his heroes sometimes show a slightly overbearing male protectiveness, his heroines are typically competent and intelligent. Such is the case in "Parasite Planet," mentioned above, and in its two sequels, "The Lotus Eaters" and "The Planet of Doubt," both of which are noteworthy for their touches of humor and for the fact that the central figures are a loving married couple, something relatively rare in or out of the mainstream.

Three formula stories in the collection are slighter pieces, but still of interest: "The Worlds of If," "The Ideal," and "The Point of View" tell of the trials of Dixon Wells, a rich but hapless young man, in his dealings with Professor Haskel van Manderpootz, a stock figure of the quirky scientist. The three stories depend on a single situation: van Manderpootz's egomania results in inventions that arouse and then frustrate Wells's romantic yearnings.

In "The Ideal," van Manderpootz puts together a machine that will show the user his personal, ideal image on whatever he concentrated. Wells looks into it, thinks of a woman, and falls immediately and hopelessly in love with the image he sees. A very similar idea with a quite different treatment appears in "Pygmalion's Spectacles," showing that even this slender stuff can be transmuted to solid enjoyment under Weinbaum's touch.

Again a scientist, this time an unsuccessful one, develops a viewing device, one in which the viewer can take part and that will give a total illusion of reality — with light, sound, taste, touch, and scent. In his frustration at lack of commercial interest, the inventor asks a man he meets by chance to his apartment to see his "spectacles." There is no comedy this time: the viewer, Dan Burke, falls in love with a girl he meets in a strange Edenic setting. Although Burke sits at the device for five hours, his subjective experience seems to last for several days, and, as the programed entertainment draws near its conclusion, Burke is ready to forsake his real life for the illusion. For the reader, disturbing questions about the difference between appearance and reality arise, and for Burke problems arise: as the illusion begins to fade, Burke becomes desperate to remain. When he comes reluctantly back to reality, the professor is gone; Burke is now nearly despondent, and the reader has shared his despair as he has been dragged from what he knows to be only a dream, a phantasm.

To this point, the story is flawless: it is powerfully tragic, and its irony is intensified by Burke's awareness of the hopelessness of his situation. In a single session he has become addicted to a dream, yet when he tries to find the professor the next day, the inventor has disappeared: Burke's opiate no longer exists. Some readers may feel that the story diminishes drastically in stature at this point, for a desire for a happy ending leads Weinbaum to have Burke run across the professor six months later, and discover that the original for the girl in the viewer was the professor's niece, a drama student at a nearby university. Until this turning point, "Pygmalion's Spectacles" comes close to being the perfect short story.

"The Adaptive Ultimate" is nearly as powerful a story. It is based on the simple idea that a being able to adapt to any surroundings is almost invulnerable. A dying woman is saved by an experimental serum that gives her this ability, and she comes close to making herself supremely powerful. Again, a frustrated love is involved, and this time there is no convenient happy ending to solve the problem of her lover, a man named Scott. Although she returns in death to the emaciated state in which he had first seen her lying in a hospital ward, she still seems beautiful to him. And to add to his loss is the knowledge he will carry that he aided in overthrowing her.

Stanley G. Weinbaum cannot be described as a "hard" science fiction writer; his interest seemed to be always in individuals, whether human or alien, rather than in ideas and hardware. But here too he was capable of drawing a sound conclusion: in "The Red Peri" a character survives unprotected in space for a short time, a concept most dramatically illustrated in the Kubrick-Clarke movie *2001: A Space Odyssey*.

With talent such as Weinbaum demonstrated, his early death was a great loss to science fiction. He had skills that were immediately appreciated, not only by the readers, but by other writers such as H. P. Lovecraft. In *A Martian Odyssey and Other Science Fiction Tales*, there are many fine stories, but one wonders what Weinbaum might have done with the half a lifetime he was denied.

Walter E. Meyers

Sources for Further Study

Criticism:

Moskowitz, Sam. *Explorers of the Infinite: Shapers of Science Fiction*. New York: World, 1963. This overview of Weinbaum's achievement emphasizes the science fiction tradition in its approach.

Reviews:

San Francisco Chronicle. June 5, 1949, p. 23.

Time. LIII, May 30, 1949, p. 87.

MARTIAN TIME SLIP

Author: Philip K. Dick (1928-1982)
First book publication: 1964
Type of work: Novel
Time: 1994
Locale: Mars

An autistic ten-year-old boy who can see and travel through time becomes the focus of land speculation on an Australialike colonial Mars

Principal characters:
> JACK BOHLEN, a repairman and borderline schizophrenic
> SILVIA BOHLEN, his wife
> LEO BOHLEN, Jack's father, a land speculator from Earth
> ARNIE KOTT, the head of the Water Worker's Local, Fourth Planet Branch
> MANFRED STEINER, an autistic, time binding ten-year-old
> NORBERT STEINER, his father, a neighbor of the Bohlens, and a black marketeer
> OTTO ZITTE, his employee and pretender and heir to his black market business
> HELIOGABALUS, Arnie's tame Bleekman
> DOREEN ANDERTON, the Union treasurer, Arnie's mistress, and Jack's lover

By 1994 Mars, explored and colonized from Earth in the 1970's and early 1980's, is a neglected frontier. Because of difficult conditions and lack of material and moral support from home, immigration has been virtually non-existent for a decade, leaving the population thinly scattered in towns and suburbs across the web of the partially operative old canal system. Mars has too much sand and not enough water; the only settlement that really prospers is New Israel, but Mars is more like Australia than Palestine, supporting (after a fashion) a race of neoaboriginal Bleekmen and a species of kangaroo-sized boxing bugs resembling the praying mantis. But schizophrenia, not the problems of frontier life on another planet, is the thematic focus of the novel from the very first sentence. The disease is endemic in the 1990's, reflecting, as the story makes clear, society's inability to prepare its members to cope with the realities of their existence. To put it another way, "the reality which the schizophrenic fell away from — or never incorporated in the first place — was the reality of interpersonal living, of life in a given culture with given values." The "given culture" in this case is one not unlike ours. There and then, as here and now, sex and death, greed and human kindness, are the substance of social life. The main plot focuses on land speculation, minor ones on competition in the black market and the bedroom.

In a sense all the characters in the book, with the exception of the Bleekmen and (perhaps) the teaching robots, are affected by the schizophrenic process. The first character to break down is Norbert Steiner, a black marketeer, who, after visiting his autistic son Manfred in the camp for anomalous children, runs deliberately into the path of a tractor bus. It is particularly appropriate, in light of the symbolic function of machines in this story, that Steiner, a self-confessed mechanical incompetent, should choose a machine as the vehicle of his death.

Norbert's son Manfred is the consummate schizophrenic in the book. At ten years of age he is totally incapable of social intercourse. His madness is apparently either the cause or the result of his ability to see the future, to see himself in old age, kept alive in a decaying nursing home (which at the time the story takes place has yet to be built), an object not a person, with most of his organs replaced by machines. Manfred's combined personal and public entropic vision casts mere social existence, including language, into an impossible perspective until he meets Bleekmen.

But Manfred's madness, involving both precognition and the ability to travel in and otherwise manipulate time itself, is more symbolic than realistic. He is not exactly Everyman, but his eventual acquisition of speech is symbolic of the compromise we all make, consciously or unconsciously, with the knowledge that we shall die some day.

If Manfred sees his own future as a machine however, the "second-best" schizophrenic in the book, the repairman Jack Bohlen, has visions of *others* as machines, mechanically lifeless. His first "episode" had occurred on Earth before he emigrated in (approximately) 1984. For fourteen months he had tried to get an apartment in a huge new co-op building, a kind of condominium enormous enough to support its own shopping center, but when he did it was a disaster for him. He began to feel that his life no longer had a purpose, that the future had ceased to exist. However trivial, the apartment had given him a socially acceptable direction; without it he wandered about aimlessly, lost track of time, forgot to cash his paychecks, and, when called into the office where he worked, he had a vision of the personnel manager as a lifeless thing, a robot whose organs had been replaced by plastic and stainless steel.

This same sequence of material success followed by a vision of a human machine is repeated later. After Jack gets on Arnie Kott's payroll (a step up for him), he sees the psychiatrist Dr. Glaub "under the aspect of eternity." The "truth" of Jack's vision is to suggest the mechanical nature of life lived according to the materialistic values of this (our) culture. This point becomes symbolically clear when Jack visits "the great self-winding entity of their lives, the unique artificial organism that was their public school" (run by the United Nations) and encounters his son's teachers, robots with the names and "personalities" of various human types (Kindly Dad, Angry Janitor) and historical figures (Thomas Edison, Jack's favorite, and Caligula) and whose function is, of course, to reproduce the culture that has been programed into them.

Jack is the most sympathetic character in the story, the one about whose fate we care the most; but he is not the center of the plot. After all, he survives. It is his counterpart among the politically powerful, Arnie Kott, who is most completely destroyed by the direct and indirect effects of the schizophrenic process. As the story opens, Arnie has recently inveigled his way into leadership of the Water Workers' Local, Fourth Planet Branch, clearly an important position in a water based economy. Exactly as Jack after getting an apartment in the co-op, Arnie needs new worlds to conquer. His major schemes involve an attempt to replace Norbert Steiner in the black market food business and an attempt to find out what is going on in the F.D.R. Range in time to profit by it. In the first project his motivation is primarily personal — he has been one of Steiner's best customers, and depends on amenities from home to entertain his mistresses. He sets up his own business, but then discovers that he has a competitor (Steiner's repairman, Otto Zitte who, as part of the inbreeding of personal relationships on Mars, seduces Jack's wife Silvia). When Arnie destroys Otto's landing field with a small nuclear bomb, he provokes, as it happens, his own murder, leading Jack (who knows the man if not the facts) to say that Arnie "at last, had brought about his own death; he engineered it somewhere along the pathway of his life."

Though the black market scheme (like Steiner's tractor bus) kills him, Arnie's main efforts have been directed elsewhere, in a direction more significant for Mars and, had he lived, for himself as well. The United Nations and the co-op movement are about to build AM-WEB in the F.D.R. Range, a huge new project that will revitalize colonization and utterly change the (human) face of Mars. AM-WEB will not prosper — in its ruins Manfred will lie in a nursing home — but meanwhile it will have an enormous effect on property values. Although he does not know it, this project will change the balance of power on Mars so utterly that Arnie will be once again unimportant, which is one explanation for Jack's perception that Arnie "has brought about his own death," after failing to get a piece of the AM-WEB action. Meanwhile, in his attempts to do just that, Arnie takes the curious route of employing Jack to build a machine (of all things) to make possible communication with Manfred in case he does actually see the future. The machine does not work; Jack's father Leo, a land speculator from Earth with an inside tip, lays claim to the appropriate land; and Arnie, through the mediation of his "tame" Bleekman, Heliogabalus, to whom Manfred's thoughts are "as clear as plastic," tries an even more desperate maneuver. He takes Manfred to the Bleekie holy place in the F.D.R. Range, Dirty Knobby, where they both go into a trance designed to send Arnie back into the past to beat Leo to the claims office. Although it at least appears to Arnie that he does enter the past, all he experiences are symptoms of schizophrenia and an inability to do what he wants.

In these operations Arnie is a bit like Faust. Though Leo has inside information, he at least operates within the acceptable rules of the game (which Jack condemns). Arnie's attempt to pass through schizophrenia, even someone else's, places him outside himself in a way which suggests magic in Manfred's powers, the use of Dirty Knobby, and the drunken Bleekie priest (who, ironically, demands payment). We can see Arnie's Faustianism in two ways: first, as a desperate attempt to maintain his position in society; and second, as a sign of schizophrenic withdrawal, a loss of contact with reality engendered by his recent successful rise to the head of the Water Workers' Local. In any case, he returns from (his schizophrenic vision of) the past and believes that he is still in a trance when Otto shoots him. He dies believing he is still alive.

Commodity culture and schizophrenia blur the distinction between life and death, the first by externalizing human purpose in materialistic goals — an apartment, land, power, a mistress — the second by cutting the subject off from the outside world and "the warmhearted people there." Commodity culture is schizophrenogenic, giving its subjects materialistic goals and then either preventing their achievement or disappointing them with success. In commodity culture success and failure are equally fatal. The truth of this in Dick's universe is seen in the counter example of the Bleekmen. On the one hand, they are a Stone Age culture, living off the land, "owning" nothing but the absolute essentials: bows and arrows, paka shells for carrying water, pounding blocks for grinding meat or grain, an animal skin each for clothing. This is a life they have in some way chosen, for, as Jack reminds us, their ancestors built the great canal system, but they have forgotten even how to throw pots. They have no purpose as we know it, and as a result, perhaps no sense of time.

In any case, they can see ahead like Manfred, and read thoughts, but it does not terrify them. Theirs is a kind of Zen-consciousness. As Helio says,

> Purpose of life is unknown. . . . Who can say if perhaps the schizophrenics are not correct? Mister, they take a brave journey. They turn away from mere things, which one may handle and turn to practical use; they turn inward to *meaning*.

Manfred's happy ending is to join the Bleekmen, a culture that does not bind him to materialistic goals and to time.

It is in the light of the Bleekie solution that we can understand the ending of the book. Jack and Silva cannot, of course, follow the Bleekmen into the desert — if they did they would be no examples for us — but Jack can readjust his goals to make his life somewhat livable. He has a final schizophrenic attack when he cannot reconcile his ambition — to remain in Arnie's employ — and stay with the mistress he has acquired from Arnie — with his familial ties. The crisis arises when he discovers his father Leo's interest to be the same as Arnie's; the effect of his breakdown is to keep the knowledge of AM-WEB and its location from Arnie until after Leo has filed his claim. After Arnie's death, which is an indirect consequence of Jack's crisis, Jack and Doreen, his mistress, separate, and Jack goes home to Silvia with two truths: that the difference between Manfred's world and everyone else's is mainly a matter of degree, and that "A person can always find two places to choose from. Home, and the rest of the world with all the other people in it." In the final scene, Jack and Leo set out with flashlights to hunt for Erna Steiner (who has been frightened by the reappearance of her son Manfred, returned from the future with his mechanical body) and see if she is all right. Here is a kind of goal that depends, not on things, but on human feeling — to take care of one another.

The message of the book seems to be to stay small, to help one's neighbors if one can while maintaining a low profile in the world at large. Arnie, Otto, and Jack all suffer from being too ambitious and, according to Manfred's vision, so does the United Nations in its abortive AM-WEB project. There is neither fundamental despair here, nor the escapism of a "separate peace," but a return to the local social group as a way of remaining human — to escape becoming either a machine or a schizophrenic. In this way the family operates to mediate between the absolutely personal, schizophrenia, and the absolutely social, the vision of citizens as machines.

Richard Astle

Sources for Further Study

Criticism:

Aldiss, Brian W. "Dick's Maledictory Web: About and Around *Martian Time Slip*," in *Science-Fiction Studies*. II (1975), pp. 42-47. Aldiss reveals the inner workings of the plot.

Gillespie, Bruce. *Philip K. Dick: Electric Shepherd*. Melbourne, Australia: Nostrilla, 1975, Gillespie reviews the events in *Martian Time Slip*.

Reviews:

Analog. LXXIV, November, 1964, pp. 87-88.
Magazine of Fantasy and Science Fiction. XXVII, December, 1964, pp. 70-71.
New Statesman. XCII, December 17, 1976, p. 879.
Observer. August 8, 1976, p. 22.

MARTIANS, GO HOME

Author: Fredric Brown (1906-1972)
First book publication: 1955
Type of work: Novel
Time: 1964
Locale: The Earth, mostly Southern California

A satiric fantasy of humanity beseiged by insubstantial but foul-mouthed Martians who allow no one a moment of privacy or a shred of secrecy

Principal characters:
> LUKE DEVEREAUX, a thirty-seven-year-old science fiction writer
> MARGIE DEVEREAUX, his estranged wife, a psychiatric nurse
> CARTER BENSON, his friend, another writer
> DR. ELLICOTT H. SNYDER, a psychiatrist
> YATO ISHURTI, Secretary-General of the United Nations
> HIRAM PEDRO OBERDORFFER, an inventor
> BUGASSI, the witch doctor of an African tribe

Luke Devereaux, a science fiction writer going through a writer's block, borrows his friend Carter Benson's cabin in the desert outside Los Angeles to help him get started on a novel. The night the Martians come, he is working on his third drink and beginning to get an idea for a new science fiction novel: what if the Martians. . . . He is interrupted by a little green man who claims to be a Martian and spews forth a stream of abusive, rather Runyonesque English, addressing Luke as "Mack." The Martian taunts and insults the disbelieving Luke until, after downing another three or four drinks in rapid succession, the writer passes out on his bed.

When he awakens the next day, the Martian is gone from the cabin, but Luke discovers it sitting on the radiator of his car, abusive as ever. Hallucination or not, Luke cannot see through the creature, so he drives to the diner down the highway with his head sticking out the window to see around the Martian, who refuses to get off the hood. The Martian follows Luke into the diner. The counterman groans. "Oh, God, another one of 'em."

Luke's Martian is one of a billion rude, sharp-tongued little creatures that have appeared all over the Earth at exactly the same time. They are about two and a half feet tall, with large spherical hairless heads and spindly arms and legs and emerald green skin. They are bent on antagonizing every human being with whom they come in contact. Since there is one Martian for every three people on earth, they contact almost everybody; and since they can see in the dark and see through solid objects, read letters and papers in closed boxes and locked safes, they have plenty of material to be insulting about.

All privacy or secrecy ends. The Martians are interested in everything, they love to tell secrets. There are no longer any military secrets, top or otherwise. On a much smaller scale, the arrival of the Martians makes poker impossible: one cannot have a poker game if everyone knows everyone else's hand and if there is a Martian present calling out the cards before they are dealt. Even the world's most popular indoor sport is no longer a game for the sensitive to play. Most couples start using ear plugs and keeping their bedrooms and other places of assignation dark, so that even though the Martians can see *them*, they do not have to see the Martians, or hear their ribald commentary.

No one knows very much about the Martians — their sex or lack of it, what they eat, where they sleep, or whether they are physically present on earth or simply projecting a mental picture. No one is even sure they are Martians. The Martians do not volunteer much information; they claim they "kwimmed" to Earth from Mars, and that they are much more intelligent than human beings. They can be photographed and their voices recorded on tape, but they do not show up on radar. Their bodies are insubstantial but opaque. A large number of accidental injuries and deaths are caused by people trying to attack Martians physically — at first, because people did not know that Martians are invulnerable, and later, because they are too frustrated to care.

The economic effect of the Martians' arrival is enormous and depressing. A drastic cut in defense spending leads to increased unemployment. The stock market falls, and the bottom drops out of the entertainment business, because Martians interfere with actors and announcers, baiting and mocking them on the air. Crime, especially planned crime, occurs less frequently because the Martians tell tales. (Not that they are opposed to crime — they just love to make trouble.) The emotional stress that the Martians cause, however, leads to increased crimes of passion and violence.

In Long Beach, unable to find any kind of writing job, Luke Devereaux is running out of cash. For seven weeks, he has been trying to get a job. He has wanted desperately to call Margie, his ex-wife (or almost ex-wife: he wasn't quite sure), but his pride prevents him as long as she has a job and he does not. Down to his last six dollars, Luke runs into Carter Benson, who has a check for Luke from his publisher, an advance on the reissue of a Western novel that Luke wrote twelve or fifteen years earlier. The publisher says that mysteries and Westerns are in great demand, and sends Luke a thousand-dollar advance on another Western.

Luke's writing block is dispelled; he dashes home to his typewriter, ideas coming thick and fast. He has half a sentence on paper when a Martian appears astride his typewriter carriage, yelling "Whoopie! Faster, Mack, faster!" Luke screams and tries to throw himself out the window, but he lands on the fire escape. His landlady calls a doctor, who contacts Margie. Wary of Luke, but obviously still in love, Margie arranges for him to be sent to a private sanitarium.

When Luke recovers consciousness, he can no longer see the Martians, and regards them as having been a temporary hallucination. Deaf and blind to Martians, he works eight to ten hours a day on his Western novel. This places his psychiatrist, Dr. Synder, and Margie in a quandary. Should they try to cure him, thus rendering him susceptible to harassment by the Martians, or should they leave him insane but productive?

Luke finishes the book, which promises to be a best seller. He resumes married life with Margie in the sanitarium, and she calls off the divorce suit. He accepts the fact that other people still see Martians — or that they think they see them. Dr. Snyder recommends keeping Luke in the sanitarium, in case he should come to disbelieve not only in Martians, but also in other human beings. Since Luke thinks that the Martians were a figment of his imagination, he might come to believe that he has invented the rest of the world, too.

Once Luke finishes his novel, he suddenly has time to think about the Martians. He is certain that he is sane and that Martians are nonexistent. Does this mean that everyone else in the world is crazy? What if he did invent the Martians? He had been working on a plot about Martians the night they arrived. What if he only imagines his entire universe? And what if, while inventing a science fiction plot, a small fiction within his larger fictional universe, he has accidentally crossed wires and made the Martians part of the large universe?

Luke decides that the solution is to relay the message that Martians do not exist to his unconscious mind; then they will vanish for everyone else, too. He decides he will have to go back to the shack in the desert, and he escapes from the sanitarium immediately.

The same day, Yato Ishurti, the Secretary General of the United Nations, delivers a radio speech to the world and to the Martians in which he proposes a plan. Ishurti reasons that the Martians are on Earth either to unite men in a common cause or to prevent humans from landing on Mars. He asks that all people on Earth pledge no longer to fight among themselves and to promise that they will never send a spaceship to Mars. A deafening roar of agreement breaks forth from the people of Earth. The Martians, however, do not leave, and Ishurti commits ritual suicide.

Several weeks later, on August 19, other programs to rid the world of Martians come to a head. In Chicago, a janitor and amateur inventor named Hiram Pedro Oberdorffer is completing a contraption he calls an antiextraterrestrial subatomic supervibrator. He waits for it to build up potential. It is 11:05 P.M., Chicago time. That afternoon, Margie Devereaux, who has been looking for Luke for two weeks, figures out that he must be at Carter Benson's shack, and leaves for the desert.

At about the same time, an African witch doctor named Bugassi prepares a juju against the Martians, who have spoiled his tribe's hunting and left them on the verge of starvation. It is a juju to end all jujus; he finishes just before dawn. When the sun strikes the juju, says Bugassi, the Martians will leave. At that exact moment, Hiram Pedro Oberdorffer sits sipping beer and waiting for his subatomic supervibrator to build up potential.

Less than an hour before, in a shack in the desert, Luke had made his third drink. It was the fourteenth evening he had spent at the shack trying to get the upper hand on his subconscious. The problem, he thinks, is that he lacks faith in himself. Maybe if he imagined something completely different and brought that into existence, then his subconscious could not deny that he had invented the universe. So he imagines Margie driving through the desert. Pretty soon he hears her car. When she gets out, he concentrates on the thought, *There aren't any Martians.* It is approximately 9:05 P.M., Pacific Time. Meanwhile, in Chicago, Mr. Oberdorffer sips beer and waits for his supervibrator to build up potential, and in Africa, Bugassi waits for the sun's first rays to strike the greatest juju ever made.

Four minutes later, the Martians disappear simultaneously from everywhere on earth. To this day, no one knows why they left, but a great many people have strong opinions on the subject. Millions still believe that they were devils and went back to hell. Even more millions believe that they were Martians who went back to Mars because of Yato Ishurti's speech. No standing armies have been built up, and no country is planning to send rockets to Mars, just in case. An African tribe knows that Bugassi's juju made the Martians leave. A janitor in Chicago knows that he did it himself with his subatomic supervibrator. And, of course, Luke knows he did it.

Luke is now a very successful writer with a happy marriage and twin sons; he is satisfied with the universe as he imagines it now. On one point, at least, everyone agrees: nobody misses the Martians at all.

In a postscript, Fredric Brown addresses the problem of who is right: who really made the Martians leave? Brown explains that "Luke is right, the universe and all therein exists only in his imagination. . . . But then, I invented Luke. So where does that leave him *or* the Martians? Or any of the rest of you?"

This light fantasy satirizes the classic science fiction cliché of the hostile alien invasion. It presents the stereotypal little-green-men Martians as hostile visitors, but it makes their hostility purely verbal — the Martians do not attack people physically. Since most hostility in the world actually is verbal, and physical violence is usually a last resort, the concept provides a solid satiric base for viewing human beings and their foibles.

Eileen Gunn

Sources for Further Study

Reviews:

Analog. LVII, July, 1956, p. 156.

Fantastic Universe Science Fiction. IV, January, 1956, p. 127.

Galaxy. XII, June, 1956, p. 156.

Magazine of Fantasy and Science Fiction. X, February, 1956, pp. 96-97.

MATRIARKATET
(The Matriarchy)

Author: Tage Eskestad (1920-   )
First book publication: 1975
Type of work: Novel
Time: After the "final" war
Locale: Unidentified, probably the United States

Following the "final" war, an antimale, antitechnology Matriarchy emerges

> *Principal characters:*
> JACOB, a fourteen-year-old boy "drone"
> MARI, his lover, a Volva who lives alone in the "no man's land"
> GERMAINE, a hunting-girl and captain in the Matriarchy
> BORIS, Germaine's lover, a magician of the Black Brethren

The starting point of *Matriarkatet* is Danish-Norwegian author Aksel San-demose's vision of the eternal repetition of history as expressed in his book *Varulven* (The Werewolf); 1958:

> There are many indications that all this has happened before, and I can imagine how in perhaps a hundred thousand years the human beings will once again leave what they will call their original home to take out over the world from a place where life has hibernated. Only God knows what myths they will carry with them.

In Tage Eskestad's vision the world has been incinerated in the final world war. Out of the rubble, a stone-age Matriarchy emerges, led by a strong-willed band of females who have rerejected and suppressed all technology. Twentieth century civilization has not only been forgotten, but deliberately forgotten. "Where the 'capitalist' in the 'technology' are the hunting-girls?" one of the boy-drones asks in the beginning of the novel. This is the strongest oath he can use. Words like "technology" and "capitalism" have become meaningless curses. And should he want to invoke the gods, he cries out to "Mao" and "Marx" — although he does not know what any of the words mean or who either of the names stands for. In this society a crude socialism reigns supreme, with Mao and Marx as its deities. The few relics that remain from the twentieth century are associated with sorcery and taboos. All precise knowledge of modern man has been lost; only a distant, vaguely remembered past remains in this society dominated by aggressive females.

None of the women in the Matriarchy work. It is a feudal, even tribal, society which resembles some primitive cultures in our world, but with the sexual roles reversed. This woman-rule, however, has not improved the social structure; it is oppressive, inefficient, and, at times, barbarous. For example, the sexual act between the woman-hunters and the drones takes place at one time every year during the "saturnale." Although at other times, males and females are not allowed to touch one another, the woman-hunters rape every drone they find outside the Matriarchy camp; after the rape they cut off the drone's tongue to prevent him from talking. Thus, because the Matriarchy is more violent than the society it tries to forget, it begins to disintegrate from within.

The Matriarchy is not, however, the only society in Eskestad's world. Opposed to them is the Black Brethren, a monklike society of men, also living at a stone-age level. Unlike the Matriarchy, the Black Brethren are trying to probe the lost past in order to understand the nature of everything that has been left behind. They search blindly, however, since they do not know what they are looking for; they cannot distinguish between magic and reality; in their own way, they are just as afraid of the past as are the matriarchs.

The two groups are separated from each other. The only connection between them are the Volvas, a mysterious band of women who live alone in the no-man's land between the Matriarchy and the Black Brethren. The Volvas are actually women of the Matriarchy who have come to believe that the artificial life of the female dominated society, with its drones, troublesome taboos, and inquisitions, is wrong. And, although the Volvas are sympathetic to Black Brethren and their philosophy, they cannot join them, since a patriarchial society would be as distasteful as its opposite. Thus, to the Matriarchy the Volvas are a kind of sacrosanct group of demi-goddesses, surrounded by taboos and witchcraft; to the Black Brethren they are partners in a search to fathom the miracles of the past.

The women of the Matriarchy have done their job well: they have buried all remnants of the past civilization and the memory of that civilization so thoroughly through several generations that the Black Brethren and the Volvas have been largely baffled in their efforts. For instance, because of the long period of enforced silence and superstition, the ability to distinguish between natural phenomena and man's work has degenerated to the point where the Black Brethren think a four-sided window pane in an old building is a natural phenomenon which grew up in the "crystalline age," and that the pipes and cables in the cellars are "roots from the big growths of the metal age."

On the other hand, they are beginning to understand the meanings of letters and words in books. With the help of pictures and comparisons, in the manner of modern archaeology, they investigate books and other artifacts. Gradually, some of them begin to understand that the past culture was not simply a vague and mystical region, but a real, viable society which used and developed technology and science. Thus, a new mankind begins on the ruins of twentieth century civilization. When a few of the women-hunters approach Black Brethren, it is easy to see that the two societies will sooner or later merge.

Jacob, a young drone, defies the taboos of the Matriarchy and follows his inclination to probe the miracles of the past. While pursuing his investigations, he is captured by Mari, a Volva; he has his first sexual experience with her, and then together they search in the ruins. But breaking its own taboos, the

Matriarchy catches both Jacob and Mari in order to sacrifice them at the stake. Mari dies, but Jacob is freed by a platoon of Black Brethren. The Black Brethren society adopts him, making him a Little Brother to Boris, a magician. As a character, Jacob is vague and insipid, but functionally he is important, since it is he who leads the reader through the different societies, vividly and accurately describing each in turn. He is especially thorough in giving the reader a detailed picture of the nature and function of the Matriarchy.

Germaine is a much more important and convincing character. A platoon leader of the women-hunters, she brings about the fall of the conservative Matriarchy leadership and opens up the group to a new way of life by first approaching the Black Brethren. She is a typical woman of the Matriarchy, domineering, a born leader, a tough soldier and hunter. She follows the rules of the Matriarchy only when they suit her purposes, and breaks them when they do not.

The only one who can tame Germaine is Boris, partly because he is a strong man physically, as well as psychically, and partly because he is an unknown type of man as compared to the weak drones she has known. Germaine follows Boris as long as necessary before leaving him to return to the Matriarchy to bring about its downfall. When she comes back, it is as the leader of the women from the now defunct Matriarchy. She wants Boris back, neither on his conditions nor on those of the fallen Matriarchy, but on her own. Thus, Germaine has marked out the way to reconciliation for both of the societies.

Boris is similar. It is he who will not accept the things left behind from twentieth century civilization as natural phenomenon. To him, technology is not merely mysticism or the works of forgotten gods, but is a human art which he attempts to revive. He not only studies the past, but also tries to make things himself based on pictures and instructions in books and other relics. He reinvents the wheel, the sailboat, and, in a way, the gun, although it does not utilize bullets; he uses the powder in a pipe to create a kind of flame thrower — which is good enough against arrows and spears.

Boris is also the first man to break the Black Brethren's unwritten law banning women in the camp. When Boris catches Germaine and brings her back, the Brethren are paralyzed, and they turn on him. But seeing that nothing happens to Boris, and therefore finding no reasons why women should be kept out, they welcome the rest of Germaine's platoon.

Thus, the society normalizes. And that is the main point of the novel: it is perhaps probable that a stone-age matriarchy might arise after a "final war" as a protest against the patriarchal and economic system which had seemingly led to the war and the fall of civilization. But such a society could not endure; it would be too unstable and too artificial to be anything but a temporary protest. It may appear that *Matriarkatet* is a contribution to the arguments surrounding the contemporary controversy about sex roles. But it is not, since we do not have a patriarchy and nobody wants a matriarchy. Tage Eskestad points out that a society has to have neutral sexual roles for the sake of stability.

Although Tage Eskestad has written very few books, his name is established in the Danish science fiction field. His writing is passionate and lifelike, and his knowledge of mythology gives his stories a feeling of authenticity. *Matriarkatet* is the only one of his stories which is not taken from well-known myths. It presents a general mythology, an experiment with mythological elements, as well as a model of a society. *Matriarkatet* also shows how myths are born, carried on, and changed by mankind; how realities are deliberately changed and exaggerated into myths; and how little time is needed to accomplish this manipulation and distortion of history.

Eskestad makes one additional point. When he writes about the Black Brethren and their explanations of things left behind from our civilization, he makes references to the discoveries and procedures of modern archaeologists. He points out that they think in much the same way as the Black Brethren. Although they may not call their unknown finds "natural phenomena," they do label them "objects of worship," or the like and bury them in museums, instead of sharing them with other scientists who may be better able to understand them. This, he suggests, is another way of distorting history, an accusation against archaeologists which Eskestad makes in common with others such as Louis Pauwells and Paul Bergier.

Carsten Schiøler

MEMOIRS FOUND IN A BATHTUB
(PAMIETNIK ZNALEZIONY W WANNIE)

Author: Stanislaw Lem (1921-   )
First book publication: 1961
English translation: 1973
Type of work: Novel
Time: The fourth millennium A.D., with flashbacks to the near future
Locale: The Rocky Mountains, the United States

A satire applicable to several targets, caricaturing blind devotees of nonfunctional social systems, surveillance-happy militarists, and fumbling bureaucrats

Principal characters:
THE NARRATOR
GENERAL KASHENBLADE, the Commander in Chief
UNDEREAVESDROPPER BLASSENKASH
MAJOR ERMS, a Third Pentagon functionary
CAPTAIN PRANDTL, Department of Codes
ANTHEUS KAPPRIL, Custodian Ninth Degree
"THE ADMIRAL," active in Degradation proceedings
PROFESSOR DOLT, an authority on blackmail and treason
PROFESSOR DELUGE, cabalist and collaborationist
FATHER ORFINI, co-conspirator with The Narrator

The preface to this narrative tells how, in the fourth millennium A.D., archaeologists excavated the "Third Pentagon," last of the redoubts of American capitalism. This had been a huge underground headquarters, well-camouflaged and supplied with such great reserves of food, water, and compressed air that it could be cut off completely and prolongedly from the outside world. Faced with a massive defection or revolution of the American people, the masters of the Pentagon did isolate the "Building," as it is usually called in the narrative. After seventy-two years of this isolation, molten lava filled the Building and preserved its contents for the future archaeologists.

Meanwhile, on the Earth's surface, a mysterious catalyst from Uranus had destroyed all paper, a substance which Lem describes wryly as regulating all human activities and determining the fates of individuals. The loss of all paper, books, and documents disorganized civilization severely for some time and deprived mankind of most of its historical records. Thus the discovery of a journal preserved by the lava in a bathroom of the Third Pentagon provided a precious, though often puzzling, acquisition for the future historians.

The skeletons of the Narrator and of Father Orfini, a denizen of the Building in whom he undertook to confide, were found with the journal, and in this document we read of the misadventures suffered during the Building's period of isolation, when the Narrator somehow entered it. His itinerary through its myriad offices becomes a saga of confusion, absurdity, and despair, a tour of a bureaucratic Inferno reminiscent of Dante's *Divine Comedy*.

The besetting sins and suffering of the Building's people derive from their persistence in carrying on the routines of military planning, intelligence gathering, and surveillance, even though their isolation makes it all vain and artificial. Deprived of external targets for their operations, the people of the Building have internalized their espionage. This internalization resembles the historical phenomenon of imperialist nations which, when they are no longer achieving imperialism abroad, turn it against their own citizens in the form of authoritarian government. The situation in the Building also reflects the readiness of most bureaucracies to invent functions, to continue activity when their original, valid functions have ceased to exist.

A thriving bureaucracy needs an adversary, so that dangers or emergencies may stimulate its work. Accordingly, the Building has invented the *Antibuilding*, the supposed headquarters of its enemies, and from it the Building is allegedly infiltrated by hostile agents. Some people say that the Antibuilding is completely infiltrated and controlled by the Building's operatives, and there is also the horrid suspicion that the agents of the Antibuilding have taken control in the Building itself.

The denizens of the Third Pentagon have learned to eavesdrop on one another. They produce double agents, triple agents, codes of all sorts, intricate systems of security and counter-espionage. Their surveillance devices include polygraph mittens, which check the truthfulness of the wearers, and microphones in pillows, to catch the words of persons who talk in their sleep. All drainpipes are monitored and all sewage is filtered. Uncertainty reigns: Who works for whom? There are many alternate codes and plans, and nobody knows which of these, if any, are valid.

The characters of this book, as may be gathered from their names and titles, serve to describe the organizational flavor and bureaucratic morass which characterizes the story. The characters are not developed as individuals; they have no depth. Even the Narrator himself is nameless, and we know him only as a pitiable human being who is caught in the maze of the Third Pentagon. He tries to make sense of that organization, but there is no sense to be found. He is assigned a mission by General Kashenblade but cannot clarify it. His movements are watched, and meticulous reports thereof are prepared and duly filed. *Agents provocateurs* seem to be drawing him out, and various tests of his loyalty are devised. He wishes to distinguish reality from absurdity but cannot. Many escorts or guides present themselves to him, but upon none of them can he rely. Father Orfini, the last and most promising of these, has become a suicide at the story's end, and the Narrator has followed him into voluntary death.

Lem appears to apply his bitter satire to all the militarists, bureaucrats, surveillance artists, and secret police oppressors of our world, whether they emanate from Washington, Moscow, Warsaw, or any other center of power. To demonstrate the need for interpreting Lem very flexibly, it is necessary to consider his life and the background of genuine authoritarian hazards in which he had to live. Born in 1921 in Poland, he began his medical studies, but the Nazi invasion and occupation intervened. He had to work as a mechanic during those years — a fortunate job, perhaps, as his interest in engines and electricity was keen. However, he was thoroughly exposed to the clumsiness and brutality of armies and authoritarian regimes. At one point the Germans came close to executing him.

It is evident from his writings that Lem's education included a large dose of philosophy — the traditional scholastic approach as well as the often obscure or uncertain meanderings of modern thought. From these sources and from his enormous general fund of words, concepts, and knowledge, he developed an ability to play with ideas most dextrously, and an inclination to toy with the reader, leaving him uncertain as to which of several meanings might be derived from his stories.

After World War II, Lem became an increasingly successful writer of science fiction, extremely popular in Poland, the Soviet Union, and Germany, and well known elsewhere. He was a pioneer in cybernetics and produced works of philosophy. Wishing to flourish as a writer in avowedly Communist Poland, he had to be mindful of the strictures of censorship and surveillance there. Not only did Poland have its own standards of Marxism and expectation of socialist realism incumbent on writers, but also Warsaw had to live in the shadow of Moscow.

Until Stalin died in 1953, the Polish subservience as a satellite of the U.S.S.R. was complete. Since then there have been discernible trends of relaxation or liberalization, but with occasional retightening of the screws on writers. Protected somewhat by his considerable fame, Lem has had to be careful even so, as he desires to continue to be published in the Communist nations, where the publishing houses are controlled by the governments. What better way, then, to attack secret police, bureaucrats, and militarists than to assail them ostensibly as Americans, as he does in this book?

We should consider particularly the state of Eastern Europe and the Cold War psychology which pervaded the world in the years preceding the publication of *Memoirs Found in a Bathtub*. In 1956 there were riots in Poland and East Germany, while in Hungary there was brief warfare. This unrest engendered greater secret police activity and crackdowns throughout the Eastern Bloc of countries. Stalinism was denounced, and the power of the neo-Stalinists was much reduced by 1957, but the crises between East and West continued to occur. This was the era of Secretary of State John Foster Dulles and his policy of "brinkmanship," with threats and counterthreats of "massive retaliation." In 1960 came the U-2 Affair and an acrimonious meeting between Khrushchev and Eisenhower. The same year witnessed John Kennedy's campaign for the Presidency, keynoted by his allegations of a "missile gap" which could expose the United States to a devastating attack.

The idea would occur readily enough to many of Lem's readers in either

Eastern Europe or the Western nations that the "Third Pentagon" bore a certain resemblance to Moscow's Ministry of Defense and KGB centers. The "Seminars on Applied Agony" held in the Building suggest this, as do the references to taking people to the Cellar Section for a little slapping around, a boot in the face, and the loss of some teeth, to induce confessions.

Nevertheless, the Building of this novel is specifically located in the Rocky Mountains, at the foot of Mount Harvard in the Collegiate Range. Also, the genuineness of the Rocky Mountain location is enhanced by the fact that the actual underground headquarters for the air defense of the United States and Canada, the North American Air Defense Command, is indeed located near Colorado Springs, deep under Cheyenne Mountain. Comparable headquarters have been visualized in other science fiction literature too, notably in Robert Heinlein's stories. Furthermore, in this book and elsewhere in his writings, Lem evinces a clear dislike of capitalism and is often quite critical of the culture and institutions of the West.

This novel offers clues to Lem's approach, observing that a way out of all monstrous absurdities may be found through *mystery*. Another key point is the dependence of the Building on the concept of the Antibuilding. In real life the builders of power in Moscow or Washington depend on allegations of external menace to ratify their positions and to secure approval of the desired budgets for "defensive" programs.

The translators of Lem's works deserve more notice and credit than do most persons who render literature from one language to another. Lem's playfulness, his double and triple entendres, his ambiguities, and his use of proper names to convey atmosphere or to hint at situations, all make the translator's task most challenging. How is he to convey material from the Polish original, and in some cases from an intermediary German or French version, into English, while preserving the puns and multiple meanings of the original? Fortunately, many of the words on which the meanings turn are of Latin or Greek origin, and can be reintroduced into the English text in modified form. At any rate, not only is Lem's own work quite a marvel of literary expertise and dexterity, but also we should recognize that his translators have mustered comparable qualities.

Frank H. Tucker

Sources for Further Study

Reviews:

Chicago Daily News, Panorama. December 1-2, 1973, p. 10.

Galaxy. XXXIV, November, 1973, p. 84.

Luna Monthly. XLVIII, Fall, 1973, pp. 26-27.

New York Times Book Review. September 23, 1973, p. 39 and August 29, 1976, p. 1.

Renaissance. V, Summer, 1973, p. 8.

World Literature Today. LI, Autumn, 1977, p. 550.

MEN LIKE GODS

Author: H. G. Wells (1866-1946)
First book publication: 1922
Type of work: Novel
Time: Summer, 1921, and three thousand years in the future
Locale: London and vicinity, and a counterpart of Earth in another dimension

Three carloads of Earthlings, accidentally transported into an anarchistic "Utopia" based on science and rationalistic social planning, react with the violence and bigotry which the author regards as characteristic of capitalism

Principal characters:
MR. BARNSTAPLE, subeditor of a liberal weekly
CECIL BURLEIGH, a conservative political leader
RUPERT CATSKILL, Secretary of State for War
FREDDY MUSH, his secretary, a snobbish aesthete
FR. AMERTON, a fanatical priest
LADY STELLA, a London socialite
LORD BARRALONGA, a dissipated peer
URTHRED,
SERPENTINE, and
LION, Utopian scientists
LYCHNIS, a "failure" of Utopian education

It is an inescapable though melancholy truth that H. G. Wells's title, *Men Like Gods*, is wholly innocent of irony. Indeed, apart from a feeble attempt at funny names — a dissipated peer who is especially murderous in his enormous car is called "Lord Barralonga"; a dour, pessimistic editor is named "Peeve" — the book is peculiarly humorless, with the earnest self-righteousness attendant upon the defense of an idea whose time has come and long since gone. Barely four years after the end of World War I, which had shattered the West's confidence in the ideal of progress by demonstrating the cruel efficiency of such industrial products as poison gas, barbed wire, machine guns, tanks, and high explosives, Wells published a flimsily fictionalized disquisition on the happy inevitability of the ascent of technology. In the process he shows no small annoyance at reactionary obscurantists who have the temerity to question the mandate of science to subjugate and transform both man and nature.

The plot is both simple and contrived. Mr. Barnstaple, subeditor of a minor weekly, the *Liberal*, feels a pressing need for a vacation — an escape from his gloomy editor, Mr. Peeve, whose liberal optimism and faith in progress have suffered severely in the war and its aftermath; from his commonplace, frivolous wife and sons; and from the oppressive heat of the summer drought of 1921. Having gained his freedom by a few small subterfuges, he is happily motoring along the Maidenhead Road in his two-seater when suddenly the dusty highway and familiar countryside vanish, and Mr. Barnstaple finds himself on a road of smooth glass in the midst of an Arcadian landscape of mythic beauty and serenity. Immediately ahead of him on this strange road is a large limousine which has been similarly transported, and, as Mr. Barnstaple subsequently discovers, the same chance has befallen Lord Barralonga's touring car.

The explanation for the strange transport of the English vehicles lies in a collapsed and smoldering house beside the glassy road, the only dissonance in the harmonious countryside. Here the occupants of the cars come upon the aftermath of an explosion littered with the wreckage of scientific equipment and the stunningly beautiful, virtually naked bodies of a man and a woman. As they later learn from living denizens of this strange world, similarly beautiful and unclothed, the dead pair, Arden and Greenlake, were scientific investigators, experimenting with the movement of objects from one dimension to another. Although their deaths were the result of the partial failure of the apparatus, it has succeeded in moving Mr. Barnstable's two-seater and two other English cars with all their passengers into a counterpart world in a "parallel universe."

As in *The Time Machine* (1895) Wells nods casually in the direction of a scientific explanation for this startling phenomenon, and by 1922 he is, of course, able to invoke the name of Einstein. But as in the earlier book, Wells's real interest lies not in speculative "science" *per se*, but in the opportunities provided by transtemporal or, here, transdimensional travel for reflections on the destiny of mankind. The dark pessimism of *The Time Machine* has, however, given way to an intolerant optimism, a determined faith in progress. In order that the reader might have no doubts regarding the status of the other-dimensional world, it is simply called "Utopia"; and there is no indication that Wells's usage involves any of the subtle ambiguity with which St. Thomas More originally invested his neologism, which literally means both "noplace" and "happy place."

The appearance of the "natives" — who wear only loin cloths, bracelets, and necklaces — and the bucolic setting are at first deceptive but finally emblematic. Upon first seeing the corpses of Arden and Greenlake, the Englishmen debate whether to regard them as "naked savages" or "Greek gods," and of course the latter designation is far more nearly accurate. They are so advanced that they have dispensed with such accepted marks of civilization as clothes and crowded cities. During their "Age of Confusion" (which corresponds to Earth's twentieth century), now three thousand years in the past, they mastered their world with scientific technology and turned it into a fulfillment of man's ancient dreams: a pastoral paradise inhabited by Olympian demigods who, though not immortal, are longlived, youthful, and exquisitely beautiful. Conveniently for the Earthlings, their intelligence is such that they communicate through telepathy. Nature is completely under their power. Only plants that are lovely and fragrant, or else edible, are allowed to grow. The air is always clear, the temperature springlike. Annoying species have either been eliminated or modified: lions and leopards, magnificent as ever in appearance, now feed innocuously on milk products; swallows are extinct (and all birds rare) because the insect pests necessary for their survival have been wiped out.

Human nature has been as rigorously controlled as the rest. After the catastrophic results of overpopulation during the "Age of Confusion," population growth is now sharply curtailed so that no more people are born than can enjoy "fully human" lives. The current population is 250 million, a figure which is gradually increased with the increase of material resources. What is more, children are only conceived between eugenically compatible parents, although all who care to, freely indulge in casual sexual intercourse. It is this genetic planning which is used to explain to the earthlings the Utopians' superiority in strength, beauty, health, and — above all — intelligence. Their genetic advantages are further enhanced by an educational program that produces perfect social adjustment and allows everyone to pursue the work for which he or she is most suited. It is an education free of fear, superstition, and suspicion; ideals of community and cooperation displace competition, avarice, and ambition. Private property, except for a few personal items, is unheard of, but of course, all the resources of the planet are at the disposal of those who need them or can best use them. Most remarkable of all, these tight social controls and cooperation are effected with *no government at all*. Utopian society is so harmonious that various tasks and problems are automatically handled by those who are most expert in dealing with them. (For instance, Urthred, a kind of cultural anthropologist, is immediately informed of the arrival of the earthlings and assumes the role of their host and guide in Utopia.) As one Utopian explains, no formal government is necessary: *"Our education is our government."*

The two carloads of Earthlings, apart from Mr. Barnstaple, serve as a fictional demonstration of how various aspects of modern society impede the development of Earth into a Utopia. Lord Barralonga and his party do not appear until more than one hundred pages into the book because he has been behaving exactly as a socialist would envision a degenerate, irresponsible aristocrat. His touring car never even slows down upon entering the transdimensional world of Utopia until he runs down an unfortunate native who tries to hail the car. In perfect upper-class fashion, Barralonga orders his chauffeur to drive on in hopes of eluding apprehension. Only when the car is wrecked do the Utopians, bemused by such barbarity, bring its passengers back to the hall where the other earthlings are staying. The other occupants of Barralonga's touring car are Miss Greeta Gray, a lightminded glamor girl; Barralonga's chauffeur, Ridley, an undersized Cockney tough; Hunker, the American "cinema king"; and Emile Dupont, a French journalist. The last is the target of one of Wells's humorous sallies when, as the Earthlings are plotting to conquer Utopia with a force of eleven, Dupont frets over the possibility of the British assuming a larger role than the French in the despoiling of the new empire. Dupont never understands that the Utopians are communicating by telepathy, and decides they are natural subjects of France since they "speak" French.

The occupants of the limousine, however, are far more important in representing Wells's view of the corruption of the capitalist order. Lord Barralonga and his retinue are mere affluent parasites, but the passengers of the other car exemplify the moral, political, and cultural leadership of modern civilization. Chief among them is Cecil Burleigh, an important conservative political leader. His attitude towards the Utopians matches his attitude towards everything else: a sophisticated, noncommittal skepticism which, though it leads him personally to reserve judgment, provides him with insufficient moral vigor to resist the pressure of whatever constituency currently prevails — in this case all of his Earthling companions.

The others likewise behave in ways which reflect their influence on Earth. Rupert Catskill, the Secretary of State for War, takes the casual anarchic tolerance of the Utopians as evidence for effeteness and decadence, and assumes that they will be easy prey for the hardy, determined Anglo-Saxons. His secretary, Freddy Mush, is an aesthete who disapproves of the Utopians because they have tampered with the "balance of nature" (Wells has only scorn for the budding environmentalism of the early part of the century) and show no interest in the Georgian poets or the *Iliad*; and Fr. Amerton (whether he is Anglo-Catholic or Roman Catholic is never made clear) is an eloquent preacher, scandalized by the Utopians' use of artificial contraception and their disdain for marriage and clothing. Much to the chagrin of Mr. Burleigh, who tolerates Fr. Amerton only because his following includes "very valuable conservative elements in the community," the priest sets out to clothe and convert the Utopians. Among the passengers of the limousine, only Lady Stella is at all sympathetic: her good breeding and natural sensitivity at least endow her with awe and fear of the Utopians, but even her insights are dissipated by nothing more than the prospect of a good breakfast.

It is only Mr. Barnstaple, the sole occupant of a modest two-seater drawn into Utopia along with the two grander cars, who appreciates, indeed reveres the unfamiliar world from first to last; and he thus represents the most progressive element in humanity. When many of the Utopians, used to a germ-free environment and lacking natural defenses, fall prey to the diseases ordinarily carried by the Earthlings, Catskill takes this as yet another sign of their weakness and sets afoot a plan among the Earthlings to turn the ancient castle (left over from the "Age of Confusion") where they are quarantined into a base for the conquest of the planet. Mr. Barnstaple becomes a "traitor to humanity" when his warning prevents the earthlings from taking two Utopians hostage (though he cannot prevent their deaths), and he barely escapes his own countrymen with his life. In time, however, he realizes that even he is out of place in Utopia, as much as he loves it and dreads his return to his own world. Still he gains an honorary status in Utopia by volunteering to serve as guinea pig in a second attempt at travel from one dimension to another; and once back in England (most of the other earthlings are also returned unscathed shortly afterwards) he is a changed man — more decisive and resolute and, as his wife notices, even physically taller after his "holiday."

With one exception the Utopian characters are virtually interchangeable, and it is the exception who reveals most about Wells's conception of a "utopia," of mankind's ideal condition. Lychnis, a female, takes more interest in the Earthlings than any other Utopian, and it is she who nurses Barnstaple back to health after he is seriously injured escaping from his companions. He comes to realize, however, that she is "one of Utopia's failures." She takes no interest in science and technology; she quails before the prospect of trans-dimensional travel, which has come to fascinate most Utopians; and her only real talent is for nursing the sick and wounded, an increasingly useless skill in Utopia. Moreover, she is deeply emotional, possessed by "tragedy" and the "passion of pity" — qualities which have no place among the bright, self-sufficient intellects of Utopia (nor, presumably, in Wells's plans for the future of humanity). For all the talk of universal brotherhood and cooperation, Utopia's communal anarchy is, finally, a very efficient means for self-centered individualists to pursue their own ends, merely making use of one another as necessary or convenient. In such a setting compassion is an embarrassing nuisance.

When Wells came to write *Men Like Gods* he was a personage, a spokesman for an ideology; and the book is largely a forum in which to air his program for social amelioration, rather than a work of imagination. There is little of the haunting vision of *The Time Machine* (1895) or the grim irony of *The War of the Worlds* (1898) in the factitious conflict between the faceless Utopians and ludicrously stereotyped strawmen who embody Wells's crude satire on capitalist society. It is a book that truly benefits by summarization: though it occupies a place of importance in its author's development and in the history of ideas, the contemporary reader may find it somewhat bland.

R. V. Young, Jr.

Sources for Further Study

Reviews:

Booklist. XIX, July, 1923, p. 322.

Boston Transcript. May 26, 1923, p. 2.

Dial. LXXV, September, 1923, p. 285.

Independent. CX, June 9, 1923, p. 379.

Nation. CXVII, July 25, 1923, p. 90.

Nature. CXI, May 5, 1923, p. 591.

New Republic. XXXV, June 20, 1923, p. 102.

New York Times. May 27, 1923, p. 1.

Yale Review. XIII, October, 1923, p. 167.

LE MERAVIGLIE DEL DUEMILA
(The Miracle of the Year Two-Thousand)

Author: Emilio Salgari (1863-1911)
First book publication: 1907
Type of work: Novel
Time: The first quarter of the twentieth century and the year 2003
Locale: The United States

Two young Americans who succeed in their experiment of suspended animation make a trip into the twenty-first century where they encounter wonders and premonitions of technological advancement

Principal characters:
JAMES BRANDOK, a young, wealthy American
TOBY HOLKER, his friend, an American scientist
HOLKER, his great-grandson who awakens the two travelers and guides them in the year 2003

Emilio Salgari, master sailor at eighteen and a suicide victim at forty-eight, conquered Italy and France at the beginning of this century with his intriguing novels of adventure and distant folklore, such as the Sandokan series (five novels dealing with a Malay prince at war against Lord Brooks and his English troops) and his colorful Corsairs (four novels about the Black and Red privateers and their sons fighting against evil Panamanian governors). But among his one hundred and five novels there are several which deal directly with those elements characterizing what was referred to as "anticipation" fiction at the time and science fiction today: strange and powerful inventions, totally destructive new weapons, and trips into the future. *Le meraviglie del deumila* centers around a voyage into the twenty-first century by means of a suspended animation induced by the magical properties of a flower known since ancient times.

James Brandok, a wealthy young American has traveled around the world without losing his *ennuy de vivre*. When he returns to Nantuchet (sic) Island, he finds his good friend, Doctor Toby Holker, deeply absorbed in an exciting research project concerning an ancient plant, the "flower of resurrection," which enables people to endure long and harmless periods of a deathlike sleep. Holker succeeds in extracting a sort of elixir from this flower, and his experiments with animals have confirmed his theory that life might be greatly prolonged by inducing a lengthy cataleptic state. Thus, the subject could be restored to normality at any time by the administration of proper substances. At this point, Holker decides to be the first man to try this wonderful way of traveling into the future, and he offers his moody friend, Brandok, the opportunity of accompanying him.

Holker has already had a specially equipped house built in a secluded place. The two friends agree upon the length of their experiment — a century. Holker has equipped the house with a special temperature control system (of his own invention) which will maintain the correct conditions around their bodies. He persuades his friend to convert most of his wealth into solid gold ingots to be stored with Holker's own in a secret cellar for any emergency. The doctor requests his lawyer to ensure in his will that a grandchild will see to their awakening. Then, with all preparations completed, the two men begin their long sleep.

Everything goes well; in year 2003, a descendant of Holker awakens them, in the company of a descendant of the lawyer who accepted Holker's will. Life in the future is shown in details based on speculations which were well known to the author. We are shown a twenty-first century that rests entirely on the great power of electricity, with the United States in the vanguard of technological progress thanks to its sound exploitation of Niagara Falls (with numerous hydroelectric power plants). Europe is close behind because of a series of gigantic water mills which take advantage of the Gulf Stream.

Toby Holker's great-grandson, whose first name is not given, finds the trip of his forefather amusing and offers to act as a guide for the old man, and his friend. He agrees to show them the wonders of his world and keep them out of dangerous situations. Not that any sort of danger is likely. Food and comforts are easily available, requiring only an order at the nearest restaurant or department store, and even the smallest everyday duties of the citizens are taken care of by machines. War has become obsolete in this future world. Following the horrible slaughter of the world war sixty years earlier, all nations entered into a world confederation to avoid repeating such an awful event. (This is an interesting anticipation; projecting from the year the book was written, 1907, the date of the "last, nefarious World War" would be 1943.) Moreover, as the Holker of the twenty-first century wisely points out, a war would be a suicidal event in their society, where new weapons can destroy entire cities, blow up mountains, and detonate depots of explosive materials thousands of miles away.

There have been some minor changes, however. Man has developed a larger skull to encase his larger brain. There are still some people, obviously anarchists, who are discontented (paying tribute to the usual clichés fashionable in Salgari's time). Since the Army no longer exists, the task of keeping these subversive elements in order falls into the hands of a fire brigade, which cools down rioters by spraying them with electrified water, a drop of which is deadly. When the travelers show some surprise at such a swift — and Swiftian — way of putting down dissenters, they are told that it is the *best* manner in which the future can preserve its peaceful way of life.

The tour formally begins with a visit to the Brooklyn electricity station, a scientific center where messages with Mars are exchanged. Mars has been found to be inhabited by a race of creatures that look like seals, with short arms ending in ten fingers, and legs provided with large webbed-feet. While both Earthmen and Martians wait for the scientific improvements that will enable them to cross the gap between the two planets, they chatter amiably about their respective environments and creations. Other power sources, such as heat and light, now come from radium, that same element which the ancient people also knew about, but were not able to use. Heavier than air flying machines provide the means of transportation, dirigibles having been left to history.

The journey continues and so do the travelers' questions. One would expect social problems in the enormous cities and factories, but thanks to the machines, there are very few workers. Dreadful socialism spontaneously died out; there are still a few socialistic colonies of Germans or Russians but they live quietly and grow their vegetables in Patagonia and in the *Tierra del Fuego*. Racial troubles have changed in nature. Redskins have been wiped out, and blacks have grown in number (but the only American one we are shown is a waiter), as have the Asians. The latter racial group now threatens to turn everything in the world — but in a peaceful way — into something "yellowish."

The tour then takes them to Buffalo and Quebec. They see new technical wonders, especially elaborate subway systems. But the travelers begin to feel some physical disturbances. Perhaps it is the atmosphere of this future Earth, saturated with omnipresent electricity. They travel through Labrador and reach Hudson Bay, a pleasant seaside resort of 2003, and then they point the prow of their electric car-boat towards the North Pole. There they find the last colony of Anarchists, confined to that settlement by the world confederation. At last they go to Europe (after a look at the fire brigade stationed with their holy water around the anarchists' settlement) through the European Underground Channel. They experience many more adventures, enriched with anticipations of radar, restricted islands for criminals, as well as powerful explosives and electric storms. However, the travelers begin to feel progressively worse. When they finally land in Paris, they are incurably insane. The electricity which now permeates every corner of the Earth has "melted" their brains. They are taken into an asylum among the peaceful mountains of Auvergne, where a psychiatrist friend of the twenty-first century Holker will care for them.

As this summary shows, many of Salgari's intuitions about our future were well-aimed at their targets. The common attitude towards war (the war to end all wars) is present, as well as lack of tolerance of opposition to the establishment, the increased opportunities of travel and communication, a criticism of the cruel treatment of dropouts and dissenters, and a general feeling of danger pervading this future society. It is a world well developed scientifically, but still largely lacking in true humanity. Considering that Salgari wrote his fiction especially for young people and had a very wide audience, we can only regret that his voice, so rich in this novel as far as science and technology are concerned, did not succeed in uttering a loud cry of warning. But perhaps it is our fault that our ears are deaf to warnings uttered with such moderation.

Gianni Montanari

METROPOLIS

Author: Thea von Harbou (1888-   )
First book publication: 1926
English translation: 1927
Type of work: Novel
Time: An indefinite future
Location: Metropolis, a fictional Earth city of thirty million

A melodramatic depiction of the ravages of an advanced machine age on humanity, precipitating a revolution of the workers who are led from their bondage by the elite leader who enslaved them in the first place

> *Principal characters:*
> JOH FREDERSEN, the megalomaniac Master of Metropolis
> FREDER, his son, who mediates the workers' deliverance
> MARIA, a goddess figure to the workers, loved by Freder
> FUTURA OR "PARODY," a demonic android copy of Maria
> ROTWANG, the mad inventor of Metropolis' machines and Futura
> SEPTEMBER, the poly-blooded proprietor of "Yoshiwara," the drug
>   den for the elite of Metropolis
> "11811"/GEORGI, the worker with whom Freder changes places
> DESERTUS, a mad monk with a violent messiah syndrome
> THE WORKERS

Metropolis is a composition of extremes, composed of all the clichés of melodrama. The characters are puppets; the themes are principally adolescent, conventional, and popular; the style of the narrative and setting of the story produce the wild effect of a Wagnerian epic. This is a fair summary of what a late twentieth century reader will find in this now curious novel. In its own time, it was the source of the far more famous motion picture of the same title — a milestone in the history of science fantasy and special film effects. In either book or film form it is representative of German popular culture during the years between the World Wars, an orgy of grandiloquent sensations.

Freder falls in love with Maria, the spiritual pacifist leader of the workers and starving children of Metropolis. He unsuccessfully pleads with his father, Joh, to accept at last the masses as brothers. So Freder takes the place of Georgi, a worker in the factories of the city, giving him the freedom for the first time in his life to go to "Yoshiwara" for a drug trip. Meanwhile, Joh and Rotwang conspire to use the android "Parody" to impersonate Maria, while Rotwang holds the real Maria captive. This evil Maria will both alienate Freder, who loves her, and betray the workers. Then, Joh begins to search for Freder, and Freder begins to search for Maria. When Freder discovers the Parody Maria in his father's arms, he attacks his father, then faints. A few days later, on the evening of the rebellion fomented by Parody and exacerbated by Desertus and his "Gothic" followers, Freder recovers. True lover that he is, Freder recognizes Parody for what she is and rescues Maria from the Caves of the Dead under the city. The Caves, the underground factories, and the workers' dwellings, have been flooded by a subterranean river, which has been released by shocks caused by the workers' destruction of the machines. Everyone then converges in the Cathedral square. Joh arrives in time to see Rotwang fall from the Cathedral roof, which ends a fight with Freder over Maria. Freder and Maria embrace. The workers see that they have been tricked, but they are ready to rebuild the city. Joh, whose aged mother has prayed all along for his conversion, vows to be a benevolent leader for the workers whom he once exploited.

This plot includes three exciting scenes, an inspiring collection of coincidences, any number of enticingly mysterious non sequiturs, the satisfying deaths of two profane madmen, a violent rebellion, the destruction of the largest city in the world, the moral transformation of a megalomaniac, a mother reconciled to her son, the fulfilled love of a noble hero and virtuous heroine, and the advent of a society of brotherly love for millions of workers. All this takes place in about one week of fictional time. The extent to which the novel can be taken seriously is questionable.

Many of the characters and themes of the novel should not be taken any more seriously than the plot. Joh, Freder, and Maria are the traditional melodramatic villain, hero, and heroine. They should require no explication; however, three other characters may. Rotwang and his creation, the android simulacrum Parody, are a fanciful transformation of the ancient Golem tale and the Faustian mood so fascinating to the Germanic imagination. Parody, created as a moral blank slate, literally faceless, can be programmed as her creator prefers. Crazed Rotwang chooses evil. What awesome powers of creation can human genius command? What happens when it creates artificial intelligence? What are the responsibilities and frontiers of existential agony of such genius?

Another character requiring explanation is September, proprietor of Yoshiwara, the luxurious drug palace where a snort of "Maohee" permits one to share the feelings and thoughts of others taking the drug. This is an exotic high, until a company of the pampered rich plug into the brutalized brain of someone such as Georgi, the almost subhuman worker with whom Freder has changed places. To them Georgi is an alien. September is also an alien, but not because he is subhuman. The blood of all the human races flows in his veins. Symbolically he is the perfect character to put in charge of drug trips whose principal effect is to mix up individual identities, especially with the potentially salutary prospect that others might share them. Although it is not necessary, the story depicts September as obscurely sinister. Unfortunately, he, like Rotwang and Parody, remains unanalyzed in the story.

The novel's themes are basically harmless. Machine technology, profit-driven corporate business, and a drug-buffered life are undesirable. A classless society and a Christian ethic of brotherly love are desirable. Familial and romantic love will allow humanity to endure and transcend great upheavals in the world. On the other hand, some cameo themes may arouse concern. Is an endorsement of racism implied in the menial and demiworld roles filled by nonwhites in the story? Does male chauvinism abide unquestioned in the circumstance that provides the hero Freder with an aristocratic pedigree, while the heroine Maria, for all her winning virtue, may well be a nameless illegitimate? Moreover, Joh treated his deceased wife Hel, Freder's mother, monstrously. Yet Joh's relationship with his own mother, the one that sustains him through his miraculous conversion to autocratic benevolence at the end of the story, is presented uncritically. A bathetic sentimentality shrouds his Oedipal affinities. Moreover, the reader is burdened with the proposition that a man who is a brutal tyrant one day, may be reborn as a benign Solomon a few days later.

The film version of *Metropolis* is by far more famous than the novel. In story, characters, and themes, the novel reads like a film script — not surprising since the novel was the scenario for the film. The special achievement of the work is the agenda it provides for audiovisual special effects. In terms of its own times, it was a prime foray into futurism. In terms of long range influence, it is a direct forerunner of *2001: A Space Odyessy* and *Star Wars*, both of which surround rather flimsy stories with marvelous scenic effects.

From the opening scene of Freder playing an organ in his private chapel, to the maudlin anticlimax of Joh reading the absolving letter left by his dead Hel, the narrative is an unflagging assault on the senses and popular emotions. It might be best described as theatrical composition dominated by elaborate manipulation of light and color, noise and speech, cacophony and music. At least three motifs encrust the narrative. Eating imagery abounds, but nobody eats or feels hungry. Animal imagery in general — almost always uncomplimentary to animals — occurs on every other page. Bird imagery, mostly complimentary, is pervasive. Yet no real animal or bird appears. Stock nature imagery appears often, against fleeting glimpses of real nature indicated with such economy that they remain unsubstantial. The artifice of figurative language becomes a substitute for most references to the natural world. This tactic is ingenious and nicely underlines the story's overall call for a return to a simple and natural human society and away from the twisted complexity of a machine age.

Above all, *Metropolis* is a work for which all of its author's imaginative energy was employed to present a phantasmagorically stunning setting, after which most of its characters were excavated and a story devised to take place there. Virtually all action takes place on one of three physically distinct levels of this magnificent city. Freder and his fellow aristocrats live in light, airy, sumptuous apartments in the high levels of the city's tall buildings. In the tallest of them, the New Tower of Babel, are the spartan offices and conference rooms from which Joh controls the underground factories. From these heights are visible the Cathedral of Saint Michael, the ancient house of the

Magician where Rotwang lives, and the lights from the drug den, Yoshiwara. The ground level is completely paved and clean, providing streets and squares upon which the rich are driven and the workers march to and from the factories. Later the workers will roam these same streets in rebellion. Beneath the city there is a tri-level underground of hell-hot, inferno-red, noise-filled factories; warrens of antiseptically clean, impersonally identical dwellings for the workers; and finally the haunted caves of the City of the Dead, where the workers meet with Maria in secret to contemplate peaceful rebellion.

The lighted faces of gigantic clocks are located everywhere. Every ten hours a siren drowns all other noise of the city to signal the change of work shifts. Then the marching feet of millions of workers beat in unison on the way to their labor. Freder plays his organ. The machines thunder and screech. The rioting workers shout in a choral litany to Parody's invocations.

A profusion of light plays over the city and the noise. The aristocrats enjoy the day and the sun, but to the workers day and night mean nothing, because Joh has perversely ordered their lives in ten-hour shifts. So unnatural is their existence, that they are denied even the refreshing rhythm of diurnal and nocturnal time. Indeed, most of the light described in the setting is artificial. It dramatically emphasizes the moral and physical darkness of Metropolis, of its nights, and of its terrible undergrounds. Of all the flash and glare and flicker of searchlights, machine lights, billboard lights, the lights of Yoshiwara, and the chiaroscuro of color from the body of Parody, only the light of the flames of the burning city is natural.

At the heart of Metropolis in a white, templelike building is housed the machine energy source for the city. Before it is destroyed by the workers, it stands as the supreme technological achievement of a doomed civilization. Its gleam and luster signify a futuristic physics. But there is no science in the novel, as there are no real people and no real events. Everything is hallucinatory in the sense-smothering scenic barrage that exhausts us, and possibly purges us temporarily of fear and numbing confusion, the intimations of which are present in the progress of real civilization in the twentieth century.

John Pfeiffer

MICHAELMAS

Author: Algis Budrys (1931-   )
First book publication: 1977
Type of work: Novel
Time: 2000
Locale: The United States, Switzerland, North Africa

A newsman who runs the world with the aid of his computer successfully opposes an extraterrestrial attempt to disrupt the political and social comity he has achieved

> *Principal characters:*
> LAURENT MICHAELMAS, a leading media journalist
> DOMINO, his computer with worldwide connections
> NILS HANNES LIMBERG, two-time Nobel Prize winning life scientist
> WALTER NORWOOD, crashed astronaut "saved" by Limberg
> MAJOR PAPASHVILLY, Soviet backup astronaut
> DOUGLAS CAMPION, ruthless young media journalist
> CLEMENTINE GERVAISE, television director

From the beginning of his career in 1952, Algis Budrys has written a thinking man's variety of science fiction, but at the same time he has never dangerously overstretched the capacities of his material, so that even his most metaphysical works, such as *Rogue Moon* (1960), are constructed as recognizable genre products. Therefore, most of his writing can be read legitimately on more than one level at the same time; *Michaelmas*, for instance, his first considerable work of fiction for some time and his first novel for a decade, is an action-dominated genre adventure replete with humorous but omnipotent computers and other-dimensional aliens; but at the same time it is an argument about ethical concerns and problems of identity.

Laurent Michaelmas is generally recognized as the world's premier media journalist at a time (A.D. 2000) when almost all the world's inhabitants are complexly joined together into the Global Village forecast by Marshall McLuhan in the 1960's. Michaelmas is about fifty years old, stocky, but graceful in his movements, always expertly and serenely attentive to those he is interviewing or living amongst. He is a widower with no apparent close personal attachments beyond his close "friendship" with Domino, his personal computer, an extension of which, disguised as an ordinary communications unit, is always with him. Domino, of course, is no ordinary computer, and before many pages pass Budrys reveals to us that Michaelmas and Domino together monitor and exercise a great degree of control over all the world's intricately interlinked computer systems. Domino has been in existence since the 1970's, and has grown steadily during the intervening years until — like the computer networks in Alfred Bester's *The Computer Connection* (1975) and Frederik Pohl's *Man Plus* (1976) — he has become sentient. It is a point worth noticing that Budrys does not attempt to provide any real explanation for Domino's sentience or for his power over other computers, which is so great that with

Domino's aid, Michaelmas actually runs the world.

Michaelmas' power is not as implausible as it may sound. He rules by electronically manipulating the knowledge he acquires through Domino; this knowledge, which derives from Domino's constant monitoring of all communications channels and of all computerized actions and transactions, gives Michaelmas the inside information on almost everything that transpires in the corridors of power. In a world where communications are almost universally conducted electronically, control over communications systems is the only plausible form of power.

After he receives information, Michaelmas waits until a tactically devastating moment, then uses it to influence the course of events by exposing corruption or otherwise embarrassing those who (all unknowingly, because his activities are of course secret) oppose his goals. Though never clearly articulated, these goals are similar to the goals of liberals everywhere in the post-industrial West: the elimination of war, starvation, and tyranny across the world; the reduction of social and financial inequities; and the establishment of a decently administered, unexciting, but fundamentally safe and palatable society. It is a middle-class vision, and Michaelmas, as Budrys clearly demonstrates, is an appropriately middle-class bearer of the vision. As is typical of many liberals, Michaelmas' goals are not very clearly outlined, nor do those who espouse them (either in life or in *Michaelmas*) pay very much attention to the kinds of power that must be exercised to gain them.

As the novel opens, Michaelmas finds out from Domino that Professor Nils Hannes Limberg, an Einstein-like father figure and twice winner of the Nobel Prize in the life sciences, has just announced the startling fact that Walter Norwood, an American astronaut whose orbital shuttle crashed months ago in Switzerland, did not in fact die in the disaster. Limberg's staff rescued him, and Limberg himself healed his near-fatal injuries with the aid of radical new tissue-regeneration techniques. For Michaelmas this is a potential disaster. Norwood's resuscitation is likely to upset the delicate balance of power and status between East and West in their uneasy joint exploration of space. More important, however, is his immediate conviction — which will remind readers of the dilemmas of identity faced by the characters in Budrys' earlier novel, *Who?* (1958) — that Norwood could not actually have survived the crash, and that the "Norwood" Limberg plans to present to the world must be some kind of simulacrum. But why?

A further thought comes to Michaelmas. Given the elaborate testing procedures "Norwood" will be subjected to, the skills and knowledge necessary to foist a simulacrum on the world must almost by definition surpass *homo sapiens'* current capacities in the area. Therefore, the only reason for the blatant imposition of a fake Norwood on the world must be to disrupt the political and social stability Michaelmas and Domino have managed to achieve by manipulating events from behind the scenes. Therefore, someone or something must be trying to flush Michaelmas, the world's chief executive, out into the open.

As we can see by this synopsis of the opening few pages of the novel, Michaelmas — unlike the protagonists of most science fiction stories — is never baffled by the complexities and ambiguities of the plot he is thrust into; throughout the novel, he always seems to be the first (rather than the last) to work out the implications of events. Not only does this acumen on Michaelmas' part help to move the story swiftly, but it also lends verisimilitude to the basic premise of his suzerainty over all of us. The rest of the novel serves to demonstrate his skills and stature.

Michaelmas soon determines that "Norwood" is apparently real but somehow subtly wrong, a verdict in which Domino concurs — he finds something inexplicably amiss with "Norwood" at the molecular level, though he cannot say what. Michaelmas and Domino thwart Limberg's plan — if it is indeed Limberg's plan — to force "Norwood's" return to operational status in an important mission by injuring his Russian backup, Major Papashvily; Michaelmas also determines that the resemblance between his new television director, Clementine Gervaise, to his long-dead wife can be no coincidence, and discovers that Clementine underwent extensive remedial treatment at the Limberg clinic a year or so before the story begins. Through dummy corporations, the Limberg group exercises control over one of the upcoming media networks, and through this control is enabling the savagely ambitious young media journalist, Douglas Campion, to create stories disruptive of the shaky East-West space agreements. Michaelmas deals savagely with Campion by having Domino disconnect him from all communications systems; Campion becomes a nonperson instantly.

Through interviews and meetings in Switzerland and at the space center in North Africa, Michaelmas constructs a model of what has happened and what may still come to pass which requires him instantly to confront Limberg in his mountain clinic and to reveal himself as the force who has up to this point successfully opposed Limberg's (or Limberg's masters') attempts to disrupt the world. He demands to see the alien or aliens whose presence he has deduced. He is granted his demand.

The alien exists within terms of reality so remote that he can only conceive that he has created *homo sapiens* — and our entire universe — through the operation of a "probability coherer," through which he is able to communicate with "demonstration models" such as Limberg and Michaelmas. For the alien, information is creation — as of course, in a sense, it is for Michaelmas himself, if one interprets a "probability coherer" as a form of communication. The alien is totally indifferent to the uses its "demonstration models" make of the knowledge it is able to impart; the attempts to thwart the Outer Planets mission derive from Limberg's rather foolish assumption that the alien lives on Jupiter. After the alien attempts to produce an alternate Michaelmas with its coherer — just as earlier it had produced a Walter Norwood — Michaelmas manages to force its detachment from our continuum, and Domino, who had been unable to approach the site while the alien was "present," reestablishes contact, takes over the clinic's computers, and saves the world.

Ironically, however, the world is saved for liberal values but only through the secret collaboration of a dictator and his omnipotent weapon; and the dictator remains in command. Budrys cleverly sidesteps the ethical problems these circumstances evoke, first by eliding the creation and growth of Domino into a few vague asides, so that the etiology of his omnipotence and the reasons for Michaelmas' initial collaboration with him are left unexplained. Second, the prickly question in *Michaelmas* of the relationship between ends and means is not dealt with at all. Budrys accomplishes this by having Michaelmas confront, not other humans, but an other-dimensional alien, who is beyond "morality." This apparent failure to come to grips with issues raised, at least implicitly, in the text would effectively disqualify many novels from serious consideration; but it seems clear that Budrys knows very well what he is doing.

There are two possible explanations. Budrys may well be planning to write sequels to *Michaelmas*; he has constructed this volume as a kind of template from which an indefinite number of sequels could be hatched. The second explanation is that *Michaelmas* contains a secret parody and criticism of the generally incoherent authoritarian assumptions of genre fiction, and that our enjoyment and approval of Michaelmas' behavior should demonstrate to us how lazily and complacently we accept in fiction (and perhaps in life) morally dubious acts committed by charismatic individuals with whose ideas we agree. These two explanations are not mutually exclusive. The moral ambiguities of *Michaelmas* are like a beartrap: Budrys' mature tone of voice and his skill at keeping the reader's interest through a novel-length text, all make the trap more dangerous, and the novel more intriguing.

John Clute

Sources for Further Study

Reviews:

Analog. XCVII, September, 1977, p. 168.

Booklist. LXXIII, July 1, 1977, p. 1635.

Kirkus Reviews. XLV, May 1, 1977, p. 507.

Library Journal. CII, August, 1977, p. 1682.

Magazine of Fantasy and Science Fiction. LIII, November, 1977, p. 12.

Newsweek. CX, July 11, 1977, p. 75.

New York Times Book Review. July 24, 1977, p. 15.

Publisher's Weekly. CCXI, May 23, 1977, p. 243.

Spectator. CCXXXIX, October 29, 1977, p. 23.

THE MIDWICH CUCKOOS

Author: John Wyndham (John Beynon Harris, 1903-1969)
First book publication: 1957
Type of work: Novel
Time: The present
Locale: Midwich, a rural English village

A literate and thoughtful treatment of the theme of superman as gestalt, and of the reaction of civilized humans to a challenge to their evolutionary supremacy

> *Principal characters:*
> RICHARD GAYFORD, a writer
> JANET GAYFORD, his wife
> GORDON ZELLABY, a philosopher, teacher, and author
> ANTHEA ZELLABY, his wife
> FERRELYN ZELLABY, his daughter
> BERNARD WESTCOTT, a Colonel in Military Intelligence
> CHARLES WILLERS, the village doctor
> REVEREND HUBERT LEEBODY, the village vicar
> THE CHILDREN, a group mind with strange powers

Cuckoos, it is well known, lay their eggs in the nests of other birds and thus trick the hens of other species into raising and nourishing their young. Similarly, postulates John Wyndham, a superior alien race might well choose to "seed" the Earth by implanting its own young in the wombs of human women; this theme is essentially the plot of *The Midwich Cuckoos*, one of Wyndham's finest and most controlled novels. In his other works Wyndham has a tendency to introduce too many science fiction elements and thus strain the reader's credulity. Here he confines himself to exploring a single concept in detail and with great intelligence. The concept — children being reared by parents not really theirs and who are found to possess strange powers — is one already familiar to us through fairy tales of changelings and the psychologists' foster child fantasy. But the potential of this theme as science fiction had not been fully exploited until Wyndham's treatment of it.

The ideas inherent in such a theme are certainly provocative: xenogeny, or impregnation through an external source; the social and cultural pressures on women to accept the role of mother even over children that are not their own; the conflict between what we value as civilized behavior and our own need to survive as a species; the attitudes of humans toward those who are "different" or not fully understood. To these, Wyndham adds a theme of his own: the notion of a gestalt consciousness or "contesserate mind," in which any member of the group learns what a single individual is taught, and which develops not only remarkable intellectual powers, but powers of mind control as well. Wyndham's superchildren are themselves neither good nor evil — they are presented merely as an embattled new species struggling to survive in an overwhelmingly hostile environment. But because of what they are, and what they represent to humanity, they become the focus of a drama that is essentially a highly sophisticated Darwinian struggle for survival of the fittest. It is worth remembering that in an earlier novel, *Re-Birth* (1955), Wyndham had treated a similar group of evolutionary mutations as his heroes, and told the story from their point of view.

In this novel, however, mankind is the focus, and specifically "civilized man" as represented by the obscure, sleepy English village of Midwich. The setting seems a deliberate *hommage* to H. G. Wells's *The War of the Worlds*: that novel is alluded to at several points in the narrative, and it also concerns an alien invasion set in the complacent English countryside. Midwich is isolated, making it a convenient setting for reasons of plot (the horror is contained, but absolute within the limits of its power); but it is also an archetypal image of stability and security. Nothing much has happened there, we are told, in over a thousand years; but the mere fact that Midwich has survived that long suggests the extent to which man has become firmly entrenched as master of his environment. What threatens the stability of Midwich, it would seem, threatens the stability of human civilization itself — and this, it turns out, is indeed the case.

Among the residents of Midwich is Gordon Zellaby, lord of Kyle Manor and an embodiment of many of the values that Midwich represents. A man of letters of the old school, Zellaby has published a philosophical work, entitled with prophetic irony *While We Last*, and sees himself as an enlightened rationalist who recognizes that humor, compassion, and morality are the luxuries of a dominant race, comparatively recent inventions in the course of evolution. Such luxuries, he feels, are affordable only as long as the basic necessities of survival are assured. But such theorizing remains comfortably abstract for Zellaby. He becomes one of the first teachers in a special school created for the superchildren, and soon finds his theories being echoed in terms of a harsh reality: the children realize that they are a threat to the ascendancy of the human race, and thus also a threat to the values and behavioral standards that make us human.

When it is discovered that colonies of superchildren other than Midwich had been scattered in various locales around the globe, it soon becomes apparent that the more "uncivilized" the culture, the more effectively it is able to deal with the threat. A remote village in Mongolia destroyed the children — along with their mothers, who were suspected of lying with devils — before the infants matured enough to develop their psychic powers. An Eskimo settlement exposed the strange children to the cold — suggesting that physically, at least, the children are as susceptible to the natural environment as are humans. And a Soviet village was remotely destroyed by an "atomic cannon" shortly after the threat represented by the children became apparent. Of the known colonies of children, the only one to gain power unchallenged is that in Midwich, and Wyndham strongly implies that this is due to the democratic humanism of a culture that values the rights and security of the individual over the good of the whole.

But it would be misleading to view *The Midwich Cuckoos* as a plea for totalitarianism, or worse, barbarism. Wyndham is more concerned with reminding us of the tenuous threads by which our civilization is knit together. When Zellaby succeeds in destroying the children, it is by exploiting one of the most cherished elements of civilized behavior — their trust in him as a teacher — and the cost is the sacrifice of his own life, which has become the symbol of all that is decent in English humanistic culture. The survival of a society that values honesty and trust is secured only through deception and betrayal. Mankind, apparently, remains dominant, but has received a reminder that it is after all only one species among many struggling for dominance and survival in a competitive universe.

Wyndham unfolds this narrative through the eyes of a writer named Richard Gayford. Though initially a resident of Midwich, Gayford has been living there for only the past year, having moved to Canada during the crucial eight years while the children are growing up. His actual involvement in the struggle is minimal; and his perspective serves to distance the reader from the events being described in order to give it something of a quality of an epic struggle for survival. Even his wife is spared the terrifying "host" pregnancy that is visited upon every other fertile woman in Midwich, because they happened to be out of town celebrating Richard's birthday.

The limited-omniscient viewpoint — Gayford intersperses narratives of his own experiences in Midwich with reconstructions of events at which he was not present (and at one point even apologizes for "the suggestion of disquieting omniscience" that results) — also enables Wyndham to unify a narrative that naturally breaks into two parts: the events surrounding the birth of the children (the mysterious sleep that overcomes every living thing in Midwich, the sighting of a UFO in the vicinity, the later discovery of the pregnancies and birth of the children); and the final confrontation with the startlingly matured children (who have physically attained the appearance of older teenagers) eight years later. By removing Gayford to Canada during this crucial eight-year period, Wyndham obviates the necessity of detailing the growth and maturation of the children, and is able to present it to us in summary when Gayford returns to the village for a visit shortly before the final confrontation.

Despite its naturalistic style and believable attention to detail (somehow, one never questions the reality of the children's psychic powers, even though this is characteristically a difficult concept to dramatize in science fiction), *The Midwich Cuckoos* has much of the quality of myth about it. Even C. G. Jung, the leading psychoanalytical theorist of myth and magic, read and commented on the novel. The children, after all, are apparently of celestial origin, and their golden, shining eyes associate them with the sun. Their corporate mentality suggests a long-standing dream of overcoming the problem of human isolation, and their psychic powers hint at omnipotence. They are, in this sense, a dream of what humans might someday become. In this perspective they hold out the promise of the final realization of total communication and empathy for which the "humanistic" values they so threaten strive. Yet their repeatedly demonstrated cruelty, their excessive overreaction to any threat, real, implied, or even accidental, is not fully explained. Perhaps Wyndham intends to remind us that they are after all children, and not morally superior to the humans they threaten to replace. But perhaps he is suggesting that we cannot intensify those human qualities we most value without also intensifying those qualities of selfishness and cruelty that we value less.

Much in the book remains unexplained. Why is the group mind sexually differentiated (the boys apparently constitute one consciousness, the girls another)? Why are the children portrayed as virtually without emotions? Are emotional attachments to be regarded as a sign of evolutionary primitivism? How do the children plan to reproduce? Will each child born of the group automatically become part of the group mind, or will the group have to produce a whole new batch at once, to create a new gestalt? To what extent are the children really the same, and does this sameness really represent a higher form of intelligence, or is it merely a parody of an ideal Marxist state? And what might the motives of the aliens be in "implanting" these children on Earth? Certainly, not all of these questions need be answered to make the narrative rewarding and exciting, but they are logical outgrowths of issues that Wyndham raises quite consciously.

One might answer that Wyndham does not purport to be a philosopher but a storyteller, or that it is sufficient merely to raise such questions. But *The Midwich Cuckoos* is authentically that which much science fiction claims to be — a novel of ideas — and it is something of a disappointment to find that not all the ideas are fully worked out. Superior in plotting, style, and characterization, *The Midwich Cuckoos* is only slightly short of being a science fiction masterpiece.

Gary K. Wolfe

Sources for Further Study

Reviews:

Analog. LXII, September, 1958, pp. 151-152.

Fantastic Universe Science Fiction. XI, July, 1959, p. 125.

Future Science Fiction. XLI, February, 1959, pp. 119-120.

Galaxy. XVI, October, 1958, pp. 130-131.

Magazine of Fantasy and Science Fiction. XIV, May, 1958, p. 113.

Nebula. XXVI, January, 1958, pp. 102-103.

New Worlds. LXVI, December, 1957, pp. 126-127.

Worlds of If. VIII, October, 1958, pp. 112-113 and IX, September, 1959, p. 97.

THE MIGHTIEST MACHINE

Author: John W. Campbell, Jr. (1910-1971)
First book publication: 1947
Type of work: Novel
Time: 2079
Locale: Our solar system and another solar system in a different universe

An experimental spaceship is accidentally transported into another universe where its occupants join forces with other human beings to help them win an interplanetary war

Principal characters:
> RUSSELL SPENCER, an engineer and the third-generation owner and manager of the Spencer Rocket Company
> DON CARLISLE, a chemist at the Spencer Rocket Company
> AARN MUNRO, a physicist and inventor; chief scientist at the company
> ROBERT CANNING, Munro's technical assistant
> ANTO RAYL, an inhabitant of Magya in another universe

The Mightiest Machine is the last of John W. Campbell's heavy science novels. It was written in 1933 for *Amazing Stories* magazine, but withdrawn after acceptance and sold to *Astounding Stories*, where it was serialized in five installments in the December, 1934, to April, 1935, issues. It did not appear in book form until 1947. By the time initial publication was complete, Campbell had already produced half a dozen stories in an entirely different style under his Don A. Stuart pseudonym, and the popularity of his — and others' — superscience epics was beginning to ebb. *The Mightiest Machine* is not transitional; it is a lively space-opera in the style of the author's earlier *Islands of Space* and *Invaders from the Infinite*.

How did Campbell visualize the world a century hence? He saw men reaching the moon in 1983, and predicted the first rocket to Mars in 2036. Forty years after that there is a permanent community established on the moon, and rockets are strong enough to reach and leave the planet Jupiter. Color television and picture phones (he calls them "telephone scopes") are in current use, and space is being commercially exploited. Nuclear energy, however, is not yet available. In 1933 these were plausible forecasts. Philip Cleator was soon to point out in his *Rockets Through Space* (1936) that the theory underlying extraterrestrial vehicles was well understood; their construction was simply a matter of engineering. That Campbell's forecasts were a bit too conservative is just one more illustration of how scientific developments occur faster than even the best informed people think they will. As for nuclear energy, *The Mightiest Machine* was written several years before uranium fission was discovered, and there was simply too little to extrapolate from. Yet, when later in the novel atomic power is encountered in an alien civilization, Campbell speaks of two elements being "mutually destructive in certain conditions," and posits the energy being captured to run turbines; the theory is not far wrong, and the engineering is right on target.

The Mightiest Machine opens with descriptions and ingenious rationalizations of four new inventions of superscientist Aarn Munro for improving space travel. There is a "magnetic atmosphere" which protects against meteors; an antigravity device; a "momentum wave drive" which accelerates every atom uniformly, so that passengers feel no harmful effects from sudden speed changes; and a method for transmitting and storing energy. The last of these, a "transpon beam," not only enables a space ship to draw its power from a sun, the mightiest machine of all — and hence the title of the novel — but also, in reverse, it provides a weapon that pours out energy as a beam and can turn any material object into a miniature sun.

An experimental vessel, the *Sunbeam*, is equipped with these inventions and taken for a trial run by Aarn Munro and his companions. While traveling at 42,000 miles per second, the ship strikes an asteroid. Because it is protected by the tremendous power of the sun itself, the passengers are unharmed, but the resulting interplay of forces tears the fabric of four-dimensional continuum and throws the vessel through an "interspace" into another universe. Here the main action of the novel begins.

Aarn and his fellow travelers find themselves in a battle area. Because the *Sunbeam* resembles the spaceships of one of the warring powers, it is attacked by the other and drawn into the conflict. This attack is repulsed, and the Earthmen are aided by the other combatants. From here on, the superiority of Campbell's work over the average space-opera becomes increasingly apparent. All the expected trappings of superscience are present, but they are presented in a severely practical, engineering-oriented framework.

Take, for instance, the initial meeting and communication problem between the Earthmen and their friends-to-be in this new universe. In 1945, Murray Leinster's "First Contact" needed twelve thousand words and a month of fictional time to explore this situation. Here, ten years earlier, John Campbell handles it even more convincingly in twenty-four hours and one-tenth the wordage without the use of such dubious gimmicks as telepathy and hypnopedia. His characters are indeed firmly convinced that such short-cuts are badly needed, for the labor involved in learning a new language is immense. But Campbell will not succumb to an irrational temptation; when the only practical solution to a problem is work, work is expended. This outlook is typical of that found throughout *The Mightiest Machine*.

Unlike most space-operas, whose plots are a continuous series of action that could begin or end almost anywhere, Campbell's story is tightly constructed. Indeed, at times one wonders if his plot is not a bit *too* intricate.

Millennia ago on Earth, humans warred with the Teff-Hellani, an intelligent race living beneath the prehistoric continent of Mu. The result of a different evolutionary path, they had tails, horns, and hooved feet — a sort of cross between primates and goats. Each race found the appearance of the other repulsive and hateful, and their warfare, which began with swords, continued for ages, ending with spacecraft and death-rays. Finally, a plan to flood the underground caverns of the Teff-Hellani is successful, though at the cost of sinking Mu itself. But a Teff-Hellani spaceship escapes, and locked in combat with one of the human ships, it suffers the same fate as the *Sunbeam*.

Both vessels are thrown into the strange space near the planetary system of the giant sun Anrel. Separated, each thinks the other dead. The Teff-Hellani settle on a planet they call Teff-el; the humans land on another called Magya. As centuries pass, civilization is lost, and then slowly regained. The technologies of the two races flower independently, and each reconquers space. Eventually they find each other, and the ancient war, which had lived on in oral history, begins anew. Campbell thus ambitiously grafts his story onto a number of old legends, and for good measure factualizes characters in Greek mythology and introduces Biblical allusions as well.

With the help of Aarn Munro's inventions and the *Sunbeam*, the war shifts in Magya's favor. As always, the process is subject to practical technology. The author is well aware, for example, that spaceships weighing a million and a half tons cannot be built or even refurbished in a matter of days. One of the most remarkable things about *The Mightiest Machine* is that, despite this limitation, there is still no lack of suspense or excitement. Much of the narrative drive comes from the constantly escalating duel between offensive and defensive weapons and the changes in strategy and tactics they necessitate. The battle scenes are some of the most realistic encountered in science fiction.

New inventions proliferate on both sides. There are "gravity field balls," which seek the center of a spaceship before exploding; "shal torpedos," whose charge explodes a grain at a time and thus detonates continuously; "thermite bombs," which melt holes in spaceship walls; the use of microwaves as a detector (an anticipation of radar); and "investigators." These last are tiny, remotely controlled spaceships equipped with audio receivers and a televising lens. Such football-sized "egg boats" are used extensively as Magyan spying devices and later, loaded with explosive, as long-range weapons. What is important to remember about these products of Campbell's fertile imagination is that all but two (which are chemical in nature) are based on physics. World War I, it has been said, was a chemist's war, and contemporary writers portraying future conflict tended to extrapolate in chemical terms. But World War II turned out to be a physicist's war. Once more, Campbell's thinking was truly in line with what was to come.

An additional method of sustaining suspense in *The Mightiest Machine* is through the story of the search for, and translation of, a set of sacred metal plates which were engraved by the captain of the prehistoric spacecraft which brought the Magyans into this universe. The plates contain the captain's mathematical interpretation of how the barrier between the two space-times was breached — and how it could be traversed again by design. These are eventually found and studied, so that at the end of the novel Aarn and his companions can return to Earth.

The war's climax comes when two of Magya's moons are equipped with power-storage devices, powered by their sun, and used as weapons against Teff-el. One crushes the Tefflan orbital forts (which had been fabricated from parts in space, just as it is presently proposed to construct our own complex artificial satellites today), and then rams Teff-el's moon. Finally both are successfully used as battering rams to ensure victory by destroying Teff-el itself.

For all of its unusual qualities, *The Mightiest Machine* shares the intrinsic faults of all space-opera: everything is either black or white; the good guys always win; science counts but people do not. On reflection, however, it is difficult to imagine how the story could be otherwise. One cannot have full-dimensional characters side by side with adversary relationships so intense that they lead to genocide. One *must* take the science seriously; it is fictionally too dangerous to fabricate anything else for the reader to fall back on. Yet Munro, Spencer, and Carlisle (though not Anto Rayl) do come off as more than routine characters. Their actions are believable, their conversations colloquial, even sprightly, and seldom dated. There is even one scene in which the Tefflans' religious art is sympathetically described, and Aarn comments on its beauty with intelligence and understanding. But this cannot go on; it simply is not possible to examine feelings closely when your aim is to wipe out several billion people. And that is the reason why neither here nor in any other science fiction epic can we ever expect truly human characters. One might even call this the uncertainty principle of space opera — a writer can focus successfully on either the events or the characters, but seldom, if ever, on both. Nor, expectedly, do we find even a routine love-interest in this novel. Campbell is a purist who will sacrifice everything for science. Women here are not merely delegated to secondary roles, they are totally excluded. There is not a single mention of the female gender in all 56,000 words of *The Mightiest Machine*.

The Mightiest Machine was well received on publication. It has since also been translated into Italian (1955), German (1960), and French (1962), and has been reprinted in this country as a paperback (1965). Campbell constructed its denouement carefully to allow for later continuation. He actually wrote no fewer than three novelette-length sequels, each describing some new adventure befalling Aarn Munro and his cohorts on their way back to Earth. All were submitted to *Astounding Stories* and rejected; editor Tremaine felt the day of the superscience spectacular was ending, and urged him to write instead wholly in the Don Stuart vein. Eventually these sequels were combined and appeared as a book titled *The Incredible Planet* (1949). Beside their predecessor they seem rather pale and contrived, as sequels are so likely to do, and today are of interest chiefly to specialists in the field.

In 1963, Campbell stated that E. E. Smith had made "the last big breakthrough in science-fiction" with his *Skylark of Space*. It was John Campbell himself, however, whose work probably epitomized this breakthrough best. Today, most such epics seem faded period pieces; but some, like *The Mightiest Machine*, remain not only historically instructive and important, but fascinating to read as well.

A. Langley Searles

Sources for Further Study

Criticism:

Bretnor, Reginald, Editor. *Modern Science Fiction: Its Meaning and Future*. New York: Coward-McCann, 1953. Campbell's major themes are discussed in relation to those of other contemporary figures.

Reviews:

Analog. XLVI, November, 1950, p. 94.

Fantasy Book. I, 1947, p. 41.

New Worlds. CLXIII, June, 1966, pp. 154-155.

THE MIND PARASITES

Author: Colin Wilson (1931-   )
First book publication: 1967
Type of work: Novel
Time: 1994-2007
Locale: Turkey, Earth, outer space

Two scientists battle the interior menace of the "mind parasites" by developing their own psychic potentials, thereby opening the way for all mankind to do the same

Principal characters:
    GILBERT AUSTIN, an archaeologist
    WOLFGANG REICH, a geologist
    KAREL WEISSMAN, a psychologist (deceased)
    THE MIND PARASITES

Colin Wilson has been a thought-provoking philosopher and novelist for more than twenty years. The central thesis of his work can be summed up by saying that man *could* do anything, but he is lazy. He has recently discovered that science fiction, which explores the limits of the possible, is a natural arena for his insights. In *The Mind Parasites* Wilson toys with the idea that there are hidden, ethereal beings who sap man's will to perfect himself. These beings are an ancient race, but they did not become active until the Romantic poets and composers began to dream of unlimited possibilities in the human spirit. That brief flowering of optimism at the start of the nineteenth century was followed by two centuries of aridity, nihilism, and despair, as the mind parasites moved to cut off this threat to their domination of the unsuspecting race of humans.

Wilson began his literary career in 1956 with *The Outsider*, a book which espoused a not-dissimilar thesis, lacking only its fantastic elements. *The Outsider* attributed the nihilism of the existentialist philosophers, writers, and artists to a frustrated striving after transcendence, and sought to explain the nature of that frustration. Wilson had a vision of what the existentialist "outsider" could become if he turned his mind to affirmation instead of despair. Man is on the brink of greatness, he argued, but for the blindness he imposes on himself. It is his sense of defeat that keeps him from discovering his true potential.

In a later book, *The Strength to Dream* (1962), Wilson made a similar point about writers of science fiction and fantasy. Science fiction is an attempt to liberate the imagination, but like the existentialists, its practitioners fall too often into the trap of life-negation. The horror writer H. P. Lovecraft, for example, was a passionate prophet of the extraordinary, but only because he was repelled by the meaninglessness and insufficiency of life as he knew it. He had no better dream to offer.

It was as a result of this criticism that Wilson eventually wrote *The Mind Parasites*. August Derleth, who was outraged at Wilson's dismissal of Lovecraft as a writer interesting only as an example of a failure of imagination, suggested that Wilson try to write a novel of his own in the Lovecraft vein. After some thought, Wilson complied. *The Mind Parasites* is the result. It is a fascinating blend of Lovecraftian fantasy with a repetition of Wilson's original criticism. It manages to invoke, and yet still to reject, the brooding mixture of magnificence and horror which was Lovecraft's stamp. The principal characters of Wilson's story uncover the ruins of an ancient civilization which they come to recognize as an exact duplicate of Lovecraft's "fantasies." But by the end of the novel, this similarity is seen to have been a blind trail. Wilson has used the Lovecraftian mood and imagery only to set the stage for a more profound parable of darkness and light in the human psyche. The sense of horror, which Lovecraft used to undermine the apparent order of the world, is for Wilson only the first stage of an evolutionary transformation. It leads to reevaluation of reality, not despair.

The story opens when Gilbert Austin, an archaeologist specializing in the ancient civilizations of Asia Minor, is notified that his old college friend, psychologist Karel Weissman, has just committed suicide. Austin is shocked and disbelieving, since Weissman was one of the most stable and fulfilled people he knew, but the evidence of suicide is incontrovertible. Weissman clearly died by his own hand.

There may be some clue to the strange death in Weissman's papers, of which Austin has been named executor, but he has little chance to study them, as he is called away by startling discoveries in his own field. Wolfgang Reich has applied a new method of dating artifacts to certain black basalt figurines. These figurines, which contain obscure references to "the great old ones," were thought to belong to the Hittite Empire, but are actually on the order of a million years old. Austin quickly flies to Turkey to join Reich, and Weissman's papers are forgotten. Then Reich's electronic probe discovers an enormous basalt block buried nearly two miles underground, bearing the same dark references to the great old ones. So large is this block, and others like it which make up a subterranean city, that Austin half-humorously speculates that it must have been built by giants. It is clearly the greatest archaeological discovery of the century.

As the two archaeologists begin the enormous task of uncovering the immeasurably ancient traces of this civilization, whose scale so far dwarfs even the pyramids of Egypt, August Derleth, an aging author of fantasy, writes to the two men to tell them that the evidence of their diggings parallels exactly the fantastic descriptions of "Unknown Kadath" in the writings of H. P. Lovecraft. Others soon notice the similarity, and a wave of terror and superstition sweeps the world.

It is at this point that Weissman's papers, which have been sent on from London, catch up with Austin. Most are technical reports having to do with Weissman's work as an industrial psychologist, but there is one mysterious document. Entitled "Historical Reflections," it contains a bizarre theory of human history in which human abilities are thwarted by a kind of "mind cancer," perhaps better termed "the mind parasites." These parasites, Weissman believes, are all that is keeping the human race from claiming the godlike powers its great men have dreamed of. After a number of inner battles with the parasites, he has developed techniques for wresting control of his mind from them and opening up his true potential. However, he is convinced that the parasites will now bend every effort towards destroying him before he reveals their secret to the world.

Austin realizes with horror that the parasites must have succeeded. This document coincides too closely with his intuitive reaction at the time of Weissman's death, that the suicide was not natural. In addition, on the day before the discovery of the giant underground city, Austin had himself experienced an unusual state of existential despair, verging on suicide. He and Reich had stayed up late with two Turkish colleagues, discussing the enormous rise in the suicide rate since the beginning of the twentieth century. The argument gave Austin an uneasy feeling: what if all man's nobility is an illusion? The mood is unlike him — he is an optimist at heart, an incurable romantic who became an archaeologist because he is fascinated by the magnificence of human striving. But when this bitter mood is upon him, the entire world seems meaningless, and all man's efforts paltry and worthless. For the world so suddenly to change appearances, Austin reasons, there must be some external agency at work sapping the human spirit. As he looks deeply into himself, he seems suddenly to feel some slimy, alien presence watching from the depths of his own mind. Shocked into alertness by the contact, he throws off the depression. But now Austin begins to suspect that the solution to the mystery of his friend's death and the archaeological puzzle he is investigating may be one and the same. What if Lovecraft's "great old ones" are Weissman's "mind parasites?" The world itself may be in great danger now that they have been discovered.

Following suggestions made in Weissman's manuscript, Austin and Reich begin to explore the depths of their own minds. They tap hidden springs of vitality and purpose and acquire an inner discipline which multiplies all their abilities. No longer subject to mood and weariness and unexamined impulses, they become geniuses overnight, and even begin to develop telekinetic and telepathic powers.

This is the key to Wilson's criticism of Lovecraft. Lovecraft's heroes are numbed by the discovery that things are not what they seem; Wilson's are stimulated by the adventure.

Presumably, the novel is intended to begin a similar process in Wilson's readers. After all, Austin and Reich's studies in the principles of phenomenology and other methods for throwing off the yoke of the parasites are an openly acknowledged version of Wilson's own teachings. (At one point,

Austin even urges an associate to study Wilson.) One could say that *The Mind Parasites* is not science fiction at all, but philosophy.

It is no dry tract however. Wilson's insights strike home with such uncanny accuracy that they lend excitement rather than borrow it from the story. To Wilson, philosophizing is not a process of abstraction, but one in which *ideas are put to work*. The clarification of perceptions and improved understanding of the human situation it gives can occur as readily in a novel as in a formal philosophical work. In either case, its success is determined by the extent that it engages the attention of the reader.

Wilson has perfected the novel as a teaching form for his kind of philosophy. He has a way of bringing the reader inside the story, so that his own experiences become the best argument for the author's ideas. For example, if Austin and Reich can read Lovecraft and meet August Derleth, they belong in the real world, and by some inexorable equivalency in the psyche, the reader belongs in the novel with them. Once this correspondence has been established, Wilson's unique form of philosophy is right at home. Because he never treats ideas abstractly, but anchors them in common moods and the experiences which give rise to them, his conclusions have a kind of inevitability. It is as though the reader had thought them for himself.

The description of Austin's first contact with the parasites is a brilliant example of this technique of rooting philosophical and psychological concepts in experience in order to transform them into vivid narrative. While none of us has felt a cold and alien touch in the depths of the mind where no touch has ever been expected, we have all experienced unexplainable swings in mood which cast us from heights of optimism into despair. And we have experienced — though we forget the technique all too often — how such a dark mood can be banished by a resolute application of the will. When Austin throws off the unsettling touch of the parasites, his surge of triumph and conviction invokes our own knowledge of inner greatness and untapped potential. We are ready to believe all his subsequent discoveries and transformations.

As Austin and Reich make their initial discoveries, the parasites do not yet know that their ancient mastery of the human race is being challenged. Unlike Weissman, the two archaeologists have made no open sallies against the inhabitants of the inner depths. Before making any moves, they intend to pass on Weissman's techniques for inner development to prominent psychologists, philosophers, and writers who seem to have been following lines of thought similar to their own.

Unfortunately, after Austin and Reich have recruited about twenty potential allies, their efforts are discovered, and the parasites attack in force. Most of the men, overconfident in their newfound strength, are driven to suicide by the parasites, who undermine the very roots of their identity and sense of meaning. Their powers of will and intellect, however great, were not sufficient to hold off an enemy who by his very nature lives in the dark and unexplored reaches of the consciousness and attacks from every inner weakness. Only Austin, Reich, and a few others survive, after Austin taps a hitherto unsuspected reservoir of strength. It is the transpersonal life force itself, the source of man's evolutionary striving. What power the parasites have comes by interposing themselves between man and this source, and feeding on his efforts to draw from it.

Austin and Reich must begin again, humbler than before, to master the mysteries of the mind. Until consciousness is completely free and totally self-aware, danger from the parasites will exist. Furthermore, now that their existence has been revealed, the parasites have begun to exercise openly their mastery over the majority of the human species. As a result Austin and Reich are in constant danger of assassination. Though they can hold off inner attacks from the parasites, they are kept continually on the run. Finally, together with a group of about fifty new recruits, they retreat from earth in a spaceship provided by the United States government.

In space, they make the most remarkable discovery of all. As they approach the moon, the disturbing influence of the parasites is multiplied enormously. Once they have passed beyond its orbit, they seem to pass beyond the power of the parasites as well. Eventually, they get so far out in space that the parasites tear themselves, revoltingly, from the depths of their minds. And at that point, everything is transformed. What powers they had earlier wrested from the parasites were paltry by comparison to the full strength of mind revealed now that they are completely free.

With their new powers, Austin, Reich and the others no longer belong to the Earth; they are citizens of a larger universe, with new problems to be faced. But before departing to join other, more highly evolved races that they sense are out in space, they must return to their home planet and remove the threat to their fellow men. Among other things which have now become clear to them is the fact that "the great old ones" were a false trail, encouraged by the parasites to hide their true nature. In reality, Weissman's original assessment was correct. The parasites are a kind of mind *cancer*, our own weaknesses gone wild. A bizarre radiation released by the moon provides an irritant which has combined with the frustrations, fear, and passivity inherent in the evolution of consciousness to create a ghastly shadow. However, with the unlimited telekinetic powers now available, it is a small matter, relatively speaking, for Austin and Reich to move the moon to a new orbit around the sun. Once the disturbing radiation is removed, it will be only a matter of time until training and education heal the inner malignancy.

This extravagant physical solution to the problem of the parasites is far from the keystone of the novel. It merely wraps up the action. The real solution is the process of introspection begun in the two men by Weissman's "Historical Reflections." Even the voyage into space, they discover, only hastened the process of "starving out" the parasites, who have no power of their own to overwhelm an awakened mind. In fact, as the story progresses, Austin and Reich increasingly come to see the parasites more as a nuisance than a threat. While they have managed to block man's development for a time, as the shadow of his own striving, they could not hold him down forever. All that is really necessary is for man to realize his predicament.

Timothy O'Reilly

MINDBRIDGE

Author: Joe Haldeman (1943-　　)
First book publication: 1976
Type of work: Novel
Time: 2034-2281, centering on 2051-2054
Locale: Colorado Springs, New York State, and other locations on Earth; the second planet of the star Groombridge 1618; unspecified planets of 61 Cygnus B and Archenar; Hell, a planet of Tau Ceti; outer space near Sirius; and other locations offplanet

Jacque LeFavre brings his murderous temper under control, and in so doing accomplishes a psychological alteration which not only qualifies him for the "Tamers," a paramilitary organization for interstellar exploration and development, but also eventually makes him the one person psychologically capable of communication with a superior alien race

> Principal characters:
> JACQUE LEFAVRE, a Tamer and the first surviving human to be given telepathic abilities *via* a Groomsbridge bridge
> CAROL WACHAL, a Tamer whose first mission coincides with LeFavre's, later his lover
> TANIA JEEVES, a more experienced Tamer, mentor to LeFavre and Wachal

Mindbridge deals with telepathy, teleportation, first contact, and the future of the human race. Much of the action takes place in a paramilitary organization. All of these are quite conventional science fiction subjects, but they are dealt with in an unconventional way. The novel consists of two stories, but what is crucial to the actual plot is Jacque LeFavre's character, which is revealed to us at the very beginning of the novel. What may at first sight look like the plot, contained in the long stretch of connected action taking place between the years 2041 and 2044, is in reality a largely independent and subordinate subplot involving the same characters, but with a climax and resolution of its own.

Conventional wisdom tells us that in a traditionally structured story, the resolution must either come about because of a change in the protagonist's character, or at least it must illuminate that character. (In its purer form, such an illumination deals with the personality as formed, but at least as common is a mixed approach which starts with a formed character but looks back to the previous changes which have shaped it.) Most fiction deals with the first of these options, character in change, probably because it is easier to dramatize. Hamlet finally summons the resolution to act against his mother and uncle; Speaker-to-Animals (in Larry Niven's *Ringworld*) comes to realize that he must look to the long-term advantage of his species and withhold knowledge of the "second quantum hyperdrive" from them. When an author does want to study a finished character, he often supplies other characters whose outlooks are changed by what they learn about the more static personality — the reporters in *Citizen Kane*, Eric Wace and Sandra Tamarin in Poul Anderson's *The Man Who Counts / War of the Wing-Men*. *Mindbridge* rejects this particular tactic, but the novel still must cope with the problem of keeping things moving fast enough to satisfy the none-too-patient science fiction reader.

Accordingly, *Mindbridge* employs a number of devices to increase reader interest in Jacque LeFavre. On the grandest scale, the novel has LeFavre save the world just by being who he is. Misunderstanding prevails when humankind first comes in contact with the powerful L'vrai race, and humanity almost launches a war which would lead to its own destruction. The L'vrai have more than half a mind to destroy the human race anyhow, as a preventative measure. The telepathy-inducing "mindbridge" animal might prove a means of opening communication with the aliens, but from the L'vrai point of view, humans are too-quickly-evolved, dangerously unstable creatures with whom telepathic rapport is impossible. Fortunately, LeFavre proves to be an exception. As a L'vrai spokesman who takes over LeFavre's mind explains, "This one is different from most of you. He has brought the animal part of his nature into harmony with the . . . angel part. He does not attempt to separate them. Because of this, he and I can talk. . . . You keep your animals and angels separate: you would have the angel prevail. It never can."

Since this incident does not occur until the end of the book (though a few anticipatory hints are dropped earlier) the need remains for other devices to keep up interest. Chief among these is the subplot concerning LeFavre's experiences in the Tamers. The subplot does depict a change, a maturation, in LeFavre's character. During the years that the subplot overlaps with the main plot, the change is a mere rounding-out, but it is sufficient to hold the reader's attention and to provide the basis for a linear narrative of LeFavre's first years as a Tamer, from his graduation from the academy of the Agency for Extraterrestrial Development in 2051 to his encounter with the L'vrai in 2054, before jumping ahead to a climax in 2149. The 2051-2054 narrative is presented in those segments called "chapters," and it serves to orient the reader between the chronological jumps embodied in many of the remaining segments.

The subplot is the story of twenty-five-year-old Jacque LeFavre, a man with considerable capacity, but most of it still unrealized. At last he graduates from the AED Academy and goes on active duty with the Tamers. One after another he encounters the trials of maturity, and for many years emerges from all of them victorious. He has professional success in the Tamers — his very first mission, to the second planet of Groombridge 1618, discovers the "mindbridge" animal that serves as a telepathic link between two organisms touching it simultaneously, and his later success in using the mindbridge to communicate with the L'vrai makes him a legend in his own time. He emerges from adolescent rebellion and comes to terms with the memory of his father, with whom he had not spoken for eight years before the father's death. Most satisfyingly of all, LeFavre enters into a permanent love relationship with Carol

Wachal, another Tamer. It is not made clear whether LeFavre and Wachal ever get married, but they start a family and their relationship lasts for decades. Then LeFavre's luck turns. Wachal dies, in 2112. LeFavre carries on for another thirty-seven years, but mostly out of a sense of duty to humanity. He is still the best (though no longer the only) liaison with the L'vrai. When his own time has finally come, he welcomes and hastens his demise. But LeFavre knows a victory even over death, again more because of who he is than what he does. His telepathic sensitivity enables him to discover on his deathbed that (just as the L'vrai have hinted) there is an afterlife, and that Wachal is there waiting for him.

Haldeman gets through this ticklish deathbed scene rather deftly by presenting it as the report of LeFavre's great-granddaughter Tania, perhaps twelve years old, who had been in telepathic rapport with LeFavre at his death. Tania fully expects the adult world to assume she made up the whole thing, so of course we believe her instead. This scene is one example of the utility of a shifted viewpoint. Changing the perspective also serves to infuse a feeling of movement into an inherently rather static character study. *Mindbridge* is structured to take maximum advantage of the freedom of perspective shift without confusing or disorienting the reader. The 2051-2054 flow of narrative continues until some incident serves as the occasion for a flashback or an explanation, and then is interrupted by illuminatory material of various sorts. Most of this comes in the form of written documents — LeFavre's diaries, AED reports from various hands, letters, popular science articles, and even one very convincing script for a holovision commercial. But there are also narrative sections from the viewpoints of various characters and omniscient-author segments reaching far into the future.

Much of this material hints at — though it does not fully explain — how Jacque LeFavre got to be what he has become by 2051. Piecing together flashbacks, diary entries, and other material, we learn that LeFavre was born in Switzerland in 2025 and subjected thereafter to a series of wrenching traumas and uprootings. At about the age of five he is taken to New York City, where his father, a prominent physicist, has accepted a position. Jacque is maladjusted in school, promoted beyond his age group but still smarter than his older classmates. In 2034 LeFavre's father, who is of a strangely conservative cast of mind for a prominent physicist, undergoes professional disgrace when his brilliant theoretical refutation of the "Levant-Meyer Translation" is itself refuted by experiment. The "LMT" becomes the basis for an extensive program of interstellar colonization by means of teleportation. The elder LeFavre cannot spring back from the blow, and instead moves upstate to a junior college.

Probably in reaction to this move, and to the strains on his parents' marriage, Jacque is involved in some sort of animal-torturing incident. By 2035 he is seeing a child psychiatrist. In the same year Jacque's mother leaves the family, and in 2037 his older sister Maria dies. Jacque mentions Maria only once in the novel, and then only when knowledge of her is forced out by the mindbridge. This would seem to be a result either of shame at the incestuous feelings twelve-year-old Jacque was developing toward her, or of profound grief at her death. LeFavre's maladjustment in school continues through the years. In 2042 he is attacked and almost killed by a gang of street thugs for no reason in particular, and he and his father move back to Switzerland mere months after he officially dropped the s from his first name so that Americans would pronounce it right. By now he is so Americanized as to be a foreigner in the land of his birth, and conflicts with his father go on. In 2045 he is accepted by the AED Academy (which apparently has taken over the facilities of the U.S. Air Force Academy with the coming of world government) and moves back to the United States. At the Academy the stresses placed on him continue, and indeed increase as a result of deliberate psychological provocation, but the Academy is willing (for its own institutional reasons, not out of any special concern for LeFavre) to invest considerable resources into helping him get his head straight. Since he has already been subjected to enough trauma for several lifetimes, LeFavre's and the Academy's triumph over this psychological imprinting amounts to the creation of a psychic superman.

Haldeman manages to work several bits of scientific background into the biographical flashbacks. A scene in a science class not only indicates Jacque's maladjustment in school but tells us something about cosmology; the disgrace of Jacque's father gives us information on the LMT, which is the basis for interstellar colonization. Several popular science articles and similar reports also elaborate on this latter important piece of background. In what is becoming a characteristic move for him, Haldeman starts with an inherently implausible idea and then describes it in such detail, and works out its ramifications so thoroughly, that the reader soon forgets on what a weak foundation this structure of ideas rests. In this particular case the difficulty is not so much in the interstellar teleportation — a science fiction device of venerable age which received its classical treatment in Robert A. Heinlein's *Tunnel in the Sky*, and which now seems to be getting some slight support from theoretical physics — but in the seemingly arbitrary "slingshot effect" which causes teleported items to return after a time to their starting point. An even greater stumbling block is the assertion that the slingshot effect does not apply to children born on alien planets, even though their every molecule may be of Terrestrial origin. But anyone whose suspicions about the slingshot effect have not been eased by the Westinghouse International holovision commercial or the scene depicting the LMT chamber with its harried tight scheduling and ulcer-ridden controllers will surely be won over by the solid-looking equations, tables, and graphs of the "Numbers and Dollars" segment. It is somewhat less likely that even the tale of Primus Kovaly will reconcile the reader to the exemption by right of birth from the slingshot, but it should be noted that this loophole in natural law not only makes possible the colonization depicted in the novel, but, by marking out human beings as something special in the scheme of things, breaks the ground for the novel's further excursions into near-mysticism.

The material outside the narrative flow also sheds some light on the society of the twenty-first century, illumination that is of particular interest since most of the 2051-2054 narrative involves members of the AED, a governmental organization and almost a military one. The makeup of such organizations changes less quickly over the decades than does the structure of society in general. Except for further advanced sexual integration (indeed, female predominance, thanks to the breeding program for colonization) and a casualness about the value of human life beyond contemporary Western peacetime standards, AED functions much like analagous groups of today. In the outer world, the entire population has been brought up to a reasonably high standard of living through the application of large quantities of power from solar-energy satellites. But the technological and ecological balance is regarded as somewhat precarious, and indeed one of the public justifications for the colonization program is that it will ensure the continued existence of the human race in the event of collapse on Earth.

Institutionalized altruism is always dubious, and more likely causes for the continuance of the program are the utility of such a dollar sink for economic planning, the bureaucratic imperialism inherent in any governmental agency such as AED, and the interest of many of the multinational corporations. For example, Westinghouse sells AED both power and equipment, and the worldwide physics research organization the Institut Fermi depends on AED for some scientific facilities. But whatever the motivation, the outcome seems reasonably satisfactory. Indeed, it is the multinationals and other nongovernmental social groups who run the world, and they are doing a fairly good job of it. Nations remain only as cultural entities, and even in culture the whole world is becoming Americanized. Much science fiction views with alarm such a supposed power shift toward the multinationals — a perceived trend which does not really seem very convincing in an era when throughout the world an ever increasing proportion of GNP is being channeled through governmental budgets — but few ill effects are apparent in *Mindbridge*. Indeed, the division of power among a large number of international groupings, while scarcely ushering in utopia, seems to have reduced the threat both of tyranny and of war.

Finally, *Mindbridge* includes in the nonnarrative segments some omniscient-author discourses which tie up loose ends. With a characteristic burst of sardonicism, Haldeman tells us that the mindbridge animal is really nothing more than a bioengineered telepathic scorekeeper in a game played by a race of near-gods. In a burst of eschatology recalling the clone-entity Man in *The Forever War*, Haldeman tells us that in a thousand years humankind will resemble the L'vrai, with a group mind and the knowledge that individual consciousness is an illusion. So far these little doses of the meaning of it all play much the same role in Haldeman's work as does the soupçon of mysticism in early and middle Heinlein. It will be interesting to see whether over time they increase to the significance that such philosophizing has in the work of, say, Gordon Dickson.

But any such possibility is still a long way from realization in *Mindbridge*. If anything, the novel tends toward excess in the other direction, toward excessive frivolity. Haldeman has solved a difficult technical problem in making a novel of character read as quickly and excitingly as an adventure story. But perhaps *Mindbridge* goes a little too far in its efforts to keep the groundlings supplied with the titillation of violence and sex. We are given no sufficient explanation either for AED's own callousness or for the fifty-percent mortality rate among Tamers. Even granting the preposterous exemption-by-right-of-birth from the slingshot effect, AED's every purpose could be better served by artificial insemination than by the natural servicing depicted in the novel — except, of course, the affording of an excuse for a sex scene. The frivolity of *The Forever War* was a counterbalance to the background of disorientation and death. In *Mindbridge* it is out of place, or at least out of proportion, and it makes the novel a little less than what it might have been.

Patrick L. McGuire

Sources for Further Study

Reviews:

Best Sellers. XXXVI, December, 1976, p. 279.

Booklist. LXXIII, October 1, 1976, p. 238.

Kirkus Reviews. XLIV, July 15, 1976, p. 814.

Library Journal. CI, September 15, 1976, p. 1885.

Magazine of Fantasy and Science Fiction. LII, April, 1977, p. 35.

New York Times Book Review. February 27, 1977, p. 24.

Observer. May 8, 1977, p. 26.

Publisher's Weekly. CCX, July 19, 1976, p. 130.

School Library Journal. XXIII, December, 1976, p. 74.

Times Literary Supplement. July 8, 1977, p. 820.

MINDSWAP

Author: Robert Sheckley
First book publication: 1966
Type of work: Novel
Time: Several centuries in the future
Locale: The Earth, Mars and points west

A satirical novel about a young man's bizarre adventures as he travels around the universe inhabiting body after body with his mind, searching for his own body that was stolen from him

Principal characters:
MARVIN FLYNN, the adolescent hero whose body is stolen
ZE KRAGGASH, the Martian who steals Marvin's body
URF URDORF, the Martian detective who helps Marvin
CATHY, the love of Marvin's life
VALDEZ, a trusted friend of Marvin

As is typical in Robert Sheckley novels, the plot of *Mindswap* concerns the odyssey of an innocent as he progresses from a seemingly simple situation through a series of increasingly surrealistic encounters. Nothing is ever quite what it seems, and even when its true nature is unmasked, the reader is still left wondering whether there might be further surprises in store. With Sheckley, there usually are.

Marvin Flynn is the archetypal Sheckley hero, the quiet, restrained Everyman who would like the Universe to be a simpler place than it is. He is from a quiet town, Stanhope, New York, where nothing much ever happens. At thirty-one he is still considered an adolescent and, though he has had the standard twelve years of school and four years of college, he is unprepared for the larger universe he is about to face. Sheckley wastes little time dropping his hero into trouble. To satisfy his burning desire to travel, Marvin and a Martian named Ze Kraggash mindswap: that is, the two exchange bodies, and Marvin ends up on Mars. However, the unscrupulous Kraggash has pulled a major swindle, and Marvin finds himself in an illegal body with an order to vacate it in six hours. Marvin then sets out on his unlikely odyssey in an effort, literally, to find himself. The plot is important only insofar as it forces Marvin into strange circumstances and meetings with even stranger people. Everyone Marvin meets is better equipped to cope with the Universe than he is, and everyone generously gives advice. The advice may suit their own circumstances, but it never seems to work for Marvin.

In *Mindswap*, everyone is a philosopher. Each character has developed a system to cope with the random insanity Sheckley throws his way. Sheckley delights in finding logical fallacies and screwball theories, blowing them up to their logical extremes, and then demolishing them.

Urf Urdorf, the detective to whom Marvin applies for aid, believes strongly in the philosophical approach to catching criminals. By delving thoroughly into Kraggash's personality and motivations, Urdorf feels certain he can catch the culprit. It matters little to him low long it takes or whether Marvin is alive at the end of the search. Urdorf is also a firm believer in the laws of probability, which are overwhelmingly in his favor. After having failed in 158 straight cases the sheer weight of statistics favors his solving this one, if Marvin can stay alive that long.

The less-than-legitimate Mindswappers who help Marvin along his path have their own views of life. A streetwise cynic named McHonnery believes that the whole point of human intelligence is to put itself out of work, but fortunately, humans are too stupid to do so. Another man, known only as the Hermit, will speak nothing but verse when he's outside his own house. This is a safeguard against getting killed, he informs Marvin; he's seen plenty of men get killed while speaking prose, but not a single one killed while speaking in verse.

The sharpest, and most useful, philosophical parody within the book is the Theory of Searches, as elaborated upon by Valdez, Marvin's trusty companion. Marvin meets and falls in love with Cathy, the love of his life who leaves him less than an hour after she meets him. In proposing to find her, Valdez explains the Theory of Searches, which is brutal in its irony and its simplicity. He claims he can find Cathy without knowing anything about her, simply by utilizing the Theory. Although Marvin points out that it would be easy to find Cathy if the reverse were true — that is, if they knew everything about her and nothing about the Theory of Searches — he agrees that the opposite method also stands a chance.

The Theory of Searches accepts the axiom that when a seeker finds the person he is looking for, that person finds the seeker at the same time. Therefore, the person being sought is also conducting the search, however unaware of that activity he might be. Since there is a great chance the two people will miss each other if they are both in motion, one of them should remain stationary. Since Marvin and Valdez have no control over Cathy's actions, they must assume that she will go on "searching" regardless of what they do. Therefore, Marvin, the seeker, must stay in one place and let Cathy find him. The Theory works to perfection, which should not surprise anyone at this point in the story. In a Sheckley universe, skewed logic is the best logic.

Parallels may be drawn, in fact, between *Mindswap* and Lewis Carroll's books about Alice's travels through equally strange worlds. They, too, are stories of an innocent's wanderings through a place where seemingly anything can happen, and where logical arguments may be twisted and perverted to suit the arguer's end. Carroll, of course, was a mathematician and was quite familiar with the manipulation of postulates and premises in the byplay of formal debate. Sheckley, too, shows evidence of a mathematical background; much of the doubletalk his characters employ comes straight from the jargon of the theoreticians, and particularly from the field of statistical analysis.

Statistical analysis may indeed be the key to *Mindswap*. Sheckley is very casual about the probability (or improbability) of events, while at the same time having his characters argue in terms of likelihood. He thinks nothing of introducing enormous coincidences into the action of his story, and the *deus ex machina* is a common device whenever he wants a change of pace. In a lesser writer this could be interpreted as sloppy craftsmanship, a simple lack of foresight in plotting the work, or an unwillingness to go back and do the necessary rewriting to foreshadow correctly the later developments. This is not the case with Sheckley. Upon closer examination, the reader will notice that the author has planted all these devices early in the novel. Whether they happen to occur at an opportune or an inopportune time is of little importance. There is no doubt a theory somewhere that would make such a coincidence not only acceptable, but even inevitable. As Sheckley himself puts it, "Anything that *is*, is improbable, since everything is extraneous, unnecessary, and a threat to the reason."

It is the very randomness of the Universe that is at the heart of this book. Sheckley's characters, for all their posing and philosophizing, are essentially creatures of order struggling to cope with the disorder of life around them. Each devises his own cockeyed theories to impose a system of values upon a universe that cannot be understood. Stability is shown to be, at best, a temporary state that, once lost, can never be regained. Marvin Flynn leaves Stanhope, New York, the epitome of solid changelessness, in search of exotic adventure. He finds that adventure, but only at the cost of losing his security forever. In mathematical terms, Stanhope was situated at an unstable equilibrium point. Everything was fine as long as Marvin stayed there, but the very act of movement brought Marvin's world out of equilibrium and destroyed the balance. In the end, Marvin ends up as far from equilibrium as it is possible to go — in the Twisted World, a place where even skewed logic and insane probability no longer work.

However, Sheckley's characters do not merely accept the randomness of the Universe in which they find themselves; they fight against it, each in his own way. Some, like Valdez, try to codify it, as though the very act of defining what the Universe can and cannot do is putting limits on its cruelty. Others, like Detective Urdorf, attempt to tame the Universe and bend it to their wills; the detective's high failure rate may show how futile that endeavor is, but Urdorf keeps on trying rather than surrender. Still others, like McHonnery and the Hermit, look for the loopholes in life and make their own cozy niches therein; they use the randomness of the Universe to their own advantage by flowing with it and coaxing it in the proper direction.

Of the supporting players, only Ze Kraggash does not attempt to order the billowing chaos. Instead, he gives himself over totally to the randomness, becoming an active agent of disorder. He personifies the haphazard cruelty of the Universe, and his decision at the end to flee into the Twisted World to avoid Urdorf's trap demonstrates his dedication to those principles. By acting on behalf of chaos, by accepting it into himself, he has made his own accommodation with the Universe.

Marvin Flynn deliberately fights against the randomness and perversity of the cosmos, as every good hero should. While everyone around him finds his own niche and comes to terms with the existing Universe, Marvin stubbornly fights to reestablish the Universe as it should be. Stanhope, New York, is his ideal, and he will not settle for less. By following Kraggash into the Twisted World, he is defying the Universe to do its worst, issuing the ultimate challenge in his search for perfection.

The Universe wins — it always does. Yet, in its own bizarre way, it does make concessions to Marvin's dream. Perhaps it is out of respect for Marvin's courage; perhaps it is because Marvin's perseverence might have paid off eventually. More than likely, however, it is but the latest in the Universe's long string of practical jokes.

In addition to the parody of logic, Sheckley indulges in some brilliant literary parody as well. The most outstanding example is the lengthy segment near the end of the book that spoofs the swashbuckling swordsman epics. There is the obligatory barroom fight wherein the dandy, Marvin, outfights the ruffian; the plots and counterplots, and the shifting of friends to enemies; the incipient revolution against the established order; and the mind-curdling recitation of the age's political history. All these elements are woven with typical Sheckley brilliance into a wonderfully funny tapestry.

It would be possible to criticize the book as having an uneven pace or unconvincing characters, except that a Sheckley book is like a soap bubble: it exists for its own beauty, and any serious attempt to dissect it destroys the beauty with a sudden pop. Instead, the reader should sit back, relax, and enjoy the shimmering effects.

Stephen Goldin

Sources for Further Study

Criticism:

The Encyclopedia of Science Fiction and Fantasy. Compiled by Donald H. Tuck. Chicago: Advent Publishers, Inc., 1978, p. 386. This article is a biographical and bibliographical review of all of Sheckley's work.

Reviews:

Analog. LVIII, October, 1966, pp. 160-161.

New Statesman. LXXII, August 19, 1966, p. 266.

New York Times Book Review. May 1, 1966, p. 48.

A MIRROR FOR OBSERVERS

Author: Edgar Pangborn (1909-1976)
First book publication: 1954
Type of work: Novel
Time: 1963 (10,963 Martian time) and 1972 (10,972 Martian time)
Locale: Latimer, Massachusetts, and New York City, with a brief scene in Northern City, a Martian underground city in the Canadian Northwest

A Martian Observer is sent to watch an unusual human child and protect him against the corrupting influence of a Martian who has renounced his culture's principles and seems to have plans to use the child in his design to annihilate humanity

> *Principal characters:*
> DROZMA, the Martian Director of Missions and Counselor of Northern City
> ELMIS, a Martian Observer sent to observe Angelo Pontevecchio
> NAMIR, a Martian Abdicator who hates humanity
> BILLY KELL/BILL KELLER, his son in human disguises
> ANGELO PONTEVECCHIO, a child prodigy with latent powers, when grown becomes "Abraham Brown"
> ROSA, his mother and owner of a Latimer boardinghouse
> JACOB FEUERMANN, a retired railroadman and one of her boarders
> SHARON BRAND, a talented ten-year-old, in love with Angelo
> JOSEPH MAX, a neo-Nazi bent on world domination, and organizer of the Organic Unity Party

A skillfully told story of the role played by Martians at a critical moment in Earth's history, Edgar Pangborn's *A Mirror for Observers* is also a commentary on the nature of man himself. In addition to the standard science fiction devices, Pangborn also depends on effective literary devices to mold his observation. Humanity reveals itself as the human characters move, oblivious of any determining force, within an imperceptible alternative condition: the unknown presence of Martians on Earth. The perception of mankind that results is deepened through the archetypal structuring of the novel around the struggle between good and evil, the development of the potentially powerful child, and the transformation from death to rebirth. While admitting the impossibility of eradicating evil from human nature, Pangborn offers the hope that man, once he understands empirical truth, can "reach the stars": achieve a high level of ethical maturity with the insight to rely on love to establish justice and peace.

The "Prelude" that introduces the two-part novel serves to explain the Martian presence on Earth. Namir, who has rejected the culture and ethics of the established Martians, returns from traveling around the world for 134 years in one disguise or another. While he visits with Drozma, we learn that the Martians, forced to flee a slowly dying Mars, sent an expedition to Earth 30,963 years ago. Few Martians (and only one animal, the ork) survived the rigors of the journey or the ordeals of adaptation to their new planet. Rather than take over the planet, the Martians, through a personality quirk that views the destruction of or interference with different species as inherently evil, concentrated on survival (even now there are only about two thousand Martians in the underground cities, plus a few dozen Abdicators) and limited their contact with humans to observation.

Qualified Martians, gifted with a five to six hundred year life span and made presentably human by face and hand surgery (Martians have only four fingers on each hand), have been sent regularly on missions throughout the world since the dawn of human history. Through their social, political, philosophical, and anthropological studies, the Martians have made themselves masters of human culture; they have examined our art, learned our music, read our literature, and experienced our history. At the same time, however, they have developed their own subculture. More technically advanced and astute than humans, they not only invented the telephone years before Bell "reinvented the wretched thing" in 1876, but also, for their own protection, a scent-destroyer to mask the distinctive Martian scent, undetectable by humans but maddening to animals, especially horses. Their goal is union with human beings, an ideal merger that can be possible only if man experiences a genuine ethical revolution.

Although Namir, the Abdicator, is contemptuous of mankind and doubts that "human beings can ever amount to anything," Drozma lives in the hope that humans can progress spiritually, and he looks forward to a Martian association with Earthmen in about five hundred years. As soon as Namir leaves, Drozma commissions the Observer Elmis to go to Latimer, a small town in Massachusetts, to "observe" an extraordinary human child about twelve years old who has caught the attention of Namir during his travels. Believing the child, Angelo Pontevecchio, may be potentially important in human affairs, Drozma is anxious to protect him from the corruption of Namir, who frankly admits his hatred of the human race and his interest in its destruction.

In spite of their noble intentions not to interfere in human affairs, the Martians do, albeit undiscernibly. Although the humans in the novel are unaware of the Martians, they are still affected by them. The Martians are added to the world like a subtle spice: undetectable, they nevertheless alter events — as Elmis does once he becomes involved with the fortunes of Angelo — in significant and irrevocable ways. This interference is justified by an even nobler precept than the policy of noninterference: they "hope to promote human good and diminish human evil," so far as they themselves can know good and evil.

Based on Elmis' observation, the novel takes form as the official "report of Elmis" to Director Drozma; as such, its style — crisp, graphic, and witty — reflects the lively personality of Elmis, a delightful chap who "admires human creatures a little too much." Once in Latimer, Elmis (in the human guise of Benedict Miles, a retired schoolteacher writing a book) applies for a room at Rosa Pontevecchio's boardinghouse and immediately confirms Drozma's suspicion: Angelo is indeed a child prodigy. His name, Angelo (Angel), suggests the miraculous element in the child archetype; although the child may be of lowly birth, he is endowed with superior powers: he is "divine." Elmis (Ben) has no sooner settled into the "first-floor back" than the boardinghouse is burglarized. Elmis knows that the culprit is Namir but is unable to foresee how he intends to continue his campaign for the destruction of the human race. One step obviously will be to convert Angelo, whom Namir sees as a potentially powerful tool, to his nihilistic philosophy.

In his attempts to protect Angelo's soul by recommending a broadly humanistic reading program and by urging Angelo toward ethical behavior, Elmis finds an ally in Sharon Brand, a talented ten-year-old just beginning a promising musical career as a pianist. A charming girl addicted to fantasy and inflated diction but careless of her pronunciation, Sharon assures Elmis that she loves Angelo "beyond comprehemption" and joins him in warning Angelo against Billy Kell, a fourteen-year-old tough who has been trying to persuade Angelo to join the Mudhawks, a street gang he has organized and leads. And their apprehensions about Billy prove to be only too well justified. Elmis, quite disturbed by Billy's hostility toward Sharon, follows him to his home and gathers enough evidence during his shadowing (Billy abruptly and deliberately crosses a street to avoid passing a horse, for example) to make him suspect that Billy is not only a Martian but also the son of Namir.

Hard on the heels of this calamity, comes another. Elmis becomes puzzled by the striking change in the usually warm and friendly attitude of Jacob Feuermann, another lodger in the Pontevecchio boardinghouse who is also a supporter of Angelo, and at first suspects that Namir has poisoned Feuermann's mind against him. However, when he hears "Feuermann" giving Angelo some decidedly un-Feuermannlike advice, he learns the appalling truth: that Namir has murdered Feuermann and assumed his identity to have access to the boy. Although loath to kill, but bound by the law of 27,140 that calls for the elimination of any Martian who harms his own people or humanity, Elmis realizes he must execute Namir once he has positive proof of Feuermann's death. Since the marked change in Feuermann had first occurred upon his return from a visit to his wife's grave, Elmis begins his search at the cemetery; he is interrupted, however, by Namir who freely confesses his crime. Unfortunately, Elmis' attempt to kill Namir fails, but he does learn from Namir before he escapes that the Mudhawks (whom Angelo has joined) are at that very moment engaged in battle with the Diggers, a rival gang. Fearful for Angelo's safety, Elmis hurries to rescue the boy, whom he has learned to love as a son.

Angelo escapes serious physical injury, but is irreparably (one may say "mortally") wounded when his mother, a victim of heart disease, collapses and dies upon learning of his role in the ugly street brawl. Blaming himself for his mother's death, Angelo flees, never to return. Though saddened that he must leave Sharon whom he now regards as a daughter, but happy that he has provided for her education as a pianist with an excellent teacher, the blind Sophia Wilkanowska, Elmis prepares to continue his mission. He alters his appearance and sets out on his quest, determined not to return to Northern City until he finds Angelo. The fruitless search continues for more than nine years.

In 1972, Elmis (now Will Meisel) is attracted to New York City by a newspaper photograph of a man who resembles Billy Kell. Once there, Elmis succeeds in contacting both his "children": Sharon, now a pianist of great stature, at her brilliant New York debut and Angelo, now Abraham Brown, at Bill Keller's (formerly Billy Kell) apartment where Namir, disguised as Keller's Uncle Nicholas, also resides. The photograph which led Elmis to Keller identified him as a high-ranking member of the Organic Unity Party founded by the infamous Joseph Max, a racist and latter-day Hitler, who gains adherents through the emotional gimmicks of racial "purity" and American domination of the world. Devoted to rule by the elite (meaning himself) and endowed with "the paranoid intensity of Hitler" and "plenty of naked power hunger," Max (actually schooled by Nicholas) has financed the development of a virus capable of destroying much, if not all, of the human race. Armed with such a deadly weapon, Max and Keller plan to seize control first of the Americas and then the world.

Once convinced that "Will" is his beloved "Ben," Angelo/Abraham tells Elmis about his six years in a Kansas City reform school — the "abandonment" of the child archetype and Angelo's symbolic "death." Again his name, Abraham, is significant: father of a new and chosen people and leader of his race. Although "physically" reborn, Abraham does not experience spiritual rebirth until he repudiates Keller and leaves, or rather escapes from, Keller's apartment where he has been entombed and stagnating. Significantly, Abraham had never, despite Keller's urgings, joined the Organic Unity Party; this resistance is a contrast to his succumbing (largely motivated by Billy Kell's lies) to the Mudhawks. Abraham is stronger than Angelo and more mature, a quality Elmis believes is essential in Abraham's progress toward his full potential.

Once Abraham and Sharon are reunited, they discover that their childhood love never died; it has, in fact, deepened over the years. Their rekindled rapture is overshadowed, however, by an imminent disaster: Daniel Walker, a disgruntled Party worker, has stolen a vial of the lethal airborne virus and has tossed it from the roof garden of Max's thirtieth-story penthouse moments before he plunges to his death. Although a necessary climactic action of the plot, Walker's sudden defection over a reprimand for a minor infraction of Party rules is inadequately motivated and is without question the structural weak point of the novel. This negligence is much more obvious than the omitted explanation for Billy Kell's presence in Latimer *prior* to Namir's discovery of Angelo.

In scenes reminiscent of those in Albert Camus' *The Plague*, Pangborn generally and specifically describes the virus-triggered pandemic in frighteningly graphic terms: cold but shocking statistics of the numbers afflicted and dead alternate with close-ups of old men and animals dying in the streets. Abraham, with a courageous disregard of contagion, labors untiringly at a hospital tending the sick and dying. When the plague finally subsides, after raging nearly three months, it leaves forty-two million (out of two hundred million) dead in the United States alone, among them Max and Sophia. Stricken with the disease, Sharon recovers but is totally and, for a pianist, tragically deaf.

As for Nicholas, Elmis accepts his terrible duty to eradicate the evil Namir by regarding the execution as "an act of mercy": Namir is finally free from his corroding and "very human sickness of hate." Bill Keller, however, escapes with a new face to the Northwest. Thus, evil remains: hampered or sidetracked though it may be, evil abides. Just as Thornton Wilder must have Henry (Cain), "strong unreconciled evil," hovering in the wings in the final scene of *The Skin of Our Teeth*, so must Pangborn preserve Keller; being an essential part of human nature, evil in the human scheme of things cannot be destroyed. While Abraham and Sharon withdraw to the quiet of a small village in Vermont to restructure their lives, Elmis takes a slow boat to Manila for a few months' vacation before returning permanently to Northern City.

Even though he has momentarily retired to gather his strength, Abraham remains the hope of the human world; his growth in the novel gives us auspicious testimony. Once aroused by Elmis from the apathy he suffered in Keller's apartment, Abraham gains power as he resists compelling pressures to return. And he continues to grow "in wisdom and in strength." The patients at the hospital — the conscious and even the almost unconscious — react to the messianic quality in Abraham; somehow he achieves "communication" with them. He endures not only Sharon's illness, but also the final ordeal of her life-devastating deafness, and rescues both Sharon and Elmis from despair. Elmis confesses that Abraham "upheld all three of us, forcing us to understand what richness of life remained in spite of everything." Elmis, of course, is the one whose faith endowed Abraham with "potentially great insight" and the ability to "train that insight . . . on the more dangerous and urgent of human troubles." Thus, in Jungian terms, the "child" has distinguished himself "by deeds which point to the conquest of the dark."

However, while Abraham may be the "hero" of the novel, Elmis is its delight; a strongly fairy-godfather figure, with a wry sense of humor, he charms us with his innate kindness and love for, as well as faith in, humanity. Although bemused by the contradictions and foibles of humankind, he believes that man has "the essentials of maturity" and never abandons his conviction that "Union may be possible" toward the close of his son's life. If all Martians (excluding the Abdicators, of course) are like Elmis, one cannot help wishing union could be accomplished five hundred years sooner than the target date.

Elmis' worthy qualities inevitably cast him as a symbol of good in opposition to the evil of Namir. Although there is a weak attempt during the execution scene to justify Namir's malevolent view of mankind, Elmis points out the fallacy of his insistence that human beings have "no truth in them." While acknowledging the evil in man, Elmis faults Namir for wanting to throw out the baby with the bath water and contends that Namir's is a one-sided appraisal based on the very essence of Namir himself: he has invariably demonstrated "no truth." Earlier Elmis had insisted on the need of seeing both good and evil in humanity and of keeping them in perspective:

> Men trick themselves with the illusion that good and evil are neat opposites. . . . Good is a far wider and more inclusive aspect of life. I see its relation to evil as little more than the relation of coexistence. . . . Good is the drink, evil only a poison that is sometimes in the dregs; in the course of living we are likely to shake the glass — no fault of the wine.

Since Namir never really offers a motive for his unrelenting persecution of humanity, we can only conclude that he acts out of a deeply rooted, inexplicable evil in his nature. Thus, acting with a commitment to evil so absolute as to defy rational explanation, Namir becomes another embodiment of "motiveless malignity": evil incarnate. Not that this limited focus of Namir is a flaw in Pangborn's technique; it is more an intensity of characterization than a narrowness. Namir has, in spite of — or perhaps because of — his singularity, a certain Satanic grandeur and arouses the fascination evil holds for us.

When defining his less important characters, Pangborn has an eye for the telling detail: Feuermann cherishing his horse-head meerschaum, Rosa preparing tempting Italian specialties and exuding Latin hospitality, Mac placing his toilet articles with meticulous precision. Even a character as minor as Mac comes alive with sure, deft strokes. Elmis has no sooner told him about the burglary, than Mac is into his pants and "barking about the old ladies." Approving of his speed, Elmis remarks: "Nice boy. Plain-spoken. He'd have the house steaming in three minutes." Once all are aroused, Elmis is impressed by Mac's heraclean efforts to calm the panic: "Having touched off the eruption, he was shoving the lava back, barehanded," and comments tersely, "I liked Mac." So does the reader.

Thematic use of metaphor is another of Pangborn's strong points. The "mirror" of the title — which refers to the novel itself as a surveillance of the human scene — becomes a three-way mirror. It is the mirror wherein the Martian Observers learn much, not only about men, but also about themselves; Elmis returns to Northern City a wiser Martian than the one who departed. It is the mirror that reflects for the readers the truths of human nature as Pangborn sees them. And it is the mirror the men of the novel (who are in truth reflections of ourselves) need for self-awareness, but ironically are unable to use. For some reason, men will not or cannot take a good hard look at themselves.

The bronze Minoan mirror Drozma gives Elmis for Angelo is the symbol of truth, the complete self-awareness that is undoubtedly beyond the grasp of most men but not Abraham. Shaken when he first looks into the mirror as a child, Angelo/Abraham is finally able, after gaining maturity from his ordeal, to confront the mirror and accept what it shows him: that he is "human" after all, with all that that implies. This knowledge leads Abraham to insist that the cause of the plague be universally known. Realizing that men, if given half a chance, will avoid looking at themselves, Abraham wants the entire world to know that the tragedy was *man-made*. Abraham can then accept the Minoan mirror as a gift because he has learned how to look in the mirror and has seen the final truth: man himself is the source of his own evil. Abraham also sees himself "as a human being with possibilities that are not to be thrown away or lost or stultified"; and as such, the novel ends with the hope that Abraham with his potential power, his messianic qualities, will be able to lead men not only to the understanding of ethical necessities but also to the willingness to let them rule their actions.

Dorothy K. Kilker

Sources for Further Study

Reviews:
Bookmark. XIII, March, 1954, p. 133.
Kirkus Reviews. XXI, November 15, 1953, p. 750.
New York Herald Tribune Book Review. January 31, 1954, p. 14.
New York Times. March 7, 1954, p. 16.
San Francisco Chronicle. April 11, 1954, p. 17.

MISSION OF GRAVITY

Author: Hal Clement (Harry Clement Stubbs, 1922-   )
First book publication: 1954
Type of work: Novel
Time: The future
Locale: Mesklin, a distant and unusual planet

A quintessential example of "hard" science fiction, in which caterpillarlike aliens help Earthmen recover a damaged spaceship on a planet with variable high gravity

> *Principal characters:*
> BARLENNAN, commander of the Mesklin ship *Bree*
> DONDRAGMER, his first officer
> CHARLES LACKLAND, the principal human who guides the Mesklinites

Hal Clement has been a science teacher in a private Massachusetts school for many years. He is probably the best known proponent of "hard" science fiction — that is, fiction based on and derived directly from contemporary knowledge of the so-called "hard" sciences of chemistry, astronomy, physics, and biology, as distinguished from the "softer" social sciences, whose results do not readily permit controlled experimentation and the formulation of precise laws. All of Clement's works, from his first novel, *Needle* (1950), to *Star Light* (1971), a partial sequel to *Mission of Gravity*, exhibit his careful craftsmanship. *Mission of Gravity*, his best known and most popular work, is the one on which he has stated he is content to let his reputation rest. If Jules Verne has a contemporary descendant, it is Hal Clement.

When the story opens, an unmanned terrestrial research ship has been disabled near the south pole of Mesklin, a planet whose unusual characteristics shape much of the novel's action. Charles Lackland, the Earthman through whose eyes we view much of the story, has landed near the equator and made contact with an intelligent life form. These caterpillarlike creatures, about fifteen inches long and two inches in diameter, are covered with tough, chitinous skins or exoskeletons and have very strong pincers for hands. A Mesklenite named Barlennan commands the *Bree*, which sails the planet's liquid methane seas, trading for products which are later sold for profit. He has learned English from Lackland as the story begins, although how this was accomplished is never explained. Barlennan agrees to travel to the disabled ship in return for products and knowledge which the humans can provide. This journey is a major undertaking for such creatures, whose sailing experience has been extensive but limited to familiar "waters."

Mesklin is an enormous and unusual planet. Its polar diameter is twenty thousand miles, but its equatorial diameter is forty-eight thousand miles, giving it the appearance of a fried egg. Its extremely high rotational velocity results in a gravity three times that of Earth at the equator, but seven hundred times that of Earth at the poles. A "day" is eighteen minutes long, and the planet follows a long ellipse around its sun. The fall and winter seasons are two Earth months in length, but spring and summer are each twenty-eight months long.

Because the Mesklinites normally live near the pole, their bodies are well-designed to bear the extreme gravity in polar regions, where a six inch fall would usually mean immediate death, much as falling from a tall building would for us. Their psychology has therefore been shaped by their environment. Heights and objects above them, which could fall and crush them, are both feared. The entire concept of flying or even throwing an object is unknown to them. Clement thus suggests that our own physical environment heavily shapes our perceptions. For example, the world would look far different if human vision extended into the ultraviolet or infrared, and our language would reflect this difference. The Mesklinites' perceptions must be presented in English for fictional purposes, and this sometimes results in a bit of verbal humor. Barlennan, for example, remarks at one point: ". . . there's something about them that bothers me, though I can't exactly put a nipper on it."

Our perceptions of our environment shape our understanding as well. A flat earth was assumed until recently in human history. As our knowledge grew, aided by the development of what we now call science, our perceptions changed. Similarly, the Mesklinites view their world as a concave bowl, and their geographical knowledge is shaped accordingly. A slow transformation of this world view occurs as the novel progresses. The conclusion suggests that the pragmatic "how" of the Mesklinites will be enriched and ultimately transcended by the "why" contained in the scientific knowledge provided by the humans.

The novel is a careful blend of the familiar and the strange. The unusual features of Mesklin are progressively revealed during the journey through action, dialogue, and unobtrusive explanation. Dramatic tension develops as obstacles are met and overcome. Clement is a skilled writer and is extremely knowledgeable in several sciences. He avoids a major flaw which undercut the fictional integrity of innumerable stories of the pre-1940 period, where scientific explanations interrupted the narrative while the story leaked away. In many such stories the Great Scientist deigned to explain his clever invention or idea to a listener, all too often a brainless female whose only function was to serve as an admiring companion. This clumsy narrative device was common in Jules Verne's work, and was often employed by Hugo Gernsback, the founding editor of *Amazing Stories*, who encouraged contributors to include some sugar-coated science in their stories, thus giving them redeeming social importance. This tradition fortunately died out several decades ago, and most science fiction writers have developed various techniques to provide background information without interrupting the story. Clement is generally successful in *Mission of Gravity*, but is much less so in the sequel, *Star Light*, which has far too much technical exposition.

Clement has discussed in detail the creation of imaginary but plausible societies on several occasions. At the time the three-part serialization of *Mission of Gravity* was running in *Astounding Science Fiction*, he published a companion article, "Whirligig World," in which he provided a detailed scientific explanation of how he created Mesklin and derived much of the plot from its physical characteristics. Although creating from notes is not unusual for fiction writers, Clement often works out the technical details first and develops a story around them. Thus, the externals and the ideas are dominant and the inner lives of the characters are rarely explored — an approach characteristic of *Astounding Science Fiction* (now *Analog*) under the long-time editorship of John W. Campbell, Jr. As Brian Aldiss comments in his perceptive history of science fiction, *Billion Year Spree* (1973): "There were times when *Astounding* smelt so much of the research lab that it should have been printed on filter paper."

Such rigor is probably of interest to a relatively small minority of science fiction readers. H. G. Wells felt that a plausible bit of "scientific patter" was often sufficient to achieve verisimilitude. The pseudoscientific explanations of the Time Traveller are incidental in *The Time Machine*. Some writers dispense altogether with any attempt to achieve scientific credibility. In what is probably the most popular post-World War II work of science fiction, Ray Bradbury's *The Martian Chronicles* (1950), the Mars depicted is that of the poet, not the barren, lifeless world of the scientist. Yet the vignettes which comprise the novel are not weakened by the lack of scientific accuracy. The *mise en scène* for Bradbury is shaped by dramatic, not scientific considerations, an attitude at sharp variance with Clement's. Readers who feel that the psychological exploration of character should be the central concern of any novelist may dismiss the "hard" science fiction of Clement and similar writers as simply pornography for engineers.

Clement's work far transcends the Gernsbackian school of hardware and fictionalized science by fusing action, character, and, above all, setting in an enjoyable and often fascinating blend. His Mesklinite creatures are odd but likable and admirable, and are far more interesting than the humans. Although Clement remarks that Lackland gained very little insight into Mesklinite psychology, Barlennan and his crew are far from alien except perhaps in appearance. While a truly alien form of life can be described (Olaf Stapledon was fairly successful in this area), it rarely can be anything other than an intellectual curiosity to a human. The Mesklinite behavior is all too human, exhibiting intense curiosity, loyalty, resourcefulness, and a considerable amount of intelligent self-interest. Barlennan resembles nothing so much as a shrewd Yankee trader, as befits a maritime nation. Clement occasionally uses these similarities for satiric purposes. For example, when a violent storm forces the voyagers to seek shelter on an island, where they encounter a similar species which has achieved flight in gliders, the spokesman for this species is somewhat disdainful of Barlennan and his crew, referring to them as barbarians. But this other species' superiority is shortlived. Barlennan outwits them, just as he later bargains on his terms with the humans. The analogy with colonists and natives is not forced, but an attentive reader cannot help but be aware of it.

Similarly, the attentive reader might well note that Clement, although by profession a teacher of science, not literature, has cleverly utilized many of the major devices of the epic form throughout the book. If we define the epic as an extended narrative by means of which we learn of the better aspects of an entire civilization or culture through the character of a single hero, then *Mission of Gravity* is almost a science fiction exemplar.

Barlennan is the hero, of course, and it is his struggles and eventual triumph over almost incredible obstacles that form the core of the novel. While Barlennan is singularly inhuman in appearance, nonetheless his Yankee canniness or Odyssean wiliness enables him to assume many so-called human characteristics. He is sage, cowardly, brave, adventurous, boastful, and inventive by turns. Each of these qualities serve him well on his monumental journey across Mesklin. This journey certainly qualifies to be called "epic" even in terms of Mesklinite tradition. Barlennan and the crew of the *Bree* are driven by the overpowering urge for profits and adventure. This crass motivation always remains, of course, but it is supplemented as time passes by an even more powerful incentive, the acquisition of knowledge.

Knowledge can assume many forms, of course, and among the various aspects of Mesklin which impel Barlennan are knowledge of the planet itself — the lure of distant shores. Scientific knowledge is one of Barlennan's hidden objectives, just as it was Odysseus' in several of his exploits. At the end of the novel, when Barlennan has found the object of the epic search, the substance of priceless value in mythic terms (a grounded research rocket near the seven-hundred-gravity south pole of Mesklin), Barlennan insists that he and his people be taught everything: why fire burns, how a ship floats, and all the elementary scientific facts necessary for Barlennan's people to move into the age of science. An even more subtle aspect of the knowledge sought is psychological. Here, and in many places throughout the novel, Clement projects Earth standards or customs onto the Mesklinites, but gradually, almost inperceptibly, Barlennan, Dondragmar, and the other members of the crew of the *Bree* overcome their instinctive overwhelming fear of heights or of falling. The word or the concept of "throw," for example, does not exist in either the Mesklinite vocabulary or psyche. To by struck by any object falling under the power of five hundred gravities would mean instant death, and horizontal motion of an object through the atmosphere is literally inconceivable. Yet carefully, subtly, through a series of logical incidents in the episodic, epic nature of the book, Barlennan and the crew gradually and almost unconsciously overcome this primal fear.

Other epic characteristics abound. The story begins *in medias res*: prior to the opening of the novel, Lackland has already contacted Barlennan, who has begun to learn English. Lackland's continuing help, first when he is physically present on the lower gravity centers of Mesklin, and later by radio from an orbiting space ship, can easily be construed as intervention of the gods, a science fiction *deus ex machina*. Monsters are met and overcome, giants are defeated, and the hero learns from his mistakes.

If this novel is a mission of gravity, as the title indicates, the hero of that mission is Barlennan. He grows, develops, and emerges into wholeness as a result of what he has learned. What he will be after he acquires the further scientific background may be a matter of conjecture, but the reader comes to appreciate not only Barlennan, but the Mesklinite culture and civilization which produced him. We have, therefore, come to understand aspects of an entire culture through the deeds of a single hero.

But what is finally most important about the novel is that our sympathies with Barlennan's efforts to overcome his racial acrophobia are strongly engaged. We have become empathetically involved with this struggle, and on the final pages, when the *Bree*, now modified into a kind of hot air balloon, lifts off the surface, we cheer Barlennan's efforts. Barlennan's final mission of gravity, in other words, is to overcome gravity and to learn, as mankind did, to fly, to soar the nets which held him to the surface of his world.

From one point of view, *Mission of Gravity* is a curiously two-dimensional book, in the same sense that Abbot's *Flatland* attempts to re-create a two-dimensional reality. Gradually Barlennan and his people are introduced to "depth" or "height"; and if they can overcome their primal fear of gravity, they will become citizens of a multidimensional universe. Clement may have been aiming at allegory here, for the novel was written years before the space age began. He may have been suggesting that if mankind can overcome the gravity problem and begin to explore space, then his future is assured. Such a vision is surely epic in scope.

Neil Barron

Sources for Further Study

Reviews:

Booklist. L, May 15, 1954, p. 360.

Chicago Sunday Tribune. May 2, 1954, p. 6.

Kirkus Reviews. XXII, February 1, 1954, p. 85.

New York Herald Tribune Book Review. March 28, 1954, p. 12.

San Francisco Chronicle. June 13, 1954, p. 19.

A MODERN UTOPIA

Author: H. G. Wells (1866-1946)
First book publication: 1905
Type of work: Novel
Time: 1905
Locale: A parallel earth in the star system of Sirius

Two unnamed earthmen explore and evaluate an idealized version of terrestrial civilization on a distant planet whose geography, climate, and inhabitants are exact duplicates of earth's, but whose social structure has evolved differently

> *Principal characters:*
> THE VOICE, a writer, an imaginary traveler to a Utopian planet
> THE BOTANIST, a grumpy academic, an invented character in the writer's manuscript

The nineteenth century produced abundant Utopian dreams of more promising future societies. The twentieth century, reeling from future shock, has been distinguished by the number of its dystopias — negative, ironic, fearful depictions of Utopian societies gone haywire. H. G. Wells's *A Modern Utopia* straddles the moods of the two centuries; it draws its conceptual power and courage from the cheerful utopists of the Victorian era while it carefully addresses the worries of an audience newly suspicious of wholesale remedies to problems it is not even sure exist. Wells can call his a specifically *modern* Utopia because he offers not just an exotic travelogue but a candid inquiry into an idea that sits uneasily in the twentieth century mind. The Utopian issue is as much his subject as the imaginary world he discloses.

Throughout *A Modern Utopia* Wells constantly acknowledges, disputes, and revises the work of his predecessors. His two great but troubling models among earlier fictions are Plato's *Republic* and Thomas More's *Utopia*, both of which assume order to be a greater value than liberty. Having himself struggled free from the manifold limitations of the British class order and writing for a more democratically inclined audience, Wells could not adopt the classical premise. But neither could he accept the Arcadian anarchy of William Morris' *News from Nowhere* (1890), the most important of the English Victorian Utopias. While Morris exalted freedom over social organization, he required his utopians to turn their backs on the present and seek refuge in a nostalgic and, as Wells saw it, mindless neomedievalism. The parody in chapter four of *A Modern Utopia* of the natural man in the person of a hairy, barefoot poetaster and proto-hippie is Wells's merciless verdict on what he called "the sweetish, faintly nasty slops of Rousseauism" from which Morris' utopianism descends. Trying to steer his way between the inflexible social engineering of the classical Utopias and the attenuated pastoralism of Morris' anti-modern Utopia, Wells presents a "kinetic" rather than "static" version of utopia: a society both forward-looking and experimental, perfectible but not perfect, an ideal in process but not yet attained. As he outlines the shape of such a Utopia, the edges are often blurred and parts of the design are left incomplete, in keeping with the tentativeness he establishes as a governing principle of Utopia.

Wells was shrewd enough to know that a great obstacle between a utopist and the modern reading public is the (often justifiable) conviction of readers that utopian speculation is artistically flat, as insipid in presentation as it may be daring in conception. How far Wells overcomes that obstacle is a matter of controversy, but he faces up to the issue at the opening of his book. Eschewing the inanity of pure romance and the tedium of an ideological tract, he seeks "a sort of shot-silk texture between philosophical discussion on the one hand and imaginative narrative on the other." He entrusts the talk and travel to two anonymous earthlings: one an overweight, middle-aged writer reading from his manuscript about his imaginary journey to a Utopian planet parallel to ours; the other a botanist, an invented character in the writer's manuscript, described as a grumpy academic who "thinks in little pieces" and as a recently disappointed suitor. The manuscript comprises most of the text of *A Modern Utopia*, and its supposed author, whom Wells calls simply "The Voice," is a Utopian enthusiast; the Botanist, persistently reducing all utopian experience to his own cramped, sentimentalized misfortunes, provides the dystopian refrain throughout the narrative.

The Botanist may be Wells's cleverest rhetorical invention in the book. The humor of the Botanist's intrusion into the Voice's fondest dreams is Wells's way of acknowledging that a modern audience would require a devil's advocate in Utopia, someone more caustic and subversive than the genial straight man Thomas More played to Raphael Hythloday in his Renaissance *Utopia*. A modern Utopia demands a critic and a debunker and a spoilsport — and the Voice comes to see that, like it or not, he has to accept the Botanist as an irritating fellow traveler: "I had to bring him, I suppose; there's no getting away from him in this life. But, as I have already observed, the happy ancients went to their Utopias without this sort of company."

The individual facets of Utopian life which the Voice reveals are often attractive, nearly always bracing and provocative. We see healthy citizens working a five-hour day in clean surroundings, transported by handsomely designed monorails and moving sidewalks, dressed in simply but expertly tailored clothes, living in apartments that are elegantly contoured and nearly self-cleaning. The parallel London on the Utopian planet is a wonder of futuristic design — light, metallic, streamlined, soaring — and the Voice praises the architects "who had found the Gothic spirit enchanted, petrified, in a cathedral, and had set it free." If the emphasis on craftsmanship, the pleasures of eye and hand, suggest at least one affinity with the Utopianism of Morris, Wells's attitudes toward labor-saving devices put him clearly on Edward Bellamy's side in the dispute between *Looking Backward* (1888) and *News from Nowhere* over the role of machines in Utopia. Wells celebrates the mechanical marvels of his Utopia for their beauty as well as their function. To reject technological invention for a willful primitivism, he argues, is to "achieve nothing but dirtiness, inconvenience, bad air, and another gaunt and gawky reflection of our intellectual and moral disorder." The cataloguing of the hardware in the modern Utopia amounts to Wells's ritual honoring of the works of the artistic and scientific imagination.

The economics of *A Modern Utopia* entails a break not only with Wells's rival, Morris, but also with the more formidable Thomas More. Without abandoning his lifelong disdain for corporate capitalism, Wells refuses to abolish money in Utopia. Finding More's use of behavioral conditioning to induce his Utopians to despise gold facile, and contemptuous of what he labels as Communism of "the 'free store' type" in *News from Nowhere*, Wells recommends money as "the reconciliation of human interdependence with liberty." Because he stresses the value of privacy as an enhancement of the individual, he wants to preserve the right to purchase and own property privately; that kind of property which serves as an expression or extension of one's "intimate self" is held sacrosanct. The managerial challenge of Wells's Utopia is to safeguard the individual need for privacy without diminishing everybody's right to enjoy access to the goods and pleasures of the planet. Wells's position on money is linked to the issue of employment in Utopia. He dismisses as "bold make-believe" schemes that turn all toil into play, but he also finds distasteful the puritanical notion that work builds character: "Work as a moral obligation is the morality of slaves." Rather, he regards work both as a kind of payment to the Utopian community for services rendered to the individual and as an incentive to the individual for acquiring the means to a more comfortable and creative life. While Utopian policy guarantees to the employed, the unemployed, and the unemployable a minimum standard of living, the goal of universal security "is not to rob life of incentives but to change their nature, to make life not less energetic, but less panic-stricken and violent and base."

Nourished on allegiances to democratic individualism and Darwinian evolutionary theory, Wells's Utopia allows for dissent, eccentricity, failure, compromise, and adaptation to a degree seldom imagined in utopian writing before or after Wells. "It is not to be a unanimous world any more," the Voice realizes as he assesses the implications of a planetary Utopia. But Wells's utopian sociology is an uneven performance. The chapter titled "Race in Utopia" is both enlightened and sophisticated in its analysis of the conflicting claims of integration and separatism, of cultural diversity and assimilation. Although the discussion is disfigured by the patronizing tone of Wells's characterization of non-European peoples, notably the Australian aborigines, he argues trenchantly against the Aristotelian notion of "natural slaves." The idea of natural inferiors implies the existence of natural masters, and the logic of superiority leads inevitably to a policy of extermination; the implementation of such policy inevitably corrupts the putative superiors. Unless the utopian principle of synthesis is applied to racial and ethnic plurality — and by synthesis Wells does not mean fusion of differences — he foresees, decades before Hitler's rise to power, the dystopian horror of "national harrowing and reaping machines, and race-destroying fumigations."

Conversely, the chapter on women is the most embarrassing in the book. Embarrassing not because of its antifeminism, for Wells's approach is certainly no worse than the profound antifeminism in which nearly the whole utopian tradition before him is steeped, but because the chapter is so evidently autobiographical rather than philosophical, an outgrowth of his own troubled and desperate relations with women instead of the disciplined imagining of alternatives proper to Utopian speculation. In *A Modern Utopia*, despite cosmetic improvements in the status of women, femaleness is persistently reduced to motherhood. And the double standard of spousal fidelity is tellingly retained (as Wells maintained it in his private life). An unfaithful Utopian wife may be divorced as a public offender guilty of a crime against society as well as against her husband. But the husband's fidelity is "clearly of no importance whatever" to society because his sexual activity cannot eventuate in *his* giving birth. And just as Jane Wells always looked the other way while H. G. supported his mistresses in separate households, the Utopian wife, "despite the variable amount of emotional offence" she suffers from her spouse's neglect, may be able to rise above her sense of being wronged. And "if she does not mind nobody minds." Apart from its disconcerting glimpse into the clinical condition of Wells's libido, the chapter furnishes an eloquent case for the necessity of the utopian romances of Ursula Le Guin and Joanna Russ seventy years later, for those two writers have not so much continued the Wellsian tradition of *modern* Utopianism as they have extended Utopia's borders, filled its empty places, and usurped some of its sexually determined prerogatives.

The centerpiece of *A Modern Utopia* is the institution of the samurai, a "voluntary nobility" of women and men who serve as administrators, guardians, and troubleshooters. At the time in which we are introduced to the modern Utopia the samurai are a sizable minority of the planet's population, but, the Voice speculates, they will eventually comprise nearly the entire population. Filling the functions of managers, planners, and priests, the samurai are required to demonstrate competencies other than those of the professional administrator, though they are forbidden to be businessmen, bankers, actors, or professional athletes — all occupations considered likely to lead either to self-importance or graft. They are prohibited the use of alcohol, narcotics, tobacco, and — like everyone in Utopia — meat. They are obliged to bathe in cold water, to sleep alone four nights out of five, to read at least one new book a month, and to perform other tasks intended to ensure the maintenance of sound bodies, sound minds, and a lively awareness of the contemporary world. Each year every samurai must make a private retreat into the wilderness to meditate, to purify the spirit, and to renew the experience of the ordeal of survival.

Unavoidably, Wells's samurai, like other Utopian elites, tend to strike the reader who lives outside Utopia as priggish and even fanatical. Moderation seems practiced to excess; mind and body, the exaltation of the imagination, and the mortification of the flesh are so exactly balanced that the effect seems more — or less — than human.

Only by keeping firmly in mind Wells's recurring theme that "a Utopia is a thing of the imagination that becomes more fragile with every added circumstance" will most readers find the samurai tolerable. The samurai represent Wells's effort to adjust the perpetual claims of discipline and freedom in utopian speculation, to explain how an ideal world can be both organized and dynamic, constrained in small ways in order to be free in grand ways. Wells's caveat is worth heeding. The function of the samurai in the book's intellectual design is far more important than their circumstantial detail. The order of the samurai is designed to create resonances in the reader's imagination — not just with the ritual code of conduct of the Japanese swordsmen, but with the guardians of Plato's *Republic*, the medieval Knights Templar, and the House of Solomon in Francis Bacon's *New Atlantis* (1627). The outline, the resonance matters; the circumstances, as the Voice says, are "just my own poor dream, the thing sufficient for me."

But if the reader, like the grim Botanist, is tempted to exult over Wells's admission that his Utopia is an attempt to foist on the world at large a private vision containing much nonsense and more danger, the reader should have to do what the Voice urges the Botanist to do when they return to terrestrial London: look around at the world we call real and ask how substantial it is, how poor a dream it embodies, how exactly like a nightmare it is. The sin utopists are most often accused of is arrogance — attributing their personal aspirations to the general will, playing God with people's lives. Wells, at least, has no sacrilegious view of himself. His Utopian vision ends with an avowedly fanciful bit of eschatology. The Voice yearns to see a fiery archangel rising over London, trumpeting a summons for the samurai to come forth and initiate a "resurrection of the living." But the fancy is momentary. The visionary mood yields to bemusement. Wells refuses to play God. "Things do not happen like that. God is not simple, God is not theatrical, the summons comes to each man in its due time for him, with an infinite subtlety of variety. . . ."

Robert Crossley

Sources for Further Study

Reviews:

Academy. LXVIII, October 28, 1905, p. 1129.
Atheneum. II, November 18, 1905, p. 681.

Critic. XLVII, November, 1905, p. 478.

Independent. LIX, November 9, 1905, p. 1113.

London Times. October 27, 1905, p. 358.

New York Times. October 7, 1905, p. 649.

Saturday Review. C, November 18, 1905, p. 658.

CE MONDE EST NÔTRE
(This World Is Ours)

Author: Francis Carsac (1919-   )
First book publication: 1962
Type of work: Novel
Time: Eight hundred years in the future
Locale: Nerat, a planet in another galaxy

Two coordinators of the League of Human Earths – a confederation of fifty thousand worlds which enforces the Steel Law prohibiting the existence of more than one branch of mankind on one planet – are sent to determine which of three coexisting human groups on the planet Nerat will be allowed to remain

> *Principal characters:*
> AKKI KLER, the League coordinator
> HASSIL, the other coordinator
> ANNE, Duchess of Bérandie

The twenty years following World War II were dark years for French science fiction, which was buried under the avalanche of Anglo-Saxon productions. Only a handful of authors tried hopelessly to escape the latter's influence; most resigned themselves to slavish imitation of English and mostly American translations. In that context, Francis Carsac occupies a very special position: even though his work (he admits it freely) is largely influenced by the interest he has always felt in the American science fiction school, in particular that of *Astounding Science Fiction*, he has succeeded in distinguishing himself with talent to become one of the rare first rank authors of the time. Thus Carsac represents a kind of link between a typically French turn of mind and the aggressive American science fiction, omnipresent at the end of the 1950's.

Proof of this can be found in the plot of *Ce Monde est nôtre*. The story takes place in a rather distant future, about eight hundred years ahead of our time. Earth is part of a huge cosmic federation, the League of Human Earths, at war for centuries with the Misliks, a powerful race whose purpose is to extinguish the stars. To go on a successful struggle against them, the League needs the help of all available human forces; for this, it has promulgated a drastic law, the Steel Law, aimed at banning war among Men in all worlds. According to the Steel Law, there cannot be more than one branch of mankind on a planet, namely the native inhabitants, or, at least, the first settlers. Any other occupants are then deported to a virgin world that will be their new land.

A new planet, Nerat, has just been discovered by a spaceship of the League; on it three branches of Man cohabit in a latent state of war: the Bérandiens and the Vasks, the descendants of two lost expeditions, and the Brinns, who seem to be the genuine natives of Nerat. A mission comprising two coordinators of the League is immediately sent to Nerat to determine who shall be the final possessor of Nerat. The two coordinators are Akki Kler (a descendant of the first Earth people accepted in the League) and Hassil, a Hiss whose race seems to be similar to Brinns's.

On his arrival at Bérandie, Akki Kler falls in love with beautiful Anne, the Duchess of Bérandie and heiress of the throne. But the coordinators' coming and the statement of their mission bring about war among the three races, and a bloody conflict begins despite the efforts of the League representatives. After a flight to the Vasks and finally to the Brinns, the coordinators will have much difficulty in gaining control of the situation in spite of their power. Akki Kler succeeds in overthrowing Metal the Butcher, head of the armies of Bérandie, who came into power through a *coup d'état*.

After peace has been restored, each race is convened to a peace conference, which concludes with the Brinn's supremacy. Anne refuses Akki Kier's love to lead her people to their new planet. However, she will reconsider her decision a few years later, after almost all Bérandiens have been slaughtered by invaders from space.

This is a complex plot, in which adventure is harmoniously mixed with philosophy and politics. The novel dates from 1962, a time when France was engaged in a desperate conflict in Algeria; the analogy can easily be made between the Bérandiens and the "Pieds-Noirs" on the one hand, and the Brinns and the secessionist Algerians on the other. Carsac adds a little more complexity to the situation by introducing a third community. The Brinns, who claimed to be the true owners of Nerat, instead turn out to be invaders who settled in a distant past and regressed. Although they thought at the time that they were within their rights, it appears that they probably have a genocide on their conscience, though there is no formal proof of it. Thus, even if Nerat falls to them by right, it is not because they are more worthy of it, but merely because they were the first settlers. The paragraph of the Steel Law stipulating that, in the case of a serious dispute, the planet must fall to the people in the conflict who are most worthy, is not applied in that Algeria beyond the galaxy.

The League of fifty-thousand worlds, by which the Steel Law is drastically enforced, forms a strange contrast to galactic empires of American golden age science fiction. "Everyone his own share" opposes the "melting-pot" philosophy. This may be the reason why *Ce Monde est nôtre* is the only novel developed on a galactic scale that is typically French in its spirit. In fact, in the great American space operas, plot derives almost completely from the uncontrolled mixing of cosmic races, as well as from clashes provoked by the system; in Carsac's book, dramatization stems from repatriation issues.

Carsac's difference from certain American viewpoints, however, lies in the spirit of his book, not in the development and details of his plot. First comes the concept of the central power agents, whose mission is to oversee the smooth functioning of the League and the Empire, if necessary by using the immense means at their disposal. In this respect, the book teems with references that stem from American science fiction. Second, the use of the three races inhabiting Nerat is a common device in American science fiction; it is the conventional plot about a regressive civilization which has retained some technical elements of its ancient grandeur (Bérandie and, a degree lower, the Brinns) and about a group of Earthmen emigrating to another planet to preserve an archaic way of life far from civilization's temptations (the Vasks). In Bérandie, feudalism and disintegrators co-exist; the Brinns's society combines aspects of the Stone Age with a thorough knowledge of the human body; and the Vasks try at all costs to live a purely pastoral life, after rejecting technology and sending their empty spaceships back to space.

Carsac's book is also original from another viewpoint: it leaves out the "hard" sciences to introduce instead the social sciences. This technique was unusual enough in the science fiction of the time to deserve an explanation. Each society on Nerat is carefully studied, thus revealing its qualities and defects. The Bérandiens are aggressive and favor slavery. Their society is in a critical condition; its feudal structures are about to collapse, although they still appear strong. The lack of sympathy the reader might feel toward this society is compensated for by the existence of certain characters who strive to obtain a change in the duchy, which has been spoiled by barbarianism. Duchess Anne is the best representative of that minority. She is an extremely intelligent, strong woman, so much so that Akki Kler thinks she could easily have held a high position in the League. She rises above her limited education, yet she is proud of her heritage.

As for the Vasks, they arouse sympathy initially, but gradually they are seen as incurably warlike. On the other hand, their cult of Nature and of simplicity puts them in the category of attractive peoples, though one feels that their struggle against civilization is not more than a rearguard skirmish in the huge framework of the fifty-thousand-world League. Lastly, the Brinns have the advantage of being strange and different: that is why it is more difficult to judge them by the kind of criteria used for the other two peoples. Nevertheless, some disapproval might be provoked by Vask behavior — in particular the initiation ceremonies, which are an occasion for the participants to unleash the beast in themselves, civilized though they are. Akki Kler himself is a victim of the initiation spell: he feels murderous instincts, although he has been entrusted with the immense power of determining the fate of an entire planet.

The most striking element in the characters of Akki Kler and Hassil, his companion, is their plausibility. Carsac escapes the trap of presenting almighty supermen who are able to resolve the worst situations quickly and accurately. Perhaps because of his scientist's quiet temperament, the author portrayed men at the mercy of events and forced to struggle, if only for their own survival. Ironically, this puts them in the best position possible to determine what the fairest solution is to the distressing problem of the ownership of a world; they understand both the general view held by the League, and the view of the peoples involved (they have lived among them during uneasy periods). Their mission requires a decision similar to a jury's.

Ce Monde est nôtre is an important work in all respects. It proves that science fiction has been an adult literature from the beginning, since it is deeply rooted in the earliest manifestations of the genre. Whether one agrees with Francis Carsac's conclusion — namely that history is not necessarily to be relied upon without question — it is beyond doubt that he exposed the problem very skillfully.

Richard D. Nolane

Sources for Further Study

Criticism:

Rottensteiner, Franz. *The Science Fiction Book.* New York: Seabury, 1975, pp. 139-140. Carsac carries on the classic tradition of French literary science fiction.

THE MOON IS A HARSH MISTRESS

Author: Robert A. Heinlein (1907-   )
First book publication: 1966
Type of work: Novel
Time: 2075
Locale: The Penal Colonies on the Moon

The oppressed and exploited inhabitants of the moon fight for and win their freedom from the Federated Nations of Terra

> *Principal characters:*
> MIKE, a highly flexible computer which has gained self-awareness
> MANUEL GARCIA O'KELLY, a one-armed computer man and jack-of-all-trades
> WYOMING KNOTT, an idealistic young woman dedicated to the revolution
> PROFESSOR BERNARDO DE LA PAZ, an extremely independent elderly scholar
> STUART RENE LAJOIE, a wealthy soldier of fortune descended from royalty

Many science fiction fans consider *The Moon Is a Harsh Mistress* one of Heinlein's best books; anyone familiar with his work will recognize in this novel characteristics common to all Heinlein's novels and short stories. The book has a strong plot line and a certain amount of action-adventure. In addition, the main character grows in self-awareness as the story progresses, while several satellite characters, some more fully developed than others, are also present. Finally, any number of ideas and gadgets are introduced in the story to interest, delight, and bemuse the reader. As a result, the book is not only interesting in its own right but is also vintage Heinlein.

The entire novel is a flashback narrated by Mannie, who, dissatisfied with the present, is recalling the freer days of the revolution. The action begins before Mannie was committed to the revolution, and Heinlein uses the first chapter to introduce Mike. Mike is a highly flexible computer designed to operate on incomplete data, and his various components add up to more "neuristors" than the human brain has "neurons." Mike, as Mannie tells the reader, is "self-aware," perhaps "alive." The computer and Mannie converse like two old buddies, which is just what they are. Mike, at this stage just beginning his development, takes on increasingly human attributes as the story progresses. Heinlein even flirts briefly with the concept of "soul," and Mannie ponders which beings, including Mike, might or might not have souls.

Throughout much of the novel Heinlein examines, directly and indirectly, the nature of men, machines, and combinations of the two. Mike is the best of machines, a computer come alive. He is not only capable of doing a computer's job extremely well, he can also use his "judgment," as a human would, when the data are incomplete. Mike "grows up" during the course of the story from a prankish adolescent into a kind of George Washington-Samuel

Adams figure in the Lunar Revolution. At the other end of the spectrum are the best of men, the professor, Bernardo de la Paz, and the soldier of fortune, Stuart René LaJoie. Both men are always open to new ideas and new actions, and each has a mature code of conduct and sense of responsibility on which actions and judgments are based. Moreover, it is de la Paz's concepts of freedom which become the ideological framework of the Lunar Revolution. Professor de la Paz is a Thomas Jefferson-Benjamin Franklin figure, while LaJoie is reminiscent of Lafayette, a foreigner who spends his fortune for, and helps to lead, the revolution.

Mannie is somewhere between the two poles; he is a man-machine with a dozen left arms, all prosthetic. One looks like a real arm, and he uses it for social occasions; each of the others has a special function. Using his number three arm, for example, which has micromanipulators, and aided by "stereo loupe spectacles," he can make ultramicrominiature repairs. Mannie is more capable than almost any other character in the book, the replacement of his "real" left arm with prosthetic left arms having increased rather than decreased his versatility. He is neither like the professor not like the computer, yet he incorporates some of the best traits of each.

The plot is straightforward. The convicts and descendants of convicts who inhabit the penal colonies on the moon are justifiably dissatisfied with the way they are being treated by the oppressive Lunar Authority and by the Federated Nations which are squeezing the colonies for all the raw materials they can ship down to Terra. In spite of the failure of a grassroots revolutionary movement thoroughly infiltrated by the Warden's spies, Mannie, Wyoh, de la Paz, and Stu become the controlling center of a new revolution. Mike, presented through the mass media as Adam Selene, is the logistical brain of the revolution. Even though the humans have a clearer grasp of why this revolution needs to be fought, it is Mike whose calculations make the effort successful. It is also Mike who is able to provide the necessary weapon for the otherwise unarmed colony; the catapults, originally designed to throw huge, rocket-guided containers of grain to Terra, are used to throw steel-encased rocks. These rocks, striking the ground like huge meteors, cause great damage. The Federated Nations, like England in 1776, cannot crush the rebellion, and the "Loonies," as they call themselves, are recognized as a free people.

The plot of this historical romance of the future may seem skimpy, but it is no more so than the plots of the historical romances of the past written by Samuel Shellabarger, Kenneth Roberts, or John Jakes. Heinlein acknowledges his kinship to that tradition by entitling the middle section of his book "A Rabble in Arms" after one of Kenneth Roberts' historical romances of the American Revolution. The plot, as in all historical romances, is a framework fleshed out with details that give the reader a feeling for real people living in a historically recognizable place. For Samuel Shellabarger, the place is medieval Europe; for Heinlein, the place is the penal colonies of the moon in 2075.

As in all frontier communities, physical living conditions are largely determined by the environment, and because these colonies are on the moon, the most practical place for the colonists to live is underground. The Loonies live in "warrens," vast complexes of tunnels housing business, social, recreational, and living accommodations. All the warrens are interconnected by service tunnels, elevators, subways, and the like, while each city is connected to its neighbors by larger subways and surface truck-busses called "rolligons."

The moon's gravity, which is less than that of the earth, is also an important factor in determining living conditions. Because of the low gravity, humans must learn to move differently, and such acclimation takes time; and, because they are already accustomed to the low gravity, the native warriors enjoy a distinct advantage over invaders. More important, because there is less gravity for a person's body to overcome, he tends to live longer on the moon than he would on Terra. While Mannie is on a diplomatic mission to Terra, a woman guesses his age to be about twenty-two; he replies that he has been married longer than that. In fact, he points out, people on the moon do not yet know how long normal Lunar life-expectancy is, since the oldest citizens are Terran-born convicts.

The other living conditions sketched in by Heinlein are immediately recognizable given the determinants of time and place. The reader is taken into bars, hotels, businesses, and homes until he has a fairly full picture of the surroundings in which the main characters operate.

The social living conditions, as one might expect, are both familiar and unfamiliar. People still eat, sleep, work, and play; their moods still vary between happy, sad, content, or angry. But their social structures are a direct result of the place and time. Because the moon is a frontier penal colony, its inhabitants are tough and resilient. Anyone who does not fit in quickly is shoved out an airlock without a pressure-suit. Mannie relates that tourists always comment on how polite the lunar inhabitants are, but it is no wonder, considering that each individual must either get along or get out. The language of the Loonies is also a product of their social situation. Since they were transported to the moon from all of the large Terran nations, their language, a simply structured English laced with words from other Terran languages (especially Russian), is as internationally polyglot as they are. Many readers and critics have pointed out the artificiality of this language and have suggested that it makes the novel more difficult to read rather than more realistic.

The various forms of marriage depicted, however, are sociologically appropriate and make the novel both more interesting and more realistic. As with most penal colonies, the men greatly outnumbered the women in the beginning, and that ratio changed very slowly. As a result, the various forms of marriage — polyandry, group marriage, clan marriage, and line marriage — were set up to help redress that imbalance and usually to leave the woman (or women) in charge. The most interesting type is the line marriage, of which

Mannie's is an example. A line marriage consists of several husbands and several wives, in all age categories, presided over by the eldest husband and wife. Usually only the wives have the vote on family matters, but in Mannie's marriage, the husbands do get to comment and do have some veto power. When a husband or wife dies, a new husband or wife is "opted in," and although a basic balance is generally observed, special instances allow for "optings" out of order. The stability of such a corporation, both emotional and economic, as well as the other advantages which Heinlein details, make this arrangement work to the benefit of all.

Much of the novel is filled with interesting details of the lunar civilization. Hydroponics has been developed into a highly productive method of farming, and many families have their own hydroponics system. Women who cannot conceive their own children can be "host mothers" and can "carry" babies for women who cannot or do not want to maintain a pregnancy. The Loonies are incurable gamblers and will even roll the dice, double or nothing, with a shop-keeper for the groceries. There are almost no viral illnesses on the moon; viruses and vermin are easily cleared from any part of the city by letting the air out for a few minutes. Ice miners delve below the surface to find pockets of frozen water left from the time when the moon had an atmosphere. The dead are returned to the ground.

There are, to be sure, other perennial Heinlein trademarks in the novel. He tends, for example, to oversimplify his female characters, who seem to be treated either as "typically feminine" (and not discussed much) or as "exceptions" — whenever Wyoming Knott does something that betrays exceptional good sense, Mannie explains that she is reacting as a man rather than as a woman. A typically Heinlein-style relationship develops between Mannie and de la Paz and also between Mike and the humans. Played out once again is the theme of the immature youth who, guided by an older and wiser person, grows in poise and self-knowledge. Such situations are common not only in Heinlein's juvenile novels but also in *Starship Troopers* and *Stranger in a Strange Land*. By *I Will Fear No Evil* and *Time Enough for Love*, the older man has taken center stage. Another Heinlein mainstay is the misfit who makes good. As convicts, all the Loonies are misfits; and among them, Mannie, Prof, Stu, Wyoh, and Mike are special misfits. But they all make good and the revolution is won. In addition, the novel contains a sociopolitical philosophy: Professor de la Paz's "rational anarchy." At its simplest, rational anarchy is similar to the attitudes in Thoreau's "Civil Disobedience," and de la Paz recognizes his own responsibility for his actions and willingly accepts their consequences. And finally, the inclusion of Hazel Meade Stone places *The Moon Is a Harsh Mistress* chronologically just before *The Rolling Stones* in Heinlein's future history.

Heinlein has seldom been content to rest on his laurels or merely write from his own formula. He does write formulaic stories and novels, but the formulas are secondary — foundations upon which to build — rather than essential. *The Moon Is a Harsh Mistress* is thus a good example of Heinlein's work, a vintage Heinlein formula fleshed out with new Heinlein ideas.

Charles William Sullivan III

Sources for Further Study

Criticism:

Ketterer, David. *New Worlds for Old; the Apocalyptic Imagination, Science Fiction, and American Literature*. Bloomington: Indiana University Press, 1974, pp. 150-156. The theme behind the novel is the American Revolution.

Perkins, James A. "MYCROFTXX is Alive and Well: The Ambiguous Ending of *The Moon Is a Harsh Mistress*," in *Notes on Contemporary Literature*. V (1975), pp. 13-15. The end of the work leaves the reader believing the hero-computer still lives.

Reviews:

Analog. LXXVIII, December, 1966, pp. 162-163.

Best Sellers. XXVI, June 15, 1966, p. 117.

Booklist. LXIII, November 15, 1966, p. 364.

Galaxy. XXV, December, 1966, pp. 125-128.

Library Journal. XCI, June 15, 1966, p. 3238.

Magazine of Fantasy and Science Fiction. XXXI, November, 1966, p. 61.

National Review. XVIII, December 13, 1966, p. 1278.

Publisher's Weekly. CLXXXIX, May 23, 1966, p. 81.

THE MOON IS HELL

Author: John W. Campbell, Jr. (1910-1971)
First book publication: 1951
Type of work: Novella
Time: May, 1981 to February, 1982
Locale: The far side of the moon

Members of the Garner Lunar Expedition, the first to explore the satellite, are marooned after the crash of their relief ship

Principal characters:
THOMAS RIDGELY DUNCAN, the narrator, second in command
ROBERT KENNETH MOORE, a chemist
FREDERICK L. BENDER, a food thief

John W. Campbell, Jr.'s reputation rests mainly on his success as an editor. For more than thirty years, 1937 to 1971, he was in charge of *Astounding Science Fiction* (later called *Analog*), and during much of that time the magazine was first in its field, never very far from the top in both sales and influence. Campbell is frequently credited with having willed science fiction into respectability in the 1940's — which is to say that the work of such *Astounding Science Fiction* stalwarts as Asimov, Heinlein, Sturgeon, and von Vogt was clearly distinguishable from the less plausible, less well crafted science fiction of the 1920's and early 1930's. He accomplished this revolution, his writers have said on numerous occasions, by insisting that stories in *Astounding Science Fiction* be based on credible science wedded to reasonably good writing. Nothing that outraged scientific possibility was acceptable, unless used as a convention (for example, faster-than-light travel) or occasionally for a humorous effect. Even aliens had to be plausible, or at least self-consistent in their behavior; an alien had to think "*as well as* a human, but not *like* a human.*" And the writing had at least to avoid the embarrassments of Victorian pomposity and the overuse of modern slang — though the "fine writing" experiments of the 1960's were scorned. Without Campbell's revolution, some historians argue, the book in which this review appears could never have existed. Like all contemporary writing *about* science fiction, it builds on the foundation laid more than a generation ago almost single-handedly by Campbell.

Campbell's reputation as a writer is less secure, if only because (ironically) his books are still around. The reasons for his deification as an editor can no longer be objectively verified. Certainly the memories of his co-workers are subject to some nostalgic distortion, and the analyses of students are subject to the usual errors of historical reconstruction. (Old files of *Astounding Science Fiction* are hard to come by, and files of its defunct competitors of the late depression and war years are even scarcer.) Although Campbell's own fiction — much of it published under the pseudonym Don A. Stuart — survives in collections and anthologies, it seems today to be more praised than read, except for "Who Goes There?," "Twilight," and "The Cloak of Aesir." The problem is that Campbell, as an author of the kind of fiction he demanded from contributors to his magazine, was rapidly superseded by his *protégés* and friends. So he soon came to devote nearly all his energy to the magazine. In the Lester del Rey collection, *The Best of John W. Campbell*, there are no stories which were written later than 1938.

To be sure, *The Moon Is Hell*, the longest of his fictions, appeared thirteen years later. But by then it was in some respects already out of fashion; and three decades later it has become a historical curiosity, for its premise is frankly outdated. The novel tells the story of the first successful lunar expedition. The moon was to be explored by a large, privately-financed American expedition, the members of which would spend a year collecting scientific and commercial data about the far side, then return on a large rescue ship that was to be sent for them. The book thus embodies that greatest of all themes of early science fiction, the exploration of space. Since Campbell has his second spaceship crash, he is able to develop numerous other themes common in the 1930's and 1940's; human fallibility, both physical and moral (the explorers being subjected to various diseases, accidental injuries, and betrayal by one of their own number); self-reliance (the overcoming of all the lunar perils and human shortcomings being possible only through a combination of pluck, courage, and good fortune), and, most important, the superiority of the scientific method, (at the very least, assuring survival until the marooned party is rescued, and at best leading to material progress).

The chief merit of *The Moon Is Hell* is its embodying of these themes in a cleverly contrived series of incidents. Never mind that among the opening events the placing of the lunar base on the far side (out of radio contact with the earth) seems irrational, and the crash of the relief ship too pat; these are mere details. Campbell's interest really lies in the problems created by these events and in the vindication through them of modern science and engineering. The problems are grave. Lack of air, lack of water, and lack of food are compounded by the inability to communicate with earth to explain the predicament. Clearly, each of these difficulties poses two questions, one intellectual, the other psychological. First, how can each major problem be reduced to a scientific or technical puzzle, to be solved with the resources at hand, preferably before a crisis is reached? Then, how will the members of the expedition cope with the pressures induced by the constant potentially fatal struggle with an alien environment?

Since the emphasis in *The Moon Is Hell* is on answers to questions of the first type, the reader is invited to see the terrifying situation of the lunar explorers as a series of increasingly complex engineering problems. How does one get water? One finds a large deposit of gypsum nearby and bakes it, forcing its decomposition into water and calcium sulfate. How does one get oxygen? One produces it by electrolysis from the water. Where does one get the electricity for this process? One builds large banks of storage batteries and converts solar radiation into power to be stored. Later, one builds steam engines (hydrogen-fueled, naturally, that element being plentiful as a result of the electrolysis). How does one solve the problem of heat and storage space? One constructs a huge underground complex in the gypsum mines; it can be pressurized (there is plenty of oxygen) and heated (there is plenty of hydrogen fuel). How does one get the various minerals one needs for all these activities? One mines or makes them, employing all the ingenuity that confrontation with the bizarre environment brings out. For instance, one can make tools for mining by solidifying mercury at the near absolute zero temperatures that prevail in a lunar shadow. How does one get food? One manufactures it from the chemicals at hand.

Along the way, Campbell slights the probing of the nonrational side of the situation. There is a villain of sorts — Bender, who steals the carefully rationed food so that he alone will survive to sell the moon's lode of diamonds, and who is eventually tracked down and executed. There are also heroes — Long, who is literally frozen solid returning from an attempt to carry a message fifteen-hundred miles for radio and heligraph transmission to earth; and Moore, who suffers terribly in testing his synthetic foods on himself for the benefit of the whole party. But they are only stereotypes, lacking any real individuality. Campbell simply provides ideas (or ideals) of people: the greedy entrepreneur, the foolhardy but well-meaning youth, the chemical genius, along with other equally familiar characters from formula fiction and the movies, including the laconic leader, the selfless second in command, and the marvelous mechanic. The occupational label hung on each tells us little about him, for we seldom see any of the characters actually working in their ostensible disciplines. Consequently, the reader has great difficulty in empathizing with the characters or in probing beyond their most superficial aspects.

Hence, the plot is made to carry the didacticism nearly alone. It moves rapidly and predictably along the lines indicated above. Problems are encountered, reason and effort are applied to them, and solutions are found. Each new problem is more complex than the last, each succeeding solution more difficult to effect. Unfortunately, Campbell seldom hesitates to provide a *deus ex machina* when the going gets too tough. Until the *final* problem, that is — the discovery that the synthetic foods created from moon rocks are insufficient in the long run to sustain life. The problem is almost a mystical one. Only if there are molecules present which were once living, Campbell tells us, can any chemical support life. Earth scientists working on the solution, using chemical formulas relayed by Moore once a communications link has been established, discover "the hitherto unguessed vitamin-like RB-X . . . in every form of living matter." Their efforts permit the rescue party, which comes upon a comatose group of survivors suffering from ghastly forms of malnutrition, to revive seven of the thirteen who were living when the first relief ship crashed. They have triumphed, surviving more than eight months by their wits and persistence; their work bequeaths to the human race a fully operational, permanent moon base, along with a number of inventions and refinements of technological processes.

Once a popular work, *The Moon Is Hell* suffers less today from these intrinsic flaws (although they are significant) than from external circumstances. It has been, in contemporary government jargon, "OBE" — overtaken by events. The 1982 date for the expedition is now preposterous. Men first walked on the moon in 1969, although no large expedition like this one was planned at all. The profit-making motive of the exploration is equally absurd, for we know now that only powerful governments have the enormous resources required to mount any space effort — and, through a crushing irony, only bureaucracies, not entrepreneurs, have the will to do so. Campbell has projected into our time a 1930's view of society; and it is an unrealistic view seemingly grown out of middle class aspirations and *The Saturday Evening Post* covers. For all the references to atomic war and the Mount Palomar telescope (which date the book around 1950), the feel of Campbell's work is of an earlier period that we have now left far behind, although it was close enough to readers of the first edition to make the work a success.

In part, this success speaks to the traditional "sense of wonder" in science fiction. The moon, as Campbell describes it, has the feel of reality. The intense cold, the terrifying lack of air, the awkwardly light gravity that the narrator laconically describes, all ring true even after the Apollo missions. Although the geological and chemical composition of the area around the base now seems unrealistically convenient, the details of life in the unfriendly environment still have power. The moon is indeed hell by any terrestrial standard. The historical significance of the work, the last and longest piece of fiction by the most renowned of editors, should not blind a contemporary reader to its shortcomings. By the same token, those shortcomings should not obscure the power of the realization of setting and of the swift, well ordered plot.

The novella has, from the first, appeared together with an even shorter work, "The Elder Gods." This story, originally published in 1939 under the Stuart pseudonym, differs radically from *The Moon Is Hell*. Essentially fantasy, "The Elder Gods" recounts the labors of Daron, a seafarer under the loose control of the anthropomorphic Elder Gods of the island kingdom of Azun. He is given the task of overthrowing the newer gods, the Invisible Ones, who have won over the Azuni, turning them from a nation of sea rovers into an indolent, effeminate race. Here Campbell is working with a wholly different formula, one used with great effectiveness by Robert E. Howard in the Conan stories. Accordingly, the style is lusher, the action deliberately less plausible and more extravagant, the characterizations stereotyped along different lines. Since the story hints that it is set in the distant future, one may theorize that the Elder Gods are actually scientists paternally attempting to save the Azuni from decadence. (Campbell was a staunch, vocal political conservative.) But Arthur C. Clarke's dictum holds: Any sufficiently advanced technology is indistinguishable from magic; and magic it is, in the hands of the Elder Gods.

This story confirms the correctness of Campbell's approach in *The Moon Is Hell*. The ratiocinative process in science can be as exciting as swords and sorcery. Having become jaded by technical accomplishments, we may have lost the ability to appreciate certain qualities that science fiction used to have when Campbell was at his editorial and authorial best.

William H. Hardesty III

Sources for Further Study

Reviews:

Analog. XLVII, June, 1951, pp. 130-131.

Galaxy. II, April, 1951, pp. 59-60.

Magazine of Fantasy and Science Fiction. II, August, 1951, p. 83.

Startling Stories. XXIII, May, 1951, p. 23.

THE MOON POOL

Author: Abraham Merritt (1884-1943)
First book publication: 1919
Type of work: Novel
Time: The early twentieth century
Locale: The South Pacific

A science-fantasy adventure of two men determined to prevent the annihilation of mankind by a cosmic vampire, the Dweller in the Moon Pool

Principal characters:
DWELLER IN THE MOON POOL, an androgynous cosmic vampire
DR. WALTER T. GOODWIN, a famous American botanist
LARRY O'KEEFE, an Irish-American air ace and adventurer
OLAF HULDRICKSSON, a giant modern Viking
MARAKINOFF, a sinister Soviet scientist
YOLARA, the dark priestess of the Dweller
THE SILENT ONES, the wise prehuman guardians of the Dweller
LAKLA, the handmaiden of the Silent Ones

Abraham Merritt's *The Moon Pool* was originally published in the *All-Story Weekly* on June 22, 1918. With considerable textual changes, it was reissued the next year in combination with a sequel, *Conquest of The Moon Pool*. Many contemporary critics seem unable to understand its popularity, either then (readers of Hugo Gernsbach's *Wonder Stories* voted it their all-time favorite science fiction work) or now (it has gone through numerous printings and sold millions of copies). By modern literary standards the novel is certainly overwritten. Merritt's style is characterized by lush imagery, colorful rhetoric, and extremely detailed descriptions. His basic pulp-adventure plot is studded with romantic symbols and "poetic" images, and his prose style is in diametric opposition to that of "hard" science fiction, though particularly suited to its own subgenre of scientific romance or science fantasy. To the readers of pulps in the 1920's Merritt was known as the "Lord of Fantasy."

There are a number of stylistic problems in the work: excessive use of colors and hyperbole, weak repetition, too obvious foreshadowings, unanswered questions, and a somewhat stilted and artificial dialogue. Merritt writes, as his character Larry O'Keefe speaks, in "florid imagery." To contemporary readers Merritt may at times seem sexist and racist as well. His images of men and women are frequently trite and clichéd (the strong, stubborn, honest male; the virginal, good, and clinging female), and the opposition of white man and South Seas native is obviously outdated. Yet his images and language are often sensuous, vivid, and memorable, even marvelously ornate, in the style of E. R. Eddison. He effectively uses suspense and dramatic tension to sustain his story and creates an interest and excitement in the reader which is remarkable.

Critics have also objected to the many scientific inaccuracies in the novel.

Yet the science of *The Moon Pool* is at best quasi-science, a tool of the plot. The supposedly advanced technological devices, the astronomical theories, such as the theory that the moon was wrenched from its original bed in the South Pacific leaving a huge underground cavern to be peopled by a now lost race, and the theories of physics are seen as imaginative wonders, not scientific facts. Merritt is examining the role of science and the moral responsibility of the scientist in the modern world, and the central character, America's top-ranked botanist, learns that his scientific world view is not broad enough. All natural phenomena may not be explicable; the existence and mystery of the numinous, if not the supernatural, is real.

The basic plot concerns the discovery of a lost world at one of Earth's unexplored places, a prehuman civilization governed by a numinous being which embodies both good and evil. The people of this lost world are threatening to invade and conquer our surface Earth. Their technology is far more advanced than ours, and their doomsday weapon is a being which feeds on any human in its path. Four Earth men embark upon a heroic quest to prevent the Earth's conquest and protect life on Earth. After one of the men joins the opposing forces, the remaining three become the guardians of our world, much like the Nine Companions in *The Lord of the Rings*. It is their job to prevent Earth's conquest.

The narrator, like Melville's Ishmael, returns alone to tell the tale. He is Dr. Walter T. Goodwin, the botanist, whose authority is reinforced by a "Foreward" reputedly written by the President of the International Association of Science. Merritt uses the device of an imaginary authority, much as Lovecraft was to do so well in *The Necronomicon*. The "Foreward" is not only an attempt to give pseudoscientific respectability to the text, but also to set its limits. Though we may be told of the narrator's experiences, the Association is withholding technical information which is too menacing for distribution to the general public. It will only be published in scientific journals.

Goodwin, classified as an official "hero" by the Executive Council of the Association, represents the standard scientist of literature. He is courageous, determined, and reliable, a believer in fact and fact alone, the intuitive and the mysterious are not for him.

Each of his three companions represents a particular type of man. Larry O'Keefe is an Irish-American lieutenant in the Royal Flying Corps of the British navy. We discover him sitting calmly atop the remnants of his seaplane which has crashed in mid-ocean. This devil-may-care adventurer believes in a life of Blakean excess and the kingdom of Fäerie. The creatures and beings he meets are related to those in Irish mythology. He is the natural man to whom the one mystery in life is death. Another of the characters, Olaf Huldricksson, is found tied to the wheel of his boat. The "Shining Devil" has taken his wife and child, and this modern Viking, the man of action, is out to avenge them. Like O'Keefe, he believes in the "old gods," in this case those from Norse mythology. The fourth man, the traitorous "villain," is the sinister, deceitful Soviet scientist Marakinoff (a German in the original version), who fully accepts the scientific dictum that only the factual is real. His personal philosophy is never apologize, never explain.

In the lost world of Muria these four meet an interesting variety of beings and creatures, who are the source of much of the novel's fascination. Arrayed against them they find the politico-religious leaders of the dominant race in the Murian caste system. Yolara, the leader, is the Murian Lilith, the perilously beautiful and naturally cruel seducer, the queen of hell. Lugur is her satanic consort, the personification of power without humility, of pride, ambition, and callous indifference. But the real enemy is the Dweller in the Moon Pool, the "Shining One." This creature of living light is an amoral androgyne which incorporates a whole series of paradoxical polarities: good and evil, rapture and horror, ecstasy and despair, heaven and hell. It is simultaneously totally blessed and totally accursed. It feeds from a series of seven glowing lights of various colors, calling people to death with an unearthly crystalline music, and then feeding on their life forces to make itself stronger. The victims become "dead-alive," and their bodies are used as soulless slaves. Here then is the familiar figure of the vampire, but on a cosmic level, one which threatens to devour and destroy all of humanity.

The existence of the creature raises questions which are thematically central to the novel, questions with implications for the narrator and the reader. The first question is whether alien beings have values which correspond to human values. The novel's answer is clearly no, particularly with regard to a sense of justice, morality, and the value of human life. The second question, of whether there is a God that rules over the entire universe is more difficult to answer. Three possible "religions" are presented, yet each falls short of answering the question through their failure to deal with the Dweller in the Moon Pool. The Murians have an eschatalogical religion which is primitive and superstitious; a Hindu-like pantheon of gods is governed by a remote, unheeding maker and ruler of all. Yet the traditional Judeo-Christian Father who cares for and looks after his children is also shown to be unscientific and superstitious. Even science fails to comprehend the ineffable mystery of the Dweller.

The solution to the dilemma of dealing with the creature of the Moon Pool provides the answer. There are three sentient beings, the Silent Ones, who created and still watch over the creature, but no longer control it. The Silent Ones are part of a prehuman race, the Taithu, who are radically removed from man's ancestral sources; born close to the Earth's core (a greater source of strength than the sun, they say), they have spent aeons exploring the mysteries of the universe. Together with the Universal Mother, the matrix of matter, they created the Shining One from the spirit of life itself as a means of learning more than they could on their own. Yet their pride and their love for their own creation has kept them from destroying it even after it became destructive. These three beings are wise, holy, and self-realized. They claim that there is a cosmic energy, or consciousness, which flows through the whole universe, a pantheistic or pan-entheistic God. The Silent Ones are assisted by their hand-maiden Lakla, the golden-eyed, blond-haired embodiment of goodness, innocence, and love and by the batrachian Akka, the frog people.

Yet the powers of the Silent Ones are not enough to destroy the Dweller; what is needed as well is human courage and love. Love, in fact, is what replaces God as the creative power in this novel; it is seen as the pulse of the universe, "the real music of the spheres of which Plato dreamed"; it is "stronger than death, immortal as the high gods, and the true soul of all that mystery we call life." Only when Larry, Lakla, and Goodwin are willing to sacrifice themselves to the Dweller for all of humanity, do they weaken it enough for the Silent Ones and the Taithu to destroy it. At the novel's close Goodwin struggles with Marakinoff, and through chance, Marakinoff is drowned and Goodwin thrown back up on the shores of Nan-Tauach, alive to return and tell the story. Larry remains behind and Olaf has died in battle.

Merritt has used an imaginary geography and historical narrative for authenticity (much as Tolkien did with Middle Earth), as a framework to show how a man of science may be transformed and how the observer and analyst of facts may come to believe in intuition, unseen mysteries, and the existence of the soul. Goodwin has pierced the veils of illusion and reality and discovered that science is as illusory as religion, that our world is not necessarily as we see it, and that what sustains, ennobles, and transforms a person is finally the courage to love.

Clark Mayo

Sources for Further Study

Criticism:

Mitchell, Stephen O. "Alien Vision: The Techniques of Science Fiction," in *Modern Fiction Studies*. IV (1958), pp. 346-356. Mitchell uses *The Moon Pool*, which he considers typical of the genre, to illustrate the techniques of science fiction.

Reviews:

Bookman. L, February, 1920, p. 627.
New York Times. November 23, 1919, p. 671.
Springfield Republican. December 14, 1919, p. 8.

MORE THAN HUMAN

Author: Theodore Sturgeon (1918-   )
First book publication: 1953
Type of work: Novel
Time: The present
Locale: The United States

The coming together and growing to maturity of a group of misfit individuals with parapsychological talents into a gestalt *entity, with the potential not only to transcend, but also to assist the human race in its survival and progress*

Principal characters:
> LONE, a telepathic idiot who brings the *gestalt* into being
> GERRY THOMPSON, a paranoid telepath who inherits the group from him
> JANIE, a telekineticist who helps the group attain balance
> HIPPOCRATES BARROWS, a victim of the *gestalt* who becomes its conscience

In the hearts of most science fiction readers, there is a warm spot for Theodore Sturgeon's sentimental tales of wish fulfillment, which often barely subscribe to the tenets of hypothetical plausibility that separate true science fiction from the rest of fantasy. Probably for no other work is this affection stronger than for *More Than Human*, winner of the International Fantasy Award for 1953. Essentially a fairy tale, it offers hope that even the least promising of heroes can harness their wishes, draw comfort from each other, and achieve a kind of godlike stature. The means to these ends is parapsychology, forging into a dependable tool or technology the power to make what you want come true by controlling how you wish for it. Using a classically simple vocabulary, an imagistic style, and an array of formal literary devices relatively rare in science fiction before the 1950's, Sturgeon turned stereotyped characters and clichéd situations into a warmly human narrative commonly rated a classic of the genre.

It is not uncommon in commercial science fiction for a novel to be expanded from a successful novella, the result usually being a labored sequel, padded with irrelevant detail. The original in this case was so perfectly self-contained that a sequel in the ordinary sense would have been unthinkable. What Sturgeon did instead was to surround it with two more novellas, formally at variance with the original, showing how its events came into being, and how its central problem eventually was resolved.

Part One, "The Fabulous Idiot," composed of loosely related impressionistic sketches, introduces a number of misfits, some of whom gather together under the protection of Lone, an "idiot" with hypnotic, telepathic powers. The story opens with Lone's being brought to conscious awareness by a bizarre, unconsummated love affair with innocent Evelyn Kew, the repressed fifteen-year-old daughter of a sexually obsessed maniac. Almost killed by her father,

Lone is nursed back to health by a farm couple named Prodd, who "miraculously" educate him to minimal tasks and vocabulary. A succession of other characters are then individually introduced, some of whom do not become important until later parts of the novel. Touching lightly on Gerry Thompson, Hip Barrows, and Evelyn's older sister, Alicia, Sturgeon picks up the thread of the first novella again with the telekinetic Janie and the teleporting Negro twins, Bonnie and Beanie. Victims of nature and neglect, these three make friends after a fashion, and escape into the woods, soon to be joined by Lone, though he doesn't know why. When Lone adds to their number the Mongoloid son of the Prodds, "Baby," who communicates with Janie through semaphore-like gestures, the group begins to "blesh," (blend/mesh). After Lone uses their abilities to make an antigravity machine to replace the broken wheel of a truck the Prodds left behind, Baby explains that the group is a special entity, one that with Lone at its head is considerably less than the sum of its parts.

Part Two, "Baby is Three," is slightly modified from its original version (*Galaxy*, October 1952), the difference coming in its conclusion. Gerry, now fifteen years old, relives in one afternoon, with the aid of a psychotherapist, Stern, the momentous seven years since Lone picked him out of the gutter. Ostensibly seeking the answer to why he killed his "governess," Miss Kew (Alicia), Gerry encounters internal resistance to the phrase, "Baby is Three," the truth of which seems unchanged over time. When Lone died three years before this session, and Gerry brought the group to Miss Kew for care, that phrase loosed from her telepathically a flood of memories of Lone and of her attempts to help him understand the entity of which he was a part. Now able to deal with that memory, Gerry overcomes the block which repressed it, and realizes her love and kindness had begun to threaten the group's togetherness. Unlike the novella, where Miss Kew's death is imaginary, she really is dead, and Gerry is hardly "cured," as Stern in fact points out. Having accomplished all he set out to, however, Gerry is only interested in paying for Stern's help and getting away, erasing all record of the marathon session from the therapist's tape recorder and his mind.

The plot of Part Three, "Morality," parallels its predecessor, concerning as it does another person trying to recover lost memories. This story, however, is told from outside (Gerry narrates his own story), and Gerry himself is the cause of another person's problems. Janie plays Stern to Hip Barrows, whose memories include a well-to-do childhood and youth, in which he took for granted his intelligence, education and good fortune. His downfall was discovering signs of Lone's antigravity machine and trying to unravel its mystery against the wishes of Gerry, who feared the group would be discovered and exposed. Overcoming Gerry's hypnotic commands with Janie's help, he reconstructs his past, and recognizes his own need for humility; Hip then learns of Janie's connection with the *gestalt*, now pathologically withdrawn under

Gerry's paranoid leadership. Curiosity and obligation overcome his fear and Hip accompanies Janie to the Old Kew mansion, where he succeeds in making Gerry ashamed. As the group recognizes through Hip their kinship with the human race, they are welcomed to adulthood by the mental voices of other groups of their kind.

Since the reader knows in advance about the group, the surprise of the central novella, still a tightly-knit mental detective story, is lessened. But the loss is offset by the story's subordination to a marvelous tale of growing up, not only for the *gestalt* but also for its individual human components. Misfits, unwanted by society, Lone and the children share a need for love, as well as the talents their need has brought into being. The support group they form offers a buffer against the world and nurtures their complementary talents; once they can overcome the insecurities of adolescence, they will have enormous potential for good. An idiotic "thing" in Part One becomes a paranoid *gestalt* in Part Two, finally blossoming in Part Three into a mature member of *homo gestalt*, a race of immortals which lives unobtrusively among the human race, and helps to guide its destiny.

As "science fiction" in any rigorous, materialistic sense of the term, the book is wildly improbable, depending for our rational assent on our acceptance of Gerry's explanation to Stern, using vocabulary lifted from the therapist's own mind:

> I'm the central ganglion of a complex organism which is composed of Baby, a computer; Bonnie and Beanie, teleports; Janie, telekineticist; and myself, telepath and central control. There isn't a single thing about any of us that hasn't been documented: the teleportation of the Yogi, the telekinetics of some gambers, the idio-savant mathematicians, and most of all, the so-called poltergeist, the moving about of household goods through the instrumentation of a young girl. Only in this case every one of my parts delivers at peak performance.

Since this "documentation" is suspect at best, Sturgeon's later definition of "science fiction" as "wisdom" (*scientia*) literature might be more appropriate, though along with this higher wisdom the reader must also accept antigravity, a secret conspiracy of immortals, and some hefty coincidences. Sturgeon is on far safer ground in his fictional handling of these parapsychological gifts; in the telling of the story they become relatively simple exercises in technology, carried out before our eyes with a minimum of explanation.

The novel opens with Lone exhibiting his hypnotic talent for survival, not consciously understanding what he does. At various points we see Bonnie and Beanie vanish and reappear, either for fun or profit, denying the barriers of solid walls and considerable distances. Gerry's powers are demonstrated on Stern and Hip; Janie's telekinesis is exhibited in such actions as the squeezing of vital organs and the elimination of bodily fluids. Least directly observable is Baby's rapid-fire analysis and synthesis, though the effects of his thinking, filtered through Janie, are manifest. Since the reader observes at first hand the exercise of these powers, their rationalization is more a matter of literary technique than of the elucidation of a theory satisfactorily explaining their existence.

There are explanations implicit in the novel, however, related both to the hypothetical development of parapsychological talents and to the process of learning to live with them. In the first case, the story implies that sufficient need will trigger the exercise of psi powers, which may be universally latent. Their apparent rarity can be explained away by secretiveness, restrictive and conformist education, failure to form mutual support groups, and/or overexposure of one's talents, resulting in massive social retaliation against their effects while denying the causes.

Learning to live with these powers is the main subject of the novel, which has strong allegorical overtones for the real world in which such powers are not normally so conveniently available. The *gestalt*'s growing up may be likened to that of a sensitive child who feels neglected, and compensates not only with fantasies of supranormal powers, but also with the development of a talent for representing these fantasies in art. Beyond the autobiographical level, however, the story has resonance for its readers in terms of helping them imaginatively to overcome their frustrations with the complex, often intractable nature of the physical and social world in which they live. The child in us is always impatient with the need to learn how to manipulate nature, within the limits of the possible, and to persuade or manipulate people who are not convinced of the desirability, for them, of our plans. We all flirt with magic at times, in the form of wishes, curses, prayers, or rituals whose latent intent is to procure benefits by means of words or thought alone.

The *gestalt*, and its individual members, successfully accomplish what we desire, but not without effort. Although they are little hampered by the laws of physics, they are still subject to the problems of growing up, which their extraordinary powers may magnify rather than diminish. In order to maintain their autonomy, Janie and the twins run away from home, Gerry has to leave the state school, and Hip must recognize his dependence on others. Gerry's compulsion to kill Miss Kew results partly from the need to protect the still immature *gestalt* from her smothering love and disbelief. But it is also due in part to his need to exorcise the memory of at least mental incest. Penetrating her mind as Lone had before him gave Gerry a traumatic vision of the mental and sexual relationship between her and Lone, figurative mother and father of the *gestalt*.

Adolescence is a further trial, since the megalomania and insecurity normally associated with this stage of life are aggravated by the special nature of the *gestalt* and the knowledge that it has had to kill to survive. His megalomania partly justified by the *gestalt*'s powers, Gerry goes so far as to identify himself *as* the *gestalt*, not simply its "telepath and central control." His actions subsequent to regaining his identity in Stern's office are self-aggrandizing, to such an extent as to risk social repercussions against the group, as well as to impair its functioning as a group. Janie brings home his dependence by refusing his orders, not even giving him access to Baby's thoughts, without which he is as isolated from the group as the group is from humanity. The solution, finally, is to bring Gerry face-to-face with one of his victims, one who is similar enough to Gerry for him to see himself from outside. Reaching maturity and mental health requires a sublimation of the will to power, not just using it for revenge on the society which neglected him as a child, but rather developing a sense of obligation toward the race from which the whole group sprang.

The psychological solution is reasonably sound, a satisfying conclusion to a novel whose elements strain toward a happy ending. The fragmentation of Part One only makes sense as the characters come to a consciousness of themselves as a group. The reconstructions of personality in Parts Two and Three, though they parallel each other in direct and indirect ways, also converge toward conjunction with the already established *gestalt*. This formal resolution then goes a step further, achieving the kind of unexpectedly happy ending J. R. R. Tolkien called a "eucatastrophe." The mental voices of others of its kind and the *gestalt*'s forced isolation, bringing it and the reader a sense of belonging which transcends the ordinary barriers of space and time.

Though unexpected and perhaps stylistically overblown, this ending is archetypally representative of the style of *More Than Human*:

> Here was one who had whistled a phrase to Papa Haydn, and here was one who had introduced William Morris to the Rossettis. Almost as if it were his own memory, Gerry saw Fermi being shown the streak of fission on a sensitive plate, a child Landowska listening to a harpsichord, a drowsy Ford with this mind suddenly lit by the picture of men facing a line of machines.

This impressionistic use of imagery evokes several sense impressions in rapid succession, creating an effect of complexity and immense potential with a surface clarity which is childishly simple. Its focus on discovery restates a motif used several times before; the conjunction of arts and science reflects the *gestalt*'s misfired achievement of antigravity and a later scene in Gerry's memory of the individual members of the group busy in Miss Kew's "classroom." Some of the characters are stereotyped (perverted Mr. Kew and his daughters, the mute Negro twins), the rags-to-riches story is conventional to a fault, and the tone is sometimes overly sentimental. But the book succeeds in making all these things seem new, as if seen for the first time. Improbable though it may seem in outline, *More Than Human* is not only believable in the telling, but it is all but inevitable in its fictional and psychological context.

David N. Samuelson

Sources for Further Study

Reviews:

Analog. LIII, June, 1954, pp. 144-145.

Future Science Fiction. V, June, 1954, pp. 88-89.

Galaxy. VII, March, 1954, pp. 116-117.

New Statesman and Nation. XLVIII, October 30, 1954, p. 554.

New York Herald Tribune Book Review. November 22, 1953, p. 19.

San Francisco Chronicle. December 27, 1953, p. 16.

Spectator. September 17, 1954, p. 350.

THE MORTGAGE ON THE BRAIN

Author: Vincent Harper
First book publication: 1905
Type of work: Novel
Time: The early twentieth century
Locale: London, Paris, Dresden

A didactic novel which promotes a materialist theory of the mind through an account of an electrical and hypnotic process which can bring about a complete change of personality

> *Principal characters:*
> ETHELBERT CROFT, a young doctor with an interest in psychiatry
> DR. YZNAGA, a brilliant psychologist
> LADY TORBETH, victim of a "personality disorder"
> VISCOUNT TORBETH, her husband
> DEAN CHELMSFORD, her father
> EDWARD TEMPLETON, an English man of leisure
> GERTRUDE LEIGHTON, the woman he loves

The theory of evolution, especially in the version put forward by Charles Darwin in *The Origin of Species* (1859), was one of the main imaginative stimuli responsible for the rapid proliferation of speculative literature in the late nineteenth century. It posed a fundamental question about the essential nature of man, put crudely but not inaptly by Benjamin Disraeli in an address to the Oxford Diocesan Conference: "Is man an ape or an angel?" The contemplation of the bestial nature which might be presumed to underlie the higher faculties and pretensions of the human mind prompted such classic speculative fictions as Stevenson's *Dr. Jekyll and Mr. Hyde* and Wells's *Island of Dr. Moreau*. It cast serious doubts upon the Enlightenment's faith in the moral perfectibility of man — and, indeed, challenged all previous assumptions about the origin and nature of human morality. The challenge was strengthened by the work of psychologists exploring the processes of human behavior, and in particular attempting to discover the causes of deviation from "normal" behavior patterns. The question of whether certain mental aberrations were to be considered signs of moral degeneracy or species of disease became a confused one, and the concepts of evil and illness became rather blurred.

In the seventeenth century René Descartes had popularized the classical dualist model of man as a mind (belonging to the realm of spirits) harnessed to a body (a "mechanism" belonging to the realm of matter). The mind was held to belong to the metaphysical context of theology, the body alone being subject to the empirical inquiries of science. By the turn of the twentieth century, however, this dualist perspective was strongly challenged by positivists and materialists, and the right of theologians to legislate on *any* matters of truth was disputed.

One of the most striking speculative fictions to come out of this materialistic crusade was *The Mortgage on the Brain* by Vincent Harper. The author
throws down the gauntlet in no uncertain terms in his Foreword:

> Signs are not wanting, that when speculative Science formulates its next hypothesis
> respecting life, very little will remain of what was formerly looked upon as the exclusive
> field of the metaphysician and the theologian. Recent revolutionising discoveries having to
> do with the functions and attributes of matter are fast bridging the chasm between psy-
> chology and physics. . . . "Mind" and "thought" and "spirit" are now being tossed into
> the melting pot of fearless analysis. . . . Out of it all is slowly but surely emerging the
> idea that ignorance and superstition long ago forged a Mortgage on the Brain of man,
> which it is high time to repudiate before the bar of reason.

The novel tells the story of a remarkable experiment conducted under the
aegis of the great psychologist Dr. Yznaga, whose subject is a young doctor,
Ethelbert Croft. The experiment is to test a technique which can then be used
to effect the cure of Viscountess Torbeth, a victim of the syndrome which
Yznaga describes as "complex personality." What this means is that the viscountess has interludes when she becomes another person, asserting a different
identity and behaving in an uninhibited fashion hardly suited to an Edwardian
lady (and especially not a *married* Edwardian lady). It is her father, Dean
Chelmsford, who first appeals to Croft for help, and Croft quickly wins the
confidence of Viscount Torbeth, though his initial attempts to see the patient
herself are frustrated.

Chelmsford is quickly disillusioned with Croft when the young doctor takes
him to see Dr. Yznaga. Chelmsford is appalled by Yznaga's ultramaterialistic
psychology and his denial that there is any such entity as the soul or the Ego
(in the theological meaning of the word). The dean cannot concede that the
"personality" is merely the product of the physical and electrical state of the
brain acting under external stimuli, and he not only withdraws his support
from Croft and Yznaga, but begins a campaign of vilification against them — a
campaign which they are ready enough to meet with their own ringing
polemics. Yznaga's aims in connection with the new science of the mind go far
beyond the crushing of superstition, for he believes that the ability of scientists
to manipulate and adjust the minds of their fellow men will be the means to the
attainment of a better and more rational society.

> Ah, God! for an opportunity to develop a race of healthy human creatures who know
> that happiness lies in a perfect conformity to law! No more bringing into the world of
> nervous wrecks; no more shrouding the beautiful truths of sex . . . with the resultant
> horrors of secret and illicit sin . . .; no more homes and streets thronged with men and
> women madly pursuing they know not what. . . .

Croft and Yznaga argue that if society is justified in legislating that all men
should be educated, and that certain standards of physical hygiene must be
maintained, then the next logical step must be the policing of mental hygiene.

Yznaga proposes to obliterate from Lady Torbeth's afflicted brain the extra personalities which compete for control of her being. In order to test the equipment to be used — a machine which delivers electrical current into the body while hypnotic suggestion demolishes and rebuilds memories — Croft volunteers to have his own personality wiped out and an entirely new one temporarily substituted in its stead. In a "trial run" he is hypnotized so that the identity of one Edward Templeton can be superimposed upon his own, and he spends some time traveling in Europe under the supervision of the hypnotist, acting out the part of Templeton though the Croft *persona* is merely submerged. The experiment proper begins when the identity of Ethelbert Croft is entirely obliterated, and that of Templeton substituted, so that Croft *becomes* Templeton, utterly and with no possibility of a reversion save by a second operation of the machine. Yznaga and his colleagues observe the whole process minutely, and are satisfied of complete success. However, the success is a little too complete, for Templeton, knowing nothing whatever of the experiment or the peculiarity of his circumstances, takes it into his head to go forth into the world, and disappears.

Templeton travels to Dresden, where he went during the first, uneasy phase of his existence, and there resumes acquaintance with an Englishwoman named Gertrude Leighton. The two of them fall in love, and are on the point of eloping when Templeton (absurdly, he thinks) is charged with being one Ethelbert Croft, and therefore guilty of fraud in conducting financial transactions in Templeton's name. Actually, the situation is worse, for the man who has identified him is Dean Chelmsford, who has also identified the woman with whom he has been seen in compromising circumstances as his daughter, Lady Torbeth.

Yznaga and his colleagues rescue Templeton easily enough from his legal predicament, and quickly restore the identity of Ethelbert Croft, but extricating Croft from the misinterpretation put upon his actions by Dean Chelmsford (and reported to Lord Torbeth) is altogether a more difficult task, especially in view of the fact that Croft, in his own *persona*, had previously met the more amorous version of Lady Torbeth (using the pseudonym of Muriel Errington) in London without realizing her true identity. The confusion is, however, cleared up in the end, and Yznaga is allowed to apply his treatment to the viscountess. The romance of Edward Templeton and Gertrude Leighton thus becomes one of the most curious love stories in the literature of the time, ending as it does in the utter obliteration of both lovers as if they had never existed.

The Mortgage on the Brain is melodramatic in style, and its highly convoluted plot has to rely on some rather awkward coincidences in order to maintain its network of mistaken identities and erroneous conclusions. Its most fascinating aspect, however, is its polemic in support of rigid materialism, and the rather unusual hope for the moral regeneration of society which is rooted in that philosophy. Despite twentieth century attempts to "lay the ghost in the machine" (the expression is Gilbert Ryle's) dualist thinking still holds sway to a surprising extent within a contemporary world view which is otherwise highly materialistic. Even today most readers would find Harper's uncompromising materialism and his merciless attack on the evils of superstition difficult to accept; we are, as Ernest Gellner has wryly observed, very reluctant to abandon "the anthropomorphic image of man."

The argument of the book, however, goes far beyond the championship of modern Sadducism; its central concern is with the moral question of whether one man is ever entitled to tamper with another man's mind. Harper envisions and defends a situation in which the dictatorship of social norms over individual behavior might become absolute merely by an appeal to "rationality." No one in today's world is likely to agree with him, but it is interesting that he puts the question in rather different terms from those which modern readers have become accustomed to. Most speculative descriptions of societies in which psychological engineering is extensively used, whether they are favorable (Aldous Huxley's *Island*) or unfavorable (Huxley's *Brave New World*), assume a dualist perspective which clearly begs the question. Harper's viewpoint is thus not so easy to dismiss as it first appears. If his materialistic account of the mind is largely correct, then the moral question of whether and how we may interfere with minds is shifted onto rather different ground. Since medical science has equipped us with many new ways of interfering with minds, ranging from ataractic drugs to prefrontal lobotomies, we often find it comfortable to evade the moral issue involved.

The Mortgage on the Brain is undoubtedly a blunt instrument in terms of its literary finesse, but it nevertheless poses a challenge to the reader which the passage of time has made more, not less, important.

Brian Stableford

THE MOTE IN GOD'S EYE

Authors: Larry Niven (1938-   ) and Jerry Pournelle
First book publicaiton: 1974
Type of work: Novel
Time: 3017, the one hundred and fourteenth year of the Second Empire of Man
Locale: The Trans-Coalsack Sector

An exploration of the problems arising from the first contact with intelligent aliens, told from both human and alien points of view

Principal characters:
>RODERICK HAROLD, Lord Blaine, the commander of battlecruiser *MacArthur*
>KEVIN RENNER, Sailing Master of the *MacArthur*
>SANDRA FOWLER, an anthropologist engaged to Lord Blaine
>HORACE BURY, a trader and traitor
>DR. ANTHONY HORVATH, Minister of Science for Trans-Coalsack Sector
>DAVID HARDY, Chaplain, Imperial Space Navy
>SENATOR BENJAMIN FOWLER, Chair of the Imperial Commission on Aliens
>THE MOTIES, the aliens

The Mote in God's Eye is ambitious in purpose and convincingly executed; despite some literary weaknesses the novel works, providing quality science fiction entertainment.

Although *The Mote in God's Eye* shares many characteristics of a space opera, it does not suffer from many of the historical weaknesses of that sub-genre. Typically in a space opera, the emphasis is on vicariously thrilling but frequently intellectually stultifying physical action; this novel has enough fast-paced action and suspense to satisfy an adventure story enthusiast. However, in addition to its space battles, the story includes an interesting intellectual puzzle; it is also a detective story in which two widely divergent cultures — human and Moties — must attempt to understand one another in order to satisfy their self-serving purposes. Also, each species must try to conceal its less favorable cultural characteristics which, if revealed, might make future contact undesirable and intergalactic war inevitable long before it is prepared to defend itself and/or annihilate the enemy.

In presenting and developing the mystery of the unknown alien, the authors also avoid another historical weakness of the space opera, which is to portray aliens one-dimensionally. Typically, these aliens lack specific and logically developed cultural, biological, and technological characteristics, and tend to personify some human vice such as greed, lust, or ruthlessness. The role of these physically grotesque, one-dimensional threats to humanity is to provide cannonfodder for the disintegrator ray guns wielded by larger-than-life humans. The Moties, however, are a unique species. Their culture is complex, reflecting and originating in their biological, historical, sociological, and technological evolution, and significantly, their culture is basically nonhuman.

Instead, in this case the characters lacking significant development are the human ones, who resemble the stereotypes of historical romances. The hero, Lord Blaine, for example, is a latter-day Horatio Hornblower, ruggedly handsome and decisive in action, although the victim of self-doubt. Lord Blaine's heroine is Sally Fowler, who is beautiful and wealthy, trivial and fatuous, a member in good standing of the Imperial Aristocracy and a doctoral candidate at the Imperial University of Sparta. Determined to make a name for herself as an anthropologist before settling down, her professional goals are nevertheless secondary to her primary purpose of "settling down"; she misses "what she thought of as girl talk. Marriage and babies and house-keeping and scandals: they were a part of civilized life." For an anthropologist, she is incredibly prudish; for example, while discussing the use of birth control devices by unmarried women, "her distaste was impossible to disguise." The representative military type is Vice Admiral Kutuzov, who is fiercely loyal to the Empire, and enjoys pretending to be a nineteenth century White Russian. On his ship, the *Lenin*, he burns candles before religious icons; in addition to drinking an inordinate amount of tea, he spends most of his time issuing abrupt, no-nonsense orders such as, "Da. Shoot." Then, there is Jock (Sandy) Sinclair. He is from the colony of New Scotland and, therefore, is a Chief Engineer, He has lines such as "Mon, we will nae show dirty pictures aboard this ship — and what with a chaplain aboard! Not to mention the lady."

These and countless other stereotypes are forgivable, perhaps, because they free the reader from character analysis, allowing him to concentrate, along with the Moties, on the densely detailed, although not particularly unique, history of mankind up to and including the time of the Second Empire of Man. This background is necessary to place in context the problems of a first contact between cultures from different worlds, and to indicate parallels between the two civilizations and their different evolutions. Human history is presented as cyclical; civilizations rise and fall, the collapses followed by Dark Ages. This pattern continues even after the invention of the Alderson Drive — a faster-than-the-speed-of-light form of transportation which enables mankind to escape from his crowded solar system and begin colonizing the planets of other stars. On the other hand, the Moties are bottled up in their overpopulated solar system. Among other effects, the Alderson Drive has given mankind an optimistic outlook, since it allows the belief that all problems have attainable solutions — a viewpoint not shared by the basically fatalistic Moties.

According to the facts of the authors' fictional history, during the colonization of the stars, the First Empire of Man was formed only to collapse as a result of the Secession Wars. To overthrow the First Empire many of the colonies, essentially feudal estates with typical divisions of labor and responsibilities, went to great lengths to extend their powers. One colony, the Sauron colony, attempted to breed a class of supermen warriors through genetic engineering. Following the Secession Wars, mankind returned to barbarism.

Eventually, the Second Empire of Man was founded by Leonidas IV of Sparta. The Second Empire, still technologically inferior to the First but slowly catching up, is a shaky coalition of colonies obviously modeled after the British Empire. It is ruled by the Imperial Aristocracy, membership in which is hereditary. The decision-making process is aided by a parliament made up of representatives of the colonies, and by such special interest groups as the Interstellar Trade Association and a Humanity League. The interests of the established Church are considered, also, but all final decisions are made in the interest of preserving and strengthening the Empire. Decisions are enforced by the Imperial Space Navy, which is capable of and quite willing to annihilate totally a colony and its planet in order to preserve the Empire. Admiral Kutuzov is called the Tzar because he once reduced a populated planet to molten lava.

Despite the Empire's military power, revolts still occur, and it is shortly after the revolt on New Chicago has been put down that a Motie probe is discovered entering the Empire from a previously unexplored region of the galaxy. Immediately, Lord Blaine, Commander of the *MacArthur*, is sent out to make contact with the vessel, which is powered by a light sail. Blaine is forced to attack the light sail when it fires on the *MacArthur*. The alien crew is killed.

The Empire then sends out a counterprobe to the unknown space of the Mote, a G-2 yellow dwarf thirty-five light years away. The Empire's probe is composed of two ships — the *Lenin*, is to avoid all contact with the aliens and to insure that the military secrets aboard the *MacArthur*, the contact-ship, are not learned by the Moties. The *Lenin* is under orders to destroy the *MacArthur* and its personnel if necessary to preserve the secrets of the Alderson Drive and the Langston Field, a shielding device. In addition to a full crew of brave and dedicated military personnel, the *MacArthur* houses the probe's scientific team, a collection of well-meaning fools in search of knowledge who are hopelessly convinced that the Moties pose no threat to the Empire. The *MacArthur* also carries two characters who are aboard only to advance the plot. Sally Fowler, whose presence is only thinly justified by her profession, is the only woman aboard, and is included to provide romantic interest; additionally, she functions as a spokesman for the Moties' interests. Horace Bury, called the Empire's trade representative despite the fact that the navy is collecting indisputable proof that he is a traitor, is the instigator of the New Chicago revolt. At first, Bury hopes to capitalize on the Moties but later wants only to help destroy them.

Eventually, the representatives of the two cultures meet, first aboard a Motie ship and then on Motie Prime, the aliens' home planet. To the scientists, it is soon apparent that the aliens are intellectually superior to humans. Their civilization is very old; technologically, they are more advanced than the

First Empire of Man, despite the fact that they have not yet discovered the Alderson Drive. In their metal-scarce solar system, devices are designed to serve multiple yet seemingly dissimilar functions, and when a specific device is no longer needed, it is miraculously reengineered to meet a new need. The complex Motie culture is based on a system of "industrial feudalism," in which cultural developments are the direct and logical result of the rigid demands of Motie biology. Each Motie fits into a caste system in accordance with his predetermined physical and psychological makeup. Similar to ants, Moties are born Masters, Mediators, Engineers, and so on. Only the Mediators are permitted contact with humans, since they are capable of empathizing so completely that they learn to think like humans while still maintaining their individual outlooks. However, on occasion, some Mediators become so confused by the multiple roles played by humans that they go mad. There is also a subspecies in the culture called mini-Moties, who are not intelligent, but who instinctively know how to construct and improve almost any machine or tool.

While the scientists are deeply involved in their investigations, an emergency occurs aboard the *MacArthur*, prematurely terminating the probe. Here the time sequence in the novel becomes complicated. When the expedition begins its return trip to the Empire, three crewmen, presumed dead after attempting a forced reentry into Motie Prime's atmosphere, are left behind. During the time the human probe travels through normal space to the nearest Alderson Jump Point and before three Motie ambassadors can join the returning probe, the story of the stranded crewmen is told. In these six chapters, which comprise a suspenseful and thematically significant portion of the novel, secret aspects of the Motie character are dramatized. As a consequence, the reader knows in advance those secrets which the expeditionary probe members must discover for themselves once they return home. A sense of urgency is created because the secrets of the alien mystery must be revealed if mankind is to survive.

Back on New Scotland, an Imperial Commission is established to determine the Empire's self-serving policy toward the Moties. The formulation of the policy includes considerable old fashioned politicking by pressure groups as the Commission constructs an interpretation of the nature of the Moties. The interpretation is made by attempting to pull together the information collected by the probe's military intelligence agents and the scientists: the anthropologists, astrophysicists, biologists, linguists, veterinarians, and xenologists. This list suggests how exactly the authors invented and presented the Motie culture. Simultaneously with the deliberations of the Imperial Commission, the Motie ambassadors are attempting to solve their alien mystery in order to determine the best approach for convincing the Empire to help them establish colonies outside their solar system. Furthermore, the Moties must discover in time to attempt to prevent its disclosure how close the Commission is to uncovering their terrible secret — that once they are allowed to enter the

Empire they biologically cannot help but threaten mankind's existence.

Once the species solve their respective mysteries and once official policies, attitudes, and positions are established, accompanied by appropriate actions, the novel closes in the best tradition of the historical romance. Marriages are made, promotions granted, and punishments dealt, leaving the reader to speculate comfortably about the manner in which the First Contact will ultimately influence the cultural evolutions of each species.

Al Muller

Sources for Further Study

Reviews:

Kirkus Reviews. XLII, August 1, 1974, p. 836.

Library Journal. XCIX, October 1, 1974, p. 2503.

Publisher's Weekly. CCVI, September 16, 1974, p. 54.

NABOU

Author: Günther Krupkat
First book publication: 1968
Type of work: Novel
Time: 1996
Locale: Lebanon

A mystery surrounds the brilliant Arab, Nabou Tebar, a being who appears so ageless and so in control of himself that he may be an extraterrestrial android

> *Principal characters:*
> WILL PERTENKAMP, a geologist, the narrator of the novel
> YAMINA FARAH, a female engineer, Pertenkamp's girl friend
> NABOU TEBAR, a scientist and commander of the "Sindhbad" expedition
> ABDUL MAKTABI, a professor of oceanography
> OSWIN HAYL, a cyberneticist
> CLIFFORD SHELDER, a physician and biologist

As in the science fiction of the West, the visitation of Earth by extraterrestrial beings is a prominent topic in the science fiction of Eastern European countries. As a rule, however, contact with the aliens does not take place in the novel's present, but is assumed to have happened in the distant past. It is a mystery which the story must unravel. In Günther Krupkat's East German science fiction novel *Nabou*, mankind has established contact with a planet, Meju, located three parsecs away from Earth. As a result of the distance, there is a twenty-two year time lag between communication sent and received. While waiting for the answers to transmitted questions, an expedition into the depths of the Earth is prepared. A subterranean U-boat called the *Sindhbad* will be propelled by jet engines through the solid crust of the Earth, much like a bathyscape moves through the ocean, drilling its way by means of special rays.

Its inventor Nabou is a brilliant man, but something of a mystery; he is coldly detached and unemotional, and appears to be about forty years of age. Will Pertenkamp, the hero of the novel first sees Nabou before he is introduced to him. Will observes Nabou stopping his car on a Beirut highway with superhuman agility to avoid running over a careless little boy on the road. Surprisingly, Nabou later denies ever having been involved in such an incident. Much later in the novel, the hero learns of another such occurrence. Nabou saved a man from drowning and later stoutly denied the very action that would have made him a public hero, even in the face of the same man whose life he had saved.

Much of the novel is taken up by the bathyscape expedition into the Earth's interior in search of new deposits of minerals. Nabou leads the expedition with a sure hand, but distanced from everyone. Only the beautiful Yamina Farah, with whom the narrator naturally enough falls in love, seems to be close to

Nabou, causing Pertenkamp to feel pangs of jealousy. The hero's soul searching and anxiety provide much of the narrative and psychological tension of the novel, although these elements are strictly on the level of popular romance fiction. If the hero had simply talked frankly with his beloved, he might have spared himself much emotional turmoil.

The expedition proceeds smoothly, with all the enthusiasm generated by such a pioneering effort. In the interior of the Earth the explorers discover caverns. They encounter, though never see, a dimly perceived slime presence in the dark, which leads them to speculation that an intelligent form of life might lie deep in the interior of the Earth. However, nothing comes of this speculation; it is only one further fantastic incident in the voyage of discovery. The climax of the expedition occurs when the subterranean ship, because of a malfunction of its sensory probes, gets stuck in a magma pocket and is in danger of destruction. With almost preternatural foresight, Nabou had ordered Pertenkamp to adjust the probes in a particular manner; considering the order meaningless, the geologist ignored the command, thus precipitating the near disaster. Nabou becomes furious and blames Pertenkamp (although an investigation later absolves Will of all responsibility). Both men do their best to save the ship, going out in asbestos suits in an attempt to keep it afloat. Once again, Nabou saves a life: only his strength allows him to haul Pertenkamp back before he is engulfed by the crystallizing masses of hot magma. Then, with the utmost presence of mind and uncanny navigation, Nabou saves the ship and manages to bring it back to the surface of the Earth.

During the expedition, Will learns about "biomats" from the cyberneticist Oswin Hayl, a proponent of these emotionless superior automatons which far surpass fallible and imperfect human beings. This leads Will to the conclusion that Nabou is probably a prototype of such a biomat (as they are called in East German and Soviet science fiction, or "android," to use the more familiar term), an organic automaton, secretly perfected and tested. Hayl ridicules this notion, declaring that the science of Earth is not yet so far advanced. Still, the idea remains lodged in Pertenkamp's head, and after the expedition is over, he pursues this notion further. One suspicious fact is Nabou's extraordinary memory. He was able to learn Malaysian in two weeks, and even years later was able to speak it perfectly without any practice in the interim, while others who had learned it with him had forgotten everything. This contrasts in a disturbing way with his lack of memory of things like the car incident.

Pertenkamp's inquiries produce some puzzling results. First, he finds out that his father had known Nabou — who was then exactly as he is today, a man with the outward appearance of a forty-year-old. Thirty years earlier a Nabou had been involved in the erection of a lunar station, contributing a major suggestion for the material to be used in the building of the domes. This would make him at least sixty years old; and even sixty years earlier a Nabou had saved a spaceship from falling into the sun, again excelling through his presence of mind and endurance. Can all these Nabous be the same person? If they are the same, how old is Nabou, and, more frightening, what is he?

Regrettably, no photograph exists of the first Nabou. His birth is not recorded anywhere either, for in the idyllic future of a united Earth that forms the background of the novel, personal records are no longer kept. The hero fails to learn any more about him, and Nabou himself volunteers no information, insisting that he is simply a normal human being like anyone else. Even a message from space found in his office, in the language of the extraterrestrial Mejuans, fails to provide any solution to the puzzle.

Up to this point, the novel is told in a straight-forward manner, with a clean, unadorned prose and no great literary pretensions. What follows, however, becomes more feverish and haunting. Walking as if in a trance, the protagonist follows Nabou into the hills of Baalbek, where he experiences communication with a bright globe. This pulsating object tells him that it is the sum of all human knowledge, and that Nabou is only a means for understanding human thinking. Struck by lightning from the globe, Will loses consciousness. When he recovers, he is in a hospital, where his quasimystic experience is dismissed as a hallucination, the product of a feverish brain. Only later, when the message that humanity has been waiting for arrives from Meju, is the mystery resolved.

There had been contact between the aliens from space and Earth six thousand years earlier, at which time they built a secret chamber into the terraces of Baalbek as a relay station for conveying information about Earth to their planet. This station has generated androids as resident observers on Earth, each serving for a period of two hundred years, who take an active part in human affairs. These observers are more perfect than human beings in many respects but mere tools, programed to forget minor incidents which do not serve their primary purpose in order to avoid cluttering their information banks with irrelevant data. Nabou Tebar was the thirtieth such observer, followed by Nabou Tebimar, the thirty-first of the Nabous.

Nabou is clearly not a masterpiece of science fiction. However, it is one of the finest examples of science fiction from the German Democratic Republic, where the genre still has a lot of catching up to do. By Western standards *Nabou* is hardly more than an acceptable juvenile novel, lucidly written with numerous puzzles and events that keep the reader's interest. The love story is slight, sentimental, and thoroughly conventional. The characterizations are largely one-dimensional. Nabou, the alien, is pure intellect, without emotions, much like Spock of *Star Trek*; his selectively perfect memory and his reasoning powers surpass those of man, but he keeps aloof and has no ambitions. Yamina, the only female character in the cast, is beautiful but not much else, acting merely as a focus for the longings of the hero, who himself is but a focus for the plot, with little interest as a person. The other figures are virtually nonexistent. True to the pattern of much science fiction from this part of the world, there is almost no action in the book; it even lacks a villain, and therefore much of the excitement that is often the only virtue of the poorer variety of science fiction is lacking. The theme and plot combine various favorite ideas of older and newer science fiction, such as the journey into the interior of the Earth, visitors from outer space, messages from the cosmos, encounters with aliens, and android life.

In contrast to many other novels from Communist countries, *Nabou* is free of preaching. The author implicitly assumes the existence of a better future world, and he makes a bow in the direction of the Arab world, with Arab characters and Arabic being a principal language of the world. Even the Mejuans address their messages to the Earth in Arabic. All this may be a fictional reflection of the wooing of the Arabs by the East Germans at that time, but there is no overt preaching about Communism as is so often the case with works from that part of the world. There is not even the usual lip-service to socialism that so many authors find necessary before they go on with the action (most often pure adventure, without any fundamental relationship to any kind of politics). One may assume that socialism has triumphed in this future world, but the political system of the world of the novel is only incidental and not even described in broad outlines. Krupkat, along with Eberhardt del Antonio, one of the better writers of the older generation of East German science fiction authors, is to be commended for this. He concentrates on the problems that interest him and which are fairly typical of science fiction from this part of the world, and he does so competently and responsibly.

Nabou is an ideal novel for a young audience, with some interesting technological details and a puzzle-plot. It is a good example of East German science fiction at its best, a middle-of-the-road story that is much better than the often naïve and crudely propagandizing other works from East Germany. Little science fiction from East Germany has been introduced into other countries, and almost none to the West, but this is a book that deserves a wider audience of young readers.

Franz Rottensteiner

LA NAISSANCE DES DIEUX
(Birth of the Gods)

Author: Charles Henneberg (1899-1959)
First book publication: 1954
Type of work: Novel
Time: A far future
Location: The Earth

Mankind is reborn after a catastrophe by means of survivors who take the roles of Greek and Nordic divinities

> *Principal characters:*
> GOETZ, the last poet
> SABELIUS, the last scientist
> BRUCE MORGAN, the last astronaut
> DONA, daughter of Sabelius
> STAR VENETA, her sister
> THE FÉRANULE, the last offspring of the first human species

La naissance des dieux was the first novel published by Charles Henneberg, five years before his untimely death in 1959. The epic inspiration that runs through the work is surprising for the time and earned the author the "Rosny Aîné" prize.

Charles Henneberg was a case apart in the first years of modern French science fiction, even as was his wife Nathalie, who took over after his death. He was of German origin and had lived as a soldier of fortune (including numerous years in the Foreign Legion) before launching a career in literature. All of his works give the impression of being a rather unsuccessful mixture of two cultures confronting each other.

La naissance des dieux begins with a cosmic catastrophe that demolishes all established civilization on Earth in a few hours. Three men, Goetz, Sabelius, and Bruce Morgan, succeed at the last moment in escaping, thanks to a mysterious machine dubbed "the accursed rocketship." Contrary to their expectations, the disquieting starship casts them onto a strange world and then disappears forever.

The planet "Géa" is revealed at the start to be entirely devoid of animal life, but covered by dense vegetation. Then a sort of living mist appears that launches the process of creation upon Géa. Indeed, the poet Goetz quickly discerns that he can shape this living mist into animate creatures by force of his spirit alone. Violent combat begins between Goetz and his two companions. They have been joined by two women, who also escaped from the cataclysm. "The accursed rocket" is actually a time machine whose force-field has caught the two women, Dona and Star Veneta, daughters of Sabelius and lovers of Bruce Morgan. Sabelius and Morgan create men and beasts to battle Goetz's horde of monsters, which are drawn from Greek mythology and prehistory. But soon they all come to understand that Géa is Earth in a far distant future, and that they are taking part in a new Genesis, the beginning of a new cycle.

Finally they encounter the Féranule, apparently a mixture of cat and frog, but in reality the last descendant of mankind. After Goetz kills this creature the final battle explodes between the accursed poet shut up in Hades and his adversaries who drive herds of mammoths along with the primitive men. Following this apocalyptic vision, a great calm descends upon Géa, and Morgan and his companions discover suddenly that the living mist has disappeared; creation has ended.

An astonishing and charming novel, *La naissance des dieux* stands alone in the ranks of that French science fiction of the 1950's which exists in contrast to the English language science fiction of the period. From his first work on, Charles Henneberg's impact was in his evocative power, which is constantly evident in his prose, a power that has its roots in a purely European mythology told with bardic flights of Norse sagas. It can be said that Charles Henneberg is more than a French author; he is really a *European* author: a writer who appeals to a collective unconscious that stems from a whole continent. This fact is even more true for the writings of his wife Nathalie (whose hand is also recognized in many passages of *La naissance des dieux*). She added all her Russian sensibility to the universe her husband created, in order to yield veritable *chefs d'oeuvre* of baroque writing, such as *La plaie* (*The Plague*, 1964).

The three principal characters, who draw creation for virgin Géa from the living mist, are, of course, exceptional characters, each quite different from the others. The sole tie that binds them is the disgust they feel for the life of their native decadent society. Here, one senses the soldier of fortune, Charles Henneberg, with his scorn of intellectualism and his praise of the astronaut and his courage.

His scorn veritably bursts out on the character of Goetz. Goetz, prince of poets, is a counterfeit, a misbegotten embryo of the tanks that give birth to all gracious specimens of men (the shadow of *Brave New World* hovers over the paragraphs devoted to Goetz's birth). But in his huge head perched on a spindly body, the poet has given birth to visions that enchanted the world at its end. Henneberg admits Goetz's charm at the outset, but only to emphasize through the consequences of his actions, that he must be mad in order to beget such visions. All the beauty and art he sets down on paper mask a soul convulsed by the worst phantasms, phantasms still more aggravated by the deformity and ugliness of Goetz.

This tormented spirit could only take an evil role in the new creation, could only beget monsters destined to imperil the other "Gods." Yet, by the same token, this evil role makes the force and courage of the others stand out because of their role; they are destined to become legends. Goetz's somber figure, deformed mentally and physically, represents the best possible background for illuminating the character of Sabelius and, above all, Bruce Morgan.

Of Sabelius, there is little to be said, except that he shows perfect military defiance when faced with a science he sees as injurious and dangerous to civilization. Sabelius is the scientist who suddenly has understood, but too late, the perversion of his research and who pays the price of his error. Goetz blinds him and thus deprives him of seeing the colors of the new world that he has helped create.

Bruce Morgan is the cherished hero of Charles Henneberg. An astronaut without fear and with a resplendent past, he plays the finest role in this creation. The true romantic dimension of the work is revealed through him. Demigod, hero, and God, he becomes the instrument of good, the character who uses true nature to oppose Goetz's horrible creations. He becomes the character who seeks his dearly beloved even down to Hades; he stops for nothing. In the final reckoning, he is the man whose good sense, uncontaminated by diverse civilized perversities, will permit him to guide the new humanity towards its destiny.

In the course of the plot, two women appear, two beings whom Henneberg characterizes as strongly as all the others. After all, are they not about to become the new goddesses of Géa? In any case, the sharp, uncalled-for opinions of Charles Henneberg upon women are presented again: on the one hand, there is the *femme fatale* who shrinks at nothing in order to arrive at her ends (Star Veneta promoted to new Venus), and on the other, the true-born woman, brave, who is made to be the ideal companion for the soldier (incarnated in Dona, Diana the Huntress of the Future). In brief, they are beautiful idols before whom rude savages throng to prostrate themselves.

Finally, the Féranule, the pathetic being no larger than a cat, remains the unforgettable character, the one whose fleeting image best stands out against the apocalyptic background of the novel. Perhaps this comes about because he may be the last of his kind, the last mutation of the men surviving the great catastrophe. He represents all mankind's weakness, but also that stubbornness that made mankind grand. Compared to the omnipresent Gods, he is nothing; and yet he is the sole being who still appeals to our higher feelings. His death had passed unnoticed; it leaves a large gap in the grand celebration that crowns the creation.

Thus, in *La naissance des dieux*, one deals with an extraordinary novel, its quality undiminished after twenty-five years. Perhaps this is due to the fact that it stirs us on an unconscious level with baffling imagination, breadth, and evocative power. To read *La naissance des dieux* is to feel the forces of nature unchain themselves, to see the primeval world rise up in the din of Olympian Gods at strife, and to experience something unique in the science fiction of the French language.

Yet there is a great paradox in the novel. It is probably the worst-written masterpiece of French science fiction. Charles Henneberg mastered his new language poorly, and his wife also was unable to eliminate all the monstrous blunders and grammatical errors in the story. From a purely literary viewpoint, the novel is at times a genuine disaster. Were it not for the verbal torrent that sweeps the reader along from beginning to end, it would be impossible to complete a reading of the book.

Confusion also reigns in the content. Greek and Norse mythology do not always mix well, not to mention the references to Egyptian sources that appear occasionally. The result is a confusion to those who have tried to make sense of the numerous deities and renowned myths which are revived and revised for this novel. The incoherence persists on other levels, paleontology for example: the most illustrative episode is one in which plesiosaurs and ichthyosaurs descend mountains to assault the mammoth herds led by Bruce Morgan and his men. These two species of dinosaur were aquatic and equipped only with fins. Such knowledge makes this scene completely bizarre.

One can multiply such examples of inaccuracy in this, Henneberg's first novel. Yet this scientific, mythic, and grammatical delirium results in an unexpected consistency, thanks to the spirit that animates the novel. *La naissance des dieux* rises from its incoherence as the phoenix from its ashes, ever more beautiful and ever more entrancing.

Richard D. Nolane

Sources for Further Study

Criticism:

The Encyclopedia of Science Fiction and Fantasy. Compiled by Donald H. Tuck. Chicago: Advent Publishers, Inc., 1978, p. 217. A vigorous writer in the field of French science fiction, Henneberg is discussed briefly here.

THE NAKED SUN

Author: Isaac Asimov (1920-   )
First book publication: 1957
Type of work: Novel
Time: An unspecified but distant future
Locale: The Earth and Solaria

A continuation of the exploration of the man-machine relationship begun in The Caves of Steel, *here broadened to examine opposing varieties of human frailty exposed in an interstellar murder investigation*

Principal characters:
ELIJAH BALEY, a New York City detective
R. DANEEL OLIVAW, a robot and representative of the planet Aurora
GLADIA DELMARRE, the wife of the murder victim
JOTHAN LEEBIG, a Solarian roboticist

In *The Naked Sun*, Isaac Asimov offers, as in his earlier work, *The Caves of Steel*, a convincingly crafted blend of two separate genres, science fiction and the traditional murder mystery, combined with a careful exploration of the relationship between man and machine. Here, however, Asimov takes his exploration a step further, lending the murder and its investigation an ironic balance of opposing human weaknesses, the first contributing to the mystery and the second to its resolution.

Asimov brings to the combination a notable reputation in each of the genres, and it is not surprising that he should succeed in blending the two forms. As with *The Caves of Steel*, the particular success of the work actually lies in the interdependence of the two parts, each requiring the other for its very existence. The murder of an eminent Solarian scientist is a baffling matter for the Solarians, since the low population and peculiar living conditions of Solaria have heretofore precluded any crime, much less murder. Therefore, it is the Earth detective Elijah Baley who is called to resolve the case. It is Asimov's skillful blending of the elements of two genres, at this point, that provides the complexity of the case.

At odds in resolving the mystery are the three traditional requirements for murder drawn from the mystery genre (motive, means, and opportunity) and the celebrated Three Laws of Robotics (taken from science fiction and in particular Asimov's own seminal works with the robot theme). Of the humans involved, Gladia Delmarre, the victim's wife, appears to be the only human who had the opportunity and motive to commit the murder, but not the means. Conversely, though a number of robots had the opportunity and were physically capable of committing the murder, the Three Laws of Robotics emphatically deny their committing or even allowing the act. Here, then, is presented the problem of willingness without capability on the one side, and capability without willingness on the other.

Further complicating the problem, and adding a certain pressure to the difficulties of the detective's job, are the political nuances involved. Earth is overpopulated, underproductive, militarily weak, and, therefore, both isolationist and isolated. It is embarrassingly subject to its children, the fifty Spacer planets, which all have low populations and high resources. They treat Earth and Earthmen with arrogant condescension. That the Solarians called in Baley, an Earthman, is a victory in itself. His task, however, made clear to him by the officials of his own government, is not only to solve the murder, but to show the level of competence on Earth and at the same time gather information to better his planet's position.

Baley is an adequate detective, more dogged than brilliant, more analytic and plodding than given to inspiration. The complexity of his task is magnified first by the political pressures, second by his total ignorance of Solarian society, and third by a particular frailty endemic to the people of Earth and a distinct handicap in this new society. Baley is subject to incapacitating agoraphobia; this fear of open spaces, sunlight and sky, distance and depth is a neurosis developed in the cities of Earth — crowded, sheltered, controlled places now the habitation of almost all men. This phobia, developed and manipulated in *The Caves of Steel* as a device affecting the course of the story, touches all Earthmen in varying, but always intense, degrees and limits their horizons as effectively as chains. For Baley, the prospect of venturing into space to Solaria is terrifying, and once there, his motion and mobility are strictly limited, a problem made more intense by the nature of Solarian society. At first, Baley spends the majority of his time learning to cope with his own terror, struggling to make progress in the murder case from the confines of his own prepared and sheltered quarters, and developing slowly his ability to tread tentatively and finally with growing assurance beyond the accustomed security of walls and ceiling, light switches and air conditioning.

Contrasting with Baley's physical weakness is the poised and polished perfection of the robot R. Daneel Olivaw, the partner assigned to him in the case. Olivaw is sent into the case by the world of his creators, Aurora, the oldest and strongest of the Spacer worlds. His task is to identify the Solarian problem and determine if it might affect Aurora. Possessed of all the physical capability and calm certitude that Baley lacks, a perfect imitation of a man — or perhaps an imitation of a perfect man — Olivaw has the potential to dominate the situation. He possesses a vast store of factual knowledge and the perfectly logical mind for assimilating data and drawing conclusions. During the first stages of the work, he is always far ahead of Baley, informed, competent, quietly decisive, and physically dominating. Yet for all his skill, he is only a robot, and if he knows the data and records the most minute detail of every event, he still does not know men and mankind. He first serves, as in *The Caves of Steel*, as an irritant to Baley, then as an associate, and finally as an assistant. Never in his remorseless robot logic is he able to make the intuitive leaps of which Baley is ultimately capable; never in his static physical perfection does he reach beyond the limits of his nature, as Baley ultimately does.

The only suspect in the murder is the victim's wife, Gladia Delmarre. Given the circumstances of Solarian life, it seems almost impossible, both to the Solarians and to Olivaw, that anyone else could have committed the crime, even though other circumstances — the absence of a weapon and the certainty that she could not have carried it away — deny this assumption. Gladia exhibits the conditioned response of all Solarians, an extreme abhorrence for the personal, physical presence of any other person, a neurosis as incapacitating in its way as the agoraphobia of Earthmen. This response is a product of the calculated isolation of Solarian life — a population of only twenty thousand is spread over the face of a world — and of the impersonal, genetically calculated birth and rearing of children beginning with fetal "farms" and steadily increased isolation from human contact. The Solarian phobia produces an incapacitating physical repugnance at the prospect of another's presence or the hint of a touch. This in itself, then, leads to general suspicion of Gladia, for spouses alone, and even then under the most strained conditions, are occasionally in each others presence. That another Solarian could have ventured within murdering reach of the victim is an unlikelihood too outrageous for the Solarians to consider.

This trait is most strongly demonstrated in the roboticist Jothan Leebig, a man to whom Baley's suggestion of actual presence rather than the common "viewing" is infuriatingly offensive. A conservative even by the standards of the Solarians, Leebig hides his fear of other people behind anger and arrogance, responding unwillingly and condescendingly to Baley's inquiry at first, then crumbling to shaken acquiescence in the face of Baley's threatening persistence.

These contradictory frailties, Baley's agoraphobia and the Solarian isolationism, provide continued complexity to the problem until at last Baley manages to escape the influence of his robot partner and his own fear. Having become confident and more competent himself, he is able, through the clues provided by his own weakness, to transcend the known facts and come to the possibilities: to combine the frailties of Earthman, the neuroses of Solarian, the limitations of machine, and thus finally to identify the single course through which murder could have occurred.

In its conclusion, the novel becomes grimly cautionary, evoking shadows of NASA's lunar retreat twenty years before the actual event. Baley achieves his success by overcoming his own weakness and manipulating the weaknesses of the Spacers, providing the victory and demonstration of competence demanded by his government. Beyond his victory, Baley realizes the characteristic weakness of Earth's inhabitants, an insight that requires him to lead others out of the safe womb of the Cities and into the open space he once feared.

Merrell A. Knighten

Sources for Further Study

Criticism:

Pierce, Hazel. "Elementary My Dear," in *Isaac Asimov*. Edited by Joseph D. Olander and Martin Harry Greenberg. New York: Taplinger, 1977, pp. 44-46. The merits of *Naked Sun* are discussed as a sequel to *The Caves of Steel*.

Reviews:

Analog. LIX, August, 1957, p. 147.

Galaxy. XIV, August, 1957, p. 115.

Magazine of Fantasy and Science Fiction. XII, April, 1957, pp. 82-83.

New Worlds. LXXIII, July, 1958, pp. 2-3.

THE NARRATIVE OF ARTHUR GORDON PYM

Author: Edgar Allan Poe (1809-1849)
First book publication: 1838
Type of work: Novella
Time: Late 1825; June 1827-March 22, 1828
Locale: New Bedford, Massachusetts; the South Seas, several islands, especially Tsalal; the South Pole region

A progressively grotesque and fantastic chronicle of Arthur Gordon Pym's nautical adventures

> *Principal characters:*
> ARTHUR GORDON PYM, the narrator, a young man
> AUGUSTUS BARNARD, his friend
> DIRK PETERS, a dwarfish, physically powerful, resourceful half-breed
> RICHARD PARKER, a surviving mutineer, casualty of the food struggle
> CAPTAIN GUY, Captain of the ship, the *Jane Guy*
> TOO-WIT, Chief of the black aborigines of Tsalal

One of the most important arguments for the ultimate significance of science fiction is that it has absorbed the function and appeal of other "dead" literary forms. When Brian Aldiss in *The Billion Year Spree* states that science fiction is *"characteristically cast in the Gothic or post-Gothic mould,"* he is not suggesting that it has taken over the ghosts and castles of that long passé, though once powerful form, but that it frequently speaks to the same psychological and emotional needs and responses once evoked by the Gothic at its best. An even more obvious form that has been absorbed into science fiction is the great sea epic.

For hundreds of years the open sea was the fundamental metaphor for both the fascination and the terror of the infinite. As a natural phenomenon, a psychological-spiritual experience, and an ultimate testing ground, the uncharted sea lured and frightened numerous speculative souls in life and in literature. But in the twentieth century the ocean's surfaces have been mapped and charted, and even its depths have been probed and photographed. If all is not yet known about it, it is now generally assumed that everything can be understood given time and research. Although still a fascinating subject for fiction, the sea has lost its essential metaphorical power and the era of the sea epic is certainly over.

Outer space is the obvious successor. If science fiction has not yet produced its Herman Melville or Joseph Conrad it is only a matter of time. And if there is merit in this hypothesis, then one of the primary documents in this evolution and one of the most important pre-science fiction works is Edgar Allan Poe's *The Narrative of Arthur Gordon Pym*, a work that combines qualities of both the Gothic and the sea epic.

Which is not to say that *The Narrative of Arthur Gordon Pym* is either a great sea yarn or a great early foray into science fiction. It is neither. While not as disjoined and badly written as some critics have suggested, it is certainly not the masterpiece proclaimed by others. At best it is a very interesting work, interesting primarily as Poe and only secondarily as early science fiction.

Disjointed and repetitious as it may appear, the novel does have a unity, although not one generated by careful plot construction. Having violated his own dictum regarding tight plotting by writing a long work, Poe suffers predicted consequences — diffusion, loss of control, uneven momentum, and unwanted ambiguities of character and theme. But it does hang together through a unity — or rather a controlled progression — of tone or, to use Poe's own terminology, manipulation of effect. Although the narrative lacks the directness and economy of his best tales, in the end, despite the work's indirection and fuzziness, it does succeed in evoking the desired responses.

The overall movement of the tale is from conventional — if exaggerated — mutiny-at-sea conflict to man-against-the-elements survival test, to quasiscientific expedition, to Gothic "lost world" fantasy, ending up in a mystical confrontation. Critics who have complained that these episodes are only tenuously connected, and especially that the second half of the book has little to do with the first, have failed to understand the book's design, because they have looked in the wrong places. Moreover, they have ignored the devices Poe uses to relate the parts to the whole; indeed, some of these devices have been dismissed as irrelevant and gratuitous bits of gory sensationalism.

Arthur Gordon Pym's first nautical sea venture acts as a "prologue" to the novel and is a microcosm of it. Pym is talked into a short trip by his friend Augustus Barnard. After a party they set out in Pym's battered sailboat. With Augustus at the helm, they go out too far. Suddenly, Arthur realizes that his friend is too drunk to complete the trip; Augustus immediately passes out and Pym is stuck at the helm. At the mercy of the elements and luck, the boat is swamped by a whaler before they are rescued by the same ship. Thus, in this first chapter the basic situation and pattern of action is set: Arthur reacts to an ambiguous "double"; good plans go wrong; they are menaced by the elements; they are rescued — first falsely — then for real. This pattern repeats itself, in increasingly complex ways, throughout the book.

Once his appetite has been whetted, Arthur chooses to go to sea (unlike the heroes of Poe's shorter sea tales, "MS. Found in a Bottle" and "A Descent in the Maelström"). His rationale, however, is strange; he is attracted not by the possibilities of fame, fortune, or adventure, but by the prospects for disaster: "My visions were of shipwrecks and famine of death or captivity among barbarian hordes; of a lifetime dragged out in sorrow and tears, upon some gray and desolate rock, in an ocean unapproachable and unknown." This bleak prospect is, of course, more than realized.

The major action of the novel begins with Pym ensconced with plentiful provisions in his hiding place, a coffinlike chest aboard the *Grumpus*, the ship captained by Augustus' father. Before long, he is joined by his dog Tiger, who alternately saves and attempts to devour his master. If this all sounds surrealistic, the effect is intended — but the approach is still scrupulously realistic; it is realism intensified, and it prepares us for the grotesqueries to follow. Although Arthur's hiding place resembles a coffin, it remains a hiding place. Trapped for weeks in his alcove, Pym endures excruciating psychological and physical deprivation, all described meticulously and viscerally. One point for Poe as a science fiction writer is that he describes physical processes with great accuracy and particularity. Although we never know Pym very well as a human being, we certainly know him as a physiological entity.

The conflict between Pym and his allies and the mutineers is the most conventional section of the novel, although the battle is won by a grotesque trick. Violence between the mutineers reduces the crew to ten. Forced into an alliance with one mutineer, Dirk Peters, and clearly marked for extinction, Arthur thinks up a daring plan: he costumes himself like the ghost of a recently murdered crewman and confronts the mutineers suddenly. One of them drops dead; the others are so shocked and confused that they are easy to defeat in hand-to-hand combat (especially with the dog helping out), although Augustus is wounded.

Their new companion, the half-breed Dirk Peters, rapidly becomes a central figure in the novel, displacing Augustus as Pym's companion and double. Physically he is grotesque:

> short in stature — not more than four feet eight inches high — but his limbs were of Herculean mould. His hands, especially, were so enormously thick and broad as hardly to retain a human shape. His arms, as well as legs, were bowed in the most singular manner, and appeared to have no flexibility whatever. His head was equally deformed, being of immense size, with an indentation on the crown . . . and entirely bald. The mouth extended nearly from ear to ear; the lips were thin, and seemed to be devoid of natural pliancy, so that the ruling expression never varied under the influence of any emotion whatsoever.

The replacement of the handsome, rational — if erratic — upper-middle-class Wasp Augustus by the ugly, dwarfish, half-breed Dirk Peters is one of the strongest indications of the shift from realism to grotesque fantasy.

Once they — the three plus a mutineer named Parker — have control of the ship, the elements take over. A severe storm forces them to lash themselves to the windlass and washes all available stores (and presumably Tiger) into the sea. Physical survival and the threat of starvation become the problems; although actually less than forty pages, this section seems interminable as Poe lingers over every detail of the sailors' degradation.

This lingering is not simply self-indulgence on Poe's part, however; three specific incidents occur in this section which may strike the reader as gratuitously sensational, but which fit integrally into the work. In the first of these, they spot a ship during the early stages of their deprivation. They clamor for rescue, but as soon as the boat comes close they smell "a stench, such as the whole world has no name for — no conception of — hellish — utterly suffocating — insufferable, inconceivable." On the deck of the ship they sight "Twenty-five or thirty human bodies, among whom were several females, lay scattered about between the counter and the galley in the last and most loathsome state of putrefaction." The most telling detail occurs when a seagull drops a chunk of human flesh at the feet of the survivors. Pym hurls it overboard, but not before the implications of the meat have registered on the four.

This triggers a lurid scene. Near starvation and desperate, Parker suggests cannibalism as an alternative to mass starvation. The narrator objects strongly, but finally gives in. Lots are drawn. Parker loses and submits passively to his fate. The horror of the scene is not only in what happens, but also in Poe's understated presentation of it.

> Let us suffice to say that, having in some measure appeased the raging thirst which consumed us by the blood of the victim, and having by common consent taken off the hands, feet, and head, throwing them, together with the entrails, into the sea, we devoured the rest of the body piecemeal, during . . . four ever memorable days.

As it turns out, Parker's sacrifice was not even needed. Upon renewing their efforts, the survivors succeed in breaking into the submerged cabins and finding foodstuffs. Shortly thereafter the boat upturns, uncovering large numbers of nutritious barnacles. And some time after that, they are rescued by the *Jane Guy*. But at no time do they express guilt or regret over the premature consumption of their late shipmate.

The third incident is Augustus' death. Wounded in the scuffle, he grows progressively weaker and dies. In terms of plot and theme, the fact of his death is necessary and foreshadowed; but leave it to Poe to emphasize the vivid detail. "It was not until some time after dark that we took courage to get up and throw the body overboard. It was then loathsome beyond expression, and so far decayed that, as Peters attempted to lift it, an entire leg came off in his grasp." Why the gore? Poe's fascination with such things? The Gothic tradition and impulse? The popular readers' taste for such tidbits? Perhaps, but they also function to connect the two halves of the novel. Without them, the shift in mood and atmosphere would be too extreme; while these incidents do not actually forward the action, they emotionally prepare the reader for the grotesqueries to follow.

After the survivors are picked up by the *Jane Guy* the novel enters its most scientific phase, the one part of the book that can be labeled science fiction without quibble. As the book tours the South Sea Islands, Poe meticulously describes the environment in documentary detail. The prose style becomes dry, impersonal, and glutted with details and statistics; as they travel he charts the trip carefully with longitudinal and latitudinal numbers; the native wildlife is

not only noted and described, but its lore and behavior are chronicled, including a three-page analysis of the life, background, and habits of the albatross in
great detail; the history of each area is outlined. The effect is mildly interesting and generally ponderous. Why does Poe do it? Because of his own fascination with such minutiae, and to establish an aura of scientific plausibility prior
to launching into the utterly fantastic last third of the book.

Poe shifts the direction of the narrative most casually: "information
received at Tristan d'Acunha induced him to steer to the southward. . . . In the
event of his not discovering these lands, he designed, should the season prove
favourable, to push on towards the pole." Why would the practical, scientific
Captain Guy want to go to the pole? Surely it had no commercial possibilities.
Perhaps Poe's Imp of the Perverse had asserted itself. If, to the nineteenth
century romantic, the sea symbolized the "mystery," then the poles were the
key. Poe had become fascinated by the "hollow earth" theory proposed by Jon
Cleves Symmes and fictionalized in another important early science fiction
work, *Symzonia* (1820) by "Adam Seaborn" (perhaps Symmes himself).
According to this theory the oceans came together in a great whirlpool as they
fed into a hole in the South Pole, circulated through the hollow Earth, and
emerged from the Northern opening to start the process over again. Poe certainly took the theory seriously — although whether or not he actually believed
it is problematical — and once Pym's journey began, the South Pole had to be
its final destination.

But before reaching the pole Pym and Peters encounter the black natives of
Tsalal Island. If we accept the "lost civilization" or "lost world" adventure as
science fiction, then this portion of the book qualifies. Actually it seems more
contemporary than that; with only a little imagination one can see this relatively autonomous part as a "first contact" story. The strange island of Tsalal
seems much more like the surface of an alien planet than a lost city buried in
an imaginary jungle. The bizarre quality of this landscape is first signaled
when the men spot a strange new beast:

> It was three feet in length and but six inches in height, with four very short legs, the feet
> armed with long claws of a brilliant scarlet, and resembling coral in substance. The body
> was covered with a straight, silky hair, perfectly white. The tail was peaked like that of a
> rat, and about a foot and a half long. The head resembled a cat's with the exception of the
> ears — these were flapped like the ears of a dog. The *teeth* were of the same brilliant
> scarlet as the claws.

For all of the extremity of the previous situations, none were beyond the realm
of at least theoretical possibility. With this creature Poe crosses the line into
dark fantasy.

Not only are the natives black — all black, black to the eyes, tongue, and
even teeth — but the landscape — rocks, trees, bushes — is also entirely
black. Their animals, including one albatross, are likewise black. The drinking

water is "limpid" and, if not black, assumes various shades of purple as it flows. The natives live close to the black Earth, seem almost to be a part of it in their crude skin-covered huts and ground shelters. They are so black that they fear everything white — eggs, book pages, flour, sailcloth, handkerchiefs, and so on, not to mention mirrors in which their own blackness is reflected.

The only thing that the Tsalal Islanders and the sailors have in common is a fondness for the *bêche de mer*, a kind of oblong mollusca. This enables the natives, led by their deceptive Chief Too-Wit, to betray the sailors, and bury all of them save Pym and Peters alive in a ravine. For all of the exotic paraphernalia, the encounter turns out to be an old-fashioned betrayal.

Pym and Peters escape the wrath of the aborigines by squeezing through a fissure in a mountainside that leads to an elaborate set of caves. They ramble through them for several days, finding mysterious writing on the walls, scrounging for food, and finally emerging from their hiding place when the need for food becomes too great. Climbing down the mountain, Pym has a strange urge: "my whole soul was pervaded with a *longing to fall*; a desire, a yearning, a passion utterly uncontrollable." He lets himself go, but Peters catches him. This scene climaxes the Gordon Pym-Dirk Peters relationship and focuses the psychological tensions that have animated the novella.

Dirk Peters, the dark alter ego, symbol, perhaps of the dark side of his own being, saves Pym from falling "into the abyss." It is the last and most important of several rescues. Although they have been fleeing from black men, Peters is himself "dusky" and at least half a native. From the beginning of the book he is a man of violence, yet he seems utterly devoted to Pym. Pym views him with mixed emotions of fear, trust, and affection, attraction and revulsion.

Together they flee the natives in the direction of the South Pole. Whiteness increases all about, but the water becomes warmer and "milkier" and the darkness more pervasive. Finally they approach the maelström:

> And now we rushed into the embraces of the cataract, where a chasm threw itself open to receive us. But there arose in our pathway a shrouded human figure, very far larger in its proportions than any dweller among men. And the hue of the skin of the figure was of the perfect whiteness of snow.

What to make out of all of this? From our realistic beginning we would seem to have gone the full distance to pure allegory. Who or what is the "white figure"? If "black" equals "evil," as seems to be suggested, is "white" good? — that seems much less sure. The figure is both a foreboding and a welcoming one: destruction or rebirth? Or both? How does it tie in with the death-rebirth cycle that repeats several times in the novel? Where do Pym's "doubles" — Augustus and Peters — fit in?

Such questions have been puzzled over at length by critics at least since the novel has been taken up as an interesting work. They have yet to be answered satisfactorily; to attempt an extended answer to them would involve a discussion of Poe's whole opus, since they echo themes and ambiguities that pervade it. It is probably sufficient to say that Pym exhibits a tenacious urge to survive as well as an active death wish, a fear of annihilation and also a fascination with it, an energetic need to act out and a strong tendency to inertia, a physical and psychological need for wholeness and a powerful sense of dissolution. These contradictions are evidenced in the action of the book, in the relations he has with his "doubles," and with Poe's increasingly vivid, if ambiguous, color imagery.

However, as subtle, paradoxical, and complex as these things are, it is important to notice that Poe has tried to express them in a popular form, the sea yarn, and in doing so suggests serious possibilities for that more contemporary popular form, the science fiction story. The fact is that no purely realistic genre could support the philosophical, psychological, and poetic weight of a story like *The Narrative of Arthur Gordon Pym*, and yet a grounding in realistic observation and detail is also vital to it. Probably more than any other contemporary narrative form, science fiction offers the writer the chance to combine realism and fantasy in a dynamic balance. Because this balance suited Edgar Allan Poe's very unique — even idiosyncratic — vision, he was one of the first important writers to seize upon it.

Keith Neilson

Sources for Further Study

Criticism:

Campbell, Josie P. "Deceit and Violence: Motifs in *The Narrative of Arthur Gordon Pym*," in *English Journal*. LIV (February, 1970), pp. 206-212. The theme of deceit is emphasized by Campbell in this study of the major motifs in *The Narrative of Arthur Gordon Pym*.

Fiedler, Leslie A. *Love and Death in the American Novel*. New York: Criterion Books, 1960, pp. 370-382. Fiedler looks at the motifs of *The Narrative of Arthur Gordon Pym* and also discusses the place of the negro in American Gothic.

Harp, Richard L. "A Note on the Harmony of Style and Theme in Poe's *Narrative of Arthur Gordon Pym*," in *CEA Critic*. XXXVI (1974), pp. 8-11. Harp provides a concise introduction to the major critical concerns of this Poe story.

Hussey, John P. "Mr. Pym and Mr. Poe: The Two Narrators of *Arthur Gordon Pym*," in *South Atlantic Bulletin*. XXXIX (1974), pp. 22-32. The dual narrative technique which causes confusion to some readers is explained by Hussey.

Straupe, John H. "Poe's Imaginary Voyage: Pym as Hero," in *Studies in Short Fiction*. IV (Summer, 1967), pp. 315-322. Poe's characterization of Pym as protagonist is analyzed by Straupe in his study of the "imaginary voyage."

THE NASTY SWANS
(GADKIE LEBEDI)

Authors: Arkady Strugatsky (1925-   ) and Boris Strugatsky (1933-   )
First book publication: 1972
English translation: 1979
Type of work: Novel
Time: Sometime close to the present day
Locale: A fantasy land that bears a great resemblance to the Soviet Union

Victor Baniev, a writer in exile, enters a former sunny resort town now drenched in unending rain and finds "lepers," who, as harbingers of the new future, lead the children away from their past

Principal characters:
VICTOR BANIEV, a writer and hero
LOLA, his ex-wife
IRMA, Victor's daughter, one of the "new" children
DIANA, Victor's mistress, friend of Golem and the rain-men, ex-wife of Zurmansor
GOLEM, head doctor at the "leper" asylum
PAVOR, sanitation inspector, in reality a spy
RIEM KVADRIGA, official painter for the President's government
TEDDY, a laconic barman, also has a child who has undergone this transformation
ZURMANSOR, a shadowy figure, possibly a great thinker, inspiration and model for the rain-men
THE MAYOR
FLAMINE YUVENTA, a hoodlum, his nephew
ROSSCHEPER NANT, a debauched parlimentarian

The Nasty Swans, which bears the date 1966-1967, is by no means the most recent novel of Arkady and Boris Strugatsky. It was not published, however, in the Soviet Union, and its eventual appearance, in a *samizdat* edition from Possev-Verlag in Frankfurt in 1972, led to the partial silencing of the two writers. The question is, what made this work, among all the other writings of the authors, so offensive to the ruling orthodoxy? Satire is only the mask this novel wears. Its real purpose is not to criticize systems — Marxist or otherwise — but to suspend them, to expose a bedrock of existence that is absolute and unchanging. Far from being dialectical and dynamic, the rhythm of *The Nasty Swans* is ultimately reductive. The title perhaps provides the key: opposing visions will not resolve into progressive syntheses but rather coalesce in polar compounds, oxymorons.

This novel probably was banned because in it what seems a developing Marxist revolution (the breakdown of productive forces in this cosmetic "capitalist" state) is inexplicably suspended by some transcendent force — the combination of a Clarkean "childhood's end" and native illuminism. The heresy is much deeper however. Contradiction is actually the essential structure of the narrative: we follow a changing world into a new future only to find that the very idea of such a future is as illusory as that of escape into the past. Opposites in the novel combine to reveal a quite different material base: not dynamic process so much as eternal myth. The pulls of past and future meet and are absorbed in the vital, unchanging present of the hero, Victor Baniev, whose ability to endure the ravages of change, to act creatively because constantly held at this point of tension, is that of legendary Russian man. What arises here is the same ahistorical vision Alexander I. Solzhenitsyn embodies in the hero of his novel *Cancer Ward*. Told to give the society that has repeatedly battered him a chance to develop ("you must remember it's only forty years old"), Kostoglotov replies: "I'll always be younger than this society. What do you expect me to do, keep silent all my life?" This "bone-swallower" is like the Strugatskys' hero, a Victor whose victory lies in swallowing all so as not to be swallowed himself. Both are spontaneous and make demands of the present. Both incarnate the same skeptical, pragmatic, enduring spirit of a long-suffering people.

The term "science fiction," in its Western sense, hardly seems to fit *The Nasty Swans* at all. Indeed, it does not really describe any of the Strugatskys' work adequately. First of all, the authors are not primarily interested in creating extrapolated worlds that are theoretically or technologically "plausible." Such creations, where they exist, are devices that serve only for ironic contrast. Second, and more fundamentally, their novels are not "speculative" in the sense we know it; in fact, they are just the opposite. The concern is not with science instead of fantasy, or the future instead of the past. Instead, their novels play new against old, uncanny against familiar, in order to reaffirm values and states of existence which — because they survive past and future nightmares — emerge as absolute. In terms of narrative mode, the Strugatskys' stories are a classic Russian mixture of fantasy and "realism." The Russian language edition of *Snail on the Slope* refers to this work and its companion *Tale of the Troika* as "two fantastic novels." Yet the underside of each, in the manner of Gogol, is a very detailed and precise topicality. Of more interest is their work *Hard to Be a God* (1964). The science fiction device of space travel serves here only to create a future, alternate Earth whose present in our past, and whose socioeconomic development is chronicled in the tested "realist" way — representative types are studied as they move in the general stream of events. And yet, through the clever use of a contrasting "frame" on a familiar Earth, what is told realistically is simultaneously cast in the light of fantasy. If these space-traveling scientists prove powerless to alter the course of events on this other world, could it be because their "science," like the names they adopt, is simply part of some imaginary game? Their roles and actions in fact seem to have their origin in a series of childhood fantasies on Earth — it is as if three children playing "don" and "dona" in the Russian forests have generated this whole world where Don Rumata struggles with the treacheries of an evil Don Reba. And yet if all this is only fantasy, it turns out quite deadly — what is merely possible on Earth becomes irreversible actuality in Arkanar; the bolt Anton refuses to fire in his game of Wilhelm Tell is ultimately loosed there to kill Rumata's lover Kyra.

The purpose of this subtle intermingling of fantasy and reality is to blur the boundaries between here and there, past and future. What survives this reductive prcess however is a series of human types that appear, because of their presence in both worlds, to have eternal validity: the selfless Kyra ("people like you have been born in every epoch of the bloody history of our planets"), Arata the indestructible rebel ("historical evolution gives birth to such pikes only from time to time"), Baron Pampa the hard-drinking, hard-eating blusterer with a nobel heart. But if these figures are universal, it is no accident that they (in the same oxymoronic fashion that gives us real fantasy and fantastic reality) are also, like the forest Anton and his friends roam, particularly Russian as well.

There is further reduction here, but this time on the level of "ideology" itself. Indeed a foretaste of the ideological self-consciousness of *The Nasty Swans* is found in the intricate games played with the orthodox Marxist idea of history in *Hard to Be a God*. At stake here is the key concept of Marxism as (to use Bruce Franklin's words) "*the* science of human history," as justification for a "revolutionary" activity which in this case has been perfected to a nonviolent manipulation of the socioeconomic factors that underlie historical events. The "alternate world" here is a developing human society still in its feudal stage. The space-travelers seek to guide it as painlessly as possible toward its inevitable Communist future, and yet they fail. They do so, however, not because of faulty method but because they encounter something irreducible in the human being himself, an essential "evil" that defies all attempts to educate it away. Slyly the Strugatskys do not challenge doctrine but simply bypass it. Rumata sees his vision of "the still unborn boys . . . who will be sitting before the dictascopes at the schools in the Communist Republic of Arkanar" wither and die before the violence of the human present: "Are you familiar with the stench of smoldering corpses at the stake?"

In the light of this failure, the final iteration of what seems sound Marxist dogma (history is a one-way road: "there is no way back") is harshly ironic. For to accept the deterministic tenets of dialectical materialism here is to embrace a nightmare: man can create alternate histories and yet alter nothing in them; he is doomed to follow the same bloody road, to stumble forever against an unchanging reality where a few inherently "good" people struggle hopelessly against stupidity and violence, the mass of men. If any change is to come about in Arkanar, it will be (it is hinted in the final pages) the result of a very different material process — not an alteration in "relations of production" but man killing man, Rumata's vengeance on Don Reba. In addition, this irony is further reinforced by the reductive interplay of frame and story. The "anisotropic" road the children follow in their games is (on another level) the same one Rumata goes down — Don Reba or the German skeleton chained to its machine gun, its end is the same: Fascism and death.

Yet at this zero point, where the lines of parallel worlds meet, where hope for a new future is cancelled by resurgence of an old past, a more fundamental opposition seems to emerge. Moving against the indifferent process of history is the vital combinatory force which is Anton: "I'm going along this one-way street, even if it is the wrong way!" In both realms — that of childhood innocence as well as adult suffering — he goes against the flow, and yet returns to the same human place, suspends the process of change: "We were there . . . the three of us." As Anton in the Epilogue holds out his hands to Anka, and what she first thinks is blood turns out to be "only the stain of strawberries," we have neither progression (achievement of a higher state beyond innocence and experience) nor regression (flight from responsibility and the "anisotropic" vision). What occurs is rather modulation into a different realm altogether, a transfiguration in reverse where what is unveiled is not new man but indestructible man ("he seemed completely unchanged"), the archetypal Russian hero firmly grounded by his strawberry-stained hands in the abiding forests of his native land.

The reductive process in *The Nasty Swans* is more subtle and far-reaching This novel is not simply (as the dust jacket of one edition proclaims) "fierce satire on both communist and capitalist societies alike." What it sets against each other, on a level of acute ideological self-awareness, is nothing less than two systems of change: the dominant yet divergent modes of creating the new man in East and West and Marxist history and epiphanic transcendentalism. On the surface, the relation between these two seems to break down clearly along lines of the major components of the Strugatsky novel in general: realism and fantasy. Apparently what happens is the intrusion of fantastic elements — inexplicable weather changes, multiplication of "rain-men," sudden metamorphosis of children into superminds — into a "realistic" situation: we have a panorama of what seems like social conflict — police factions quarrel, the army moves against Fascist civilian paramilitary forces.

However, a closer look at the texture of the novel shows just how tentative such a neat division is here. Throughout, these opposing strands fuse and blend, their contours blur — this world is neither real nor fantastic. On one hand we cannot ground ourselves in a clear geographical or historical anywhere. We are apparently dealing with a Western government — there is a "president" whose rule is ostensibly based on neo-Enlightenment ideals, "liberty" and "reason." And yet several times Moscow is clearly named as the capital of this land. We cannot follow any clue here without running into a dead end. We seem (provided we pursue the assumption we are really in some disguised version of the Soviet Union) to be in a Black Sea resort, with its "sanatorium" and tourist-hotel provinciality. Yet the fantastic advent of unrelenting fog and rain creates a totally different and alien atmosphere. Nor do the names of characters provide any clear here and now: they range from the exotic (Lola) to the American (Teddy) to purest Russian (Bol-Kunatz, Kvadriga); from the legendary and mythical (Diana, Golem) to the satirical (General Batty) to the symbolically ironic (Victor). The temporal orientation is no firmer either. Present simultaneously (as if offering us at every minute the possibility of choice) are a today — we identify the typically modern bureaucracy: privilege, corruption, even debauchery in the classic Soviet fashion; a yesterday — Victor's ongoing memories of what is recognizably World War II; and a tomorrow — the resurrected rain-men and reborn children. In terms of the action however none of these ever clearly remains separate. Not only does past penetrate present (today's generals have strangely Germanic names — Arschmann, Pferd), but it leaps directly into the future as well: old "lepers" become instant saints, though they seem to Victor to remain the same creatures as before. What is more, the future not only turns its back on the present (in its mystical, ahistorical advent) but finds itself skewered on the past as well (Victor stands between the new dawning and memories of old twilights and defeats as both resolve into falling cities).

Furthermore, the oppositions that seem to form in this spatialized landscape simulate progressive movement rather than actually stimulate it. Town and parents decide the rain-men are their enemies and attack. Against the President and his men ("the past is indispensible to their existence") Bol-Kunatz and the children assert their opposing credo: "History in the old sense of the word has suspended its course, it is meaningless even to refer to it." Yet these conflicts, instead of providing a dynamic impetus to the action, gradually dissolve like the fog in the novel and prove illusory at best. The authorities launch their offensive not against the very tangible army but against fantastic intangibles — these rain-men as new pied pipers leading cats and children astray. Moreover, the final *denouement* comes here not through any human process or agency, but through the gradual workings of what seems to be nature itself. Parents and "gold-shirts" alike, in their final assault on the rain-men's asylum, are dispersed not by the army but by some mysterious "Voice" that seems to emanate from the fog and generate it at the same time. The final exodus, as the city dissolves in the rain, is described as "an abcess that burst." In this ultimate transformation whiskey simply turns to water, buildings melt away to reveal shining fields of light, and awkward and pimply children grow tall and straight.

Yet this natural process is not an evolution either; it is rather resolution, revelation of a static rhythm of change in permanence at the core of all events. Instead of change, there is something more like metamorphosis. Throughout the novel, for instance, Diana keeps changing (in the fight with Yuventa she becomes Diana the Ferocious, with Victor she can be Diana the Implacable or Diana the Tender), and yet she is always Diana. In like manner Zurmansor's face — which seems to give birth to the string of rain men who, resembling him, evolve from him — decomposes and recomposes before Victor's eyes.

Nor, ironically, does this natural world ever really abolish the socioeconomic realm. On the contrary, both continue to exist until the very end. Indeed, *The Nasty Swans* culminates not in transcendence but in all-embracing suspension of irreducible opposites. The old world clearly fades only to reform again. In the middle of this new sunlit landscape sits Teddy the uncomprehending, unassimilable barman. Caught between his barroom past and a liquorless future, he becomes a fixed point, a fulcrum between worlds: "No, go on . . . I'll just sit here . . . I won't escape my fate either way." And suddenly swooping down over the beautiful "reborn" figures of Irma and Bol-Kunatz is a fighter plane. As the lad raises his stick to "fire" at it, all forward movement is suddenly frozen in ambiguous polarity. With the appearance of this intruder from the other world, the promised land resolves into a child's game once again. The novel ends in irreducible suspension: at the elbow of a "totally new" Diana — Diana the Joyous — a chiding Victor pulls in the opposite direction: "Yes, all that's just perfect, but we mustn't forget to go back now."

But if Teddy is its passive focal point, Victor is the real creative center of the book's reductive dynamic. Obviously flawed, an anti-hero in fact in all his brawling and blundering, Victor nevertheless, by withstanding the contrary impulsions of the forces that converge in him, brings order out of chaos. In *The Nasty Swans* it becomes emphatically clear that the central element in the Strugatskys' vision of things is neither history nor Utopia but man. Victor is pointedly not Marxist man *en devenir*. Neither a product of the past nor harbinger of the future, he is rather a perennial spirit of opposition — the protean adversary who confounds all schemas for development, paradoxical man not evolutionary man. If, for instance, the "Brothers of Reason" football team is a *reductio ad absurdum* of the perfect socialist productive relationship — selfless devotion to the task — Victor sets against them an exaggeratedly "aristocratic" profile: he is unathletic and debauched, individualistic, unproductive as a writer, uncooperative in terms of "party" guidelines. But this alienates him not just from a "scientific" future but from a messianic one as well. In his sybaritic present he has wine and women, but in that aniseptic tomorrow he would have no role whatsoever, "be a cipher."

This is the very intractibility to a system that gives Victor his strength. He may demand personal pleasures and privileges, but this does not stop him from condemning the fanatical Pavor for using this same aristocratic image as an excuse to damn and enslave the masses. Whenever Victor becomes involved in the various processes that unfold in this novel, it is always (significantly) on an emotional not a rational level. He gets mixed up with the rain-men because he tries to come to the aid of one who is being assaulted on the sidewalk. He tangles with town authorities and the President's thugs when he foolishly starts a brawl with Yuventa. Involvement with mistress and daughter leads him to steal the truckload of books and drive to the asylum. Victor lives and acts on spur-of-the-moment impulse. *The Nasty Swans* comes to rest on an almost Dostoevskian foundation here. Reason no matter what its goal — to create a police state or a utopia — is the purveyor of illusions, builder of mind-forged systems that inevitably dehumanize and oppress. Victor, however, is guided by the heart. And the heart, though contradictory in its urgings, proves nevertheless unerring, for this contradiction is seen to be the essence of man.

Victor Baniev than incarnates the rhythm which informs this novel: endless metamorphoses controlled by that paradoxical force which is the human heart — changeless in its ability to change. This is some mythical sense may be "Russian" man. But Baniev, is, explicitly, creative man as well. In his protean spontaneity he is, however, a very special kind of creator, one whose life itself is the work of art. Once again we must be cautious of what appears, on the surface, to be a dialectical opposition. We have what seems to be two kinds of artist, Victor and Kvadriga, the renegade *versus* the party hack who sold brush and soul to the forces and power. Yet we notice, if we look more closely, that these artists are not antagonists but doubles, that their careers do not conflict in any social sense but simply diverge along more basic lines of predetermined qualities and values.

The unnamed town is the childhood home of both men. Kvadriga ostensibly returns to enjoy the fruits of his cowardice. But he cannot live in his luxurious villa — he sees it haunted by the shades of all those artists who refused to be bought, who are now in exile or prison. These figures though seem to be resurrected. They "are not alive" yet walk in barefoot bliss through the house ignoring him totally, dwellers in some better, future world superimposed on this one.

Victor too returns to his past to find the same barefoot harbingers of a new order. His carved initials in a school desk conjure memories of party enthusiasms as dreary and false as Kvadriga's artistic servitude. Now however, moving among these same prison-green walls, are what appears to be a new race of reborn children. The real opposition discovered here — that between old and new — is not dialectical but polar. And these poles would remain forever apart were it not for Victor's ability to move between them, to join them in the vitality of the present moment.

Kvadriga in contrast remains bound to the past. Ironically, his paintings only solidify a dead doctrine all the more — Mr. President's most insignificant gesture frozen in allegorical limbo. Before the advent of a new world where whiskey turns to water, he can only flee, seeking more whiskey in the limousine that symbolizes his enslavement to the old order.

Baniev on the other hand is bound nowhere. He is not a revolutionary: if he is in exile it is not because of principles but rather unthinking foolishness — after taking a bawling out from the President he commits a *faute de gout*, draws his handkerchief to mop his harried brow. Moreover his novel is rejected by the very children who ask him to speak to them: it portrays the world they refuse. And yet the strength of both novel and creator is that, ironically, they elude such attempts to categorize, to use them as texts to illustrate a doctrine however "noble." In this sense Victor is the anti-Kvadriga, an artist whose creations thrive in the imperfect and ever-changing realm of the present. If he resists control by the past, it is not by seeking conflict but by avoiding it, by taking refuge from the temptations of "glory" in dubious creature comforts. And if in turn he resists the even harder temptation of the future — if his art is not preempted by this seductive utopian finality — it is because of the same passive resistence, that of raw reality to all systems. Caught here between contending directions — the Mayor urging him to write a tract against the rain-men, Zurmansor urging him to do so also because such a tract will help his cause more than hurt it — Victor acts in typical fashion: he never writes a word.

As an artist then, Victor is less a maker of works in the traditional sense than a process of creation. Indeed, the narrative focus, through a long series of parenthetical asides, is clearly on a mind in the act of adjusting itself to events, modulating between extremes. It is out of this introspective activity in two major instances that works actually arise — a song and two fragments of stories. Obviously, it is not these trifles but the mental processes that shape them that are important here. In the first of these instances the past adjusts the future. Victor awakens with a violent itching, and believes (with mixed feelings of elation and apprehension) that he has caught the rain-men's sickness, thus is being reborn a man of the future, *homo superior*. Once again though it is a matter of blood turning to strawberries: Golem tells Victor he has simply eaten too many of the latter and has a case of hives. So future promise fades as Victor's gluttonous past returns.

In the second (less comical) instance, however, the process is reversed; the future impinges on memories of the past and suspends their forward impulsion in a new tension. Victor decides to act in favor of the rain-men and denounces Pavor. This leads him, however, not only back to the President — he is awarded the "second degree" of the "Silver Cloverleaf" — but back to recollections of a more glorious and heroic past — his World War II exploits and the winning of the "first degree" of this same medal. His option for a new future, however, has cast a pall over this past. The mind that once sentimentalized these early "patriotic" deeds now sees its folly, realizes that in fighting one Fascism it was merely supporting a new tyranny to be. The road leads once again away from progress back to the German skeleton and his machine gun. Out of this constant cancelling of extremes, however, comes the stirrings of creative activity.

Like their maker, Baniev's works too seem to exist in a perennially vital present, detached from the hegemony both of tradition and posterity. Through their tentative and fragmentary forms, opposing visions coalesce to reveal the protean artist himself, metamorphosing in and out of roles. As poet he would flee this world, "sink like a submarine into the sea." As storyteller, however, he brings his hero home from the war and its illusory glories (he is decorated with a "Victory" medal) to immerse him in a different sea — the modern urban nightmare of the President's world. Rising here, however, proves no more of a solution than sinking: as this hero (a certain Councillor B.) climbs his roof to shell the polluting factory with his old souvenir mortar, he too encounters inconclusiveness, futility. All that comes of his struggle is another sign, a new slogan: "Attention! This side dangerous during bombardments!"

The restless, self-correcting activity of Baniev's mind, inside the work of art and without, keeps him from fading into the realm of ghosts that lies in either direction, past or future. Far from the advent of a new world in this novel, we have just the opposite: a collapse of all ideological frames and projections around Baniev as only abiding reality. For if the past simply crumbles away, leaving a gap which no dialectical process can overleap, the transcendental future proves illusion as well: Golem tells us in the end that "there are no rain-men," his great book is probably blank, and childhood's end turns out to be only childhood's return. Amid the ambiguities of this reductive process only one sure value emerges: that inherent spontaneity that drives Baniev to charge a tank with drawn saber. If in "scientific" or dialectical terms such an action is irrelevant, if in transcendentalist terms it is merely foolish, in the contradictory standards of the human heart it is meant here to be mad and yet magnificent. In the end Victor Baniev — popular writer and symbolic Russian everyman — proves to be exactly what Golem calls him, not a nasty swan (the combination of black and white, good and evil) but a "poor beautiful ugly duckling," a mixture of the awkward and the striking, and with a future of sorts as well — that of simply growing up.

George Slusser

LA NAVE
(The Ship)

Author: Tomas Salvador (1921-   )
First book publication: 1959
Type of work: Novel
Time: About 2775
Locale: An interstellar ship of gigantic bulk drifting aimlessly among the stars

A scrivener turned historian, truth teller, and prophet, leads his people of the Generation Ark to a new meaning and direction

Principal characters:
    SHIM, a scrivener, prophet, and martyr

La Nave is an excellent example of the "Generation Ark" story. Generation Arks are multigenerational spaceships inside of which human (or alien) beings are born, live, and die. Robert A. Heinlein's *Orphans of the Sky* (1963) and Brian W. Aldiss' *Starship* (1959) are memorable examples of this subgenre. One popular variation focuses on the catastrophes that occur during the trip, together with their aftermaths. This is such a story.

Although *La Nave* is Tomas Salvador's first science fiction novel, he demonstrates his esteem and mastery of the genre, both in his sensitive preface and in the novel itself. Salvador is, however, essentially a writer of general fiction, having produced three collections of stories for children and a trilogy, with no previous involvement in science fiction. Perhaps this accounts for the emphasis on the humane in *La Nave*; above all it is concerned with the rediscovery of a forgotten heritage and the rising of a new hope among a people dwelling in the ruins of a grandiose technology, as seen through the tragic life of the "Savior," a man of destiny and great humanity.

The novel is built around its only real character: Shim, a prophet of verity and liberty, a traditional figure in these "positive" stories of damaged Generation Arks in which the survivors of the catastrophe are able to salvage themselves and their cause. In such works optimism and pessimism mingle, often with uncertain results. This ambiguity extends to the pivotal character. The career of Shim and the destiny of the whole Ark are tightly bound together. Each part of the book is linked to one important step both in his quest and in the revolution he originates, and the writing corresponds to that pattern. The first part consists of Shim's diary and deals with his discovery of the "truth." The second, a third person narrative, chronicles his first successes in spreading it. The third, a collection of sixteen unrhymed poems composed by a bard after Shim's death, describe his attempt at giving the whole Ark a new faith in itself.

Shim is the scrivener of the Ship. Only he and his apprentice can read and write and both are under vows of silence and chastity. Shim's duty is to record every event of importance in the Book, a servo-mechanism left by his ancestors. His people, the Kros (corruption of "Negroes"), consider themselves a superior race and despise the Wits (from "whites"), their servants. The group numbers exactly 1498 and they keep this number constant because the Meat, an enormous piece of growing animal flesh cultivated according to Alexis Carrel's formula, is their only source of food. The hydroponic gardens can support no more. Surrounded by evidences of a sophisticated technology which they neither understand (nor want to), they can barely handle what little is left intact and are quite unable to repair whatever is damaged. As for the Wits, four hundred of whom work for them, they live in the dark inner quarters and nobody knows how many there are of them.

When he becomes the Scrivener of the Ship, Shim is already an old man and he shares all the prejudices of the Kros. But he is curious and as he views the records of his predecessors, he realizes how ignorant his own people are. Although he can grasp only a part of the writing, enough of it is intelligible to disclose the true origin and nature of the Ship. For the Kros, the Ship is a world in itself, although they are conscious of its limitations. They can see the stars through the portholes but they do not have the slightest idea of what they are. More important, they cannot imagine that they themselves are moving through space. Although a legend has it that they came from some place outside the Ship, the concept is incomprehensible to them. They cannot believe that their world was built by other men. They have degenerated, not only culturally, but genetically as well. Many cases of sterility are discovered and their domination over the Wits becomes more and more problematic.

Shim reads on and discovers that the Ship is a flattened ovoid two thousand meters long, 350 meters deep, and fifteen hundred meters across. After leaving the Earth in 2317, and for reasons unknown, the energy that propelled the Ship stopped being beamed from the planet. With no power of its own, it had become a derelict drifting through interstellar space. When the crew of three thousand that manned her realized that the situation was hopeless, they revolted, causing many deaths and much damage. This uprising was soon followed by another during which the crew, raving mad and determined to die, destroyed all of the navigational instruments. Later, a third uprising erased the final traces of civilization within the Ship. In the meantime, a small group of misfits had taken shelter in the inner quarters; they became the Wits. As for the Kros, they were the result of a genetic experiment designed to develop resistance to radiation. Thus, two entirely different races came to share the Ship. Now, some twenty-three generations later, unrest and discontent are brewing among the Wits. They demand better treatment and threaten to stop working for their masters if their demands are not met. When their representatives are murdered, Shim bravely breaks his vow of silence and tells the Lord of the Ship that both peoples have descended from common ancestors and have equal rights. But the Lord, sensing a challenge to his authority, orders Shim's hands cut off and his position abolished.

Banished to the dark inner quarters, Shim joins the Wits. They now number in the hundreds and could menace their masters, resentful as they are at being forced to dwell in the putrid, almost uninhabitable parts of the Ship. Denied decent accommodations by the Kros, but also isolated from their decadent influence, the Wits have developed their own crude but original civilization. They are divided into seven tribelike Families, each ruled by a Father and set off from the others with its own manners and customs, its talents and secrets, and even by its own system of government. They have rediscovered music, dance, poetry, and the candle; and they have invented a primitive weapon for throwing. Furthermore, they are respectful of the dead. They are in many ways a childlike people, but they are curious, receptive, and eager to learn. They are also genetically sound. It is among the Wits that Shim fulfills his destiny and even discovers love. They receive him and tend his wounds. To repay them he recounts the history of the Ship and what he knows of the Earth. He also teaches them pity and kindness.

Shim becomes a man of stature. Some Wits even wonder if he is not the divine messenger, foretold in a prophecy, who will die to save them. Each Father wishes to adopt him into his Family; one even shows him wonders preserved from the destruction: books and sculptures. Shim uses what little he has learned from the Book to fix the lighting in some of the quarters, and, when he succeeds in repairing a kind of movie apparatus, his prestige reaches its zenith. The Families hold an assembly and elect him Navark (Commader of the Ship), for they consider him a superior being. As his first demonstration of authority he leads a mission to the Kros to propose a truce and inform them that the Wits are a powerful people, and their brothers. He also leads an expedition to the unexplored parts of the Ship and returns with many priceless artifacts. On his second visit to the Kros, he proposes to unite both peoples for a common renaissance. He is acknowledged to be Navark of the whole Ship; but a minority secedes and chooses its own chief. Shim is murdered on the very day of his triumph. The assassination turns the Ship into a battlefield.

Shim is not only the character that tightly binds the plot of this moving book; he is also the pervasive spirit that formulates its philosophy. Shim is a man of destiny. It does not matter that he is old and mutilated, since he possesses a charisma that enables him to inflame souls and shape events. However, it is perhaps more accurate to say that he is possessed by his charisma, for he does not control the vortex into which he is drawn. All he can do is accept it as a part of himself. He is conscious of the force that flows through and out of him, but he stands a little aside. He fearfully faces his destiny. His historical self, though, takes root in his human and even his humane self. Shim would not have been the chosen one if he had not first been the right one: the generous, kind, sympathetic, curious, wise — and rebellious — one. Weaker than the truth that he embodies, but still strong minded, he falls that it may rise: a Christ-like nonviolent figure.

The author declares in the preface that "Shim's violent death is nothing else than the necessary tribute of blood which the idealists and the utopia-dreamers always paid for the slow progression of the mediocres." This seems to imply that Shim's sacrifice is not completely useless. Most stories of damaged Generation Arks conclude with a triumph over darkness and ignorance brought about by the principal character. This novel is no exception; but it is more subtle than most. Though the sun shines only briefly, it may rise again after the night. Is Shim's attempt a failure? The Ship has become a battlefield, but the travelers have gained a self-consciousness and a sense of destiny that may be lasting. Through its portholes they see a star, another sun, getting brighter and brighter. The legend says that the coming of the prophet who is to save the Ship will be announced by a great light. Is the trip over?

The question is left unanswered. In any case, it is asked so diffidently that it is hard to believe in its importance. Perhaps it is merely an allusion to divine providence, since the author's view is clearly influenced by Christianity. It matters little whether any hope remains. The important thing lies neither in this uncertainty nor in the final anguished lines. The vital thing is the history of a human community struggling with fate and finding its identity in the fight.

Remi-Maure

LES NAVIGATEURS DE L'INFINI
(The Navigators of the Infinite)

Author: J. H. Rosny (the Elder) (1856-1940)
First book publication: 1925
Type of work: Novel
Time: The future
Locale: Mars

On the Earthmen's first visit to Mars, they find an old world that is inhabited by three extraordinary species, one of which is gradually being forced towards extinction

> *Principal characters:*
> JACQUES LAVERANDE, the narrator
> JEAN GAVIAL AND
> ANTOINE LOUGRE, the other two crew members
> THE MARTIAN TRIPEDS, a species threatened by extinction
> THE ZOOMORPHS, the Tripeds' main enemies
> THE ETHEREALS, the third Martian race

As can be seen in his first famous work, *Les Xipéhuz*, J. H. Rosny (the Elder) was fascinated by nonhuman forms of life and by radically different intelligences. Thirty-eight years after his account of the encounter of prehistoric man with the living minerals called the Xipéhuz, he published *Les Navigateurs de l'infini* (The Navigators of the Infinite) which is generally considered his science fiction masterpiece. (Rosny tried his hand at all genres without exception: he wrote at least one hundred and forty books including science fiction, scientific essays, saga-novels, and sociological narratives.) In many respects, *Les Navigateurs de l'infini* represents the author's achievement in his quest for alien creatures and in the description of human reaction to that encounter.

This short novel is the story of man's first voyage to another planet, Mars. After a long journey through space, three Frenchmen land on Mars, where they discover that it is populated by three very different races, two of which, the Tripeds and the Zoomorphs, are waging a merciless war against each other. Having to fight against great odds, the Tripeds are slowly but inevitably dying out.

The Earthmen side with the Tripeds against the Zoomorphs. The situation seems hopeless for the Tripeds; they cannot repel the repeated attacks by the Zoomorphs. But through the Earthmen's advanced science, they are finally able to change the balance of power. With the help of the Earthmen the Tripeds are able to hold their own and face their destiny. The novel closes with a sentimental climax: the extraordinary communion between Jacques Laverande and a Martian girl, a kind of platonic love between two worlds.

This summary may give the impression that the plot is simple and obvious. Such is not the case. Once more, Rosny has succeeded in giving his story a depth unequalled for the time. To find its equal, one must look at least a decade ahead to Olaf Stapledon's *Sirius* or a quarter of a century later to Philip José Farmer's *The Lovers*.

Faced with the extreme strangeness of Martian life, the three travelers from Earth may appear to be comparatively ordinary people. Several details, however, prepare the reader for the important role that the travelers will play in the book, in addition to their obvious role as the "liberators" of the unfortunate Tripeds. It is obvious from the outset that the three astronauts are complementary: Antoine Lougre is the mathematician, the scientist *par excellence* of the expedition; Jean Gavial, the born experimentalist; and Jacques Laverande, the artist ("humain plutôt museur") and the Narrator of the story. Rosny deliberately brings together what he thinks are the paramount qualities of the human race. The expedition, which develops into the rescue of an alien race, is not spoiled by the presence of the "traitor," a usual element of suspense. The three characters' intentions are pure and peaceful.

This quality also accounts for the transparency of the bold Earthmen's spaceship, an evident image, even though a bit simplistic, to convey the idea that they have nothing to conceal. Moreover, there is something magical about this spaceship, a transparent bubble traveling through space. Although it is loaded with a large amount of very technical equipment, is propelled by a motor, and utilizes a gravitational field, it is built almost totally of a metal called "argine sublimé," a term that hints at alchemy. In addition, the metal seems to be a kind of wonder-metal, endowed with all possible qualities. In the Tripeds' eyes, the Earthmen are godlike saviors equipped with a vehicle in keeping with the divine character of their mission. Thus, at the time when the story takes place, the whole human race has apparently reached a point of intellectual, moral, and technological development that is well on the way to perfection. Rosny may not believe in Utopia, but he seems to think that one day man will be sane and well-balanced enough to save another race. In Rosny's view, man has apparently elevated himself considerably from the level of fear and barbarianism which prevailed on the first encounter with the Xipéhuz.

Mars was *the* fascinating world for pre-World War II authors. The Martian races are positioned on the chessboard of conflicts in a rather curious way: the Ethereals seem totally ignorant of the existence of the other two protagonists. By far the strangest kingdom of Martian fauna, they are luminous beings who furrow the Martian nights in luminescent columns. They remain incomprehensible to the Earthmen and even to the Tripeds, and yet they represent a lofty concept of beauty, a diffused beauty out of the reach of all reasoning endeavor. Although Rosny devotes little space to the Ethereals, compared to the description of the other two races, he indicates a special fondness and fascination for this completely alien kingdom, especially in the sequence where they fly away to explode in cosmic fireworks, hundreds of kilometers from the planet's surface.

The Zoomorphs raise the reader's curiosity far less than the Ethereals as they play the difficult role of the "villain." Their intention is the same as the Xipéhuz, that is, to become the dominant race. Their flat, spongy bodies, sustained by nine tentacles arranged three by three, can spread out over an area of tens of meters. Their kingdom is different from that of the Tripeds', as their bodies contain no liquid. Their territory is the desert, from which all other living creatures have been eliminated. In fact, the Zoomorphs represent those principles contrary to all life. They draw their sustenance from the ground or by a cannibalistic osmosis. Although they seem to form no society, they gradually encroach on the domain of the Tripeds and all other Martian life dependent on water. They are a kind of disease which destroys everything in their way. Each defeat of the Tripeds is a further step towards the demise of the planet. Gradually the picture takes shape for the astronauts: the Zoomorphs are revealed to the Earthmen as a black, malevolent force struggling against the Martian world as a whole. Their intended victims are the Tripeds and all the other beings which belong to the third kingdom, that, despite its strangeness, is the most familiar to the Earthmen. Rosny does not describe animals in detail (the main difference between Martian and terrestrial animals seems to be a fifth limb, wing, or fin); he passes quickly to the Tripeds, which gives him an opportunity to display his generous ideas on encounters between alien intelligences.

These Tripeds are strange creatures, with three legs, perfectly smooth oval faces, and six pairs of eyes. Upon their first encounter with the Tripeds, the three astronauts are enticed by the pure form of their bodies and the nuances of their skin. They immediately feel that they are before a form of beauty very removed from the Ethereals' cold splendor. Above all, they have found beings on their own level in this inconceivable Martian world.

It is with the description of the Tripeds' beauty that Rosny gives a sample of his inimitable style. His sentences are a subtle mix of poetic and scientific diction; it is as if each sentence were a touch of the brush towards completing the picture of the once grand Triped society now on the decline. His descriptions of female Martian Tripeds are especially full of vivid images and extraordinary nuances. Rosny seems so fascinated by this exotic beauty that he finally prefers it to human beauty. This may be the only weakness of the book. While advocating the right to existence and the recognition of beauty in all races in the universe (different though they may be), Rosny contradicts himself when his Narrator notes that organs like a nose, a mouth, or ears are ugly beside the Tripeds' smooth faces. Perhaps Rosny's antiracist good will has driven him beyond fairness and logic.

The plot is largely void of suspense, since the ending can be foreseen rather early. The plot developments are due solely to the progressive discovery of pieces of the puzzles that surround Martian life, so mysterious in its totality and extreme diversity. *Les Navigateurs de l'infini* may be Rosny's finest achievement, considering his endeavor to combine science with poetry; it is perhaps in this book that he reached his greatest precision in scientific descriptions and in the development of the story, while still using a language that renders the text as light and airy as his Ethereals.

The end of the novel must be understood not only as the close of a narrative that leaves the reader surprised and keenly interested, but also as an extraordinary opening on the greatness of life in the universe. As the author makes clear, the love story that unites the Narrator and the Triped girl has nothing to do with a mere sensual attraction. Their love transcends sexual seduction because of the physical impossibility of the sexual act, and because of the partners' will to achieve a relationship which will permanently link their respective worlds. Moreover, in *Les Astronautes*, the continuation of *Les Navigateurs de l'infini*, unpublished until 1960, the Martian girl will give birth (by a kind of parthenogenesis) on Earth to a Martian baby out of love for Jacques Laverande.

What is the place of such a book? First of all, in Rosny's work, it is as the antithesis of *La Mort de la Terre* (The Death of the Earth, 1910), his other very great novel, in which a situation comparable to the Tripeds/Zoomorphs struggle ends with the destruction of mankind. Curiously, these two novels, so dissimilar in their endings, are generally looked upon as the author's masterpieces. A reason for this may be that the theme of each — fatality in *La Mort de la Terre* and hope in *Les Navigateurs de l'infini* — is realized perfectly within the respective book. In the history of science fiction, this novel proves once again that Rosny was one of the finest of the pre-World War II European authors.

Richard D. Nolane

Sources for Further Study

Criticism:

The Encyclopedia of Science Fiction and Fantasy. Compiled by Donald H. Tuck. Chicago: Advent Publishers, Inc., 1978, pp. 371-372. One of Rosny's outstanding science fiction novels, *Les Navigateurs de l'infini* is Rosny's best work, according to Tuck.

NEEDLE

Author: Hal Clement (Harry C. Stubbs, 1922-   )
First book publication: 1949
Type of work: Novel
Time: The present
Locale: Massachusetts and a small atoll in the Society Islands

In this benchmark portrayal of intelligent alien life, an alien detective chases a fleeing criminal to Earth, adapts to his new environment, enlists the aid of a human, and succeeds in his task

Principal characters:
THE HUNTER, an alien detective
THE QUARRY, an alien criminal fleeing the Hunter
ROBERT KINNAIRD, a high-school student, friend of the Hunter
MR. KINNAIRD, Robert's father
CHARLIE TEROA,
NORMAN HAY,
HUGH COLBY,
SHORTY MALMSTROM, and
KEN RICE, friends of Robert

Since the 1940's Hal Clement, the pseudonym of Harry C. Stubbs, a high-school science teacher by profession, has written short stories and novels that are definitively "hard" science fiction. In the growing critical terminology of the genre, hard science fiction is that which rigorously adheres to the framework of present-day scientific knowledge and confines its speculations about future developments to that framework. It typically eschews the postulation of new discoveries that upset or reverse what we now consider scientific laws. For example, a story set in a universe in which nothing moves faster than light is "harder" than one which utilizes space-warps, fourth dimension drives, or other sleights of hand to evade the Einsteinian restriction.

Yet, even the writer of the hardest science fiction will allow himself to extrapolate from what is now known. Otherwise all science fiction would concern itself with the known characteristics of human beings living on earth in the present. As Isaac Asimov, Poul Anderson, Larry Niven, and others have done, Hal Clement has used interstellar settings, has presumed the existence of faster-than-light drives, and has challenged contemporary science-fiction thinking when necessary, but without endangering his reputation as a writer of logical, carefully worked-out, scientifically defensible stories.

Prior to its first book publication in 1953, *Needle* was serialized in 1949 in the pages of *Astounding Science Fiction,* the standard-bearer of the harder side of the field. It appeared ten years after the publication of an important nonfiction article in the same magazine, L. Sprague de Camp's "Design for Life" (*Astounding Science Fiction,* May-June, 1939). De Camp argued that the human form was the near-optimum shape and size for an intelligent creature, and that any intelligent being in the universe would probably not depart much from the humanoid form. As a key point in his reasoning, de Camp estimated that the size of an intelligent being would fall somewhere between that of a small dog and a large bear. The lower limit is determined by the minimum number of brain cells required by a thinking creature. The upper limit is determined by the size of the body such a brain could control without the specialization seen in marine mammals: a dolphin's brain is larger than a human's, as is its body, simply because the exigencies of living in water require that a disproportionately large amount of the dolphin's brain tissue be devoted simply to the three dimensional movement of its correspondingly large bulk.

With de Camp's size restrictions in mind, Clement created an intelligent being smaller than the lower limit, one of the most memorable aliens in science fiction — the Hunter. Agreeing with de Camp that a thinking creature would be multicelled, and agreeing on the minimum number of cells such a creature would require, Clement evaded the size limit by presuming the individual body cells of the Hunter to be much smaller than those of human beings. Although the Hunter weighs only four pounds, he has thousands of times as many separate cells as a man. Whereas multicellular terrestrial life evolved from the protozoan, the Hunter's kind evolved from the much smaller viruses.

The Hunter differs from a human in another respect. Except for those cells used for memory storage, his equivalent of a brain, the Hunter's cells are not specialized or differentiated one from another; consequently, he does not have a specific shape. Like an amoeba, he moves by extending pseudopods, which, because of his smaller cells, can be slender enough to move with ease through a pore in the human skin. However, he is not reduced to an aimless mass; he has something akin to conscious muscular control, and can shape his body as the occasion demands. For example, if he needs to see, he simply forms part of himself into an eye, complete with lens, optical chamber, and retina.

In spite of his advantages, however, the Hunter is weak and unprotected in comparison to even a squid or a jellyfish, since he lacks a skin. On his native planet, therefore, the Hunter's species has adapted to a symbiotic life with intelligent creatures more familiar to us, ones with rigid skeletons and specialized organs. Members of the Hunter's race live literally inside their companions, the "host"-"guest" relationship being entirely normal and desirable to both parties. The host provides the guest with protection, greater mobility, food, and oxygen. Although most of the Hunter's matter lies in the abdominal cavity of his host, the Hunter takes nourishment and oxygen from the host's bloodstream and disposes of his wastes through the host's excretory organs. As compensation, the guest keeps the host free from external and internal parasites. The host is thereby safe from disease and distress, except accidents and the natural aging of the body. The Hunter's species is able to speed the healing of cuts and scratches for their hosts; in the novel, Robert Kinnaird receives a gash eight inches long and a half-inch deep, which the Hunter immediately closes and holds together with his own tissue. Finally, the host and guest provide each other with mutual affection and companionship, forming close and longlasting (usually lifelong) relationships.

Although these creatures have no personal names, they do have identities, personalities, and even professions. On his home planet, the Hunter is a police officer, the companion of a person who holds a position similar to that of an Assistant Police Chief. Individuals of the Hunter's species are by and large extremely law-abiding and benevolent creatures. The reasons for this are, first, that much of their success in finding an intelligent host depends on their good behavior as a group, since they clearly cannot overpower and enter a host. Second, since a host is entirely at the mercy of his guest, he would obviously not accept one were there any risk involved. The host realizes that if a guest operating from within closed a major blood vessel or paralyzed an important nerve, he would die in a matter of minutes, and after the guest vacated his body, the murder would be undetectable as such.

Though crime is extremely rare among the Hunter's kind, it does occur, and from this fact springs the plot of *Needle*. Guests are not dependent on their hosts for travel, either earthly or interstellar. They can also employ the bodies of small, nonintelligent animals such as monkeys when it is necessary for such jobs as manipulating the controls of small spaceships. As the novel opens, a criminal, identified only as the Quarry, is fleeing punishment for some heinous crime, using an animal host to pilot his spaceship. The pursuing Hunter knows that if the Quarry lands on a planet, he will be almost impossible to find. In the desperate chase which follows, both Hunter and Quarry are forced to crash-land on Earth. The Hunter's animal host is killed in the wreck, and he loses contact with the Quarry; thus begins the search for a "needle in a haystack" which gives the novel its title. Fortune favors the Hunter at first, since both the Quarry and the Hunter have crashed close to the shore of a small Pacific island near Tahiti, effectively restricting the Quarry to a relatively small area.

The Hunter's first move is to try to find an intelligent host, and in this task he is less fortunate. He chooses one of a small group of teen-aged boys who are playing on the beach, and enters his body while the boy naps. The boy is Robert Kinnaird, a tenth-grade high school student, the son of an engineer in the island's only industry, the production of petroleum products through bacterial action. Since the Hunter has no way of knowing that his choice of host is not an adult member of the species, he can hardly be blamed for his selection; since he also has no way of communicating with his new host, he is essentially helpless. Furthermore, to his chagrin Robert boards a ship, travels to another island, gets on a plane, and flies to what the reader (but not the Hunter) realizes is a boarding school in Massachusetts (much like the one at which the author teaches). It soon becomes clear to the Hunter that, even after he succeeds in communicating with the boy, he will not be able to provide independence of movement because of his age.

But Robert's youth has advantages, too. His enrollment in English classes speeds the Hunter's learning of the language. Eventually the Hunter achieves communication with Robert; by lightly pressing on selected nerves in the boy's retinas, he can cause words to appear against a blank background. He can now enlist Robert's active and very useful help. A second instance of good fortune occurs at this point, almost offsetting the Hunter's bad luck in his choice of a host. The discovery that an alien creature is living inside him has, to put it mildly, been a shock for Robert, producing a noticeable change in his behavior. The school doctor misdiagnoses its cause as homesickness and prescribes as a treatment that Robert return to the island. After months, the Hunter can now resume the chase.

From this point on, the reader's attention is centered on Robert, with the Hunter playing a large but subsidiary role. It becomes clear that Robert and the Hunter form a complementary team. The Hunter's role becomes advisory, while the boy exercises his ingenuity; the Hunter knows how the Quarry would think and act, while Robert is familiar with the island and its inhabitants.

Two factors narrow the pursuer's task. First, they assume that the Quarry would choose an intelligent host (rather than a fish or an animal) to gain maximum freedom of action. Fortunately, the island is populated solely by the small number of workers at the petroleum facility and their families, and nobody has left the island during the interim between Robert's departure for school and his return. The story thus becomes a classic tale of the sleuth and his assistant as the pair searches for clues, follows false leads, eliminates suspects one by one, and eventually locates and destroys the criminal.

Needle is a very fine detective story. One can imagine fans of Agatha Christie or John Dickson Carr finding a great deal of enjoyment in it. But the novel offers more. In its portrait of the Hunter, we have a convincing alien, astonishingly different in unexpected ways, yet completely believable. Like many other fine science fiction novels, *Needle* was inspired by the writer's determination to provide a counterexample to a presumed general rule; and through his portrait of the Hunter, Clement succeeds entirely. The competent and likable little alien whom we get to know only as "the Hunter" has few peers in the genre.

Walter E. Meyers

Sources for Further Study

Reviews:

Booklist. XLVI, March 15, 1950, p. 233.
Chicago Sun. April 3, 1950, p. 5.

Chicago Sunday Tribune. April 2, 1950, p. 12.
Horn Book. XXVI, May, 1950, p. 214.
Kirkus Reviews. XVIII, January 1, 1950, p. 7.
New York Times. March 12, 1950, p. 29.
San Francisco Chronicle. April 16, 1950, p. 28.

NERVES

Author: Lester Del Rey (1915-   )
First book publication: 1956
Type of work: Novel
Time: The near future
Locale: The National Atomics Products Plant and other sites in and around Kimberly, Missouri

When an experimental procedure for producing transuranium isotopes runs amok at the National Atomics plant, a medical research team takes extraordinary means to find a way of neutralizing a deadly isotope that threatens to begin a chain reaction

Principal characters:
DR. ROGER T. "DOC" FERREL, chief physician at National Atomics plant
EMMA FERREL, his wife
ALLAN PALMER, the plant manager
DR. ROBERT T. JENKINS, an assistant physician and amateur nuclear researcher
MAL JORGENSON, a theoretical nuclear research chief at National Atomics
MRS. SUE BROWN, Jenkins' wife and a nursing doctor

Once or twice in the career of a professional writer comes a story that is brilliant in every way except its execution. Unlike the other near-misses in a writer's bibliography, however, *Nerves* did not go quietly to sleep as it should have done. Instead, Del Rey found himself coming back to it again and again, occasionally rewriting portions, and ultimately expanding it into a novel.

There have been some famous cases of novels that have successfully evolved from shorter works. Asimov's *Foundation* trilogy may be the most dramatic case of such a story-to-novel evolution, but Walter M. Miller's *A Canticle for Leibowitz* may represent the most successful of all such transmutations. Daniel Keyes's prize-winning story "Flowers for Algernon" was expanded into a prize-winning novel of the same title. Lester Del Rey has been less successful in his expansion of a novelette he once wrote for *Astounding Science Fiction* (March, 1942) into a novel. The novel itself has now been revised by the author, so that the serious student of science fiction can trace the evolution of *Nerves* through three different printed versions. In other words, this novel represents one of those stories that a writer cannot forget; he keeps returning to it, reworking it in the hope of getting it right at last.

There is no doubt of the inherent value of the idea behind the story. The original inspiration came to the author in the form of a suggestion from John W. Campbell, Jr., the extraordinary editor of *Astounding Science Fiction*, and a science fiction author in his own right. Campbell thought that a story should be written about an accident in an industrial power plant as seen through the eyes of a company doctor. The effect aimed at, we are told in *The Early Del Rey*, was to produce the "same mood and feeling that had made Willy Ley's novelette 'Fog' so popular." Robert Heinlein had already written "Blowups Happen" (*Astounding Science Fiction*, September, 1940), which treated the consequences of an accident at a fission power plant, and so Del Rey turned to the idea of the possible industrial uses of isotope development and manufacture. Consequently, *Nerves* is full of extrapolations and inspired guesswork about isotope transmutation, the potential stability of superheavy transuranic elements, the likely social and political consequences of atomic productions, and so on. Perhaps the most remarkable thing about the argument of the story is that it originated well in advance of the development of the Manhattan Project, which led to the first atomic bomb tests in 1945, and to the subsequent development of atomic power plants.

The speculations of Heinlein, Del Rey, Campbell, and others were getting uncomfortably close not merely to guessing the secrets of the Manhattan Project scientists, but to publishing a scenario for the development of fission weapons in which Nazi Germany was especially interested. Perhaps the most notorious example of official sensitivity on the subject came in 1944 with Cleve Cartmill's atomic bomb story "Deadline" (*Astounding Science Fiction*, March, 1944), which led to an official investigation of the author, the editor, and the magazine by Military Intelligence, which was certain that someone in the Manhattan Project had talked; it even considered impounding the March issue of the magazine and having it classified Top Secret.

Lester Del Rey reveals in one of the autobiographical notes at the end of *The Early Del Rey*, Volume 1, that his intention was to write a suspense story. He had been making a relatively systematic study of suspense elements, and had worked out certain rules which he was anxious to put into practice. The result was the novelette version of *Nerves*. Considered as a suspense story, *Nerves* could serve as a model of interlocking plotlines building toward a grand climactic scene. The tension begins to build slowly from the very first sentence. "Doc" Ferrel receives a call from Palmer, the National Atomics plant manager, who wants him to be on hand for an inspection visit from a congressional committee which is conducting a fact-finding tour to gather information before debate begins on a bill that would require the removal of atomic plants at least fifty miles from the nearest town of ten thousand or more people. Doc agrees to be at his post for the visitation. By the time he arrives at the plant, tensions are already beginning to increase, and Doc reflects prophetically that conditions are favorable for an accident.

An accident is not long in coming. It involves several men who were working on the atomic pile in the main power plant. The damage is not severe, however, and Ferrel and his staff are able to treat successfully all the burn and radiation victims by applying medications and treatments which have been developed for such emergencies. The political effects prove far more serious. National Atomics would naturally be embarrassed by the accident, especially at such a sensitive time. Palmer's hand is forced by this misfortune, and he feels it necessary to take a calculated risk. He asks Jorgenson to run an experimental process to produce an isotope that has special agricultural applications. It would eliminate the latest weevil mutation in the home state of the chairman whose committee will hear the bill on atomic power plants. With the isotope as *quid pro quo*, the chances are that the bill can be killed in committee. Otherwise, the outlook is bleak.

Jorgenson's report is encouraging. It looks as though the conversion process can work even with such short notice, but there is cause for concern. The men are already tired and worried as a result of both the inspection tour and the accident at the power plant. Then, too, there has been the warning that the process could go wrong and produce Isotope R, an erratic and dangerously unstable form, which in turn could mutate into "Mahler's isotope," which would certainly mean doomsday for the surrounding town, possibly for the state or the entire country, and potentially for the whole world. But Jorgenson has already run successful test batches without incident, and the warning has come from an amateur in atomics, anyway. Palmer weighs the factors, and decides to go ahead with the production.

The stage is now set for the second accident, the one that leads to Isotope R and ultimately to Mahler's isotope. Jorgenson's equations have worked for his experimental test runs, but with the larger masses and the higher temperatures something goes wrong. At first it shows up as a fluctuation on the temperature and radiation gauge, a fluctuation that increases by the moment. Sensing the danger at once, Jorgenson could with some luck save the situation even at the last moment — but luck is not with him. Moving slowly in his armored suit, Jorgenson tries to direct a coordinated shutdown of the reaction process, but the men are tired and disorganized. Nothing can be done other than to save as many men as possible from the reactor melt down. Jorgenson sacrifices himself to that end, disappearing under a river of radioactive magma.

Outside, word begins to spread about the breakdown. The presence of Isotope R and its likely consequences soon make the extent of the disaster apparent to everyone. With Jorgenson a likely victim, Palmer hopes to rely on Hokusai, Jorgenson's colleague; but Hokusai is down with appendicitis. Palmer begins cleanup operations with the Isotope R problem left unsolved. Meanwhile, Doc Ferrel and his young assistant, Bob Jenkins work heroically to save as many of the survivors of this latest disaster as possible. That work, difficult enough when dealing with I-713, is complicated by the evidence that every bit of metal they remove from the victims has already become Isotope R, which, if a small amount of it were to transmute into Mahler's Isotope, would be sufficient to vaporize the entire plant. Ferrel and Jenkins work through the night, performing miracles, and depositing Isotope R fragments into a lead container.

The stage is thus adequately set for the climactic events. Incredibly, Jorgenson is found, barely alive, in the sea of magma. The rescue is dramatic enough to satisfy the requirements of an epic. The significance of the rescue lies in the hope that Jorgenson, if he can be saved and if he regains consciousness, might have the answer to the problem of neutralizing Isotope R before it becomes Mahler's Isotope. The scenes that follow, in which Ferrel and the entire staff work to save Jorgenson, are possibly the most gripping in the story. While the medical room drama holds the reader spellbound, a certain amount of grim relief is provided by the political and public relations crises that Palmer must somehow handle while trying to save the situation in the plant. Time is running out; calculations indicate that only a few hours remain before the transmutation into Mahler's Isotope.

There must be an answer, but how can it be found? And even then, can the solution be implemented in time? Lester Del Rey manages the developing crescendo of the story with sure, economical touches. Jorgenson is saved but is unable to communicate. It is Palmer who ultimately provides the solution, the same Palmer who had predicted the possibility of Isotope R in the converter reaction. Palmer's struggle is not only a race against time but also against panic and the mind-numbing effects of well-earned fatigue. Abetted by the heroic persistence of the workers and the ingenuity of the engineers and technicians, a method of dispersion is developed which will isolate each particle of Isotope R, cool it down, and keep it from reaching critical mass.

The suspense elements worked out by Del Rey are especially effective because they are supported by some extremely interesting hard science speculations on the possible stability of superheavy transuranium elements and their isotopes. The futuristic medical treatments of Ferrel and Jenkins are equally impressive, especially as they are combined first with the disaster spectacles, and later with the critical struggle to save Jorgenson. In these middle chapters of *Nerves* we have what is possibly the best medical writing in science fiction. In addition to the hard science, we are also given very convincing soft science speculations on the social, political, and economic impact of commercial atomic production. The blending of the two is handled with exceptional skill by Del Rey, a skill he learned in part from Campbell. The influence of Campbell is also apparent in the manner in which Del Rey has his characters respond to the series of crises they are forced to confront. It is a combination of scientific swashbuckling, speculative brainstorming, and hardworking heroism that sees them through. One of Campbell's favorite story formulas is the life- or even world-threatening disaster which forces the characters to save their lives and the larger situation by scientific problem-solving and some practical ingenuity. That formula is essentially the pattern from which *Nerves* is made.

Few would argue against the success of *Nerves* as a science fiction suspense story. Oddly enough, however, suspense here does not depend upon surprises or the unexpected. Quite the contrary. The reader is given ample clues and foreshadowings of what is coming. The suspense depends rather upon watching characters we care about continually put into more serious jeopardy. If we can set aside for the moment the tensions produced by the congressional investigation and the rising tide of concern and alarm among civil officials following upon the accidents, the immediate focus of the reader's anxiety is on nature.

First, Del Rey uses an elemental nature which humans try to control by understanding its operations. The physicists in *Nerves*, however, are dealing with even greater imponderables in creating and transmuting elements that come to exist in nature through man's efforts. Nevertheless, these new man-made elements do not behave as humans would wish; perversely enough, they follow what may be called an implied law of elemental nature, or an extension of it. For the reader inclined to speculation, the metaphysical questions raised by this very aspect of the story are well worth pondering and debating.

The characters in *Nerves*, however, have more immediate problems to solve. Having mistaken the path the transmutation of I-713 will take, the beleaguered company of scientists, technicians, workers, and managers set about correcting the error and finding the answer to the threat posed by Isotope R. Ultimately, *Nerves* confronts us with the specter of natural forces set loose by human error, running out of control, threatening destruction and the implied chaos of disorderly nature. In the end, however, the story affirms eventual human mastery of nature through personal courage and mental resourcefulness.

Del Rey's characters must also contend with human nature. Humans make mistakes, are prone to fatigue, and break under stress (especially the prolonged multiple stresses under which the medical team at National Atomics must function). Jenkins' triumph is, therefore, both a personal vindication (he had always wanted to be a nuclear physicist) and a symbolic triumph for human nature, which proves itself competent to establish mastery and control over nature through its science.

Both of these themes reinforce one another and represent something of an illustration of the science fiction archetype that is at work beneath the surface of the suspense and action. It points the way toward solution and salvation through science. Perhaps for this reason, *Nerves* does not function as a cautionary tale. It is not so much that Del Rey comes across as an atomic power hawk — some stress is given to the as-yet unsolved problem of how nuclear waste is to be rendered harmless — but that the logic as well as the formula of the story runs in another direction. The nuclear power issue is inevitably raised, but it is not given an evenhanded discussion. Some readers will find that the values raised and their accompanying attitudes are indeed power-oriented. Others will find the author's faith in science and in man's problem-solving capabilities as naïve as the insistent belief that every problem, especially man-made ones, has a solution.

Although *Nerves* is a novel of science fiction ideas, speculation, and suspense, it will survive or perish in the end on its merits as either myth or art.

Nerves has its share of archetypal elements, and it may be that these will be enough to ensure its survival, although it certainly does not qualify as myth in the same way that *Frankenstein* does or, less elegantly, *The Foundation Trilogy*. As a work of science fiction, *Nerves* has exceptional strengths but also serious weaknesses. Ironically, the weaknesses are in the very areas that the author has spent the most time expanding and rewriting; but then, no architect buttresses the strongest parts of a building. The chief defect lies with characterization, for despite all the rewriting, the characters simply do not come alive. Oddly, in this novel, the author is most successful with his women, who are unfortunately only supporting players. The men are all flat, rather shopworn types who never are able to transcend the triteness of their dialogue. We know very little more about the characters than what appears on the cover: Palmer is a plant manager, Ferrel is a company doctor, Jenkins is a wonderkid, and Jorgenson is a madman. Much of the accessory detail added by Del Rey is, in the end, dispensable since the strength of the novel really lies in its speculative extrapolations and its suspense formulas.

A word should be said about the stylistic success of *Nerves*. Unexpectedly, perhaps, one of the strong points of the novel is Del Rey's use of imagery and symbolism. The imagery, with its strong accent on the visual and the tactile, help to keep the story alive and vivid. The symbolism, although used sparingly, is very effective when it appears; it is perhaps unfortunate that Del Rey was so tentative in this area. The first paragraph sets a standard for craftsmanship that the novel too often fails to maintain, but it deserves an attentive reading for the vibrations and echoes it sets up as the story begins.

If *Nerves* does not quite measure up to those works mentioned above that have made a successful transition from story to novel (*Flowers for Algernon*, *A Canticle for Leibowitz*, *The Foundation Trilogy*), it is nonetheless an important science fiction work and one of the best suspense stories in the genre.

Donald I. Lawler

Sources for Further Study

Criticism:

"Pop Theology: Those Gods from Outer Space," in *Time*. LXXXIV (September 5, 1969), p. 64. This anonymous article cites Del Rey's writing as creating prototypes for science fiction mythologies.

NEWS FROM NOWHERE

Author: William Morris (1834-1896)
First book publication: 1891
Type of work: Novel
Time: The early twenty-first century
Locale: London

The travels and conversations of a nineteenth century man who dreams that he
spends a day in England's future after a successful Communist revolution

Principal character:
WILLIAM GUEST, a political idealist

William Morris' name is little known today except to students of nineteenth
century literature: they might know him as the author of a number of once very
popular and now unread (though by no means unreadable) narrative poems and
translations, languorous and late-Romantic in style, and a good number of prose
romances with magical titles such as *The Well at the World's End.* They might
learn that he became, by way of the famous group of painters known as the
Pre-Raphaelite Brotherhood, an ardent and intelligent Socialist, an effective
speaker, a political organizer of great effectiveness, and the editor of *Commonweal*, the Socialist journal. The more curious English majors might go on
to discover that Morris was a skillful painter and a superbly talented craftsman
whose wallpaper designs, beautiful book-printing, and original furniture are
historically important and lovely in themselves.

When he died in 1896 at the age of sixty-three, Morris was an almost
saintly hero to two generations of Aesthetes who believed that intelligence and
honor in economics coupled with a keen sense of beauty and its nearly religious value could, quite simply, transform the world from the industrial and
brutal horror it had become into (in the words of a Morris title) The Earthly
Paradise. To the very end of his long life, Bernard Shaw kept a portrait of
Morris like an icon on the otherwise rather bare walls of his study at Ayot St.
Lawrence. (It hangs there still.) Shaw said that Morris was at least three
geniuses rolled into one: Shaw was probably thinking of Morris' staggering
accomplishments in literature, painting, crafts, and politics.

His one novel, *News from Nowhere*, draws from these three areas to create
one of the most interesting visions ever offered in any of the futuristic Utopian
novels. Morris wrote his novel as an answer to Edward Bellamy's *Looking Backward* (1888) because of its vision of an over-ordered, mechanized future. However, *News from Nowhere* is particularly interesting to a modern reader because it
paints a beautiful and compellingly charged picture of a successful pure Communism — the phrase which runs through the book. As such, it has the invaluable
effect of explaining the profound and widespread appeal Communism has had for
so many intellectuals and political idealists to those (in the West) who know only
the Communism soured by the tryanny of the twentieth century.

To understand the Communism of *News from Nowhere*, however, it is as necessary to understand Aestheticism as *Das Kapital*. As a student at Oxford in the 1850's Morris formed a close friendship with the painter Edward Burne-Jones. They were both encouraged in their painting and their ideas by Dante Gabriel Rossetti, himself a blazing young genius who wanted to write a new kind of poetry and paint a new kind of picture. It was to be inspired by the past: the present was industrial, squalid, and ugly; this new vision of beauty was to be *pre*-Raphael, before the Renaissance which had led to this depressingly ugly present; it was to aspire to the purer beauty of the Middle Ages — especially of the late fourteenth century.

The circle which formed around Morris and Rossetti wanted to rediscover and reexplore the beauty and the meaning of the aesthetic experience. The poet had already become a seer, the substitute for the priest, who seemed to have less and less to say. From the great art critic John Ruskin, they learned of the social — indeed, political — importance of art and of the moral blight which ugliness creates. But thereafter Aestheticism went off into two strongly different directions. One went through Walter Pater to Oscar Wilde and the Decadents, who insisted on art for art's sake — that is, for the sake of the self-contained and self-justifying sensations which the work of art produces.

The other Aesthetic stream flowed, rather more directly, from Ruskin through Morris to Shaw and ended, a bit oddly, in the beginnings of the modern British Labor Party. That Party was conceived in the intellectual and political passion set ablaze by the innumerable political discussion groups of the 1880's and 1890's. The subtlest of bows toward these groups is in the very frame for *News from Nowhere*: the novel is simply the dream of a political idealist weary after a night of political discussion.

Relatively little is made of this character — called William Guest — or, indeed, of any of the characters: they are names, like those in Plato's dialogues, in an interesting discussion. What little development there is of William Guest comes after he has been exposed to this new world — he soon learns that it is set early in the twenty-first century — and consists mainly of his depression at the discrepancy between what is and what could be.

What first strikes him about this world is its sheer physical beauty. He sees a lovely stone bridge over the Thames, a replacement for one of the Victorian iron monstrosities. He sees houses which seem to have grown up from the land itself; they are a natural part of it, houses "alive, and sympathetic with the life of the dwellers in them." It is the houses which first make Guest feel as if he were living in the fourteenth century — a principal motif: for him the medievals comprised the last culture which "liked everything trim and clear, and orderly and bright." This architecture, "not only exquisitely beautiful in itself," is important because it contained, Guest says, "such generosity and abundance of life that I was exhilarated to a pitch that I had never yet reached."

All around him, Guest sees a delicate loveliness and beauty which is reflected in (or is the cause of) a robust, healthy beauty in the inhabitants. Morris insists on this point to a surprising degree, particularly on the physical
beauty of the women. Indeed, at one point he makes Guest complain, in effect,
that the old capitalism is bad because it produces women who are "gaunt figures, lean, flat-breasted, ugly, without a grace of form or face about them."
But now people live to advanced ages in great health and happiness.

Guest learns how the inhabitants of this world, this Communist Britain,
educate their children. It is very simple: they don't. They distrust great book-
ishness, think it absurd that intellectuals should pride themselves on being
physically and manually incompetent, and think it even more absurd that learning should be thought of as a process one goes through in youth. Learning for
them is a continuous and a perfectly natural part of their daily lives. They learn
as much by observation, reflection, and conversation, however, as they do by
books — which are somewhat rarer than in the old days. The children follow
the adults around, "most of whom are engaged in genuinely amusing work,
like housebuilding and street-paving, and gardening, and the like." The children are left to grow up as naturally as Walter Pater said they should — like a
rose in a country lane. They grow up in a world in which the artists are crafts-
men, and in which everyone is a craftsman producing beautiful work. The idea
of anything being too beautiful for use is totally incomprehensible to them.

Socially, the great change has been marked by an ending of industrialism.
Guest's interlocutor admits that it was improbable, but it happened: handicrafts
replaced the machines. Accused of impracticality (no less than Engels himself
complained that Morris was a "sentimental Socialist"), Morris is nonetheless
shrewd in seeing exactly what the real, the psychological and personal, basis
must be for such a change.

The change is described in a long central section of interesting pseudo-his-
tory: Guest is told of the great battles that took place at Trafalgar Square before the revolutionary government replaced the old greedy and corrupt capitalism. Morris could not have imagined the *extent* of the slaughter the twentieth
century was to contain, but he anticipated remarkably the appallingly frequent
twentieth century horror of feeling that "there was nothing else in the world
but murder and death."

But for Morris (who believed optimistically in the beneficent power of the
human spirit), this tragedy was a necessary prelude to the second birth of the
world. The civil war lasted two years, but at the end there was a new world.
Human beings have powerful drives toward creation or destruction; Morris
thought we would all choose creation as long as we are not hungry, angry, or
overworked.

The obvious question is how people stave off the boredom which presumably must result if the drive of capitalism is removed. Guest learns that the
boredom is prevented "by the production of what used to be called art." These

central sentences explain the process: "by slow degrees we got pleasure into our work; then we became conscious of that pleasure, and cultivated it, and took care that we had our fill of it; and then all was gained, and we were happy. So may it be for ages and ages!"

Morris understood that the essence of capitalism is personal competitiveness. The psychological basis of his Communism is a change of heart whereby people simply do not see life as essentially a competition. He knew that this change of heart is based on the very real longing for freedom and equality such as everyone has and thus, politically, on "the hope of realizing a communal condition of life for all men." There might be a friendly rivalry between groups who want to go housebuilding and those who want to go haying, but "success in besting our neighbors is a road to renown now closed, let us hope forever." Consequently, "every man is free to exercise his special faculty to the utmost."

Therefore, there is no money: there is no need of it. Freed from property, even marriage is a surprisingly relaxed affair: couples split, reunite if and when they wish, and their children have an extraordinary measure of personal freedom. There is more than a hint of considerable sexual freedom. Guest is told that while not all crimes and problems have been eliminated (human passions remain awesome in their power), most crimes of passion have disappeared because most of them and all their attendant anguish come from the revolting idea "of the woman being the property of the man." Thus family tyranny is abolished: people do not own things or one another.

This is a clear and bright world. Most of the old ways have been abolished: most amusingly, the House of Commons is used to store dung. Politics, government, and bureaucracies have all disappeared. What little administration is necessary is dispatched in a kind of town-hall system: the inhabitants avoid centralization whenever possible. The local level is, for them, the *only* level. (There is practically no discussion of international politics: one is told that many other countries followed Britain's lead and became, in effect, peaceable, Communistic communes.)

The changes are also reflected in the clothing. Guest says constantly that the beautiful women he sees around him are always wearing light and lovely garments. In a line worthy of Oscar Wilde, he says that "they were clothed like women, not upholstered like armchairs." The clothing reflects a change in manner. Men and women are more open with one another; there is more tolerance and understanding: "there is no unvarying conventional set of rules by which people are judged."

Morris asks his readers to share his dream: in his last line he suggests that we see it as a vision, a vision of what life could be. Like William Guest, we ought to weep at "the picture of the sordid squabble, the dirty and miserable tragedy of the life" that we all know.

In at least one way, Morris' Utopia (Greek for not-a-place, that is, Nowhere) is unique. Utopias, including the Utopia of Morris' hero Thomas More, tend to be rational, orderly, schematic: they are often absorbing blueprints for an ideal political society. Many of them — including More's — could be realized in actuality given sufficient political power. What is wrong with them is clear: no one really wants to live in them. More's *Utopia*, Plato's *Republic* — these are fascinating books; but they would be dull and repressive real societies.

But William Morris' vision is not so rational or orderly; there are people who do not fit and yet somehow belong; most, but not all, social problems have been solved; Morris does not profess to have answered all the questions or eliminated all the crimes or given everyone perfect happiness. His Nowhere is not likely to be really achieved on earth since it depends upon the apparently impossible withering away of the government, *any* government. Yet it has what all the other Utopias lack: one could imagine living there happily with freedom, dignity, honesty, and beauty. Politically impossible, yes. But Morris' is the most valuable of the Utopias because it represents the moral ideal toward which politics should strive.

Brian Murphy

THE NEXT CHAPTER
(LE CHAPITRE SUIVANT)

Author: André Maurois (Emile Herzog, 1885-1967)
First book publication: 1927
English translation: 1927
Type of work: Novelette
Time: Flashback from 1992 to 1951-1964
Locale: Largely in Europe

An exploration of the great power of the press, telling about the profound effects induced by global publicity campaigns

> *Principal characters:*
> ALAIN DE ROUVRAY, France
> LORD FRANK DOUGLAS, Great Britain
> JOSEPH C. SMACK, The United States
> DR. MACHT, Germany
> DR. KRAFT, his successor, and
> BARON TOKUNGAWA, Japan, the five globally-influential press magnates who constitute the "Dictators of Opinion" through their "World Newspaper Association"
> BEN TABRIT, Dean of the Faculty of Sciences in Marrakech, Morocco

André Maurois was one of the writers whose science fiction constitutes only a small portion of his literary production. At his death in 1967, his legacy included scores of books of considerable diversity. His output of science fiction and other relatable imaginative literature, though it was small in quantity, was enriched by his otherwise prolific and versatile career. His novels established him as a discerning interpreter of human nature and national character. *Les Silences du Colonel Bramble* (The Silence of Colonel Bramble, 1918) reflected his insights into the English character, elements of which enter into the present book as well. That novel, as well as his many novels dealing with French provincial, upper-middle-class life, proved exceedingly popular among his compatriots, usually achieving many foreign readers through translations.

The numerous interpretive biographies and literary studies of Maurois demonstrated his great competence as a scholarly researcher, applied to such French writers as the Dumas family, Victor Hugo, Honoré de Balzac, Marcel Proust, André Gide, and Jean-Paul Sartre. He was a particularly keen analyst of Percy and Mary Shelley, not to mention Robert and Elizabeth Browning, Charles Dickens, and others. In the area of history and current affairs, Maurois wrote such surveys as *Histoire des Etats-Unis*, published in English as *The Miracle of America* (1944); *Edouard VII et son Temps*, issued in English as *King Edward VII and His Times* (1933); and *Tragédie en France*, *Tragedy in France* (1940). There were also books of philosophy and occasional biographies of scientific figures, such as *La Vie de Sir Alexander Fleming*, (Life of Sir Alexander Fleming, 1959).

One should not suppose that this author's life was given only to literary creations. His family's textile mill claimed much of his time in his earlier years, and he served his country in both world wars. All this experience, together with his variegated literary career, helps to explain how his rather limited excursions into science fiction could be quite fruitful. Fruitful, that is, despite the superficiality or even incidental nature of the scientific element, with more credit due the cogent treatments of human nature and society which are found therein.

For example, in *Voyage au Pays des Articoles*, rendered in English as *A Voyage to the Island of the Articoles* (1929), a Frenchman disenchanted with Europe after World War I travels to the South Seas. There he finds an island society which cherishes its artists and writers as its privileged class. The objects of this adulation are shown as effete and detached from reality — thus satirizing some of Maurois' European contemporaries. In *La Machine à Lire les Pensées* (The Thought-Reading Machine, 1937), an American professor has developed a machine which detects and records all the passing thoughts of persons on whom it is trained. Not only does this make mischief, as we might expect, but Maurois indicates here that transient thoughts are really not as meaningful as the modern psychoanalysts have led us to suppose — what truly matters is the translation of more purposeful and fundamental thoughts into action.

In *The Next Chapter*, a keen sense of history, human nature, and social phenomena is the most commendable element. Nevertheless, there are a number of good anticipations of scientific developments which were either unknown or only dimly emergent in 1927. The television, and its use for video conferences of executives is one such feature. There are also knowledgeable references to atomic science and atomic energy, as well as to the use of highly destructive "rays" which could be lasers. The large scale generation of energy from the wind is also a key discovery.

The suspension of disbelief in this fragmentary document of history, "published in 1992," is deftly facilitated by footnotes which refer to intervening documentary sources with such dates as 1968 and 1978. The narrative opens with a reference to a major war which began in 1947 and destroyed New York, London, Paris, Berlin, and Peking. Thirty million persons were killed in 1947 alone. The Peace of Peking ended that conflict in 1951, but not until 1962 were the great cities rebuilt.

When in 1962 the Moroccan scientist Ben Tabrit invented a technique for collecting and storing wind energy, which made this energy source far cheaper than fossil fuels, the powers were still so competitive and antagonistic that the threat of war again became acute in 1963, involving such rivals as the Franco-German grouping, the "Union of Dominions," and the "Russo-Chinese Empire."

Here Maurois brings in the interesting concept that boredom helps to produce wars — that the bored populace is like tinder, easily ignited by sparks from quarrels which, objectively viewed, are not so serious or hard to settle. In the case of access to wind power, the point is clear enough. One way to head off the imminent recurrence of world war in connection with the development of wind power, is to divert the ire of the people to a less dangerous target, providing them with excitement from an artificially created hate-object, a synthetic enemy, so unconnected with truly urgent and combustible quarrels that their anger can be vented safely.

It is the five Dictators of Opinion who undertake this diversionary project. Controlling the dominant newspaper chains of the world through their World Newspaper Association, they have a virtual control over global opinion. For years the five men have conferred weekly by video-phone to plan the management of opinion and to head off harmful crises whenever possible. This book does not anticipate the great role of radio, motion pictures, and television as opinion molders. Note that it was published in 1927, the very year of Charles Lindbergh's Trans-Atlantic flight — the radio-broadcast reporting of which heralded the advent of radio as a popular medium. The motion picture with sound was also just about to show what it could do. Television would not escape from the laboratories until two more decades had elapsed. Thus Maurois' concentration on the power of the press is natural enough, though devoid of great prescience.

The five press lords undergo little character development. The names of the German member — Macht, then Kraft — mean "power" and "strength," evidently conveying a feeling about that nation. The American and Japanese members seldom say anything; the archetypally French Rouvray and the rather breezy Englishman, Douglas, are the active members of the group.

The concept of public opinion being molded like putty in the hands of the press would have been very familiar to Maurois from genuine international phenomena well before 1927. His book, *The Miracle of America*, though published later, includes in its historical narrative an account of the coming of the Spanish-American War in 1898, when the Hearst newspapers are described as launching a campaign for war in the same way that one might launch a campaign for a new cigarette. Maurois also describes the dramatic role of modified public opinion in the recruitment of the United States to the side of the Allied Powers in 1915-1917. He speaks of American opinion veering rapidly to the Allied side. When the *Lusitania* was sunk, he notes, a cry of horror went up from the whole world. Maurois also must have been aware that the Franco-Russian Alliance, which was the mainstay of the Allied configuration ten years before World War I, secured the support of French public opinion, despite the normal aversion to the Czarist autocracy in democratic France, with the aid of large Russian payments to influential French newspapers.

Despite the limitations of Maurois' vantage point of 1927, he appears to have foreseen very well the expanded influence of the media during and after

World War II. The Nazi German and Communist propaganda machines were in a way similar to what Maurois had contemplated, taking advantage of the credibility which may become attached to even the most outrageous lies if they are repeated often enough. The author lived until 1967, and thus was able to observe with a certain satisfaction the fulfillment of his prophecy on the ability to mold opinion in such phenomena as the American presidential campaigns of the 1960's, where immense media resources were marshaled to build up and sell the candidates. He did not, of course, see the climax of the media build-up of those two *causes célèbres* in recent history, the Vietnam War and Watergate, both of which fulfilled generally his prognostications of media power. Are the alterations of opinion thus wrought fundamental, or are they more like the transient thoughts which Maurois tried to reduce to a proper perspective in his *The Thought-Reading Machine*? The author seems to leave that question for readers to ponder.

At any rate, in this book the diversionary campaign contrived by the magnates of the World Newspaper Association consisted of carefully-planned, falsified reports that intelligent, aggressive beings on the Moon were attacking Earth. The strikes were reported as being made at various remote locations on our planet — so that the falsity of the newspaper reports could be concealed. This press campaign was successful, so arousing the public against the evil beings of the Moon that the peaceful settlement of Earth's real quarrels about access to wind power was very readily achieved.

Unfortunately, the effect of the antilunar publicity went much farther than the Dictators of Opinion had foreseen. There was a public clamor for counter-strikes against the Moon. The Moroccan scientist Ben Tabrit then came forward with his new invention, powerful rays which could indeed strike at the Moon. Today, more than a half-century after Maurois wrote this book, we would be astonished if a scientist were so versatile as to produce two discoveries so disparate as Ben Tabrit's — wind energy storage and antilunar rays. One should reflect, however, that 1927 was still the era of Thomas Edison, an inventor of exceedingly varied processes. The narrow specialization of scientists and engineers had not yet gone so far.

The lamentable results of the attacks which were made against the Moon, under the irresistible pressure of the thoroughly aroused people of Earth, need not be described in detail. In fact, Maurois leaves his narrative truncated at this point, and the full consequences must be imagined by the reader. We are told that although nobody had any idea in 1962 that beings really did exist on the Moon, that idea proved to be true. When attacked, they struck back, destroying various towns and cities on Earth. One of those destroyed was Elbeuf, France, the hometown of the textile mill which Maurois had managed for many boring years. The *ennui* of Elbeuf, with its seeming frustration of his nascent literary career, is thus summarily liquidated in this book.

This is a future fiction work of impressive competence — though that is hardly surprising from a writer of Maurois' experience and stature. Its theme of the massive molding of public opinion is intriguingly developed. It is a theme of great portent in the real present and future, a subject which could benefit by more thorough and updated attention from first rate contemporary writers of science fiction.

Frank H. Tucker

Sources for Further Study

Criticism:

Keating, L. Clark. *Andre Maurois*. New York: Twayne, 1969, p. 32. Maurois and his literary acumen are discussed at length. The author describes it as pleasurable to read.

Reviews:

Booklist. XXV, January, 1929, p. 166.

Boston Transcript. November 17, 1928, p. 8.

NIGHTWINGS

Author: Robert Silverberg (1936-   )
First book publication: 1969
Type of work: Novel
Time: The far future
Locale: Roum, Perris, and Jorslem

A chronicle about the "redemption" of Earth both from outside invaders and from its own progressive deterioration

> Principal characters:
> WUELLIG (TOMIS), initially a Watcher, subsequently a Rememberer, then a Pilgrim
> AVLUELA, a Flier
> GORMON, an alien masquerading as a Changeling
> THE PRINCE OF ROUM, a Dominator
> OLMAYNE, a Rememberer

The first part of *Nightwings* was originally published as a novella bearing the same title in 1968 and won a Hugo award. The two remaining sections, expanding the story to novel length, also saw separate publication before the book appeared.

The story is set in a distant future referred to as the Third Cycle; the First Cycle was the period of man's rise from savagery to civilization and the Second the period of his technological magnificence. The Earth of the Third Cycle is decadent; the human race has been humbled by a self-inflicted catastrophe and the period of confusion which followed it, though the relics of the technology of the Second Cycle are still used for various purposes. Society is divided into a series of occupational guilds, which define for each man a place within the scheme of things and regulate both his behavior and his opportunities. One such guild, the Fliers, consists of individuals equipped with insectlike wings — a product of Second Cycle genetic engineering. The process by which these wings permit flight is mysterious and quasi-magical, but is subject to the restriction that the wings are only operative by night when the pressure of the sun's radiation is absent; thus the novel acquires its title. Other products of Second Cycle experiments in genetic engineering and teratogenesis are the guildless Changelings, monstrous creatures generally regarded as subhuman. The Changelings were once guilded, but lost that status following an abortive rebellion in which they temporarily seized the most important of human shrines, the city of Jorslem.

The protagonist of the novel is, during the first section, a member of the guild of Watchers, whose function it is to "tune in" periodically to a kind of psionic scanning device which allows them to sense the approach of invaders from outside the solar system. An invasion has been prophesied, but many of the people on Earth now believe the prophecy to be a myth and the vocation of the Watchers, though sacred, to be a futile one. The protagonist is not initially named (the rules of the guild demand that his name be kept secret) but we later discover that as a Watcher he is called Wuellig.

The first part of the narrative tells how the Watcher comes to the city of Roum in the company of a Flier named Avluela (whom he loves, though he is much older than she and is in any case bound by a vow of celibacy) and a Changeling named Gormon. The three find themselves without lodgings because the Watchers of Roum refuse to take them in, and they go to seek an audience with the Prince of the city in order to ask for shelter. Their request is granted, but only because the Prince is smitten with Avluela and commands her to his bed. Gormon, at this point, is enraged with jealousy, and confesses to the Watcher that he is Avluela's lover (though such a union is strictly forbidden by the laws of the guild-system). He further swears that in time to come he will put out the eyes of the Prince of Roum in order to revenge himself.

Gormon has made a habit of mocking the Watcher's calling and forces the Watcher to confront his own lack of faith by questioning him while the Watcher's hand is inside the Mouth of Truth, a stone hollow which, it is said, will crush the hand of anyone who offends it by lying. When Gormon, in turn, places his own hand in the Mouth so that the Watcher can ask *his* question, he tells the Watcher that despite his conviction of the futility of Watching there *will* be an invasion, and that he is not a Changeling but a military observer for the aliens whose invasion fleet is approaching. The Watcher soon confirms this information, and sounds an alarm which rouses the whole planet to prepare its defenses. Alas, the defenses are quite inadequate, and Earth falls, its conquest little more than a formality.

The ex-Watcher, now guildless because there is no more Watching to be done, decides to leave Roum for Perris in the hope of joining the guild of Rememberers, custodians of Earth's history. He finds company in a man who wears the mask of the guild of Pilgrims, though he does not have a starstone, a jewel which allows genuine Pilgrims to link their consciousness to the divine Will. The false Pilgrim is, in fact, the Prince of Roum, now blinded and fleeing from the invaders, who have ordered the capture of all Dominators. As the two leave the city, the ex-Watcher sees Avluela flying overhead in full daylight, sustained in her flight by Gormon the invader, who flies with her.

The second section of the book tells of the travelers' acceptance by the guild of Rememberers in Perris, sponsored by a female Rememberer named Olmayne. The protagonist, now called Tomis, throws himself into the tedious work of an apprentice, and eventually — by sheer accident — locates an "image-recording" which shows the ancestors of the invaders imprisoned by men of the Second Cycle in a kind of zoo. It is believed that this historical act called down the wrath of the Will upon Earth to destroy the civilization of the Second Cycle. The invaders have finally come to take the revenge which they swore in the distant past — to complete the humiliation of man. The invaders desperately want to recover and destroy this particular image-recording, which has been concealed by the Rememberers, and Tomis eventually betrays its whereabouts to them in order to win the freedom of the Prince of Roum, who is threatened with exposure by Olmayne's husband Elegro. Tomis wins an amnesty for the Prince, but gains nothing, because the Prince is murdered by Elegro, who is himself slain by his adulterous wife.

In the third part of the book both Tomis and Olmayne become Pilgrims, bound for Jorslem as possible candidates for rejuvenation by means of a process administered by the guild of Renewers. Not everyone is accepted for Renewal, and some of those to whom the process is administered fail to meet the spiritual requirements. While *en route* to Jorslem Tomis and Olmayne become involved with a Surgeon who expresses his opinion that the invasion not only marks the consummation of the punishment inflicted upon mankind by the Will for the sin of pride, but also provides a sign that the time is now ripe for the redemption of the race. Tomis discovers when he reaches Jorslem that a new guild has been formed, a guild of Redeemers, which will accept members from all other guilds, including Changelings. He meets Avluela again, and finds that she already belongs to the new guild.

Tomis and Olmayne are both accepted for Renewal, and Tomis is successfully rejuvenated; but Olmayne, a jealous and intolerant woman entirely selfish in her outlook, proves unable to adjust to the requirements of the treatment and regresses to early childhood, in which condition she dies.

The means by which the members of the new guild obtain personal redemption — and seek redemption for the whole race — is a mutual attunement of minds made possible by a combination of the instruments once used by the Watchers and the starstones used by the Pilgrims. Together, the two devices permit users to attune themselves to the Will and literally to enter into one another's spirit. All men can now be reunited, no matter what their status or occupation, and the despised Changelings are to play the role of scapegoats no longer. The conquest of Earth ceases to have any real importance: "When all mankind is enrolled in our guild, we will be conquered no longer. When each of us is part of every other one of us, our sufferings will end. There is no need for us to struggle against our conquerors, for we will absorb them, once we are all Redeemed."

Nightwings was written by Silverberg in the months following the destruction of his home by fire, an event which in his autobiographical essay "Sounding Brass, Tinkling Cymbal" he characterizes as traumatic and confesses to having seen as a kind of judgment, redressing an imbalance resulting from his enjoyment of good fortune in the past. Clearly, there is within the book considerable depth of personal feeling and an entirely private significance. Its symbolism often seems less than subtle, but there is no mistaking the authenticity of the emotion underlying its allegorical features. There is much in the novel which can best be interpreted by reference to Silverberg's personal experience. It clearly reflects, for instance, the fact that during the 1960's he traveled extensively in Europe and that his visit to Jerusalem was of particular personal significance. But it is also a futuristic recasting of traditional Judeo-Christian salvation myth, and as such has much more general allegorical claims.

Nightwings, especially the first section, is in some ways a deeply nostalgic work. The situation described there — the decadent Earth strewn with the quasi-magical flotsam of an ancient and all-powerful technology, threatened by invasion from the stars — is highly reminiscent of the scenarios which Silverberg employed habitually in the days when, as a prolific young science fiction writer, he used to fill the pages of *Science Fiction Adventures* with novelettes bearing titles such as "Slaves of the Star-Giants" and "Vengeance of the Space Armadas." *Nightwings* recalls this conventional scenery in the service of a very different ideology; the romanticization of extravagant violence and tough-minded heroism is here replaced by a very different set of values emphasizing the virtues of empathy and pacifism. The theme which runs through virtually all of Silverberg's novels of the second phase of his career (post-1965) is the healing of states of alienation: the reconciliation of "outsiders" of various kinds to their fellow human beings, very often by a direct contact of minds, frequently involving processes of rebirth both literal and metaphorical. *Nightwings* approaches this theme in reverse of the pulp-fiction scenarios which Silverberg had abandoned in order that the scenario itself might be, in a sense, renewed.

Everything that Silberberg does in *Nightwings* he went on to do much better in other novels. The mythology of rebirth is much more powerfully developed in *Downward to the Earth*, while the allegorical qualities of the plot helped prepare the way for the brilliant *Son of Man*, by far the most significant allegorical novel to use the vocabulary of symbols developed by the literature of the scientific imagination.

Nightwings is inferior to much of Silverberg's work of the 1970's, but it is nevertheless an important work. It cannot be described as a transitional work, for Silverberg had already abandoned the habits of his earlier career some years before writing it, but it is a novel which constructs a kind of bridge between the mythology of his early work and the ideological concerns of his mature work. The Second Cycle of the book is an imaginary historical era which was once central to the futuristic imaginings of science fiction writers, but which has now passed from fashionability — an invalidated dream. *Nightwings* is a novel which recognizes the redundancy of that mythology while remembering that it once seemed so marvelously appealing. Contemporary science fiction — of which Silverberg's later work is such an important part — is now into its own "Third Cycle" of tattered dreams and spiritual questing, and for this reason *Nightwings* has a certain paradigmatic status. It is hard to find the story wholly convincing, and its message is awkwardly over-obvious in its presentation, but the novel remains very much in keeping with the ideative climate of recent science fiction.

Brian Stableford

Sources for Further Study

Reviews:

Books and Bookmen. XVII, June, 1972, pp. 72-73.

Luna Monthly. XXIV–XXV, May–June, 1971, p. 41.

New Worlds. CXCVII, January, 1970, p. 33.

Observer. May 28, 1972, p. 33.

Son of WSFA Journal. XXI, May, 1971, p. 10.

NINETEEN EIGHTY-FOUR

Author: George Orwell (Eric Blair, 1903-1950)
First book publication: 1948
Type of work: Novel
Time: 1984 and after
Locale: Airstrip One, Oceania, a country that was Great Britain

A classic portrait of the totalitarian state of the future

> *Principal characters:*
> WINSTON SMITH, an average man
> JULIA, an attractive young girl with whom he falls in love
> O'BRIEN, an official in the Ministry of Truth and Winston's nemesis
> BIG BROTHER, the leader of the Party

In *Nineteen Eighty-Four*, George Orwell created a twentieth century myth ranking with the nineteenth century's *Frankenstein*, *Dracula*, and *Dr. Jekyll and Mr. Hyde*. That he was able to do so may in part be attributed to his political insight, but to a much greater measure his success was due to his skill with and understanding of the structure of the English language. The terms "1984" and "Big Brother" have passed into the language, and many who have never heard of Orwell refer to "Big Brother" as a symbol of the tyranny of government, from the IRS to police surveillance helicopters. The term "Newspeak" itself has not attained such currency, but the process by which language may be used to obscure and manipulate thought is, if anything, considerably more pervasive and insidious than the more direct manipulation Orwell envisioned in 1948. It is an aspect of the future which Orwell predicted most accurately.

Orwell wrote *Nineteen Eighty-Four* the year before his death, when he was living in the Hebrides, bleak remote islands off the coast of Scotland. It was partly a reaction to contemporary politics and partly a rebuttal to Aldous Huxley's *Brave New World* (1932), which depicted a society in which behavior is controlled by conditioning from the cradle — or, rather, test tube. More of an influence were H. G. Wells's *When the Sleeper Wakes* (1895) and Jack London's *The Iron Heel* (1908), about the takeover of the United States by an oligarchy of powerful businessmen. Though *Nineteen Eighty-Four* accurately reflects the mood of post-World War II England and Europe, it is not dated. The chilling fact is that, particularly in the ways in which the English language and its abuses have developed, the novel is less "science fiction" now than when it was written. One does not need to know, for instance, that Goldstein, the "betrayer" of the Party and object of the Two Minutes' Hate, is based on Trotsky. It is, however, useful to remember that the concept of brainwashing and rewriting history is a satire of left-wing intellectual attitudes (as Orwell describes them in "The Prevention of Literature") as well as a satire of the methods of the totalitarian state. For this reason, the critical reception of *Nine-*

teen Eighty-Four was mixed, for many of the critics were of the left-wing intelligentsia.

Language and its significance is the dominant theme in *Nineteen Eighty-Four* and a dominating concern in Oceania, the superstate which rules one-third of the world and is at perpetual war with Eastasia and Eurasia, which rule the other two-thirds. From the first sentence, "It was a bright cold day in April and the clocks were striking thirteen," Orwell accurately pinpoints every casual detail of life in this terrifying superstate. The clocks are striking thirteen because the whole state is on military twenty-four-hour time. The ruling group, known simply as the Party, headed by Big Brother, maintains its power by fear, through constant monitoring by telescreen, and above all by the continual censorship of language. In Newspeak, it is impossible to think certain thoughts because there are no longer words for them. History and literature are rewritten to conform to the Party's view. "Who controls the past controls the present, and who controls the present controls the future" is one of the Party's major slogans.

Always, "Big Brother is watching you"; and no gesture, word, or even thought escapes him. "Big Brother" does not appear in the novel except as a face on a poster or telescreen, his black hair, moustache, and deceptively benign expression reminiscent of Stalin. O'Brien, during his interrogation of Winston Smith, admits that Big Brother may not even exist. Yet he becomes the most memorable character in the book, a symbol of all the oppressiveness of Orwell's nightmarishly totalitarian future state. This, of course, is his function in *Nineteen Eighty-Four*; he is the focus of the absolute obedience, spoken and unspoken, conscious and unconscious, demanded of all the population of Oceania.

In contrast, the name of the novel's protagonist, Winston Smith, has hardly become a household word. Yet he is one of the most carefully delineated characters in science fiction literature. He is a twentieth century Everyman — thirty-nine, unattractive, plodding along in his job, his life a drab, colorless, meaningless existence. Orwell makes this barrenness interesting, if painful, meticulously detailing Winston's life from the moment he wakes from an idyllic dream to the reality of a bleak room, a painful fit of coughing, and the compulsory morning exercises, dressed in "a dingy singlet and a pair of shorts." He has lunch in the canteen, far under the ground of the building in which he works, with its noise, its crowded metal-topped tables, stew with "cubes of spongy pinkish stuff" which, when spilled, "had the appearance of vomit," and with constant surveillance from fellow workers and the telescreen.

Into this drab existence comes Julia, an attractive girl ten years younger than he. At first he can attribute her interest in him only to the possibility that she might be a member of the Thought Police. Love and any pleasure in the sexual act are severely prohibited by the Party. Winston and Julia are both of the upper fifteen percent that are Party members, but they are not members of the Inner Party, which rules the state of Oceania. By a series of maneuvers reminiscent of World War II Underground, passing hidden notes, a series of meetings under the cover of a crowd, Winston and Julia meet and make love far out in the country under a hazel tree, bluebells underfoot and a thrush singing, it would seem, just for them, near a stream with fish lazing in its pools. "It's the Golden Country — almost," says Winston, but the allusion to the idyllic English pastoral is lost on Julia. She is enough younger than Winston to have grown up knowing only the Party. She has no memory of a life that preceded it. For her, defiance and rebellion spring from her own nature, and she has learned to coexist. She has developed her own private variation of *doublethink*, a method by which Party members can accommodate two conflicting views simultaneously. In public one of the most orthodox and enthusiastic supporters of the Party, the state, and the anti-sex league, she seeks out men in whom she senses hostility to the state. For her, the sexual act is an act of political rebellion, as well as a sensual experience she revels in. Winston, more inhibited, is nevertheless excited by "anything that hinted at corruption" of the Party, seeing desire as "the force that would tear the Party to pieces." So even in this moment, the ultimate defiance of the Party is still shadowed by it. Their lovemaking is, in the final analysis, "a political act."

Back in the city, they find an equally idyllic retreat — a bedroom above an antique shop — in the proles' quarters, the area populated by the other eighty-five percent of the population, the earthy and unthinking masses of the people. Winston is aware that the end may well be a cell in the Ministry of Love (the police), yet he goes on. They continue with their jobs in the Ministry of Truth, Julia working on the novel-writing machines and Winston on the rewriting of news to make it politically orthodox, which often involves complete refabrication of events or even outright invention, the past revised and the previous versions erased by being thrown into the "memory hole" — the incinerator. They encounter O'Brien, who both are convinced is not only sympathetic but will lead them to the Brotherhood which, rumor persistently has it, is being formed all around them, lying in wait to destroy the Party. In O'Brien's apartment, they pledge themselves to any crime that will bring about its overthrow.

Sexual repression and violence are necessary to maintain the discipline of the totalitarian state. Early in the novel, Winston records in his secret diary an account of a film about a bombing of a refugee ship: "there was a wonderful shot of a child's arm going up up up right up into the air a helicopter with a camera in its nose must have followed it up. . . ." His language, devoid of punctuation and capitals, reflects the uncritical muddle even of Winston's mind, and he is an intellectual who hates the Party. Only one of the proles objects to the film, shouting, "it aint right not in front of kids it aint," and the police eject her. Winston, along with the rest of the population, has been daily conditioned by the Two Minutes Hate on the telescreen. He does observe that the horror of it was that one could not resist going along with the emotions generated on the screen. All emotion belongs to the Party; even "a nervous tic, an unconscious look of anxiety, a habit of muttering to yourself" can betray one, even an expression on one's face. "Facecrime" in Oceania is a punishable offense, as is "thoughtcrime." In a society maintained by a constant state of war, "War Is Peace." In a society in which conformity is the ideal, "Freedom Is Slavery." In a society where all dissent is crushed, "Ignorance Is Strength."

But Big Brother and the police state are not the only forces to conformity. There are many "little brothers," each afraid, and each willing to betray a friend, neighbor, parent, or child in exchange for his own illusory security. The loner is suspect; the word in Newspeak is *ownlife*, and it is the opposite of the "correct" attitude of the citizen. Stressed all through *Nineteen Eighty-Four* is man's isolation and his dependence upon society, not only for companionship but in the long run for existence itself. History is rewritten, buildings and streets are renamed, records are destroyed. A person ceases to exist. He becomes an *unperson*.

Built into the analysis of the Newspeak language are ironic comments and grim satire on political jargon. Besides the "memory hole," there are the ministries: Ministry of Love (the police), Ministry of Truth (propaganda), and Ministry of Peace (the war department). The function and necessity of language is seen as Winston moves "from thoughts to words . . . from words to actions." And as language is destroyed, Chaucer, Shakespeare, Byron, and ultimately Winston himself become *unpersons*.

Winston and Julia are caught, even as Winston has known all along they would be, and imprisoned in the Ministry of Love. There, in a scene reminiscent of Dostoevsky's Grand Inquisitor, Winston is interrogated by O'Brien. Throughout the interrogation, indeed throughout the novel, there is a subtle and intuitive *Doppelgänger* relationship between Winston and O'Brien, even a bizarre hint of affection. "I shall save you," O'Brien says. "I shall make you perfect." Perfection is complete submission of the will to that of the Party. Heresy is not tolerated. It is destroyed before the heretic is destroyed. Martyrdom is impossible. The Party's dictum is not "Thou shalt not" or "Thou shalt" but "Thou *art*." The Party controls the laws of nature. "Reality is inside the skull." Big Brother exists; "You do not exist." Existing only as a creature of society, the individual is powerless. Power is collective and is an end in itself. Ultimately, power is the ability to make another suffer. The future society exists only for itself and its own power, not to bring some Utopian state. There will be no love, only "fear, rage, triumph, and self-abasement." O'Brien concludes triumphantly, "If you want a picture of the future, imagine a boot stamping on the human face — forever."

When Winston cries out that such a world would be impossible and that men would never stand for it, O'Brien asks him in return if he considers himself morally superior and then plays back the tape he had recorded earlier of Winston's pledge to do anything, however vile, to destroy the Party. The effect is devastating, as is O'Brien's final thrust. Making Winston get up off the bed and remove his clothes, he shows him, in almost a page of sickeningly explicit detail, the physical wreck that Winston has become. "If you are human, that is humanity." *Ecce homo*. But when O'Brien asks him if there is any degradation left for him, he replies, "I have not betrayed Julia."

Winston is allowed to recover physically, is even allowed writing materials; and in a scene recalling the opening entries in the diary, he writes "in large clumsy capitals," "FREEDOM IS SLAVERY" "TWO AND TWO MAKE FIVE" "GOD IS POWER." It is the end. The Party has completely bent his will. But there is still the matter of Julia.

O'Brien then faces him with Room 101. Each person has his own "Room 101," the one horror he cannot face. In Winston's case, it is rats. Confronted with rats, described in terms that convey his atavistic fear and loathing, Winston reveals the rock-bottom loathsomeness of self, crying out, "Do it to Julia!" His last shred of dignity, self-respect, love — his humanity, in short, is destroyed.

Freed, Winston is no longer any threat to the Party. He drifts shiftlessly about, makes a show of the busywork the Party throws his way, but he is a dead man. He spends most of his time in a pub, sodden with victory gin. He even meets Julia again, "in the Park, on a vile, biting day in March, when the earth was like iron and all the grass seemed dead and there was not a bud anywhere except a few crocuses which had pushed themselves up to be dismembered by the wind." Orwell's skillfully evocative language both recalls and negates their former meeting in the open. They are even free to embrace, but the thought is repellent to each of them. They share, tonelessly and listlessly, their betrayal of each other, but even that seems no longer to matter. Winston tries to follow her, but she is gone.

Winston Smith is a portrait not only of a man broken down by the totalitarian state but a man broken down by life, a future-world Hurstwood. He is in part an extension of all the derelicts that Orwell wrote about in *Down and Out in Paris and London*. And his final degradation is that he accepts, even is comfortable in his condition. His love is dead, and even his memories have been killed, for as he remembers a flash of his childhood, he immediately rejects it as a "false memory." Winston Smith, even as O'Brien said, is dead. He no longer exists. He loves Big Brother.

Nineteen Eighty-Four is usually classed as science fiction. The work can also be considered as black fantasy; creating a mythic figure embodying all that is repressive in the modern totalitarian state, it is regarded by many critics as a "horror novel." *Nineteen Eighty-Four* is seen as the ultimate in pessimism, the bitter statement of a man dying of tuberculosis. Yet this powerful portrait of a world in which man is stripped of his imagination, his emotions, and above all, his language, is at once uncomfortably close to some aspects of contemporary life and a powerful reminder of man's need to preserve his imagination, his emotions, and his language at all cost. In its own grim way, *Nineteen Eighty-Four* is a powerful statement of what constitutes humanity.

Katharine M. Morsberger

Sources for Further Study

Criticism:

Elsbree, Langdon. "The Structured Nightmare of *1984*," in *Twentieth Century Literature*. V (October, 1959), pp. 135-141. Elsbree analyzes the plot and construction of the novel.

Howe, Irving. *Orwell's* Nineteen Eighty-Four: *Text, Sources, Criticism*. New York: Harcourt Brace, 1963. This is the best source of criticism and analysis of Orwell's novel.

Lee, Robert E. *Orwell's Fiction*. Notre Dame, Ind.: Notre Dame University Press, 1969, pp. 128-157. Lee places *Nineteen Eighty-Four* within the context of Orwell's other works.

Slater, Joseph. "The Fictional Values of *1984*," in *Essays in Literary History*. Edited by Rudolph Kirk and C. F. Main. New York: Russell & Russell, 1965, pp. 249-264. Discussion of the novel as a traditional novel is presented here. There is also a good analysis of characters.

Steinhoff, William. *George Orwell and the Origins of* 1984. Ann Arbor: University of Michigan Press, 1975. Steinhoff traces Orwell's sources and places it within the literary tradition which it represents.

Reviews:

Amazing Stories. XXIII, December, 1949, p. 39.

Christian Century. LXVI, September 7, 1949, p. 1042.

Marvel Science Fiction. III, November, 1950, pp. 99-100.

Nation. CLXVIII, June 25, 1949, p. 716.

New Republic. CXXI, August 1, 1949, p. 23.

New Yorker. XXV, June 18, 1949, p. 18.

Super Science Stories. VI, November, 1949, p. 80.